THE

THE **BOBBS-MERRILL** COMPANY, INC.
A SUBSIDIARY OF HOWARD W. SAMS & CO., INC.
Publishers · INDIANAPOLIS · NEW YORK

THE SOUTHERN FRONTIER

SOUTHERN
FRONTIER

by JOHN ANTHONY CARUSO

Maps by NEIL E. BOLYARD

For these admirers of The American Frontier Spirit:

RUEL ELTON FOSTER
ERNIE BEVAN McCUE
ROBERT FERGUSON MUNN

Books by JOHN ANTHONY CARUSO

THE AMERICAN FRONTIER
 The Appalachian Frontier
 The Great Lakes Frontier
 The Southern Frontier

Contents

THE SOUTHERN FRONTIER

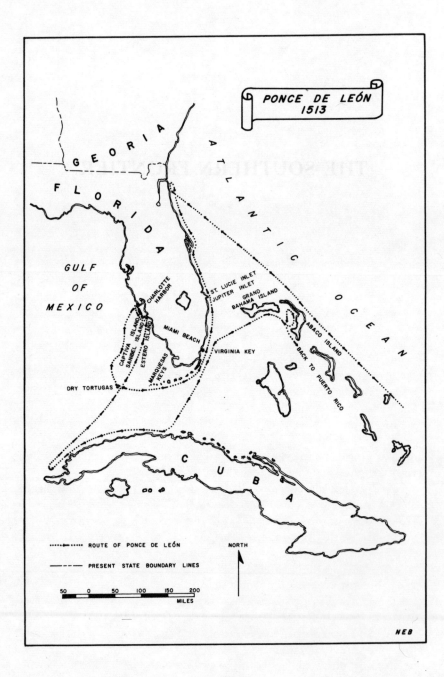

PONCE DE LEÓN
1513

GEORIA

FLORIDA

ATLANTIC

GULF
OF
MEXICO

OCEAN

CHARLOTTE
HARBOR

ST. LUCIE INLET
JUPITER INLET

GRAND
BAHAMA ISLAND

MIAMI BEACH

CAPTIVA ISLAND
SANIBEL ISLAND
ESTERO ISLAND

ABACO ISLAND

VIRGINIA KEY

BACK TO PUERTO RICO

MARQUESAS KEYS

DRY TORTUGAS

C U B A

C U B A

ROUTE OF PONCE DE LEÓN

NORTH

PRESENT STATE BOUNDARY LINES

50   0   50   100   150   200
MILES

NEB

The Fountain of Youth

DON JUAN PONCE DE LEÓN PERHAPS FLUSHED WITH MINGLED ANGER AND impatience when, on April 2, 1513, he found that shoals and sand bars along the coast forced him to anchor his three ships more than three miles offshore in only forty-eight feet of water. He might easily have regained his usual serenity had he known that he was about to open the earliest frontier in American history. But for the present that frontier promised neither the gold nor the fertile lands he sought. All that could be seen from the topmast of his large caravel was a silent region of sandy beaches and groves watered by small rivers that flowed into the sea. Five days he waited, avoiding the possibility of grounding on some bank or bar, before favorable winds enabled him to land somewhere between what is now St. Augustine and Jacksonville Beach. He took possession of the land, which he thought was an island, in the name of his king. And he christened it Florida because he discovered it during the Easter season, which was celebrated in his native Spain as the Easter of Flowers.[1]

Don Juan left no record of the ceremonies that attended his discovery. The Spanish chroniclers, too, are silent. The engaging Antonio de Herrera gave us the fullest account of the discovery that we have, but he mentioned neither cross nor stone engraved with royal arms, no proclamation summoning the natives to pay homage to the king of Spain and to embrace the true faith, and no priest to celebrate Mass.

Unfortunately, the chroniclers of later ages could not fill this unfinished picture with details of their own making. Did Don Juan wear a uniform, civilian clothes, or armor battered in his many military campaigns? Did he express long and earnest gratitude to God, or did he repeat the simple prayer he had heard Columbus utter twenty years before? Did he grasp the unfurled banner of Castile in his left hand while with sword in his right he took possession of the new land in the name of his king? Don Juan did himself and the art of historiography a disservice by failing to provide posterity with the answers to these questions.

Vanity and love of wealth seem to have been the motivating forces of his life. But a man may attain immortality even by vanity and love of wealth, if these complement a vital purpose and unbounded courage. Already in his early fifties, Don Juan had reached that stage of life when most men would gladly exchange its introspection and serenity for the joys and frivolities of youth. In addition to wealth and new lands, Don Juan sought the Fountain of Youth with fearless zeal. As though he were sure of ultimate success, he never bothered to provide us with the date of his birth. Nevertheless, we learn that he was of ancient noble blood, and that he first saw the light of day around 1460 at San Servás de Campos in the kingdom of León. One of his ancestors had acquired the name of León by marrying Doña Aldonza de León, a daughter of Alfonzo IX and sister of that Ferdinand who was canonized for wresting Seville from the Moors.[2]

Ponce—as they called him in Spain—was already widely known for his valor and experience in Moorish campaigns when in 1493 he sailed with Columbus to Española, which today is Haiti and the Dominican Republic. He soon helped Governor Francisco de Bobadilla quell a native uprising. Nine years later, when Nicolás de Ovando arrived in Española to supercede Bobadilla, Ponce put down the revolting Indians of Higuey Province and captured their intrepid chief Cutabanamá. Ovando rewarded him for his services by appointing him lieutenant in the village of Salva León, where he began a plantation and raised cattle and horses. The regional Indians soon interrupted these worthy labors by regaling him with tales of much gold in the neighboring island of San Juan de Boriquien, now called Puerto Rico. Ponce retold the tales, perhaps with glowing variations, to Ovando, who gave him permission to search the island for its reported treasures.[3]

Crossing to Puerto Rico in a small caravel, Ponce presented himself to the native chief, who exchanged names with him in the Indian manner and conducted him graciously through the island. They found "small treasures," which Ponce sent to Ovando. At the same time, Ponce started a settlement, where he built a storehouse and a fortification of rammed earth. Then he returned to Española to report to Ovando, leaving two Spaniards and some trusty Indians to manage the plantation and livestock in his absence.[4]

In the spring of 1509 Ponce returned to Puerto Rico, where he led another campaign against rebelling Indians. His remarkable greyhound, Bezerillo, could understand the Indian tongue and could distinguish warlike from peaceful Indians. Because the Indians were more afraid of two Spaniards with Bezerillo than a hundred Spaniards without him, his master granted him a half-share of booty more than that allotted to each of his crossbowmen. This hunting with greyhounds, which resulted in the coining of a new word, *aperrear*—to cast to the dogs—quickly brought what the Spaniards were pleased to call pacification, an euphonism that enabled them to conceal their usual process of indiscriminate slaughter and enslavement. Ovando rewarded Ponce by appointing him governor and chief justice of the island.[5]

But Ponce was not destined to remain in Puerto Rico for long. King Ferdinand, finding that Ovando had, in making his appointments, contravened the rights of Diego Columbus, who had inherited his father's property, removed Ponce from office and bestowed it on Cristóbal de Sotomayor. But Ovando, when he returned to Spain, persuaded the king to restore Ponce to the governorship of Puerto Rico. As soon as Ponce learned that he had been restored to office, he seized Juan Cerón and Miguel Díaz, who had been serving as Sotomayor's chief justice and sheriff, respectively, and sent them to Spain in chains, to answer charges of malfeasance in office. A little later the Indians, infuriated by the arbitrary acts of Cerón and Díaz, massacred Sotomayor and eight other Spaniards. Ponce promptly suppressed the revolt, only to learn that the Spanish courts had upheld Cerón and Díaz.[6]

Ponce then realized that his future lay elsewhere. A man of considerable wealth, he planned an expedition to seek new lands, and especially the Fountain of Youth, on the island of Bimini, which the Indians told him lay north of Española.

Man has always striven to renew himself. Even in our enlightened age, countless persons seize on every new advertisement of a patent medicine or a cosmetic as avidly as flies seize on a grain of sugar, though they have little doubt that it promises infinitely more than it can perform. How much more susceptible were people in the sixteenth century! Superstitious and unlearned, they readily accepted as truth every yarn reported from the remote and mysterious New World. Legends of the Fountain of Youth, however, had their origins in the Middle Ages. That elusive philosopher-king, Prestor John, whom many of his contemporaries sought in vain, reported to the king of France and the Pope in his mystifying letter, which appeared in Europe seemingly out of nowhere, that he had bathed in the Fountain of Youth six times and in consequence had reached the age of five hundred sixty-two.[7] Sir John Mandeville found the Fountain in Asia and indulged in its rejuvenating waters with bacchanalian abandon.[8] Peter Martyr filled his chronicle of the New World with tales of Amazonian women, mermaids, singing fish, and alligators that exhaled perfume. He argued with more heat than logic that the Fountain of Youth was certainly a possibility, that wise men, indeed, were less skeptical of its existence than the unlearned.[9]

The Indians, too, had their Fountain of Youth. They located it in Haiti, in Cuba, even on the northern shore of South America. Later when Ponce failed to locate it in Florida, the Spaniards hid their disappointment and chagrin by poking fun at him in all quarters. Every chronicler from Oviedo to Fonteneda, copying one another's errors and legends, neglected Ponce's solid achievements to make space for facetious references to his credulity. The sarcastic remarks they wrote in their declining years bespoke their disappointment, or fear, that the Fountain would be found too late to do them any good.

King Ferdinand perhaps thought he had nothing to lose and possibly much to gain by issuing on February 23, 1512, a capitulation or patent authorizing Ponce to discover and settle the island of Bimini. But the king was too practical and too shrewd a businessman to place much confidence in the Fountain of Youth; he perhaps chuckled to himself as he named Ponce *adelantado* or governor and directed his scribe to state in the patent that the primary goal of Ponce's expedition was gold and new lands. He also made certain that the expedition would pay for itself by charging its expenses to the explorer under promises of great rewards in titles and profits. And Ponce should be lord of all he surveyed save for one restriction: he must not trespass on lands which might belong "to the most serene king of Portugual, our own very dear and much-loved son." Later the Indians of the island should be protected and Christianized and civilized—a process which all too often meant enslavement. The patent allowed Ponce three years to complete the expedition, specified the royal rights to what precious metals might be found, and requested a report of conditions on the island as soon as it should be discovered. The king concluded his patent by directing Diego Columbus to assist Ponce in fitting out the expedition.[10]

Fortified with this royal grant, Ponce returned to Puerto Rico and bought a caravel in which he proceeded to Spain, where he made preparations for his expedition. But Ferdinand regarded Ponce so valuable in controlling the rebellious Indians of Española that he asked him to defer his voyage. Not until early in the following year was Ponce free to fit out and supply three ships—a brigantine, a large caravel, and a galleon. Adhering strictly to the spirit of his patent, he enlisted neither priests nor monks to convert the Indians nor to administer to himself and his men in case of need.[11]

On March 3, 1513, he sailed from San Germán to Aguadillo, Puerto Rico, whence he steered northwestward in the hope of finding Bimini, which most historians have recognized as the present island of Andros in the Bahamas. Passing among these islands, which were then called the Lucayos, he eventually reached San Salvador, the place of Columbus' first landing. Refitting one of his ships, he crossed the bay to the windward of the islands. Then on Easter Sunday, March 27, he fringed islands and shoals to arrive at present Abaco Island. Finding it uninhabited, he continued northwestward for three days until an increasingly rough sea forced him to change his course.[12] At noon on April 2 he anchored at the spot where we first met him.

2

Six days later he resume his journey northward. By now he perhaps had noticed a cooling in the weather and had become convinced that he could assure success for his expedition only by planting a settlement as quickly as possible in warmer climate. So on the following day, availing himself of favorable winds, he turned southward. He saw nothing significant enough to report until April 21, when, just below the St. Lucie River, he discerned some Indian huts. Seeing no natives, however, he continued southward and, between present Jupiter Inlet and Palm Beach, encountered the swift-flowing Gulf Stream which drove back his ships. The large caravel and the galleon, which were nearest shore, dropped their anchors; but the wind was so strong that it strained their cables and drove the brigantine, which was farthest from shore, beyond sight in clear weather.

Here Ponce first saw Indians, males and females, whose only clothing consisted of palms woven in a kind of plait over their genitals. Seeing the two vessels anchored close to shore, the Indians ran toward the beach as they called to the Spaniards. Ponce, with some of his men, accepted their invitation. But no sooner were the Spaniards ashore than their hosts began to grapple with them and to steal the small boat in which they had come. While the Indians themselves suffered little harm, their darts and arrows tipped with sharp bones wounded two Spaniards. Under cover of darkness Ponce collected his men, returned to his ships, and sailed to a river, which he named Rio de la Cruz—now Jupiter Inlet—where he erected a commemorative stone cross, secured wood and water, and waited for the brigantine to return. Suddenly sixty Indians attacked the Spaniards, who repelled them and captured one of them for the purpose of obtaining information about the coast and country and of training him as an interpreter.[13]

When the brigantine returned, Ponce, still searching for Bimini, doubled present Jupiter Light, which he called Cabo de las Corrientes because of the force of the current, and continued southward along the coast until he reached two islands, one of which he named Santa Marta, now Virginia Key. On May 13 he left Santa Marta and the other island, Pola, and sailed for the Marquesas, a hundred forty-five miles distant. The Florida Keys he named Los Martires, because the high rocks from a distance resembled a group of men writhing with pain.[14]

From the Marquesas, Ponce sailed to the Dry Tortugas, where he changed his course from west to north and northeast, perhaps because he had not seen any sizable land mass for several days. On May 23 he touched just north of present Charlotte Harbor in the country of the Calos Indians, then sailed southward to present Captiva and Sanibel islands. Continuing to present Estero Island, he took water and wood and careened his caravel. Somewhere he learned that a chief named Carlos—or a name that sounded to him like Carlos—was reputed to own much gold in his domain at the southwestern tip of the peninsula. Yet Ponce distrusted the natives and ignored them when they motioned to him to come ashore. Whereupon they paddled to his ships. When they saw him attempting to change his anchorage, they thought he was preparing to sail and grasped the cables of his ship as though to hasten him on. This started a fight during which some Spaniards, rowing ashore, captured four women and destroyed two leaky canoes.[15]

Next morning, while the Spaniards awaited a favorable wind to sail for Carlos's domain, an Indian paddled to the ship and surprised them by requesting them in their own language—which he had learned when he lived in Española—to remain so that the chief could barter gold for their articles. Needless to say, the Spaniards agreed. Soon Indians appeared in twenty canoes, some of which were fastened together in pairs. As they approached, they divided their flotilla. Some shot arrows or hurled darts at the ship, while others made for the anchors which they tried to weigh in vain. When they attempted to cut the cables, Ponce sent a boatload of his men against them. As the Indians turned and ran, the Spaniards killed a few of them and captured four, two of whom Ponce released and sent to the chief with a message of peace.[16]

Next day some Spaniards in a boat met a few Indians, who informed them that their chief would arrive in the morning to trade with them. By this subterfuge the chief gained time and gathered men in eighty well-equipped canoes. Later that morning they began a fight that lasted all day; but, fearing crossbows and cannon, they kept at such a distance that their arrows fell abortive into the water. At last, seeing that they could do the white men no harm, they went away. On June 14 Ponce sailed from the island, which he called Matanza, from *mata*, meaning to kill, in commemoration of his murderous battle with the Indians.[17]

A week later Ponce reached the Tortugas, as he now named these islands, because during the night he and his men captured one hundred seventy turtles and fourteen seals or manatee, which they called *lobos marinos*, meaning sea-wolves. Another week of sailing found them along the northwestern coast of Cuba, though they were ignorant of their whereabouts. On July 1 Ponce, still searching for Bimini, headed for Los Martires and eventually arrived at Tequesta Point, which is today Miami Beach. Thence he continued his search for Bimini, navigating among the Bahamas until he reached a small island on which he found an old woman whom he took on board as a guide. Naming the island La Vieja, meaning The Old Woman, he sailed to Great Bahama, where he found Diego Miruelo with a boat from Española bound for what may have been an unlicensed expedition. Sailing back and forth among the Bahamas, Ponce refitted his ships and sent one of them under Ortubia to search for Bimini while he himself returned to Puerto Rico. Here Ortubia eventually joined him and informed him that he had visited Bimini, but that he had found no rejuvenating spring on it.[18]

So ended Ponce's first expedition. Though he found neither gold nor slaves, he discovered the Bahama Channel through which explorers made passage from Havana to Spain. The expedition, too, contributed to our knowledge of Indian character.

3

A truly great man is never discouraged by the object of his failure; he attacks it with intensified determination and sometimes with wider ambition. Ponce wasted no time in returning to Spain and in obtaining from the king a patent that empowered him to colonize Bimini and Florida and to Christianize the Indians. But all this lay far in the future. Just now the king commanded him to undertake the pressing matter of subduing the ferocious Caribs, who were again wreaking much suffering and death on the growing Spanish settlements.[19]

Meanwhile other adventurers visited Florida. In 1516 Diego Miruelo arrived from Cuba in a single vessel, traded iron and glass toys for gold with the natives, and returned to his starting point. Next year Francisco Hernandez de Córdoba, driven from Yucatan to Florida by stormy weather, anchored near Charlotte Harbor and then sailed to Havana. Two years later Alonzo Álvarez de Pineda, sent by Francisco de Garay, governor of Jamaica under Diego Columbus, searched for a strait or passage, mapped the coast of present Texas, then known as Amichel, and discovered the mouth of the Mississippi, which he called Espiritu Santo, twenty-two years before Hernando de Soto crossed it at or near Sunflower Landing, Mississippi.[20]

By this time Ponce de León, tiring in his attempt to conquer the stubborn Caribs, withdrew to Puerto Rico and prepared his second expedition to Florida. In February, 1521, he sailed with two ships, two hundred men, fifty horses, and a number of domestic animals and farm implements to cultivate the soil. Monks and priests accompanied him to undertake the missionary work in accordance with his patent. He landed near Charlotte Harbor, where eight years before he had first heard of Chief Carlos, and where the Indians had attacked his ships. Since that time, Spanish slave-hunting raids along the coast had filled the Indians with hatred for white invaders and with undying determination to keep their freedom. They attacked Ponce as soon as he began to build houses, wounding him in the thigh and killing several of his men.

Eventually the Spaniards, unable to make headway, took to their ships with their wounded leader and sailed for Cuba. On the way one of the ships was lost and later fell into the hands of Hernán Cortés, conqueror of Mexico. A few days after his arrival in Cuba, Ponce died of his wound, leaving the mystery of the Fountain of Youth still unsolved.

Over the sepulcher in Puerto Rico, where his body was interred, his sorrowing countrymen, inspired by a part of his name, raised this epitaph in Latin:

Here lies the bones of a LION
Whose deeds were mightier than his name.[21]

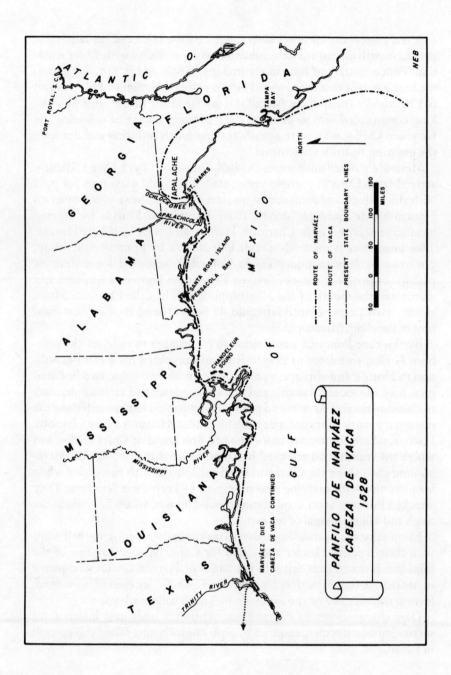

ATLANTIC O.

NEB

PORT ROYAL, S.C.

FLORIDA

GEORGIA

TAMPA BAY

APALACHE

ST. MARKS

OCHLOCKONEE R.

APALACHICOLA RIVER

NORTH

ALABAMA

MEXICO

SANTA ROSA ISLAND

PENSACOLA BAY

MISSISSIPPI

CHANDELEUR SOUND

GULF

MISSISSIPPI RIVER

LOUISIANA

NARVÁEZ DIED

CABEZA DE VACA CONTINUED

TEXAS

TRINITY RIVER

ROUTE OF NARVÁEZ

ROUTE OF VACA

PRESENT STATE BOUNDARY LINES

50   0   50   100   150

MILES

PÁNFILO DE NARVÁEZ
CABEZA DE VACA
1528

2

In Search of Eldorado

Eldorado! the golden man! this chimera played a major part in the creation of the great Spanish empire. Zealous searcher of Eldorado, which came to mean the Golden Land, was the *conquistador* or conqueror who reflected the most conspicuous hereditary and environmental characteristics of his age. His ancestors had waged successful warfare against the Moors for nearly eight hundred years. This pattern of life had engendered in the conquistador the religious fanaticism, the overbearing pride, the barbarous cruelty, and the sublime courage, or, perhaps, the foolhardiness, that enabled him to defeat his heretic enemy, to preserve his Christian faith, and, in 1492, to unify his country.

This coincided with other events to prepare him for his great mission in history. In 1453 the capture of Constantinople by the Moslems saw the eventual decline of the prosperous commerce carried on by the Italian city-states with the Near East and emphasized the need for a new route to that region at the western end of the Mediterranean Sea. Spain, enjoying geographic proximity and an intensely vital national life, naturally took the lead in the discovery and conquest of the New World. The conquistador with his military prowess, his fervid imagination, and his religious fanaticism was the ideal agent to hispanize and Christianize the boundless lands he discovered and explored.

His program of conquest entailed three basic drives: gold, glory, and gospel. Only the thirst for gold needs elucidation here. Though Spain had rich mines, she enjoyed no privileged place in the growing world commerce because of her tortuous mountain terrain, her poor highways, and her want of navigable streams. Only by gaining access to the easily transportable gold and silver of America could she hope to gain her equilibrium in world trade. Small wonder that she bent her magnificent energy to secure possession of great quantities of precious metals, which were universally acceptable in facilitating commercial exchanges and credits.

In his search for gold the conquistador clutched at rumors of fountains of youth, enchanted islands, Amazons, and Eldorados that seemingly existed everywhere in the two American continents. From the early decades of the sixteenth century persistent rumors of mysterious kingdoms of fabulous wealth and power hypnotized the conquistador and lured him through limitless jungles and incredible dangers.

The legend of Eldorado was quite a simple one. On certain feast days a Chibcha chief of Guatabela, in the mountains of present Colombia, had himself covered with gold dust which, amid flamboyant ceremonies, he washed off in a supposedly holy lake while he emptied into it a gigantic golden bowl filled to the brim with sapphires, diamonds, golden bracelets, and emeralds. Such was the simple legend of Eldorado; but in the neurotic mind of the conquistador it assumed fantastic proportions; he transformed it into a Golden Land, which he constantly sought in vain. Yet this madness had the redeeming quality of helping immeasurably to piece together the greatest modern empire in America.[1]

No conquistador loved gold more than Lucas Vásquez de Ayllón, an *oidor* or superior judge of Española. In 1520 he sent Francisco Gordillo with a caravel to explore the mysterious land to the north. Gordillo in the Bahamas fell in with Pedro de Quexos, who also commanded a caravel, and joined him in a slave-hunting expedition. In June, 1521, about the time that Ponce de León was driven from Florida, Gordillo and Quexos landed in the vicinity of the Cape Fear River on the present coast of North Carolina and took formal possession of the region, which the Indians called Chicora. They won the confidence of the natives by dressing two of them, a man and a woman, in doublet and hose; then they invited one hundred fifty more on board, shipped their anchors, and sailed for home. On the way one of the caravels was lost. The other reached Santo Domingo, where Gordillo and Quexos were greatly chagrined to learn that Ayllón condemned as unauthorized their seizure of the Indians. Concurring in this opinion, Diego Columbus ordered that the Indians be set free and returned to their native land, thereby winning their everlasting gratitude. Meanwhile some of the captives sickened and died of grief and hunger, while others preferred to eat dogs, asses, and even the dead animals they found along the walls rather than the food that the Spaniards set before them.[2]

Ayllón detained one of them, an imaginative fellow whom he had baptized with the name of Francisco Chicora, and whom he took to Spain. There Francisco regaled Peter Martyr and Oviedo with the marvelous tales that they preserved in their histories. Encouraged by his yarns of a race of men with inflexible tails, of a king named Datha who had become a giant by softening and stretching his own bones in childhood, and of domesticated deer that lived in the houses of the natives and generously provided them with cheese and milk, Ayllón requested and obtained from Charles V a patent to visit Chicora, which was reputed to be a land of fabulous wealth. But three more years passed before he was able to sail in six vessels and a large boat or tender with five hundred men and women, a small number of Negro slaves, and three Dominican friars who were to convert the Indians.

Landing in the vicinity of the Cape Fear River, which he optimistically called the Jordan, he set his men to work to replace a ship he had lost in entering the river, while he himself designed an open boat that had one mast and that could be propelled by both oars and sail. Exploration by land and sea convinced Ayllón and his followers that the place was unsuited for settlement. Furthermore, Francisco Chicora and other natives deserted him at the first opportunity, rendering him helpless to talk to the Chicorans and to convince them of his friendship. So he moved southward along the coast until he came to the Pee Dee River, which he called the Gualdape and where, in a flat country surrounded by marshes, he began the settlement of San Miguel de Gualdape.[3]

The winter proved unusually severe. The settlers soon ate up their food. Then exposure and disease made them too weak to catch the fish that abounded in the river. Ayllón himself, weakened by hardships and privations, succumbed to fever and died on St. Luke's Day, October 18, 1526. The survivors quarreled, permitting an adventurer named Gines Donzel to seize leadership of the colony. With the support of Pedro de Bazan, he collected a party of malcontents, seized and imprisoned the military and civil officials, and exercised authority with a high hand over both his comrades and the Indians. Quarreling with two of their followers, Donzel and Bazan determined to kill them; but their plans went awry when one night some of the Negro slaves revolted, set fire to Donzel's house, and seized him and Bazan. Set free, the rightful leaders executed Bazan and imprisoned Donzel and his comrades. Then, placing Ayllón's body in one of the ships, they started with one hundred fifty sick and destitute survivors for Santo Domingo.

As they made their way slowly homeward, seven of them died from exposure and another from pulling the flesh entirely off the bone of his frozen leg. The icy winds and sea tossed the small vessels like chips of wood and then overturned and sank them. And Allyón, says Oviedo, found his sepulcher in the sea, "where have been and shall be put other captains and governors."[4]

2

Ayllón's failure only intensified Spanish determination to explore and settle Florida. The champion of these aspirations was Pánfilo de Narváez, a native of Valladolid who in the New World had acquired considerable wealth and with it a rugged determination to keep it. Bernal Díaz, who knew him in Mexico, describes him as a tall man with a fair complexion, a red beard, and a voice so resonant it seemed to come from a cave. In 1520 he had been sent to Vera Cruz to arrest Hernán Cortés for disobeying orders to return to Haiti. From that mission, Narváez returned minus

Cortés—and minus one eye. The remaining one became a flaming eagle eye that fascinated his followers with its half-glowering, half-appealing look.[5]

Obtaining a grant from Charles V, Narváez, in June, 1527, sailed with five ships to Santo Domingo from the port of San Lucar in Spain. He had six hundred colonists and soldiers, among whom were priests, Franciscan friars, Negro slaves, and the wives of certain members of the expedition. His officers included Father Juan Suárez, superior or commissary of the friars, Alonzo Enríque, comptroller, and Álvar Nuñez—better known by his cognomen Cabeza de Vaca, meaning Cow's Head—treasurer and high sheriff. Cabeza de Vaca came of an ancient and noble family. One of his ancestors, a humble shepherd named Martin Alhaja, placed a cow's head at the opening of a mountain pass to indicate a passage through the defile to the king of Navarre, who was leading a campaign against the Moors. In commemoration of this favor, which enabled him to win the campaign, the king ennobled Alhaja's descendents and changed their name to Cabeza de Vaca.[6]

At Santo Domingo, where he tarried to obtain horses for the expedition, Narváez met a series of reverses. A hundred forty of his men deserted to the lure of gold in Peru and Mexico. Then a hurricane wrecked two ships that he had sent to Trinidad under Cabeza de Vaca. The remaining four ships weathered the storm, but their crews were so terrified that they persuaded Narváez to postpone his departure until spring.[7]

In the latter part of February, 1528, Narváez sailed for Havana with five ships, including a brigantine he had recently purchased at Trinidad. But the pilot grounded the ships on the shoals, necessitating a delay of fifteen days. Then, rounding the western extremity of Cuba, he ran into a high south wind that, by raising the water over the shoals, enabled him to escape. Weathering several more storms, the ships sailed for Havana; but before they reached that bay a high south wind drove the ships off course to an inlet near Tampa Bay. There Enríque with a few men landed, found a village in which they held a conference with the Indians, and traded them trinkets for venison and fish. Next day Narváez himself landed only to find that the natives had fled. His men, ransacking every hut, were chagrined to find only one gold ornament and some fish nets. On the following day, April 16, in the presence of some of his men, the notary, the monks, and officers of the expedition, Narváez raised the royal standard and read this proclamation, which a very learned jurist and member of the Council of the Indies had written for the occasion:

In the name of his Catholic and Caesarian Majesty, Don Carlos, King of the Romans and Emperor ever Augustus, and Doña Juana, his mother, Sovereign of León and Castile, Defender of the Church, ever victorious, never vanquished, and ruler of barbarous nations, I, Pánfilo de Narváez, his servant, messenger, and captain notify you to the best of my ability that God Our Lord, one and eternal, created heaven and earth and one man and one woman from which have sprung and shall spring all mankind. In the four thousand and more years of its existence the world has become so populous that men have had to scatter in different directions and divide themselves into kingdoms and provinces in order to subsist. God put all these nations under one man, called Saint Peter, as master and head of the human race, regardless of place, law, religion, or belief. And He commanded him to make his capital at Rome, the central part of the world, and permitted him to judge and govern all people including Christians, Moors, Jews, Gentiles or whatever creed they professed.[8]

The proclamation, alluding to the Demarcation Line of 1493, by which Pope Alexander VI decreed most of the New World to Spain, stated that one of Saint Peter's successors had made a gift of islands and mainland to Ferdinand and Isabella and their successors. The present ruler, Charles V, had, therefore, been proclaimed in this domain, most of whose inhabitants had received and served him, as good subjects should, and had obeyed his religious men who, disdaining reward or material consideration of any kind, had gladly brought the Word of God to them. The proclamation urged the natives to do likewise.[9]

It enjoined on them, moreover, the necessity of understanding and reflecting on what Narváez told them and of recognizing the supremacy of the Church and Charles V. Should they agree, they would be received with love and charity, would be free to do as they pleased, and would not be required to become Christians save "when informed of the truth you desire to be converted to our Holy Catholic Faith." But he warned them that, should they show hostility, he would invade their country, make total war on them, and enslave them and their wives and children and dispose of them as the king saw fit.[10]

With this solemn farce Narváez, with the remainder of his men, moved inland on the forty-two of the eighty horses that had survived the rough voyage from Santo Domingo. By evening they reached a very large bay where they remained overnight. Then, returning to camp, he sent the brigantine up the coast to search for a harbor that the pilot said he had seen but could not now find. Narváez instructed the pilot of the brigantine, in case he failed to find the harbor, to sail direct to Cuba, secure a vessel that had been left at Trinidad, and return with both ships full of supplies to Florida. Narváez himself, with a larger party, advanced along Tampa Bay and eventually met and captured four Indians who guided them to a village where they found unripe corn and a number of boxes, each of which contained a corpse covered with painted deerskins. The villagers indicated by making signs that they had found the boxes in a Spanish vessel wrecked in the bay. Father Suárez, believing that the boxes and their contents represented some kind of idolatrous practice, had them burned.[11]

The villagers told Narváez that Apalache, a province far to the north, teemed with gold. He rested for two days, then, deciding to march to this Eldorado with most of his men, returned with his party to the coast. There, in a council of his officers, he announced his plans. He would send the fleet up the coast to Mexico, which he erroneously thought was nearby, and would march with his officers, their wives, the friars, and all but a hundred of the colonists to Apalache. This plan Cabeza de Vaca opposed, saying that they should stay with their ships until they found a harbor which they could occupy and hold. The pilots, he added, were uncertain of where they were, and the supplies were so limited that each man would have to subsist on such inadequate rations as a pound of biscuit and a pound of bacon. Nobody, he concluded, knew anything about the country or about its inhabitants or whether food could be found along the way. All save Enríque agreed with Cabeza de Vaca, but Narváez had made up his mind and would not swerve from his purpose.[12]

The women, of course, voted with the majority, on the side of safety. Their leader strode up to Narváez and warned him that neither he nor his men would ever return. When Narváez requested the source of her opinion, she replied she had received it from a Moorish woman of Hornachos. His eagle eye burned brighter as he chided her and Cabeza de Vaca for being afraid to venture inland, and he ordered him to take command of the ships. Cabeza de Vaca declined, saying that while he felt that the expedition would fail, his honor required him to share its hazards with his comrades. Narváez then charged his lieutenant, Caravello, with the ships, which soon sailed away. The leader of the women advised them that, since they were convinced their husbands would never return, they should in no way worry about them but should look out for new mates from among the men on board. Unhampered by convention, they speedily did so. Perhaps their leader's choice "fell on some one more ready than her previous spouse to heed her prophetic warning."[13]

3

With three hundred armed men mounted on armored horses, Narváez plunged into the wilds of Florida. The standard-bearer led the glittering horsemen to the Withlacoochee River, which they crossed on crude rafts. They subsisted on biscuit, bacon, and shoots of young palms. Soon they met a force of two hundred hostile Indians, six of whom they seized. The captives led the way to their village, where the Spaniards found an abundance of corn ready to be harvested. Here they stayed several days while their leader sent two parties under Cabeza de Vaca downstream to investigate the possibility of a harbor. Finding none, Cabeza de Vaca returned. Narváez then resumed his journey toward Apalache, following the direction in which the Indians had pointed. One day they heard strange music and presently saw approaching a group of Indians playing flutes that, like whistles, had no stops. Behind them, on the shoulders of another Indian, rode their chief, Dulchanchellin, who wore a painted deerskin.

Narváez told him by making signs that he intended to go to Apalache. The chief, replying in the same manner that the inhabitants of Apalache were his enemies, offered Narváez assistance and then joined him. That night they came to a river, probably the Suwannee, which the Spaniards crossed with the help of the Indians and improvised boats. One horseman drowned in attempting to swim the river. His horse was rescued only to be killed, roasted, and eaten. Next day they came to the chief's village, where he provided them with grain; but that evening Dulchanchellin, warned of approaching enemies by an arrow that zinged near him at a watering place, fled with his followers into the wilderness and never returned.[14]

Next day when the Spaniards resumed their journey, they captured three or four Indians whom they forced to serve as guides. Hitherto they had traveled through open woods of pine and oak, across shallow lakes with sandy bottoms, and over hummocks and polluted swamps of live oak. That landscape gradually changed. Now they came to a forest full of deer, rabbits, bears, mountain lions, geese, ducks, herons, partridges, hawks and falcons. They got their first glimpse, too, of an opossum, which Cabeza de Vaca describes as "an animal which carries its young in a pocket in its belly, and while they are young they are there carried until they can seek food, and if perhaps they are out looking for food and some one appears, the mother will not flee until she has got them in her pocket."[15]

What intense disappointment, what agonizing gloom seized the weary and half-starved travelers as they approached Apalache! No great and gleaming city of stone, no perfumed forest which they imagined rivaled that of Mexico, no signs of gold and gems met their happy expectancy. What they saw was a wretched huddle of forty thatched huts divided by narrow and crooked and filth-ridden paths. Cabeza de Vaca, with nine horsemen and fifty infantry, attacked the village. Meeting no resistance, they entered and found only women and children. The men were either hunting or had gone on the warpath. The Spaniards squatted and, surveying the dismal scene with angry eyes, spat and upbraided their patron saints. Their only booty was corn and piles of deerskins.[16]

Narváez sent out three exploring parties which confirmed reports that Apalache was the largest village of that country, but that it lay amid impassable lakes, marshes, fallen trees, and tangled underbrush. The warriors soon returned and tried to regain possession of their village. Though they were repulsed, they constantly harassed the Spaniards. Equipped with bows composed of hardwood and strings of deergut or deerskin with reed arrows pointed with snake teeth, fish bone or flint, they practiced incessant guerrilla warfare, which killed many Spaniards together with their horses. The arrows, whizzing and thudding from nowhere, inflicted on the Spaniards deep double wounds by splitting on the meshes of their mail coats. Each day they spent in Apalache increased their misery. They ate up their stores of food which, because of circumstances, they were unable to replenish.

One day an arrow picked off Don Pedro, an Aztec prince from Tex-cuco who had faithfully followed his friend Father Suárez. Don Pedro had led an army across the lakes that surrounded Mexico City, had tri-umphantly scaled high walls, had come out unscathed from many bloody battles; but all his luck, all his intrepidity melted before the dead aim of an unseen sharpshooter in wild Apalache. His death plunged his com-rades into the profoundest discouragement. Of what use was all their bravery, all their military skill against the guerrilla warfare of their ene-mies? Their frustrations found expression in sour jests by their campfires. Miguel de Lambreros, whom the king had commissioned lord lieutenant of the first town they should establish, protested mockingly Cabeza de Vaca's collection of the royal share in gold mines.[17]

For twenty-five days they endured this misery. Then Narváez deter-mined to turn with his men southward to Aute, perhaps on the present site of St. Marks and nine days' march from Apalache. The Indians told them that there they would find maize, beans, pumpkins, fish, and even friendly Indians. There, too, was the sea with its prospect of relief. Might not their ships, guided by some saint's instructions to the pilot, be waiting there to take them home? But their departure for Aute was as dreadful as their sojourn in Apalache. On the first day they saw no Indians; but on the next, while they were fording a lake which had many logs and water that rose to their chests, they were deluged with arrows from the wooded shore. Men and horses fell with grave wounds. The guide was captured. Those who escaped injury emerged from the lake and charged the In-dians who, however, leaped into the water and swam to shore, then con-tinued to shoot from fallen trees and underbrush. Later Cabeza de Vaca vividly described their peril:

> In this conflict some of our men were wounded, for their armor was of no use. That day some men swore they saw two oaks, each as thick as a man's lower leg, pierced entirely through by the Indians' arrows— no small wonder, considering the strength and skill with which they shoot them. I myself saw an arrow that had pierced the stump of an elm to the depth of half a foot. What Indians we had so far seen in Florida were archers. Since they are so large of frame and go naked they seem from the distance like giants. They are marvellously pro-portioned, very lean of figure, strong, and agile. Their arrows are as thick as a man's arm, eleven to twelve hand-spans in length, which they shoot at two hundred paces with so much sureness that they miss nothing.[18]

In such constant peril they toiled toward Aute. One day a hidalgo named Avellaneda, going back to the rescue of his servant boy who had cried for help, fell with an arrow that almost passed through his neck at the edge of his cuirass. He later died of his wound. Next day they reached Aute, where they buried Avellaneda. To their amazement they found the village deserted and its houses burned, though plenty of corn, beans, and squash remained to be harvested. For two days they rested. Then Narváez sent Cabeza de Vaca with sixty men—ten cavalry and fifty infantry—to look for a harbor. Feasting on oysters, for which they gave thanks to God, Cabeza de Vaca and his men traveled until vespers along Apalache Bay with its low, marshy shore rising softly from the lagoons and then descended to the shallow gulf. For two more days they followed the reefs, bars, and islands of the coast which they regarded as much sea as land. Eventually, blocked by the Ochlockonee River, they returned to Aute, where they found Narváez and many others sick, perhaps of malaria. The Indians had, by attacking them during the night, added immeasurably to their misery. Nevertheless, since the sea was their only way of escape, they set out for the mouth of the Apalachicola River. Impeded by the sick and those who were becoming ill in increasing numbers, they inched toward their destination, only to find they had none. Even in different circumstances they could hardly have moved with so many of them sick.

Their physical and mental suffering soon bred councils of despair. The mounted men plotted to desert their leader and the infantry and the sick. But the hidalgos—those who, coming from better families, had learned unforgettable lessons of loyalty in Spain—went to Narváez with word of the plot. Far from punishing the plotters, he dissuaded them from their course by pointing out the shamefulness of abandoning their king, their captain, their sick and helpless comrades at such a critical hour. They resolved to share the common fate of the others.[19]

Narváez then asked their advice as to what they should do to get out of a country that had caused them so much misery. They told him to build ships. This seemed an impossible task. None of them had any knowledge of shipbuilding; they had no tools, no iron, no forge, no tow, no resin, no rigging; they had no food with which to sustain themselves. But misfortune is the measure of human resourcefulness. Next day one of them expressed confidence that he could make bellows from wooden pipes and deerskins. In their desperation anything that promised relief appeared workable. They urged the man to undertake the project while they made nails, saws, axes, and what other tools they needed from stirrups, spurs, and crossbars. To provide food for the shipbuilders and their assistants, they planned to make four raids on Aute with what few horses and men would be available and to kill a horse every third day. The raids led to many "quarrels and contentions with the Indians" but brought in six hundred forty bushels of maize. They collected many palmetto branches for their fiber and husk and twisted and prepared them for use in place of tow for the boats.[20]

On August 4 they began their Herculean labors with only one carpenter among them. How many devices and ingenuities they employed, how many defeats and triumphs they experienced, no man can know. In making the bellows they had to use sheath knives, bone needles, and gut threads and had to seal the seams with evergreen pitch. In making the pipes they had to fell straight saplings, split them into four pieces, and whittle them down to shape after cutting away right angles. The tool-makers, before they could begin their work, had to build kilns in which to reduce wood to charcoal and had to make earthen molds in which to melt their iron and steel. Still, they had no hammers and anvils with which to work the metal and no tongs with which to hold it. Perhaps they solved this problem by removing the hot metal with clay-covered ladles, then dropping it in water to temper it to steel. Their ax-heads must have been dull and brittle, their saws, thick and inflexible with teeth that, even with the persuasion of muscle and with the fury of de-spair, must have made grudging impression on pinewood knots. Yet in just seven weeks they built five boats, each calked with palmetto fibers and stretching between thirty and thirty-two feet. A Greek answering to the redundant but picturesque name of Doroteo Teodoro pitched the boats with a resin he obtained from pine trees. They made ropes and rigging from the tails and manes of their horses, sails from their shirts, and oars, which they considered necessary, from the juniper that grew around them in abundance. Vigorous searches rewarded them with stones for ballast and anchors. From legs of horses they removed one-piece skins and tanned them to make canteens in which to carry their water.[21]

At last, on September 22, they boarded their five boats, which perhaps resembled square-ended scows or barges. Starvation and Indian attacks had reduced their number to two hundred forty-three. In the first boat was Narváez with forty-five men; in the second, Alonzo Enríque and Fray Juan Suárez with an equal number; in the third, two officers with forty-eight men; in the fourth, two officers with forty-seven men; and in the last, Cabeza de Vaca and the quartermaster, Alonzo de Solís, with forty-nine men. The boats were so burdened that their sides were only six inches above the water and so crowded that the men hardly had room to move. They named the harbor they were leaving Bahia de los Caballos, meaning The Bay of the Horses, in memory of the mounts they had killed and eaten. Naked or half-dressed in deerskins, they moved along the coast, prolonging their miseries with a little dried deer meat and with water that oozed from their horsehide canteens. Commending their souls to their favorite saints, they turned in what they thought was the direction of Pánuco which in their ignorance of geography they believed was nearby.[22]

They continued to move along the coast, floundering and pulling loose among the bars and shallows and occasionally passing a village of native fishermen, whom Cabeza de Vaca described as "a poor, miserable lot." A group of Indians fled at the sight of the white, bearded men, leaving their five canoes on the beach. From these canoes the white men con-structed waist-boats that enabled them to raise the sides of their barges about sixteen inches above the water. They passed another village where they feasted on a large quantity of dried mullet with their roes. Their scant provisions dwindled, and their water became useless as their canteens rotted. Eventually they arrived at an island, perhaps Santa Rosa Island, where they encountered a storm.

Finding themselves without water, they were afraid to resume their voyage. Since they had not drunk for five days, their thirst was unbearable; some of them in their desperation began to drink salt water from which four or five of them became so crazed that they died. As the storm continued into the sixth day, they began to realize that, unless they stirred, they would all die of thirst. So they chose to venture out to sea, preferring the possibility of dying from drinking salt water than of their own parched breath. Commending themselves to God, they hauled in the stones that served as anchors and pulled in the direction of a canoe they had seen. At sunset God rewarded them for their fortitude by directing them to the calm and shelter of Pensacola Bay.[23]

Here, unusually tall and well-proportioned Indians in many canoes invited them to their village, which stood nearby at the edge of the water. The Spaniards, seeing that their hosts were unarmed and friendly, followed them and jumped out on the shore. Before each of the huts, which were built of matting laid on wooden frames, were many clay pitchers full of water and much cooked fish. The Indian chief, dressed in a cloak of marten skins so fragrant that it reminded Cabeza de Vaca of amber and musk, recognized thirst in the wild eyes of his guests and waved them to drink. With a gesture he then invited Narváez and his officers to his hut, where he gave them fish. Narváez in turn gave the Indians maize; they wolfed it down and asked for more. Narváez obliged them, then presented their chief with many trinkets. All went swimmingly until, in the middle of the night, the Indians suddenly attacked their guests and killed three of the sick scattered along the shore. In the chief's house, they struck Narváez in the face with a stone, whereupon some of the Spaniards clutched at the chief until his braves rescued him and hustled him out of the door, leaving his antagonists holding his fragrant marten cloak.[24]

In the teeming darkness they all embarked save Cabeza de Vaca with fifty men, who remained to cover the retreat. Three times the Indians attacked his force, each time so furiously that they forced it to retreat more than a stone's throw. Not one of them escaped injury; Cabeza de Vaca received a wound on the face. Fortunately the wounds were slight, for the Indians had few arrows. After the second attack fifteen Spaniards under three officers stealthily followed the retreating Indians through the dark and formed an ambush. When the Indians attacked again, the hidden Spaniards surprised them so effectively that they turned and fled.[25]

Next morning the Spaniards used the wood of the more than thirty canoes they had destroyed to build fires by which they warmed themselves against a chilling north wind. In the morning, when the wind sub-

sided, they resumed their voyage. Enduring three days of thirst, they
reached Mobile Bay. Seeing Indians in a canoe, they hallooed to them in
a friendly manner. When the Indians approached his boat, Cabeza de
Vaca made a sign of a thirsty man drinking. The Indians agreed to take
his jugs and fill them with water. But Doroteo Teodoro was desperate
with thirst; suddenly he cried that he could endure no more; he clamored
to go with the Indians. And, disregarding the rebukes of his leader as well
as the remonstrances of his friends, he took a Negro and hurried with
him into the canoe. The Indians agreed to leave two of their number as
hostages. That night they returned, without jugs and without Doroteo
and the Negro. They cried some words to their detained friends, who
would have plunged into the sea had not the Spaniards caught them.
Whereupon the Indians fled, leaving the Spaniards very dejected over
the loss of their two comrades.[26]

Next morning a large group of Indians appeared in canoes and asked
the Spaniards to return their hostages. Cabeza de Vaca replied that he
would deliver them as soon as they surrendered Doroteo and the Negro.
With the Indians had come five or six chiefs—handsome and well-proportioned men with long and loose hair and clad in marten skins with
fancy patches of fawn fur. By making signs they requested the Spaniards
to go with them, promising water and food and to release Doroteo and
the Negro. But the Spaniards noticed that the Indians in canoes were
beginning to gather around them with the intention of preventing them
from escaping by blocking the inlet. This danger they avoided by hastily
dropping their barges to the inlet, where they continued to expostulate
with the Indians. Neither side would reach an agreement. The Indians
then began to hurl clubs and stones and to threaten to shoot arrows at
the Spaniards, though they had no more than three or four bows among
them. They continued to attack until noon, when a strong wind forced
them to shelter their canoes.[27]

Continuing westward, the Spaniards met the shoal water of Lake
Borgne which, as it increased, forced them to retrace their course. Gradually they groped their way into Chandeleur Sound and along the islands
of the same name until they reached a point of land that formed one of
the lips of a mighty river. This was the Mississippi.

We have now reached the geographic limits of this book. Cabeza de
Vaca had scarcely begun his astonishing odyssey. For the next seven
years he was to wander overland before finding a haven in Mexico. As
for Narváez, his days were numbered. He soon joined Cabeza de Vaca.
They dipped their jugs, drinking the first fresh water in days. Their
hunger intensified, they disembarked on an island to parch their corn,
which for the past two days they had eaten raw. When they found no
firewood, they attempted to cross the river, but for two days they struggled in vain against the current and rising north wind. On the third day,
a little before dawn, fires and columns of smoke rising from the shore
advised them that the Indians were giving warning to the regional tribes.

The fear of peril in the darkness kept them from landing until morning. But that night a strong wind separated their boats forever.

On November 6 three of the boats, one of which carried Cabeza de Vaca, wrecked on an island—Galveston Island or one near it, which Cabeza de Vaca called Malhado, meaning Bad Luck. The commissary and the friars wrecked on the mainland farther west. Narváez in his boat hugged the coast as he moved westward. One day he saw some of the castaways of one of the boats making their way painfully on foot. He landed some of his crew to lighten his boat, then took on the castaways and ferried them across a bay that cut off their route. Dropping a stone for an anchor, he spent that night with the cockswain and a page, who was dangerously ill. That night a wild wind swept his boat out to sea with neither water nor food aboard. And Narváez like Allyón found eternal rest in a watery sepulcher.[28]

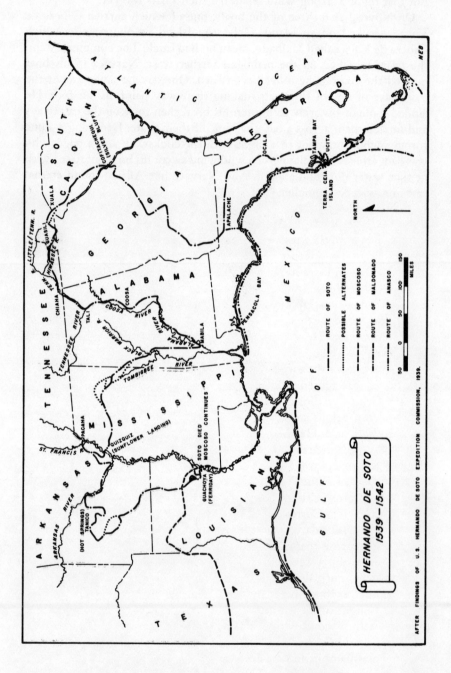

HERNANDO DE SOTO
1539-1542

AFTER FINDINGS OF U.S. HERNANDO DE SOTO EXPEDITION COMMISSION, 1939.

ROUTE OF SOTO
POSSIBLE ALTERNATES
ROUTE OF MOSCOSO
ROUTE OF MALDONADO
ROUTE OF ANASCO

MILES
50   0   50   100   150

NORTH

Hernando de Soto

IN AUGUST, 1537, ÁLVAR NUÑEZ CABEZA DE VACA ARRIVED IN LISBON WITH glowing tales of his adventures and with discreet intimations of the wealth he had found in Florida. All Spain gaped and gasped at his incredible odyssey. He charmed by suggestion or inference rather than by statement or admission. He would break off in the middle of a sentence—just when his hearers expected him to impart some confidential or intriguing information. He was a master of evasion. Pressed by questions, he would reply with an air of solemn mystery: "That's something that has to be reserved for the ear of the emperor. I have sworn not to divulge certain facts." He hinted that he had found finely tailored garments among the Indians of Florida; he intimated that he had seen much gold and silver and precious stones; he implied that Florida was the richest country in the world. He soon began to believe, and he led his hearers to believe, his romantic tales of Eldorado.[1]

Among his listeners was Hernando de Soto. Soto—for that is the correct usage of his name unless it is given in full—had planned an expedition to Florida before Cabeza de Vaca returned to Spain. But Cabeza de Vaca's tales as well as Cortés' sensational success in Mexico strengthened Soto's belief that Florida was another Eldorado. His love of gold was a deeply-seated neurosis that could be cured only by a change of heart. He was thirty-six or thirty-seven years old—a man with flaming black eyes and a handsome, curly-haired head that he always carried with magnificent pride. Everybody made room for him, despite his moderate girth and height. Caught off guard he would smile agreeably, only to rebuke such levity with a scowl while he shot guilty glances all around him. More deeply read in horses and arms than in books, he sought praise for his expert horsemanship and military gifts, which he thought were brilliant. He had so much confidence in his own judgment that he never entertained the thought of error. He brooked neither the opposition of his enemies nor the interference of his friends; he listened intently to all arguments, examined all available facts, only to repudiate them all in favor of his own instincts—which unfortunately were not always unerring. He was only half a military leader—he knew when to advance but knew not when to retreat. No danger, no hardships, however great, could embitter him, could sicken him, as much as the thought of defeat.

Oddly enough, his inflexible temperament made possible more generous qualities: frankness, sanguineness, and infinite trust in all men. As a commander he was prompt in emergency, resourceful in strategy, fiercely brave in battle. But embedded with these strengths were rashness in attack and carelessness in disposing for defense—weaknesses that often brought him to the brink of disaster. He always banked on his ability to extricate himself by some bold or brilliant stroke.

2

Historians have waged bitter verbal warfare among themselves over his birthplace—was it Xerex de Badajóz or Villa Nueva de Barcarrota? Each side has claimed new and undisputable evidence at irregular intervals. None seems to deny, however, that he was a gentleman by all four counts, which means that his grandparents on both sides were of noble blood and therefore eligible for the Order of Santiago, to which Charles V admitted him just before he departed on his expedition to Florida. A succession of adventures in early manhood brought him fame and fortune. With a rusty sword as his only possession, he accompanied Pedrarias de Ávila to the West Indies, served under him in Nicaragua, and eventually married his daughter Isabel, thereby becoming the brother-in-law of Balboa, discoverer of the Pacific Ocean. Later he followed Francisco Pizarro to Peru, where he won fame by helping him capture the Inca ruler Atahualpa and the royal stronghold of Cuzco. As his share of the spoils, he received a large fortune which enabled him to establish in Spain a fine house equipped with stewards, ushers, equerries, and pages—in short, "all the glitter and pageant of the household of a rich nobleman." Seeking high office, he gladly lent Charles V considerable sums with reasonable rates of interest.[2]

In the early spring of 1537 Clarles V issued an *asiento* or contract appointing Soto *adelantado* of Florida. Soto was authorized to raise five hundred men "with the necessary arms, horses, munitions, and military stores." He was granted a tract of land twelve leagues square anywhere in Florida that touched neither seaport nor chief town. He was permitted to import free of duty one hundred Negro slaves, a third of whom should be women. The emperor, capitalizing on the cumulative experience he derived from dealing with the treasures of Mexico and Peru, included a provision granting himself half of all the gold, silver, jewels and pearls, and other objects that should be found in burial places, sepulchers, Indian temples, and localities where sacrifices were made to idols and to other secret places. In addition, the emperor should retain his customary one fifth of all the ransoms obtained from chiefs and headmen. The remainder should be distributed among the conquerors. Lawyers, as fomenters of litigation, were forbidden to enter the country. Priests were to accompany the expedition "for the instruction of the natives of that province in our Holy Faith." The *asiento*, finally, established a hospital for the poor and supported it by all fines imposed by courts of justice.[3]

Soto's call for volunteers brought an enthusiastic response from all parts of the Iberian peninsula. Numerous young spendthrifts from among the nobility sold their estates, their horses, vineyards, and olive orchards, their plate and jewelry, their towns of vassals, to participate in an adventure that they confidently believed would help them replenish their coffers. Among the Portuguese who assembled to follow Soto was the Gentleman of Elvas—he left no other certain identification—whose chronicle of the expedition is one of the fullest and most vivid in the entire literature of Spanish exploration. The volunteers, wrote Elvas, assembled at Seville, but lack of space on the ships forced Soto to turn down many of them. Mustering them again at the port of San Lucar, he noticed that the Portuguese among them

> . . . turned out in polished armour, and the Castilians very showily, in silk over silk, pinked and slashed. As such luxury did not appear to him becoming on such occasion, he ordered a review to be called for the next day, when every man should appear with his arms; to which the Portuguese came as at first; and the Governor set them in order near the standard borne by his ensign. The greater number of the Castilians were in very sorry and rusty shirts of mail; all wore steel hats or helmets, but had very poor lances. Some of them sought to get among the Portuguese. Those that Soto liked and accepted were passed, counted, and enlisted; six hundred men in all followed him to Florida.[4]

Early in April, 1538, Soto, amid great festivity, sailed from San Lucar with a fleet of seven large and three small vessels. Banners fluttered in the breeze; artillery boomed from every ship; trumpets blared; and Soto, with his adored Doña Isabel at his arm, flushed with joy as favorable winds urged his vessels to his magnificent odyssey.[5]

In the latter part of May he reached Cuba and went to Santiago, where he spent almost a year collecting horses, bloodhounds, Irish greyhounds he planned to use in pursuing Indians, a herd of thirteen pigs, salt meat, Negroes, Indians, and domestics. Then he marched his army to the port of Havana, whence it would sail, while he himself visited all the settlements over which he was now governor. Finally, on May 18, 1539, he sailed for Florida, leaving his wife Isabel in Cuba and the government of the island to his friend Juan de Rojas.[6]

3

A dropping wind prolonged his journey until Whitsunday, May 25, when his ships anchored at Tampa Bay. For the next five days shoals forced him and his men to keep to their ships a league from shore in four fathoms of water. Florida, under the brilliant sun, lay like an enchanted land. The sandy shore with its innumerable shells spread like a silver bar between the emerald, white-crested waves and the deep verdure of the wilderness farther inland. The sword-shaped leaves of the royal palmettos, crested with pyramids of silvery blossoms, towered along the inner shore. Patches of live oaks deep in the wilderness were to remind the Spaniards of olive groves in their native land. Here and there hordes of sweet bays and red azaleas and yellow jasmins obtruded like hosts of gaudy butterflies on gray cypresses and magnolias. Squadrons of Spanish curlews, their silvery-white plumage roseate in the sun, turned and tacked high in the sky, and loons pierced the wilderness with their eerie, laughing cries as they whirled over swampy lakes.

From their ships the Spaniards at night saw curl after curl of smoke rise along the shore and dwindle to specks of fireflies. They knew the nearest Indians were passing fiery warnings to the tribes farther inland. To the natives these invaders with their pale and bearded faces, their hard, clanging suits, and their floating castles—which grew ominously larger and larger as they rose and fell with the waves—portended evil, black magic, defeat, death. Soto paid no heed to their warnings. Impatient to land, he boarded one of his brigantines and, without waiting for the larger ships, which could not follow because of the shoals, made for shore. Recklessness characterized his campaign from its inception.[7]

The Indians fled at his approach. Immediately he pushed imprudence to the brink of folly by going deer-hunting. Five days later, when his army landed on Terra Ceia Island, he led it along the bay through swamps and across fords until he came to the village of Ucita, which consisted of eight large huts of timber and palm leaves. On a mound thrown up artificially for defensive purposes stood the chief's house and a kind of temple on the roof of which perched a wooden fowl with gilded eyes. To prevent a surprise attack, Soto ordered some of his men to cut down all the surrounding trees and dense thickets within range of a crossbow-shot from the encampment. At every strategic point along the paths he placed sentinels and kept horsemen in readiness to support them at the first shout of alarm. That night, under the torch's flare, he found on the dust flooring of the chief's house a small string of pearls. The fire used in boring them for beads had ruined them, but "to him they were typical of the jewelled chain of the future which should link him with greatness to his life's end and as long after as men's tongues should wag."[8]

He sent scouting parties to explore the neighborhood. Soon they reported that the Indians were agile and fearless and expert fighters, and that ponds, swamps, and underbrush made the country almost impassable. One party brought back four women and six wounded men, one of whom soon died. Another party brought in a man—a white man! He said his name was Juan Ortiz. He had been with a group of Indians who fled as Baltasar de Gallegos, leader of the party, approached. Naked, feathered, and painted like his companions, Ortiz had run forward with outstretched arms, crying to the lancer who was about to run him through: "For the love of God and the holy Mary, don't kill me!" The lancer, astonished at hearing these words from one who he thought was an Indian, stayed his lance, while Ortiz explained in halting Castilian—he had not used the language for eleven years—that he came of a good family of Seville and that he was the last survivor of Narváez's expedition. Gallegos escorted him to Soto, who embraced him and supplied him with a suit of soft velvet, a suit of armor, and a good horse.

He told a story so strange that the Spaniards gaped in amazement. The chief Ucita, who bestowed his name on his village, had captured him and tied him to the stake to burn him. But Ucita's daughter, like Pocahontas with Captain John Smith, took pity on his sufferings and begged for his life. The chief spared him, but made his life so miserable that he longed for death.

Fertile in methods of torture, Ucita put Ortiz to watch the Indian burial grounds from the wolves and lynxes that infested the region. The corpses reposed in rough boxes on scaffolding. Ortiz on the very first night heard the pad of feet, the clatter of scattered timbers, the crunch of bones. He ran swiftly in the direction of the noises and aimlessly threw one of the four darts that Ucita had given him. Next morning the Indians found the corpse of a little boy and, a little farther on, a dead wolf with a dart in its side. Ortiz, learning that the dead boy was the son of one of the chiefs, expected death. Instead Ucita began to treat him with grudging tolerance. Some time later Ortiz again found himself in imminent peril. Ucita told his daughter he wanted to sacrifice Ortiz to appease one of the many evil spirits. Again the girl saved Ortiz' life by warning him and even protecting him while he made his escape. He took refuge with Ucita's enemy, Mocozo, who treated him kindly. And when the Spaniards appeared, Mocozo, keeping a promise he had made to Ortiz, allowed him to return to his people. He was on his way to join them when he met Gallegos' scouting party.[9]

Ortiz told Soto that he had seen neither gold nor jewels, but that he had heard of a rich country about ninety miles inland. He sent Gallegos with fifty horsemen and twenty or thirty footmen to a nearby chief, Paracoxi, who told him of a province called Ocale that was so rich that its warriors wore golden hats like casques. By this subterfuge the Indians were certain of ridding themselves of their unwelcome guests. The gold-crazy Soto sent all his ships save a few pinnaces back to Cuba for more provisions which would enable him to prolong his stay in Florida. Preceding or accompanying the ships went Vasco Porcallo de Figueros.

This quixotic fellow, who boasted he could count more gray hairs on his head than could any other member of the expedition, had come out to capture slaves for his mines, but swamps and forests had rendered his mission futile. His inability to pronounce the name of one of the villages, Hirihigua, intensified his conviction that Florida was no place for him. His soldiers heard him murmur to himself: "Hurri, harri, hurri, higa, burra coja, hurri, harri, may the Devil take the land where the first and most continuously spoken names I have heard are so vile and infamous."[10] Some readers of this book may sympathize with him.

On August 1 Soto marched northward toward Ocale, leaving at Tampa a small force under Pedro de Calderón and food for two years. The procession, which included five hundred fifty lancers, crossbowmen, arquebusiers, a number of priests and Dominican friars, pigs, and two hundred horses, advanced over low and thicketed country full of bogs and swamps. The horses, weighted down with armor and heavily accoutred riders, mired and floundered. The men crossed several small rivers on logs while they swam their horses. The sows had farrowed. Their refractory piggies, scattering in all directions, forced on the horsemen and dogs a ragged and disorganized advance. One day a rabbit started up in the long grass and stampeded the horses. The laughing and singing adventurers quickly recovered them and called the tract of water where the incident took place the Lake of the Rabbit.[11]

The next few days sobered and then depressed them. Under the blazing sun several of the foot soldiers collapsed, and one man died of thirst. But a little farther on they cheered when they saw maize in the fields. They noisily set about making bread, pounding the corn in wooden mortars with a pestle and, when it became flour, sifting it through their shirts of mail.[12]

When they neared Ocale, their leader, impatient to ascertain what treasure, if any, could be found there, rode recklessly ahead with an escort of only ten men. They found no trace of gold. So they turned to making their corn into flour. Feasting on freshly baked bread and opossums, which Elvas described as "little dogs that do not bark," they stayed in Ocale until August 11. Then they resumed their march, arriving on August 18 in Caliquin, which, they learned, Narváez had visited eleven years before. Dispirited by that leader's ill-starred expedition, they begged Soto to return to Cuba. Soto's reply was as cryptic as it was emphatic: he would not go back until he had seen the rich country which, he believed, lay near at hand.[13]

Soto now first employed the policy of obtaining possession of the local chief and of keeping him as a hostage. One day Gallegos rode out with bloodhounds to capture Indians to serve as guides and rounded up seventeen of them. Among them was a young daughter of the chief. Her father, a handsome, young, and magnificently built warrior arrayed in all of his savage panoply of head feathers, soon appeared and requested that his daughter be freed. In reply, Soto persuaded him to accompany the expedition until it should reach the next province. But at the next village the chief's subjects requested Soto to release him. He put them off by explaining that their chief was a guest, not a prisoner. Unsatisfied with this explanation, the Indians laid secret plans to rescue the chief.

The minor chiefs begged for a parley to discuss the matter further—a ruse which, Ortiz explained to Soto, gave them time to conceal their best bowmen in the long grass around the village and, at a signal from the hostage, to kill the white leader and his men. Soto aborted this ruse by concealing his horsemen, each armed and mounted, in his own lodging; then he gave them orders and waited for the Indians to attack.

The Indians, numbering four hundred, stationed themselves in the forest that surrounded the village and sent two of their men to Soto to ask him again to release their chief. In reply, Soto took the chief by the hand and, accompanied by six foot soldiers, one of whom was a trumpeter, approached the Indians as though he intended to give him up. At this juncture one of Soto's officers, Luis de Moscoso, who impatiently awaited his signal, saw suspicious movements in the tall grass and, without waiting for the blast of the trumpet, shouted the war cry of the Spaniards: "Santiago! Up and at 'em!"

Mounted on Azeituno, his spirited white stallion, Soto with his men charged the Indians, who had now collected on the plain, and routed them before most of them could string their bows. A moment later, however, Azeituno, riddled with arrows, thumped with his master to the ground. Soto rose uninjured and raced to battle. A few Spaniards were wounded. Some of the Indians jumped into one pond and some into another, where they concealed their heads under water lilies. That night some of the Spaniards observed the phenomenon of water lilies slowly and silently moving shoreward over the moonlit surface of the water. They rushed into the water up to their horses' breasts and drove the Indians back. Next morning Soto's native guides whacked the Indians on their heads with paddles and pulled them by their hair out of the water. Spanish forges never worked so busily as on that day.[14]

Undeterred by their failure, the Indians soon hatched a new plot. One day the chief, who had been exempt from menial labor and even enjoyed the privilege of sitting with Soto at table, suddenly punched him with full force in the face, bathing his teeth in blood. This was the signal for revolt. The chief sprang upon Soto to strangle him but instead received from him such a punch on the nose that blood flowed profusely into his mouth and down his chin. With cudgels and hammers and cooking pots and pestles the Indians, howling for blood, bashed out the brains of four soldiers before their comrades could quell the revolt. To discourage any other rebellious attempt on the part of the Indians, Soto made a frightful example of his captives. He turned the young braves over to those of his soldiers who had good chains and could be trusted. The older braves he condemned to death. He had these wretches taken out into an open space in the middle of the camp where, at his com-

mand, his Ocale Indians shot them down with arrows. One gigantic warrior seized his captor, Saldagna, by the neck with one hand and a thigh
with the other, lifted him above his head, and dashed him to the ground.
He would have stomped Saldagna to death had not halberdiers finished
him off. Even so, he found a nobler death than had his comrades.[15]

4

The bruised army limped ahead. On October 6 it reached the province
and village of Apalache, whence Narváez had, twelve years before,
turned toward the sea. Finding the village rich in maize, pumpkins, and
other vegetables, Soto made it his winter quarters. He sent out a party
under Juan de Añasco to bring up Calderón and his small force from
Tampa Bay. At about the same time, he dispatched Francisco Maldonado
to find a suitable port to the west. Maldonado eventually returned with
a story that terrified everybody save Soto. He reported that he had discovered a beautiful bay—Pensacola Bay—but also traces of a stark tragedy. There along the shore by amethystine waves he saw glistening white
objects scattered like heaps of pearls in the sun. This was the Bay of
Horses, and the glistening white heaps were the bones and skulls of the
mounts that Narváez and his men had been forced to slay. The discovery
greatly depressed Soto's men. Were they destined to a similar fate? Even
though Narváez had been a brave soldier, had he not perished with all
but two of his men? Soto's followers, filled with fear, implored him to
turn back. His answer was characteristic; he would find the golden country he sought or, failing in that search, would perish rather than return
to bear the possible humiliation of seeing himself outdone by some other
conquistador who, by greater perseverance, might discover another Peru
or Mexico in the great interior. So he sent Maldonado to the pinnaces
that remained at Tampa Bay, with instructions to sail to Havana for
more provisions and to meet him at a designated time during the summer
at Pensacola Bay.[16]

On March 3, 1540, Soto left Apalache for Cofitachequi on the Savannah River, probably at or near present Silver Bluff, South Carolina. Toil-
ing through swampy country and across the Ockmulgee, the Oconee,
and the Ogeechee rivers, they passed a number of Indian villages that
seemed great improvements over those they had recently seen. Elvas
describes one of these villages as he gives a vivid picture of Indian
society:

> The houses of this town were different from those behind, which
> were covered with dry grass; thenceforward they were roofed with
> cane, after the fashion of tile. They were kept very clean: some have
> their sides so made of clay as to look like tapia. Throughout the cold
> country every Indian has a winter house, plastered inside and out, with
> a very small door, which is closed at dark, and a fire being made within,

it remains heated like an oven, so that clothing is not needed during the night time. He has likewise a house for summer, and near it a kitchen, where fire is made and bread baked. Maize is kept in a *barbacoa*, which is a house with wooden sides, like a room, raised aloft on four posts, and has a floor of cane. The difference between the houses of the masters, or principal men, and those of the common people is that, besides being larger than the others, they have deep balconies on the front side, with cane seats, like benches; and about are many *barbacoas*, in which they bring together the tribute their people give them of maize, skins of deer, and blankets of the country. These are like shawls, some of them made from the inner bark of trees, and others of a grass resembling nettle, which, by threading out, becomes like flax. The women use them for covering, wearing one about the body from the waist downward, and another over the shoulder, with the right arm left free, after the manner of the Gypsies: the men wear but one, which they carry over the shoulder in the same way, the loins being covered with a *bragueiro* of deerskin, after the fashion of the woolen breech-cloth that was once the custom of Spain. The skins are well dressed, the color being given to them that is wished, and in such perfection, that, when of vermilion, they look like very fine red broadcloth; and when black, the sort in use for shoes, they are of the purest. The same hues are given to blankets.[17]

On May 1 the Spaniards arrived at Cofitachequi. Soon they saw approaching a young girl whose easy dignity of bearing excited their admiration. She announced that she was the niece of the *cacica* or princess who ruled the province. She explained that her aunt had remained at home to prepare for their reception and informed them that a canoe would soon arrive to carry their leader across the river. Soto made a courteous reply, and the girl returned to her aunt.[18]

The princess, being every inch a woman, quickly changed her mind. Instead of allowing Soto to come to her, she decided to go to Soto. Carried on a chair, which was covered with delicate white cloth woven from mulberry bark, the red-skinned Cleopatra appeared before her Antony in rich furs and feathers. A pearl necklace wound thrice around her neck. Her men of state stood around her, and behind them was a fleet of canoes laden with gifts for the visiting prince. Soto was so enchanted by her beauty, intelligence, and grace he never thought of asking her name. She made a speech of welcome, unstrung her largest pearls one by one, and made a sign to the interpreter, Ortiz, to give them to Soto. Ortiz suggested that the pearls would receive added luster should she agree to give them to him with her own hands. She replied with sweet coyness that her sex forbade such levity. This further enchanted Soto. He assured her through Ortiz that presenting the pearls to Soto as a ceremonial gift, as a sign of good will, would never besmirch her modesty. She smiled, rose from her seat, and approached Soto, who gracefully accepted the string of pearls. Then he drew off a ring and presented it to her as a sign of peace. She accepted it with disarming grace.[19]

In turn, she lavished on the strangers all the comforts she commanded. She put half of her houses at their disposal; she sent them wild turkeys, dried venison, maize, walnuts, and mulberries; she presented them with blankets and furs. Soto remained unsatisfied. He asked her about gold and silver. She replied by having some ores brought in. Much to his disappointment, he found that she had mistaken copper for gold and mica for silver. Yet he found some consolation. One of his soldiers caught a pearl between his teeth while he was eating an oyster. The man offered the pearl to his leader who, however, declined it, telling him to buy horses with it when they got back to Havana. He asked the princess about pearls. She replied that, should he care to open the burial grounds, he would find many more and that, in some deserted towns nearby, "he might load his horses with them."

Soto took her at her word. He immediately went with his secretary and chronicler of the expedition, Rodrigo Ranjel, to the burial grounds, which yielded him three hundred fifty pounds of pearls woven together in the figures of babies or birds. But the two men also saw something that made them gasp with shock. What did their disturbed eyes fall upon? Relics of Ayllón's expedition—Biscayan axes of iron and rosaries of jet beads! The pearls, however, quickly restored their equanimity.[20]

Still Soto was not satisfied with loads of pearls. He wanted gold; he wanted a treasure such as he had found in Peru; he wanted the satisfaction that comes with success; he wanted to shine before his countrymen, before his beloved Isabel, before his king. He therefore frowned on the proposals of his men to begin a colony on the site of Cofitachequi. He decided to move on to the rich province of Chiaha, which the princess had described to him. Though she had treated him with courtesy, with unfailing kindness, he planned to take her along to use her authority to secure carriers and to keep them after he had secured them. Here was an odd, perhaps a demented man, who placed mere pearls and gold above all else; the princess felt that no good could come from him; she planned to shake him off as soon as she could. She knew too well how difficult was the role he would ask her to play. When she declined his invitation, he put her under guard and forced her to march on foot with her female slaves. Elvas disapproved of such ungallantry; he wrote of it in his journal for all future ages to read.[21]

Marching on an Indian trail along the Savannah River, Soto and his men reached Xuala, perhaps in the extreme northwestern part of Oconee County, South Carolina. When he found no gold there, he became so disgusted with the region that he turned sharply north and crossed the Blue Ridge Mountains into Cherokee country. By this time the princess had managed to escape. One day, obtaining permission to go behind the bushes for a moment with her slaves, she took off with "a cane box, like a trunk, full of unbored pearls." Soto, perhaps feeling some compunction for having forced her to accompany him, let her go. Elvas later learned that she was living with an escaped Negro slave as his wife.[22]

Leading his men along Cullasaja Creek to the Little Tennessee River, which he crossed near Franklin, or possibly, at Nicholas Ford, Tennessee, Soto reached Guasili, a town on the Hiwassee near the mouth of Peachtree Creek. Thence they continued southwestward to Chiaha, on the Tennessee River, where they were hospitably received by its chief. Still searching for gold, they hastened their departure southward to Tali, then to Coosa, the chief town of the Lower Creeks, on the river of the same name.

In October they came down the Alabama River to the province of the Mobile Indians and met the chief of the tribe at a town in the upper part of Monroe County, Alabama. He was a giant, perhaps seven feet tall, with a fine and comely figure. Sitting under a large umbrella made of deerskins quartered red and white so skillfully that it looked from a distance like taffeta, the chief, who gave his name as Tuscaloosa, received one of Soto's officers, Moscoso, with contemptuous gravity and with eyes downcast. Soto then approached him and attempted to dissuade him from his attitude by taking him by the hand, drawing him to his feet, and addressing him felicitously as he sat with him on a bench. In vain—the chief retained his sulky demeanor even when the Spaniards tried to entertain him with jousting and horse races. His only show of civility was a grumbling permission to some of his subjects to perform dances which, says Ranjel, "were very much in the fashion of rustics in Spain."[23]

At nightfall the chief prepared to depart, but Soto detained him and asked him for carriers. The chief scoffed at the idea that he, lord of all the region, should be restrained; men served him, he said haughtily, rather than he served men. To which Soto replied by taking him into custody.[24]

Tuscaloosa became Soto's most formidable enemy. While the chief made a show of conciliating his captors by furnishing them with four hundred carriers, he secretly sent messengers to summon his braves. The trusting Soto gave him a scarlet cloak, some buckskins, and a heavy-boned horse that could bear his great height and weight. Most Indians were terrified by horses, for they had never seen them. Not so Tuscaloosa—he mounted the horse with fierce joy, as though he were riding a lion or a tiger. The reaction of the animal must have been somewhat different; it had never known a rider whose feet almost touched the ground.[25]

Tuscaloosa planned to entice Soto to the fortified village of Mabila, which stood perhaps between the Alabama and Tombigbee rivers in present Clarke County, Alabama, where he could more effectively deal with him and his men. He promised him another hundred men and women as soon as they should arrive in that village. But this time Soto was a little wary; he sent a few soldiers to ascertain the temper of the Indians in Mabila. When, on October 18, Soto arrived in the village,

Moscoso met him outside the stockade and informed him that the Indians planned trouble—that they had concealed a large number of weapons and warriors in the houses. Soto could see for himself that the Indians had demolished the outer fortifications to make room for a clear field and to leave the Spaniards no cover should they try to storm the place. Despite Moscoso's warning, Soto rashly entered Mabila with a few officers, soldiers, and a couple of priests. No sooner had the Spaniards stepped into the stockade than Tuscaloosa posted sentinels at the two narrow entrances to prevent their departure. At the same time, he attempted to conceal his belligerent intentions by having fifteen women dance native dances. Then, suddenly assuming his blatant arrogance, he demanded immediate release. Soto replied by requesting the promised porters and servants. Whereupon the chief jumped to his feet and, shaking off Soto's placating gestures, stamped off to confer with the other chiefs.[26]

After giving him ample time to return, Soto sent two men to bring him back. Tuscaloosa bellowed a refusal to them. On returning, they noticed that cabins were crowded with braves, and they advised Soto to retire while he could. Needless to say, Soto refused. At this juncture Gallegos tried to detain one of the minor chiefs by holding onto his cloak. The chief slipped the garment over his head and left it in Gallegos' hands as he continued on his way. His Latin dander up, Gallegos, with sword in hand, ran after the chief. As the chief still refused to stop, Gallegos slashed at him, lopping off an arm. Then he darted into the cabin in which Tuscaloosa had retired and attempted to drag him out. Moscoso, understanding the difficulty of his friend's task, attempted to help him; but, seeing the cabin filled with braves, he backed to the door, shouting: "Baltasar, come out, or I shall have to leave you. I can't wait any longer." On hearing the noise, the Indians swarmed out. Soto and his men ran for one of the entrances. Before Soto could reach it he fell or was knocked down. His men rescued him while they desperately cut their way outside, where two horsemen, Ranjel and De Solís, reinforced them. Then all of them charged the Indians back. Ranjel received twenty arrows in his quilted doublet, but Gallegos and Moscoso managed to escape unharmed through one of the entrances. Meanwhile, Soto attempted to rally his men, but he gathered so few of them that he was forced to withdraw to the plain. When the Indians pursued them, the Spaniards pretended flight, luring their foes into the open field. There they wheeled their horses around and charged their pursuers. By this time Soto had succeeded in collecting his men in four divisions of infantry with which he surrounded the village, while behind them he posted his cavalry at various points to cut off any Indians who tried to escape.[27]

They plied axes against the stockade and then set it on fire, while the Indians shot arrows down on them. Several times the besiegers pressed through gaps they had made only to be beaten back by the raging valor of the defenders or by a strong wind blowing in their faces. Again and again they swung their axes; again and again they banged themselves against the stockade. Sweat streamed down their bronze and bearded and agonized faces and mingled with blood as they exerted themselves around a circle of flames. After several hours of this exhaustive fighting, they withdrew in order to drink at a nearby pond. They could taste the gore that tinged the water.[28]

Late that afternoon the Spaniards succeeded in getting far enough inside the stockade to apply their torches to the huts of wood and straw. Instantly the flames leaped up, forcing into the streets those who had been shooting from the lofts. Women of all ages and boys as young as four fought in their frenzy beside the desperate warriors of the tribe or hanged themselves or leaped into the blazing huts rather than be captured.[29]

In less than an hour the village was a mass of smoldering ruins. Still the Indians showed no sign of surrendering. So Soto brought up his cavalry which hacked its way into the enclosure with lances, swept from end to end, and returned. But the Indians kept shooting from the height of the stockade until the halberdiers brought them down. An arrow pierced as neatly as an augur through the wooden lance of one of Soto's officers, forming a cross with it without splitting it. Another arrow whizzed into Soto's buttock but he had no time to pull it out. Standing in his stirrup, he continued to lead his men.[30]

Spanish lance and saber and fire eventually triumphed over Indian bravery. Hardly a native escaped unscathed. Just before nightfall the last three defenders came out with the women who had danced for Soto that morning. They crossed their wrists to show that they were ready for manacles; they made signs to the soldiers to advance and take them prisoner. But, as soon as halberdiers went forward, the three warriors jumped to one side and began shooting at them. The halberdiers killed two of them. The remaining Indian ran back, clambered on the stockade, whipped the cord from his bow, tied it around his neck, and, leaping forward, hanged himself.[31]

Soto lost twenty men in this battle. One hundred forty-eight others received nearly seven hundred wounds by Indian arrows. About two thousand Indians perished, including Tuscaloosa and his son, who was nearly as tall and strong as the chief. Hundreds of other natives, though wounded, managed to crawl to the safety of the high bushes that surrounded the village.

The conquerors stayed a month in Mabila, recuperating from their wounds, which they dressed with the fat of the dead Indians. Word soon reached Soto that Maldonado had returned from Havana with ships and provisions to Pensacola Bay, six days' journey away. Instead of rejoicing at this information, Soto kept it to himself. He feared not death but defeat—feared that his troops would mutiny should they learn of Maldonado's presence nearby; feared the possibility of losing his prestige and of becoming a laughingstock before his countrymen and, even more humiliating, before his king, should he return to Cuba without gold and silver; feared, in short, of taking the misstep that would ruin the flattering image he had drawn of himself. Maldonado waited his appointed time and then sailed to Cuba, bearing no word of its governor and only silence to Doña Isabel.[32]

On December 9 Soto moved northwestward across the Black Warrior River and, a week later, across the Tombigbee River to a Chickasaw village in the present state of Mississippi, where, finding abundant fruit, he went into winter quarters. One night three Indians stole into his camp and killed his hogs. The Spaniards caught and killed two of the thieves and cut off the hands of the other and sent him back to the chief. At about the same time, Indians caught four Spaniards burglarizing some huts. Severe with friends and enemies alike, Soto condemned two of the Spaniards to death and deprived the other two of their properties. At the last moment, however, Ortiz saved the lives of the condemned men by subtly translating the complaints of the robbed Indians into pleas of mercy.[33]

5

In March, 1541, Soto, about to resume his journey, asked the Chickasaws for male carriers and women. The Chickasaws, "considering this an insult to be wiped out with blood," surprised the Spaniards in their camp during the night and set the camp on fire. The Spaniards, bewildered by the noise and blinded by the smoke and flames, ran in all directions as they tried to find their arms or to put saddles on their horses, some of which snapped their halters and stampeded or were burned to death in their stalls. By now the confusion was so great that the Spaniards fled; but God, says Elvas, favored them by temporarily depriving the Indians of their vision, thereby rendering them unable to discern what they had done and making them believe that the beasts "running about loose were the cavalry gathering to fall upon them."

Soto, mounting his horse, struck down one of the Indians with his lance; but, having forgotten in his haste to tighten the girth of his saddle, he soon fell, though he was not hurt. Eleven Spaniards and fifty horses perished. Many of the men were naked and suffered cruelly from the cold. They passed the night mumbling curses as they lay tossing and turning in their efforts to keep warm by great fires. The shivering and hungry army soon left for the next village, where they busied themselves making saddles and lances from ash and grass mats to protect their naked bodies from the cold.

Early in May they advanced to present Sunflower Landing in northwestern Mississippi, a level country of many marshes and thick woods. One day their complaints lessened, their spirits brightened, and their eyes widened with excitement and admiration. Before them flowed a magnificent river! It was the largest river they had ever seen in the New

World. It was swift, muddy, and very deep; it swept down in its wide path huge masses of driftwood from countless prairies; it contained such fish as the Spaniards had never seen in any of the rivers of their native land. Elvas wrote that the river was so wide that a man standing on one bank would be unable to distinguish a man from a beast on the other. Soto admiringly called it El Rio Grande de la Florida, meaning the Great River of Florida. The Indians, with their gift for metaphor, called it Mississippi, Father of Waters.[34]

Soto's adventures west of the Mississippi are not germane to this volume and will be told in few words. Like the knight in Poe's poem, he continued his feverish search for Eldorado, even though it should take him over the Mountains of the Moon and down the Valley of the Shadow. Marching into the present state of Arkansas, he reached the province of Pacaha, near the mouth of the St. Francis River, whose chief he found at war with the chief of Casqui. Soto conquered Pacaha, reconciled its chief with the chief of Casqui, and entertained them at dinner. The chief of Casqui rewarded Soto by giving him his daughter. Whereupon the chief of Pacaha did his erstwhile rival one better by giving Soto two of his sisters, whom Elvas describes as symmetrical, tall, and buxom. With these damsels to temper his anxiety with temporary joy, Soto pushed on westward to the province of Tanico, near Hot Springs, Arkansas, and then, turning southeastward, marched to or near the present towns of Arkadelphia and Camden, where he decided to spend the winter. Rain or snow, which fell almost continually, made travel dangerous—almost disastrous. Furthermore, Indians in the villages through which he had just passed told him that the village in which he sojourned, Autiamque, lay near the sea. By now he had remaining only about three hundred men and forty horses. Some of the mounts were lame and made a poor show of cavalry; some, for lack of iron, had gone without shoes for over a year. In the spring Soto planned to march to the sea, where he would build two brigantines, one to be sent to Mexico and the other to Cuba for the purpose of informing his wife and his friends of his whereabouts and of obtaining funds from the sale of some of his property to refit another expedition. Fortunately, Autiamque, which its inhabitants had abandoned at Soto's approach, furnished the Spaniards with plenty of food—more maize, beans, walnuts, and persimmons than they could eat. So, with the help of their shackled slaves, they busied themselves for the next three months building a high palisade around their camp, hauling wood for fires, and trapping rabbits to supplement their vegetarian diet.[35]

Early in March, 1542, Soto broke camp and led his men in what he thought was the direction of the sea. In the ensuing five weeks they experienced much misery and privation. Juan Ortiz had died in Autiamque, depriving Soto of his only medium of communication with the natives. Sometimes the Spaniards became entangled and lost in thickets; sometimes, in their endeavor to find a ford, they wandered up and down and retraced their steps for several days; sometimes snowdrifts impeded their progress or halted it altogether. At last they arrived at Guachoya, a village perhaps near Ferriday, Louisiana, on the Mississippi River. Soto sent Juan de Añasco with a small group of men down the river, to try to ascertain the distance to the sea. Eight days later, Añasco returned to tell him that he had seen no sea but only miles and miles of the river's tide, bayous, and swamps. Not even the Indians he had captured on the way could tell him of any sea.[36]

So Soto's dream of Eldorado was dashed on the rocks of reality. His failure to find gold was to him a great bereavement. His body gradually wasted away, while his spirit sank lower and lower under a fever of torment. Then, suddenly, he regained his old temerity. From his straw pallet he dispatched to the neighboring chief a message calling himself the Child of the Sun and demanding carriers and provisions.

The chief replied that the Child of the Sun should be able to dry up the river between them. "Then," said the chief, "I will believe you. . . . If you desire to see me, come where I am; if for peace, I will receive you with special good will; if for war, I shall await you in my town; but neither for you nor for any man will I set back one foot!"

Soto, burning with fever, could only curse his weakness. By now full realization of failure had combined with physical debility to set off paranoid feelings; he became convinced that the defiant chief and the neighboring Indians planned to destroy him, and he resolved to strike the first blow. At his command his soldiers fell on the unsuspecting natives. The screams and cries of women and children deafened the Spaniards, who cut down a hundred warriors and allowed scores of others to escape with severe wounds that might strike terror into those who had concealed themselves. Amid this horror Hernando de Soto, the fearless conquistador, the proud *adelantado* of Cuba, sank pitifully toward death. On May 20, feeling that the end was approaching, he called a meeting of his officers and, with their full approval, chose Moscoso to succeed him. Then, having made his last will and confession, he died.[37] Destiny had raised him high only that it might all the more cast him down.

Fear of Indian uprisings forced the Spaniards to give the Child of the Sun a secret burial. Telling the Indians that he had ascended to the sun, they took his body out in a canoe to midstream where, under cover of darkness, they let it sink to the bottom. A whispered order and one deep answering note from the water—was this a fitting requiem for Hernando de Soto?

Moscoso and his men wasted no time in deciding to reach Mexico by land. Crossing Louisiana into Texas, they marched into the country of the Naguatex Indians, then swept southward across the Trinity River, only to abandon his plans at the approach of winter in favor of returning to Guachoya, where Soto had died. Resolved to descend the Mississippi, they built seven brigantines, in which they sailed on July 3 for the sea. Reaching it seventeen days after their departure, they sailed down the Gulf of Mexico to the mouth of the Pánuco River, one hundred fifty miles north of Vera Cruz. Antonio de Mendoza, who had succeeded Cortés as viceroy of New Spain, received them warmly and offered them the hospitality of the country. At last, dressed in deerskins dyed black and carrying their packs on their backs, they reached Mexico City, where they went directly to church to give thanks for their preservation and to partake of the sacraments which had long been denied them.[38]

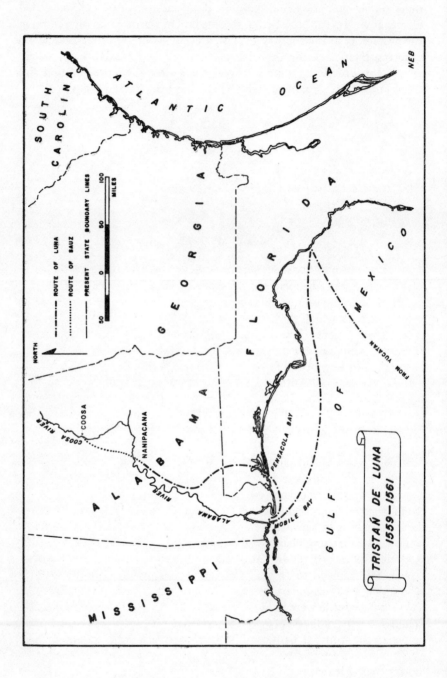

Florida: Stage of Spanish Tragedy

THE PERILS AND PRIVATIONS WHICH MOSCOSO AND HIS COMPANIONS EN-dured by no means dampened their ardor for recounting their adventures and even enlarging on them. Everywhere in Mexico City they spun webs of adventure in which they imagined themselves enmeshed. They glamorized Ortiz' rescue; they dwelled with flights of fancy on the princess of Cofitachequi and her pearls; they painted glowing pictures of Coosa, where they had been well fed, and where one or two of them had dallied with Creek damsels. Antonio de Mendoza was so anxious to extend his sway over Florida that he offered Moscoso funds to fit another expedition. Moscoso refused. The Northern Mystery may have inspired his imagination, but it proved inadequate to stir his feet one step in that direction.[1]

Since Charles V had failed to seize Florida by the sword, he planned to conquer it by the cross. He perhaps implanted this idea in the mind of Fray Luis Cancer, a devout and learned Dominican who was living in the convent of Santo Domingo in Mexico City. Here he heard stories of the hundreds of Indians Cabeza de Vaca and Soto had enslaved. Perhaps he heard the clanging chains of slavery as loud as if he had been present. Doubtless he was stirred by stories of faith preached by fire, sword, and rapine. He resolved to free the natives from Spanish oppression with God's love. As a missionary, first in Española and then in Puerto Rico, he had seen how futile were his attempts to spread religion in regions swiftly depopulated by ruthless conquerors. So he had gone to Guatemala, where he began the study of native languages under Bishop Bartolomé de Las Casas, who had established himself there with a small band of Dominican monks from Mexico.

Las Casas taught Fray Luis more than declensions and conjugations in the Indian languages; he taught him something of wisdom and patience and love, something of spiritual teaching "that went beyond a mere reverence for crosses and recitations of Aves and Paters, such as was, alas! at times the only missionary equipment of his less gifted companions."[2]

At that time one of the provinces of Guatemala was known as *Tierra de Guerra*, meaning Land of War, because its inhabitants were so fierce and warlike that they had forced the Spaniards to return three times "with their hands up to their heads." This province Las Casas, Bishop of Chiapa, determined to conquer, "not in corselet or mail and with the clash of swords," but with cross in hand and "feet shod with the preparation of the Gospel of Peace." That he might work unimpeded toward this goal, he persuaded the governor of Guatemala to forbid the province to Spaniards for five years. Then he sent Fray Luis, who meanwhile had learned the language of the natives, to request the chief for permission to come there. Along with his gentle words Fray Luis brought little gifts, trinkets, mirrors, and beads of bright colors, which he knew would bring delight to the chief and his people.

The chief readily assented. And the Land of War eventually became the Land of the True Cross, where no Spaniards lived save a few Dominican monks, and where Indians morning and evening chanted sacred songs to the accompaniment of the same flutes and drums that formerly had aroused them to frenzy against their white enemies. For this spiritual conquest Fray Luis received the title of *Alvarez de la Fé*, meaning Standard Bearer of the Faith.[3]

But Fray Luis was not satisfied to remain a standard bearer in a peaceful land. He longed for a country that presented a formidable challenge. So he went to Mexico City, where he could find the latest reports of newly discovered lands. The stories Cabeza de Vaca and Moscoso told him impelled him to bear his standard to Florida.[4]

2

Fray Luis found kindred spirits in three monks of his own Order, Gregorio de Beteta, Juan García, and Diego de Tolosa. Ignorant of direction and distance, Fray Gregorio and Fray Juan had made three or four unsuccessful attempts to reach Florida by land. Now they were ready to try again by sea, and Fray Luis decided to capitalize on their enthusiasm before it cooled. Encouraged and accompanied by Las Casas, he went to Spain to obtain royal permission to realize his ideal. Thanks to his zeal and to the influence of Las Casas, permission was soon granted. He was authorized to establish a mission at some point in Florida where Spaniards had not spilled Indian blood and to return to that region the Indians whom Soto had enslaved and whom Moscoso had scattered in various parts of Guatemala.[5]

In 1548 Fray Luis embarked from Seville and arrived with surprising speed in Vera Cruz, where Viceroy Mendoza received him gladly and, in compliance with royal orders, gave him a ship and all he needed for his enterprise. In the following year Fray Luis in company with Fray

Gregorio, Fray Diego, Fray Juan, and a lay brother named Fuentes, sailed from Vera Cruz. At Havana he took on board a converted native girl named Magdalena who was to act as his interpreter and guide.[6]

In the evening of Ascension Day the ship, searching the shore for a port, anchored in the vicinity of Tampa Bay. Despite the hostile demonstration of some Indians, Fray Luis and Fray Juan and Fuentes went ashore in a small boat and passed the night on an island a little distance from the mainland. They made a fruitless search for a suitable harbor, then returned to the ship, which sailed back to the first landing place. No place in Florida could have been more unfortunate. The natives there had never forgotten Soto and his cruelties and had vowed never to give another white man an opportunity to repeat them.[7]

As the Spaniards entered the bay they saw some empty huts and behind them a forest in which nothing stirred. Fray Luis, seeing and thinking no evil, permitted Fray Diego and Fuentes and Magdalena to land. As Fray Diego climbed a tree to survey the country, one Indian after another until they numbered fifteen or twenty ran out of the forest. Disregarding the pilot's warning, Fray Luis, fearing that the Indians would slay Fray Diego, sprang into the water up to his belt. Reaching the beach, he fell on his knees and asked God for grace and assistance. Then, seeing the Indians approach, he took out of his sleeves some of the trinkets he had brought, for, he wrote later, "deeds are love and gifts shatter rocks."

The gifts pleased the Indians. They allowed the monks and Fuentes and Magdalena to kneel among them and begin the litanies. To Fray Luis' joy, the Indians kneeled or squatted also. When the litanies were only half over, the Indians rose. Fray Luis, too, rose and sat down with them in a hut, where they told him of a harbor about a day and a half's journey away. Reassured by their actions, Fray Luis saw no harm in permitting Fray Diego, Fuentes, and Magdalena to remain with the Indians and journey to the port by land. He himself returned to the ship for more presents; but when he came back he found no trace of his comrades. He searched for them until sunset, then returned to the ship. Next morning he resumed the search with Fray Gregorio, but they found that the Indians had disappeared. Returning dejectedly to the ship, they sailed for the harbor of which the Indians had spoken, hoping that their friends had preceded them there. An inexperienced man, the pilot took eight days to find the harbor and eight more days to enter it.[8]

On Corpus Christi day Fray Luis and Fray Juan went ashore and celebrated Mass between them. Next day Fray Luis and Fray Gregorio again searched for their friends in vain. They were about to return to the ship when they saw an Indian coming out of the woods. He was carrying as a token of peace a rod topped with white palm leaves. Behind him was another Indian who called in broken Spanish: "Friends, friends; good, good."

As the Indians approached the monks they made signs with their hands, while they called out: "Come here, come here; sword, no; sword, no."

"We are good men," Fray Luis tried to say in their language.

Apparently they understood him, for they shouted back the words. The two monks cautiously approached, received the rod with the palm leaves, and requested the Indians to give back their friends. The Indians agreed and the friars returned to the ship.[9]

Next day all three friars went ashore. Indians waded out to them, bringing fish to trade for trinkets. One of them begged from Fray Luis a small wooden cross, kissed it reverently, as he had seen the monks do, and hurried with it to a woman. She, too, kissed it and passed it on to other Indians. Fray Luis, wading inshore, discovered that the aforementioned woman was none other than Magdalena. He had not recognized her because she had removed her clothes and had rejoined the tribeswomen. She told Fray Luis and Fray Juan, who had just come up, that their comrades were safe in the chief's house.

Full of joy at the expectation of recovering Fray Diego and Brother Fuentes, the three friars returned to their ship, where they learned to their sorrow that Magdalena had lied. Juan Muñoz, one of Soto's soldiers who had remained in captivity among the Indians, had escaped from his master and had reached the ship in a canoe in the absence of the friars. Now he explained to them in Spanish, which he had almost forgotten, that the Indians had killed Fray Diego and Fuentes; yes, he added, he himself had held Fray Diego's scalp in his hands![10]

The friars shook with alarm. They implored Fray Luis to forsake his mission; they reminded him that the ship was leaking, that their fish and meat had spoiled and had been thrown overboard, that their drinking water was scarce, that so many of the crew were down with fever, that the sailors were ready to mutiny, and that some of them were willing to take the ship ashore. All these pleas were vain. Where his comrades had fallen, replied Fray Luis, there he would remain, there he would gather the fruit of his labor, there he would win over the Indians to the true faith.[11]

He spent Monday, St. John's Day, writing letters and perhaps adding the introduction and final paragraph to that portion of his journal on which this narrative is based. Tuesday a storm, in which Muñoz saw the intervention of God, prevented Fray Luis from landing. Wednesday, sailors brought the boat to shore, despite lashing winds and roaring waves. The friars and Muñoz saw Indians grouping on the bank around the slope of the beach. Ignoring Fray Gregorio's entreaties, Fray Luis began his preparations to land.

"Is the slave there?" called the Indians.

"Here I am," replied Muñoz, standing up in the boat that was about to take them to shore. "Do you want to kill us as you have killed the others? You will not kill us, because we know what you have done."

At this the Indians became confused.

"Be silent, brother," said Fray Luis to Muñoz, "do not provoke them."

"No people in the world could be more enraged than they are," said Fray Gregorio to Fray Luis. "For the love of God wait a little; do not land."

But Fray Luis would not listen. Throwing himself into the water, he soon reached land. He called for a small cross he had forgotten in the boat.

"Father," said Fray Gregorio, "for God's mercy, will not your Reverence come for it, as there is no one here who will take it to you, for these people are a very evil lot."

Instead of returning to the boat, Fray Luis, his eyes filled with the vision of heaven, walked along the beach toward a hillock where the Indians had gathered. As he approached them, he threw himself on his knees and prayed for a few moments. Then he began to climb the foot of the hillock. An Indian came forward, embraced him, and, taking him by the arm, urged him forward. Indians surrounded him and pushed him to the foot of the hillock. One of them snatched his hat, another struck him in the head with a club and knocked him down.

"*Hay vala*," cried Fray Luis. He was about to say more when a blow and then another interrupted him forever. The Indians then sent a shower of arrows against the boat, but it managed to escape.

Unwilling to remain any longer in those parts, Fray Gregorio urged the pilot to sail for another region on the Florida coast. The pilot refused, saying that the ship was unfit for a new voyage. So they set sail for Havana, but, acting on the advice of the pilot, they steered for Mexico instead. On July 19 they reached Vera Cruz.[12]

3

In 1555 Emperor Charles, depressed by political and diplomatic reverses and tortured by arthritis, gout, syphilis, and indigestion, resolved to interpose a little religious contemplation between himself and the grave. "Fame," he muttered as he abdicated and sought a Spanish monastery, "is a whore who reserves her favors for the young."

His son and successor to the Spanish throne, Philip II, was a meager man with bandy legs and a puny chest. His body was like a human cage which, however small or narrow, contained a soul that would have felt pinched even on a flight to heaven. Charles loved action and achievement; Philip indulged repose. Philip showed all the vices and none of the virtues of his father. He imagined that the world revolved on his windy proclamations. He concealed a paucity of thought under a plenitude of verbal obscurity. To a correspondent who awaited him in the next room, he wrote a lengthy letter on a subject that a man of sense would have answered in six words. He welcomed ambassadors—only to answer their questions with monosyllables. A religious bigot, he hated Protestants more intensely than his medieval forefathers had hated Jews and Moors. Yet he was unworthy even of his religious ardor. While during the day he affected an air of piety and regal dignity, at night he often disguised himself as a peasant and stole away to spend many hours in some bawdy house.[13]

Philip inherited his father's power and dreamed his father's dream of crushing the Reformation. Instead it spread. The enterprising Huguenots, whom Philip called "Lutheran heretics," became more and more powerful in the domestic policies of France. They soon threatened Spain's possessions in the New World. Year after year they sailed in increasing numbers between French ports and Newfoundland. Some of them were pirates who preyed on Spanish shipping. They sacked Spanish ports in the islands; they darted down on Spanish treasure ships; they invaded Havana and seized Chagres on the Isthmus of Panama. The ships of a Huguenot mercantile firm in Dieppe once attacked a Spanish treasure fleet from Peru, capturing nine of its ships. The remaining ships brought to Seville a paltry 280,000,000 maravedis or something less than £2,000,000.

To protect its vessels from sea robbers, the Spanish government in 1543 adopted the fleet system or armed convoy under command of an admiral and a vice-admiral. The fabulous amounts of precious metals brought home from Mexico and Peru necessitated an escort of an armada of from eight to sixteen and, eventually, as many as ninety galleons. But even formidable convoys failed to stop the French from raiding Spanish settlements. In 1554 while France and Spain were at war, François le Clerc—better known as Pié de Palo, meaning Peg-Leg—and his intrepid Huguenot lieutenant Jacques de Sores pillaged Santiago de Cuba, collecting 80,000 pesos in booty. Next year Peg-Leg surprised Havana and, after wringing every possible jewel and coin from its inhabitants, destroyed the port.

In view of these events Philip II justly feared that large portions of his New World possessions might readily fall into the hands of French heretical seamen. On their way to the Azores and Spain his slow-moving treasure ships from Mexico and Cuba sailed past Florida through the Bahama Channel, which Ponce de León had discovered in 1513. Philip feared that the French would, in case of war, plant a colony on the Florida coast near the channel so that they could seize any Spanish vessels that came in sight. He proposed to preclude such a possibility by colonizing the peninsula.[14]

Despite the failure of Father Cancer's mission Philip II resolved to continue his policy of conquering Florida by the cross. In this endeavor, Luis de Velasco, who had succeeded Mendoza as viceroy of New Spain and who showed his humanitarianism by freeing fifty thousand Indian slaves in his first official act, received strong support from the archbishop of Mexico and the bishop of Cuba, whose diocese included Florida.

In 1555 the archbishop of Mexico beseeched Emperor Charles V by letter to provide and command "by such means as may appear most just, that Florida and her people come to the knowledge of their creator, since we have it so near at hand, and know the numberless people which are lost therein from having none to preach to them the Holy Gospel."

Next year the sober-minded and somewhat pacific viceroy urged Philip, now king of Spain, to reduce Florida to the faith. At about the same time the more practical bishop of Cuba suggested that, since native wives were now scarce in Cuba, the Florida damsels should be brought over to Havana to fill the need, for, he said, the destruction of the native population by the whites had gone so far that "an Indian who could get a wife eighty years old thought himself in luck."[15] Conditions seem to have changed somewhat since the New World was in its swaddling clothes.

4

These authoritative and persistent appeals intensified Philip's plans to colonize Florida against possible French occupation. Toward the end of 1557 he ordered Velasco by letter to appoint a governor for Florida "to the end that the natives thereof who are without light of the faith may be illuminated and instructed in it, and that they and the Spaniards who reside in those lands . . . may become established and have homes and means of living." Philip also pointed out that "the French came quite near to Santa Elena nearly every year to buy from the Indians gold, pearls, marten skins, and other things." In view of this danger he ordered an expedition to colonize Florida at two points, one undesignated and the other at Santa Elena on the present South Carolina coast.

Philip entrusted this task to Velasco who, desiring more definite information than he had yet received about Florida, sent Guido de las Bazares with three vessels and a party of sixty soldiers and sailors to select a harbor and to reconnoiter in the region of Santa Elena. Bazares discovered Mobile Bay, which he named the Bay of Filipina in honor of the king and which he recommended as a suitable port. The severity of the winter season forced him to give up his plans to explore the South Carolina coast. He promptly returned to Mexico.[16]

In the first half of the following year Velasco completed preparations for the voyage. As leader of the expedition he chose Tristán de Luna y Arellano, who had been Coronado's second in command in the Cíbola enterprise eighteen years before. A wealthy man, Luna was able and ready to put up his own money to augment the generous appropriation soon to be made by the king. He was, moreover, "a very worthy Christian, a man of clean life, and a servant of his Majesty." He counted also the esteem of the highest officials in New Spain for his character and goodness of person.[17]

During the first half of 1559 Luna completed preparations for the expedition. The flattering reports that survivors of the Narváez and Soto expeditions had spread throughout the country had attracted hundreds of volunteers to the new enterprise. At last, early in May, it departed in great splendor for Vera Cruz, where thirteen ships awaited to transport it to its destination. Led by Velasco, it advanced in regular marches along high mountains and down the coastal valleys, its magnificent chain consisting of five hundred cavalry, arquebusiers, shield-bearers, crossbowmen, one thousand colonists and servants, monks, many women and children, and a number of Florida Indians who had come to Mexico with the escaped Spaniards of former expeditions. Some of the two hundred forty horses in the expedition carried ammunition and supplies of corn, biscuit, bacon, dried beef, cheese, oil, vinegar, and wine. Tools for building and digging, axes and mattocks for the farmers, and cattle for breeding—Viceroy Velasco had included everything that he believed necessary to assure a glorious success for the expedition and of course for himself.[18]

On June 11, with salvos and prayers and the royal standard flashing in the breeze, they sailed away for present Pensacola Bay, which Maldonado had discovered during Soto's expedition nineteen years before. For seventeen days the fleet enjoyed fair weather; then contrary winds blew them to the reefs off the northeast coast of Yucatan and killed one hundred of their horses. They threw the dead animals overboard and headed northeast for the Florida coast. Refurnished with water, wood, and grass, they sailed westward to Filipina Bay, only to return to Pensacola Bay, which Luna believed the better of the two harbors. No storm, he boasted, could damage his ships in such a well-protected port. Furthermore, they saw no trace of Indians save for a few miserable fishermen's huts along the shore.[19]

This propitious beginning encouraged Luna to choose a high point overlooking the harbor as the site of his first settlement. Here he would build a large town; here he would erect a palace with a battlement which would face a gate at each of the approaches to the city and would protect the people in case of attack. He sent one of the galleons to Mexico to inform the viceroy of his safe arrival and to request him to send more horses and supplies. Mindful that he had provisions for only eighty days, he sent out two parties to search for food. One party, led by two captains and accompanied by the vice-provincial, Fray Pedro de Feria, went up the Escambia River, which flowed into Pensacola Bay. The other, which included two officers and Father Domingo de la Anunciación, advanced by land. Finding nothing of value to the expedition, both parties remained in the interior longer than the three or four days they planned to spend there. When they ran out of provisions, they trudged painfully back to camp.[20]

But their hunger and failure proved only the prelude to innumerable misfortunes. Dire tragedy soon befell them in Pensacola Bay. On the night of August 19, less than a week after their arrival, a terrific hurricane broke over the harbor which Luna and his pilots had declared free of hazard and destroyed the ships with great loss of life. It smashed to pieces five of the larger ships, a galleon, and a bark, killing many men, women, and children. One of the caravels, flung like a chip of wood by an angry hand, landed in a grove of trees more than the distance of a cannon shot from the edge of the sea. The colonists, hurrying to examine the stranded vessel, found not a pin missing from her cargo. Father Anunciación opined that the storm could not have swept the caravel so far. This, he said, was clearly the work of demons. Whereupon many of the terror-stricken sailors swore they had seen evil spirits striding the low, racing, black clouds.[21]

The colonists lived on the cargo of the stranded caravel. Luna wasted no time in sending four companies of cavalry under Mateo del Sauz to explore farther inland than the earlier parties, while he himself stayed with the rest of his party in the vicinity of the harbor. Sauz marched his men through a desolate and uninhabited wilderness until he came to the large and deep Alabama River. They passed a few settlements along its banks to a much larger village, Nanipacana, where they found maize, beans, and other vegetables.

In the fields that surrounded the village they encountered a few Indians whom they summoned and treated with kindness, giving them ribbons and glass beads. Through interpreters they learned that Soto, seventeen years before, had partly destroyed the village and driven away its inhabitants. After exploring the neighborhood Sauz sent sixteen of his men to inform Luna of what had happened. Having eaten all his food and having suffered a fever from the miasmic climate of the gulf coast, Luna was happy to depart with over a thousand colonists by land and water for Nanipacana, leaving a lieutenant with fifty men and Negro slaves to hold the port.[22]

5

When they arrived in Nanipacana, which Luna renamed Nanipacana de Santa Cruz, they learned that its inhabitants had fled with most of their food supplies. Within a few days the colonists devoured the small amounts of corn Sauz had uncovered. Then they kept alive by eating acorns, a painful diet even when ground and soaked first in salt water and then in fresh to lessen the bitterness. Some of the sad-eyed mothers roamed as far afield as their strength and daring permitted, gathering leaves and twigs of trees with which to succor their crying and distressed children. To alleviate these dire circumstances, Luna, in the spring of 1560, sent Sauz with a hundred and fifty infantry to search for food in Coosa, which the Indians had described as a rich province to the north. Fathers Anunciación and Domingo de Salazar went along as spiritual advisers. For forty-three days, averaging less than six miles a day, they trudged through barren country, sustaining themselves with some herbs and blackberries which were beginning to ripen, some nuts, and some intolerably bitter acorns. Some of them, finding the leaves of the trees unedible, boiled and ate the leather straps of their accoutrements, while others ate the lining of their shields and their boots, "not a sorry mouthful at such a pass." Some died of starvation, some of the poison grasses they had eaten. Since famine would confront them in Nanipacana as well as on the journey, they plodded on through the uninhabited pine barrens and sand hills of present southern Alabama, sometimes following an Indian trail and sometimes marching aimlessly. In June they came to a grove of chestnut and walnut trees which provided them with an abundance of nuts. Giving thanks to God, the tatterdemalion party toiled on in better spirits to a town near a large river, perhaps the Coosa, in present Coosa County, Alabama.[23]

Unwilling to alarm the town's inhabitants, they camped on its outskirts, where they later built bowered shelters. Next day Sauz sent interpreters to greet the Indians and give them presents. To this benevolence the Indians responded by bringing them maize, vegetables, and fruits. The Spaniards in turn assured them that they intended them no harm; that, on the contrary, they wished to treat them kindly. But the Indians, having had some painful experiences with Spaniards under Soto, were suspicious of their hungry guests. To get rid of them, they resorted to the trick of decking out one of their fellow villagers as an ambassador from Coosa and sending him to the Spaniards. Carrying a wand adorned with elegant feathers as a symbol of peace, the sham ambassador invited them to his country. They were completely deceived. Greeting him lavishly, they followed him until, on the following day, he vanished. The Spaniards then recognized the fraud but decided to continue their journey. Within a few days they arrived at Coosa, a town of thirty huts on the Coosa River, in present Talladega County, Alabama.[24]

The Indians showered the Spaniards with hospitality. Provided with maize for themselves and their horses, the Spaniards sojourned there for three months while Father Anunciación and his companion "tried to admix something of religious instruction" among their hosts who, however, remained entirely unimpressed. At that time they were thinking only of war with the Natchez, their traditional enemies whose villages lay along the Yazoo River. The chiefs held a parley and then asked Sauz to assist them against the Natchez. Sauz was so impressed by one of the chief's eloquence that he gave him two captains, fifty foot soldiers, and some horsemen. The tireless Father Anunciación accompanied them.[25]

Next day some three hundred braves, armed with bows as tall as themselves and carrying quivers of feathered arrows tipped with poisoned flints, assembled before their headmen in a formation of their own conception. Suddenly the headmen raced headlong through the Spanish camp and Indian squadrons to the chief, lifted him on their shoulders and, howling and shrieking, carried him to the steps of a platform that rose nine feet high near the camp.

The chief mounted the platform and paced to and fro with grave solemnity while his braves grouped themselves below. One of his attendants handed the chief a fan of multicolored feathers with which he pointed three or four times toward the province of the Natchez in the manner of one taking an altitude of the sea. The attendant then handed him some seeds which he placed in his mouth. Once more he pointed with his fan in the direction of the Natchez as he ground the seeds between his teeth. Then, spitting the seeds out as widely as he could, he cried: "Friends, be comforted, for our expedition shall be a success, our enemies shall be vanquished, and their forces shall be destroyed like these seeds I have crushed in my mouth." Amid shouts of approval he descended the platform, mounted his horse, and rode at the head of his braves against his enemies.[26]

Eventually they arrived at a great river in the vicinity of a large village. The chief requested his Spanish auxiliaries to omit the customary evening trumpet call for the Ave Maria so that he might surprise the village; but on entering it he was disappointed to find that its inhabitants had fled. In the middle of the town he found a stake around which were scattered skulls and scalps of Coosa warriors. These ghastly trophies of Natchez victories so incensed the Coosa chief and his men that they ran like madmen through the village, looking for any object on which they might wreak their vengeance. In one of the huts they found a Natchez who had been unable to flee because of illness. They bloodied him with clubs. Father Anunciación, seeing him near death, tried in vain to convert him. The battered Indian paid no heed to him whatever, thereby "surrendering his soul miserably to the devils who had borne away those of his forefathers."

The Coosa next set fire to the town, only to extinguish it when Spaniards protested that it would destroy their food and threatened to desert them. That night the Indians celebrated their victory with dancing, singing, and discordant flute-playing. To the Spaniards in Coosa the chief sent a quantity of maize, so that they could witness the promising rewards of courage and the good fortune of their ally.[27]

Leaving a garrison of Spaniards and Indians in the village, the war party advanced rapidly but found no trace of their enemies in the wilderness. The chief explained to his Spanish auxiliaries that the Natchez feared them and had fled to safety to their villages on the faraway Yazoo or even across the Mississippi River. The Coosa and their white allies pursued the Natchez to the great river and frightened them into submission with their show of strength. The Natchez agreed to pay tribute to the Coosa who, moderating their indignation, negotiated with them.

The Coosa chief, who had remained on the other side of the river with Father Anunciación and other Spaniards, majestically received the Natchez leaders and heard their disculpation in which they laid their errors to bad counselors, asked for pardon, and promised to be friends thereafter. The chief pardoned them, saying that the Spaniards had recommended clemency and mercy, and accepted their offer to pay a tribute of chestnuts, walnuts, and other fruits to the Coosa three times a year. So the Coosa and the Natchez patched up their differences without much bloodshed.[28]

6

The victorious war party returned to Coosa. Sauz sent Captain Cristóbal Ramirez y Arellano, Luna's nephew, with ten cavalry and six infantry
to Nanipacana while he himself, with the rest of his troops, remained in
Coosa, where food was abundant. Twelve days later Ramirez and his
men sighted Nanipacana. They fired two volleys from their arquebuses
to give notice of their approach. Receiving no answer, they wondered
whether their friends had been killed or had gone elsewhere. Looking
around, they found broken barrels and cases and a Spaniard hanging from
a tree. Believing that the colony had fallen to Indian treachery, they withdrew to a hillock for the night.

Next morning they entered Nanipacana to find it deserted. On a tree
they saw a notice: DIG BELOW. Following this direction, they unearthed
a jar that contained an account of occurrences in the colony during their
absence and its decision to return to Pensacola Bay. Rejoicing that their
friends were still alive, they marched briskly to the harbor, a journey of
one hundred twenty miles which they accomplished in just three days.
The colonists greeted Ramirez and his men with embraces and shouts
of joy.[29]

At Nanipacana the colonists had indeed endured great suffering. Starvation and disease had demoralized them to the extent that Luna had to
apply severe punishment for all kinds of disorders. The married soldiers
had drawn up a formal petition in which they bewailed their misfortunes
and pointed out that, since the Indians appeared unwilling to accept
Christianity, the venture was a failure. Luna had commanded them in
the name of the king to keep silence under penalty of death; but the discontent continued and soon embraced the entire colony.

Touched by heart-rending appeals and the pitiful truth behind them,
Luna had called his staff into a desperate council of war at which they
eventually agreed to return to the port. No sooner had they arrived
there than Fray Pedro de Feria obtained from Luna permission to go to
Havana and, if necessary, to Mexico for necessary supplies. Doubting
that Fathers Salazar and Anunciación were dead, Feria left for them a
box containing a little flour with which to make sacramental wafers. The
priest sailed with two small ships, taking with him all the other monks
and some married soldiers who had left their families either in Cuba or
in Mexico. A few days later they arrived in Cuba to find that its governor
had no supplies to give them. But he gave them a ship in which they proceeded to Vera Cruz, thence to Mexico City.[30]

7

In their miserable camp at Pensacola Bay, most of the colonists, sick
as well as sound, openly expressed disgust with the expedition and spoke

with determination of returning home. Luna was just as determined to remain. From Sauz he received letters requesting him to march with the colonists to prosperous Coosa. But the colonists, championed by Jorge Cerón, the camp master, flatly refused to go, saying that they were too weak from hunger and that they lacked food and arms for the journey. Cerón advised Luna to send a single captain with twenty-five or thirty men to get food. The leader countered by condemning them for their laziness and negligence and by insisting that they all proceed to Coosa. Luna said:

"If I return to Mexico, people who have assured the viceroy that the province of Coosa is most fertile will demand proofs of its barrenness which I must either produce or lose my honor. Will I be able to uphold it if I refer merely to those letters which describe the land as being more uncultivated than poor, or if I quote the soldiers who have returned and are at variance according to their individual character? I want to go personally to Coosa to disillusion myself so that I may disillusion others, and learn the reason either for the change or for the deceit which has been practiced. Who can persuade himself that Spaniards would remain there if it were as bad as it has been painted?"[31]

To which Ramirez, who had gone over to Cerón against his uncle, replied:

"So miserable is the province of Coosa that it could not support the two hundred Spaniards if the spoils of the war with the [Natchez] had not produced a plenitude of maize, beans, and bear grease. Before that, in order to live, we gathered up all the maize in the territory, but it was not enough, for the Coosa as well as ourselves suffered intense hunger. Some of the barrenness can be attributed to depopulation—in fifty leagues there is no considerable settlement. Those which are to be discovered are so small that they resemble scattered hovels rather than villages. Thus we see that the province of Coosa is extolled in New Spain for no other reason than that it is distant. And I am certain that if it is decided the army must go there, everyone will perish, for it is impossible to withstand the adversities of such a march."[32]

Luna replied that the two hundred soldiers in Coosa could not have stayed where they were had they been worse off than the colonists at Pensacola Bay. As soon as Coosa consumed all its provisions, he said, they could advance to the province of the Natchez which according to reports had an abundance of fruit. But Jorge Cerón and his followers, who had conceived a dread of Coosa and a corresponding love of Mexico, lost no opportunity to discredit their leader and surreptitiously sent messengers to recall the soldiers under Sauz. Meanwhile, Luna had issued an edict commanding everybody to be ready to march toward Coosa; but Cerón and his mutineers constituted the majority and easily flouted it.

In November, amid growing irritations and useless recriminations, Sauz and his men arrived at Pensacola Bay after an absence of seven months. With him were Fathers Anunciación and Salazar who had failed to Christianize the Indians. Only one dying Indian woman had requested baptism from Father Salazar. While they deplored the absence of the other monks, they deplored even more the dissension between Luna and Cerón. They failed in all their attempts to bring them together. On Palm Sunday, 1561, Father Anunciación confessed himself and prayed for peace. Luna, Cerón, and the soldiers gathered to celebrate the solemnity of the occasion and Father Anunciación began to say Mass. Before consuming the Blessed Sacrament he turned to the congregation, holding the Host upright above the paten. Amid the expressions of surprise at this novelty Father Anunciación paused; then, his eyes filled with tears, he lifted his voice and asked Luna to come forward. The governor rose at once and went in front of the altar, where he remained kneeling in expectation of what Father Anunciación required of him.

"Do you believe that this Blessed Sacrament, which I hold in my unworthy hands, is the true body of Our Lord Jesus Christ, Son of the Living God, who descended from heaven unto earth to redeem us from the power of sin and the Devil?"

Astonished by this proceeding and ignorant of what was intended, Luna replied: "I do believe it."

"Do you believe that this same Lord will come again to judge the living and the dead so that He may reward the good and punish the bad?"

"Yes, I believe it."

"Then if, as a loyal and true Christian, you believe in the Real Presence in this Blessed Sacrament of the Supreme Judge of us all, how, without fear of His judgment, do you permit the existence of the many wrongs and sins which offend Him and which we have suffered and wept over for these five months past? It is your duty as the superior to correct them and to read in your heart whether hatred, disguised as zeal for justice, plays any part in your indignation. The last ray of the Divine Light which you have before you will allow you to distinguish between the two emotions. You witness the innocent perishing along with those you hold guilty, and you wish to combine the punishment of some with the injustice you inflict upon the others. How will you be able to explain yourself on the terrible day of Judgment if to your own detriment you abhor and rob all of us of the peace for which, for the sake of men, God made Himself man? Do you wish to deprive us of this felicity and further the artifices of the Devil, the Father of Discord?"[33]

He said more, full of spirit and doctrine, in which he urged harmony. He spoke so effectively that no sooner had he turned toward the altar with the Host than Luna, deeply touched, rose and retired to hear the remainder of the Mass. After the Holy Sacrifice Luna stood up, gazed around at the people in the church, and said in a loud voice:

"Gentlemen, from the time I left Mexico, I have not intended to offend anyone; I have endeavored only to discharge the obligation under which the king has here placed me to the best of my judgment, which is based upon the wisdom of others wiser than I. However, if in the present dissension I have been at fault, with all my heart I now ask your pardon for the wrong which malice or my own ignorance may have caused, and I pardon any who may have offended me."[34]

With these words he burst into tears which served like ink to write and sign his pardon. Cerón knelt down before Luna and tearfully asked him for forgiveness. The officers followed with expressions of loyalty and love, "whose fire," says Dávilla, "had ignited not only the straw, but also the wood, which the devil had cut from the mountain of mercy." The reconciled colonists began immediately to devise a remedy for their miserable condition, but they were so demoralized, so famished, and so sick that they were unable to arrive at a decision.[35]

Fortunately succor was at hand. Viceroy Velasco, heeding Father Feria's appeal, had sent Ángel de Villafañe to replace Luna and to move the colonists to Santa Elena, which Philip II thought more practical for his purpose than Pensacola Bay, for he wanted a "window to the Atlantic," where he could watch the French should they venture too far south of Canada. On Holy Tuesday, March 14, 1561, Villafañe arrived in the harbor with two ships. With him came Fray Gregorio de Beteta, who had been with Father Cancer to convert the natives of Carolina to Christianity. Villafañe provisioned the garrison at Pensacola and then set sail for Santa Elena. At Havana, many of his followers deserted him; but in May, with the remaining colonists he reached the Carolina coast. He explored as far as Cape Hatteras but found no site he considered suitable for colonization. So he abandoned the project and returned to Española in July. A ship was soon dispatched to remove the garrison left at Pensacola Bay.[36]

When he learned of Villafañe's failure, Philip II decided against any further attempts to colonize Florida for the time being. He was assured, "as to France, because the French as yet had not made any firm foot hold on American soil. The steady increase of French fishing vessels in Newfoundland waters failed to impress him. He could not foresee that not the pot of gold but the beaver was to lead to the solution of the Northern Mystery and to spread colonies from the Atlantic to the Pacific."

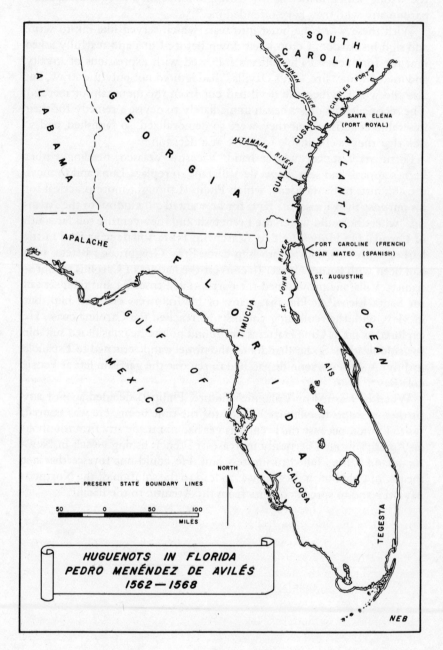

SOUTH CAROLINA

ALABAMA

GEORGIA

SAVANNAH RIVER

CHARLES FORT

CUSABO

SANTA ELENA
(PORT ROYAL)

ATLANTIC

ALTAMAHA RIVER

GUAL

APALACHE

FLORIDA

FORT CAROLINE (FRENCH)
SAN MATEO (SPANISH)

ST. JOHNS RIVER

ST. AUGUSTINE

TIMUCUA

GULF

OF

OCEAN

MEXICO

AIS

NORTH

CALOOSA

- - - PRESENT STATE BOUNDARY LINES

50   0   50   100
MILES

TEGESTA

HUGUENOTS IN FLORIDA
PEDRO MENÉNDEZ DE AVILÉS
1562 — 1568

NEB

The Huguenots in Florida

GASPARD DE COLIGNY, LORD OF CHATILLON-SUR-LOING AND ADMIRAL OF France, owned one burning ambition: to restore his country to her former glory. Civil war, rising from religious differences, had, during the past several years, destroyed her army, crippled her navy, and deprived her of her allies. Coligny planned to stabilize and then to strengthen her position among nations by wresting world supremacy from Spain. He hated that country not only because she had humiliated France but also because she had persistently intrigued against his co-religionists, the Protestant Huguenots.

Availing himself of the prolonged enmity between the French royal House of Valois and the royal House of Habsburg in Spain, Coligny, though leader of the Protestant party, was able to obtain the spiritual and financial support first of Henry II, then of Charles IX and other leading Catholics of France, in his scheme to seize the Spanish treasure fleets and to capture Santo Domingo, Nombre de Dios, Havana, and other Spanish possessions in the Caribbean. Such successes would enable him to establish in America colonies for Huguenot refugees. Unfortunately for this sect, the places he chose for his scheme were Portuguese Brazil and, later, Spanish Florida, in both of which they were trespassers. The Treaty of Cateau-Cambrésis between France and Spain in 1559 defeated Coligny's plans to attack the Spanish possessions in America, but it failed to lessen his determination to plant a colony in Florida under Jean Ribaut and, later, René de Laudonnière.

Early in 1562 one hundred fifty men, most of whom were Protestants and old soldiers, gathered at Havre in response to Coligny's call for volunteers. On February 6 they sailed in three small ships under Jean Ribaut, a skillful sailor and devout Protestant who three years earlier had served Coligny in a diplomatic mission which he fulfilled with honor to himself and to his country. Though they were journeying too late to encounter any danger from the outgoing Spanish fleet and too early from the returning one, he took the precaution to escape possible observation by avoiding the Canaries and the Azores, the customary route of the enemy ships. And, instead of making for the coast of Canada, he cut across the current of the Gulf Stream and, on April 30, reached the eastern shore of Florida a little north of the present site of St. Augustine.

Coasting northward, he found himself on the following day at the mouth of the St. Johns River, which he called the River of May for the month in which he had discovered it. In a boat he and a small group of his soldiers rowed to the shore where they met Indians who received them "with gentleness and amitie." Their chief delivered an oration and then presented Ribaut with chamois skins in token of friendship. Next day Ribaut erected near the mouth of the river a stone column on which were engraved the arms of France.[1]

Continuing northward, Ribaut passed nine "rivers," perhaps sounds or inlets along the Georgia shore, to which he gave the familiar names of the streams in his own country. And, while he journeyed, he entertained more Indian chiefs, one of whom, says Laudonnière, presented him with

> . . . a plume or fanne of Hernshawes feathers died in red, and a basket made of Palmboughes after the Indian fashion, and wrought very artificially, and a great skinne painted and drawen throughout with the pictures of divers wilde beasts so lively drawen and portrayed, that nothing lacked but life. The Captaine to show himself not unthankfull, gave him pretie tinne bracelets, a cutting hooke, a looking glasse, and certain knives. . . .[2]

At another place Indians greeted them by entering the water up to their armpits and bringing them "many baskets full of Maiz, and goodly Mulberries both red and white."[3]

Still sailing northward, Ribaut came to a "great river," present Port Royal Sound, South Carolina, which he believed was the Jordan that Ayllón had discovered and described thirty-five years before. He called this place Port Royal—a name it still bears. Three leagues up the sound, which at its mouth was three miles wide, Ribaut anchored his vessels and erected another column to indicate that the country was a French possession. Ranging the woods, they found them full of game:

> Turkeycocks flying in the Forrests, Partridges gray and red, little different from ours, but chiefly in bignesse. Wee heard also within the woods the voyces of Stagges, of Beares, of Lusernes, of Leopards, & divers other sortes of Beasts unknown to us. Being delighted with this place, we set our selves to fishing with nets, & we caught such a number of fish, that it was wonderfull.[4]

Ribaut's primary object was exploration, not immediate settlement. But so many of his men expressed their delight in having found such a

beautiful country that he decided to ascertain whether they were willing
to remain and hold Port Royal for their king. Mustering them on deck,
he pointed out that many men of lowly station had, by their virtues,
achieved wealth and fame. He recalled Aelius Pertinax who, though a
slave, had by his valor earned such admiration from his countrymen that,
step by step, he was able to make himself Emperor of the Romans. He
recalled, too, Agathocles, son of a simple potter, who from early manhood applied himself so diligently to military life that he became King of
Sicily, and who immortalized himself by commanding his servants to
serve him at table vessels of gold and silver and others of earth, thereby
showing that the dignity he enjoyed had come not from his father but
from his own genius.

   These inspiring words filled his men with enthusiasm. Scarcely had he
finished his speech than they came forward and eagerly offered their
services for the new colony. He selected twenty-eight of them, chose as
their leader Albert or Aubert de la Pierria, and built for them a long cabin
which he christened Charles Fort in honor of their king Charles IX. This
he surrounded with a bulwark, armed with eight pieces of artillery, and
supplied with ammunition and food for several months. Then he informed his followers of his intention to sail for France for more ships and
supplies, promising to return in six months. On June 11 they saluted his
departure with a salvo of artillery.[5]

2

   The French at Charles Fort quickly completed their defenses. Then
they began to explore around the rivers and swamps and forests, visiting
Indian chiefs who loaded them with presents and feasted them on
hominy, beans, and game. One of the chiefs, Audusta, invited them to the
religious festival of Toya, chief god of the tribe. They accepted eagerly.
Going to the village, they found groups of women sweeping the great
circular area where the ceremonies were to take place. The festival soon
got under way. The villagers, painted and trimmed with rich and multi-
colored feathers, marched to the chief's house, where they placed themselves under three Jawas or high priests who, dancing while singing a
lamentable tune and beating a drum, entered the circular area—only
to run like unbridled horses into the woods. During this ceremony,
Indian women wailed and cried while they gashed the arms of young
girls with sharp mussel shells and flung the blood into the air with dismal
yells of "*He Toya!*"

   To the Frenchmen these weird ceremonies were very funny; they
began to laugh—a sacrilege which the chief punished by shutting them
up in his hut. One of them, however, managed to escape and hid behind
a thicket, where he witnessed the entire performance. When it ended, he
approached an Indian boy and asked him by signs why the Jawas had run
into the woods. The lad replied that the Jawas had invoked Toya, sum-

moning him by magic to speak to him. The Indians ended the religious festival by ravenous feasting, which more than made up for the three days of fasting that preceded the festival. The Frenchmen, released from the hut, feasted with equal zest.[6]

They then returned to Charles Fort—and hunger. Again they applied to the chiefs; again the chiefs graciously fed them. But the land was too poor and the harvest too small for the chiefs to continue their generosity. They told the Frenchmen that two chiefs, Ovade and his brother Covexis, ruled in the south and that their domain abounded in maize and beans. Whereupon Pierria, the French leader, sent four soldiers in a small boat to Ovade, who received them graciously and loaded their boat with food. This plenitude, however, proved as fleeting as April snow. No sooner had they returned to Charles Fort than their house burned down so quickly that they were able to salvage nothing save a small quantity of maize. Audusta helped them build another house, but he could not provision it.

To arrest the possibility of starving, Pierria sent a few soldiers in a canoe to Covexis, who received them as courteously as had his brother. Not only did he provide them with food but assured them that, as long as his cornfields yielded harvests, they would not want. As a parting gift, he presented them with crystals, pearls, and some pieces of silver. In reply to their inquiry about the silver, he informed them that it had been extracted from certain mountains located within ten days' march from the province.[7]

Rejoicing at the prospect of wealth, they returned to Charles Fort, only to learn that their comrades had mutinied against Pierria and had murdered him. With each adversity Pierria had grown harsher, until he began to threaten with death anyone who dared disobey him. Then he hanged a drummer who aroused his displeasure and banished La Chere, a fine and large soldier, to an uninhabited island three leagues from the fort where he left him to starve, though he had promised to supply him with food. At last the soldiers, seeing his violence increasing with each passing day and fearing for their lives, plotted to kill him. One of them whom Pierria had cursed and beaten for some imaginary offense ran him through.[8]

They rescued La Chere from his island, then chose Nicholas Barré, a sanguine and able man, as their new leader. He quieted dissension, dissolved rancor, and restored peace among them. But six months passed without any sign of Ribaut or the reinforcements he had promised to bring with him. The men grew restless, disgusted, depressed; they tried to escape the gloom of the forest and the thought of famine by dwelling on the cabarets, the dances, and the damsels they had known in France. They regarded Florida as a boundless prison. How could they escape it? How span the huge Atlantic to their freedom? Not one of them knew how to build a boat; but necessity, says Laudonnière, proved "maistresse of all sciences."

Ribaut had left them some tools. Putting them to use, they felled trees which they sawed, nailed, and pitched with pine oil. The Indians, anxious to get rid of them, furnished them with ropes and cordage twisted from the bark of trees. They made sails from shirts and bed coverings. Then they loaded the boat with the guns which had been left for their defense, their tools, and what ammunition remained to them, stored it to the best of their ability with provisions obtained from the Indians, and set sail for France. At last, fair winds filled their patchwork sails, permitting them to hold their course. But suddenly the wind died away; a breathless calm overtook rickety ship and ocean.[9]

For twenty days the ship stood on a still sea while provisions dwindled until each man was reduced to twelve kernels of corn a day. When the corn was gone they boiled and ate their leather shoes and jerkins and tried to slake their thirst with salt water and their own urine. Several men died. The survivors, though dizzy with exhaustion, though crazed with thirst, performed the endless labor of bailing out the water that gushed through every seam. Suddenly heavy winds rose and increased to a gale, tossing the helpless ship mercilessly among the monstrous waves, then throwing her on her side. The desperate voyagers, deluged with brine, clung to spars and cordage until the ship, as though by a miracle, righted herself. Then one of them begged his comrades to take heart: should the wind hold, he prophesied, they would see land within three days.

Encouraged by his words, the men waited for three more days without eating and drinking. Land failed to appear; they became more depressed than ever. In this extremity of despair they began to throw wolfish glances at one another, whispering that one of them should, by his death, rescue the others. Better that one should be eaten than that they should all perish. Eventually all eyes fell on La Chere, whose name, ironically, means Dear One and who, for all his starving on his island, was still a man of ample physique. They caught him, killed him, quartered him, boiled him, and ate him. Soon they sighted land. Crazy with delight, they allowed their ship to drift hither and thither with the tide. But a small English bark rescued them. Its captain gave them food and drink, landed the most feeble in France, and took the rest prisoners to Queen Elizabeth, who needed men for an expedition she planned to send to Florida.[10]

3

Ribaut's failure by no means discouraged Admiral Coligny in his plans to weaken Spain by planting a Huguenot colony in Florida. He planned another expedition, but before this could be launched circumstances in France forced him to turn his energies elsewhere. Civil war, fomented in the interest of religion, brought France to the brink of disaster. Coligny, embroiled in the fratricidal struggle, could give no assistance to Ribaut and his comrades at Charles Fort. Ribaut served in the war until the Peace of Amboise in March, 1563, when he went to England where he

sought and obtained an interview with Queen Elizabeth. Unwilling to
risk King Philip's displeasure, she refused Ribaut her immediate help but
encouraged him to undertake the enterprise himself, promising him half
of all he found and reminding him that Florida lay along the route of the
Spanish treasure ships. As an added inducement, she granted him a pension of three hundred ducats and a house.

Ribaut, anxious to succor his followers at Charles Fort, frowned on
delay. He joined and supported Thomas Stukeley, an English adventurer
who was preparing to sail for Florida with five vessels. When Queen
Elizabeth got wind of the enterprise and forbade it, Ribaut planned to
seize the vessels with the help of three French pilots and sail with them to
France. He was discovered, seized, and imprisoned.[11]

The advent of peace allowed Coligny to renew his efforts to colonize
Florida. Since Ribaut was still in prison, Coligny selected as commander
of the new venture René de Laudonnière, who had accompanied Ribaut
on the first expedition. Though Laudonnière was a skilled sailor, he
lacked Ribaut's firmness of character and presence of mind. On April 22,
1564, Laudonnière sailed from Havre with three ships, the *Isabella*, the
Little Briton, and the *Faulcon*, which were well armed to resist attack by
sea and to afford protection for the future colony. The colonists numbered three hundred, including one hundred twenty soldiers, one hundred
ten sailors, artisans of every description, servants for the soldiers, pages,
and four women, one of whom was to serve Laudonnière as chambermaid
and housekeeper. Four of the party were members of the French nobility
and four had been with Ribaut during the first expedition. Still another
member of the party was Le Moyne de Morgues, a gifted artist who gave
us a series of vivid pictures of the country and its inhabitants as well as
one of the most descriptive accounts of the expedition.[12]

The fleet skirted the English coast, turned south to the Canaries,
crossed the Atlantic to the Bahama Islands, and on Thursday, June 22,
struck the Florida coast in the neighborhood of present St. Augustine.
Finding the place unsuitable to his purpose, Laudonnière sailed south to
the St. Johns River where he and a few of his friends went ashore.
Saturiba, chief of the region, whooped and clamored a welcome. He conducted them to the sand knoll where stood the column Ribaut had
erected. The Indians held it in such reverence that they had crowned it
with evergreens and placed offerings of maize on the ground around it.
Arriving at the column, the Indians kissed it and invited the Frenchmen
to follow suit. Desiring to win their friendship, the Frenchmen did their
bidding.[13]

Saturiba then took Laudonnière by the hand, as though he wanted to
tell him some great secret, and showed him the neighborhood. At the
chief's request one of his sons presented Laudonnière with a piece of
silver. This delighted him so much that he returned to show it to the
colonists. Next morning Laudonnière, with a friend, Ottigny, and a
small group of soldiers set out to explore the region. They greeted

Saturiba who, dressed in a decorated deerskin and surrounded by his guard, sat under a great arbor. Then they sailed three leagues up the river to a bluff, where Laudonnière rested while Ottigny and the soldiers explored. What a delightful place for repose! The bluff was crowned with palms and cedars "as red as blood" and with bay trees so fragrant that, says Laudonnière, "balm smelleth nothing like in comparison." Beneath, through the shaggy boughs of the cedars, he could see the glistening sea fill the horizon. He thought the place so pleasant that "those which are melancholicke would be inforced to change their humour."[14]

Ottigny and the soldiers ranged the neighborhood until they met four Indians who invited them to their dwellings. The Indians carried Ottigny and a few of his comrades on their shoulders while the others walked a narrow trail that led straight to the dwellings. There the Frenchmen beheld a wonderful spectacle. In one of the huts sat a very old man who assured them that he was the father of five generations and that he was two hundred fifty years old! Opposite him sat his father, shrunken to a mere anatomy and seeming "rather a dead carkeis than a living body." His age was so great that

. . . the good man had lost his sight, and could not speake one onely word but with exceeding great paine. Monsieur de Ottigny having seene so strange a thing, turned to the younger of these two olde men, praying him to vouchsafe to answere him to that which he demanded touching his age. Then the olde man called a company of Indians, and striking twise upon his thigh, and laying his hand upon two of them, he showed him by signes, that these two were his sonnes: again smiting upon their thighes, he showed him other not so olde, which were the children of the two first, which he continued in the same manner untill the fift generation. But though this olde man had his father alive more olde then himselfe, and that both of them did weare their haire very long, and as white as was possible, yet it was tolde them, that they might yet live thirtie or fortie yeeres more by the course of nature; although the yoonger of them both was not lesse then two hundred and fiftie yeares olde.[15]

So wrote Laudonnière with Gallic ebullience. If Florida had no Fountain of Youth, it had at least the Garden of Eternal Life on Earth. Unfortunately, their morals failed to correspond to their gift of longevity. One of Laudonnière's comrades called them "the greatest thieves on earth, for they steal as well with the feet as with the hands."[16]

On returning to the mouth of the river, Laudonnière again saw Saturiba. How, asked the French leader, had he come by the piece of silver he had given him? Saturiba replied that he had taken it during a war with his traditional enemies, the Thimagoans, who dwelled several days' journey up the St. Johns. Pleased with the prospect of obtaining wealth, Laudonnière promised Saturiba military assistance against his enemies.

Then, returning to his ships, Laudonnière sailed up the coast in search of a suitable place on which he could build a fort. Near a bluff on a broad, flat knoll that rose a few feet above the right bank of the river, where it narrowed to less than a half-mile in width, Laudonnière found a spot almost inaccessible from the shore. Here he decided to build Fort Caroline, named in honor of his king, Charles IX. At daybreak his men, assembling at the sound of a trumpet, gave thanks to God "for our favourable and happie arrivall," sang a psalm, and started their duties.

Gradually the fort, in the form of a triangle, rose with a trench and turf battlements on the land side, a palisade on the river side, and a sand-and-fagot bastion which contained a magazine for the ammunition. Within the fort, on its river side, Laudonnière built himself a house, which had one door opening toward the river and another to the court of the palisade. With the assistance of Saturiba's warriors, who had come to watch the Frenchmen work, they thatched the fort and house with palm leaves in the native fashion. Seven pieces of artillery guarded the fort on its river sides. In an adjacent meadow Laudonnière built a bake oven, a storehouse, and several outhouses.[17]

4

Fort Caroline stood in a thickly populated region. All around dwelled the Timucuans whose influence and language extended through the center part of the peninsula. They were a tall, well-proportioned people with a complexion between olive and copper. Men and women went naked, protecting their bodies from the heat of the sun by rubbing them with cocoanut oil. The men, many of whom were corpulent, painted the skin around their mouths blue and tattooed their arms and thighs with a certain ink they extracted from an herb. They pricked the ink, which left an indelible color, into the skin with thorns. They trussed up their long hair on the top of their heads and wore loincloths made from tanned deerskins. The warriors wore feathers, leaves, or grasses around their heads or covered them with masks made of the skins of wild animals. They adorned their chests with engraved disks of gold and silver and painted on their faces red and black designs which in wartime gave them a fierce appearance. Though they practiced pederasty, they by no means neglected their "daughters of the sun," as they called their prostitutes. Their abstemiousness, even in festivity, greatly impressed the French, who attributed their longevity to it. Laudonnière thought them deceitful and treacherous, though he praised their courage in fighting.[18]

The women, who allowed their hair to grow down to their hips, were remarkably agile and strong. They climbed trees rapidly, could swim in broad rivers while each carried a child, did their household chores, planted corn, and participated in public ceremonies. During pregnancy they lived apart from their husbands, eating only bread untouched by man. Both men and women allowed their toenails and fingernails to grow long. They sharpened their fingernails to points so that they might dig them into the foreheads of prisoners or tear skin down over their faces to wound and blind them. They pierced the lobes of their ears through which they passed small oblong fish bladders. These they dyed red and then inflated. Among the Timucuans were many hermaphrodites who carried the provisions when the Indians went on the warpath, transported the sick, cared for those who had contagious diseases, and prepared the dead for burial.[19]

The chiefs, who were called *paracusi* in peace time and *urriparacusi* in war time, were united in a number of confederacies under a supreme chief. The tribes were constantly warring with one another. Saturiba was quick to realize the advantage of enlisting the support of the Frenchmen in his feuds with other chiefs.

Among the most influential members of Timucuan society were the shamans, who combined the functions of the physician and the magician. They consecrated the arrows used by warriors and hunters, induced rainfall, found lost objects for their owners, recited incantations over ears of corn, piles of beans, and baskets of fruit, foretold the future, and cured the sick with incantations and herbs and drugs which they carried in a jug. The shaman cured certain ailments, such as indigestion, by puffing furiously on his pipe and producing billows of smoke that passed through the nose and mouth of his patient and made him vomit. The shaman cured other diseases by cutting with a sharp shell into the skin of the forehead of his patient, sucking out his blood and spewing it into an earthen or gourd receptacle. Pregnant women drank the blood of young men to strengthen their milk and to make their unborn children brave and energetic.[20]

On certain days, especially with the coming of warm weather late in February or early in March, the shamans met with their chief in a public place to deliberate on important matters. As soon as the supreme chief sat down on the projecting chair that served as his throne, each of his shamans approached and saluted him twice while with uplifted hands he exclaimed: "Ha, he, ye, ha, ha!" and blessed the assembly and a potation of *casina*, an intoxicating but nourishing beverage made from the leaves of a certain root which was strained and served hot. The chief drank first, then the others in succession according to their ranks. The councils which followed were very deliberate and well advised. In urgent matters the chief always consulted his shamans.[21]

The Timucuans knew no personal God. They worshiped only what they saw and could understand: the moon and the sun. The annual sun worship, which they celebrated at the end of February just before they planted, was a colorful and solemn ceremony. They killed the largest stag they could find and skinned it neatly, keeping its horns intact. Then they stuffed the skin with choice roots and hung the horns, neck, and body with long garlands of delicious fruits. Amid music and song they carried the stuffed and adorned skin to a meadow or valley, where they hung it on a high tree, with its head and breast toward the sunrise. The chief, standing with his shaman under the tree, offered prayers to the sun, beseeching it to bring to their lands such good things as those they now offered it, while the common people, standing somewhat apart, made their responses. Then the chief and the worshipers saluted the sun and departed, leaving the deer's hide there until the next year.[22]

The Timucuans practiced human sacrifice. On the day of the sacrifice a firstborn son was led to the sacrificial altar before which his mother knelt and covered her face with her hands in sorrow. Her principal female friend or relative then offered the child to the chief while the women who attended her danced with demonstrations of joy in a circle around the stump. The woman who held the child danced in the middle as she sang the praises of the chief. The official of the sacrifice, who was dressed in rich feathers, stood amid five attendants. As soon as the dancing ceased, he stepped up to the sacrificial altar where, in the presence of the assembly, he sacrificed the child.[23]

Timucuan superstitions were numerous and unrelieved by civilized humor. The person who drank out of another's cup after eating bear meat never fell sick. A body tremor indicated that somebody was coming or that something was about to happen. The hooting of an owl brought luck. A quick whistle ended a storm. Women washed themselves with a certain herb to recall an absent husband. They induced men to fall in love with them by coloring their palm-leaf hats with a certain vegetable dye and propitiated the moon and sun by exposing corn at the door of their houses and by refusing to eat the first fruits or the first ear of corn of the first harvest gathered from a newly cultivated field.[24]

Monogamy was the general practice. A chief sometimes allowed himself two or three wives, though he willed his belongings only to the children of his first wife. Widows selected some occasion on which they approached their chief with loud demonstrations of sorrow and called on him to avenge the deaths of their husbands, to support them in their widowhood, or to permit them to remarry after the period of mourning expired. When they received his assent, they went to the burial place, cut off their long hair below their ears, and scattered it over the graves of their husbands together with weapons and drinking-shells of the dead. They were forbidden to remarry until their hair had grown long enough to cover their shoulders.[25]

The chief who wished to marry selected the tallest and most beautiful of the daughters of his principal men. Four men brought her to him on a litter which they carried on their shoulders and which was covered with skins of wild animals and canopied with palmetto leaves and boughs. On each side a man shielded her from the sun with large screens or fans. In front trumpeters blew on instruments made of bark hung with oval balls of silver, gold, and tinkling brass. Behind walked a small number of beautiful girls, dressed in skirts made of pendent Spanish moss and adorned with pearl necklaces and bracelets, each of whom carried a basket of fruit. Behind them came the bodyguards.

The chief, seated on a platform built for the occasion, received her and motioned her to a chair on his left. Then in the presence of his principal men, who sat below him on long benches at either side of his platform, the chief congratulated the girl on her good fortune and told her why he had chosen her as his wife. She returned coy answers while she waved a fan. Then young girls, whose hair was tied back of their heads and fell over their shoulders, danced in a circle to the tinkle of trinklets tied on belts while they sang the praises of the chief and his bride and lowered and raised their hands in unison.[26]

The death of a chief plunged his subjects into the deepest gloom. They mourned him by fasting three days and three nights and cutting off half of their long tresses. They also placed his drinking shell on his grave, planted arrows on it, and burned down his house with all of his household goods. For six months a group of women, selected for the purpose, mourned him by howling three times a day—at dawn, noon, and twilight.[27]

The chief usually began tribal warfare by planting on the roads arrows with locks of hair fastened to them. Saturiba, however, had his own way of declaring war. He assembled his warriors in a circle with a fire at his left and two large vases of water at his right. Entering the circle, he gave various demonstrations of rage and then let out a horrible yell in which his warriors joined as they struck their hips and rattled their weapons. Then Saturiba lifted one of the vases toward the sun while he worshiped it and prayed that the blood of his enemies be poured out like the water he was about to scatter. He flung the vase high in the air. As the water fell down on his warriors he shouted to them: "As I have done with the water, so I pray that you may do with the blood of your enemies." Then he quenched the fire with the water in the other vase and shouted: "So may you be able to extinguish your enemies and bring back their scalps."[28]

Before the battle began, the chief asked his shaman to disclose the strength and whereabouts of his foes. Le Moyne once saw a sorcerer, who boasted more than one hundred and twenty birthdays, borrow a shield from one of the Frenchmen, lay it on the ground, and draw around it a circle inscribed with strange characters and signs. Then he knelt down on the shield so that no part of his person touched the ground and began a low recitation accompanied by wild gestures. In a short time he was seized with convulsions and with such violent contortions that "he was hardly a human being; for he twisted his limbs so that his bones could be heard to snap out of place, and did many other unnatural things." Then he quickly regained his normal self but in a very fatigued state and with an air of astonishment. Stepping out of his circle he saluted the chief and told him the strength and whereabouts of his foes.[29]

In warfare each chief followed his own devices. Saturiba preserved no order in his ranks; his men marched along one after another as they saw fit. But another chief, Outina, marched his warriors in regular ranks. Only he and his swiftest young men, acting as scouts and vanguard, were painted red. Heralds shouted military orders. At sunset the army halted, rested, and camped, with the chief and his bodyguard accompanying the center of the field. The hermaphrodites carried the food, which consisted principally of *casina*, bread, honey, and roasted corn.[30]

The victors dragged off the braves they killed in battle and scalped them with "reeds sharper than any steel blade." They dried the scalps over a fire and hung them up. After the victory they cut off the legs and arms of the slain, broke the bones, dried the yet bleeding limbs and, suspending them on the ends of their spears, carried them back in triumph to their villages. There they celebrated their victory by crowding around a circle where, with solemn ceremony, they affixed the scalps and other trophies to tall poles set in a-row in the ground. Within the circle stood the shaman, holding in his hand a small image and muttering imprecations against the enemy. Opposite him knelt three men, one of whom marked each word of the imprecation by beating on a flat stone in front of him with his club while on the other side his companions sang to the accompaniment of rattlers made from dried seeds.[31]

5

No sooner had René de Laudonnière completed Fort Caroline than he sent Ottigny up the river in a boat to establish peaceful relations with Thimagoa who was Saturiba's "most ancient and natural enemy" and who was chief of a large domain rich in gold and silver. Mindful of his military commitments to Saturiba, Laudonnière hid from him his real intention. Serving as guides with Ottigny were two Indians who, thinking that they were about to fight Thimagoa, had joined the adventure with the gaiety of two men going to a wedding. Twenty leagues up the river they approached Thimagoa's village and saw, a short distance in front of them, three canoes full of his people. The two Indians became feverish with excitement; their eyes glimmered as they snatched their pikes and swords; but Ottigny bore slowly and coolly down on the canoes and gave their occupants ample time to paddle to the river bank and escape to the woods.

Ottigny landed, placed a few trinkets in the deserted canoes, and withdrew to a distance. The Thimagoan Indians took heart and, step by step, returned to their canoes. Ottigny asked them by signs whether they had any gold and silver. They replied that their country had none, but that they would guide him to a region rich in both metals. Ottigny, observing their reticence, became suspicious of them and wanted to return to Fort Caroline; but one of his soldiers protested that they should stay until they ascertained the facts for which they had come. Ottigny then permitted the soldier to continue with the guides for a specified time.

When the soldier failed to return, Laudonnière sent Captain Vasseur with a few men after him. As they sailed up the river they saw two Indians on the shore beckoning to them to visit their village. Vasseur assented. Led through corn fields and palisades, they soon reached the village, where they met Mollua, a petty chief who seated them in the place of honor and feasted them on fish and bread. When they had finished eating Mollua identified himself as one of Outina's vassals. He described Outina, head chief of Thimagoa, as so wealthy that his warriors wore armor of gold and silver plate. Greatly impressed, Vasseur promised to help Mollua in any war against his enemies, not knowing that these included Timucuans and therefore Saturiba. To strengthen this commitment Mollua replied that each of Outina's vassals would be happy to reward each Frenchman with a heap of gold two feet high from their mine in the Appalachian Mountains.

With such encouraging news, Vasseur and his men hurried homeward, passing the night with a minor chief who, believing that they had subdued the village of Thimagoa, showed the greatest delight in their presence. Vasseur encouraged the Indians in their delusion until one of his hosts ended by asking the Frenchmen by signs how they had conquered the village. Vasseur replied simply that he had surprised and routed them with incredible slaughter. This was too general an explanation to satisfy the chief; he asked for details with such persistence that at last the sergeant, François de Caille, drew his sword and, pretending to re-enact his deeds of valor, pursued and thrusted at his imaginary Thimagoans until they fled to the woods. This bit of gasconade convinced the chief; he led the Frenchmen to his hut and loaded them with *casina*.[32]

On July 29 the *Isabella* sailed for France to obtain reinforcements, leaving Laudonnière with two hundred colonists, a hundred fifty of whom were soldiers. Soon Saturiba began to press Laudonnière for the help he had promised against Thimagoa. Laudonnière, wishing an alliance with the more affluent Outina, aroused Saturiba's displeasure by putting him off. At last Saturiba, impatient of delay and learning from his soldiers of Laudonnière's duplicity, went on the warpath against Outina, defeated him and, loaded down with scalps and prisoners, returned home in triumph.[33]

Laudonnière pretended indifference. Furthermore, he decided on the policy of making an enemy in the hope of gaining a more powerful friend in the future. To strengthen his plans he asked Saturiba to give up to him some of the prisoners so that he in turn could return them to Outina; but Saturiba stubbornly refused to deliver them to one who had broken faith with him and left him to fight alone. Whereupon Laudonnière attempted to intimidate him by sending to him a group of soldiers who sounded their drums and trumpets and fired salvos from several pieces of bronze

cannon. Saturiba's braves fled in terror, but the chief himself received
Laudonnière with serene good will. While Laudonnière fatuously counseled him to make peace with the enemy, Saturiba, though deeply offended and brooding vengeance, loaded him with presents. At this juncture a severe thunderstorm destroyed the cornfields and killed the birds
in the fields. Saturiba, mistaking the storm for a cannonade directed
against his dwelling by the French, withdrew in intense anger from the
neighborhood. He soon declared war on Outina. Laudonnière, believing
that the only road to the gold mine in the Appalachian Mountains lay
through Outina's province, sent a Swiss ensign, Arlac, with ten soldiers
to the assistance of that chief, enabling him to defeat his enemies.[34]

In the ensuing days Laudonnière faced graver difficulties with his
own people. Idleness and failure to realize their golden dreams engendered discontent and conspiracy and dissension among many of them.
They began to gather in cliques and parties, nursing each other's anger
and blaming all of it on their leader. They complained that he had put
them on half-rations, that his promised reinforcements and supplies had
failed to arrive, and that he was snobbish toward everybody save Ottigny,
Arlac, and a few other officers. Their complaints changed to thoughts of
conspiracy when one La Roquette claimed that he had discovered by
magic a gold and silver mine up the river. It was so rich, he said, that it
would yield each of them a share of two thousand crowns and fifteen
thousand crowns for the king. He found a ready ally in Le Genre who
was "exceeding desirous to enrich himself in those parts" and who bore
Laudonnière a grudge for refusing him permission to return to France.
In a secret meeting, Le Genre and his followers agreed that Laudonnière
was preventing them from gaining riches and that they should kill him.

At this juncture Laudonnière caught a severe cold and was confined to
his house. Availing himself of Laudonnière's illness, Le Genre tried to
persuade the druggist to put arsenic in his medicine. When the druggist
refused, LeGenre concealed under Laudonnière's bed a barrel of gun-
powder which, however, was discovered. Whereupon Le Genre fled to
the woods, whence he wrote repentent letters to his leader, begging for
forgiveness.[35]

On September 4 an adventurer named Captain Bourdet arrived with
a small ship from France. A few months later, when Bourdet prepared
to return home, Laudonnière persuaded him to carry back seven or eight
of the troublemakers. In their stead Bourdet left an equal number of
pirates who proved worse than they. These scoundrels joined some of
Laudonnière's men, stole one of his barks, and sailed on a plundering
excursion to the West Indies. They soon seized a small Spanish ship off
the coast of Cuba, plundered a deserted village, abandoned their bark for
a better boat, which they hijacked, and, missing Matanzas, landed in a
smaller harbor called Arcos, where they were discovered and captured.[36]

Meanwhile, Laudonnière faced open revolt at Fort Caroline. On a Sunday morning in November, while he entertained Ottigny in his home, one

of his officers handed him a note embodying the grievances of the mutineers. La Caille, who was a friend of Laudonnière and who carried the
note to him unwillingly, advised him to defend himself against the grievances while his friends undertook to pacify the men and return them to
obedience. Accepting this advice, Laudonnière ordered all the soldiers to
assemble on the fort parade on a specified day. With Ottigny by his side,
he came out and saw some thirty of his officers, soldiers, and gentlemen
volunteers waiting before the building with fixed and somber countenance.

La Caille, advancing, began to read, in behalf of the rest, a paper which
he held in his hands. It opened with protestations of duty and obedience,
next came complaints of hard work, starvation, and broken promises, and
a request that they be allowed to sail in one of his ships to the West Indies
and South America, where each of them hoped to enrich himself.
Laudonnière refused their request, though he promised that, as soon as
he completed defenses of the fort, he would conduct a search for the
Appalachian gold mine, and that meanwhile he would send two small
vessels along the coast to barter for provisions with the Indians. Though
they seemed contented with these promises they endeavored to enlist
new supporters.[37]

The promise of riches made their task supremely easy. They soon numbered sixty-six of the best soldiers in the fort. Their leader, Fourneaux,
whom the Catholic chronicler Barcía calls "a great hypocrite and a tale
bearer," drew up a paper which they all signed and which they pressed on
La Caille to deliver to Laudonnière. When he boldly refused to have anything to do with the plot, they resolved to kill him; but his roommate,
Le Moyne, the artist, who also had refused to join them, learned of their
intention and warned him. Le Moyne fled to the woods.[38]

Next day Laudonnière lay ill in his home. Fourneaux, with twenty
arquebusiers, forced himself to Laudonnière's bedside and, holding a
cocked pistol in his face, cursed him and demanded permission to sail for
New Spain. Nothing daunted, Laudonnière reminded them that they
lacked the means to undertake such an expedition and that they had better change their minds. Replying angrily that they lacked nothing, they
forced Laudonnière to put on his clothes, then carried him in chains to
the ship in the harbor. They seized arms and ammunition, disarmed the
loyal soldiers, and took control of the fort. Fourneaux then forced Laudonnière to sign their passports and to grant them additional sailors and
a pilot. The mutineers finished two ships on which carpenters had been
working, armed them, and on December 8 set out in them on their
piratical adventures.[39]

No sooner were they gone than Ottigny and Arlac released Laudonnière and took him to the fort. He reorganized his command and appointed new officers while his men completed the fort and built two new
ships to replace the stolen ones. On March 25, 1565, an Indian brought
them word that a ship lay in the harbor. Laudonnière sent La Caille with

thirty men in a small ship to ascertain who the strangers were and what they wanted. Finding a Spanish brigantine, La Caille suspected it contained the returning mutineers and hid his men at the bottom of his ship. When he approached the brigantine, he found that his suspicions were justified. He seized the chief mutineers and brought them to Laudonnière, who was waiting for them at the river's mouth.

They told a pitiful story of their adventures. Off the coast of Cuba one of the ships captured a brigantine loaded with *casaba*. Seeing that it was a bigger vessel than their own roughly-made bark, they transferred their belongings to it and steered for a village in Jamaica, where they plundered and caroused for a week. Re-embarking, they fell in with a small vessel which had on board the governor of Santo Domingo. They asked the pilot of the captured vessel how they could reach Jamaica, where they expected to barter food for the merchandise they found on board. The pilot readily offered his services, directing them toward Jamaica, which was then a Spanish port, where they might entrap themselves while he gained freedom for himself and his companions. As they neared port, they forced one of the prisoners to address the governor of the island a letter asking for food, and foolishly sent the pilot with two of the prisoners to deliver it. The answer was not long in coming. At daybreak on the third day three armed vessels bore down on them in the harbor and captured and killed all of the pirates save Fourneaux and twenty-five others who escaped to sea by cutting the moorings of their brigantine.

Unfortunately for them, the pilot, Trenchant, had joined them against his will. Now, eager to rejoin his leader at Fort Caroline, he steered the brigantine to the Florida coast while the pirates were asleep. Great was their anger when they discovered their dilemma, but, having no provisions save a few casks of wine, they decided to surrender. But first they would have one last and glorious fling. Opening a few casks of Spanish wine, they drank until, mingling mirth with desperation, they began to enact their own trial. One of them agreed to personify their judge; another, Laudonnière. They called witnesses who presented testimony for either side.

"Say what you like," said one of them who had heard the council for the defense; "but if Laudonnière does not hang us all, I will never call him an honest man."[40]

In reality the pirates *were* court-martialed and found guilty. Fourneaux and three others were sentenced to be hanged.

At the last moment one of the condemned men appealed to the soldiers: "Comrades, will you stand by and see us butchered?"

"They are not comrades," retorted Laudonnière. "They are mutineers and rebels."

At the request of his soldiers, they were shot rather than hanged, and their bodies were strung up on gibbets at the mouth of the river.[41]

6

The colony sustained the evil of mutiny only to face the scourge of famine. The Frenchmen, like the Spaniards before them, became so obsessed with the dream of finding gold that they overlooked the necessity of providing for their stomachs. During winter and early spring, the Indians lived in the forest; they could provide the colonists with neither maize nor beans. Yet the Frenchmen planted no crops of their own. For a few months they lived on the supplies that Laudonnière had laid by; then, in May, they began to feel the first gnawings of famine. Their faces grew haggard; they began to drag their emaciated bodies over the scorching sand; they stretched, listless and wretched and homesick, under the shade of their barracks. The few fish that Indians sometimes brought them only intensified their hunger. They dug for roots; they gathered sorrel in the meadows, praying for supplies from home, hoping for maize and beans from the Indians. None came from either source. Unable to work, they feebly wandered to the top of the bluff, where their leader had dreamed of a new land of Canaan, and stared into the glimmering sea for some trace or sign of rescue.[42]

For many days they watched in vain. Gold and conquest no longer interested them; they thought now only of returning to France as quickly as possible. With the energy of despair, they began to build a boat for the voyage, and they planned to add two decks to the brigantine in which the mutineers had returned. And while they worked and planned, they subsisted on berries they gathered in the forest and on the roots of palmettos that grew along the river banks. The Indians, seeing them reduced to starvation, lost all fear of them. They demanded a shirt for a fish. A complaint of its excessive cost brought a churlish reply: "If you think so much of your merchandise, eat it, and we will eat our fish." And the Indians would begin to laugh and mock the colonists "with open throat."[43]

Since Laudonnière would derive no further advantage from continuing friendly relations with Outina, he paid heed to the wishes of his men to seize that chief and hold him as a hostage for the food they so greatly needed. Taking fifty men who could still bear the weight of their armor, he sailed in two barges up the river to Outina's village, surrounded his mud-plastered palace, and seized him amid the yells and howlings of his subjects. Taking him to one of the barges, Laudonnière demanded a supply of corn and beans as the price of his ransom.[44]

His capture filled the region with alarm. Bands of angry warriors, painted for war, thronged to the chief's village from all parts of his domain. The forest rang with their threats, while the women, gathering at the river bank, moaned, cried, and gesticulated in despair. But they offered no ransom from fear that, as soon as it was paid, their chief would be killed. Outina, learning that Saturiba had offered a handsome bribe for his person and that his subjects were about to choose his son or a relative whom he hated to succeed him, induced his captor to make another attempt to exchange him for maize and beans. Laudonnière agreed, put him on a ship, and carried him to his village where they found the Indians waiting with gifts of bread, beans, and fish. They promised them as much food as they needed, as soon as their chief was released. Laudonnière released Outina and received in his place two hostages; but when Ottigny and Arlac, with a strong detachment of arquebusiers, set out to receive the promised supplies, they found the corn coming in slowly and the warriors mustering fast and concealing themselves in the underbrush between their village and the shore. The Frenchmen, growing anxious, urged the chiefs to greater alacrity in collecting the promised ransom. They replied: "Our women are afraid, when they see the matches of your guns burning. Put them out, and they will bring the corn faster."[45]

Several of the officers went to see Outina, who in return for the kindness his captors had accorded him, warned them that he could no longer control his enraged subjects. He said he had seen arrows stuck in the ground by the side of the road, a sign that they had declared war. In the face of impending peril, Ottigny resolved to return to the ships. His soldiers, each shouldering a sack of corn, marched through the rows of huts that surrounded Outina's palace, while Arlac went ahead with eight matchlock men. As Arlac approached the wooded area that separated the village from the shore, concealed Indians raised a war whoop and sent a deluge of arrows and stones clanging against the breastplates of his men who fired back, killing several of their assailants. The remaining Indians retreated to the protection of the forest and attacked again, hooting like owls, screaming like cougars, and howling like wolves. When the Frenchmen threw down their bags of maize and took up their arquebuses, the Indians eluded death by dropping flat on the ground. Then, as the Frenchmen charged with their swords, the Indians fled, showering arrows on flanks and rear. Two Frenchmen were killed and twenty-two wounded.[46]

Having succeeded in carrying off only a few bags of maize, the Frenchmen were soon again in want. And the Indians added to their misery by killing two of the carpenters, thereby forcing delay in the completion of the ship. With the energy of despair, they destroyed the houses around the fort, converting the woodwork into charcoal. To obtain timber they tore down the palisade of the fort on the riverside, leaving it defenseless.[47]

On August 3, while they pushed these preparations with feverish haste, Laudonnière, tormented in mind, frustrated in ambition, and bitterly disappointed at the complete failure of his colony, went for a walk on a little hill. Suddenly he saw something that thrilled his weakened body. Fluttering over the horizon were four sails "rising like gulls in the sun." Then he saw a ship and another and another! He hurried word to the fort below. It electrified the languid and despairing men; they rose and danced for joy; they leaped and sang and laughed as though possessed.[48]

But doubt mingled with their joy. Were the strangers friends or foes? Were they Spaniards or Frenchmen? They were neither. They were English, and their captain was John Hawkins, the seadog who had been marketing a cargo of Guinea Coast blacks in the islands where, with sword, matchlock, and culverin, he had forced the Spaniards to meet his prices and to sign testimonials that he had behaved like a peaceful merchant while in their ports. He had been sailing along the coast for fifteen days in search of water. He sent a Frenchman named Martin Artinas, who had accompanied Ribaut in his first expedition and who had readily found employment with the English adventurer, to ask Laudonnière to permit him to refill his empty casks. Artinas brought along a present of two flagons of wine and some wheaten bread. Laudonnière, having tasted no wine for seven months, found it very refreshing, and he generously divided it among his soldiers.

Next day Hawkins himself came to see Laudonnière, who received him and entertained him in the dismantled fort. The enigmatic Hawkins, who could be as overbearing as he was generous, shook his head when he saw the vessels in which the Frenchmen planned to embark; he offered to take them to France in his own ships. But Laudonnière, not knowing whether France was at peace or war with England, was afraid to trust this man, who professed to love and serve God while he kidnaped blacks and packed them on his ships so close to one another that they could scarcely breathe. Laudonnière refused the offer, thereby precipitating among his men such a turmoil that he was constrained to call a council at which they decided to purchase one of Hawkins' smaller ships. Hawkins, far from resenting Laudonnière's suspicions, agreed to sell him the ship he wanted at whatever price he would name. And he threw into the bargain fifty pairs of shoes for the barefooted soldiers. Laudonnière was deeply touched. To him Hawkins was "a good and charitable man, deserving to be esteemed as much of us all as if he had saved all our lives."[49]

A few days later Hawkins, having left two Englishmen at Fort Caroline as hostages for the fulfillment of the agreement between himself and Laudonnière, sailed for England. Laudonnière had his supplies and those left by Hawkins stored aboard the ship and waited to sail to a favorable wind for his beloved France.[50]

On August 28, just as wind and tide became propitious for the voyage, two captains, Vasseur and Verdier, saw approaching a fleet of seven ships. Intense excitement again pervaded the fort. Laudonnière sent out an armed boat to ascertain whether the ships were friendly or hostile, then took the precaution of assembling his soldiers. Through the sweltering day, through the dreary night watches, the colonists waited in vain for a report from their messenger; then, on the following morning, the ships, bristling with arms and crowded with men wearing morions on their heads, moved past the outposts on the bluff without offering a reply to the sentry's eager inquiry. One of the sentinels, unable to control his suspense at these mysterious movements, fired at them a shot that fell abortive in the water. As the ships continued to advance in silence, Laudonnière hesitated no longer. At his command his men trained two small fieldpieces at the approaching ships. He was about to give an order to fire on them, when he recognized on one of the ships a man with a beard of luxurious growth. Suddenly his anxious look became one of radiance, as though the sun had suddenly broken through rain clouds. He uttered an ejaculation of delight, and his soldiers replied with a volley of welcome and a resounding cheer. Laudonnière knew only one man in the world with such a beard: Jean Ribaut![51]

The two men embraced each other again and again. Then Ribaut took Laudonnière aside and told him that returning ships had brought to France letters accusing him of arrogance, tyranny, cruelty, and a plan to establish an independent colony. He explained that he knew now that these accusations were unfounded but that they had prompted his unusual and startling precautions. Then he handed him a letter from Coligny, who required him in friendly terms to resign his command and to return to France to clear his name. Laudonnière declined with much dignity Ribaut's plea to remain. The false reports preyed on his mind, bringing on a fever that lasted eight or nine days. During this time, Ribaut landed his supplies and pitched his tents. Before long the River of May swarmed with new life. But now, when they thought they were at rest, a new misfortune searched and pursued them. Amid the light and cheer of renovated hope, a cloud of blackest omen gathered on the horizon. At half-past eleven on the night of Tuesday, September 4, some soldiers who had been walking on the beach brought Ribaut word that they had seen six ships steering in the direction of Ribaut's flagship, the *Trinity*, and her three companions. They could plainly see large cannon on the ships that drifted toward them in the gloom of evening. On the stern of the largest ship flew the yellow-and-red flag of Castile and León.

Pedro Menéndez de Avilés

PHILIP II WAS ENTIRELY AWARE OF WHAT THE FRENCH WERE DOING IN Florida. His ambassador to France, Francisco de Alava, kept him informed of every move they made. He knew of Laudonnière's voyage to Florida; he knew of the French piratical acts; he knew of Ribaut's departure with supplies and reinforcements. From Normandy, from Brittany, from Nantes, from Bordeaux, from Bayonne the ambassador received and relayed to his master reports of the arrival of armed vessels destined either for Florida or to rob the Spanish treasure ships from the Indies. The ambassador protested repeatedly to Coligny and Queen Catherine. They cajoled him with empty promises: the pirates and robbers would receive condign punishment. The queen's real design was to let her subjects arm themselves as they pleased, so long as she could profit by them.

Philip II regarded the presence of Fort Caroline so near to Havana and on the path of his treasure ships as an imminent menace to New Spain. Fray Domingo de Noriega, Commissary General of New Spain, clearly stated its importance in a letter to the king: "The sum of all that can be said in the manner, is that they put the Indies in a crucible, for we are compelled to pass in front of their port, and with the greatest ease they can sally out with their armadas to seek us, and easily return when it suits them." Noriega urged Philip to act before Coligny could send Ribaut to relieve the colonists at Fort Caroline. "Seeing that they are Lutherans," he wrote, "it is not needful to leave a man alive, but to inflict an exemplary punishment, that they may remember it forever."

Still Philip hesitated. He wanted to gain Queen Catherine's support to oust the Huguenots from Florida. But Catherine's hands were tied. Though she needed Philip's support to maintain her position of power in France between Catholics and Huguenots, she was unwilling to gain it at the expense of losing the support of French Catholics who had caught Coligny's vision of a great, rich, glorious France. She therefore temporized. To Alava's protests she replied through Burdin, secretary to her son, Charles IX, that Ribaut's ships in no way menaced Spanish possessions and that, indeed, they were bound for the country known as "the Land of the Bretons," which France had discovered over a century before.

Such quibbling failed to deceive Alava. "Why do you want us to talk this nonsense?" he asked Burdin. "Whether you call it the Land of the Bretons or the Mountains of Hercules, as the queen does, the province where the vessels of our king are going is the same which we call Florida, and you call New France, to which it is requested that none of the subjects of your master go."

Burdin insisted: "The French discovered the Land of the Bretons a hundred years ago, as can be seen by the maps of the newly discovered provinces."

Alava remained undeceived. "Now we have proved that the land you call Land of the Bretons and we Florida is one and the same, and you mean to say that you first discovered it, so that the issue turns on the right of your king to it, and not that it is a different country from Florida, where the French are going, as may be gathered from your king's answer, and what you yourself are saying."[1]

Philip entrusted the task of driving the Huguenots from Florida to a sea-soldier who had rendered signal and distinguished services to his country: Pedro Menéndez de Avilés, Knight of the Order of Santiago, Commander of Santa Cruz de la Zarza, and Captain General of the Fleet. He was descended from an ancient family of Asturias, where, says one of his admiring biographers, "earth and sky bear men who are honest, not tricksters, truthful, not babblers, most faithful to their king, generous, friendly, lighthearted, and merry, daring, and warlike."

Menéndez seemed to have a few of the less attractive of these virtues; the rest were thrust upon him after he gained fame and fortune. From boyhood he was ungovernable and fierce. The rugged mountains of Asturias mothered a continuous brood of rovers and intrepid crusaders who responded to the spell of the sea before they reached their teens. Menéndez proved himself more than a mere product of his environment: he ran away when he was only eight. A relative with whom he lived found him in Valladolid, brought him home, and discouraged his running away again by betrothing him to a girl two years his senior. Nothing could be more disquieting to one of his temperament than the approaching prospect of domestic bliss. So, when he was fourteen, he ran away again, embarking with eighteen or twenty men in a tender which soon attacked a well-armed French ship. In the encounter Menéndez' boat was so greatly damaged that his crew at first wanted to surrender, but he urged them on with such valor that they took on renewed confidence. The Frenchmen did not dare to board it. They permitted it to escape to the safety of Galicia.[2]

In the next two years Menéndez continued to fight French corsairs.

Then, returning home, he bought a ship from the sale of a part of his patrimony and, at the command of Charles V, pursued the French corsair Jean Alfonse, who had enriched himself by capturing about a dozen Spanish ships off Cape Finisterre. He attacked Alfonse, who died of a wound, and rescued five ships which the corsair had seized. Charles V, admiring his success and intrepidity, commissioned him to fight corsairs even in peacetime and granted him and his descendents all he should capture. In this enterprise he was so successful that Charles appointed him Captain General of the Fleet. This position, which Charles wrested from the jurisdiction of the House of Trade, enabled Menéndez to impose on naval officers the discipline necessary to assure the treasure ships prompt and safe passage of their sea routes. The House of Trade soon found an opportunity to avenge itself on the man who had been instrumental in depriving it of one of its most important functions. On his return from a successful journey to America, it seized and imprisoned him on the pretext that he had exceeded his instructions, but the king quickly established his innocence.[3]

Early in 1557 Philip II appointed Menéndez captain general of a powerful fleet to pursue pirates and protect the other fleets and the coasts of Spain and Flanders. During the war with France, Menéndez' prompt arrival in Flanders with troops and supplies contributed largely to the victory of St. Quentin. Two years later he commanded a fleet that brought Philip back to Spain. A storm soon broke over the ships; some foundered; some, to save their cargoes, were lightened; some lost rich tapestries and treasures; Philip himself was almost drowned. On landing in Spain, Philip asked Menéndez to what he attributed the storm. With his reply he characterized himself as well as his king: "For many months all Spain has prayed for Your Majesty, beseeching our Lord to conduct you in safety to your realm. During that season the devils could do you no harm; but when Your Majesty landed the prayers ceased, and thereupon they found the opportunity to work what evil they could."[4] The king marveled at his admiral's facile wisdom.

Philip put Menéndez in command of an armada bound for New Spain and instructed him to return in fifty days with what treasure he could collect. Learning that treasure was already on its way to Spain, Menéndez stayed in New Spain for ten months—long enough to disobey his king and to accumulate a fortune. Once more he sailed to the New World; once more he returned with a rich cargo. This time he fell into the clutches of his old enemies in the House of Trade; they arrested and imprisoned him on charges of disregarding regulations, of having exceeded his authority, and of having connived at smuggling a large quantity of money. Menéndez went whining to the king, who commanded the judges of the House of Trade to pass judgment on the prisoner. They kept him in prison for twenty months and then sentenced him to pay a thousand ducats. Philip restored his command, though he remitted only half of his fine—an act indicative either of his guilt or of the king's greed.[5]

Menéndez kissed Philip's hands for the graces he had bestowed on him. He asked for just one more favor—could he please be permitted to search for his only son, Juan, who had been shipwrecked near the Bermudas? Philip not only assented but promised him whatever he needed for the project. His generosity, however, was motivated less by his esteem for Menéndez than by pressing reasons of state. He wanted Menéndez to survey the entire Florida coast, exploring its inlets and bays for possible suitable harbors. Menéndez, whose thoughts until now were far removed from such mundane matters as the settlement and conquest of Florida, readily fell in with the royal wishes, saying that he knew of nothing more important in the whole kingdom: "Florida is a land so vast, and in such a good latitude and climate for all kinds of produce, that settling there would of necessity bring the discovery of excellent things." By this terrestrial path he led his king to the celestial: "Even if nothing should be found, my lord, the country is filled with millions of savage Indians, without faith or law, totally unenlightened by religious truth." Such circumstances, he continued, filled him with so much pity and sorrow that he would gladly forego any other undertaking "for the settlement and conquests of those extensive regions."[6]

This zeal, whether real or false, delighted Philip. Without hesitation he empowered Menéndez to conquer and convert Florida, but at his own expense. The king would lose nothing; his servant might gain something.

By a contract of March 20, 1565, Menéndez received the title of marquis and *adelantado* of Florida with a grant of land twenty-five miles square. His colonists were to number five hundred, of whom one hundred must be soldiers, one hundred sailors, and the rest stone-cutters, carpenters, locksmiths, sawyers, and smiths, all equipped with arms. Two hundred of the colonists must be married. He was to take four Jesuit priests and ten or twelve friars of whatever Order he saw fit. He was to parcel out the land among the settlers, establish at least two towns, each with a port and with not less than a hundred persons. To assist him in establishing the towns, in cultivating land, in planting sugar cane, and in manufacturing sugar, he was privileged to transport to Florida five hundred Negro slaves, a third of whom were to be women. He was enjoined to allow in the colony neither Jew nor Moor nor Marrano nor anybody contaminated with heresy. He must submit a detailed report of the Atlantic coast from the Florida Keys to Newfoundland. Finally, he must drive the French heretics from Florida by whatever means he saw fit.[7]

Menéndez made preparations for his enterprise with such fierce energy that within a few months he realized a force of two thousand six hundred forty-six persons, "not mendicants and vagabonds, but . . . the best horsemen of Asturias, Galicia, and Vizcaya," and a fleet of twelve vessels, most of which averaged from sixty to seventy tons. His flagship, the *San Pelayo*, nine hundred tons, was regarded as one of the finest ships of the day. He was so anxious to thwart and ruin Ribaut and to destroy Fort

Caroline that every day seemed a year. Chafing at the delay, he sailed from Cadiz on June 29, leaving the smaller vessels of his fleet to follow in their best speed. He touched the Canaries, steered for Dominica where he added another ship to his squadron and appointed the officers of the expedition, and, without waiting for his smaller ships, which had not yet reached Puerto Rico, set sail for Florida.[8]

2

On August 28, St. Augustine's Day, Menéndez sighted the River of Dolphins, which Laudonnière had visited two years before. Seeking the French, he rowed ashore with fifty arquebusiers and presently met in the woods a band of Indians who, singing and lifting their arms skyward as though in adoration, informed him that his enemies were fortified twenty leagues to the north. Sailing in that direction, he discovered a beautiful harbor which he named St. Augustine in honor of him on whose festival he had sighted land.

On September 4, as he continued northward, he saw four ships anchored near the mouth of the St. Johns River. These were the *Trinity* and three other of Ribaut's ships which he had left at the mouth of the river because they were too large to pass the bars safely. Resolving to attack the French before they could chase and outsail him, Menéndez slowly bore down on them. But while his crews watched the decreasing space, while three leagues still remained between them and their prize, black clouds with violent thunder and lightning overtook them and soon drenched them with warm rain. That night, at ten o'clock, the sky cleared; the wind began to stir again; and Menéndez pressed on. He had given orders to approach the French ships bow to bow, then to board them at daybreak in order to forestall them from possibly burning their own ships and escaping to shore in row boats. The French fired repeatedly, but their bullets were aimed too high and fell harmlessly between the masts of the Spanish ships. Menéndez kept doggedly on his course until he drew up the bow of the *San Pelayo* between that of the *Trinity* and another of Ribaut's ships. The world seemed shrouded in silence. Suddenly a trumpet blast was heard from the deck of the *San Pelayo*. A French trumpet replied. Then Menéndez with great courtesy called across the darkness:

"Gentlemen, from where does this fleet come?"

"From France," answered somebody on Ribaut's flagship.

"What are you doing here?"

"Bringing infantry, artillery, and supplies for a fort which the king of France has in this country, and for others which he is going to make."

"Are you Catholics or Lutherans?"

"We are Lutherans of the new religion, and our general is Jean Ribaut."

They asked who he was and whose fleet he had brought with him.

"I am Pedro Menéndez, General of the Fleet of the King of Spain, Don

Philip II. I have come to this country to hang and behead all Lutherans whom I shall find by land or sea. My instructions from the king are so precise that I have power to pardon nobody. These commands I shall fulfill, as you will see. At daybreak I shall board your ships and if I find any Catholic on them he will be well treated; but every heretic shall die."

They interrupted him with curses: "If you are a brave man, don't wait until tomorrow. Come on, and you'll see what you'll get!"[9]

When they continued their curses, Menéndez lost his temper and ordered his trumpeter to sound the call to arms. The sailors at his command slackened the cable to board the French ships. Seeing his sailors hesitate, Menéndez leaped down from the bridge to hurry them, though they could work no faster because the cable was wound on the capstan. The French, seeing him coming, quickly cut their cables, hoisted sail, and fled. Menéndez pursued them, but they were such adroit devils in running and maneuvering that he failed to catch up with them. Eventually giving up the chase, he returned to St. Augustine, where he found three ships debarking troops, guns, and supplies.

With the help of slave labor, the first ever recorded in the United States, two of his officers dug a ditch around an Indian communal house that stood near the shore and bulwarked it with logs and sand. This was the origin of St. Augustine, the oldest city in the United States. As soon as the work was finished, Menéndez took full possession amid the booming of cannon, the blaring of trumpets, and an assemblage of Indians looking on with mingled curiosity and awe. The chaplain, Mendoza, crucifix in hand and chanting *Te Deum Laudamus*, advanced to meet Menéndez and his men. They knelt and one by one kissed the crucifix.[10]

Meanwhile Ribaut, on arriving at Fort Caroline, held a council of war in which he and his officers resolved to push against St. Augustine. On September 10 he crowded his ships with four hundred soldiers and two hundred sailors. Before sailing they opened two casks of wine to celebrate the victory they anticipated. Inferring that the Spaniards were false Christians, they cried: "Drink to the head of Don Pedro and the convert Moors and Jews with him. We shall punish them by hanging them from the yardarms so that they will not come again to look for us in this land." That same day Ribaut sailed, leaving Laudonnière with two hundred forty men to guard the fort.[11]

Next day at dawn he found Menéndez trying to pass the bar and to land a sloop and two boats filled with men and artillery from one of his larger ships. The Spanish leader, finding himself in peril, cried to Our Lady of Utrera that the heretics were upon him and begged her to send him a little wind. Our Lady of Utrera not only obliged him but, says Mendoza, "herself seemingly came down upon the vessel." The wind was so strong that Menéndez easily crossed the shoals of the sand bar to safety. Next day he saw Ribaut's ships, their decks black with men, hover off the entrance of the port. But Our Lady of Utrera still accorded

Menéndez her loving care; she blew the breeze into a gale and the gale into a tempest so severe that it forced the French ships to seek shelter as they tossed wildly in the raging sea.[12]

And Our Lady of Utrera inspired Menéndez to undertake a bold stroke. He would march overland with five hundred men and attack Fort Caroline while its defenders were absent! He had a Mass said to the Holy Ghost for guidance, then told his officers that their responsibility and obligation were so great that he feared they might abandon the enterprise in fright. When he revealed his plan, they expressed fears and doubts and complained; but he remained adamant. This, he told them, was a holy war against Lutherans; they must fight it with fire and blood, "not only because of the orders we carry, but also because they seek us with a determination to put an end to us, so we may not implant the Holy Gospel in these regions and so they can spread their own abominable and disastrous sect among the Indians." The sooner they punished the heretics the quicker they would serve the interests of God and their king. Despite his convincing arguments, his officers held long disputes about the enterprise before they reluctantly agreed to approve it. Menéndez then made the necessary preparations for the campaign.

On September 16, amid thundering drums and blaring trumpets and tintinnabulating bells, he heard Mass with all his men save Juan de San Vicente, who complained of a bellyache and a painful leg. To the requests of some of his friends to join them, San Vicente replied: "I'm waiting, by God, for news saying that all our people have been beheaded, so that those of us who stay here can set out in the three ships and go to the Indies, for there is no reason we should all die like beasts."[13]

The soldiers marched in a grave mood toward their destination. Their guides were Jean François, one of three French prisoners, and two Indian chiefs who had quarreled with the French at Fort Caroline six days before. A company of twenty Asturians and Basques, under Martín de Ochoa, with their axes blazed a path through forest and swamp, while Menéndez directed them with a compass. On the third day they found themselves in a thick pine forest, less than a mile from Fort Caroline. A heavy rain had converted the ground into an impassable swamp. Knee-deep they sloshed their way around the swamp, their clothes soaked and heavy with water, their food spoiled, their powder wet, their bodies aching from strain and lack of sleep. Menéndez, pike in hand, led the way and shared in every labor. Those who could not swim were carried across the deep water on pikes. Sometimes, when they rested, they huddled in shivering groups, cursing the enterprise and its author. Menéndez heard a lieutenant say aloud to his comrades:

"How we have been taken in by this miserable Asturian who knows no more about land warfare than an ass! By God, if it had been up to me, he would have been given his deserts the day he set out from St. Augustine on this damned trip!"

Menéndez paid him no mind.

All night he prayed to God and the Virgin. Then, two hours before breakfast, he summoned his officers and asked them:

"Gentlemen, what decision shall we make now that we find ourselves tired, lost, without ammunition or food, or hope of helping ourselves?"

Their reply expressed dejection and disgust: "What is the point of wasting time swapping opinions instead of retreating immediately to St. Augustine, eating palmettos as we go? To delay is to increase the difficulty."

Menéndez admitted justification of their anger but entreated them to let him speak his mind—not to persuade them to accept his plan but to enable them to arrive at the best advice. In the past they had accepted his judgment; now he wanted to follow theirs. With these temperate words he regained their confidence.

"Tell us how you would be served," they said, "and we will be very glad to hear your argument and will give our opinion."[14]

He presented his plans with such convincing eloquence that they agreed to follow him. They prayed on their knees in the swamp; then, guided by Jean François, whose hands were tied behind with a rope held by Menéndez himself, they made for the fort, groping and stumbling in the dark among trees and roots and underbrush. While they followed a narrow path, they lost their way and began to retrace their steps. Menéndez ordered them to halt and stand where they were until morning. At daybreak Jean François recognized the ground. The fort, he said, lay beyond the bluff. Menéndez climbed the height to reconnoiter. He saw the river and some houses, but the rain, the dimness of early morning, and the intervening buildings prevented him from seeing the fort.[15]

He sent Ochoa and the camp master, Pedro Menéndez Valdés, to reconnoiter. A French sentinel saw them and asked: "Who goes there?"

"Frenchmen," they answered as they closed with him.

Ochoa knocked him down with a sheathed sword, wounded him, took him prisoner, and finally had to kill him. Menéndez, hearing the shouting and thinking that Valdés and Ochoa had been discovered, shouted the battle cry which his countrymen for generations had used against the Moors:

"Santiago! Up and at 'em! God's with us! Victory!"

Down the path they rushed pell-mell until they reached Ochoa and Valdés who shouted: "Brothers! Follow my example! The Lord is with us!"

Ochoa, running back toward the fort, found two Frenchmen in their nightshirts and killed one of them. Laudonnière's trumpeter, mounting the rampart, saw the Spaniards coming toward him and sounded the alarm. Aroused from sleep, the Frenchmen rolled out of their beds, some half dressed, some quite naked, and ran outside. Laudonnière, running out of the fort in his shirt, grabbed his sword and target and began to call his soldiers together; but, seeing that the fort was already lost, he and a soldier named Bartholomew entered the courtyard of his house. Here his pursuers would have captured him had they not stopped to cut the cords of a tent over which they had stumbled. Escaping behind Ottigny's house, Laudonnière sprang through an opening on the side of the fort and fled to the woods.[16]

Le Moyne that night had served as one of the sentinels. This artist, returning to his house, laid down his arquebus and, though drenched to the skin, threw himself into his hammock and fell asleep. Screams and sounds of blows soon awakened him. Jumping to his feet he rushed out to see what had happened. Two Spaniards came toward him with drawn swords but failed to attack him. Seeing that the enemy had seized the arsenal, he turned back and ran toward one of the embrasures, leaped into the ditch, and escaped to the forest.[17]

An old carpenter, Nicolas Le Challeux, was on his way to work with a chisel in his hand. Seeing Spaniards rushing toward him, he turned tail and ran as fast as he could. A pikeman chased him, but, he wrote later, "by the grace of God my strength was doubled—poor old man that I am, and grey-headed. I leaped over the rampart, which I could not have done if I had thought about it, for it was eight or nine feet high. Once over, I raced toward the forest." When he was about a bowshot from the woods, he turned his face toward the fort and, seeing nobody following him, paused to listen to horrible sounds of slaughter and to see the victorious Spaniards plant three flags on the ramparts. Having by now abandoned all hope of seeing his friends again, he put his trust in God and plunged deeper into the forest. He would find no greater cruelty, he wrote later

... among the wild beasts. My misery and suffering made me sigh and weep. I saw on earth no other hope than that the Lord in his special grace might deliver me beyond man's hope. In a voice of sorrow, I prayed unto God, saying: "O God of our fathers and Lord of all consolation, Who has commanded us to call upon Thee even from the lake of Hell and the pangs of death, promising Thy swift aid, show unto me, for the hope that I have in Thee, what path I might take to come to the end of this miserable age, plunged in the gulf of sorrow and bitterness. Give me, feeling the effect of Thy mercy, the assurance that I have conceived in my heart of Thy promises. Let it not be taken away by the cruelty and furious rage of the wild beasts on the one side, and of Thy enemies and ours on the other. For the enemy seek our death more because Thy Holy Name is called upon among us than for any other thing. Help me, O God; assist me, as I am afflicted that I can call no more."[18]

While he prayed, he struggled through briars and thorns under tall trees. Suddenly he heard noises made by several weeping and complaining men. Confident that God would help him, he went up to them and found that they were fugitives like himself. They commiserated, then considered what they should do to save themselves. One of them advised that they return and surrender themselves to the Spaniards.

"How do we know that if we yield ourselves to the mercy of the Spaniards," he asked, "they will not show us mercy? Even though they kill us, we shall suffer only for a time. For they are men, and it may be that once their fury is appeased they will compromise with us. Otherwise what should we do? Is it not better for us to fall into the hands of human beings than into the mouths of wild beasts, or to die of hunger in a strange land?"

Most of them agreed with him and even praised his council. But Le Challeux begged to differ.

"Let us not be willful," he said, "as to trust in man more than in God, Who maketh those that are His to live, yea, even in the midst of death; and Who giveth always His help when man's hope fails."

Despite his admonition six of them left and made their way to the Spaniards, who hewed them down with swords and halberds and dragged their bodies to the river, where the victims of the massacre were flung in heaps.[19]

Meanwhile, Le Moyne had joined a soldier named Grandchemin. Hoping to reach the small vessels anchored behind the bar, they toiled all day through the woods and rested that night in a swamp overgrown with reeds. Tired and hungry and despairing of his circumstances, Grandchemin began to upbraid Le Moyne and said he wished to go back and surrender. Le Moyne tried to dissuade him in vain. When they came in sight of the fort and heard the sounds of rejoicing and the general uproar of the Spaniards, Le Moyne stopped and said to his companion:

"Friend, let us not go there yet; let us stay away at least for a while: God will open ways of safety for us about which we now know nothing, and will bring us out of danger."

But Grandchemin refused; embracing Le Moyne, he bade him farewell. The artist, anxious to learn what fate awaited Grandchemin, made his way to a place nearby from which he could watch him. He saw Spaniards arrest Grandchemin; saw him fall on his knees and beg for his life; saw them hack him to pieces; saw them carry off the dismembered pieces of his body on their spears and pikes. He wept bitterly as he plunged deeper into the woods.[20]

Meanwhile, the Spaniards had rushed into the fort, killing every Frenchman they could find. Even Menéndez quaked before the frightful slaughter. For he feared that his men might contract heresy from too close contact with the Huguenots, and that God would punish him should he permit his soldiers to treat women and children cruelly. Frantically he ordered his men to spare all women as well as all children under fifteen years.[21]

Jacques Ribaut, son of the absent French commander, sailed up the river in the *Pearl*, rescuing as many of his countrymen as he could. The Spaniards, drunk with victory, clamored for the lives of the Frenchmen on the ship. But they found to their disgust that rain had put their cannon out of commission. So they sent Jean François and a trumpeter to summon Ribaut to surrender. Ribaut refused, though he was so timid and irresolute that he allowed François and the trumpeter to depart unharmed. Then Menéndez sent Ribaut a message in which he promised to spare the men on board should they agree to surrender themselves and their luggage. They replied that no war had existed between France and Spain when, six months before, their king had ordered them to make the voyage. They felt, therefore, that they had done nothing wrong, had made no demands on anyone.

"We have kept the king's command inviolate," they said, "so you cannot assert that we are the cause of the slaughter you have made against all the rules of warfare—for which our hearts bleed. In another time and place you may suffer for this deed. As for giving up our ship, as you demand, you could more easily take our lives. And if you think to constrain us, we will employ the means that God and nature have given us to defend ourselves."[22]

Menéndez fumed at such defiance. With his permission, his soldiers crowded on the river bank, where they had piled the corpses, shouting insults to those on the ship, tearing out dead men's eyes, and hurling them toward their enemies on the points of their daggers. Menéndez turned the guns of the captured fort against Ribaut's ships and sank one of them in shallow water, where Spanish soldiers recovered it before its cargo was damaged.[23]

The crew of the sinking ship rowed to the *Pearl*, which dropped a small distance down the river to two other small vessels. These had just arrived from France with supplies which enabled Ribaut to remain longer in the river and rescue more of his countrymen.[24]

So completely had Menéndez surprised the fort that none of his soldiers was killed, and only one was wounded. A hundred forty-two men, women, and children were killed in and around the fort. In addition, six drummers and trumpeters and fifty women were made prisoners. Larroque, in a book which he wrote in 1572 and published fourteen years later, stated that Menéndez hanged some of his prisoners and placed above them this inscription in Spanish: "I do this not to Frenchmen but to Lutherans." Other historians believed and repeated this story, which in turn gained credence among the French people. Unsubstantiated by any witness, it may be apocryphal.

The fugitives, exhausted, famished, and half naked, plodded through the forest amid terrifying lightning and thunder and crippling rain. Laudonnière, hoping to find Ribaut's ships, searched for the river until, burning with fever, he could go no farther; he stood in water up to his shoulders, hardly able to draw his breath. Next morning he saw Le

Challeux and six other men approaching. With his chisel, which never left left his side, he cut down a pole with which to assist his comrades to cross deep and swift streams that channeled the swamp. By clinging to the pole and giving it a vigorous push, each man managed to struggle to the other shore, where he grasped reeds that grew along the bank. Other fugitives joined them to swell their number to twenty-three. Two of them, by climbing tall trees, discovered one of the smaller of the French ships commanded by a Captain Maillard, who saw their signals and sent boats to their rescue.[25]

They were so exhausted that few would have escaped had not their comrades waded to their armpits among the rushes and borne them on their shoulders. Laudonnière was so feeble that one of the soldiers had to hold him upright to save him from drowning in the marsh. As soon as the fugitives had recovered their strength, they held a council in which they decided to return to France. Before they sailed, they saved a few more stragglers from the swamp. On September 25 two of the ships turned their prows toward France, only to separate on the following day. Jacques Ribaut, with Le Challeux and his party, eventually reached La Rochelle. The other vessel, with Laudonnière abroad, was driven by foul weather into Swansea Bay in South Wales, where Laudonnière fell ill again. He sent a portion of his men to France with the ship. With the rest, he went to London, whence he returned to France to report to the king.[26]

3

After resting briefly at the fort, which he rechristened San Mateo because he had captured it on Saint Matthew's Day, Menéndez hastened back to St. Augustine. His prolonged absence had depressed its garrison, which feared that he and his men had been killed. Imagine the garrison's elation when, on September 24, they saw a soldier approaching and shouting at the top of his lungs: "Victory! Victory! The French fort is ours!" Menéndez had given him permission to run forward with the glad tidings. The chaplain Mendoza embraced the soldier and promised him a reward. Then Mendoza ran to his house as fast as he could, put on a surplice and the best cassock he had, and, holding a crucifix, went out and met Menéndez before that worthy reached the door. Then followed four priests, each bearing a cross, and women and children, weeping or laughing and chanting *Te Deum Laudamus* and offering up a thousand praises to God for so great a victory.

When the procession ended, Menéndez sent out two armed boats to the mouth of the St. Johns to prevent Jacques Ribaut from joining his father while returning to France with the news of the Spanish attack. When he learned that Jacques had already sailed he abandoned his plan and dispatched a single vessel with supplies to Fort San Mateo. A few days later, while he was taking his *siesta* in a hammock, a small group of

Indians brought him word that they had seen a French ship wrecked on the coast toward the south and that those who had escaped from her were on the banks of a river they could not cross. Menéndez immediately sent forty soldiers to ascertain their position while he himself, disguised in a French costume with a cape over his shoulders, followed with twelve soldiers in a boat. In the distance he saw the campfires of the Frenchmen and advanced toward them. A Frenchman, seeing him, swam out to meet him. Menéndez asked him to identify himself and his comrades.

"Followers of Ribaut, Viceroy of the King of France," replied the Frenchman.

"Are you Catholics or Lutherans?"

"All Lutherans."

Menéndez informed him that Fort Caroline had fallen and convinced him by showing him some of the spoil he had taken. The Frenchman swam back to his comrades but soon returned and asked Menéndez for a ship and sailors to return to France. Menéndez replied that he was waging war of fire and blood against heretics and that, therefore, he could grant them no safety. To all their pleading he had only one reply: "Surrender your arms and place yourselves at my mercy, that I may do with you as Our Lord may command me."

The Frenchman took these terms to his comrades, who sent him back to Menéndez with an offer of five thousand ducats in return for their lives. Menéndez indignantly replied that the sum was more than enough for such a poor sailor as himself but that mercy would be shown for its own sake and not for price. The starving Frenchmen saw no alternative but to yield themselves to his mercy. They surrendered their banners, their arquebuses and pistols, their swords and targets, their helmets and breastplates. Then Menéndez sent twenty of his men to bring the prisoners to him, ten at a time. When the French officers arrived, he conducted them to the rear of a sand hill.

"Gentlemen," he said, from custom rather than from sincerity, "I have few soldiers and they are inexperienced. You are many. If you go unbound, it would be an easy matter for you to take your revenge on us for the people we slew when we took the fort. It is therefore necessary that you march the four leagues from here to my camp with your hands tied behind you."[27]

Each group as it landed was fed, tied, and led behind the sand hill. When, at the close of day, all of them were brought together, Mendoza, admitting to himself that he was "a priest with the bowels of a man," begged Menéndez to spare the "Christians," that is, Catholics, among them. Menéndez spared ten Bretons who said they were Catholics and four carpenters and calkers of whose services he had great need. They were put on one of the boats and taken to St. Augustine. The rest were ordered to march thither by land. Menéndez walked ahead until he reached a hummock, where he paused long enough to draw a line with his spear in the sand. Then he went on. At dusk, as the last faint flush of the sun faded from sea and sky, the Frenchmen arrived at the spear line in the sand. There the Spaniards fell on them, killed them, and slashed off their heads. At dawn Menéndez reached St. Augustine.[28]

The next few days brought him great anxiety. He heard that some of his ships were lost and that others were scattered or lagging on their way. Only a part of his fleet had reached Florida, and, of this, a large part was still at Fort San Mateo. He knew that Jean Ribaut could not be far off, and that he could hope to defeat his superior numbers only by surprising them. Next day Indians brought him word that Ribaut with two hundred men was in the neighborhood of the place where the two French ships had been wrecked. Having lost their provisions, they subsisted on roots and grass and impure water collected in the holes and pools along their route. Menéndez resolved to capture them by repeating the tactics of his previous exploit. He sent a group of soldiers by land while he followed with a hundred fifty additional troops.

Reaching the the inlet at midnight, he again ambushed himself on the bank. Next morning he could see the French on the other side. The French, too, saw their enemies and offered them battle. They displayed their banners and sounded their fifes and drums. Menéndez ignored them. Instead, he ordered his men to sit down to breakfast while he with three officers walked coolly along the shore. This attitude brought the desired effect. The French blew a trumpet of parley and showed a white flag. Menéndez replied in the same manner. Ribaut then sent out a sailor who shouted across the water that a Spanish envoy should be sent over.[29]

"You have a raft;" replied Menéndez, "come yourselves."

But a French sailor saw an Indian canoe on the Spanish side, paddled to it and back unmolested, and presently returned with Ribaut's sergeant-major, Le Caille. He told Menéndez that the French numbered three hundred fifty and wished to return to the fort. He begged for boats to aid them in crossing the water.

"Brother, go with God's blessing, and deliver the reply which has been given you. If your general wants to come and speak with me, I give my word that he can come and go in safety with as many as four or six companions if he cares to bring them, or with the members of his council, so that he can choose the advice which best suits him."

The Frenchmen took this message to Ribaut, who that afternoon crossed over with eight of his men in a canoe. Menéndez met them courteously, offered them food and wine, which they scarcely touched, and then led Ribaut to the reeking spot in the sand where lay the corpses of his slaughtered comrades. By showing him a part of the plunder, Menéndez convinced Ribaut that Fort Caroline had fallen.

"What has happened to us, may well happen to you," said Ribaut. "Since your king and my king are brothers and friends, you should also be a friend and give us the ships we need to return to France."

When Menéndez equivocated, Ribaut begged leave to consult his officers, saying he would return as soon as they decided on what course they should take. Within three hours he was back with word that some of his people were ready to surrender but that many refused.

"They may do as they please," said Menéndez, dryly.

In behalf of those who wished to surrender, Ribaut offered Menéndez a ransom of a hundred thousand ducats.

"It grieves me very much to lose such a fine ransom and prize," said Menéndez, "for I have a pressing need of this aid to help in the conquest and settlement of this land, which, in the name of my king, is in my charge, as is the implantation of the Holy Gospel."[30]

Thinking that Menéndez could scarcely afford to forgo such a prize, Ribaut asked and obtained leave to discuss the matter with his officers. Next morning he returned with word that two hundred of his men had withdrawn from the place, but that the remaining one hundred fifty would surrender. And he handed over two royal standards, his sword, dagger, buckler, pistolet, gilt helmet, and a seal which Coligny had given him to stamp the decrees and titles he might issue. At Menéndez' orders one of his officers brought over the Frenchmen in groups of ten. All of them save Ribaut were led behind the sand hill where their hands were tied behind them while they were asked:

"Are you Catholics or Lutherans? Are there any who wish to confess themselves?"

Though Ribaut, whose hands were still free, replied that they were all of the Huguenot faith, sixteen of them, including drummers, fifers, and four German youths, declared that they were Catholics. They were spared. "*Domine, memento mei,*" sang Ribaut. When he had finished his psalm he turned to Menéndez:

"We are of the earth and to earth we must return. Twenty years more or less matters little."

Menéndez ignored him. He turned him over to his brother-in-law and biographer, Solis de Merás, and to an officer named San Vicente, with orders to kill him. San Vicente asked him for his fine felt hat, and he said:

"You know how captains must obey their generals and execute their commands. We must bind your hands."

This done, he walked a few steps with his prisoner until he suddenly struck him with his dagger and Merás drove his pike through his breast. Then they hacked off his head.[31]

Four days later Menéndez exultantly reported the massacre in a letter to his king:

I put Jean Ribaut and all the rest of them to the knife, judging it to be necessary to the service of the Lord Our God, and of Your Majesty. And I think it a very great fortune that this man be dead; for the King of France could accomplish more with him and fifty thousand ducats, than with other men and five hundred thousand ducats; and he could do more in one year, than another in ten; for he was the most experienced sailor and corsair known, very skillful in this navigation of the Indies and of the Florida coast.[32]

That night Menéndez returned to St. Augustine. Some of his men condemned him for his cruelty; others praised him for his mercy; all quarreled over their opinions.* Don Bartholomé Barrientos, Professor at the University of Salamanca, wrote an explanation of the matter which is celebrated for its uniqueness:

> He acted as an excellent inquisitor, for when asked if they were Catholics or Lutherans, they dared to proclaim themselves publicly as Lutherans, without fear of God or shame before man; and thus he gave them that death which their insolence deserved. And even in that he was very merciful in granting them a noble and honourable death, by cutting off their heads, when he could legally have burnt them alive. . . . He killed them, I think, rather by divine inspiration, than through any counsel of the human understanding, for he had no wish that his own people by touching pitch, should be defiled by it.[33]

But Menéndez had not yet completed his mission. Indians brought him word that a group of Frenchmen had fortified themselves on the coast southward, near Cape Canaveral. The Frenchmen were those who had refused to surrender. From pieces of the wrecked *Trinity* they were building a ship, in which they hoped to return to France. Menéndez quickly sent to Fort San Mateo for reinforcements which he augmented with his own soldiers. Leading a united force of two hundred fifty men, he pushed southward along the shore with such merciless speed that some of them dropped dead from wading night and day through the loose sands.

When the French saw them coming, they fled in panic to the forest. Menéndez burned the fort and incompleted ship, buried six guns which the Frenchmen had abandoned in their flight, and sent a trumpeter to summon them to surrender, promising them their lives. Their captain, with three or four others, told the messenger that they would rather be devoured by Indians than surrender to Spaniards. They took refuge in Indian villages. The rest, famished and trembling with cold and exhaustion, surrendered. This time, Menéndez saw fit to keep his word. Finding that some of the prisoners were Navarese of noble blood, he treated them with great kindness, gave them clothing, and seated them at his own

---

* Menéndez' massacre of the Huguenots has aroused considerable controversy among Catholic scholars. Fathers John Gilmary Shea and Joseph Woods and subsequent Catholic commentators have condemned it; Father Michael Kenny, among others, has condoned it. As a narrative historian, my purpose was simply to give an objective account of the massacre.

table. The sailors messed with the sailors and the soldiers with the soldiers. Under the influence of the priests, they soon renounced their errors and returned to Catholicism.[34]

On the back of Menéndez's dispatch, Philip made characteristic comment on everything his lieutenant had accomplished: "As to those he has killed he has done well, and as to those he has saved, they shall be sent to the galleys." Later he sent Menéndez a typically prolix letter in which he expressed gleeful approval of all his deeds:

> . . . as for the judgment you have executed upon the Lutheran corsairs, who have sought to occupy and fortify that country, to sow in it their evil sect, and to continue from there to robberies and injuries which they have committed and are still committing, wholly contrary to the service of God and of me, we believe that you have acted with entire justification and prudence, and we hold that we have been well served.[35]

4

In March, 1566, five and a half months after his departure from Florida, Laudonnière arrived at Moulins, where Charles IX was then holding court. There Laudonnière met Jacques Ribaut who blamed him for the disaster in Florida. He was especially critical of his failure to man a sufficient garrison when he could easily have strengthened it with two hundred men, and of his carelessness in allowing himself to be surprised while he slept.

Nevertheless, all Frenchmen united in their clamors for vengeance against the Spaniards. As soon as they returned home, Ribaut, Laudonnière, and Le Challeux had published accounts of the massacre. Le Challeux's account, published in May, went through two editions in the same year. That same month the widows of the victims went to Paris, where they demonstrated noisily before the royal palace. Then, in August, another deputation of a hundred twenty widows journeyed all the way from Normandy to Paris to ask the queen to take action against Spain. Though Catherine and her son deeply sympathized with their outraged subjects, their interests were so involved with those of Spain that, to conceal any semblance of countenancing a public demonstration against their ally, they were compelled to accord the widows a cool reception and then to send them back to their homes. Unable to lift her hand against the massacre of her subjects, Catherine sought relief for her outraged feelings in persistent but respected complaints to Philip for his cruelty, while she pressed him to punish Menéndez. But Philip, holding the whip hand, replied that had he permitted an invasion of his domains Indians would have been encouraged to rebel, that Florida was too important a locality to the navigation of his vessels to permit to it to foreigners, that France had been forewarned to stay away, and that the French in Florida had sunk Spanish ships. Catherine, fearing that Philip would declare her an enemy of her religion, dared not go beyond complaints and angry words. She was helpless to avenge the wrong.[36]

But Dominique de Gourges could and would. He was the scion of a distinguished Roman Catholic family who had served in Italy, where Spaniards had captured him and forced him to work as a galley slave. To this grievance he now added that of his nation: he would avenge both. Probably with the blessing of the queen and Coligny, and ostensibly to engage in the slave trade, he sold his property, borrowed money from his brother, who like him had served as a galley slave in Italy and who now held a high post in Guienne, and equipped three small vessels with a complement of one hundred arquebusiers and eighty soldiers, all well armed. On August 22, 1567, he sailed to the Indies, where he spent a short time trading with the natives and replenishing his food and water supply. Then he steered for Cape San Antonio, on the western end of Cuba, where he collected his men and addressed them with Gascon eloquence. Disclosing his true purpose, he inveighed against Spanish cruelty, pointing with angry rhetoric to the massacre at Fort Caroline and St. Augustine.

"What disgrace," he thundered, "if such an insult should pass unpunished! What glory to us, if we avenge it! To this I have devoted my fortune. I relied on you. I thought you jealous enough of your company's glory to sacrifice life itself in a cause like this. Was I deceived? I will show you the way; I will be always at your head; I will bear the brunt of the danger. Will you refuse to follow me?"

A chorus of cheers greeted his question; they clamored to advance against the Spaniards at once; but he persuaded them to wait until the full moon lessened the danger of crossing the Bahama Channel. When the moon rose they sailed, coasting along the north until, as morning broke, they anchored at the mouth of the St. Marys River. Armed Indians, mistaking them for Spaniards, thronged the shore to prevent them from landing. Gourges, summoning a trumpeter who had been in that region and who knew the Indians well, sent him ashore with many gestures of friendship. As soon as they recognized him, they yelped with delight and danced with joy. Among them was none other than Saturiba, an old friend of the French. Gourges told him that he had come as a friend to present him with gifts. Saturiba was so pleased that he summoned a grand council at which he presented Gourges with a French boy, Pierre Debray, sixteen years old, who had escaped from the fort and had lived with the chief. Debray told Gourges that the Spaniards were four hundred strong and that they were well provided with ammunition and supplies. Saturiba offered Gourges his services. The Spaniards, he said, had treated his people cruelly, had driven them from their cabins, had stolen their corn, had raped their wives and daughters, and had killed their children. Gourges, delighted at this outburst against the

Spaniards, disclosed his plans to deliver them from the tyranny they had suffered.

"I came here," he said, "only to reconnoiter the country and make friends with you, then to go back and bring more soldiers; but when I hear what you are suffering from them, I wish to fall upon them this very day, and rescue you from their tyranny."

The soldiers applauded his words with thunderous cheers.

"But you will do your part," said Gourges; "you will not leave us all the honor."

"We will go," replied Saturiba, "and die with you, if need be."

"Then, if we fight, we ought to fight at once. How soon can you have warriors ready to march?"

The chief asked three days for preparation. Gourges cautioned him to secrecy in order to surprise the Spaniards.

"Never fear," replied Saturiba, "we hate them more than you do."[37]

Gourges confirmed the alliance by distributing among them gifts, which included knives, daggers, looking-glasses, hatchets, rings, bells, all of which they received with eager faces and tawny outstretched arms. Availing himself of Gourges' liberality, Saturiba pointed to his shirt and indicated a desire to own it; indeed, he begged one for each of his men as a kind of uniform for festivals and councils and even for their graves after death. As soon as Gourges met their request, they stalked around him, fluttering in the spoils of his wardrobe.[38]

He sent out three scouts to ascertain the strength and position of the Spaniards. When, at the end of three days, they returned, Saturiba with his braves departed for the mouth of a small river or creek, where Gourges with all his soldiers and sixty of his sailors in two boats joined him and pressed with him toward the Spanish fort. All day Gourges with ten arquebusiers reconnoitered among trunks of trees, fallen logs, tangled vines, and small streams, defying their own weariness in their feverish effort to locate the fort, only to halt before an impassable stream. Disappointed, he began to retrace his steps when an Indian offered to lead him by a better but longer route along the shore. Without waiting for his soldiers to rest, Gourges ordered them forward. The Indians, more skilled in woodcraft than their white friends, continued on the shorter route through the forest.[39]

At dawn they all met on the bank of a creek beyond which lay the fort. Gourges could see the Spaniards working on its defenses, which were slight and unfinished. As soon as the tide had fallen sufficiently to make the creek fordable, he selected a spot where trees concealed his approach and ordered his men to cross the creek. Tying his powder-flash to his morion or steel cap and holding his arquebus above his head with one hand and his sword with the other, each man waded in waist-deep water, cutting his shoes and wounding his feet on the sharp edges of the oyster shells that covered the bed of the creek. Before them stood their guerdon.

"Look!" cried Gourges to his men. "There are the robbers who have stolen this land from our king; there are the murderers who have butchered our countrymen! On, on! Let us avenge our king! Let us show that we are Frenchmen!"

He commanded his lieutenant, Cazenove, to attack the entrance with thirty men, while he with the remainder of his troops advanced to a low platform alongside the fort where the Spaniards had begun to dig a ditch. The Spaniards had just finished their lunch and were picking their teeth when they heard a startled cry:

"To arms! To arms! The French are coming! The French are coming!"

The voice was that of the cannonader who, mounting the platform, had seen the French striding toward him with their heads lowered. One of Saturiba's headmen ran toward the platform and drove his pike through the cannonader from breast to neck. By this time the Spaniards were pouring out of the fort, still uncertain whether to fight or to retreat. Gourges heard Cazenove shouting from the gate that the Spaniards were escaping by it. Whereupon Gourges with his men ran to the gate and caught sixty Spaniards between his group and that of his lieutenant. Not one of the sixty Spaniards escaped save those who were captured.[40]

The victorious leader returned to the first blockhouse and prepared to attack San Mateo. He made eight ladders and sent Indians to ambush themselves on both sides of the fort, while he himself followed with part of his men. The Spaniards, seeing the motley army of savages and whites approaching, fled to the woods where groups of Indians, leaping from ambush and raising their hideous war cry, cut down all of them save fifteen whom Gourges saved for the more inglorious finish he planned for those he had captured at the fort. He ranged the pallid wretches before him and said:

"Did you think that so vile a treachery, so detestable a cruelty, against a king so potent and a nation so generous, would go unpunished? I, one of the humblest gentlemen among my king's subjects, have charged myself with avenging it. Even if the Most Christian and the Most Catholic kings had been enemies, at deadly war, such perfidy and extreme cruelty would still have been unpardonable. Now that they are friends and close allies, there is no name vile enough to brand your deeds, no punishment sharp enough to requite them. But though you cannot suffer as you deserve, you shall suffer all that an enemy can honorably inflict, that your example may teach others to observe the peace and alliance which you have so perfidiously violated."[41]

With these words ringing in their ears, they were swung from the branches of the same trees on which they had purportedly hanged the Huguenots, and over them was nailed the inscription, burned with a hot iron on a tablet of pine: "I do this not as to Spaniards, nor as to Marranos, but as to traitors, robbers, and murderers."[42]

Thus, Gourges fulfilled his mission. At his request the Indians burned the fort while he returned to his ships. Before he sailed, he assembled his men and requested them to thank God for their victory.

"My friends, let us give thanks to God for the success He has granted us. It is He who saved us from tempests; it is He who inclined the hearts of the Indians toward us; it is He who blinded the understanding of the Spaniards. They were four to one in forts well armed and provisioned. Our right was our only strength; and yet we have conquered. Not to our own swords, but to God only, we owe our victory. Then let us thank Him, my friends; let us never forget His favors; and let us pray that He may continue them, saving us from dangers, and guiding us safely home. Let us pray, too, that He may so dispose the hearts of men that our perils and toils may find favor in the eyes of our king and of all France, since all we have done was done for the king's service and for the honor of our country."[43]

On May 3, 1568, they sailed for home. Their exploit, though romantic, lacked the fullness of poetic justice, for the chief offender escaped punishment. At that moment Menéndez was high in favor at court, where night after night he regaled approving listeners with tales of his murderous exploits in Florida. As for Gourges, he was so well received at home that Spies, the Spanish ambassador to England, was mobbed and threatened as he passed through Bordeaux on his way from Spain to Paris. On June 25 Alava notified Philip II of the defeat of the Spaniards and four days later word of it reached the Spanish court. Alava protested the outrage committed by the French. Catherine merely remarked:

"See how they have only just written me that they have taken Florida?"

"I assure Your Majesty," wrote Alava to Philip, "that she did it with a manner which showed her great joy."

Spies, in his report to Philip, stated that the artillery that the French had captured in Florida had been ordered to be returned to Spain. To Philip all this was small consolation.[44]

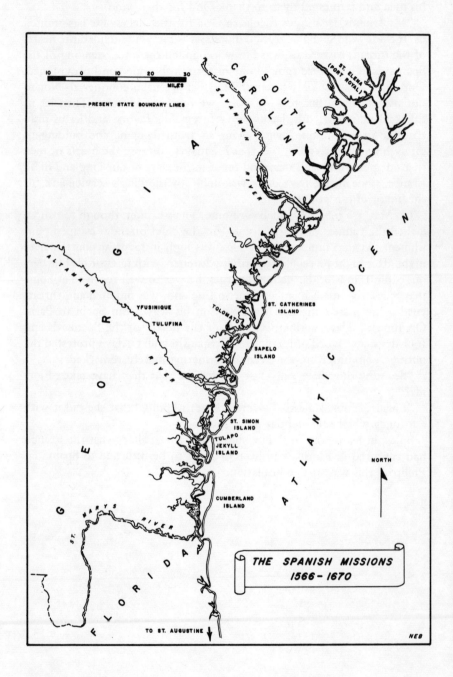

THE SPANISH MISSIONS
1566 - 1670

The Spanish Missions

IN SEPTEMBER, 1566, A FLEMISH PINNACE ANCHORED NEAR THE MOUTH of the St. Johns River. It carried the first Jesuit missionaries to Florida. Their leader, Father Pedro Martínez, got into a small boat with nine Flemings and a Spaniard and rowed ashore to ask the Indians the direction of St. Augustine. But the season of storms had begun. No sooner had the pinnace touched shore than a violent tempest drove it out to sea. Martínez, not daring to penetrate the interior for fear of the Indians, had no choice but to await the arrival of another vessel or the return of his own; but eventually, impelled by hunger, he and his companions got into the boat in which they had rowed ashore and followed the coast line in a southernly direction.[1]

Such was the inauspicious beginning of the Jesuit mission to the West Indies. Menéndez himself had been instrumental in its coming. Deeply moved by the great need of providing the Indians with religious instruction, he had appealed to Philip II to use his influence in that direction. The king in turn wrote to Francisco Borja, Duke of Gandia and Propositor General of the Jesuits, directing him to appoint twenty-four members of his Order as missionaries in such parts of the Indies as the Royal Council should designate. Unable to send so many, Borja did the next best thing, selecting three men of strong character and sound scholarship: Fathers Pedro Martínez and Juan Rogel and Brother Francisco de Villareal. Late in July, 1566, they sailed from San Lucar aboard a Flemish hooker in company with a fleet bound for New Spain. As they neared the coast of Florida, a violent storm separated their ship from the rest of the fleet. Though they landed only a few leagues from St. Augustine, they were unable to find any natives. So they coasted northward until, becoming desperate from lack of food, Martínez with the nine Flemings and the Spaniard, whose name was Flores, went ashore.[2]

In a hut they found a very large fish, of which they took half. As compensation, they left some strings of glass beads and a cape belonging to Flores. Next morning they met five Indians. Martínez pointed to his mouth to signify that he and his companions were hungry. They understood, for they went away and soon returned with a few fish. Martínez with a scissors cut out some figures from the parchment of a book and presented them to the Indians, who received them with wide-eyed pleasure. Eventually an Indian who was perhaps a hundred years old informed them by signs that they would find a Spanish settlement only after they had passed three villages at the mouths of three rivers. They went on, passing the mouths of two rivers and searching for a third, until, on September 28, they reached a small island called Tacatacuru, now Cumberland Island, where they saw four Indians fishing. Martínez and Flores, eager to go on without delay, remained in the boat; but the Flemings with a gesture of bravado sprang ashore. Suddenly Martínez and Flores, seeing one of the Indians running away, suspected some trickery. And within a few minutes appeared forty Indians, some of whom surrounded the boat and flung themselves aboard. They grasped three of the Flemings and Martínez by the shoulders, hurled themselves with them into water, beat them, and dragged them ashore. Flores, however, fiercely defended himself by biting off a piece of the hand of an Indian who tried to drown him. Free of his assailant, he hastily set out to sea with the six Flemings just as Indians, wading waist-deep in the water, wounded three of them with a volley of arrows.[3]

Martínez knew now that he was about to win a martyr's crown. As soon as he put foot on land, he raised resigned and supplicating hands toward heaven. That instant an Indian bashed in the monk's skull with a war club. By his death he fulfilled the desire he had expressed in Seville to Father Lobo, famous preacher of the Franciscan Order: "O, Father Lobo, what anxiety I feel to shed my blood at the hands of the barbarians, in defense of the faith, and with it to wash clean the shores of Florida!"[4]

The Flemings, desperately hungry and not knowing where they were, dropped anchor at the mouth of the San Mateo River. Some Spaniards, discovering the vessel in their flight, sent word to Menéndez, who was overcome to hear of the death of Martínez and the wounding of three of his companions as well as the loss of the bulls and licenses of Pius V, which authorized the conversion of the Indians under the tutelage of the Jesuit Order. Hopeful that the Flemish hooker with Father Rogel and Brother Villareal on board had not been lost, he sent one of his servants with a vessel to Puerto Rico, Santo Domingo, and Havana to search for it. He found the hooker in Havana, where it had taken refuge, and the missionaries in good health. Menéndez soon escorted them to the province of Carlos, in southwestern Florida, where he built a blockhouse, a house for the converted sister of the chief, Doña Antonia, and a chapel in which the priest could say Mass. Rogel gave instruction to the soldiers, who had long been deprived of the sacraments.[5]

Menéndez, meanwhile, had returned to Spain, where Borja granted his request for the priests he needed in Florida. At the same time Menéndez concluded with the Council of the Indies a bargain by which it paid his expenses of the galleon *San Pelayo* and other expenses he had incurred over and above those of his contract. The king appointed him governor of Cuba and gave him two hundred thousand ducats to defray part of the expenses of the voyage to Florida. On March 13, 1568, he sailed from San Lucar with ten missionaries led by Father Juan Bautista Segura, a native of Toledo and a former rector of several Jesuit colleges. Weathering a violent storm in the Bahama Channel, they arrived in Havana, whence they sailed to Florida.[6]

The missionaries labored assiduously in the province of Carlos. They preached in Tocabaga, north of Tampa Bay, and, by means of an interpreter, in the province of Tequesta, on the Miama River mouth at Biscayne Bay. Menéndez ordered Rogel to Santa Elena, on the present site of Port Royal, South Carolina, where he ministered to the settlers, the soldiers, and the natives. In the village of Orista, which consisted of about twenty dwellings, Rogel built a church and a house in which he lived with three Indian boys as assistants, one of whom, Juan, had so sweet and obedient a disposition that the priest could find no occasion to "remind him of the wholesome fear of discipline."[7]

Rogel was happy to find that the natives of the province were more rational than those of Carlos. They were neither base nor cruel nor thievish; they were monogamous; they preserved cleanliness in their homes and order in their gardens; they spoke truth, sought peace, loved justice. Rogel promised himself a full spiritual harvest. He applied himself so assiduously to their language that in six months he could converse and preach to them on such basic matters of faith as the unity of God, His power, His love of good and hatred of evil, reward and punishment, immortality of the soul, and universal resurrection. The artlessness and mental range of the Indians often fell short of understanding his theological abstractions. "Did God have a wife?" He dismissed their question with a faint smile. And they listened to him with such attention that he offered hearty thanks to God.[8]

Slowly, however, he realized that his preaching had made little headway. With the approach of winter they deserted him and scattered through the woods in search of acorns and game. To discourage their wanderings, he gave them hoes to help them in cultivating the soil. Though they gladly accepted the hoes, they soon began to regard them as implements of slavery. Their ancient customs proved stronger than their civilization and Christianity; they soon scattered over the surrounding country. And Rogel, heavy of heart, returned to those few who remained to teach them some of the precepts of his beloved Catholic faith.[9]

But he soon became involved in new difficulties with them. He attempted to explain to them the mystery of the Trinity and the reason for venerating the Cross. At first they listened to him with much devotion. Confident that they were ready to accept more difficult theological abstractions, he told them that they could not become sons of God unless they declared themselves enemies of the devil, author of all evil. The Indians, thinking that he was condemning one of their gods, became so incensed that they turned their backs to him and mocked at everything he said. The devil, they replied, was the best person in the world; he made men fearless and brave. This disgusted Father Rogel, who doubtless was "not unwilling to associate the Prince of Evil or any other potentate of unrighteousness with their gods." Yet he was reluctant to leave them. In return for their promise to accept Christianity, he offered to live among them; but they all refused with some trivial excuse. So he returned to Orista, where he found the inhabitants enjoying a great feast on the banks of the Savannah River.

"I have come," he said to them, "from the land of the sunrise, brought here by concern for your welfare as fellow beings, to seek your salvation. For your good alone, and without benefit to myself, I have endeavored to teach you, bestow gifts, and help you. You have seen how I have given whatever you have asked, though you have given me nothing. I have taken neither my sustenance nor sustenance for my Brothers from you—an effective proof of how much I care for you and love you, if my having come from such distant lands and voluntarily suffered so many hardships for your sake were not enough. I have been solicitous to teach you; and when it seems that you are beginning to learn, you mock my Doctrine without fear of punishment from God, who makes manifest that Doctrine; for it is in His name that I proclaim His Holy Faith. If you should care to learn the Doctrine sincerely and put aside the error in which you live, I shall remain until you are instructed. If not, I shall have done my duty by this warning and shall return to Spain."[10]

"If you care so much for us," responded their spokesman, "why do you leave us? You do not speak truth."

The Indians became angry and began to mistreat Rogel by word and deed, while he tried gravely but gently to assuage them by qualifying his words as much as possible. Eventually they allowed him to go back to his house and chapel. Despairing of their barbarity and promising to return when they were willing to hear him, he demolished chapel and church and, packing his few books, returned to Santa Elena. Later he sailed for Havana, taking with him Father Antonio Sedeño and some boys whom he wished to educate in the Jesuit college established there in the previous year.[11]

In Havana the priest found Governor Menéndez, who had just returned from Spain with provisions for Florida. He also brought letters from Propositor General Borja, one of which enjoined Father Antonio Sedeño to continue his work in Florida, even though it should promise little hope of succeeding.

Sedeño soon embarked with Rogel, Villareal and Menéndez for Santa Elena, but long before he reached that settlement he had opportunity to exercise his charity. During the voyage most of the soldiers became so sick that they permitted him no rest. And on his arrival they came down with a contagion. Most of them recovered, but Sedeño and Villareal, weakened by their unresting ministrations, failed to recuperate, despite their use of the remedies which had proved efficacious with their comrades. Thereupon Menéndez sent them back to Havana in the face of their protests. But the pilot was so careless and the sea so stormy that the ship wrecked on some shoals. Everything on board was lost save the passengers who reached shore in a very weakened condition and began trudging toward an Indian village. The inhabitants greeted them with howls and showers of arrows, which doubtless would have finished them had not the soldiers been able to defend themselves with some arms and ammunition they had salvaged. Very hungry, wounded, and tired, they reached St. Augustine, where they slowly recovered from their calamities.[12]

2

Undaunted, Father Segura planned new missions with greater zeal. Withdrawing his missions from Guale and Orista, he turned his attention to the Indian villages of Ajacán in the Chesapeake Bay region of Virginia. In 1561 some soldiers in Villafañe's ill-fated expedition had, in the practice of the time, abducted the brother of a chief of that country for the purpose of teaching him Spanish to enable him to serve them as an interpreter in their conversations with his people. At the end of the expedition Dominican monks had taken him to Mexico, where they presented him to Viceroy Luis de Velasco who had him baptized and gave him his name. Later the viceroy had taken his godson to Spain and presented him to Philip II, who clothed and perhaps educated him. Then Menéndez brought him back to Havana, where he met Father Segura. Handsome, well-proportioned, and seeming a devout Catholic, Don Luis easily won the admiration and trust of his benefactors. They banked on his assistance in settling the land and in converting Indians to Christianity. Their faith in him was entirely misplaced. His conversion had not been genuine. He sought to assuage his troubled conscience by planning to betray the missionaries.[13] He proved a Judas in the guise of a Timothy.

The missionaries, believing in his fervid and earnest promises to secure the support of his brother, the chief of Ajacán, in converting the natives of that region, named him to accompany them to their mission. In January, 1570, Father Segura in company with Don Luis, Father Luis de Quiros, and Brothers Sancho Zaballos and Gabriel Gómez sailed to Santa Elena, where they spent several months planning the proposed mission to Ajacán. On August 5 they sailed from Santa Elena for Chesapeake Bay with seven companions including Father Luis de Quiros, Brothers Gabriel Gómez, Sancho Zaballos and Pedro de Limares. Bad weather and difficulties in finding the region of which they were in search prolonged the journey, during which the Jesuits were compelled to share their provisions with the crew of the ship. By the time they approached their destination, they had consumed all their flour and half of their four barrels of biscuit. Discovering Chesapeake Bay, they ascended it until, on September 10, they arrived at the province of Ajacán, where they entered and sailed up the James River as far as College Brook and unloaded.[14]

Two days later Fathers Quiros and Segura wrote to Juan de Hinistrosa, governor of Cuba, expressing surprise at their finding the country of Don Luis "in quite another condition than expected, not because he was at fault in his description of it, but because Our Lord has chastised it with six years of famine and death, which has brought it about that there is much less population than usual."[15]

The corn of the scant harvests had been eaten; the wild fruits on which the natives subsisted had perished; and they were reduced to eating roots and herbs "obtained with great labor from the soil, which is very parched." The Indians received Don Luis with primitive manifestations of joy, as though he "had risen from the dead and come down from heaven." The chief, who lived some distance away, invited the missionaries to baptize his three-year-old son, who lay gravely ill. Segura sent one of his comrades to administer the sacrament.[16]

In their letter to Hinistrosa the missionaries had dwelled pleadingly on the absolute necessity of dispatching a vessel to their succor during March or not later than the beginning of April "so that we can give seeds to the tribe for planting." Since they proposed to establish their mission nearby, they included instructions on how the relief expedition should find them:

> . . . from the time it is understood that the frigate is to come with the help requested, one or two Indians will be sent with a letter to the mouth of the arm of the sea, along which any ship coming must sail. Thus, when they see the ship, they will make a large smoke signal by day and a fire at night. Furthermore, the people there will have a sealed letter of yours and they will not return it until they receive another like it, which is to be a sign that those who come are friendly and are the ones who bring the message . . . our letter will carry information about the way which must be followed in entering and serve as a guide.[17]

Finding themselves without supplies, they built a hut of logs and branches in which they might have shelter and say Mass. Don Luis remained with them, serving them as interpreter and teacher. They spent most of the winter waiting patiently but vainly for the relief expedition. In February, Don Luis left them under pretense of preparing a place for their reception and returned to the village of his brother. They were now reduced to searching the forest for herbs and roots on which to subsist.[18]

When Don Luis failed to return at the designated time, Segura sent Father Quiros and two of the brothers after him. They marched to their martyrdom. Don Luis had already planned their death. He received them with a great show of friendship, promising to return on the following day, and Quiros and his two comrades believed him. That night, as they were returning to their hut, Don Luis with a band of Indians followered them and soon overtook them. Quiros, unable to see Don Luis' companions because of the darkness and supposing him to be alone, greeted him in a friendly manner. The only reply was a shower of arrows, some of which entered Quiros' heart and killed him. While Don Luis stripped the priest of his cassock and put it on, his companions with their clubs beat the two brothers. One of them soon died. The other, with blood running from his battered head, fled to the woods and hid himself. Next morning, however, the Indians found him, killed him, and burned his body together with that of the other missionary.[19]

But Don Luis had not yet fully realized his savage purpose. Fearing that the remaining missionaries would defend themselves with the few hatchets and knives that served them in their daily offices, he decided to kill them also. As soon as Segura saw him approaching in Quiros' cassock, he knew that his end had come. Don Luis asked him for the hatchets and knives, saying he wanted to cut some wood for him. As the missionaries handed these to him they knelt before the improvised altar and each, as he prayed softly, received a single blow on the head from an ax. Only one of them escaped—the little boy Alonso, who was saved by Don Luis' brother and on whose account rests the description we give here. The Indians lacked the humanity to bury their victims in the crude chapel. But, impressed or unimpressed, they lacked neither the resolution to burn the chapel nor the sacrilege to dance over its ashes.[20]

Meanwhile, in the fall of 1570, Governor Hinistrosa in Havana received the letter written by Quiros and Segura. He provisioned a small ship and, in the spring of the following year, sent it to Ajacán under Vicente Gonzales and Brother Juan Salcedo. Seeing none of the signals they expected and unwilling to land without some word from the missionaries, they grew suspicious and stayed on the ship. But the Indians saw them. Disguised in the cassocks stolen from their victims they tried to induce the missionaries to go ashore by shouting: "Come, here are the Fathers you seek!" This macabre ruse, however, only confirmed their suspicions. At this juncture two of the Indians swam out to the ship, where they were seized and dragged aboard for Havana. To avoid the full force of the Gulf Stream, the ship returned along the coast, close to land. One of the Indians, availing himself of this circumstance, jumped overboard and was never seen again. The other Indian reached Havana in chains; but fear of punishment sealed his lips.[21]

By this time Menéndez had returned with settlers and supplies to St. Augustine. As soon as he learned from Father Gonzalez that Segura and his companions had been murdered, he immediately resolved to punish the offenders. He sailed to Santa Elena, picked up Rogel and Villareal, who had journeyed there from Saint Augustine, and some soldiers, and proceeded to Ajacán in a small but swift ship. On reaching the bay, Menéndez with thirty soldiers landed and seized a number of Indians who, to save their own lives, readily charged Don Luis with the massacre. Menéndez told one of them, who was a chief, that he would punish those he had captured unless Don Luis surrendered. The chief volunteered to bring in the renegade within five days. But when at the end of that time the chief failed to appear, Menéndez ordered that eight of the condemned Indians be hanged from the yardarm of the ship. Before they died, Rogel with the assistance of the boy Alonso, who had returned to the missionaries and served as their interpreter, converted them to Christianity. Rogel wanted to go inland with some of the soldiers to recover the bodies of the martyrs; but Menéndez, unwilling to divide his men, refused him permission. So the expedition returned to Santa Elena, whence Rogel and his companions continued to Havana.[22]

On learning of the death of Segura and his companions, Propositor General Borja recalled the Jesuits from Florida. Father Pedro Sánchez, whom Borja placed over the Jesuits in Havana and Florida, ordered them to Mexico. With their departure Florida reached the lowest ebb of its colorful history.

3

In 1574 Pedro Menéndez de Avilés returned to Spain, where he died. The ensuing decade brought a shocking indifference in the spiritual and temporal needs of Florida. Few priests remained in the peninsula to say Mass and to administer the sacraments. But gradually, with the coming of the Franciscans, the picture changed. These sons of Giovanni de Bernadone, better known as St. Francis of Assisi, succeeded where the sons of St. Dominic and St. Ignatius had failed. Their first real missionary activity in Florida began in 1584, when Father Alonso de Reynoso arrived there with eight friars. This Junípero Serra of the Atlantic coast was a devout and zealous man who combined crusading zeal and invincible persuasiveness with profound knowledge and inspired teaching. He returned to Spain, where he recruited thirteen more friars for missionary work in Florida. When he arrived with them in St. Augustine, Governor Pedro Menéndez Marqués, a nephew of his predecessor, greeted them with this poem:

> *Padres Franciscanos pues habeis venido*
> *De los remotas partes del Oriente*
> *A ocupar este seco y pobre nido,*
> *A donde absconde el sol su roja frente,*
> *Lo que con humildad a todos pide,*
> *Prediqueis a estos indios de Occidente*
> *Que tienen al demonio por amigo*
> *Y a Dios que los creó por enemigo.*

Franciscan Fathers, so you have come
From the distant parts of the East
To settle this poor and barren nest
Where the sun's fair face is hid.
What humbly now I beg you all
Is to teach these western tribes
Who look upon Satan as a friend
But their Maker, God, regard as foe.[23]

The friars, equipped with mattresses, blankets, and pillows, went to various Indian towns and began their work. By this time St. Augustine had become a flourishing town with public buildings, a parish church, and well-cultivated gardens. But in 1586 Francis Drake, with twenty-three hundred men, after leading a successful raid on the Spanish Main, landed at Fort San Juan de Pinos, near St. Augustine, for the purpose of surprising its garrison. The Spaniards, correctly believing that Drake had a force numerically superior to their own, fired a few shots and then abandoned the fort for St. Augustine, where a larger garrison was stationed. Drake and his men then advanced on the town while its inhabitants fled to the surrounding countryside. The Englishmen, finding the town deserted, burned it to the ground. Then they sailed for Santa Elena to destroy it also, but a rough sea and contrary winds prevented their landing. They continued northward toward Virginia.[24]

In view of these circumstances and the possibility of new raids, Father Reynoso pressed his superiors for more missionaries. The appointment of a new governor, Domingo Martínez de Avendaño, gave fresh impetus to missionary work. The Council of the Indies, responding to his appeal for more friars, sent twelve Franciscans under Father Juan de Silva. In 1594, provided with certain vestments, cruets, missals, bells, and other items of necessity in a church, they reached St. Augustine, where they presented themselves to the Superior, Fray Francisco Marrón. Believing that the Indians of Guale, in present eastern Georgia, were "ripe for the harvest," Marrón assigned to it six of his best men—Pedro de Corpa, Miguel de Auñon, Francisco de Velascola, Blas Rodríguez, Antonio Badajoz, and a lay friar. Avendaño himself escorted them to their posts to protect them from possible danger and to commend them to the various tribes. In this task, however, he contracted a tropical disease. Feeling his end was near, he offered up his soul to God and chose as his successor Gonzalo Méndez de Canzo, a forceful and experienced seaman whose primary ambition was the conversion of the Indians.[25]

The missionary at Tolomato was Father Corpa. Stern, quick-tempered, and frank, he constantly reprimanded those of his charges who practiced polygamy. One of the leading offenders was Juanillo, son of the chief of Guale and an exceedingly arrogant, quarrelsome, and warlike young man. Corpa told him in no uncertain terms that, since he claimed to be a Christian, he ought to act like one and put away all of his

wives save the one to whom he was lawfully wed. This injunction
Juanillo wrathfully disdained. Whereupon Corpa deprived him of his
hereditary office as head *mico* or chief and bestowed it on a certain
Don Francisco who was long past the age when the attractions of Indian
damsels had any meaning for him.

Highly incensed, Juanillo left the mission without Corpa's permission
and soon collected around him a group of pagan Indians. He reminded
them that the Franciscans were only the vanguard of a general wave of
Spanish immigration that eventually would deprive them of land as well
as liberty. He added that the Franciscans discussed peace and brother-
hood but that they planned to make themselves rulers and masters of
the Indians. He concluded that their only means of survival against a
Spanish invasion was to kill the missionaries.[26]

They greeted his words with jubilant shouts. Decorating themselves
with feathers and war paint, they betook themselves to Tolomato and
on the following morning, September 13, 1597, hid themselves in the
church to realize their murderous intent. When the unsuspecting priest
opened the door of his church, they killed him with a blow from a stone
hatchet.

Next day, while exulting over Corpa's body, Juanillo gathered the
chiefs of many Indian villages and harangued them on his warlike plans.

"The friar is dead," he said. "He would not have been killed had he
let us live as we did before we became Christians. Let us return to our
ancient customs and prepare to defend ourselves against the retribution
the governor of Florida will attempt against us. If he has his way, on
account of this friar, it will be as severe as if we had done away with all
of them. Because of the friar we have killed, he will attack us the same
way he would on behalf of all of them."

They applauded his words, agreeing that Governor Canzo would
doubtless try to take the same revenge for one that he would for all.

"Well, then," continued Juanillo, "if the retribution inflicted for one
will not be less than for all of them, let us take back the liberty these friars
steal from us with their promises of treasures they have never seen—
in expectation of which they assume that those of us who call ourselves
Christian will put up with this mischief and grief now.

"They take away our women, leaving us only the one and perpetual,
forbidding us to exchange her; they prevent our dancing, banquets, feasts,
celebrations, games, and warfare, so that by disuse we shall lose our
ancient courage and skill inherited from our ancestors. They persecute
our old folks, calling them witches. Even our work annoys them and they
want us to cease on certain days. When we are disposed to all they wish,
still they are not satisfied. It is all a matter of scolding us, abusing us,
oppressing us, preaching to us, calling us bad Christians, and taking away
from us all the joy that our forefathers got for themselves—all in the
hope that we will attain heaven. But these are delusions, to subjugate us
by having us disposed to their ends. What can we hope for, unless to be

slaves? If we kill them all now, we shake off the heavy yoke from that moment. Our courage will cause the governor to treat us well; in case, that is, he doesn't come off badly beforehand."[27]

The multitude agreed with his views. Cutting off Corpa's head, they placed it on a pole near the harbor as a trophy of victory. His body, which they threw in the woods, was never found.[28]

They went to Father Blas Rodríguez' hut in Tupique and told him they had come to kill him.

"My children," said the priest calmly, "for me it is not a difficult thing to die, for the death of the body will come, even though you be not the instrument of my death. Every hour we must expect it; in the end we shall have to die. What hurts me is your loss and the fact that the Devil has been able to make you commit so great an offense against your God and Creator; it hurts me, likewise, that you are so ungrateful for the work which I and the other Fathers have undertaken in your behalf in order to teach you the way to heaven."[29]

Tears gathered in his eyes as he continued:

"Look, children, you still have time, if you wish to depart from your evil intention; God, our Master, is most merciful and He will forgive you."

Seeing them adamant in their evil purpose, the priest begged them to let him sing Mass. The Indians checked their ferocity and, granting his wish, reclined on the floor of the hut. When he had finished the Mass, he distributed his slight effects among them. Then, turning to his executioners, he knelt and repeated the generous, self-abnegating petition: "Forgive them, for they know not what they do." He had scarcely uttered these words than he received a mortal blow from the hatchet of one of the chiefs. Without a sense of blasphemy or a moment of hesitancy they threw his body into a field to be consumed by wild beasts and carrion birds. Much later an old Christian Indian took up the decomposed body and reverently buried it on a high and wooded hill.[30]

Exulting in the easiness of their crimes, Juanillo and his followers dispatched a messenger to the chief of St. Catherine Island to kill its two missionaries, Fathers Auñon and Badajoz. But the chief, being well disposed toward the friars, sent a courier to warn them. The messenger, either from fear or treachery, returned with a spurious answer. Then the chief himself went to warn the priests who, however, replied that, as men of God, they had no choice but to die for Him. The chief retired, but soon Juanillo and his followers swept down on the two missionaries and killed them.[31]

Juanillo then led his followers against Father Velascola on the island of St. Simons. The monk was such a large and powerful man that the Indians greatly feared him. Learning that he was just returning by boat from St. Augustine, they hid in a clump of trees near the bank of disembarkation, where, on his arrival, they seized him by the shoulders and killed him with stone hatchets and tomahawks. Then they pounded his body and cut it up beyond recognition to make sure he would not revive to fight them.[32]

From St. Simons they went to Jekyl Island, where Father Dávila had established a mission in the village of Tulapo. Striding up to his house, they pounded for admission. Instead of opening the door, Father Dávila hid himself in a palm thicket. There the Indians hunted him and, in the brilliant moonlight, saw him crouching in a coppice. Instantly three arrows quivered in his shoulders; but one of the Indians, who was perhaps a chief, protected him, took him naked and wounded to some infidel Indians of an interior village, where he made him serve as a slave.[33]

Encouraged by his successes, Juanillo planned to attack Cumberland Island, even though it had a Spanish garrison and lay near St. Augustine. The chief of the island, Don Juan, was himself a candidate to the same office as Juanillo and therefore hated him. Juanillo, gathering a large supply of arrows, planned to make short shrift of his rival and of his Spanish friends. But he reckoned without destiny's capricious hand.

Landing on October 4 in the port of San Pedro, he and his men spied a brigantine nearby and presumed correctly that it carried supplies for the monks and reinforcements for the garrison. They hesitated; they drew back; then, suddenly, they heard the desperate howling of a dog. This aroused Don Juan's old Indian servant, Jusepe, who, thinking the dog was howling at his master's horse, ventured out to call it. As soon as they heard him Juanillo's men shot five arrows in his shoulders and back. Though critically wounded, the old servant crawled back to get his bow and arrows, but he was too weak to draw. By now Don Juan and his braves were aroused from sleep; dashing down to the canoes, they seized them and then fiercely attacked Juanillo's men, who fled in all directions.[34]

Meanwhile, one of the missionaries of the island, Father Pedro Fernandez Chozas, aroused by the pandemonium outside, ran from his house to the church where, he later declared, he put on his vestments and began to celebrate "the Mass of my glorious and Seraphic Father, St. Francis, for it was on his feast day."[35] Then he and the other missionary, Father Francisco Pareja, sent the soldiers on the brigantine to Canzo with a letter begging him for immediate protection. As grim evidence of the shocking revolt, they sent with the letter Father Velascola's cloak.

Though ill, Canzo, as soon as he received the letter, took measures against Juanillo. With the approval of the church dignitaries on the island, he sent Sergeant Juan de Santiago with a dozen soldiers to protect the friars and the Christian Indians. Ten days later Canzo led a hundred fifty light infantry to San Pedro, where he began a series of punitive expeditions. To Guale and Tolomato he sent a reconnissance force of twenty-two men under Captain Vicente Gonzalez who, however, alarmed the Indians so much that they fled to the mountains or hid in the forest. He succeeded, however, in capturing an Indian who stated that most of the friars had been murdered, though he disclaimed any connection with the murderers. He also disclosed that Juanillo and his followers had gathered on the island of Ospo. To that place Canzo rushed for a surprise attack at dawn. As soon as they landed on the island his men were attacked and some of them were wounded, but Canzo pressed forward, burning village, public buildings and granaries, and sparing only the church, which miraculously still stood. Proceeding to Tolomato, he burned all its houses and sent Alonso Díaz to investigate and, if possible, to take some native alive.

Finding the village deserted, Díaz burned it to the ground. He saw a hand protruding from a grave and, uncovering it, found the burial place of two murdered Franciscans. Exhuming the bodies, he identified them as those of Father Miguel de Auñon and Brother Antonio Badajóz. Their legs and arms had been broken. The feet were tied together. The corpses emitted such a terrific stench that the soldiers could not transfer them but identified them for later removal by placing a modest marker over their grave.[36]

To several rebellious villages Canzo sent soldiers who burned everything in sight. On November 11, seeing the futility of pursuing the rebellious Indians into the interior, he returned to San Pedro. At this juncture he learned that Father Dávila was living near the village of Tulufina, where the Indians held him in captivity. Canzo, advancing into the province of Guale, sent word to its inhabitants that he was coming to rescue the friar. He offered rewards for his release. The Indians, after imprisoning the friar for several months, freed him that he might bring them water and firewood and keep birds and animals from the seeds and the ripening corn. Sometimes they turned him over to some Indian boys who amused themselves by using him as a target in archery practice. Sometimes they teased and abused him. Once they asked him to make powder and bullets for ten arquebuses they had captured, perhaps from the Spaniards. He refused, saying that he did not know how.

"Do not excuse yourself," they replied, "you do know how."

"I have no books," insisted the friar, "because you have taken them away from me."

"We will bring them."

So saying, they brought him a breviary, a copy of the *Summa*, and a copy of *The Prayer Book of Religious*. Though he tried to explain that these were the wrong kind of books, they continued to press him to fulfill their request until he made them understand that he lacked the necessary materials. To him the books were a source of consolation. He hid them in the hollow of an oak tree, where he often went to read them.[37]

Eventually they tired of his suffering and of his almost divine patience; they clamored to burn him alive. As they tied him to a stake and began to heap up wood around him, they pressed him to embrace their gods and espouse one of their women. His only reply was a mild rebuke. At this juncture a squaw came forward with the proposal that they save the priest and exchange him for her son, who was a prisoner in St. Augustine.

Though they granted her request, they would not let Dávila go until one of Canzo's captains arrived with three hundred men and threatened to massacre all of them and burn their crops. Greatly alarmed, they handed over the long-suffering priest, who soon returned with the captain and seven Indian prisoners to St. Augustine.

Dávila was so changed that at first nobody recognized him; then everybody received him with boundless sympathy. The good friar, however, refused to testify against his enemies, saying that, in cases so criminal, he must refrain, in accordance with the canons of his office, from implicating innocent people. One of the witnesses was an Indian lad of seventeen named Lucas, who admitted he had been present at the murder of Father Blas Rodríguez. Such testimony proved damaging to himself; Canzo, unable to prove guilty any of the other witnesses, resolved to put him to death as an example of what punishment awaited those who murdered missionaries. He decreed that Lucas "leave the jail where he now is . . . with a rope around his neck, his hands tied behind him, and with a loud voice his crime must be proclaimed to the public; that he be taken to the gallows, already prepared for this purpose, and that there he shall be hung by the neck and strangled until dead."[38] The sentence was duly carried out.

Canzo also issued a decree enslaving any of the Guale Indians that might be captured; but the king strenuously rejected it as unjust. Whereupon the governor released the captured Indians but kept a careful watch over them. As they made their way homeward, he sent a contingent of eighteen soldiers under Alonzo Díaz de Badajóz on a reconnaissance mission. This officer found the Indians in a repentant mood. Some of them, including chiefs, accompanied him on his return to St. Augustine and found employment in the Spanish service.[39]

The governor now took steps to reward his friends and to placate his enemies. Touched by the poverty of his Timucuan neighbors, and mindful of their aid in withstanding the recent rebellion, he reduced the tribute in grain for each married man and, as a token of obedience, demanded an increased tribute from each single man. The faithful Don Juan he rewarded with the sum of two hundred ducats.[40]

Yet Juanillo retained many of his followers. One of these was Don Francisco, whom Father Corpa had chosen *mico* of Guale instead of Juanillo. Far from feeling grateful to the Spaniards, Don Francisco joined Juanillo. He and Juanillo led their followers into the interior of Guale and fortified themselves in the village of Yfusinique. In October, 1601, Canzo, learning of their whereabouts, sent Diego de Cárdenas and Sebastian de Ynclán, an Indian interpreter, to enlist the support of the chief of Asao in assaulting them. The chief quickly called up his warriors and set out for Yfusinique, where he found the rebels strongly entrenched.

Before attacking them he sent Juanillo and Don Francisco a message promising to refrain from attacking the fort if they surrendered. They chose to defy him. Whereupon Asao attacked with such murderous energy that many of its defenders were killed. Among them were Juanillo and Don Francisco, whose scalps Asao ordered cut off and carried down to St. Augustine to be exhibited to the Spaniards with pride. With their deaths the revolt collapsed. The Indians, after three years of warfare, returned to dig and plant around St. Augustine, certain that peace once more prevailed in Guale and along the northern border.[41]

4

In 1604, Canzo's successor, Pedro de Ibarra, accompanied by Father Pedro Ruíz and a force of infantry, journeyed in an impressive ship to the Guale villages along the coast and inland. Everywhere the Indians pledged their allegiance to him while they gloated over his gifts, which included coarse woolen cloth, hats, looking-glasses, knives, hatchets, and spades. While Father Ruíz sang Mass and dedicated new churches, Ibarra, through interpreters, made numerous speeches in which he promised more missionaries. Within a month Ibarra succeeded in reconciling the rival tribes and in clearing the ground for renewed missionary activity in the recently rebellious province.[42]

The promised missionaries, seven in number, arrived in St. Augustine at the end of 1605 and proceeded to their assignments, which embraced large parts of present Florida and Georgia. There they made innumerable converts and petitioned their mission guardian in St. Augustine, Father Blas de Montes, for a bishop to administer the sacrament of confirmation to Indians as well as second-generation Spaniards. Father de Montes in turn interceded with King Philip III, who authorized an episcopal visitation to Florida. The task fell to the newly consecrated Bishop Fray Juan de las Cabezas Altamirano, whose spiritual jurisdiction embraced Cuba, Jamaica, and the mainland provinces. In the middle of March, 1606, he arrived at St. Augustine in a ship that flew the colors of Spain over an English pirate ship, the first bishop ever to visit Florida.[43]

He began his work propitiously during the Lenten season. On Holy Thursday he blessed the Holy Oils and Chrism; on Good Friday he meditated and prayed; on Holy Saturday he ordained twenty young men, Spaniards and Indians, to the priesthood. On Easter Sunday, he confirmed three hundred fifty men, women, and children. So began his renowned visitation, which lasted six months and which carried him to the remote Timucuan province of Nombre de Dios, to Cumberland Island, and to the inland village of Guale. Everywhere he was welcomed with open arms as he confirmed thousands of Indians and Spaniards and admonished them to grow in grace by way of "charity, joy, peace, patience, benignity, goodness, longanimity, mildness, faith, modesty, continency, and chastity."[43]

Altamirano's visitation blessed and strengthened the missions of Guale and Timucua so much that they began a half-century of difficult but unimpeded growth. Missions rose everywhere in the remote province of

Apalache, where the Franciscans made a thousand Indian converts. In July, 1612, arrived a contingent of twenty-one Franciscans under Fray Luis Geronimo de Oré, a native of Peru who enjoyed wide fame for his theological learning. In the same year, at a general chapter of the Franciscan Order in Rome, Florida was established as a province with the name of Santa Elena and with Fray Juan Bautista de Capilla as first provincial.[44]

A peaceful people have no annals. The very sketchy Fransiscan annals of the succeeding years attest to a routine of conversions, baptisms, and confirmations in the widely scattered missions. Only one event temporarily disrupted the peaceful progress of God's work. In 1656 the great chief of Apalache, San Martín de Ayacocuto, revolted against the new governor, Diego Rebolledo, an arrogant, tactless, and inexperienced tyrant who projected the hate he felt for himself toward monks and Indians alike. He insisted on posting soldiers in some of the missions and ordered the Indians to supply them with corn. The soldiers, by taking Indian squaws and girls, aroused intense jealousy among them and created a delicate situation for the monks. The governor met their protests with characteristic arrogance. Instead of removing the soldiers he augmented them.[45]

Indian resentment gradually increased. One of the chiefs complained that Rebolledo forced his people to come to St. Augustine burdened with grain like pack mules and horses. Their resentment became uncontrollable when, early in 1656, Rebolledo, harkening to rumor that pirates had appeared along the coast, furiously began to collect troops for the defense of St. Augustine. Stretching his authority, he ordered the chiefs of Timucua and Apalache to bring three bags of corn on their shoulders to St. Augustine and to provide themselves with food for the journey, which required eight days' marching.

The chiefs, regarding themselves as lords of the regions, protested the indignity and vassalage which Rebolledo's orders entailed. When the governor replied by backing his demands with bayonets, the Indians took up arms, killing the treasurer, Francisco Menéndez, and others. The missionaries sided with the Indians. While Spaniards and Indians killed one another in the fields, monks and governor reviled one another in the mission. The Franciscan provincial denied Rebolledo's allegation that he had forced the Indians to transport provisions on their backs. True, the monks required Indians to carry some slight sustenance for the missions, but they never punished them by death if they failed to do so. Rebolledo claimed that he always paid the Indians for their work. The monks countered by showing that he had paid them for only twenty-five days of the ninety-six they had labored on the presidio at San Luis. The governor counterclaimed that the priests had sold for a profit the food brought over from Havana. How could they, retorted the indignant monks, when they had brought only a few bottles of wine, a little sugar, and articles for their convents which the Indians neither bought nor needed?[46]

After eight months of fighting, Rebolledo sent his friend, Sergeant Major Adrien de Canizares, with sixty men to put down the rebellion. Canizares, at Rebolledo's request, spread the lie among the natives that the monks and especially Fray José de Urrutia were responsible for the rebellion. The friars, however, showed that they had dispatched timely warnings of the impending revolt with the request that it be rescinded. For this crime against the peace Canizares garroted eleven Indians one by one. His action infuriated the tribesmen to further frenzy and destruction. Now feeling justified in their course of action, they retaliated and destroyed many missions. Six missionaries, fleeing to the coast, boarded a vessel for Havana, only to die in a tropical storm. Yet the missionaries who remained in Florida continued their work without interruption until, in 1670, the English appeared at Charleston and began a long and bitter fight against Spanish rule on the Southern Frontier.[47]

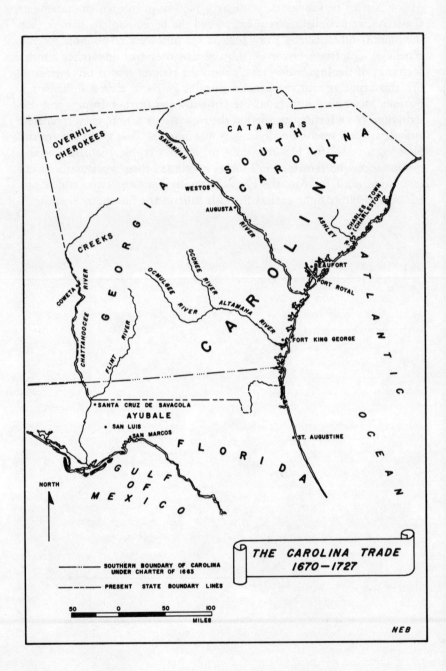

OVERHILL CHEROKEES

CATAWBAS

SOUTH CAROLINA

GEORGIA

CAROLINA

SAVANNAH

WESTOS

AUGUSTA

RIVER

ASHLEY R.

CHARLES TOWN (CHARLESTON)

BEAUFORT

PORT ROYAL

CREEKS

COWETA

CHATTAHOOCEE RIVER

FLINT RIVER

OCMULGEE RIVER

OCONEE RIVER

ALTAMAHA RIVER

FORT KING GEORGE

•SANTA CRUZ DE SAVACOLA

AYUBALE

• SAN LUIS

SAN MARCOS

FLORIDA

•ST. AUGUSTINE

ATLANTIC OCEAN

GULF OF MEXICO

NORTH

SOUTHERN BOUNDARY OF CAROLINA
UNDER CHARTER OF 1663

PRESENT STATE BOUNDARY LINES

50   0   50   100

MILES

THE CAROLINA TRADE
1670—1727

NEB

The Carolina Trade

EVEN IN ITS EARLY DAYS CHARLES TOWN, LATER CHARLESTON, SOUTH CARO-
lina, was a bustling emporium of traders and trappers. Their caravans
of between twenty and thirty horses equipped with merrily tinkling
bells plodded down the narrow streets of the town to the wharves on the
bay, where their Indian or Negro slaves loaded innumerable deerskins
or beaver skins on packets bound for London. The shops of such prosperous merchants as Benjamin Godin, John Bee, and Samuel Eveleigh
were freshly stocked with English woolens in bright colors, strouds, and
duffels, and with all the trinkets that would fill the packs of traders on
their return journeys to the distant Indian tribes. The leading taverns,
Charlton's and Bowling Green House, were filled with roistering traders
and trappers who gambled away much of their earnings while they drank
astonishing quantities of rum, brandy, wine, and English beer. Then, in
about a week or ten days, they were gone to trade again with the Choctaw or Chickasaw, or both, in skins that were often inferior to those of
animals in the northern forests.[1]

But the earliest business of the Carolina traders was the Indian slave-
trade. Though other colonies trafficked in Indians captured in an endless
succession of wars, none reached the commercial proportions of Carolina.
Her fabulously daring traders and explorers often penetrated the wilderness as far as the frontiers of Florida and Louisiana to operate among
tribes close to the rival colonies of France and Spain. Among them none
was more fearless than Dr. Henry Woodward. That doughty young
Englishman unwittingly became the discoverer of a spacious river and
the founder of an empire when, in October, 1674, he crossed the Savannah, which he mistook for the St. Johns, and entered into a trade agreement with the Westoes. The chief of this tribe had sent ten of his men
to Charles Town to invite him to their country, and he had departed
with them during raw, drizzling rain which fell intermittently until, a
week later, they reached their destination.[2]

At the river bank, which Woodward later described as a chalky cliff, they met two Indians who took them in a canoe to the other side. The chief courteously entertained Woodward with a dinner "of those things they counte rarietys amonge them." As soon as the rain ceased, the chief took his guest six miles upstream to his capital, a sizable village which stood near the present site of Augusta, Georgia. Woodward fired his gun into the air in salute, and the village responded with a shout of welcome and a volley of from fifty or sixty small guns. Then about a hundred Westoes, dressed in "their anticke fighting garb," received him with considerable commotion and escorted him to the chief's hut. Because they had never seen a white man, they pressed around him with much noise and curiosity. They examined his features, his dress, every move he made. He looked up to discover that some Indian boys, whom he termed "smaller fry," were making openings in the roof of the hut to get a good look at him. He listened with pretended gravity and solemn nods while the chief made a long speech. All its eloquence was lost on him save that of its accompanying gesticulations, which seemed to tell him that the Westoes were a very powerful people and that they wanted friendship with the English. That night they oiled his eyes and "joynts" with bear grease, presented him with several deerskins, and set before him enough food to satisfy "at least half a dozen of their owne appetites."[3]

Next morning he examined their village, which was built in a haphazard manner and consisted of many long houses with tops and sides of bark. On long poles that rose above the roofs of their houses, he saw scalps of their Indian enemies. He observed that the inland side of the village was protected with a double palisade and the river side with a single one. On the river bank, he counted nearly a hundred canoes, which the Westoes used in warfare and to traffic along the river. He noticed that they were well provided with arms, ammunition, and cloth which they traded for deerskins and young Indian slaves with Virginia tribes at certain times of the year. He stayed with them for ten days, during which time he arranged for the English colony at Charles Town to trade deerskins and furs for guns and cloth. So he made them allies of the English against the Spaniards and against Indian tribes allied with the Spaniards. Ten of the Indians accompanied him homeward, killing, during a heavy rainfall on the way, "two large she beares." On arriving near Charles Town, he sent them home without granting them the courtesy of allowing them to visit the town. They agreed to return in March with more deerskins, furs, and "young slaves."[4]

Though young in years—he was only twenty-eight—Dr. Woodward was no tenderfoot among frontier vicissitudes. Nine years earlier he had landed in the prosperous English colony of Barbados as a medical student who had not completed his course but who still strove to broaden the crude scientific knowledge of his day. He had envisioned Barbados as the pot of gold at the end of the rainbow. Instead, he found it full of sugar planters and laborers but bare of opportunity. Disappointed, he eventually sailed with Sir John Yeamans, governor of Barbados, to the newly established colony along the Cape Fear River, in present North Carolina. There he found the opportunity for the greatest adventure of his life. With twenty other men he sailed under Captain Robert Sandford on an expedition southward along the coast. They explored inlets and bays and rivers, all of which Captain Sandford later described with pictorial dexterity. They rowed a considerable distance up Ladinwah Creek and ranged

> . . . through very spacious tracts of rick Oake land, and yett Wee were not past the Oyster bankes and frequent heepes of shells, nor the salt water. Att my returne downe the River I sent some ashoare to range on the West side who did instantly affirme that the lands there were of an equall excellency with the best of those Wee had other where viewed, and that they believed itt an impossible injunction to be putt to march to the end of the tracts.[5]

Finally they reached Port Royal, where Jean Ribaut had established his ill-fated colony and where the Spaniards had kept a mission and a garrison until Sir Francis Drake drove them away. Here Captain Sandford met an Indian chief, Shadoo, who invited him to send some of his men to spend the night in his principal village, which was some distance away. Curious "to know the forme, manner, and population of the place," Captain Sandford selected four men, including Woodward, to accompany him. On their way to the chief's residence they

> . . . crossed one Meadowe of not lesse than a thousand Acres, all firme good land and as rich a Soyle as any, clothed with a ffine grasse not passing knee deepe, but very thick sett and fully adorned with yeallow flowers; a pasture not inferiour to any I have seene in England. The wood lands were all of the same sort both for timber and mould with the best of those we had ranged otherwhere, and without alteration or abatement from their goodnes all the way of our March.[6]

As soon as they arrived in the village, Shadoo received them with great courtesy and conducted them to a large round house at the entrance of which stood a dais. Here Shadoo sat with his wife. Around the dais were low benches filled with men, women, and children. In the center of the house was a fire mounted on a great heap of ashes and surrounded by a trench. Shadoo beckoned the white men to him and presented them with skins, while his attendants signified friendship by stroking their shoulders with palm branches. All around were fields of corn. The landscape was fruitful with peach trees and fig trees and grapevines. The white men remained in the village for several hours; then, escorted by a sizable group of Indians including Shadoo, they returned to the ship, which soon sailed to resume exploration.[7]

Sometime later Sandford returned to Port Royal. The chief of that place was most reluctant to let the Englishmen go. When, he asked, did they expect to return? He wanted the English to settle among them to protect them from the cannibalistic Westoes.

When Sandford promised to return in ten moons, the chief handed over his nephew as a hostage to be returned at that time. Sandford in turn decided to leave with the Indians one of his own men to learn their language. Woodward, probably attracted to the idea of making himself very useful to the Lord Proprietors at Charles Town by making a careful study of the country and its tribes, volunteered for the mission. Whereupon Sandford agreed to remain in Port Royal until morning to attend a venison feast which the chief wished to give in his honor and to see if the Indians would remain constant in their intention.

Taking Woodward and the young Indian with him to the town, he requested its inhabitants to approve the arrangement he and the chief had conceived. Then Sanford in the presence of the chief and his wives delivered Woodward over to the Indians. They received him with such demonstrations of joy and thankfulness that Sandford had no doubt of their desire for friendship and society. The chief bade Woodward sit on the throne beside him and presented him with a large field of maize. Then he brought him the comely sister of the Indian hostage to feed him and sleep with him.[8]

Woodward waited month after month for the Englishmen to return. One day Spaniards arrived from St. Augustine in large canoes. Learning of his presence, they quickly made him prisoner and returned with him to St. Augustine. There he found favor. He lived with a friar, became a Catholic, and was appointed physician of the town. He studied Spanish character; he weighed the strengths against the weaknesses of the Spanish Empire; he slowly learned some Spanish—and he planned to escape at the first opportunity. This came in 1668, when the pirate Captain Robert Searles paid Florida a visit.

Searles sacked St. Augustine and, during the ensuing confusion, released all of its English prisoners. He took Woodward to the Windward and the Leeward islands. There the young physician shipped as surgeon on a privateer in order to defray his expenses to London to see Lord Ashley, founder of the Carolina colony. On August 17, 1669, the privateer met a hurricane that picked it up and tossed it on the island of Nevis like a toy paper boat in several pieces. Woodward was one of the few men who survived and was cast ashore on that island. At the end of the year, a fleet under Joseph West picked him up and took him to Port Royal, where he became a conspicuous figure. His knowledge and influence among the Indians was so great that, as we have seen, the colony in 1674 sent him to negotiate the treaty with the Westoes.[9]

Just like all men of achievement, he made enemies. His own impulsiveness proved his undoing. Learning that two of the leading men of the colony were slave traders who proposed to undertake a mission to the Westoes, he warned that tribe to take precautions against the possibility of enslavement. The aged chief innocently disclosed Woodward's warning to the slave traders who, of course, wasted no time in accusing him of plotting with the Westoes against the colony. Its proprietors forthwith stripped him of his office as Indian agent and outlawed him.[10]

Deprived of Woodward's guiding hand, the Westoes soon fell out with the Carolinians. The latter enlisted the support of the tribe living along the Savannah to war against the Westoes, who by 1682 were practically exterminated. Meanwhile, Woodward had returned to England and had persuaded Lord Ashley to grant him a commission to venture westward beyond the Savannah into the lands of the Creeks and open up trade with them. By the summer of 1685 he returned from England and led a half dozen men to the Chattahoochee, where he introduced himself to the great chief or "emperor" of Coweta, near present Columbus, Georgia. Woodward's presence there soon precipitated a struggle with the Spaniards, who claimed the region for their king. The commander of the garrison in Apalache, Antonio Matheos, was an officer of energy and spirit. Hastily collecting two hundred fifty mission Indians and a force of Spaniards, he advanced up the villages of the Lower Creeks to teach the English upstart a lesson he would never forget. As Matheos approached the Ocmulgee River, Woodward decided to play with him a game of hare and hound: he hid his men in the woods, leaving behind him an impudent, ironical note pinned to a tree:

I am sorry that I came with so small a following that I cannot await your arrival. Be informed that I came to get acquainted with the country, its mountains, the seacoast, and Apalache. I trust in God that I shall meet you gentlemen later when I have a larger following. September 2, 1685. *Vale*.[11]

Finding the English hare too clever for him, the Spanish hound vented his frustration by destroying a half-finished fortification which the Indians had been building under Woodward's direction. Then Matheos posted spies and returned to St. Augustine. Scarcely had he turned his back than Woodward and his men emerged from their hiding places in the woods and resumed their trading in beaver skins and deerskins. The spies soon carried the news to their master, who in December returned in a huff to the very spot where he had hoped to crush his English enemies. This time he had positive orders from Governor Cabrera to seize Woodward at all cost and to burn the villages that had supported him.

Marching overland to Sabacola el Grande, he crossed the Chattahoochee and then advanced by circuitous trails in his endeavor to surprise Woodward. But again the wily trader eluded him. The ponderous Spanish commander with his clanging infantry failed to conceal his movements from Woodward's swift and alert scouts. The few Indians he managed to see in the villages claimed that everybody—men, women, and children—had gone hunting. Instead of fighting a decisive engagement, Matheos encountered only rustling leaves, the murmuring Chattahoochee, and an occasional inquisitive Indian. This time he assuaged his anger by confiscating from an English blockhouse at Palenque five hundred deerskins, twenty-three beaver skins, eight pairs of socks, and a few other articles of clothing. Then he burned the blockhouse and returned home.[12]

Again Woodward and his men emerged from their hiding places and resumed their trading with the Indians. But at the end of a successful season he contracted a fever and lay helpless in the village of Casista. Some of his men returned to Charles Town. Woodward, unable to throw off his illness, had some of his Indian friends bear him homeward on a litter. Even his high fever failed to dampen his business ardor; he had his train loaded with skins for the Carolina market. But illness, though it perhaps took his life, was now a lesser adversary than the Guale Indians who, friendly to Spain, murdered four of his men as they journeyed toward Charles Town. Then they seized one hundred eight deerskins, two hundred beaver and otter hides, and nine buffalo hides.[13]

The inhabitants of the villages Matheos had burned soon bent the knee to him, begging without pride and charging their treachery to ignorance of English chicanery. With this piece of ignominy Woodward fades from the stage of history.[14]

2

His passing by no means discouraged the English from advancing toward the Chattahoochee. The new governor of Florida, Diego Quiroga y Losada, who succeeded Cabrera in 1687, resolved on a conciliatory policy with the Indians. Even this failed to discourage the English. When they kept coming in, Quiroga found he had no choice but to send soldiers to capture them. But his constant marching up and down the Chattahoochee proved no deterrent to English resilience. So Quiroga ordered one of his best officers, Captain Primo Rivera, to build a permanent fort on the river. In four months, Rivera raised a stronghold with a stockade, a parapet, a ditch, and four bastions. Its garrison, under Captain Fabián Ángulo, consisted of twenty Spanish infantry and twenty loyal Apalache warriors.[15]

The fort greatly impressed the Indians. Meeting in May, 1688, at Coweta, they declared that they had only one word and one heart and that both were Spanish. They promised Ángulo that they would support him in keeping the English out. But Spanish policy failed in its very inception. Many of the Indians, resenting the burning of their towns and the presence of the fort in their country, fled from Spanish domination and joined the Yuchi on the Ocmulgee. Thither the English promptly followed them. They referred to the Ocmulgee River as Ocheese or Yuchi Creek and to the Indians who dwelled on its bank as the Creeks.

To the Spaniards, Yuchi and Apalachicolas were synonymous terms.

The garrison was short-lived. In 1691 it was removed to meet threats of pirate attacks on St. Augustine. Ángulo not only destroyed the fort but filled in its ditch. The English retaliated by inciting the Indians to attack Spanish missions in Timucua and Apalache. And the Indians, who nearly always preferred English to Spanish goods, complied with their request. To this contemptuous challenge the Spanish governor, Laureano de Torres, responded in 1695 by dispatching seven Spaniards and four hundred Indians against the marauders, many of whom were captured.[16]

As the eighteenth century opened, Carolina and Spain entered into a lively dispute over possession of the Apalachicola country. Hitherto the center of the Carolina trade had remained at the forks of the Altamaha. Now bold traders penetrated to the Tallapoosa and to the Alabama, where they formed an alliance with the Chickasaw, who furnished them with captives as slaves. These advances, which brought Carolina a lucrative fur and slave trade, prompted Governors Thomas Smith and Joseph Blake to lay claim to the entire Apalachicola country.

To Laureano de Torres, this claim was preposterous; he laughed; he choked with rage; he laughed again. But the English grew greedier with each new slave and fur the Chickasaw sold them. Governor John Archdale was a Quaker, but the peaceful complexion of his faith did not prevent him from forbidding Spaniards in the Apalachicola country. Meanwhile, the English met a more formidable enemy in the French, then Spain's allies, who had established themselves at Biloxi on the Gulf coast. This only reinforced English greed for conquest. In 1702 Governor James Moore decided to strike the first blow for English Control of the Mississippi Valley. In an address to the Common House of Assembly he urged "the takeing of St. Augustin before it be strengthened with French forces." He added: "This wee believe will open to us an easie and plaine way to Remove the French (a no less dangerous enemy in time of peace than warr) from their settlement on the south side of the Bay of Appalatia."[17]

The outbreak of the War of the Spanish Succession, known in America as Queen Anne's War, with England on one side and France and Spain on the other, provided Governor Moore with an opportunity to attack St. Augustine. He persuaded the Yuchi to invade the Apalache country, where they burned the villages of Santa Fé before they were driven off by Spanish forces. Moore then turned to deal St. Augustine a double blow. He planned to attack it by sea while Colonel Robert Daniel was to attack it by land. Daniel took and plundered the town, burning a library because it contained a collection of Greek and Latin Fathers and a Bible written in Latin. Governor Zuñiga retired with his forces to the safety of the fort.

Meanwhile, Moore with his ships had spread devastation along the coast. On the island of San Marcos he burned three churches and convents. Three missionaries fell into his hands, but their Indian converts fled to the safety of the fort in St. Augustine. On October 22, 1702, Moore joined Daniel with fourteen or fifteen ships and attempted to reduce the fort; but its defenders bravely stood their ground.

Moore, needing heavy artillery in his desperate attempt to reduce the town, sent Daniel to obtain it in Jamaica. No sooner had Daniel departed than two Spanish ships with large guns appeared near the mouth of the harbor. Their presence induced Moore to raise the siege. He hastily burned his ships and returned to Carolina by land. Before he withdrew, he wreaked his vengeance on the town he had failed to conquer by burning down its parish church and the church and convent of the Franciscans. Daniel, standing in for the harbor of St. Augustine on his return, was astonished to find that the siege had been raised. He extricated himself from his trap with great difficulty.[18]

Discredited by his fiasco, Moore soon resigned his post. But his successor, Sir Nathaniel Johnson, gave him an opportunity to retrieve his lost reputation by a new campaign against the Spaniards and their Indian allies. With the aim of establishing its Indian system of trade, the Carolina assembly in December 1703 sent Moore with a thousand friendly Indians and fifty whites to drive the Spaniards from the frontier province of Apalache.

Crossing the Ocmulgee, Moore, on January 14, 1704, attacked Ayubale, a square fort defended by nearly two hundred Indians under a militant friar, Ángel de Miranda. To their assistance rushed Captain Alonso Días Mexía with thirty Spaniards and four hundred Indians from the presidio of San Luis Patali, near present Tallahassee. Twice they repulsed Moore, but in the evening they ran out of ammunition and had to surrender. Moore was glad to win an unquestionable laurel. He had never heard, he wrote later, of a "stouter or braver thing done," which "regained the reputation we seem to have lost . . ."

But victory made him vengeful. He had many of his prisoners stripped naked, tied to stakes, and burned, while he subjected Mexía, who was wounded, to the indignity of watching his doomed friends from his stocks. Father Parga met a crueler fate: they burned him, beheaded him, and hacked off one of his legs. To escape such cruelties, most of the Indian towns surrendered to Moore. But that uniformed brute had not yet glutted his vengeance. Advancing on the presidio of San Luis Patali, which still held out, he offered its commander to give up Mexía, Father Miranda, and four captive soldiers in return for its surrender; but he demanded a ransom for the men he would free; and when they could not produce it he burned all of them at the stake. Two of his Indian victims showed in prayer and exhortation the heroism of Christian martyrs. Of the fourteen missions in the region Moore spared only one: it bought immunity with the church ornaments and ten horses loaded with provisions. At last, Moore retired eastward with fourteen hundred mission Indians, a hundred of whom were enslaved and the remainder established safely on the Savannah River between Charles Town and the Apalachicola allies.[19]

Father Juan de Villalba soon went with others to the ruined towns, each of which presented a scene of unparalleled horror. Bodies of men, women, and children lay everywhere, some scalped, some half-burned, some hanging from stakes. Among the ruins of San Luis Patali, Father Villalba found Father Mendoza's half-burned body, his hands and partly melted crucifix sunk into his flesh. Father Parga's mutilated body he carried to the mission of Ybitacuche, where he buried it. Father Miranda's remains he never found.[20]

Moore's campaign dealt a paralyzing blow to the Apalache missions. Even so, the missionaries refused to leave the charred region; eventually they gathered at San Marcos, on the Gulf Coast, where they remained for many years. But the English were now free to live and trade among the eleven Creek towns along the Ocmulgee River. Yet they were not content to remain there; in 1707 they moved on to Pensacola, which they destroyed with the assistance of their Tallapoosa allies, though they failed to capture the fort itself. Later in the year, they again invested Pensacola; but they withdrew when a French and Indian force under Bienville rushed to its relief.[21]

At this juncture Thomas Nairne, official leader of the Carolina traders, devised a plan by which he hoped to drive the French from Mobile and extend the trade to the Mississippi. The Carolina assembly approved his scheme, but it fell abortive when the Indians refused to support it and when the French threatened to strike at Charles Town. Thereafter the frontier policy of Carolina "lacked the aggressive and imaginative qualities which Nairne . . . imparted to it." Soon it began to sag under the strain of poor management, licentious traders, and the skilled diplomacy of the French in Mobile. The Chickasaw remained loyal to the Carolinians; the Choctaw favored the French. Before long these two tribes began a bitter feud. The Carolina assembly, fearing that it would endanger the trade, in 1711 sent Captain Theophilus Hastings with thirteen hundred Creek Indians into the Choctaw country, where they burned many villages, killed many people, and took many prisoners.[22]

The Treaty of Utrecht, which ended Queen Anne's War in 1713, left Pensacola and Mobile in French hands. But the Carolinians, seizing on the failure of the treaty to mention the Southern Frontier, continued to assert their old inclusive claims which they based on their charter and on the Indian trade. The French found them as uncomfortable neighbors in peace as they had been in war. The French governor of Louisiana, Cadillac, tried in vain to obtain Governor Craven's support to establish a general peace among the Indians, English, and French, to "withdraw his traders from the natives that had first traded with the French; and to comply with the spirit of the peace by preventing those traders from instigating slave-catching raids among the French allies."[23] The English could no longer threaten Mobile, though they continued their efforts to displace the French in the Mississippi Valley.

Early in 1715 occurred an Indian war so formidable that it threatened Carolina with total destruction. The tribes collectively known as the Yamasees were the chief instigators of the war, though every tribe in the region played a part in it. The Yamasees had settled in what was known as the Indian Land, a vast tract extending from their village, Pocotaligo, in the north to the Altahama River in the south. Dwelling between Carolina and the outlying tribes and Spaniards who succeeded one another along the Savannah, the Yamasees had served the English colony well in raids against the missions on the islands off the coast of Georgia and St. Augustine.[24]

But, in time, the greed of the English for their land turned their invaluable friendship to bitter hate. Since the beginning of the eighteenth century, the Carolinians continued to expand in the Indian Land, establishing large rice plantations along the Savannah and large ranches in the plain to the west. The Yamasees eventually regarded this white avalanche as a threat to their existence. They protested to the Carolina authorities who, anxious to keep them as a contented buffer tribe between the colony and their Spanish foes, ordered the squatters from the Indian Land. Most of them ignored the order. But the Yamasees nursed keener resentments. The Carolinians subjected them to all kinds of humiliations and cruelties: they stole their horses and canoes; they ravished their women and carried them away. The traders moreover often forced them to buy goods, made them drunk and then loaded them with goods for which they could not possibly pay, and seized their relatives and held them until they discharged their debts.[25]

The Spaniards gained their friendship by sympathizing with them and deprecating their malefactors. A year before the war began Nairne and other traders living in Pocotaligo noticed that several of the chiefs often journeyed to St. Augustine and returned loaded with gifts. John Fraser, an honest Scotch Highlander who lived and traded with them, often heard them speak of the kindness the Spaniards accorded them. One received a hat, another a jacket, still another a coat trimmed with silver lace. Some braves received hatchets, others knives, and nearly all of them guns and ammunition. The Indians told Fraser that the Spanish governor had accorded them the great honor of allowing them to dine with him at the same table.[26]

About nine days before hostilities began, Sanute, an Indian attached to Fraser's family, told Mrs. Fraser that all of the English were wicked heretics, that they would go to hell, and that, if the Yamasees followed them, they too would go to that horrible place. He then told her that his people had chosen the governor of St. Augustine as their king and would follow him soon in a war in which all the English would perish as in a great fire. He advised her to inform her husband to return with their family to Charles Town as quickly as possible. On receiving this information Fraser went to Sanute and asked him to explain how the Spaniards could war on the Carolinians while they were at peace with Great Britain. To which Sanute replied that the Spanish governor had told him that Spain would soon declare war against Great Britain. Fraser took Sanute's advice and returned with his family to Charles Town.[27]

But Nairne, as official Indian agent to the Yamasees, remained in Pocotaligo. On April 14, the day before the Yamasees began their bloody revolt, Nairne and other traders noticed that their Indian friends were cold toward them. Nairne asked their chief to explain their attitude. The chief replied with a casual air that they had no complaints; that they intended to go hunting in the morning. So Nairne went to sleep with his usual tranquility.

He had a rude awakening. Frenzied shrieks and cries brought him and his fellow traders to their feet to behold a wild band of Indian madmen, ghastly in red and black paint, dancing like demons risen from hell. Then, with equal ease, they rushed upon the white settlers in Pocotaligo, killing about ninety of them. A man named Burrows, who was a captain of militia, by swimming one mile and running ten, escaped with two wounds to Port Royal and alerted the town. Another trader, whose name is unknown, hid in a marsh near the town, watching his friends being tortured, until nightfall when, stripping himself to look like an Indian, he walked unmolested through the town and to safety. Nairne was less lucky. He was seized, tied to a stake, and burned in a slow fire, while his enemies picked his body with hundreds of lightwood splinters that slowly seared his flesh. He died on the second day of his torture.[28]

Meanwhile the inhabitants of Port Royal, about four hundred in number, boarded a boat which the Carolinians had recently captured from smugglers. As it sailed for Charles Town, Indians came to the shore and fired at it, but it was too far away from them to cause any damage. On learning of the massacre Governor Craven called out the militia of Colleton County, proclaimed martial law, laid an embargo on all ships, and obtained from the assembly authority to impress men, arms, ammunition, and stores, and to arm trusty Negroes. He dispatched agents to Virginia for military assistance, which came too late, and to Massachusetts to purchase guns. He ordered a ring of garrisons around Charles Town and on nearby plantations to repel possible Indian attacks.[29]

By now every Indian tribe save the Cherokees had joined the Yamasees in their war against the English colony. They were divided into two possible groups: the southern tribes numbering about six thousand bowmen, and the northern tribes numbering between six hundred and a thousand bowmen. The northern invaders soon penetrated the plantation of John Keane, about fifty miles from Charles Town, and murdered him and his family and employees. Another planter, Thomas Barker, collected ninety horsemen and advanced against the enemy; but his Indian guide led him into an ambuscade where he and several of his men were killed. The rest retreated. This triumph permitted four hundred

Indians to advance to Goose Creek, where seventy white men and forty Negroes determined to defend themselves in a crude fort they had just completed. But they became discouraged when the Indians attacked them, and they agreed on peace terms. The triumphant Indians entered the fort and butchered its garrison. Then they advanced on the town, only to retreat before the Goose Creek militia under a brave man with the ironical name of Captain George Chicken.[30]

Governor Craven, ascertaining that the Cherokees had remained neutral, sent an army of three hundred men under Colonel Maurice Moore to their country to pursuade them by a show of force to join the English. Moore advanced on an old trading path along the left bank of the Savannah and then up the Tugalee to the village of the same name, where he called on its chief, Caesar, for assistance. Caesar hated the Creeks and wanted to destroy them; but the Lower Cherokees, who lived in the mountains of present northeastern Georgia, had friends among the warring tribes and hesitated to join the English against them. Only the Overhill Cherokees, who lived along the northern Georgia border, backed Caesar and clamored for war against the Creeks, their ancient foes.[31]

At this juncture the Creeks sent runners to inform Moore that they were sending representatives to confer with him. Eventually their spokesman appeared, but they conferred not with Moore but with the Cherokees. Colonel Moore and his men waited anxiously, ready for any eventuality. Suddenly they heard war whoops; they readied their guns; they rushed to the spot where the conference between the Creek spokesmen and the Cherokees was going on. Then and there Moore discovered that the Cherokees had killed the Creek agents in cold blood.

Moore learned the reason for their bloody deed. The Creek agents, instead of talking peace, had tried to persuade the Cherokees to join the war against the British. But Caesar's influence had prevailed; sensing danger, he struck first. His unhospitable treatment of his Creek guests redounded to Moore's salvation. Hiding in the forest were between two hundred and five hundred Creeks, ready to pounce on him as soon as the Cherokees agreed to join them. Moore moved quickly with his army and a force of Cherokees to surprise the concealed Creeks who, however, proved even more agile than they in getting away.[32]

The support of the Cherokees as a kind of bulwark against the Creeks proved a major factor in crushing the Yamasee conspiracy. Governor Craven, too, did his share, fighting the invading hordes in their own thickets until they began to fall back to Saltcatchers where they had pitched their main camp. Here English and Indians fought a sharp and bloody battle in which bullets and arrows shot from behind trees and bushes claimed equal honors in destruction. Craven kept his troops at the Indians' heels and eventually chased them from their villages on Indian Land, then across the Savannah River, then from the province entirely.

The defeated Indians fell back to St. Augustine, where they were received amid the ringing of bells and the firing of guns, as though they were marching triumphantly home from the battlefield. They established themselves in villages around St. Augustine, where they were furnished with everything they needed and with everything they requested, for many months. Charles Town meanwhile enjoyed a less hollow celebration. Its refugees returned to their plantations and Craven entered it in triumph to receive the applauses and the blessing that his courage, his conduct, and his success in the campaign merited.[33]

3

The Yamasee conspiracy shocked the colony into a sense of its insecurity and led it to take stringent measures to strengthen its southern defenses. Among the favored measures was the creation of a buffer state. In 1717 Sir Robert Montgomery, a Scotsman, secured from the Lord Proprietors a strip of land extending westward from the Savannah to the Altamaha. He called it the Margravate of Azilia for reasons known only to himself.

In a pamphlet entitled *A Discourse Concerning the design'd Establishment of a New Colony To the South of Carolina In the Most delightful Country of the Universe*, Montgomery stated that the "native excellencies" of Azilia almost equaled the "virgin beauties" of Paradise of which he seemed to have inside knowledge. He located it "in the same latitude with Palestine herself, that promised Canaan which was pointed out by God's own choice to bless the labours of a favourite people." He pictured the whole country as a vast square in the center of which, on another square, would lie his capital. In its exact center, surrounded by ramparts and forts, he would build his palace in which he would rule as the first Marquis of Azilia. Around him he would gather his gentry who, assisted by white laborers, would be devoted, not to the extension but to the cultivation of their estates. The dangerous use of Negroes or Indians would be unnecessary. This Garden of Eden would yield an abundance of rice, coffee, tea, figs, currents, almonds, olives, mulberries, and cochineal.[34]

Sir Robert was so enthralled by his own rhetoric that he overlooked the sober reality that Azilia would be thrust up against Spanish guns. His readers were more earthy and failed to respond to his utopian call. By 1720 his colonists faded and his dream of Azilia faded with them.[35]

In the following year Governor Francis Nicholson, with the approval of the Board of Trade in London, adopted the more practical measure of occupying the present region of Georgia by building a fort on it. For this task he chose Colonel John Barnwell, who since Nairne's death had served as chief agent and adviser of the Indian system. Barnwell, however, was unable to secure the hardy soldiers, young skilled craftsmen, carpenters, and smiths he needed. He had to content himself with twenty-six inexperienced men and a few scouts whom he sent to the mouth of the Altamaha. In his absence they besotted themselves with rum. When he eventually reached them, he faced the Herculean task of trying to keep them sober long enough to help him explore the country and to send them wading waist-deep in swamps for cypress timber. On the northern branch, formerly occupied by an Indian tribe, eventually rose a gabled blockhouse to which Barnwell gave the name of King George.[36]

The Spanish governor at St. Augustine, Antonio Benavides y Bezán, protested the presence of the fort to Nicholson, while the Spanish ambassador in London, Jacinto, Marqués de Pozobueno, held a diplomatic tussle with the Duke of Newcastle, head of the government. When these protests fell on deaf ears, Benavides dispatched Francisco Menéndez Marqués, auditor of St. Augustine, on a diplomatic mission to Nicholson.

Acting on the orders of his superior, the Spanish emissary proposed to Nicholson that their countries settle their difficulties by treaty. He requested a suspension of arms, the return of certain Negro and Spanish prisoners—and the motive for the construction of the disagreeable Fort King George. Nicholson replied that he had no authority to make a treaty. He availed himself of the occasion, however, to resent charges that he had mistreated Spanish prisoners and to request the return of runaway slaves and prize ships taken since the end of Queen Anne's War. So Menéndez returned empty-handed to Benavides who, in his report to the Council of the Indies accused Nicholson of planning to capture St. Augustine and to command the Bahama Channel.

The Council of the Indies received this information with bitterness. It instructed the Marqués de Grimaldi, secretary of state, to dispatch to the Board of Trade a memorial declaring Fort King George an affront to His Catholic Majesty and demanding its destruction. But the Board of Trade, standing on the treaty signed between England and Spain in 1670, replied that the Altamaha, on which the fort lay, belonged to England and that the safety of the territory and navigation of the river necessitated its presence. So the matter stood until 1727, when the English abandoned Fort King George. This, however, was not because of Spanish protests but because of mutinous garrisons and the destruction of much of it by fire.[37]

Early Louisiana

On JANUARY 26, 1699, A FRENCH FLEET CONSISTING OF TWO FRIGATES, *La Badine* and *Le Marin*, a flagship, the *François*, and two ketches anchored near the Spanish unfinished stone fort of Santa María de Galve, at present Pensacola, and announced its presence by firing five cannon shots. A thick fog prevented the commander of the fort, Andrés de Arriola, from clearly seeing the French ships, prompting him to reply to the salute with three shots charged with ball. When the fog lifted, he saw the fleur-de-lis flying from the masthead of the flagship. Though his country and France were at peace, the Spanish commander, obeying royal instructions, readied the fort and two vessels in the harbor for possible action; but the day passed without incident.

Next morning the *François* fired a blank shot while her commander, Pierre Lemoyne, Siegneur d'Iberville sent a message with a few companions in a boat to the fort. To present as formidable an appearance as possible, Arriola stationed all of his soldiers at their posts, hiding their half-naked bodies by arranging them in such a manner that they showed only their heads over the parapet of the fort. He received the French boat on the beach, allowing on shore only the messenger and one of his comrades, whom he escorted to his headquarters where he had assembled his officers. The messenger brought word that his leader had come at the command of his king to reconnoiter the coast of the Gulf of Mexico. He sought permission to enter the bay to obtain shelter for his ships and fuel and water for his return voyage to France, and he offered to supply the Spaniards with what provisions they might need from ships under his command.

In his penned reply Arriola regretted that strict orders from the king prevented him from permitting any foreign vessel from entering the harbor. In view of the friendly relations that existed between their countries, however, he offered the services of his sergeant-major and of a good pilot to help the vessels anchor at a safe place along the coast, where

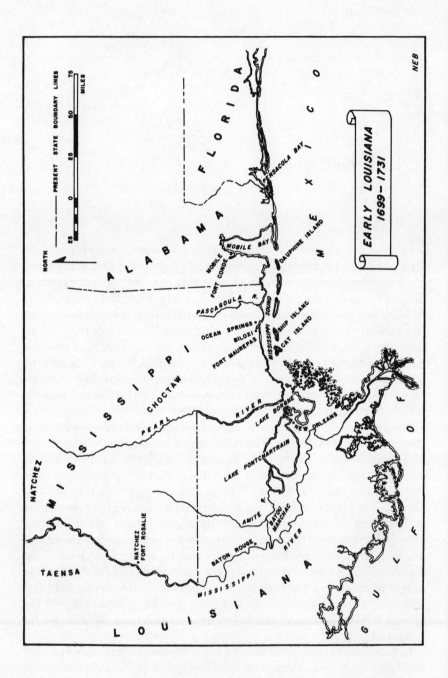

EARLY LOUISIANA
1699 - 1731

they could secure the wood and water they sought. Accordingly, when the messenger prepared to return to the flagship, Arriola sent the pilot and several other men with him.

Iberville received them warmly and told them that the expedition consisted of one thousand well-equipped men with a large number of cattle and horses and abundant supplies. The French leader then sent Arriola another message in which he repeated his request. Arriola replied that his "hands are tied, and that, just as your Lordship tried to serve your king, so I should strive to fulfill scrupulously what my master commands me to do." Whereupon the French fleet, without further ado, took its departure.[1]

Iberville's daring and romantic enterprises had already earned him the sobriquet of "the Canadian Cid." He was a large man with a trim waist, "muscles of steel, and the springy catlike tread of an athlete." His most conspicuous ornament was a profusion of curling yellow hair which fell long over his broad shoulders and which framed refined though large features. His eyes, blue and penetrating, glowed with resolution and self-reliance and mirrored a calculating intelligence. One who knew him well characterized him "as military as his sword and as used to water as his canoe."[2]

He was the third of the eleven sons of Charles Lemoyne, Seigneur de Longueuil, a distinguished soldier of Lower Canada. Iberville showed qualities of leadership from early boyhood. He was a proud, impulsive, generous, intensely loyal, and patriotic lad who excelled in sports and games of all kinds. The toys of the militant Lemoyne brothers, who are better known by their estates than by their Christian or family names, were the steep rocks, the towering pines, the gnarled cedars, and the wild game of their native land. Their interests in frontier sports increased and broadened with their ages; they hunted, fished, and went canoeing and snowshoeing; they developed their muscles while they grew in resolution, self-reliance, and initiative.

Iberville espoused every honorable cause with fortitude, endurance, courage, and quick intelligence. One or more of his brothers, in warm emulation but definitely under his guidance, either hunted with him or supported him as an associate or served him as a subordinate in each of his expeditions. Life on the French frontier filled them with hatred for the rival English and Dutch colonies and with implacable bitterness toward the Iroquois. In France as well as in Canada their family name spelled bravery. They were known far and wide as the Canadian Maccabees.[3]

The first scene of Iberville's remarkable adventures was the icy shores of Hudson Bay, where the English had planted a number of trading posts in defiance of the French, who claimed the region by right of a charter granted forty-three years before the one conferred by the English king, Charles II. Even before the two countries went to war in Europe they began to skirmish for possession of these posts in America.

In 1686 the French authorities in Canada sent Chevalier de Troyes with a band of thirty-three Frenchmen in half-savage, half-civilized attire and sixty-six plumed and painted Indians to drive the English from the James Bay extension of Hudson Bay.

Iberville and his two brothers, Sainte-Hélène and Maricourt, were in the party. It meandered on snowshoes from near Montreal up the Ottawa River across frozen rivers and through dense forests for a distance of six hundred miles to Lakes Nemiscamingue and Abitibi. The piercing cold, the perils from wild animals, the skulking Indians, the exhaustion of the long journey—all these had no terrors for these sons of Hercules, who subsisted largely on game, or, when that became scarce, on the bark of trees, and who slept in holes they dug in the snow or in shelters of bark built by large fires. Without cannon, without the necessary accoutrements for serious war, they advanced with quixotic foolhardiness to assail stockaded and bastioned forts.

At Lake Abitibi they built canoes and waited until its ice cakes melted and sent its network of rivers leaping down into the bay. Then with their dexterous paddles, they fended their canoes away from threatening rocks or masses of ice that raced down the stream with them or after them or were blocked like masses of glistening granite against obstructions in the river. Dodging fallen trees and mastering cataracts and ice jams, they rushed into the Moose River, where Iberville's canoe was swamped in a swirl of the waters and two of his men drowned—possibly with Father Sylvie's quick absolution. At the risk of his life, Iberville pulled two of his men ashore.[4]

One day, while he was serving as scout, he saw the first English trading post in the distance. That night he and his men cached their meager provisions and clothing and stole around the post, measuring the height of its walls, examining its splits through which muskets would be thrust, and noticing with delight that its unsuspecting garrison had plugged the protruding cannon. Then they slipped away as silently as they had come.

Next night, while Troyes with the main force distracted the attention of the garrison, Iberville and his men battered the main gate of the post with the trunk of a huge tree. Before it fully yielded and while the sleeping sentinel staggered forward to defend it, Iberville leaped inside. Suddenly the gate closed, making him a prisoner. In the teeming darkness he swung his sword left and right to defend himself against possible crouching soldiers until he saw in the gloom the glitter of a lantern from the stairs above. He fired in that direction; its groaning owner toppled with it to the ground. At that moment his own men gained entrance to the post and crowded around him. The dazed and feeble garrison, sensing the futility of trying to resist these wild men from nowhere, quickly surrendered with its twelve cannon and its three thousand pounds of powder.[5]

These supplies enabled Troyes to attack Fort Rupert, six days' journey away. He sent Iberville in canoes to the fort while he dispatched to it Sainte-Hélène with fifty men in a ship that had been found undefended at the Moose River. Near the fort Iberville saw a ship. He resolved to capture it. Up the stern his men crawled like wildcats. The man on the lookout, suddenly awakening, sprang at Iberville who, however, cut him down with a single stroke of his sword. Up the hatch came tumbling the crew, the first three of whom were sabered as soon as they showed their heads. The next man, who was none other than the governor of the territory, surrendered the ship. Iberville and his men then hurried ashore, advanced on the fort, climbed its roof, hacked holes in it, and hurled hand grenades down on the room below. One of these struck a woman. Iberville and Father Sylvie leaped down to her rescue and tended and consoled her while the fort surrendered.[6]

Late that summer Iberville advanced three hundred miles against Fort Albany, which thundered its forty guns simultaneously and then surrendered. The victors found 50,000 crowns' worth of peltries but no food. Iberville solved this difficulty by allowing the prisoners to shift for themselves while he and most of his men made for the St. Lawrence, leaving Maricourt with a few veterans to guard the fort.[7]

In the following year Iberville appeared at Fort Rupert, where he captured an English ship. And in the ensuing months, he fluttered from place to place in the bay, capturing more English ships and taking them and their crews to Quebec. When France declared war against England, Iberville, supported by the navy as well as Canadians, intensified his raids. He volunteered in an expedition that planned to capture Schenectady before the English could fortify themselves in that town and could receive reinforcements. This force, consisting of one hundred ten Frenchmen and ninety-six Indians, left Montreal in the dead of winter on moccasins or snowshoes that permitted them to flit like ghosts over the snow without being detected.

The town, awakened by the horrible yelps and yells of the approaching Indians, improvised a garrison that offered keen resistance until its enemies battered down the doors of the fort. The victors butchered the defenders and set fire to the fort while they guarded it against possible surprise. Sixty persons were killed and twenty-seven were taken prisoners. The French commander ordered his soldiers to spare the minister, an inoffensive Dutchman named Tassemakers who had come to Schenectady after serving in several other posts, but he was killed before he could be recognized. The mayor, John Sanders Glen, fled across the river; he was pursued and captured; but his good reputation spared him his life. The victors, knowing that word of the fall of Schenectady would soon reach nearby Fort Orange and would quickly bring vengeance, set fire to it and started for the St. Lawrence. A force of a hundred forty Mohawks and Mohegans attacked them on the way and took twenty scalps.[8]

Iberville then returned to Hudson Bay, where he captured more English ships laden with furs. Almost as soon as he reached Quebec he sailed for France to request Louis XIV to permit him to attack Fort Nelson in Hudson Bay, which the English still held. The king granted his request. Whereupon Iberville sailed on the *Envieux*, but when on October 18, 1692, he reached Quebec he discovered to his chagrin the impossibility of attempting to break through the ice of the straits. The authorities, knowing the folly of keeping such a man idle, commanded him to attack instead the fort of Pemquid, which stood on the coast of Maine between the Penobscot and the Kennebec rivers.[9]

Iberville sailed zealously up to the fort with the intention of taking it by surprise; but when he learned that deserters had alerted its commander, he wisely withdrew. At this juncture his brother arrived in Quebec with a commission authorizing them to organize an expedition against Fort Nelson. Thither, over a sea made perilous by ice jams, they sailed with one hundred twenty Canadians and some Caughamanga Indians in two ships.

Fort Nelson bristled with heavy guns and stone throwers but had an inexperienced commander. Iberville fortified his position and then called upon the fort to surrender. Its commander, finding himself without fuel and with no prospect of obtaining any during the winter, capitulated. The victors found numerous provisions and settled down to enjoy them until the ice broke up. But their happiness soon turned to tragedy. Scurvy broke out among them, killing nine Canadians and ten sailors. The ice intensified their misery. Not until July 28 could they weigh anchor with only one hundred fifteen men, some of whom were unfit for service. Even then Iberville delayed his departure. Hoping for the arrival of English ships, which would give him an opportunity for battle, he stayed at Fort Nelson until September, then started for Quebec. He left behind him sixty-four Canadians and six Iroquois with ammunition and stores for a year. But he failed to reach Quebec. Head winds on the coast of Labrador beat him back toward France, and on October 9 he staggered into the harbor of La Rochelle with his scurvy-stricken crew.[10]

Everywhere he heard that the king was making great preparations to raid Placentia Bay, Newfoundland, where French defenses were crumbling. Governor Frontenac urged Louis XIV to circumvent these plans by sending ten or twelve armed ships to seize Boston, but the king was skeptical of success and refused. Instead, he ordered that the English be driven from Fort Pemquid and their posts in Newfoundland and Hudson Bay. So Iberville was sent to Pemquid, where he learned that three English ships awaited his arrival at the mouth of the St. John's River in New Brunswick. Enthusiastically accepting the challenge, he fired on one of the English ships and tore away her mast. The other ships escaped in the fog.[11]

Anchoring at Pentagoet, he met Baron de St. Castin, a French nobleman who had married an Indian girl and who pledged his support in the battle for Pemquid. On August 13, 1690, Iberville arrived in sight of the fort, while St. Castin, who had preceded him, readied two mortars and a cannon, and opened fire. Though in a precarious position, the commander, Chubb, refused to surrender until Castin warned him that his Indian braves could not be restrained from indiscriminate slaughter of their enemies if he waited for the fort to fall. This warning proved more effective than the roar of cannon. Chubb hauled down his flag and surrendered his garrison of ninety-two men. Iberville burned the fort to the ground.[12]

Early in September Iberville sailed for Newfoundland, just as a fleet of seven English ships approached the harbor. In Newfoundland he found that the English were in possession of a number of posts, nearly all of which were in the eastern side of the island, and that they were carrying on an extensive and lucrative trade, chiefly in fish. The French, on the contrary, were cooped up in Placentia Bay under a grasping and avaricious governor. Insanely jealous of any superior authority, the governor resented Iberville, though he grudgingly consented, after repeated quarrels with him, to assist him in driving the English from St. John. In their plans they were entirely successful: they entered the town in triumph and razed it to the ground. The governor then returned to Placentia, while Iberville set out with his men on snowshoes to drive the English from their posts in the north.

With reinforcements under his brother, Sérigny, they sailed to Hudson Bay, where floes wrecked one of their ships with the loss of her crew. Iberville, having lost sight of his other ships but confident of their safety, kept on to Fort Nelson, where he saw, early on the morning of September 4, three ships about three leagues to leeward. He signaled them but when they failed to reply he realized that they were British. Though he was one against three, and though he had scarcely a hundred serviceable men, he bore down on them. While the enemy cannon roared, killing one of his men and wounding seventeen others, he continued to bear down on the *Hampshire* until the *Hampshire* bore down on him. Then he ran up under her lee, yardarm under yardarm, and poured in broadside after broadside, though her companion ships raked him fore and aft, making his deck a tangle of rigging and splintered spars, all blood bespattered, where mangled bodies were rolling helplessly. The gunners of the two ships that were locked in their death grapple could see each others' faces through the smoke as the fierce battle continued. Suddenly a wild scream broke silence on the English ship; she sank in a cold whirlpool with two hundred thirty valiant men. Not one of them was saved.[13]

Iberville swung around his battered hulk toward the second English ship which quickly struck her colors and surrendered. The third ship escaped. Iberville would have pursued her immediately, but he could not: he found his rigging cut, his shroud in shreds, his pumps broken, and water gushing through seven holes that enemy shells had torn close to the water line. He repaired the damage as quickly as possible and started in pursuit of the ship; but she had disappeared in the fog. He returned to Fort Nelson, only to encounter a terrible night storm that crippled the cables of his ship. With her seams leaking and with hard ice floes, driven by high winds, gashing her hulls, she managed to run ashore, where, when the storm abated, she landed some of her men. The rest found themselves in desolate rocks without food and even without the means of lighting a fire. Knowing that the fort had ample provisions, they put their mortars in position and summoned it to surrender. The arrival of French ships settled the matter. Without striking a blow, Fort Nelson hauled down her flag. Iberville left his brother to guard the fort and sailed away to France.[14]

He told Louis XIV he was weary of his work in the north. He had captured every fort, time and time again, only to see the careless Frenchmen almost hand them over to the enemy. What he wanted was something that would be more than a useless expenditure of blood. He proposed that France should establish a fort at the mouth of the Mississippi, which La Salle, in 1682, had explored and claimed and named for his king, Louis XIV.

For some years after La Salle's tragic death in Texas, France, warring elsewhere against Spain and England for mastery of North America, forgot Louisiana. The Treaty of Ryswick, in 1697, ended the shooting war but started the cold war for colonial supremacy. France, having control of the St. Lawrence valley of Canada, the Great Lakes region, and the Ohio and upper Mississippi River, dreamed of settling and fortifying the lower Mississippi to keep it from falling to Spain or England. We have seen how England, through her trade with the Indians, was expanding from Carolina west to the Mississippi and south to Florida. Though the Treaty of Ryswick recognized each of the three powers as possessor of the territory it controlled when the war began, none of them was content; each coveted its neighbor's property and wished to take it as soon as the treaty could be repudiated.

During all this time, some leaders in France and Canada continued to urge the settlement of the lower Mississippi valley. In 1694 Henri de Tonti, La Salle's friend and companion, offered his services to settle Louisiana, which, he pointed out, could be used as a base for an attack on Mexico, as a depository for the fur trade and lead ore of the Illinois region, and to prevent the English from seizing the territory. Three years later Sieur de Rémonville, a Canadian nobleman and friend of La Salle, urged France to organize a company that should settle Louisiana as soon as possible to forestall the English, who were on the point of seizing the mouth of the Mississippi. In the same year Tonti published *La Salle's Last Discoveries in America* in which he described the geography, the Indians, and the mineral wealth of the Mississippi Valley. Widely circulated in France, it revived interest in forgotten Louisiana.[15]

Louis XIV's secret agents soon learned that England was planning to establish a colony in Louisiana. Dr. Daniel Coxe, who had served as a court physician to Charles II, had acquired possession of an ancient patent that Charles I had granted to Sir Robert Heath and of a larger grant to Lord Maltavers. These two patents composed an enormous area called Carolana which extended from sea to sea between the thirty-first and the thirty-sixth parallels. Coxe planned to settle a colony of French Hugenot refugees who were thronging to England and to the Protestant countries of northern Europe. Spain, too, was interested, and in October, 1698, sent a force under Andrés de Arriola from Vera Cruz to secure both Pensacola Bay and the mouth of the Mississippi. France, then, should waste no time.

Count Pontchartrain, minister of marine, held a conference with French and Canadian leaders in which they planned to send a ship directly from France to beat the two competitors to the prize. In his search for an experienced and valiant naval commander, his gaze fell on Iberville, who wasted no time organizing his expedition. He collected two hundred colonists and a company of marines on two frigates, *La Badine* and *Le Marin*, and on October 24 sailed from Brest. On reaching Santo Domingo, he picked up the flagship, *Francois*, under a former pirate, Laurent de Graff, who served as pilot for the remainder of the voyage. Iberville coasted along the shore of Western Florida to Pensacola, where, as we have seen, he discovered that the Spaniards had already taken possession of the region.[16]

He moved westward. On January 31 he anchored off Mobile Bay. Unwilling to risk his ships in unknown water, he sent an officer and his brother Bienville in one ketch and another officer in the other ketch to examine the bay, while he sent still another officer in a bigger boat to survey the mainland. The latter soon reported that bad weather had prevented him from landing. So Iberville with two of his brothers went ashore where they spent the night in heavy rain. Next morning, when the sky cleared, they explored until another rainfall forced them to seek shelter on Dauphin Island, which Iberville called Massacre Island because he found sixty skeletons there. That night a wild storm arose, preventing him from continuing his search for a suitable harbor, though the long line of reefs and island protected his ships and boats from damage. Rounding a headland, he ran into a tempest and made for land.

There, while his men bemused themselves hunting bustards and ducks, he went with his brothers to the mainland at present Cedar Point. Following the shore for some distance, they came to a tall oak which Iberville climbed. From this vantage point, he could survey the extent and nature of the land to the north. He saw the mouth of a river tumbling its muddy waters into the bay but no contour of the coastline that would lead him in that direction. All around him the land appeared fertile, with forests of oaks, elms, pines, and nut trees and with carpets of flowers similar to those he had seen in Santo Domingo; yet this assuring aspect offered him no solution to his problem. Next morning, when the weather cleared again, Iberville continued westward. A strong wind blew him past Horn and Dog islands to Ship Island, so called for its silhouette on the horizon, and to Cat Island, where they found numerous raccoons which they mistook for "wild cats."

On February 10 Iberville anchored off the northern shore of Ship Island, whence three days later he went to the mainland with Father Anastasius Douay and a small group of his soldiers. Discovering tracks of Indians on the shore, they stayed that night on the spot, sleeping in a crude hut they built. Next morning they sought the Indians, leaving behind two axes, two pipes, and some odds and ends to attract them to the hut and to show their friendly intentions toward them. At a small bay they saw Indians paddling desperately in a single canoe toward shore. Jumping into a canoe that they had brought with them, Iberville and his comrades pursued and overtook the Indians just as they reached shore. The Indians, mistaking the Frenchmen for Spaniards, dashed into the forest, leaving behind an ailing chief. Iberville treated him with great kindness, building him a hut, bringing him food and doing everything to win his friendship.[17]

Meanwhile Bienville and two Canadians had pursued other Indians, had caught several of them, and had won their friendship by giving them gifts. By offering themselves as hostages, they persuaded two of the Indians to board *La Badine*. Iberville had guns fired for their education as well as for their amusement and dined them royally. At their invitation Iberville returned to shore, where they accorded him their usual form of salutation, rubbing their hands on their heads and bellies and on those of their guests and then raising them toward heaven. Iberville, hoping to seal their friendship, replied in kind. Then all of them went to Bienville's camp, where they smoked calumets while the Indians received axes, blankets, shirts, knives, and numerous other gifts which struck their fancy. That evening Iberville had wine and whiskey served to the Indians, but he was amazed to find that they were much less fond of these drinks than were their northern brothers.[18]

With his vessels safely in harbor, Iberville pursued his plans of ascertaining the mouth of the Mississippi and of planting a settlement on one of its banks. No longer fearful of an English expedition, he sent de Graff with his *François* back to Haiti and thence to France to bring word of the Spanish settlement at Pensacola.[19]

Returning to *La Badine*, Iberville sent two ensigns to explore the Pascagoula River, which emptied into the Gulf a short distance from his anchorage, while he started westward with Bienville, Sauvole, Father Douay, and a force of fifty men in two longboats and several bark canoes. He rowed along the shore of Ship Island, then Cat Island, then southward through the archipelago that covers the Gulf just south of the entrance of Lake Borgne. For several days he threaded his way through the labyrinth of islands, beating against head winds, struggling against torrential rains and amid thunder and lightning, and anchoring at sunset off some island to pass the night.

On March 2, as his ships scudded before a northernly gale with gun-wales awash, he saw a line of rocks projecting from the coast. Approaching them in the growing darkness, he could make out a rift in the line stretching across his course. Chancing his way through the rift, he entered that branch or delta of the Mississippi known as North Pass. Observing a change in the water, he tasted it and found it fresh, though it was thick and muddy. And what he thought were rocks were really petrified logs and driftwood which untold generations had blackened, the current had piled up, and fluvial sediment had cemented and then chiseled into a rocky palisade. Next day, Shrove Tuesday, Iberville ascended the delta to the main stream, where rushes and reeds gradually gave way to trees. Climbing one of these, he surveyed the surrounding region—a vast tract of canebrakes and rushes stretching as far as he could see. He fired salutes; he was greeted by a deep silence. He continued upstream, keeping a sharp watch for what Indians might be wandering along the river banks. By now the wind had died down; the sailors had taken up their oars.

On March 7 Indians began to appear, only to run away in panic as the white men approached. Two Indians in a single canoe paddled vigorously to the shore and fled into the woods; others appeared and fled also; then one curious fellow dallied long enough to be captured. The white men showered him with gifts, thereby inducing his comrades to join him. Iberville persuaded one of them to lead him to their village. Its chief, clad in bearskins and his face smeared with mud to enhance his appearance, offered Iberville an unusually long calumet embellished with multi-colored feathers. Being no smoker he took a small puff at it and passed it on to his comrades. Then the chief sat down in one of Iberville's boats and led the way to a place where his braves and some of their wives had assembled to accord the strangers a proper welcome. As Iberville stepped ashore, the Indians greeted him with their customary abdominal caress, which he returned. In a clearing he saw, mounted on two forked sticks and guarded by a brave, the large calumet he had given to the Indians he had met on Mississippi Sound.

The Indians brought food, an unpalatable concoction of sagamite, beans, and Indian corn cooked in bear grease, which they wolfed down as much from repugnance as from hunger. In turn, Iberville gave them whiskey which, even when diluted with water, proved too strong for them, and needles, mirrors, and knives. The young men of the village then danced and yelled to the sound of pebbles rattling in gourds, while Iberville interrogated the chief, who was strutting about in a superb blue coat Tonti had given him, about the surrounding tribes scattered along the lower Mississippi. Bienville, who had managed to pick up a few Indian words, assisted his brother in his query. Partly by signs, partly by words of mouth, Iberville learned that the Quinipasses were living in a settlement eight days' overland journey to the northeast. Iberville also ascertained a point of geography which had perplexed him for some time. He had read in La Salle's account of his expeditions that the Mississippi somewhere in its course was divided into two channels, both of which emptied into the sea. Anxious to find this fork, Iberville asked the chief and his braves innumerable questions. They assured him that the great river had only one channel and proved their point by stating that Tonti in his voyage to and from the delta had passed their village.[20]

Continuing his voyage upstream, Iberville came to a collection of huts in which many of its inhabitants lay ill with smallpox. Iberville and his comrades, nevertheless, tarried among them long enough to allow Father Douay to celebrate Mass and to present them with trinkets and their chief with a pair of red stockings, two shirts, and a scarlet jacket with gold lace trimmings. The Indians in turn gave the explorers some dried meat of which they ate sparingly, and a number of buckskins with which they patched their shoes.[21]

Early next morning, March 16, they rowed upstream to present Scott Bluff, Louisiana, where they saw on the east bank a pole painted red and adorned with heads of fish and bears as a kind of sacrificial offering. This pole marked the boundary between the Bayagoula and Houma tribes; they were so jealous of one another that they shot on the spot anyone caught hunting on the wrong side of the boundary. The Indians called the marker *Istrouma*, which the French translated "Baton Rouge," the present name of the capital of Louisiana.[22]

On March 18 the explorers rowed past Profit Island, where the river swings around in a loop, almost in a circle, bringing its banks close together. The eroded banks permit the river to form a channel that swings to the westward and that is separated from the loop. Here, at the False River Cut-Off, the Indians told the explorers that they could save a day's journey by dragging their boats across the intervening neck of land. This they did in two days, reaching a place just north of present Tunica Island, where they picked up a trail to one of the Houma villages. A delegation of its leading inhabitants met Iberville and, much to his discomfort, presented him with a calumet, which he passed to his friends. The Indians feasted them and danced for their enjoyment.[23]

Finding himself short of provisions, Iberville started on his return journey to his ships at Cat Island, four hundred miles away. Descending with the current, he made excellent time. Next day he found himself at the village of the Houmas, where he learned that the Mugulasha, a tribe farther down the river, had a letter which Tonti had written to La Salle fourteen years before. The Mugulasha chief gladly exchanged the "speaking bark," as he called the letter, for a good ax. He included a prayer book in which was written the name of one of La Salle's men. These items tied loose historical threads together to confirm French claims to the Mississippi save for Spanish prior rights established by Soto in 1541. Iberville meanwhile had journeyed eastward with a few men through the Bayou Manchac to Amite River and to lakes which he named Pontchartrain and Maurepas in honor of the minister of marine and one of his sons. Iberville reached his anchorage at Cat Island just a few hours before his brother Bienville.[24]

Casting about for a suitable location on which to establish a colony, Iberville selected a fair, sandy glade of raised coast on the eastern shore of Biloxi Bay. In making this choice he doubtless reasoned that France with a fort on the Gulf could control its northern shore as well as the mouth of the Mississippi. On four square acres near present Ocean Springs, Mississippi, he built Fort Maurepas. Protected in its sides by deep gorges or gullies, in its front by water, and in its rear by a dense forest, it contained all the natural advantages of a formidable stronghold or bulwark against attack.

Iberville strengthened its rear, which he thought its weakest point, with an entrenchment that ran to the gullies. The fort had four bastions and twelve pieces of artillery. Deer Island almost concealed the gulf beyond. The bastions looked out over sand as white as silver, over a broad expanse of water that recalled the Mediterranean, and over majestic live oaks and splendid magnolias in whose branches birds of brilliant plumage sang incessantly. Fort Maurepas was to Mississippi what Jamestown was to Virginia and Plymouth Rock to Massachusetts.[25]

2

On May 4, four days after Fort Maurepas was completed, Iberville sailed for France with the *La Badine* and *Le Marin* to enlist new colonists and to obtain fresh supplies. He left a garrison of seventy men and six ship-boys under his friend, Sauvole de la Villantry, with his brother, Bienville, as second in command. Acting on Iberville's orders, Sauvole sent Bienville with five men and a chief of the Bayagoulas for his guide to explore the interior. On August 24 the party journeyed to the Colapisses, whose domains embraced the present sites of Lewisburg, Mandeville, and Fontainbleau on the northern shore of Lake Pontchartrain. There Bienville and his companions learned that, just two days before, two hundred Chickasaws under two Englishmen had attacked one of the villages. This, says Gayarré, was "the harbinger of the incessant struggle which was to continue for more than a century between the two races, and to terminate by the permanent occupation of Louisiana by the Anglo-Saxon."[26]

Bienville rested for two weeks, then voyaged to Pascagoula bay and river, explored Round Island, Mobile Bay, and, at its mouth, Dauphin Island. Encouraged by the friendly reception he received everywhere, he ventured to Bayou Plaquemires and Bayou Chetimachas, which his brother had described for him. Then he turned his ships and descended the river. On September 16, when he arrived a few miles below the present site of New Orleans, he met the *Carolina Galley*, an English frigate under Captain Bond—not Bank or Banks or Barr as he is called by historians who rely solely on French sources.

Bond, in the employ of Dr. Daniel Coxe, proprietor of the Carolana grant, had prudently spent the winter of 1698-99 in Charles Town and had in the spring resumed his voyage. Coasting along the gulf from Florida Cape to Rio Pánuco, he had reached the Mississippi on August 29 and had ventured upstream for about a hundred miles. Bienville, with characteristic audacity boarded the *Carolina Galley* and discovered that Captain Bond, who received him hospitably, was one of his old antagonists from Hudson Bay. The most widely accepted version of this incident states that the English skipper explained that he was exploring the banks of the river to select a spot for a colony. Bienville told him that Louisiana belonged to Canada and that the French had already established several settlements on the river. This was a little wide of the truth; but in diplomacy, Bienville knew, veracity is often a synonym for lunacy. As evidence that a settlement was nearby he offered his own presence with such smaller boats as canoes. Bond believed him and sailed back. At this place the river makes a considerable bend. The event associated with it became known as the English Turn—*détour des anglais*, which the elated Bienville might have preferred to render *tour des français*.[27]

But Fort Maurepas was in no mood for rejoicing. Six months had passed without any word from Iberville. Meanwhile, the garrison and the few colonists suffered unspeakable hardships. The weather was so cold that "water, when poured into tumblers to rinse them, froze instantaneously, before it could be used." But the colonists suffered less from the unusually severe weather than from their own pride and laziness. Many of them were Canadians called *coureurs de bois* whose chief occupations were hunting and trapping; they knew nothing and wanted to know nothing about farming; they failed to raise crops to replenish the supplies which had been brought from France. They preferred to explore the region in search of gold and other precious metals, while their homes swarmed with alligators and snakes that terrified and jeopardized their women and children.

Sauvole despaired of relief. "Unless a gold mine is discovered," he wrote, ironically, "the king will not be compensated for his services." Though they still loved their beautiful country and its magnificent trees, birds, and flowers, they desponded pitifully from hunger and disease; they longed for Iberville's return, which would dispel the gloom that pervaded the little colony.[28]

Imagine their joy, therefore, when on December 7 they heard signal guns booming from the direction of the sea. At last friends were coming to their rescue! The colony rushed down to the shore, where it lingered for days that seemed like weeks for Iberville's appearance. Finally, on the morning of January 6, 1700, they heard cannon fire from Surgéres Island, about fifteen miles from the fort, announce Iberville's arrival. Soon appeared two vessels, *La Renommée*, fifty guns, and *Le Gironde*, forty-six guns, proudly flying the fleur-de-lis and, says the poetic Gay-arré, "approaching as near as the shallowness of the beach permitted, folded their pinions, like waterfowls seeking repose on the crest of the billows."[29] The fort saluted Iberville with volleys of musketry, while the colony shed joyful tears as it cheered.

Iberville brought more settlers, an appointment for Sauvole as governor of Louisiana, and instructions' "to breed the buffalo at Biloxi, to seek for pearls, to examine the wild mulberry with a view to silk, timber for ship-building, and to seek for mines."[30] To explore the mines in the country of the Sioux, far to the north, Iberville brought a geologist, Pierre le Sueur, who had taken part in Canadian explorations and had brought back with him a quantity of blue and green earth which he claimed contained copper.[31]

Learning that the British had attempted to establish a settlement on the banks of the Mississippi, Iberville wasted no time in taking precautionary measures to forestall them from any further attempt. On January 17 he departed with Bienville to a spot eight leagues below the English Turn, where he planned to build on his return a substantial fort which received the name of Boulaye, perhaps from the old French word *boulaie*, meaning a plot of beech trees. Continuing upstream, he reached Baton Rouge, which marked the boundary between the two chief Indian nations of the region, the Bayagoulas and Houmas. Then he returned to begin construction of Fort Boulaye.

One day while he and his companions were so engaged, they saw a canoe sweeping down the river toward them. It was occupied by eight men, one of whom was apparently their leader. Imagine what greeting they extended him when he identified himself as Henri de Tonti! He had heard of the establishment of Louisiana and had come down from the Illinois country, of which he was governor, to ascertain if he could be of some assistance. He had come with twenty-two men, most of whom had stopped at the Bayagoula villages to exchange their supply of beaver skins for merchandise.

Iberville, learning that the missionary, Father Montigny, was still alive among the Natchez, saw the possibility of friendly relations with that tribe. Placing the fort under one of his officers, Sieur de Maltot, he sent Bienville with a large detachment upstream, while he followed with a few men in a felucca. At a portage Iberville fell in with Le Sueur who was going to the copper mines of the north and who accompanied him to the village of the Bayagoulas. Iberville stayed with them for several days, giving them presents and cotton seed which was the first to be planted in Louisiana. He also composed their differences with the Houmas and made himself acquainted with their country. Then he journeyed with his brother toward the Taensas, where he met Father Montigny, who had built himself a house and was about to build a church. On March 22 Bienville began his journey back to Fort Boulaye, while his brother and Father Montigny continued upstream to the Taensa village, where they were well received. But they saw there the saddest and most frightful spectacle of their journey:

> A sudden storm burst upon us. The lightning struck their temple, burned all their idols and reduced the whole to ashes. Quickly the Indians assembled, making horrible cries, tearing out their hair, elevating their hands to heaven, their tawny visages turned toward the burning temple, invoking their Great Spirit with the howling of devils possessed to come down and extinguish the flames. They took up mud, with which they besmeared their bodies and faces. The fathers and mothers then brought their children and, having strangled them, threw them into the flames.[32]

This horrified Iberville so much that he had his men take the children away from their parents; but seventeen had already perished in the flames.[33]

Shortly afterward Iberville returned to Fort Boulaye, which he placed under his brother with twenty-five men. Then he continued downstream to Fort Maurepas, whence on May 28 he sailed for France.[34]

That summer yellow fever struck Fort Maurepas and Biloxi, killing many of the colonists. Among the victims was Sauvole. The sorrowing Bienville immediately left Fort Boulaye and assumed command of Fort Maurepas.[35]

In December 1701 Iberville returned to Louisiana with two ships, *Le Renommée* and *Le Palmier*, bringing badly needed supplies and a large number of colonists. An operation for an abcess in his side delayed him in Pensacola until March 1702, when he returned to Fort Maurepas. He announced that in November, 1700, Philip V, grandson of Louis XIV of France, had been proclaimed King of Spain, and that henceforth the two countries would act in harmony. The king, moreover, had instructed him to erect a new fort on the Mobile River and remove the colony to that place to be nearer their Spanish friends. In the absence of the Spanish commander, Iberville convinced the second in command, Francisco Martínez, that the proposed fort would enable the two nations to present a unified front against their common enemy, England. Ill health, however, prevented Iberville from inspecting the site of the fort. So he sent his brother, who left Fort Maurepas under Dugue de Boisbriant with twenty men. Fort Louis de la Mobile was much larger than Fort Maurepas. Three hundred seventy-five feet square, it contained four bastions each of six cannon that protruded outside in a half circle. Within the fort were a chapel, a guardhouse, a warehouse, and quarters for the commander and his officers. Outside the palisade, on the banks of the river, were the barracks for the soldiers and the Canadians.[36]

No sooner was the fort completed than Tonti returned from the Illinois country with several Choctaw and Chickasaw chiefs. Iberville, who was now recuperating from his illness, seized the opportunity to ween them from their friendship with the English. For the purpose of impressing them with the wealth and influence of the French, he loaded them with gifts while he expressed joy at seeing them peacefully disposed instead of destroying one another in continual warfare. But he said he was disappointed to learn that the Chickasaw allowed the English to dupe them. The sole aim of the English was to enslave and sell them outside their country; he knew of some English traders who had bought some Chickasaw from their captors for that very purpose. He advised the Chickasaw to break with their English friends; if they refused, he would arm the Illinois, their arch-enemies.

Passing from threats to cajolery, he offered, in return for their compliance to his wishes, to build between themselves and the Choc-taws a trading post where they could always exchange furs for mer-chandise at reasonable prices. The chiefs accepted his offer; they promised to abandon their English friends in return for suitable trade concessions. Iberville sealed his bargains with them by giving them mus-kets and ammunition and a great variety of trinkets. Furthermore, he told the Chickasaw that he would order his Indian allies to stop molesting them and that, in return for their influence in inducing their neighbors to abandon the English for the French, he would request the Illinois to release Chickasaw prisoners. Iberville promptly fulfilled his promises.[37]

On April 22, less than a month after he had signed the peace treaty with the Indians, Iberville departed for France, never again to return to the struggling colony he had done so much to establish. He was destined never to witness the results of his labors. He expected to return to Louisiana in the late summer of 1703, but illness and military duties in the War of the Spanish Sucession kept him in France. Not until the spring of 1706 was he able to depart with a fleet with which he planned to drive the English from the West Indies. He attacked and captured the island of Nevis of the Lesser Antilles and then sailed for Cuba; but yellow fever had already weakened his body. On July 9, 1706, he died while his ship was lying before the port of Havana.[38]

Meanwhile the warlike Sioux had forced Le Sueur and his men to abandon their mining operations in the north. Without mines, the French government which, unlike Iberville, had never stressed the impor-taince of domestic life and agriculture, regarded the colony as a failure. On her forts and colonies along the gulf and lower Mississippi, France had spent large sums without securing any material returns. Yet Iberville and Bienville had succeeded in laying the foundation stones of Biloxi, Mobile, and New Orleans. In these places, says Dunbar Rowland with nostalgic charm, "something heroic, something indescribably sweet of Iberville's day still lingers, the distillations perhaps of suffering and sorrow that came of great sacrifice and unremitting toil and effort. But it was not for this dauntless herald of a glad day to realize any portion of his dream. To him and others of his day it wore the face of failure."[39]

3

Bienville succeeded his deceased brother as governor of Louisiana. He was just twenty-six years old. For more than forty years thereafter he was to guide the destinies of the struggling colony his brother had founded. The difficult position in which he found himself required genius or an indomitable stubbornness; he could offer it only tactful patience, great courage, and fierce tenacity. The first decade of his administration was brimful of dissension, mercy, starvation, and death. Only the friendship of the Spaniards at Pensacola occasionally relieved the colony of its gloom. They sent Bienville provisions from Florida and Mexico, while he reciprocated with soldiers to repulse the English in the siege of St. Augustine. Otherwise the colony would have collapsed.

The home government kept the colonists so busy searching for mines and pearl fisheries, and in trying to domesticate the buffalo for their "wool," and to raise silk worms, that they had to depend on vessels from France to provide them with food. The soldiers wore skins rather than their shabby uniforms. They numbered one hundred eighty, "all armed with their guns." The colonists, who were in rags, consisted of "twenty-seven families that have only three little girls and seven young boys one to ten years of age." They subsisted on acorns, a little corn they raised, and wild game, fish, and fowl. They lived in eighty rickety wooden houses covered with palmetto leaves or straw. They had raised nine oxen, "five of which belong to the king and four to private persons"; fourteen cows; four bulls, one of which belonged to the king; five calves; one hundred pigs; three goats; and four hundred hens.[40]

Gayarré epitomized early Louisiana as "a Shakespearian mixture of the terrible and the ludicrous." The terrible aspect we have seen; the comical aspect was the threatened insurrection of twenty young "females veiled, pious, and virtuous" whom the king had sent to make his colony respectable and to anchor the settlers down with families. Bienville housed them in Mobile until husbands could be found for them. They quickly developed an aversion, not only for the tatterdemalion, unkempt, and scrawny men but also for corn mush. They began to inveigh bitterly against the Bishop of Quebec whom they accused of enticing them away from their comfortable homes "under the pretext of sending them to enjoy the milk and honey of the land of promise." Enraged at having been deceived, they swore to fight their way out of the colony "at the first opportunity."[41]

More venomous than these frustrated petticoated rebels were the com-Roulleaux de La Vente. La Salle, a nephew of the great explorer, had missary, Nicholas de La Salle, and the curate of Mobile, Father Henri settled with his family on Dauphin Island early in 1702. He soon proposed a code of laws which Bienville rejected as unsuitable to the colony. Greatly angered, La Salle joined La Vente in attacking Bienville and in requesting Pontchartrain in France to remove him from office.

Gayarré describes La Salle as a fat, short, sleek man "with bloated features and oily skin," and as "a true representative" of the toad, though "certainly to him the traditional legend of a jewel in the head could not be applied." His cold, grayish eyes squinted dully like those of a pig; indeed, "as he strutted along, one was almost amazed not to hear an occasional grunt." For hours "his prosy voice carried to his hearers . . . the same insane, insipid flow of bombastic phrases, falling on the ear with the unvaried and ever-recurring sound of a pack-horse wheel in a flour-mill." In his "delirious" self-esteem he was "as complete a financier, as skillful a statesman, as great a general, and, above all, as profound a legislator, as ever lived."

La Salle soon wrote to Pontchartrain, accusing Bienville and his brother Chateauguay of every kind of misdeed, and branding them as thieves and rogues who squandered the king's property.[42] He also attacked Barrot, the colony's apothecary, whom he had failed to win to his side, as "no better than a fool, a drunkard and a rogue, who sold the king's drugs and appropriated the money to his own purpose."[43]

Bienville in turn accused La Salle of making mistakes in his accounts and of recently acting like "a common thief in refusing to repay his brother the expenses of a voyage to Havana made expressly for the purpose of bringing back provisions."[44] As for La Vente, Bienville denounced him in a letter to Pontchartrain as a violent and insecure man who had talked constantly of leading the colonists to revolt. Bienville went on to charge the priest with breaking up families, insulting women, baptizing children in the nude outside the church, and writing to Pensacola for flour, falsely stating, as the Spaniards themselves acknowledged, that the governor was starving the colonists to death. Bienville concluded that though La Ventre stirred up everybody against him by his calumnies, "he did not blush to keep an open shop where his mode of trafficking showed that he was a shrewd compound of the Arab and the Jew."[45]

As the quarrel spread, the colony became divided into two hostile camps. Nerves jangled under disappointment and famine until "everybody fumed, shouted, and flung himself at his desk." Father Gavier, who sided with Bienville, wrote to Pontchartrain, expressing his intense disgust and anger that a priest should have the audacity to poison the colony with his outrageous lies. Boisbriant, too, sided with Bienville, though he regretted that the governor saw fit to disapprove as below his station his love affair with the woman in charge of the twenty girls whom the Bishop of Quebec had sent to Louisiana. Boisbriant meekly submitted to the judgment of his leader; but the scorned woman, with more than hellish fury, complained to Pontchartrain in measured terms of what she called "an act of oppression." She concluded her observations with this sweeping indictment of Bienville: "It is therefore evident that he has not the necessary qualifications to be governor of the colony."[46]

This flood of contradictory denunciations finally stirred Pontchartrain to action. He appointed a Norman, Nicholas Daneau, Sieur de Muys, to succeed Bienville as governor of Louisiana and Diron d'Artaguette to succeed La Salle as commissary and to examine and improve conditions in the colony. Pontchartrain ordered the two men to hold an inquiry into the accusations brought against Bienville and, if these proved him guilty, to convey him to France as a prisoner. Bienville received secret warning of what was about to happen and asked for a leave of absence. This was needless worry, for he was destined to keep his position. Muys died in Havana before he reached his destination, and Artaguette undertook the investigation alone.

Now that the colonists faced the possibility of losing Bienville, they suddenly became alive to his merits; they unanimously subscribed to Pontchartrain a petition in which they expressed their satisfaction with the governor's administration. They supplicated Pontchartrain not to deprive them of such a wise and faithful governor. And Artaguette vindicated Bienville entirely. To La Salle all this was very distressing; "but his spleen was worked into a paroxym of rage when he was informed that his successor . . . had made a report to the king, in which he declared, that all the accusations brought against Bienville, were mere slanderous inventions, which rested on no other foundation than the blackest malice." Though deprived of his office, La Salle could still eject his venom. He wrote Pontchartrain that "Artaguette was not deserving of any faith or credit; that he had come to an understanding with Bienville, and that they were both equally bad and corrupt."[47]

Artaguette found the colony in a deplorable condition. The Canadians still roamed the woods instead of showing a disposition to settle down. Food was very scarce; during the winter of 1709 many of the colonists were obliged to live mainly on acorns. When Artaguette requested them to relieve the distress by cultivating the land, they replied that they could live well by hunting and that, being unmarried, they saw no need of building homes. Artaguette then took steps to change the deplorable situation. He wrote to Pontchartrain suggesting that forty comely girls be sent to the colony without delay and requesting peasants to teach the Canadians the rudiments of agriculture, a few companies of soldiers to provide the colony with a measure of security, and officers to train the soldiers. He stated that the married and settled people lived in slothfulness for which they excused themselves by saying that they saw nothing permanent in the colony and that they would begin to work just as soon as the king sent more troops and colonists.[48]

In 1711 a great flood forced the settlers to move to the present site of Mobile, eight leagues above the entrance of the river. That fall Artaguette returned to France, where he told Pontchartrain that his colonial enterprise was losing investments and that the colony needed a new policy.

Unbeknown to Artaguette, Louis XIV had already resolved on a change. Unable to finance the colony, he decided to turn it over to an individual or a company. His choice was Antoine Crozat, who on September 14, 1712, obtained a fifteen-year grant to operate the colony of Louisiana, which, according to Iberville's proposition, included the immense region

. . . bounded by New Mexico and by the lands of the English of Carolina, all the establishments, ports, havens, rivers and principally the port and haven of the Isle Dauphin, heretofore called Massacre; the River of St. Louis, heretofore called Mississippi, from the edge of the sea as far as the Illinois; together with the river of St. Philip, heretofore called the Missouri, and of St. Jerome, heretofore called Ouacache [Wabash or Ohio] with all the countries, territories, lakes within land, and the rivers which fall directly or indirectly into that part of the River St. Louis.[49]

Crozat enjoyed the monopoly of working and exploiting all the mines of precious metals that might be discovered in his domain, provided he pay the king one fourth of their produce. The grant declared him perpetual owner of all the lands he should cultivate, all the buildings he should erect, all the factories he should establish. For these advantages, he was obligated to send annually to Louisiana two ships with contingents of colonists. After nine years he was to assume the expenses he incurred in running the government of the colony, including those of the garrison and of its officers. Meanwhile, the king was to pay fifty thousand livres as his share of the expenses of Louisiana, which was to be governed in accordance with the laws, ordinances, customs, and usages in the viscounty of Paris. The government of the colony was to consist of a council identical with that of Santo Domingo and Martinique. The grant virtually made Crozat supreme lord of the colony. It was like a royal farm with Louis XIV as the landlord and Crozat as the farmer.[50]

Antoine Crozat was born of peasant stock on a large estate in Toulouse. The lord of the estate was so impressed by his intelligence, honesty, and good looks that he adopted him and sent him to school. At fifteen he became a clerk in a commercial house, eventually bought a half interest in it, and married his partner's daughter. On the death of his father-in-law, he found himself sole owner of the firm and one of the richest merchants in Europe. As such, he lent large sums of money to the king, who rewarded him by making him Marquis du Chatel. But with wealth and honor came tragedy. His wife died, leaving him with a beautiful and talented daughter, Marie Anne, who fell in love with a young nobleman, "the sole pillar of a ducal house, connected with all the imperial and royal dynasties of Europe." One day Crozat heard a rumor that the young duke was about to enter into a matrimonial alliance with one of the most powerful families in Europe. Fearing that his daughter would never survive "the withering of her hopes," Crozat went to see the young duke's mother. She reminded him of his peasant origin and of the historic importance of her House, which claimed emperors and kings and was indissolubly bound up not only with the annals of France but also with the history of Europe and Asia.

"You deserve infinite credit," she told him, "for having risen to the summit where you now stand. You have been ennobled, and you are one of the greatest merchants of the age, but you are not yet a Medici!"

The mention of that Florentine family, which had made itself one of the rulers of Europe, inspired Crozat to acquire a vast domain so that his daughter, too, might enjoy the position to marry into the nobility.[51]

Crozat chose as governor of the colony Antoine de la Mothe-Cadillac, founder of Detroit, who on June 5, 1713, arrived at Dauphin Island with Jean-Baptiste du Clos or Duclos, commissary in place of Artaguette, and with officers and twelve husband-seeking girls from Brittany. Bienville, whose knowledge of the colony was considered indispensable, was retained as lieutenant-governor. The new governor was born of an ancient Gascon family that for several centuries had "been sliding down from the elevated position which it had occupied." Symbolic of his desperate circumstances was his dilapidated residence, which he called a castle but which from a distance presented to any unprejudiced observer "some unlucky resemblance to a barn." To the boys of the neighborhood this "solitary tower . . . dressed in a gown of moss and ivy" was known as "Cadillac's Rookery," an epithet that caused its ruined owner no end of humiliation. This, however, he concealed with an air of infinite arrogance. On Sunday mornings he liked to strut to church in full dress, his ponderous wig, "which spread like a peacock's tail," seemingly "alive with conscious pride at the good luck it had of covering a head of such importance to the human race." His nose epitomized his arrogant bearing. It was *retroussé*,

> which seemed as if it had hurried back, in a fright, from his lips, to squat in rather too close proximity to the eyes, and which, with its dilated nostrils, seemed always on the point of sneezing at something thrusting itself between the wind and his nobility. His lips wore a mocking smile, as if sneering at the strange circumstances that a Cadillac should be reduced to be an obscure, penniless individual.[52]

Perhaps he believed that, after all, modesty is often a kind of apology that common men demand of the wise for their wisdom.

Now, at the age of fifty-four, he looked back on his life with a gnawing bitterness engendered by a host of disappointments and reverses and by a wife who made no secret of her hatred for him. In 1677, at the age of nineteen, he had entered the army, serving as a cadet and then as a lieutenant in the regiment of Clairembault. Six years later he migrated to Port Royal, now Annapolis, Nova Scotia, where he built a house in which he lived until his marriage at Quebec to Marie Thérèse Guyon. Then he took his bride to his grant in what is now the state of Maine. In 1689 he returned to France.

During his absence, British soldiers looted and burned his house at Port Royal. Word of this misfortune reached him while his ship foundered on her return to Canada; but he derived some consolation for his loss and for his discomfort when Governor Frontenac named him commander of Michilimackinac. As a rendezvous for *coureurs de bois* and fur traders, this old mission of the Jesuits "savored little of its apostolic beginnings"; indeed, it reeked of brandy and abounded with squaws. Cadillac naturally aroused the resentment of the Jesuits, who accused him of debauchery and described the fort as a "combined cabaret, gambling den, and a place which they would blush to describe by its proper name, where women learned to regard their bodies as merchandise."[53] The commander defended his policy by explaining that brandy and squaws attracted Indians and therefore prevented the English from seizing the profitable fur trade.[54]

In 1697, when France abandoned her western forts, Cadillac returned to Canada. Thence he sailed for France, where he laid before the ministry his plan to erect on the Detroit River a post that would protect the western fur trade from the possibility of falling to the English. Pontchartrain accepted his plan. In June, 1701, Cadillac journeyed to his destination with fifty soldiers, fifty *coureurs de bois*, and one hundred Indians in twenty-five canoes loaded with provisions, goods, ammunition, and tools. On high ground protected by water on three sides Cadillac built Fort Pontchartrain du Detroit, meaning Fort Pontchartrain on the Strait.

The Jesuits resented Cadillac for luring the Indians away from Michilimackinac and accused him in their reports to Governor Vaudreuil of deprecating their Order, underselling the merchants of Montreal, compelling his blacksmith to shoe his own horses free, giving his soldiers only one-twenty-fourth of a pot of liquor at a time, and granting licenses to bushlopers. Vaudreuil, who had succeeded Frontenac and who, unlike him, favored the Jesuits, summoned Cadillac to Quebec to answer charges. Thanks to his eloquence and sincerity, he was acquitted and returned to Detroit in triumph.

But he soon faced more serious trouble. In 1706, while he was in Quebec, the Sieur de Bourgmont, whom he had left in command of Detroit, supported the Miami in a quarrel with the Ottawas. But the Ottawa chiefs, still wishing to maintain peace with the French, restrained their young men from attacking the fort and sent a soldier and Father Constantine, a beloved Recollet missionary whom they had captured, to inform Bourgmont that they were warring only against the Miamis. Unfortunately, hotheaded braves killed the two emissaries as they arrived at the gate of the fort. Cadillac, anxious to heal the breach between the two warring tribes for the good of Detroit, failed to comply with Vaudreuil's orders to treat the murderers with severity. Thenceforth, Cadillac's prestige in Detroit waned. In 1710, by refusing to feed and clothe his garrison at his own expense, he quarreled with Vaudreuil. Whereupon the governor withdrew all the troops from Detroit and removed its commander. In the following year Crozat appointed Cadillac governor of Louisiana.[55]

He had been told that the colony was a land of milk and honey. Much to his chagrin he found it "a wretched country, good for nothing, and incapable of producing either tobacco, wheat, or vegetables." He described Dauphin Island as consisting of

> . . . a dozen fig trees that are very fine and that produce black figs. I saw three pear trees of wild stock, three apple trees of the same sort, a little plum tree about three feet in height that had seven poor plums on it, about thirty feet of grapevines and nine clusters of grapes in all, some of rotten or dry grapes and the rest somewhat ripe, about forty feet of French melons, a few pumpkins: that is the "terrestial paradise" of Artaguette . . . "the Pompona" of Rémonville . . . their memoranda and their relations are pure fables. They are spoken about what they have not seen at all and they have too readily believed what was told them.[56]

The colonists quickly won his contempt. Dipping his pen in bitterer ink, he wrote:

> According to the proverb, "Bad country, bad people," one can say that they are a heap of the dregs of Canada, jailbirds without subordination for religion and for government, addicted to vice principally with the Indian women whom they prefer to French women. It is very difficult to remedy it when his Majesty desired that they be governed mildly and wishes that a governor conduct himself in such a way that the inhabitants may make no complaints against him. Until the present these people have remained in this condition; the question is to reform them. With what favor will they receive this reformer? Disorderly monks to be sure reject their abbot when he seems to them severe and speaks to them of reform, but their rejection is always based on some poor pretext.[57]

He had come to Louisiana primarily to make money by discovering mines, "not to superintend and foster the slow and tedious progress of civilization." He lost his temper, therefore, when he received positive orders to assist Crozat's agent in establishing trading settlements or posts on the Wabash and on the Illinois. He never penned a more bitter reply:

> I have seen Crozat's instructions to his agents. I thought they issued from a lunatic asylum, and there appeared to me to be no more sense in them than in the Apocalypse. What! Is it expected that, for

any commercial or profitable purposes, boats will ever be able to run up the Mississippi, into the Wabash, the Missouri, or the Red River? One might as well try *to bite a slice off the moon!* Not only are these rivers as rapid as the Rhone, but in their crooked course, they imitate to perfection a snake's undulations. Hence, for instance, on every turn of the Mississippi, it would be necessary to wait for a change of wind, if wind could be had, because the river is so lined up with thick woods, that very little wind has access to its bed.[58]

Bending all his energies and turning every sou at his command toward the discovery of mines, he sent Canadians in every direction on exploratory parties; but search as they might they found no trace of precious minerals. Cadillac soon found himself without funds to continue his enterprise. He asked Duclos for money to resume his "researches"; but the commissary replied that the treasury "had been pumped dry."[59]

"Well, then!" retorted the frustrated governor, "what is the use of your being a financier, if you cannot raise money by borrowing, and what is the use of my being a governor, if I have no funds to carry on the purposes of my government?"[60]

Duclos replied by asking him to show his accounts for all the funds he had used and for all the goods and trinkets he had distributed among the Indians. Cadillac indignantly refused. Instead he dashed off to Pontchartrain a letter informing him of this outrage, "which in his opinion was a demonstration of the wild notions that had crept into the colony."[61]

Duclos countered by sending Pontchartrain a complaint of his own. In this he stated that Cadillac was

. . . too crafty for me and that he is capable of frustrating the most appropriate and the best planned measures that I could take for the good of the service, from the moment that I was no longer in favor with him. It is this that makes me take the liberty of asking you as a favor, my lord, to please recall me to France and to be so kind as to grant me there the post that your Lordship intended to give me . . . before I have thought of coming to [this colony], a thing that I certainly should not have done if I had known the character of . . . Cadillac to the same extent that it was unknown to me.[62]

Pontchartrain persuaded him to stay on.

Discouraged by his failure to find mines, Cadillac resolved to seek prosperity for the colony by inaugurating commercial relations with New Spain. To that colony he dispatched a ship. But England by the Treaty of Utrecht, which ended the War of the Spanish Succession, forbade Spain to permit the French any license of permission to trade or navigate among her American colonies. So the viceroy of New Spain turned back Cadillac's ship. To this rejection he added the sting of supplying the crew with provision to return home.[63]

Nothing daunted, Cadillac took steps to accomplish his aim by overland traffic. Assembling 10,000 francs worth of merchandise, he entrusted it to a fearless adventurer, Louis Juchereau de St. Denis, with orders to deposit it with the Natchitoches and then to continue to New Spain. St. Denis and his men ascended the Red River, deposited the merchandise at the assigned village, and marched to the country of the Asinai where La Salle had been murdered. There they found no white men save a few Spaniards who were as naked, as destitute, and as nomadic as the Indians.

With the assistance of Indian guides, they eventually reached the Presidio of San Juan Bautista, known also as Presidio del Norte, which stood on the banks of the Rio Grande. Its commander, Captain Diego Ramón, whom the chronicler Pénicaut erroneously called Pedro de Vilesca, received them cordially, provided them with lodging at the fort, and invited St. Denis and his friend and physician, Medar Jalot, to his residence. Ramón entertained them for several days before he asked St. Denis to state his business. The Frenchman explained that Cadillac had sent him to establish commercial relations between the two colonies. Ramón replied that only his immediate superior, Gasparo Anya, governor of Coahuila, whose residence was nearly two hundred miles away, could grant him such a concession, but that he would send a messenger to him immediately and that they should await his answer. St. Denis accepted this gracious invitation—and for sentimental reasons. He had fallen in love with Ramón's granddaughter—Manuela de Sánchez y Ramón—and she with him. She confided her feelings to her grandfather who, far from waxing angry, was delighted.[64]

Anya eventually summoned St. Denis to his residence, received him cordially, and informed him that he must take his request to Fernando de Alencastre, Noroña y Silva, Duke of Linares and Viceroy of New Spain in Mexico City. St. Denis agreed to do so, though he postponed his journey until the following year. Doubtless his thoughts were now far from ideas of trade, far from the merchandise he had left with the Natchitoches, far from Cadillac's possible irritation. Several months slipped by before he journeyed with forty mounted men and an officer to the viceregal court. And there capricious destiny frowned on him. The viceroy scanned his papers, handed them back to him, and peremptorily ordered him off to a dungeon, where he languished until, three months later, some French officers in the service of Spain, hearing that a relative of the great Iberville through marriage was in prison, interceded for him and secured his release.[65]

The viceroy expiated for his error by giving him a purse of 300 piastres, lodging him in a commodious and comfortable apartment, and inviting him frequently to his table. He grew so fond of him that he offered him a position in the Spanish army. The French officers, too, urged him to join them, pointing out that the rich provinces of Spain presented better inducements than those of impoverished France. The viceroy even promised him the command of a company of cavalry with a salary that would have induced any impecunious gentleman who had no military commission in Louisiana but who served merely as a volunteer. But nothing could move him. At last the viceroy, with some show of impatience, said to him:

"You are already more than a half-naturalized Spaniard, since you are to be married to Manuela, the eldest granddaughter of Don Diego Ramón, when you return."

"I will not conceal from you," replied St. Denis, "that I love Manuela, since it has been told to Your Excellency, but I have never fancied myself as worthy to marry her."

The viceroy urged him to accept the commission offered him, saying that Don Diego would be proud of him and would be delighted to give him his granddaughter in marriage. But St. Denis was obdurate. So was the viceroy. He presented St. Denis with a thousand piastres, saying as he laughed that he hoped Manuela would have more power than he in persuading him to remain in New Spain. But St. Denis was unable to obtain from him permission to establish trade between Louisiana and New Spain. Next day the viceroy presented him with a fine bay horse and ordered an officer with ten mounted men to escort him back to Anya.

When eventually St. Denis arrived at his destination, he met Jalot, who had won the admiration of the region by curing many people of such diseases as quartan fever and dysentery. They journeyed together to the Presidio of San Juan Bautista, where they found Ramón in a great predicament. The Indians of four villages had been badly treated by Spanish soldiers and had packed up their traps and gone away. This greatly distressed Ramón, who depended on them to feed his garrison. St. Denis assured him he would bring them back. He and Jalot soon overtook them. Tying a white handkerchief to a stick, St. Denis approached them and warned them in Spanish, which they understood, that the region to which they were going was inhabited by harsh and cruel tribes and promised them that, if they agreed to return, he would ascertain that they would never again be molested.[66]

He easily persuaded them and returned with them to the fort, where Ramón assured them that henceforth any Spaniard who entered their reservation would be put to death. Soon St. Denis and Manuela were married amid such magnificence as the presidio had never known before that day. He remained with his wife for six months. Then, beginning to think that Cadillac might be anxious about the merchandise left among the Natchitoches, he set out without his wife, who was big with child, for Louisiana, with a promise, which he kept, of returning and taking her and their child to their new home in Louisiana.[67]

Cadillac was distraught to learn that his plans for commercial relations with New Spain had broken down. He sought compensation for his failure by planning a fort among the Natchez, who showed some dispo-

sition to trade with the Carolinians and who had recently murdered four
Canadians. For this task, Cadillac chose Bienville. Yet the two men had
never been more unfriendly. Cadillac had a daughter who had fallen in
love with Bienville. The young woman plainly showed her sentiments
through her eyes, but Bienville "was wrapped in respectful blindness."
She made her love so apparent that "at least it flashed upon Cadillac's
mind." He sent for Bienville, offered him "the olive branch of reconciliation, and by slow degrees gave him to understand that the god Hymen
might seal the bond of their amity." Bienville bowed low in respectful
appreciation of the offer but quietly informed Cadillac "of his firm determination, for reasons best known to himself, forever to undergo the
mortification of celibacy."[68] But Bienville in a letter to his brother revealed his real reason for rejecting the marriage proposal: "I do not see
ahead how I could provide for a wife or provide for myself, for our
governor is very stingy. He has not offered me a glass of water since
. . . he has been here."[69]

Some historians suggest that Cadillac deliberately planned to ruin
Bienville by sending him to conquer the fierce Natchez with an inadequate force. He was about to depart when he learned that the Natchez
had taken the warpath. Cadillac himself was responsible for their bellig-
erency. He had scornfully refused to smoke the calumet they had offered
him and they had deduced from his boorishness that he planned some
stroke against them. So they pillaged Crozat's warehouse and killed all the
Frenchmen they caught traveling up and down the Mississippi. Though
he made all haste to march against them, Bienville asked Cadillac to give
him the eighty men whom Pontchartrain had originally assigned to him
for the task of conquering the Natchez. But Cadillac gave him a force of
only thirty-four men whom he augmented with fifteen sailors when
Duclos and Crozat's agents joined Bienville in protesting the impossibility
of constructing a fort and waging war against a tribe that could muster
eight hundred warriors. With this small force in eight pirogues, Bienville, in April, 1716, rowed to the Tunicas, eighteen leagues below the
Natchez, where the missionary, Father Davion, advised him that both
tribes planned to kill him. Concealing any anxiety he might have felt, he
assembled the Tunica warriors and told them that he intended to build a
post where they could trade their peltry for merchandise and that they
should do him the favor of sending some of their tribe to announce his
arrival to the Natchez. With this request they complied.[70]

Bienville went to an island in the river on which he began to build a
trading post. While he was so occupied, three Natchez representing their
chiefs arrived and presented him with a calumet. He waved it aside, saying that they could get some of his soldiers to smoke it, but that he himself, being a great chief of the French, would smoke only a calumet presented to him by their sun chiefs. They replied that their chiefs would
be happy to visit him. And in a few days he saw approaching four
pirogues in each of which were four men standing and smoking a calu-

met and three sitting under parasols with twelve swimmers around them. The sitting men were Natchez chiefs, whom Bienville invited to his tent, which they entered while they sang and passed a calumet over Bienville's head and feet, then over their heads and his stomach, and then over their stomachs as a sign of friendship. He disdainfully pushed the calumet aside, saying that before he would accept it he wanted to hear their speeches and know their thoughts.

The chiefs, disconcerted by his disdain, went outside and lifted their calumets toward heaven, while one of them, the great priest of the temple, looked at the sun and invoked it in prayer as he raised his arm over his head. Then they re-entered the tent and again offered Bienville a calumet. The French leader, pretending boredom with their ceremonies, asked them how they expected to compensate him for the Canadians they had murdered. This stunned them; they hung their heads in shame. Bienville had them put in irons and conducted to the prison prepared for them. They refused water and food; instead, they began to sing a death song. That night Bienville ordered some of his men to fetch the great chief Great Sun and his brothers, Stung Serpent and Little Sun, and assured them that he would save their lives if they agreed to return to their villages and kill the murderers and bring back their heads, which could be identified by their facial tattoo patterns. This unpleasant task was assigned to Little Sun, who returned five days later with three heads.

Bienville found that one of the heads was that of an innocent man. He quickly summoned the chiefs, upbraided them, and had the rejected head thrown at their feet. Greatly disturbed, they confessed that they had killed the innocent man because his brother was one of the murderers and had escaped. Bienville then expressed displeasure at the incomplete and insufficient number of heads. Learning that a chief named White Earth was leader of the movement against the French, he placed the great chief of the temple and two warriors under guard and sent them to the Natchez village to bring back the culprit's head.[71]

At this juncture Stung Serpent came down with yellow fever. Bienville had his irons removed and summoned him and his brothers and questioned them again regarding the conspiracy against the French. They replied that they had taken no part in the councils at which White Earth had, at the instigation of the English, agreed to trade with them and to kill the Canadians. Bienville released them. Several days later the great chief of the temple and the two warriors returned without White Earth's head. Instead, they brought a young chief who told Bienville that the Great Chief, supreme leader of the Natchez, was an uncle of White Earth and had refused to give him up. He added that he had brought with him to the four men who had committed the crime. They declared their innocence until six warriors testified to their guilt. Bienville had the guilty men bound and taken outside the fort, where they were clubbed to death.

June arrived with a flood that inundated the island and made living quarters in the fort uncomfortable. Humidity and heat that engendered fevers brought down half of Bienville's men. In view of these circumstances he resolved, inasmuch as the Natchez occupied a bank of the Mississippi, to make peace with them. He summoned the imprisoned chiefs and warriors and made known his terms. They must promise to kill White Earth as soon as they found him and deliver his head to the French officers at Natchez. They must restore all they had stolen and force their men to pay in skins and provisions whatever they had wasted. They must pledge their nation to cut two thousand five hundred *pieux*, thirteen feet and ten inches long, of acacia wood and transport them to make a fort on a designated spot on the Mississippi. And, finally, they must furnish bark from three thousand cypress trees to cover the buildings in the fort before the end of July.[72]

The chiefs and warriors accepted these terms with almost regal grace, swearing by the sun that henceforth they would remain friendly to the French. They urged Bienville to smoke the calumet. While he placed small value on their hollow assurances, he pretended to believe them genuine. He refused, however, to smoke with them until their nation had ratified his terms. With the departing Indians he sent Major Pailloux with three soldiers to witness ratification of the treaty. On June 7 nine old men came with great ceremony and pomp to Bienville and offered him the calumet, which he accepted and smoked. The Indians adhered strictly to the terms of the treaty. They furnished the timber; they labored with great zeal in cutting the ditches; they raised the parapets and bastions; they covered the barracks, the storehouse, and the magazine with bark. Stung Serpent lent invaluable assistance by sending Bienville a hundred fifty men to transport all his baggage, ammunition, and provisions from the Tunicas to the Natchez.

On August 25 Bienville raised the fleur-de-lis over Fort Rosalie, named in honor of Madame Pontchartrain, and moved in with his troops. He stayed only three days. Then, seeing no signs of hostility among the Indians, he left Pailloux in command of the fort and departed for Mobile, which he reached on October 4. He found the frigates of the season in the harbor with significant dispatches. Louis XIV was dead. Pontchartrain was no longer in power. The Duke of Orleans had been appointed regent during the minority of Louis XV. The Marine Council, which had supplanted the minister of marine, had appointed Bienville commander pending the arrival of the new governor.[73]

During his absence, affairs in the colony had gone from bad to worse. Cadillac characteristically expressed his deep concern and frustration in a letter to Pontchartrain:

Decidedly, this colony is a monster without head or tail, and its government is a shapeless absurdity. The cause of it is, that the fictions of fabulists have been believed in preference to the veracity of my declarations. Ah! why is there in falsehood a charm which makes it more acceptable than truth? Has it not been asserted that there are mines in Arkansas and elsewhere? It is a deliberate error. Has not a certain set of novel-writers published that this country is a paradise, when its beauty or utility is a mere phantasm of the brain? I protest that, having visited and examined the whole of it with care, I never saw anything as worthless. This I must say, because my conscience forbids me to deceive his Majesty. I have always regarded truth as a queen, whose laws I was bound to obey, like a devoted knight and a faithful subject. This is, no doubt, the cause of my having stuck fast in the middle of my career, and not progressed in the path of promotion, while others who had more political skill, understood how to frame, at my expense, pleasing misrepresentations. I know how to govern as well as anybody, but poverty and impotence are two ugly scars on the face of a governor. What can I do with a force of forty soldiers, out of whom five or six are disabled? A pretty army that is, and well calculated to make me respected by the inhabitants or by the Indians! As a climax to my vexation, they are badly fed, badly paid, badly clothed, and without discipline. As to the officers, they are not much better. Verily, I do not believe that there is in the whole universe such another government.[74]

These circumstances only intensified Cadillac's frustrations; he lived in daily fear of rebellion. At last his fears became so real that he took refuge in Dauphin Island where he issued a proclamation stating that, in view of the rebellious and seditious attitude of the people, of their quarrels and duels, of their bad tempers, drunkenness, and loose women, he prohibited all common people from wearing swords or carrying weapons under penalty of one month's imprisonment and a fine of 300 livres, which would be applied to the construction of a church. The people countered by founding an "order of chivalry," electing Cadillac, in a solemn meeting, grand master with the title of Knight of the Golden Calf. With pretended solemnity they informed him that they wished to bestow this great honor on him in appreciation of his wonderful achievements and of his researches for precious metals.[75]

Those mockeries infuriated him. He was preparing to repress the disorders in the colony when he received from Crozat a letter blaming him for all the evils of which he had complained. At the bottom of the letter was this note from the minister of marine: "The governor, Lamothe Cadillac, and the commissary, Duclos, whose dispositions and humors are incompatible and whose intellects are not equal to the functions with which his Majesty has instructed them, are dismissed from office."[76]

Cadillac welcomed this letter as an anodyne that relieved him of his misery. And Bienville was destined to hold his second governorship for less than a year. On March 9, 1717, arrived Espinay, the new governor, and Hubert, the new commissary, with three companies of infantry and fifty colonists. Espinay brought to Bienville the compliments of the king, the decoration of St. Louis, and a royal patent to Horn Island, on the coast of present Alabama.[77]

Nothing is so intolerable to an egotist as another egotist. Bienville and Espinay, being much alike in personality, grew jealous of each other and quarreled, each creating a powerful faction that kept the colony in constant turmoil. Crozat, finding that conditions under Espinay were "likely to move as lamely as before," in the beginning of August, 1717, asked the king to relieve him of his monopoly. By this time the troops in the colony had dwindled to one hundred twenty men. Such a handful of men could hardly defend Louisiana against the encroachments of Carolina traders, who had won over the Choctaws and were winning over the Natchez to their side. Crozat, moreover, had lost hope in the colony. In vain had his agents attempted to trade with New Spain by land or by sea; in vain had been his expensive researches for mines and pearl fisheries. And his efforts to establish trade with the Indians had proved unprofitable; it hardly paid enough to keep the posts in repair.[78]

Only discord seemed to thrive in Louisiana. The scattered population of the colony hated Crozat's monopoly and therefore united their energies to defeat it. His officers were so engrossed by their own selfish interests and by their petty quarrels that they had no time to formulate a constructive program for the colony.[79]

John Law's Mississippi Company

No sooner was Louisiana returned to the king than it passed over to John Law. In August, 1717, that fabulous manipulator of finance was instrumental in establishing the Company of the West for the principal purpose of exploiting the colony. By its charter it enjoyed the exclusive privilege of uniting the commerce of Louisiana with the fur trade of Canada for a period of twenty-five years. It granted Louisiana full sovereignty "on the condition only of liege homage to the king of France and of a crown of gold of thirty marcs at the beginning of every new reign." The colony could levy troops, equip vessels of war, construct forts, establish courts, raise garrisons, and wage war in defense of its complete liberty of commerce. The company had its own resplendent banner: on a green and silver field a river couchant leaning on a golden horn of plenty, which had an azure top with golden fleur-de-lis and a golden device supported by two Indians and a crown *tréfleé*.[1]

John Law's life had been as changeful as passing clouds—now assuming fantastic shapes, now roseate with the rays of the sun, now black with the expectation of a storm. He was born in 1671 at Edinburgh, Scotland. His father, a wealthy banker, supplied him with generous sums which he spent at gambling tables and race tracks and in convivial and amorous escapades. When he was twenty, he widened his sphere of enjoyment by moving to London, where he conquered elite society with his wit, his gracious manners, and his handsome face. A born mathematician, he theorized that gambling was a science in which any player could certainly win if he possessed knowledge of its mysterious laws, which uninformed people called luck. Unluckily, he depleted his resources before he completed his researches. His losing streak melted with his guineas. And he added to his embarrassment by running through Edward Wilson, better known as Beau Wilson, in a duel over the affections of a high-born lady who had compulsively invited him to sleep with her and who, on every occasion, insisted on concealing her identity with a mask.

Tried for murder, he was found guilty; but the gratified lady had powerful friends at Court; she contrived to have Law's jailor bribed or drugged. Law fled to Amsterdam, where the British Resident, following instructions from home, employed him and kept a sharp eye on him. He studied the operations of the Amsterdam bank, which served as "a permanent cash deposit for those merchants obliged to put their money in and leave it there, because drafts and wholesale contracts above a certain sum were payable only in bank money, that is to say, by a simple transfer from the account of the creditor to that of the debtor."[2] He discovered that the bank made money by investing its deposits and that its confidence played an important part in its financial success.

He reflected that money consisted of metal and an imprint of the government. Metal could not be created, but the imprint could be multiplied on paper. And the imprint, he reasoned, was the true money because it represented such assets as land, labor, and commerce. For the next seven years Law peddled these monetary ideas in Scotland, England, Italy, and Germany without success. Finally he went to France, which faced bankruptcy, thanks to Louis XIV's vainglorious wars and social extravagances. The regent, ready to clutch at a straw, accepted Law's services. On May 7, 1716, Law established a private bank "which would introduce, with the utmost prudence, the use of bank notes, hitherto unknown in France."[3]

The bank was successful from its inception. Law had now only to maintain the credit he had established. This he did by founding the Company of the West. The disharmony and subsequent failures in Louisiana were generally not known in France. The colony, indeed, was still greatly esteemed for its reported magnificence and fertility, its abundant products, and its rich mines which were said to be more extensive than those of Peru and Mexico. Law, using the anticipated wealth of this vast colonial empire as security, was supremely confident that his bank would underwrite and eventually pay off the national debt. Soon the bank became the main repository for royal funds; its administration by private directors and shareholders was anomalous; and in December, 1718, the regent and Law converted it into a royal or national bank. Law remained as director.[4]

The popularity of the bank continued to increase; but the shares of the Company of the West attracted few persons and remained below par. Undaunted, Law took steps to attract public attention to the company by promoting its speculative dealings and by publicizing its great potentialities. With the permission of the regent, he absorbed into the company two other French trading corporations—the East India Company and the China Company—and gave his enterprise the magnificent title of the Company of the Indies, which became better known to contemporaries and posterity alike as the Mississippi Company. Law then hired a host of promoters who published many pamphlets which described Louisiana "with all the perfections they could invent." They pointed out that the

Mississippi Company with its markets in all parts of the world was bound to produce results commensurate with its importance. They predicted large profits for stockholders and, in consequence, unlimited prosperity for France. They pictured the soil of Louisiana as so fertile that it needed only the scratch of a plow to produce the richest harvests. In its forest grew, at every season, all the known fruits of the world; luscious pears, peaches, and apples fell in heaps on cool shores and on velvety banks of bubbling streams. A thick carpet of flowers in endless variety perfumed the land to its very borders. Great herds of cattle "in the primitive vigor and gentleness of their antediluvian perfection" thundered across the colony in every direction. The rivers and lakes were stocked with fish "so abundant that they would suffice to nourish millions of men and so delicious that no king ever had any such on his table."[5]

Even more enticing were Law's imaginary gold and silver mines. No tedious process was necessary to work the gold mines, for their surfaces were strewn with lumps of the precious metal. Even the lakes and rivers of the colony, when they were filtered, yielded priceless deposits of gold. As for silver—it was so abundant that it had little or no value; it might be used in the shape of square stones to pave the public roads. These singular properties extended even to some of the flowers. One of these gathered dew that by morning became a solid diamond that dropped to the stem where, "in unrobed splendor," it reflected "back the rays of the morning sun."[6]

To defray the expenses of the Court and of the advertising campaign, the regent authorized Law to issue another lot of shares. To the original 200,000 shares were added 50,000 shares that sold at 500 livres each, producing 25,000,000 livres. But so great was the enthusiasm of the gullible public that the shares were issued at 1000 livres each. Only those who owned five of the old or "mother" shares could buy the new or "daughter" shares. All shares not subscribed within twenty days were to become the property of the company. These "tricks of the trade" aroused much excitement. And Law heightened it by announcing that he would pay a semi-annual dividend of 6 per cent, making a yearly income of 12 per cent. His artifice had the desired effect. Soon the shareholders were reputed rich; the poorest beggar could, by proving that by some windfall he had become the owner of a single share, rise "to the importance of a wealthy man and command the largest credit." Gayarré poetically described the frantic infatuation that seized Frenchmen in all walks of life:

Lands, palaces, edifices of every sort, were rapidly shifted from hand to hand, like balls in a tennis court. It was truly a curious sight to behold a whole chivalrous nation turned into a confused multitude of windling, bawling, clamorous, frantic stock jobbers. Holy cardinals, archbishops, bishops, with but too many of their clergy, forgetting their sacred character, were seen to launch their barks on the dead sea of perdition to which they were tempted, and eagerly to throw the fisherman's net into those troubled waters of speculation which were lashed into fury by the demon of avarice. Princes of the royal blood became hawkers of stocks: haughty peers of the realm rushed on the Rialto and Shylock-like exulted in bartering and trafficking in goods.[7]

That summer the shares skyrocketed. By August they had risen far above 1000 livres each. Those who had bought them at this price already realized a large profit; but those who had bought them at 300 livres and at 500 livres each gained much more. This colossal boom made Law the most sought-after and courted man in all France. Large crowds gathered in front of his sumptuous house and jostled one another in order to catch a glimpse of him. One day the English ambassador, Lord Stair, saw hundreds of people besieging Law's house, though its doors were locked to everybody. Some forced open one of the doors, others leaped over the wall into the garden and entered the windows, still others climbed to the roof and dropped down the chimney into Law's study. Many others resorted to a variety of ruses in their efforts to talk to him. One night a lady who had failed to obtain an invitation to dine with him at the house of a friend stationed herself in front of it and made her coachman and footman shout "Fire!" While Law and his friends rushed out of the house, the lady sprang from her carriage to buttonhole him, but he saw through her ruse in time to elude her.

In their pursuit of riches women gladly abandoned all feeling of decency and delicacy. One afternoon Law received several ladies. Having spent most of the day in numerous interviews, he asked to be excused for a few minutes to heed an urgent call of nature. "*Oh, si ce n'est que cela,*" replied one of them, "*cela ne fait rien. Pissez toujours, et écoutez-nous!*" Always obliging with the ladies, Law bowed. And, while they talked, he nonchalantly relieved himself.[8]

At another time an elderly lady rushed toward him from a crowd, begging him for an allotment of shares. She intended to say, "*Faites-moi une concession,*" but, in her excitement, her tongue slipped drolly: "*Faites-moi, je vous en prie, une conception.*" The old rake, who had sown his seed in many different soils, smiled at her seeming request to make her pregnant. "*Madame,*" he replied with characteristic wit, "*vous venez trop tard. Il n'y a pas moyen à présent.*"[9]

He had pledged himself by his charter to send annually to Louisiana six thousand white people and three thousand Negroes. The question of slaves was easily solved. On December 15, 1718, the Mississippi Company was authorized to absorb the Senegal Slave Trade Company. In the summer of the following year two ships, *Grand Duc du Maine* and *Aurora*, brought to the colony about five hundred slaves who were stationed at a slave-trading post at present Algiers, Louisiana, where they were distributed to the colonists.[10]

But Law encountered great obstacles in his efforts to find settlers for the colony. As a foreigner he had no idea of the reluctance of Frenchmen to migrate. In vain did he distribute over France, Italy, Germany, and

Switzerland circulars praising Louisiana as a newly-found paradise. The Swiss authorities warned their countrymen against any agents who should urge them to migrate to "the Island of Mississippi, lately discovered." Law extricated himself from his dilemma by persuading the French government to release men and women from jails and houses of correction on their promise to marry and live in Louisiana. They were hurriedly married, chained together, and dragged toward the ports, an experience which Gayarré describes with gruesome vividness:

> Guarded by a merciless soldiery, they, on their way to sea-ports, filled up the public roads of France like droves of cattle, and as they were hardly furnished with means of subsistence or with clothing by their heartless conductors, who speculated on the food and other supplies with which they were bound to provide them, they died in large numbers, and their unburied corpses, rotting above ground, struck with terror the inhabitants of the districts through which the woebegone caravan had passed. At night they were locked up in barns, when any could be found, and if not, they were forced, the better to prevent escape, to lie down in heaps at the bottom of ditches and holes, and sentinels were put around to watch over them.[11]

At the ports the emigrants sometimes had to wait for months before ships sailed. Then the largest possible number were packed like matches in a matchbox on ships ranging in size from fifty to seven hundred tons. The emigrants, moreover, had to make room for their utensils and boxes of food and supplies and barrels of drinking water. After a journey ranging in length from six to nine weeks, the survivors, who sometimes constituted only one-fourth of their original number, reached Louisiana—if they had been fortunate enough to elude pirates who made their headquarters in that region of the world.[12]

Law's arbitrary methods in obtaining emigrants aroused so much indignation among the public that the regent saw fit to suspend them. To arouse genuine interest in the colony Law hit upon a master stroke. He engrossed two huge tracts for himself, one of which lay at or near the junction of the Mississippi and Arkansas rivers and the other below the English Turn. He encouraged his friends and agents to follow his example, promising to raise their properties to duchies, counties, and marquisates. Most of them did not go themselves to Louisiana, though each sent from fifty to two hundred of his dependents to cultivate his holdings under the orders of an intendant.[13]

Law also took steps to develop his properties with emigrants from Switzerland and from both banks of the Rhine. He issued in those regions several pamphlets in German. One of these, published in 1720, described Louisiana as bounded on the east by Florida and Carolina and on the north by Virginia and Canada which was said to extend perhaps to the "Polum Articum." It stated that an adventurer named "Christophum Columbum" had enticed many people to desert "Europam" for "Americum," especially those regions which remained undiscovered. It lauded the soil, which it stated was capable of producing annually four crops that in abundance staggered the imagination. It averred that wild game was plentiful, perhaps unlimited. It quoted imaginary emigrants who, on returning temporarily to France, reported countless leopards, bears, buffaloes, deer, "Indian hens," snipe, turtle-doves, partridges, "wood-pigeons," quail, beavers, martens, wildcats, parrots, buzzards, ducks, "prairie chickens," and nameless other fowl. It promised that the return of any investment in the colony would be fabulous:

> If one gets 300 acres of land for 100 Reichthalers, then three acres cost one Thaler; but, if the benefit to be derived and other "prerogatives" of such lands are considered, then an acre of this land, even if not culti-vated, is worth about 100 Thalers. From this basis it follows that 300 acres, which as stated already, cost 100 Thalers when purchased, are really worth 30,000 Thalers. For this reason one can easily understand why these shares may yet rise very high.[14]

Such seductive passages convinced the most skeptical readers. Law's astute agent, Elias Stultheus, a Jew from the Rhine country, had no diffi-culty in recruiting Germans and Swiss by entire parishes together with their mayors and provosts. In 1720 four thousand colonists including French as well as Jews, Germans, and Swiss arrived at Dauphin Island in seven ships, one of which carried Stultheus and a cargo of supplies and farming implements valued at 1,000,000 livres. But for fifteen months an accumulation of sand in the channel and at Biloxi prevented Stultheus and his followers from proceeding to Law's properties. Many died from hunger or from eating poisonous plants. The arrival of six hundred Negroes from Guinea and of French emigrants bound for the conces-sions of various French noblemen only intensified the prevailing suffer-ing, discontent, and confusion.

Everyone demanded small boats in which to reach shore; Stultheus alone demanded thirty. When these were not forthcoming the colonists blamed Bienville and reported him to the regent, who threatened to dis-miss him. But Law valued his experience. Though he had never seen the governor and was destined never to see him, he defended him vehemently and persuaded the regent to give him another chance. Law also sent Bien-ville an intelligent intendant, Duvergier, and a brilliant engineer, Le Blond de la Tour, who with Bienville's consent built another port, New Biloxi, four leagues farther west and on dry, healthy ground. Old Biloxi was soon abandoned.[15]

2

On April 19, 1719, news reached Louisiana that France, discovering a plot by the Spanish ambassador at Paris to overthrow the regent, had declared war on Spain. Bienville, who had always coveted Pensacola for reasons of expansion, now seized on circumstances to prepare an expedition against that Spanish port. He called a council of war which agreed to attack Pensacola at once. He and his brother Chateauguay collected eight hundred Indians and whites, while another of his brothers, Sérigny, who had just arrived from France, prepared to bombard the port from the sea. On May 14, at ten o'clock in the morning, Sérigny entered Pensacola Bay with four ships and demanded surrender of the fort. The governor, Juan Pedro Matamoros, ignorant that war existed between his country and France, indignantly refused.

Whereupon Sérigny began a cannonade that lasted five hours but wrought no damage. Then the governor sent to Sérigny an officer who, inquiring about the reason for the attack, learned for the first time that Spain and France had declared war in the previous January. Finding himself too weak to withstand a siege, Matamoros surrendered on condition that the French ships should send him and his garrison of four hundred men to Havana. Sérigny, having found little supplies in the port and having been obliged to feed his men as well as his prisoners, consented to the request. But no sooner did the ships arrive in Havana than their crews were seized. The governor of Cuba, Gregorio Guazo, moreover, appealed for aid to the viceroy of New Spain while he diverted to Pensacola an expedition that he had planned to send against the English in Carolina.

The viceroy, who had already received word of the disaster from the Franciscan superior at Pensacola, immediately ordered recruits and directed seamen and ships to speed to Vera Cruz. At about the same time five Spanish vessels arrived in Vera Cruz. The viceroy, infinitely pleased with what he considered a manifestation of God's favor, sent the five ships and seven others with eight hundred fifty men to recapture Pensacola. In that port the Spaniards encountered two French frigates of about the same size as those they had recently captured. They attacked them and then boarded them. The passengers and crew of one of the frigates, seeing that it was about to be captured, set fire to it and then took to their boats in which they reached shore. The other frigate surrendered. Then the Spanish vessels surrounded Pensacola, bombarded it, and summoned Chateauguay to surrender. Chateauguay hauled down the French flag and gave up with three hundred fifty men. Indeed, he could do nothing else. Half of his garrison had deserted and the rest refused to fight just as they had previously refused to work. While the Spaniards sang *Te Deum Laudamus* in gratitude for their victory, Chateauguay and his comrades were sent to Havana.[16]

The Spaniards quite naturally resolved to follow up their victory by attacking Mobile. But they moved so slowly that they allowed Bienville ample time to receive them. Fearing that the Spaniards would return, he had sent his most intrepid officer, Louis Juchereau de St. Denis, to mobilize the Indians while he himself prepared Mobile for defense. St. Denis immediately sent runners to summon the braves, who came trickling into his camp from their villages on the Mississippi, along the bayous of the gulf, and in the northern woods. They had little time to train or prepare for battle. On August 13 three Spanish brigantines under the command of Antonio Mendieta hove in sight of Dauphin Island and, confident that enemy forces were weaker than his own, sent to Sérigny a letter demanding immediate surrender. Mendieta announced his intention of conquering the entire colony; he vowed vengeance for the prisoners taken at Pensacola; he had time, he fumed, for neither mercy nor diplomacy.[17]

Sérigny refused to surrender. At first Mendieta's advance was as burning as his language. He captured two small boats packed with needed supplies. Then, receiving reinforcements, he pressed with his fleet into the harbor and blockaded it. There he found, much to his chagrin, the French frigate *Philippe*, advantageously ensconced behind a point of land and supported by four batteries on shore. Resolving to flank the fort, Mendieta began to sail up the Mobile River, where he seized five small boats and where he landed a part of his forces; but the French under Sérigny fired on him from the *Philippe* and from the shore batteries, preventing him from achieving his aim. And now St. Denis, with an army of Indians and whites, attacked Mendieta from behind the natural barricade of the forest, killing a few of his men and capturing many others. Among the prisoners were eighteen Frenchmen who had deserted at Pensacola. For want of an executioner, Bienville had them tomahawked for taking arms against the king.[18]

Two days later the rest of the Spanish squadron arrived at Dauphin Island, where it remained for two weeks, firing at the *Philippe* and at Mobile without doing any damage to either. Then, on August 26, the Spaniards withdrew. Five days later Bienville was elated to learn that a French fleet of five ships had arrived under Count Champmeslin. Bienville and his brother Sérigny immediately went to meet Champmeslin, who held with them and his officers a council of war in which they agreed to recapture Pensacola. Though they wanted to realize their plans before Spanish vessels could arrive from Vera Cruz, they were obliged to wait fourteen days while half of the cargo of one of the ships was unloaded to make room for the water and wood they needed for the campaign and to give the Indians time to obtain their provisions and assemble them. At the completion of these preparations regular troops joined Champmeslin on his boats, while Bienville with a company composed mainly of volunteers sailed for Perdido Bay, where St. Denis awaited him with five hundred Indians.[19]

Meanwhile the Spanish commander of Pensacola, Alfonso Carrascosa, anticipating a French attack on the town, had put a hundred fifty Negroes to work to strengthen his defenses. But the Negroes feared the possible arrival of the French whom they had deserted. They continually saw ghosts of Frenchmen coming and when Carrascosa attempted to reassure them they fled like goats to the top of a hill where they could not be captured. Carrascosa, nevertheless, succeeded in strengthening the fort on Santa Rosa Island while he derived some comfort from the arrival of a brigantine from Vera Cruz. But his supplies were so low and his soldiers so sick that his officers advised him to abandon the place before they all died. Carrascosa refused, saying that his orders forbade him to make the unseemly and culpable decision of abandoning a place which had been restored with so much difficulty.[20]

Such were conditions in Pensacola when, on September 17, Champmeslin arrived before that port with his fleet. He immediately opened fire on the small fort that guarded the eastern end of the bay. The fort defended itself as best it could for two hours, until two sloops, a brigantine, and a pirogue which were giving it some assistance were forced to sail away. The sloop soon ran aground, but the brigantine and the pirogue managed to escape. By now St. Denis's white men had bombed the ships and the newer or larger fort that guarded the western shore of the bay, while his painted Indians, decked in their feathered headgear and yelling their terrifying war whoops, assisted them with endless streams of arrows. The fort and ships were soon demolished. Torn to pieces, Carrascosa's ship began to founder while her deck ran with the blood of her dead or wounded crew. Spanish courage overawed even the French who, says Barcía, "grieved that such brave men, worthy of eternal renown, must die without having been able to win victory."[21]

Champmeslin sent Carrascosa a message exhorting him to surrender and praising his valor and spirit. Seeing the impossibility of escape either by land or sea, Carrascosa, after some reluctance, struck his colors and surrendered as a prisoner of war. Soon the governor, Juan Pedro Matamoros, followed suit. Champmeslin accorded Carrascosa the respect due to a valiant man. He refused to accept his sword in recognition of his gallant defense. To Matamoros he gave less courteous treatment. He refused his offered sword; instead, he ordered a common soldier to take it as a rebuke and sign of contempt for the governor's lack of courage in defending his post. Champmeslin rewarded the Indians by permitting them to plunder the larger fort, though he forbade them to scalp any of the prisoners. These included thirty-five French deserters. They were tried by a military court. Twelve were hanged from the mast of one of the recaptured French ships and the rest were sent to the galleys. The other prisoners were sent to Havana, though their officers were retained as hostages pending the release of Chateauguay and his men.

Champmeslin soon returned to France, leaving the colony without a fleet. To discourage any attempt on the part of the Spaniards to recapture the fort, he ordered most of it destroyed. All the soldiers returned to Mobile save one officer and a handful of men who were instructed to cannonade the Spaniards should they return, spike the guns, burn the few remaining buildings, and fall back on Mobile. The Spaniards never returned. Early in the following year a treaty of peace returned Pensacola to Spain. Chateauguay with his men were released and journeyed to

France, where he was decorated with the cross of the Order of St. Louis. He soon sailed for Louisiana bearing a similar decoration for St. Denis.[22]

3

In January, 1720, John Law was appointed Controller-General of Finance for the kingdom of France. This was the height of his prosperity; his decline and fall rapidly followed. Needless to say, his "system" carried the germs of its own destruction. Tales began to filter through to France that Louisiana had neither gold nor silver mines, that large areas of it were barren, and that its inhabitants were dying of starvation or disease or both. So shareholders learned to their dismay that their shares were worthless old rags, that they had no representation or backing. The crafty among them began to change their shares for cloth, spices, or jewelry; began to sell their notes for specie and to send it out of the country. The Prince de Cōndi, who had enriched himself by Law's financial hints, sent to the bank three wagons which were what he estimated he required to haul away the gold he hoped to obtain by exchanging his notes. Many others followed his example. In a short time, the country was drained of 500,000,000 livres in specie.

Law became alarmed and had the regent pass decrees forbidding goldsmiths to make, sell, or display any object made of gold or silver, forbidding anybody to wear diamonds, pearls, or other precious stones. In the next eight months the regent passed no less than thirty-three decrees to fix the value of gold and silver, to preserve and to increase the metallic circulation, and to limit the amount of gold and silver which might be converted into plate and jewelry. No payment in gold and silver could be made save for small sums. The standard of coin was kept in the most bewildering state of fluctuation, while the value of bank notes was decreed as invariable.[23]

On May 21, 1720, Law, with the consent of the regent published a decree that spelled his doom. It successively devaluated money and shares. A bank note valued at 100 livres was to be reduced by July 1 to 80 livres and lowered gradually until, by the end of the year, it would be worth only 50 livres. In the same manner shares in the Mississippi Company were to be reduced in value from 9,000 livres each, a price arbitrarily fixed for them, to 5,000 livres.[24]

Needless to say, the edict produced widespread public indignation. The man in the street felt as if he had lost half of his riches; he was unaware of the worthlessness of what he retained. His confidence in notes and shares was shattered; he rushed to convert them into substantial assets. Every rich man saw himself in desperate circumstances, every poor man saw himself reduced to beggary. The circulation of paper at this time was 2,235,085,570 livres; it was suddenly reduced to nothing. The outcry became so prodigious that the regent, becoming alarmed for himself as well as for Law, repealed the obnoxious edict. This was poor psychology. The edict was bad enough; its revocation was worse. Once confidence is shaken it is seldom restored. Angry mobs surrounded Law's house in the Place Vendôme, breaking its windows with rocks and stones and shouting deprecations and curses and insults at the author of their woes. Many people fought with one another; some were trampled to death.

At last the regent was forced to relieve Law of his office, though he continued to receive him in private and offered him consolation for his seeming severity. "I am like the fabulous hen who laid the golden eggs," remarked Law ruefully, "but which, when it was killed, was found to be like any ordinary fowl." Saint-Simon says that Law accepted with singular patience all the abuse hurled at him but that during his last days in France he became increasingly irritable. Trembling for his life, he kept himself behind locked doors. But even there he felt unsafe. Men and women sent boys to spy on him and to report every move he made. So he contrived to seek sanctuary in the Palais Royal. One who saw him there described his complexion as that of a dead man; no doubt he wished himself dead at times, or at least on the Mississippi or in Louisiana.[25] He soon left France, wandered over Europe, and, in 1721, returned to England. Later he returned to the continent and settled down in Venice, where he died in dire circumstances on March 21, 1729.

Yet in his last years Law was safer than he knew. After his resignation his "system" was the subject of numerous lampoons and much ribald verse. This was an excellent sign; the French seldom kill those whom they satirize. The story of his system was jestingly retold in pasquinades of which the following is an example:

> *Lundi j'achetai des Actions;*
> *Mardi je gagei des Millions;*
> *Mercredi j'arrangeai mon Menage;*
> *Jeudi je pris un Equipage;*
> *Vendredi je m'en fus an Bal;*
> *Et Samedi a l'Hôpital.*

> My shares which on Monday I bought
> Were worth millions on Tuesday, I thought,
> So on Wednesday I chose my abode;
> In my carriage on Thursday I rode;
> To the ball-room on Friday I went;
> To the workhouse next day I was sent.[26]

The public quickly changed its estimate of Louisiana. The land of promise became "a terrestial representation of Pandemonium." It was now a country of marshes, lagoons, swamps, bayous, fens, bogs, endless prairies, and inextricable and gloomy forests peopled with every "monster of the natural and of the mythological world." As if by black magic, its horses were reduced to the size of sheep, its cattle to that of rabbits, its hogs to that of rats, and its fowl to that of sparrows. So oppressive was its heat, it deprived men of their mental and physical energies. Gifted men were turned into mediocrities and mediocrities into idiots.[27]

4

This picture was, of course, too depressing; the colony was really making excellent progress. John Law was gone, but his handiwork, the Mississippi Company, remained for eleven more years. Though it had ruined its creator, it had blessed its creation. The concessions at last had sufficient laborers. They produced rice and Provence figs and Spanish oranges in great abundance. Thanks to the agricultural ingenuity of the German and Swiss immigrants, their farms grew larger and increasingly fertile. The Mobilians worked assiduously, gathering their resin and their tar. Karl Friedrich von Arensburg, a German who had fought under Charles XII of Sweden and who, on migrating to Louisiana, had gallicized his name to Charles Frederic d'Arensbourg, wrote to his brother-in-law, a retired captain living in Danzig, to come and bring his furniture with him.[28]

By now Louisiana had a new capital. Law, on Bienville's recommendation, had searched ceaselessly for a suitable port. Several places had been considered and then rejected as inadequate. Bienville had always believed that the capital of the colony should be located on the Mississippi, which would give it direct communication with the French settlements and trading posts in the Illinois region. Bienville had, in the time of Espinay, chosen a spot on one of the most beautiful curves of the river. Its advantages were threefold: it lay in the center of the new concessions; it was situated only thirty leagues from the mouth of the river; and it had direct communication with Lake Pontchartrain by means of the bayou of St. John. Bienville had named the projected settlement New Orleans in honor of the regent—the sole tangible memorial of that indolent and sybaritic ruler. Some of the purists objected strongly to its name. "Those who coined the name *Nouvelle Orleans*," wrote Father Charlevoix, "must have thought that Orleans was of the feminine gender. But what does it matter? The custom is established, and custom rises above grammar."[29]

Work on the new settlement began sometime in the early spring of 1718, when Bienville sent a few convicts to work clearing the land. But New Orleans had a very slow and precarious beginning. The two or three huts that the convicts built on ground infested by alligators and snakes were soon flooded out. Nothing daunted, Bienville urged on the laborers to work faster; he even contemplated building a dike strong enough to protect the growing settlement. For three more years, however, he could accomplish nothing of any importance. Everybody in the colony seemed to oppose New Orleans. The entire council of Louisiana, the colonists of Mobile, the traders of Biloxi, and the boatmen of Lake Pontchartrain—

all, for purely mercenary reasons, preferred disorder to harmony. They realized that their financial returns were proportionate to the sufferings of the people. Even Le Blond de la Tour, the chief engineer, an energetic but unimaginative man, frowned on the new project and gave all his attention to New Biloxi. But in Adrien de Pauger, the assistant engineer, Bienville found an able ally. Willful and choleric, Pauger disagreed loudly with La Tour's contention that New Orleans was quite futile because of the presence of sand bars at the mouth of the Mississippi. He averred that simple and inexpensive operations which he was most willing to undertake would not only remove the existing sand bars but prevent the development of new ones. With Bienville's blessings and assistance, he soon realized his plan. As soon as the sand bars were removed, he sent ships up the river.[30]

In May, 1722, the *Aventurier*, which belonged to the Mississippi Company, arrived in Biloxi with a message approving Bienville's plans to transfer the seat of government to New Orleans. La Tour accepted defeat with embarrassed grace. Thenceforth he supported Bienville and Pauger in their plans, which he had pigeonholed. He instructed Pauger to call together immediately as many workmen as possible. Then he requisitioned the *Aventurier*, boarded her, and on June 10 sailed for a triumphal entry of New Orleans; but adverse winds, dead calms, and tempests denied him a pleasure which he never merited.

Eventually he reached New Orleans, where he set thirty-eight men to work clearing the ground, killing alligators and snakes, and building huts. But severe labor and the high cost of living soon drove them away. La Tour tried to remedy the situation by reducing the price of beans from twenty-five to five *sols* a pound and by invoking a decree that forbade, under pain of two hundred livres fine, the selling of "French beef" at more than two *sols* a pound and that reckoned a pound of native beef at two *sols*, a quarter of buck at two livres, a capon at forty *sols*, a small fowl at twenty *sols*, and eggs at fifty *sols* a dozen. These praiseworthy efforts were vain. New laborers came but would not stay. "At this rate," complained La Tour, "the buildings will not be finished under eighteen months."[31]

These delays, however, proved most fortunate. On September 11, a terrible equinoctial storm broke over the little town. It destroyed the maturing grain, the church, the hospital, and thirty-four huts, and tossed three ships to the shore and nearly wrecked them. At Biloxi several vessels were lost; at Mobile, the rice crops were destroyed; at Natchez, plantations were damaged and some of the houses of the planters blown down. The bayou of St. John rose three feet; the Mississippi rose eight feet. In consequence the lack of provisions became acute and famine stalked the land. Bienville saved the powder by transferring it to a dovecote which he had built to afford himself a few luxuries. The widespread havoc, however, failed to disturb La Tour. "All these buildings were temporary and old," he wrote, "not a single one was in the alignment of the new town, and they were to have been pulled down. Little harm would have been done, if only we had had shelter for everybody."[32]

The planning of the new town was excellent. It was a checkerboard with straight and comfortably wide streets. Facing the sides of a square in the center of the town stood the government buildings, the church, the hospital, and the markets. The dwellings were of a single story, raised a foot from the ground on identical piers or blocks and roofed with bark or thin boards. Instead of glass, which was impossible to transport by ship, the colonists covered their windows with a thin linen that admitted sufficient light. A drainage ditch surrounded each square or island. This was usually divided into five lots, each of which had a yard and garden.[33]

Pauger was justly proud of his creation. "If I had not taken upon myself all that could be done to overcome ill-will," he wrote in September, 1723, "things would not yet have got beyond the stage of sending ships into the river, and the principal seat would have remained at Biloxi, where the country could not provide sufficient food, as it does here."[34] One of the Ursuline nuns who managed the hospital stated in a letter to a friend or relative that she had heard a popular song in which the appearance of New Orleans was compared favorably to that of Paris. She added that the town was growing rapidly and predicted that in time it would become as large as any of "the principal towns of France."[35]

The arrival of hundreds of marriageable young girls presaged for the colony a steady increase of population. Important among the prospects or instincts that stirred them was that of establishing homes. Collected by heads of religious institutions from convents and schools and houses of correction, they arrived under Ursuline nuns who guarded them until they could find husbands. Because they carried an outfit of clothes in a little chest or trunk called *casquette* in French, they were known as the "casket girls," though this term is properly applied only to those who arrived in Louisiana in 1727. The first group of these girls numbered twenty-three and landed at Mobile fort. The second group arrived at Dauphin Island in 1719. On January 8, 1721, arrived *La Baleine* with the third group, numbering eighty-eight, under three nuns, Sisters Gertrude, Louise, and Bérgere. Each had her trunk which, says Pénicaut,

> consisted of two suits of clothing, two skirts and petticoats, six laced bodices, six chemises, six headdresses, and all other necessary accessories, with which they were well provided so that they could be married as quickly as possible in legitimate wedlock. This merchandize was soon distributed, so great was the dearth of it in the country; and if Sister Gertrude had brought ten times as much of it, she would have found a market for it in a short time.[36]

The girls quickly found husbands.

The next group was known as *les filles à la casette* because, before embarking for Louisiana, each had received from her king a small box containing her trousseau. As soon as they landed, they were placed in a house guarded by a sentinel. During the daytime young men were permitted to see the girls, and each could select one he liked; but after dark they were not allowed to enter the house. The cargo proved inadequate for all the suitors who presented themselves. The last girl caused serious trouble. Two young men were ready to fight a duel for her, though she was no Dulcinea and acted more like a guard than a girl. But the commander settled the quarrel by making them pull straws.[37]

Bienville was not present to witness the steady growth of the colony. In 1723 the Mississippi Company, learning of much disharmony and dishonesty among its officials in Louisiana, sent Jacques de La Chaise as intendant to uncover the thieves, grafters, and usurers who had robbed the king's stores and to remove and punish officials who had failed to perform their duties. La Chaise, nephew of the great Father La Chaise, confessor of Louis XIV, "was a solid block of honesty." Arriving in Louisiana in April, he found that dissension among the officials and quarrels among the colonists were paralyzing the colony. The tracts of land, which had been hurriedly and carelessly surveyed, "overlapped or had been sold to several persons or, at least, had been so senselessly laid out, that one owner had to pass over the land of another to reach his own." All this "was as productive of peace as if several families, living in the same house, all use the same entrance, or must pass through one another's rooms . . . to get to their own."[38]

La Chaise, who was not very bright, declared "in energetic tones" that "he was going to put an end to plundering." So he greeted every official, including Bienville, with innuendoes and inferences and expressions of suspicion. This so infuriated Bienville that, though he privately held a low opinion of every official save Pauger, he began to support them secretly and to place obstacles in the intendant's way "wherever and whenever he could." This caused a division of the colonists into two factions: *la grande bande*—the big gang—which went along with La Chaise—and *la petite bande*—the little gang—which opposed him.

Finding himself blocked on all sides, La Chaise leaped to safety by sending to France frantic letters requesting that Bienville be recalled. Eventually France bowed to his wishes. Bienville received orders to return to France and defend himself of the charges of which he was accused. So, early in 1725, he went docilely with his brother Chateauguay to Mobile and Dauphin Island, where they found the *Bellone* about to sail for France. While they were rowing toward the ship, she sprung a leak and sank with a consignment of 60,000 crowns. They returned to New Orleans, where they remained until, several months later, they sailed on the *Gironde*, which arrived in France in August. Meanwhile Boisbriant had been appointed temporary commander at New Orleans. Bienville lost no time in preparing his defense; but his twenty-four years of service and the deaths of his seven brothers in the navy, which he recalled, failed to reinstate him. None of the Lemoynes were permitted to remain in Louisiana. But the king, in recognition of Bienville's services, granted him a pension of 3,000 livres. He was not to see Louisiana again for nearly nine years.[39]

5

Bienville's successor was Bouche de la Pérrier, a young marine officer who had served with distinction in the War of the Spanish Succession and had commanded faithfully several ships of the Mississippi Company. He was a very nice fellow; he approved of everybody and everybody approved of him. In accordance with his instructions, he reached an understanding with La Chaise, thereby eliminating the discord that had been harmful to the colony. Being even more prudent than his instructions, he failed to punish guilty officials on the ground that loyalty to him was unimportant so long as they showed loyalty to their work and made themselves useful. Turning blind eyes and deaf ears to his scheming subordinates, he occupied himself with the construction of a huge levee that extended eighteen miles above and below New Orleans to protect the region from frequent floods; he constructed, too, a canal connecting Lake Pontchartrain with the Gulf; and he dredged the channel of the Mississippi and deepened it to allow ocean-going ships to disembark at New Orleans. All of which was to his credit; but unfortunately for him he lacked that knowledge of Indian character, which was so essential to his post.

Never trust a man who approves of everybody; seldom is he a strong personality; Pérrier had next to none. In 1729 he appointed to the Natchez village a certain Chepart who aroused the fury of its inhabitants by his rank injustice and his petty tyranny. They brought him to trial before the council of the colony, which was about to dismiss him; but Pérrier, who believed his tale of innocence, rescued him and restored him to his command. This eventually proved the undoing of both men.

Fort Rosalie, which dominated the village of Natchez, was a stockade that included a redoubt overlooking the Mississippi, a chapel, a presbytery, and a shed roofed with bark and surrounded with a galley under which stood the tobacco presses. The estates or concessions there were prosperous. The brownish green of the sweet potatoes, the tobacco planted in rows, and the figs and other fruit trees delighted Chepart who, returning from New Orleans puffed up with triumph, planned to appropriate for himself the most prosperous of the Natchez villages, White Apple, which was located six miles from Fort Rosalie and which belonged to one of the chiefs or suns, as he called himself, because, like the other chiefs, he descended from a man or woman who made him believe he came from the sun.

Chepart ordered the chief to vacate the village within a few days. The chief protested that he had lived in his village as many years as he had hairs on his head and that, therefore, he had every right to remain there; but wishing to avoid further trouble, he withdrew to consult with the elders of the tribe. After lengthy discussions the elders and the chiefs conspired to massacre the French, but agreed to refrain from disclosing their plans to their women who were as fond of gossiping then as women are now, and many of whom, moreover, had joyfully slept with white men. They also agreed to form in the temple a bundle of twigs equal in number to the number of days that would intervene between that day and the day on which they planned to attack, to draw from it a twig each day, break it, and throw it aside, and to commit this task to a discreet man. But thought of the massacre produced so much uneasiness on the faces of the plotters that it aroused the suspicion of Tatooed Arm, wife of the Great Chief, that something drastic was afoot; and, with much wailing and many exhortations, she induced her son, who was one of the plotters, to disclose his plans to her.

Horrified at the prospect of the massacre, Tatooed Arm warned some of the Indian mistresses of the Frenchmen but cautioned them to refrain from disclosing the source of their information. Then she stopped one of the soldiers, whom she met on the road, and told him to warn Chepart of the plot. Far from giving credence to this information or profiting from it or, at least, investigating and cautiously sifting the matter, Chepart accused him of cowardice and had him put in chains. He took no precautions of defense for fear of giving the Natchez the impression that he lacked courage and that he was afraid of them. Meanwhile Tatooed Arm went to the temple and took from the bundle several twigs to advance the date of the attack so that any Frenchmen who might escape might warn their countrymen in other settlements. She sent several more soldiers to warn Chepart who, however, accorded them the same reception as he had the other. Then he went with several of his friends to eat and drink and sleep with Indian women in White Apple. In the small hours of the morning he returned, befuddled and sleepy and worn, to Fort Rosalie, where he dispatched his interpreter to ascertain whether the Great Chief intended to lead an attack against the French. The Great Chief, though young, hoodwinked the interpreter into believing that the Natchez were peacefully disposed. So Chepart congratulated himself for having disregarded the warnings sent to him. And he went to his house near the fort to sleep off the effects of his carousal.[40]

On the fateful day, November 26, 1729, two or three Indians, loaded with corn and poultry, visited each settler and, pretending to be about to leave on a great hunt, traded with him for a musket and powder, offering him higher prices than usual. At about the same time a small group of Indians seized a number of small ships for their merchandise as well as to check the French who might want to embark and save themselves. The Jesuit missionary, Father du Poisson, was on his way to New Orleans in the interest of his mission of whites and Indians. Stopping at

Natchez, he celebrated Mass and then carried the blessed viaticum to
a sick parishoner. As he was leaving, a chief named Big Leg seized him,
threw him to the ground, and shot him dead.

By now shots were heard everywhere. The turmoil reached Chepart
who, seated in his chair, was watching with pipe in mouth some dancers
with unflagging interest. He gave one terrified leap and instead of trying
to defend himself ran out into the garden. Through the stockade he had
a glimpse, before dying like a dog, of the ground covered with corpses
and of a great heap of heads just outside the shed. He blew on his whistle
to summon the garrison; but it no longer existed save for one man who,
at that moment, was putting wood in the bake-oven and who hid himself in the chimney. An Indian rushed at Chepart and killed him with
one shot. The Indians spared only the Negroes, the young girls and
boys and the women who were not pregnant. The pregnant women they
slashed open, tore out their unborn infants, and flung them before their
very eyes to the dogs. The prisoners were quartered in a house situated
on an elevation, under guard of several warriors. From there they saw
a part of the tragic scene: how some women defended their husbands,
how others tried to avenge them, and how these heroines were sacrificed
to the vengeance of the Indians who, according to their custom, spared
only the young in order to enslave them. About two hundred perished.
Only about twenty escaped to the woods, most of them bleeding from
their wounds. While the massacre was going on, the Great Chief sat
quietly under the tobacco shed of the Mississippi Company, placidly contemplating the circle of gory heads, including Chepart's, which were
placed before him. When the Natchez were assured that no more Frenchmen remained at the post, they burned it to the ground, while they drank,
sang, danced, and insulted the memory of their dead victims.[41]

One of the Frenchmen, though gravely wounded, fled to the Yazoos,
whose chief received him cordially, supplied him with food, dressed his
wound, and furnished him with a pirogue in which he continued to New
Orleans. The chief requested him to tell Périer that his tribe would
remain faithful to the French; but he soon broke his promise. The Natchez loaded him with gifts and goaded him to attack the French post in
his region. His braves massacred the commander and seventeen of his
men and killed Father Souel, the missionary. He spared only four women
and seven children, whom he enslaved.[42]

A few days after the Yazoo massacre, Father Doutreleau, missionary
of the Illinois country, traveled with five friends down the Mississippi
on his way to New Orleans. Reaching the mouth of the Yazoo on New
Year's Day, 1730, they disembarked and improvised an altar to celebrate
Mass. When he was about to begin, some Yazoos appeared, approached
them in a friendly manner, and took their places behind the Frenchmen,
who were ignorant of the Yazoo massacre. During the *Kyrie Eleison*, a
shower of bullets fell on the priest and his friends as they knelt around
the altar. Father Doutreleau was struck in the arm. Seeing one of his

friends fall dead at his feet, he knelt down to await another volley. Bullets whizzed around him without hitting him. He seized the chalice and paten and ran in his vestments to the river, where two of his men, who thought him dead, had just left the river bank in a canoe. Pursued by Indians, he waded into the water and scrambled toward his friends.

As he turned his head he was shot in the mouth, but his friends dragged him into the canoe and paddled frantically toward Natchez. When they saw that village in ruins they hurried downstream, ignoring Indians who shouted to them to come ashore. Amid a shower of bullets, which fortunately fell short of their mark, they sped on to the country of the friendly Tunicas, where they dressed Father Doutreleau's wound and bandaged the fractured thigh of a soldier. The priest and two men proceeded in the canoe toward New Orleans, leaving the other men on shore. "*Au revoir!* I'll come back right away to be your chaplain!" he called as he waved them adieu. He was as good as his word; he left New Orleans before his wounds were healed.[43]

Word of the massacres had already reached Pérrier, who immediately sent Captain Le Mervilleux to warn settlers living on both sides of the river and to build palisaded forts for their protection. He sent Sueur to urge the friendly Choctaws to attack the Natchez. Regarding the Natchez as their bitterest enemies, the Choctaws responded with incredible alacrity. Seven hundred of them under Sueur attacked the Natchez on January 29, 1730, rescuing fifty-nine women and children and a tailor and carpenter and one hundred six Negroes and Negresses with their children. At the cost of two men killed and seven or eight wounded, they captured eighteen Natchez braves and lifted sixty scalps. Seeing themselves attacked by formidable numbers and regarding defeat as certain, the remaining Natchez fled to two palisaded forts where they spent the night dancing the dance of death.[44]

Meanwhile another officer, Loubois, led against the Natchez village a force of eleven hundred Frenchmen, three hundred Red River Indians, and the Choctaw braves who remained under Sueur. Loubois fired continuously at the palisade without damaging it. Next day he bombarded the fort from closer range but again he failed to crack its defenses. Then, his ammunition almost exhausted, he sent toward the fort five Frenchmen bearing a white flag. The Natchez attacked them, killing three and capturing the rest. Fighting desperately, they advanced against the French and were about to capture their cannon. But one of the officers, Artaguette, with five men, drove them back. At last, on February 25, the Natchez agreed to free their prisoners; but they had no intention of surrendering. Suspecting treachery, they sought to provide for their escape during the suspension of hostilities. When, on the following morning, the French approached the fort to receive the prisoners, they discovered to their amazement that the Natchez chiefs and braves, together with their women and children and booty, had decamped during the night, leaving a small guard with the prisoners.[45]

A few days later Loubois advanced to the bluff on the river bank and began a terraced fort which he garrisoned with one hundred twenty men and fortified with several cannon. Then he dismissed his Indian allies and, leaving the new fort to one of his officers, departed with his troops and the prisoners to New Orleans. But the Natchez were by no means subdued; they committed other outrages; and Pérrier, receiving reinforcements from France, again marched into their country. But they had been hiding for nine months; Pérrier could not find their fort, which they had built in extremely marshy country, until a Natchez lad of twelve, who had deserted his tribe, led him to it. That same day, January 20, 1732, Pérrier attacked the Natchez who, in a transport of rage, counterattacked; but the grenades of their enemies so terrified them that they retreated back into the fort. Whereupon Pérrier bombed the quarters in the fort reserved for women and children, who screamed in terror; and the men, seized with grief for the loss of their loved ones, surrendered.[46]

The French granted them a parley until the following day. But, under cover of darkness the braves tried to escape; most of them were discovered and driven back to the fort. Those who managed to escape joined a group of hunters and departed with them to the country of the Chickasaws, allies of the English. Among the Natchez prisoners were the Great Chief, Tatooed Arm, several warriors, and many women and children. The French carried their prisoners to New Orleans, where they were confined. Later they were sold as slaves in Santo Domingo.[47]

The Natchez tribe disappeared; but so had the funds of the Mississippi Company. Early in 1731, therefore, it requested the king to take back its charter. In the following spring, the king issued a series of orders which ended the company's control of Louisiana. Pérrier remained as governor of the colony for another year; but new Indian troubles disgusted him and he resigned and returned to France. Bienville, the only man who could handle the Indians, returned to his old position.[48]

Georgia: Frontier Utopia

TOMOCHICHI, CHIEF OF THE YAMACRAWS, WAS A PEACEFUL AND AMIABLE man. Not by natural endowment, but by a perverted necessity. He had, in his younger days, been a courageous, even an aggressive warrior. But his native tribe, the Lower Creeks, had expelled him, perhaps because he persisted in his plans to found a new nation. So he had gone off like another Romulus with his few followers to establish his capital on a bluff which received the name he had given to his tribe. But though free he felt insecure; powerful and unfriendly tribes lived all around him; and now that he was over ninety years old he could no longer hope to conquer or even forestall them. So when, in February, 1733, he saw a small group of white men land at the foot of Yamacraw Bluff and clamber up cheerlessly toward his village, he hastened to welcome them and make them his friends.[1]

Their leader, James Edward Oglethorpe, had come with William Bull and a few other men to choose a site for the first permanent settlement of a new colony. Oglethorpe was lucky that day. He met not only a friendly chief but also a half-breed woman, Mary Musgrove, wife of John Musgrove, a renegade South Carolina trader. Because she spoke English, she established between Tomochichi and Oglethorpe a friendship that lasted until the old chief's death. Returning to nearby Beaufort, where he had sent his colonists, Oglethorpe brought them in four small boats to Yamacraw Bluff. There, at the edge of a pine forest above the reddish Savannah that curves like a sickle as it winds into the sea ten miles away, he sheltered them for the night in four tents made of boards and boughs. On that day, February 12, 1733, Oglethorpe founded the utopian colony of Georgia.[2]

He was forty-four years old—a noble man with a thin but stubborn strain of self-righteousness and hypocrisy. He denied to others what he desired for himself. Though he strictly prohibited rum in his colony, he drank countless bottles of it himself, together with much wine and

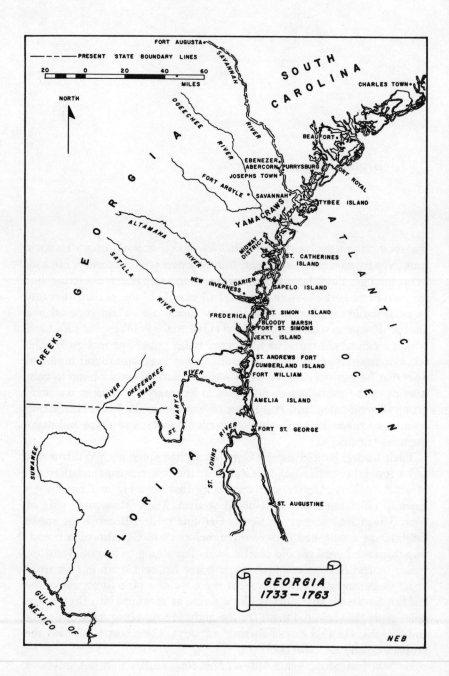

FORT AUGUSTA

— — — PRESENT STATE BOUNDARY LINES

20   0   20   40   60
MILES

NORTH

SOUTH CAROLINA

CHARLES TOWN

SAVANNAH RIVER

OGEECHEE RIVER

BEAUFORT

EBENEZER
ABERCORN PURRYSBURG
JOSEPHS TOWN
FORT ARGYLE • SAVANNAH
PORT ROYAL

YAMACRAWS

TYBEE ISLAND

G E O R G I A

ALTAMAHA RIVER

MIDWAY DISTRICT

ST. CATHERINES ISLAND

A T L A N T I C

SATILLA RIVER

NEW INVERNESS
DARIEN

SAPELO ISLAND

FREDERICA
ST. SIMON ISLAND
BLOODY MARSH
FORT ST. SIMONS
JEKYL ISLAND

CREEKS

RIVER

OKEFENOKEE SWAMP

ST. MARYS RIVER

ST. ANDREWS FORT
CUMBERLAND ISLAND
FORT WILLIAM

AMELIA ISLAND

O C E A N

SUWANEE RIVER

FLORIDA

ST. JOHNS RIVER

FORT ST. GEORGE

ST. AUGUSTINE

GULF OF MEXICO

GEORGIA
1733 — 1763

NEB

beer. He seemed to know what was good for him, for he was overripe when he finally died. Though he glowed with eloquence when he was among intimate friends, he fumbled and stumbled over his sentences in making a public address or moralized so laboriously that his audience yawned and temporarily parted company with consciousness. He forbade slavery in Georgia, saying it was against the gospel while enriching himself as a director of the Royal Africa Company.

He had divided his life between military service, which brought him no distinction, and philanthropic pursuit, which was to win him immortality. Leaving Oxford before he took a degree, he entered the army and served in the War of the Spanish Succession. Soon after the Treaty of Utrecht, which ended the war, he served for five years under Prince Eugene of Savoy. Then he returned to England where, on the death of his brother Theophilus, he inherited a considerable estate at Westbrook, which brought him financial independence and comfort. He was not destined, however, to enjoy the indolence of an affluent country gentleman. In 1722 he was chosen to Parliament from the town of Haslemere, which was located near his estate. Yet he took no active part in parliamentary affairs until 1729, when he was chosen chairman of a committee that investigated the conditions of the prisons. The harsh treatment with which inmates were treated doubtless won his sympathy for the unfortunate and oppressed.

On January 13, 1732, he made a speech in the House of Commons in which with many clichés and much moralizing he expressed sympathy for the persecuted Protestants of Europe and strongly advocated that something be done for their relief. He enjoyed ready outlets for his stern and uncompromising humanitarian instincts. He was a member of the Society for the Propagation of the Gospel in Foreign Parts. He served zealously on a council of fifty that sought to support and educate homeless children. He defended seamen against the evils of impressment. He supported the Moravians in their quest for financial assistance. And he championed a parliamentary resolution that sought to relieve the poor of certain of their more burdensome taxes.[3]

His sympathy toward debtors probably originated in the hideous death of a friend, Robert Castell, a scholar and amateur architect who had written and illustrated an able work on ancient villas. A scoundrel named Bambridge had in a very short time extorted large sums of money from Castell. When Castell, in a resurgent tide of pride, refused to submit to further exactions, Bambridge had him committed to Corbett's, one of the foulest prisons in England, where he died of smallpox. Oglethorpe investigated the case and, consumed with righteous fury, described jailed people as "a slow fire and hectick fever to consume the vitals of the state." As a member of Parliament he forced an inquiry that he himself conducted, which exposed the horrible conditions of most English prisons. He found them full of good, honest folk who, as victims of temporary bad luck, had failed to pay their bills. His report created a sensation that resulted in many diversified reforms. Later he claimed that his investigations had resulted in the liberation of ten thousand unfortunates.[4]

Unluckily, most of these released debtors were no better off out of prison than in. England was so crowded that it could offer them neither employment nor housing. The freed men found that they had exchanged freedom for starvation, that Oglethorpe's humanitarianism had, by the very conditions that existed in England, created only a new form of suffering. For these people Oglethorpe projected a colony in America—a colony which, at the same time, harmonized with the imperial destinies of the English government. The age of Oglethorpe and Addison and Walpole was also the age of Chatham and Wolfe and Clive. The government and Oglethorpe agreed that the projected colony would serve England in her imperialistic designs while it would provide better opportunities to thousands of unfortunate and oppressed Englishmen as well as foreigners. Humanitarianism and religious tolerance had combined with mercenary considerations to establish a southern post that should serve as a buffer state between the English colonies and the Spanish colonies on the eastern coast of North America.[5]

Many Englishmen shared Oglethorpe's dream. One of these was Dr. Thomas Bray, a minister who had founded the Society for the Promotion of Christian Knowledge and the Society for the Propagation of the Gospel in Foreign Parts, popularly known as SPCK and SPG respectively. He was interested, too, in numerous philanthropies for the relief of poor families by means of colonial settlements, by building parochial libraries in Great Britain, and by Christian education of Negroes in the West Indies. From a friend, Abel Tassin D'Allone, he had acquired a bequest of £900, which he added to a grant of £5000 he had received for his project from an estate successfully defended against its fradulent heir. In 1723, Dr. Bray, being old and infirm and fearing that his death would mean the end of his benevolences, organized the Associates of Dr. Bray to carry on his work. When Dr. Bray died in 1730, one of Oglethorpe's friends, John Viscount Percival, became the most influential of the Associates. To him, Oglethorpe applied for help in carrying forward his plan for a colony in America.

At Percival's behest the Associates petitioned George II for a tract of land "on the south-west of Carolina for settling poor persons of London." On June 9, 1732, George II granted them a charter that established the province of Georgia between Savannah and the Altamaha rivers and between the head springs of these rivers due west to the Pacific. The charter placed the colony for twenty-one years under a corporation "in trust for the poor." The president of the corporation was Viscount Percival, who in the following year was made the first Earl of Egmont in recognition of his new office. The seal of the corporation which bore the motto *Non Sibi, Sed Aliis*—Not for Themselves but for Others—and which showed on one side a group of silkworms at their work, expressed the benevolence of its members in refusing any grant of land or any emolument whatever for their services. The obverse side of the seal represented two figures separated by a design, "Georgia Augusta." Each had a cap of liberty, a spear in one hand, and a horn of plenty in the other, and they leaned on urns which were emblematic of the boundary rivers mentioned in the charter.[6]

Oglethorpe bent all his energies toward realizing his dream. He faced a stupendous task. While others gave to the project their leisure, their prayers, or their wealth, Oglethorpe gave his endless patience and unremitting industry in sifting from among thousands of applicants healthy Protestants who, though unfortunately caught in the dilemma of debt and unfairly thrown into jail by stringent English law, had yet led moral, sober, and just lives. They had to show their willingness to work, which in a wilderness of wholly undeveloped resources, on a frontier between barbarism and civilization, needed strong and fearless people. The requisites of availability were perforce able bodies, good characters, open records, and willing, resolute dispositions. Thirty-five families were selected, numbering one hundred fourteen men, women, and children. Among them were carpenters, bricklayers, mechanics, and farmers, all of whom were needed to make homes and farms in the wilderness they must conquer. Dr. Henry Herbert, an Episcopalian minister, volunteered to go along to minister to the religious needs of the colonists. Nicola Amatis, a native of Savoy, Italy, was instructed to teach them the culture of the silk, which the Trustees planned as a major industry.[7]

On November 17, 1732, they sailed from Gravesend on the *Ann*, a vessel of two hundred tons under Captain John Thomas. Oglethorpe invited Dr. Herbert and Amatis to share a cabin prepared for him at his personal expense. At Madeira the vessel stopped to take on five tuns of wine for which that island was famous. The calm sea and occasional unfavorable winds protracted the voyage during which two small children died. But these were the only exceptions in an otherwise happy and anticipatory voyage.[8]

On January 13, 1733, the emigrants reached Charles Town, where their leader allowed them to go ashore for ten hours to stretch their legs, to see the town, and to enjoy a reception given by Governor Johnson. Next day he sent them to Beaufort while he himself and William Bull and a few other men set out in small boats for Yamacraw Bluff where he met Tomochichi and Mary Musgrove. Then he collected the emigrants on the bluff and delivered them a speech. He had never been a charming speaker; he leaned as always on clichés and the moralizing that characterized his addresses in Parliament. That morning he was unusually solemn as he reminded them of their duties as founders of the colony; he told them that they could expect to reap only what they sowed. Adverting to his favorite topic of moralizing—rum—he requested them to refrain from drinking it, not for the sake of themselves but for the sake of the Indians. He hoped, he said, "that through your good example, the settlements of Georgia may prove a blessing and not a curse, to the native inhabitants."[9]

Then he set them to work. To each man he assigned a special task. Some plied axes, some worked with hoes and shovels, some unloaded the ship by means of a crane, some ran up temporary board shelters, and some began the construction of a stronghold, Fort Argyle, on the eastern extremity of the bluff. Colonel Bull, with a crew of four expert carpenters he had brought from Charles Town, laid out the town, which they called Savannah, in an orderly design that favors it even today.

The colonists of Charles Town were so delighted to have them that they gave them horses, cattle, sheep, hogs, and rice, while the South Carolina assembly voted them £2000 in the currency of that colony and later increased this amount. The other English colonists regarded the founding of Georgia as an auspicious event. Thomas Penn, proprietor of Pennsylvania, presented the colony with a gift of £100. The governor of Massachusetts congratulated Oglethorpe profusely and prayed God to bless him. In March a native of Charles Town visited Savannah and published an account of his visit in the local newspaper. This stated that

> ... Oglethorpe is indefatible, takes a vast deal of pains, his fare is but indifferent, having little else at present but salt provisions. He is extremely well-beloved by all his people; the general title they give him is Father. If any of them is sick he immediately visits them and takes a great deal of care of them. If any differences arise he is the person who decides them. Two happened while I was there and in my presence; and all the parties went away to outward appearance, satisfied and contented with his determination.
>
> He keeps a strict discipline. I neither saw one of his people drunk or heard one of them swear; he does not allow them rum but in lieu gives them English beer. ... There are Four Houses already up but none finished; and he hopes when he has got more Sawyers, which I suppose he will have in a short time, to finish two Houses a Week. He has ploughed up some Land, part of which he sowed with Wheat, which is come up and looks promising. He has two or three Gardens which he has sowed with divers sorts of seeds, and planted Thyme, with some other Sorts of Pot-herbs, Sage, Leeks, Skellions, Celery, Liguorice, etc., and several Sorts of Fruit Trees. He was palisading the Town round, including some Part of the Common, which I do suppose may be finished in a Fortnight's time. In short he has done a vast deal of work for the Time, and I think his Name Justly deserves to be immortalised.[10]

But Oglethorpe wanted more than the love of his friends; he sought, too, the friendship of his potential enemies, the Lower Creeks, who had once driven his friend Tomochichi from their tribe. With the assistance of Mary Musgrove, he accordingly summoned them to a conference, which began on May 20 at his residence in Savannah. The chiefs formed a procession led by a medicine man bearing a fan of white feathers in each hand as a symbol of peace. Then followed the Creek chiefs and Tomochichi and his wife Senauki, attended by a picked retinue of twenty men who shouted and danced as they approached Oglethorpe. The medicine man showed his friendship for Oglethorpe by stroking his cheeks gently with fans. They ate and drank and smoked the peace pipe.

When the conference opened, the leading Creek chief, Long King, a very tall and old man, stood up and began a long speech in a stentorian voice accompanied by graceful gestures. He who had given breath to the English, he said, had also given breath to the Indians; He who had made both had given more wisdom to the English; and He who dwelt in heaven and earth and all around had sent the English to instruct them. Long King therefore gave up to the English his right to all the land he did not use. This was not only his opinion, said Long King, but that of the eight towns of the Creeks, each of whom had agreed to send their chiefs with skins, which was the only wealth they possessed. As he ended his speech, the chief of each of the eight towns brought up a bundle of buckskins and laid it at Oglethorpe's feet. Then Long King thanked him for his kindness to Tomochichi whom he characterized as a good man and a brave warrior, though his own people had banished him.[11]

The next speaker was Tomochichi who, coming in slowly with his followers, bowed very low and said to Oglethorpe:

"I was a banished man; I came here poor and helpless to look for good land near the tombs of my ancestors, and the Trustees sent people here; I feared you would drive us away, for we were weak and wanted corn; but you confirmed our land to us, gave us food and instructed our children. We have already thanked you in the strongest words we could find, but words are no return for such favors; for good words may be spoken by the deceitful, as well as by the upright heart. The chief men of all our nation are here to thank you for us; and before them I declare your goodness, and that here I design to die; for we all love your people so well that with them we will live and die. We do not know good from evil, but desire to be instructed and guided by you that we may do well with, and be numbered amongst, the children of the Trustees."

So saying, he offered Oglethorpe a present. This was a buffalo skin painted on the inside with the head and feathers of an eagle. "The feathers of the eagle are soft," he said, "and signify love; the buffalo skin is warm, and is the emblem of protection. Therefore love and protect our little families."[12]

The next speaker, Yahou-Lakee, chief of Coweta, stood up and addressed Oglethorpe as follows:

"We are come twenty-five days' journey to see you. I have been often advised to go down to Charles Town, but would not go down because I thought I might die on the way; but when I heard you were come, and that you were good men, I knew you were sent by Him who lives in Heaven to teach us Indians wisdom: I therefore came down that I might hear good things, for I knew that if I died on the way I should die in doing good, and what was said would be carried back to the nation, and our children would reap the benefit of it. I rejoice that I have lived to see this day, and to see our friends that have long been gone from amongst us. Our nation was once strong, and had ten towns; but we are now weak, and have but eight towns. You have comforted the banished, and have gathered them that were scattered like little birds before the eagle. We desire to be reconciled to our brethren who are here amongst you, to call the kindred that love them out of each of the Creek towns, that they might come together and make one town. We must pray you to recall the Yamasees that they may be buried in peace amongst their ancestors and that they may see their graves before they die; and their own nation shall be restored again to its ten towns."[13]

The Creeks ceded to England the region between the Savannah and the Altamaha rivers as far as the tide waters flow on the islands of the coast, from Tybee to St. Simon, reserving for themselves only the islands of Ossabaw, Sepalo, and St. Catherines, with a suitable camping ground at Savannah whenever they should choose to visit their white friends.

In ensuing months Oglethorpe planned a scouting expedition to what he called the "Southern Frontiers" for the purpose of ascertaining what defenses the colony needed against possible encroachments from the Spaniards in Florida. On January 23, 1734, he left Savannah with fourteen white men and two Indians in a scouting boat commanded by Captain Ferguson and accompanied by a yawl loaded with provisions, ammunition, and camping equipment. Sailing on inland streams, they explored creeks and sounds, the islands of Ossabaw, St. Catherines, and Sepalo, and the northern branches of the Altamaha River. On January 26, during a severe rainstorm, they landed on "Albany Bluff," off St. Simon Island, where they sought shelter and dried themselves under a large live oak. Here, for the first time, Oglethorpe saw the site he later selected for Fort Frederica, where he was to spend much of his ten years in Georgia and where he was to build the only house he ever had in the colony. Continuing their journey, they reached an island directly south of St. Simon which Oglethorpe named Jekyll in honor of his friend, Sir Joseph Jekyll, Master of the Rolls, who, with Lady Jekyll, had donated £600 to Georgia and had in other ways been a great benefactor and friend of the colony. Continuing southward, Oglethorpe's party explored a part of the mainland. Then they turned their boats homeward, visiting the site of abandoned Fort King George. On February 8, they reached Savannah.[14]

2

The time had come for Oglethorpe to return to England. He sought solutions to problems associated with the establishment of the colony.

The location and financing of forts, the building of public buildings, towns, and roads, the relationship of the Indians to the colonists, the enactment of colonial laws and regulations, and the soliciting of new emigrants—all these required his presence in Parliament of which he was still a member. He had, moreover, to make a full report to the king and to the minister of colonial affairs. In the latter part of March, therefore, he entrusted the general affairs of the colony to Thomas Causton, his storekeeper and bailiff, and sailed to Charles Town whence, after a short sojourn, he embarked on the British transport *Aldborough* for St. Helens on the Isle of Wight. With him was Tomochichi, his wife, his son Hillispilli, his nephew Towanahowi, and five Creek chiefs with their attendants and their interpreter. In England the Indians "created great excitement and interest from the nobility down to the rabble in the street who at times almost injured the red men in their stampedes to see them." Towanahowi gladdened everybody by reciting the Lord's Prayer, which he had learned during the voyage, both in his own language and in English.[15] Oglethorpe was received like a conquering hero. Special resolutions were passed in acknowledgment of his services; medals were struck in his honor; and poets paid homage to him with odes in the style of Alexander Pope, the literary lion of the day:

> . . . Let nervous Pope, in his immortal lays,
> Recite actions, and record thy praise;
> No brighter scenes his *Homer* could display
> Than in thy great adventures we survey.
>   . . .
> Thy great example shall through ages shine,
> A favourite theme! with poets and divine;
> People unborn thy merits shall proclaim,
> And add new honours to thy deathless name.

Another poet, perhaps Samuel Wesley, celebrated Tomochichi:

> What stranger's this? and from what region far?
>   This wondrous form, majestic to behold?
> Unclothed, but armed offensive for the war,
>   In hoary age, and wise experience old?
> His limbs, inured to hardness and to toil,
>   His strong, large limbs, what mighty sinews brace!
> Whilst truth sincere, and artless virtue smile
>   In the expressive features of his face—
> His bold free aspect speaks the inward mind,
> Awed by no slavish fear, from no vile passion blind.
>   . . .
> Thine with thy OGLETHORPE'S fair fame shall last,
> Together to Eternity consigned,

In the immortal roll of heroes placed,
   The mighty benefactors of mankind;
Those heaven-born souls, from whose high worth we know
The Deity Himself best imaged here below.[16]

At Kensington Palace the Indians were presented to George II, who received them as he sat on his throne. The Creek chiefs wanted to appear in the skimpy costumes of their native country; but, at Oglethorpe's insistence, they donned more appropriate dress. Their faces were variously painted in the manner of their country, some black, some red, some in several colors, some with triangulars and half-moons and bearded arrows. Tomochichi and his wife were attired in scarlet trimmed with gold.[17]

"This day," said Tomochichi to the king, "I see the majesty of your face, the greatness of your house, and the number of your people. I am come for the good of the whole nation called the Creeks, to renew the peace which we long ago had with the English. I am come over in my old days, although I cannot live to see any advantage to myself. I am come for the good of the children of all the nations of the Upper and Lower Creeks, that they may be instructed in the knowledge of the English."

He handed the king a gift.

"These are the feathers of the eagle," he said, "which is the swiftest of birds, and which flieth all around our nation. These feathers are a sign of peace in our land, and have been carried from town to town there; and we have brought them over to leave with you, O great king, as a sign of everlasting peace.

"O great king, whatsoever words you shall say to me, I will tell them faithfully to all the kings of the Creek nation."[18]

To which His Majesty graciously replied:

"I am glad of the opportunity of assuring you of my regard for the people from whom you come, and am extremely well pleased with the assurances you have brought me from them, and accept very gratefully this present as an indication of their good disposition to me and my people. I shall always be ready to cultivate a good correspondence between them and my own subjects, and shall be glad of any occasion to show you a mark of my particular friendship and esteem."[19]

These festivities were unfortunately marred by tragedy. One of the Creek chiefs developed smallpox, of which he died only three days after his audience with the king. Fear of contagion kept everybody away from his funeral save Tomochichi, three of the Creek chiefs, the church warden, and the grave digger. Wailing in the custom of their tribe, Tomochichi and his companions conveyed the dead chief, who was sewed in two blankets, to St. Johns Cemetery at Westminster and buried him together with his glass beads, his feathers, and his silver money.[20]

Oglethorpe alleviated their bereavement by taking them to his home at Westbrook and entertaining them there for two weeks. Then, as they emerged from their period of depression and mourning, he took them to Putney, where Lady Dutry entertained them lavishly. Later, at Lambeth, they visited the Archbishop of Canterbury, who received them with great tenderness and exhorted them to embrace Christianity. From Lambeth they went to the college of Eton, which gave its students a holiday, and then to Hampton Court, where they reviewed the royal apartments and walked through the royal gardens. Tomochichi won all hearts by his venerable age, his wit, and his gracious manners. Everybody who met him was impressed by his keen observations, his pertinent enquiries, his mature judgment, and his liberal views. He expressed surprise that such short-lived people as the English should build themselves such long-lived buildings. He urged that established rules be maintained in any bartering between the colonists and the Indians, that no white man should trade with an Indian without a license from the trustees, and that a storehouse should be built in every principal Indian village. Such measures, he pointed out, would preclude the possibility of frauds and therefore of animosities or quarrels between his people and the colonists. The trustees assured him that his requests would receive the attention their importance merited.[21]

After spending nearly four months in England, the Indians were anxious to return to their villages in Georgia and tell their friends of the things they had seen and of the lessons they had learned during their sojourn. But the public still maintained a lively interest in them. Wherever they appeared, huge crowds followed them, grasping their hands, making them numerous gifts, and showing them every mark of friendship and civility. The gifts they received exceeded £400 in value. The artist Verelst painted an oil portrait of Tomochichi and his nephew. It showed the old chief in furs and the boy holding an eagle in his arms. Prince William, thirteen years old, gave Towanahowi a gold watch with the admonition that he call on Jesus Christ every morning when he looked at it. The Indians were particularly delighted with the royal barges that appeared on the Thames on the Lord Mayor's Day and with Prince William's taking his riding exercise with the Horse Guards.[22]

On October 30 the Indians departed in the king's coaches for Gravesend, where they boarded the transport *Prince of Wales* which soon embarked for America. Oglethorpe remained to prepare for his return voyage and to serve his term in Parliament which, through his influence, passed several important laws for Georgia. To help finance this "Great Embarkation," as it was called, Parliament appropriated £26,000. Oglethorpe attended several meetings of the trustees with whom he planned to establish in the southern part of the colony a settlement named Frederica, in honor of Frederick, Prince of Wales. Eleven hundred persons applied for permission to settle in Georgia. All of them were rigidly examined. Neither drunkards nor other "notoriously vicious persons" were accepted. The selected persons met the requirements of what the trustees called "the best characters."

Because Oglethorpe and the trustees believed that the colony should be in a position to defend itself as well as neighboring South Carolina, they had the emigrants formed into little brigades and had them drilled daily by sergeants of the Royal Guards. The trustees agreed to pay their passage to Georgia and arranged that during the voyage they were to have four beef days, two pork days, and one fish day. In addition, each man was to receive "a watch coat; a musket and bayonet; a hatchet; a hammer; a handsaw; a shod shovel or spade; a broad hoe; a narrow hoe; a gimlet; a drawing knife; an iron pot, and a pair of pot hooks; a frying pan; and a public grindstone to each ward or village."[23] For his maintenance in the colony for one year he was to be supplied with

> ... 312 lbs. of beef or pork; 104 lbs. of rice; 104 lbs. of Indian corn or peas; 104 lbs. of flour; 1 pint of strong beer a day to a man when he works and not otherwise; 52 quarts of molasses for brewing beer; 16 lbs. of cheese; 12 lbs. of butter; 8 oz. of spice; 12 lbs. of sugar; 4 gallons of vinegar; 24 lbs. of salt; 12 qts. of lamp oil, and 1 lb. spun cotton; 12 lbs. of soap.[24]

The women and children were allowed practically the same maintenance as the men save that each received only 260 lbs. of beef or pork, 6 quarts of lamp oil, half pound of spun cotton, and were forbidden beer. Children between the ages of seven and twelve years were considered "half a head" and were given one-half the allowance, while those between the ages of two and seven years were listed as "one-third of a head" and received one-third of the allowance.[25]

Each freeholder who agreed to clear and cultivate his land was promised fifty acres which was to be held in "tale male." Oglethorpe, knowing the degrading effect of rum on the Indians, prohibited its use in the colony. He thought, too, that Georgia had too warm a climate for hard liquor, though few of his contemporaries and none of his successors agreed with him. One of his contemporaries, indeed, believed that the restriction produced the opposite effect of that which was intended:

> In the first place, we were cut off from the most immediate and probable way of exporting our timber (the only poor prospect of export that we could ever flatter ourselves with) to the Sugar Islands, rum being the principal return they make: In the second place, the experience of all the inhabitants of America will prove the necessity of *qualifying water with some spirit*, and it is very certain, that no province in America yields water, that such a qualification is more necessary to, than Carolina and Georgia and the usefulness of this experiment has been sufficiently evident to all the inhabitants of Georgia who

could procure *it*, and use *it* with moderation: A third reason which made this restriction very hurtful to the colony, was, that though the laws were in force against it (which put it in the power of magistrates to lay hardships upon every person who might be *otherwise* under their *resentment*) yet great quantities were imported, only with this difference, that, in place of barter or exchange, the ready money was drained from the inhabitants: and likewise, as it is the *nature of mankind* in general, and of the *common sort* in particular, more *eagerly* to desire, and more *immoderately* to use those things which are most restrained from them, such was the case with respect to rum in Georgia.[26]

Another of Oglethorpe's contemporaries, who stated that he wrote without "Byass," blamed the prohibition of rum for "a plague of sickness" that infested the colony. It has caused "inflammatory Fevers of various kinds, both continued and intermittent; washing and tormenting Fluxes, most excrutiating Cholicks and Dry-Belly Achs; Tremor; Vertigoes, Palsies, and a long Train of painful and lingering nervous Distempers. . . ."[27]

Another unique law of the trustees prohibited Negro slavery. In this policy, however, they were not motivated by any sympathy for the slaves. As director and later deputy general of the Royal African Company, Oglethorpe himself sold slaves far and wide and reaped a large profit. But he stated that in the case of Georgia slavery was incompatible with the philanthropic spirit in which the colony was founded. The charity settlers could not hope to buy slaves themselves and could not ask their benefactors to purchase slaves for them. Oglethorpe also feared that the presence of slaves would degrade white labor; the colony would quickly be denuded of its natural defenders if farmers were at liberty to leave their work and let their slaves do it for them. Slaves, indeed, were a positive danger to the colony. Not only were they unacceptable as soldiers but they could desert to the Spaniards in St. Augustine.[28]

The trustees planned to turn their commercial attention principally toward raising silk and making wine, enterprises that required no slave labor. In his writings Oglethorpe rested his objections to slavery in Georgia on moral grounds. "There is an honest reluctance in humanity," he once wrote, "against buying and selling, and regarding those of our own species as our wealth and possessions." At another time, he wrote that slavery was "against the gospel, as well as fundamental law of England."[29]

In October, 1735, Oglethorpe, ready to return to Georgia, set out for Cowes to join the emigrants who numbered 257 and who included about eighty German Lutherans, better known as Salzburgers, under their leader Baron von Reck, twenty-five Moravians under Bishop David Nitschman, and Oglethorpe's friends, John and Charles Wesley, Benjamin Ingraham, and Charles Delamotte, and his servants. Contrary winds delayed them for several weeks. Finally, on December 10, they sailed in two vessels, the *Symonds*, and the *London Merchant*, which were convoyed by a man-of-war, the *Hawk*, until a gale separated it from the other ships. On February 5, 1736, they entered the Savannah River and anchored opposite present Cockspur Island. Leaving the emigrants at this place, Oglethorpe went to Savannah, where he was welcomed by its inhabitants and by a salute of twenty-one guns.[30]

3

Georgia was a utopia not only for the poor and unemployed but also for persecuted sects in and outside of England. The first group that applied for admission to the colony was the Lutheran sect known as the Salzburgers. Since the days of the religious wars they had been living in the mountains and valleys of the Archbishopric of Salzburg in Austria. Though they pretended Catholicism, they secretly read their Bibles and followed Protestant traditions. Archbishop Leopold Anton, discovering their religious duplicity, angrily resolved to drive them from his archbishopric. Whereupon they hastily applied for aid from Protestant countries and for their right, under the Treaty of Westphalia, to have three years in which to dispose of their property. Three hundred of them met at Schwarzach and swore to remain loyal to their faith.

Archbishop Leopold Anton countered by issuing in October, 1731, a decree ordering all members of the reformed religion or of the Confession of Augsburg to leave the province of Salzburg within eight days and never to return on pain of confiscation of their property or even death. Though he later extended this limit, many of them had to leave their homes in the dead of winter without any idea of where they were going. Some of them applied for assistance to the Protestant city of Augsburg. Reverend Samuel Urlsperger, pastor of the Lutheran church of St. Ann in that city, heard their pleas and arranged with a member of SPCK and the trustees of Georgia to send fifty of their families to Georgia. At the same time, SPCK offered to pay their expenses from Augsburg to Rotterdam, where they could board an English ship, while the trustees arranged for their transportation and settlement from England to Georgia. George Bancroft painted a pathetic picture of their joys and sufferings during their pilgrimage from Augsburg to Rotterdam:

On the last day of October, 1733, "the evangelical community," well supplied with Bibles and hymn-books, cathecisms and books of devotion, conveying in one wagon their few chattels, in two other covered ones their feebler companions, and especially their little ones—after a discourse of prayer and benedictions, cheerfully, and in the name of God, began their pilgrimage. History need not stop to tell what charities cheered them on their journey, what towns were closed against them by Roman Catholic magistrates, or how they entered Frankfort on the Main, two by two in solemn procession, singing spiritual songs. As they floated down the Main, and between the castled crags, the vineyards, and the white-walled towns that adorn the banks of the Rhine, their conversation, amid hymns and prayers, was of justification and of sanctification, and of standing fast in the Lord.[31]

At Rotterdam they met two of their chosen ministers, John Martin Bolzius and Israel Christian Gronau, both of whom had conducted charitable work in the Latin Orphan House in Halle. They had consented to relinquish their lucrative and honorable positions to accompany the Salzburgers—forty-seven of them—to minister to their spiritual needs in Georgia. A voyage of six days brought them to Dover, where several of the trustees visited them and gave them a dinner of roast beef and plum pudding. On January 8, 1734, the Salzburgers, under their leader Baron George Frederick von Reck, sailed on the *Purisburgh* for their new homes in America. Two months later, they reached their destination. "God blessed us this Day," wrote von Reck on March 10, "with the Sight of our Country, our wish'd-for Georgia, which we saw at ten in the Morning; and Brought us into the Savannah River, and caused us to remember the Vows we made unto him, if He did through his infinite Goodness bring us thither."[32]

All Savannah greeted them with loud huzzas and cannonading which the sailors answered in kind. The Indians touched von Reck with their hands in testimony of their delight at his arrival with his people. All of them save their ministers and their physician, Dr. Zwelfer, were lodged in a tent pitched on Johnson Square. The others lodged with Dr. Samuel Quincy, minister of the colony. The colonists asked Oglethorpe to conduct them to a place with diversified topography and with plenty of water. Oglethorpe soon obliged them. Accompanied by an Indian guide, he and von Reck, on March 14, made an arduous journey, partly by water up the Savannah and partly on horseback, to "a crooked little stream which chose to run twenty-five miles to the Savannah when a straight cut would have been six miles." Here were fine meadows in which much hay could be made with little trouble. Here were woods of cedar, walnut, pine, cypress, oak, and many myrtles whose berries produced a green wax for candles. Here grew an abundance of sassafras and indigo and China-root. The earth, wrote their leader, was of "several sorts, some sandy, some black, fat and heavy, and some of a claiey nature. The first is good for potatoes and Pease; the second for all sorts of Corn; and the Third to make Bricks, Earthen Ware, etc." He noticed with delight that the region teemed with eagles, wild turkeys, deer, wild geese, hares, partridges, and buffaloes.[33]

Here the Salzburgers built their first settlement, which they called Ebenezer, that is, Rock of Strength. Some of them came to build houses for their women and children, some came to stay in two tents at Aber-

corn while they began a road to Ebenezer, some took their baggage on
sledges drawn by four horses which Governor Johnson of South Carolina had given them. The road, which ran through twelve miles of forest
and which had seven bridges, was completed in just ten days—a record
which aroused the admiration of their less enthusiastic English friends.
As soon as they all arrived in Ebenezer they drew lots, cleared the land,
and sowed their vegetables and grain. Ten days later they completed a
wooden chapel in which they gave thanks to God.[34]

But tragedy soon shook the infant settlement. Surrounded on three
sides by low swamps, it was often flooded and generated malarial fever.
"The People in *Abercorn* as well as in *Ebenezer*," wrote Bolzius, "are
troubled with Loosenesses. It is thought that drinking too much in hot
Weather, is the Reason of it. They are too bashful to tell it in the Beginning when the Evil might have been prevented. Some have had great
Benefit by our Physick." But "physick" proved ineffectual in stemming
the illness, which carried away a goodly number. At last Bolzius and
Gronau, in despair, went to Savannah to confer with Oglethorpe on the
propriety of changing the location of the town to a more salubrious
place. Oglethorpe, who had recently returned from England, went to
see them and, pointing out that their moving would obviate all their past
labor and would present new inconveniences and hardships, tried to encourage them to remain; but when he saw that they were determined
he allowed them to move a few miles to "Red Bluff," so called from its
reddish clay, at the junction of Ebenezer Creek and the Savannah River.
The old town "quickly disintegrated and soon degenerated into a cow-
pen—the first of Georgia's dead towns."[35]

Early in 1736 another group of Salzburgers migrated to Georgia on
the ship that brought Oglethorpe back from England. They, too, settled
in New Ebenezer, which by 1741 boasted more than a thousand inhabitants. Small groups of Salzburgers settled in nearby Bethany and
Goshen and a few built homes in faraway St. Simon Island. Under
such leaders as Bolzius, Gronau, Hermann Henry Lemke, and Christian
Rabenhorst they prospered in farming and silk raising. Before long they
had accumulated enough money to pay their pastor a comfortable salary
and to support orphans and old people. During this period of the trustees,
they represented the largest non-English group in Georgia.[36]

Another group of persecuted Protestants that found refuge in Georgia
was the Moravians, who were the followers of John Huss, known as the
Morning Star of the Reformation. Though they called themselves *Unitas
Fratrum*—the Unity of Brethren—they eventually became known as
Moravians, because most of them originally came from Moravia, the
central province of present Czechoslovakia. In the early part of the
eighteenth century, the remnants of this sect, which based their rule of
faith and practice in the works of Jesus Christ, gathered on the estate of
their young leader, Count Nicolaus Ludwig von Zinzendorf in Saxony,
where he founded a great religious and educational center at Herrhut.

When the Saxon government restricted refugees from Bohemia and Moravia, Zinzendorf petitioned the trustees to allow his followers to migrate to Georgia to spread Christianity among the Indians. Though the trustees knew that the Moravians were conscientiously opposed to war and even to bearing arms, they granted five hundred acres of land and two lots in Savannah to their leaders Bishop August Gottlieb Spangenburg and Reverend David Nitschmann. The Moravians, however, were not charity colonists; they came to Georgia at their own expense as servants of Count Zinzendorf, though they borrowed money from the trustees which they later returned.[37]

Zinzendorf was unable to leave Europe for his grant on the Ogeechee River near Fort Argyle. Instead, he sent ten of his followers under Bishop Spangenburg. They landed in Savannah where they awaited the arrival of more Moravians. Though the trustees had been hesitant to grant the first group of Moravians permission to colonize in Georgia, they were so impressed by their quiet industry and piety that they permitted others to come. On October 31, 1735, the second group, consisting of men, women, and children, arrived in Savannah under David Nitschmann. They, too, preferred Savannah to settling on their tract on the Ogeechee River. Both Spangenburg and Nitschmann soon saw that Georgia was no place for their people. They became very unpopular when, in 1737, they firmly refused to give either their names or their numbers in a house-to-house enrollment of every able-bodied man in defense of a purported Spanish invasion of Savannah. Hailed before Bailiff Causton, they reminded him that the trustees had granted them exemption from bearing arms. Causton warned them that if they persisted in their attitude they would risk the possibility of being killed and having their houses burned by enraged Englishmen. They realized then that they had better leave Georgia.

When the Spanish menace passed, Causton, admiring their industry and piety and wishing to keep them in the colony, became more conciliatory toward them; but Spangenburg, who had gone to Philadelphia, wrote to the trustees asking permission to move with his people to Pennsylvania. Permission granted, they began to leave in 1737. By 1740 no Moravian remained in Georgia. Egmont, who had been most kind to them, summed up their sojourn in Georgia as follows: "It were to be wished they had ever gone, for though they be a very religious and painstaking people, yet that principle of not fighting is a very bad one in a new erected colony."[38]

Faring better than the Moravians were the Jews who, however, migrated to Georgia without Oglethorpe's blessings. The Inquisition in Portugal drove many of her Jews to England, where the Seraphic Congregation in London, which consisted of many men of wealth and influence, did all they could to help them. Three members of this congregation—Francis Salvador, a director of the Dutch East India Company, Anthony da Costa, the first Jewish director of the Bank of England, and

Alvaro López Suasso, known as Baron Suasso—secured a commission from the trustees "to take subscription and collect money for the Purposes of the Charter." Soon the trustees learned that these wealthy Jews planned to use the money they collected to send some of their people to Georgia. Fearing that the presence of Jews in Georgia would prejudice the entire colony in the eyes of the English government in particular and Englishmen in general, they requested the commissioners in January, 1733, to return the collected money. The commissioners refused. They had already sent forty-three of their people to Georgia. Oglethorpe, displeased with their presence in the colony, consulted lawyers in Charles Town to ascertain whether he could send them back to England. When he learned that he could not, he gave them lots in Savannah.[39]

That summer, during his absence in Charles Town, some colonists bought rum at the trading post of John and Mary Musgrove at Purrysburg, South Carolina. At about the same time, these settlers became desperately ill with "burning fevers or else bloody Fluxes attended by Convulsions and other terrible Symptoms." One of the sick men was a carpenter named Milledge, who on his deathbed told Oglethorpe that he had become ill on the day after he drank the rum he had bought at the trading post. Oglethorpe was immediately convinced that the rum had caused the illness. In the absence of a doctor, he recruited women with some experience in nursing to tend the sick and dying. They gave their services until they, too, became ill or died. Indian roots and rhubarb and diascordium and laudanum failed to stem the epidemic. At this juncture another group of Jews arrived in Savannah. One of them was Dr. Samuel Nuñez. Though the Jews were unacceptable to the trustees, Dr. Nuñez went immediately to work, refusing pay for his services. He applied on the sick cold baths and gave them cooling drinks and other remedies that restored them to health. "Next to the Blessing of God and the new Regimen," wrote Oglethorpe, "I believe one of the greatest Occasions of the people's Recovery had been, That by my constant watching of them I have restrained the Drinking of Rum."[40] But one of his contemporaries saw with admirable objectivity that the colonists owed their recovery to Dr. Nuñez' medical skill: "They had a good Physician with them and behaved so well as to their morals, peaceableness and charity, that they were a reproach to the Christian Inhabitants."[41]

4

Leaving his brother in Savannah, Charles Wesley, early in March, 1736, accompanied Oglethorpe to the new settlement of Frederica, where he took up his duties as private secretary to the governor and as Secretary of Indian Affairs. Charles owed much to Oglethorpe. The trustees had become displeased with the conduct of Samuel Quincy, resident minister of the colony, and had discharged him. Oglethorpe and other trustees then had searched for a strong, competent minister to preach to both the colonists and the Indians. They were attracted to John Wesley, a Fellow of Lincoln College, Oxford, who, though only in his early thirties, was already famous for his piety.

Approached with this offer, John agreed to become the required evangelist in Georgia and to endure the hardships of frontier life. Charles wanted to accompany his brother to America. To promote peace and happiness between the brothers, Oglethorpe offered the position of private secretary to Charles while the trustees appointed him Secretary of Indian Affairs and minister of Frederica. But a difference of opinion on morals and religious matters had already engendered considerable enmity between Charles and Oglethorpe. Instead of attending to his official duties, Charles spent most of his time among colonists, trying to settle trivial disputes which won him nothing but their enmity. He was totally inexperienced in human nature, intolerant with anybody who disagreed with him, and so obsessed with what he considered worldliness that he froze with indignation or blushed with anger when in his opinion anybody deviated from what he called "the straight and narrow." Needless to say, what others considered Oglethorpe's tolerance and liberalism filled Charles with disgust. Oglethorpe, on his side, was impatient with his secretary's tactlessness, though he recognized him as a young man of unyielding Christian faith. He tried to keep him out of trouble by giving him as many chores as he could find. One day Charles complained in his journal that he was dead-tired from writing letters for Oglethorpe and that he would not spend "six days in the same manner for all Georgia."[42]

Soon he had more legitimate reasons for complaining. One Sunday, while he was in the middle of a sermon, a bullet whizzed by him and lodged in the wall of the church. He felt sure that the bullet had been aimed at him. Because Oglethorpe had forbidden shooting on Sundays, the constable ran out of the church, found that the man who had fired the bullet was Dr. John Hawkins, physician of the colony, and jailed him.

Behind this ugly incident were two married women—Dr. Hawkins' wife and her friendly enemy, Mrs. Welch—both of whom were in love with Oglethorpe. They believed that the Wesleys—John in Savannah and Charles in Frederica—were responsible for Oglethorpe's puritanism, which prevented them from converting Georgia from a haven for the unfortunate to a garden for sensuous pleasures. They determined to drive the Wesleys from the colony by putting them at odds with their leader. Mrs. Hawkins in particular hated Charles. During the voyage to Georgia, John had converted Mrs. Hawkins to Christian living; but his brother sensed her hypocrisy and quarreled with him for persistently believing that her repentance was genuine and for permitting her, therefore, to receive Holy Communion. Mrs. Hawkins, being a clever and strong-willed woman, easily made Mrs. Welch her tool, though each was extremely jealous of the other. "Let us supplant these parsons," said Mrs. Hawkins to Mrs. Welch, "and we shall have Mr. Oglethorpe to ourselves."[43]

Her plan was quite simple. At her request, Mrs. Welch—whom Charles described as "a blockhead"—went to him and confessed that she as well as Mrs. Hawkins had committed adultery with Oglethrope. Charles believed her, rationalizing that the women's relations with Oglethorpe accounted for the kindness he had shown them during the voyage. Then the two women went to Oglethorpe and informed him that Charles was slandering them and charging them with adultery.[44]

Oglethorpe, too, believed them and was very angry with his secretary. Mrs. Hawkins, moreover, went to her husband, begging him to defend her honor—which he did by firing that bullet at Charles in church. Then she blamed her husband's imprisonment on Charles and insulted and threatened him every time she saw him. He recorded her bitterness and scurrility in his journal:

> She said she would blow me up, and my brother, whom she says is the cause of her husband's confinement; but she would be revenged, and expose my d——d hypocrisy, my prayers four times a day by beat of drum, and abundance more, which I cannot write, and thought no woman from Drury Lane could have spoken.[45]

Charles was so distraught over her attitude toward him that he came down with a mysterious fever. Yet he continued his duties. Oglethorpe summoned him and charged him "with stirring up people to leave the colony." When Charles vehemently denied the charge, Oglethorpe, wishing to hush up the scandal, "spoke of reconciliating matters." Reluctantly, he again summoned Charles.

"Pray, sir, sit down," he said. "I have something to say to you. I hear you have spread several reports about me and Mrs. Hawkins. In this you are the author of them. There is a great difference in telling such things to another and to me. In you who told it to your brother, 'tis scandal; in him who repeated it to me, 'tis friendship. My religion does not, like the Pharisees', consist in long prayers, but in forgiving injuries, as I do this of yours, but that the thing is in itself a trifle and hardly deserves a serious matter; though I gave one to your brother because he believed the report true. 'Tis not such things as these which hurt my character. They would pass for gallantries and rather recommend me to the world."[46]

Again Charles denied that he had spread the reports. To prove his innocence he summoned Mrs. Welch who, trembling from fear of being severely punished, confessed that, being in love with Oglethorpe, she had invented falsehoods to gain John Wesley's support "to throw out Mrs. Hawkins, and so make room for" herself. With this confession Oglethorpe's animosity toward his secretary faded like a black cloud before the sun. Charles wrote that Oglethorpe "seemed entirely changed, full of his old love and confidence in me."[47]

"Are you satisfied?" asked Charles.

"Yes, entirely," replied Oglethorpe.

"Why then sir," said Charles, "I desire nothing more upon earth."

And from that moment Charles gradually regained his health. Oglethorpe thought best, however, to exchange Charles for John. But Charles was unhappy in his official duties; he wanted to devote himself entirely to religious matters; he confessed he had had enough of "drawing up bonds and affidavits, licenses and instructions for the traders" by day and writing letters for Oglethorpe from nightfall until one in the morning. So, on July 25, 1736, he sent in his resignation which Oglethorpe accepted with a show of reluctance.[48] In the following February, Benjamin Ingraham followed Charles back to England, leaving only John Wesley and Charles Delamotte "to labor in the Lord's vineyard in Georgia."

Meanwhile, John Wesley was having social troubles of his own. Since his arrival in Georgia, he had seen much of Sophia Hopkey, Mrs. Thomas Causton's niece, a girl of eighteen who in beauty and intellectual charm recalled the famed Héloïse. John gave Miss Sophy, as he called her, French lessons while he converted and united her to his church. He eventually fell in love with her; but his good friend, Charles Delamotte, excited his apprehension by doubting the sincerity of Sophy's religious conversion. Yet Wesley greatly desired her company. Once, when he was obliged to go from the village of Irene to Savannah for an hour, he wrote that he

. . . groaned under the weight of an unholy desire. My heart was with Miss Sophy all the time. I longed to see her, were it but for a moment. And when I was called to take boat, it was as the sentence of death; but believing it was the call of God, I obeyed. I walked awhile to and fro on the edge of the water, heavy laden and pierced through with many sorrows. There One came to me and said, "You are still in doubt what is best to be done. First, then, cry to God, that you may be wholly resigned, whatever shall appear to be His Will." I instantly cried to God for resignation. And I found that and peace together. I said, "Sure, it is a dream." I was in a new world. The change was as from death to life. I went back to Irene wondering and rejoicing; but withal exceeding fearful, lest my want of thankfulness for this blessing, or of care to improve it, might occasion its being taken away.[49]

He concluded that marriage would probably obstruct his plans to convert the Indians. Furthermore, he rationalized, "he could not be strong enough to bear the complicated temptations of a married state."[50]

A few days later, he saw Sophy in his garden.

"I am resolved, Miss Sophy, if I marry at all, not to do it until I have been among the Indians."

Naturally piqued, mortified, and furious, she replied:

"People wonder what I can do so long at your house; I am resolved not to breakfast with you any more. And I won't come to you any more alone."[51]

Again Delamotte cautioned him against marrying Sophy, saying as he shed many tears that he could not in that event live in the same house with him.

"I have no intention of marrying her," said Wesley.

But Delamotte was skeptical. He told Wesley that he ought to make up his mind one way or another, for he was "losing ground daily." Next day they appealed for an answer "to the Searcher of hearts." Accordingly, they resorted to drawing lots. On one they wrote "Marry," and on another, "Think not of it this year," but after they had prayed to God to give them a "perfect answer," Delamotte drew a third lot on which was written, "Think of it no more." Instead of the agony he expected, Wesley said cheerfully, "Thy will be done." They cast lots again to ascertain whether Wesley ought to converse with Sophy any more. God told him: "Only in presence of Mr. Delamotte."[52]

Four days later he learned that Sophy was keeping company with William Williamson. This was his first knowledge of her interest in Williamson. Greatly shocked, he called on Mrs. Causton who intercepted him by blandly asking him to publish the banns of marriage between her niece and Williamson. He sickened at the thought that she would marry somebody who, he felt, would make her unhappy; yet he confided in his journal that he could not bring himself to save her by marrying her himself. He soliloquized: "Either she is engaged or [she is] not; if she is, I would not have her if I might; if not, there is nothing in this show which ought to alter my preceding resolution." Then he thought: "She is engaged, but conditionally only. Mr. Williamson shall marry her, if you will not." But he trembled at the thought of losing her and, in so doing, letting her lose her soul also: "I should have incurred any loss rather than she should have run that hazard, of losing her body and soul in hell."[53]

He wrote a note in which he asked her to see him in the garden. When she arrived, he asked her:

"Are you fully determined?"

"I am."

"Take care you act upon a right motive. The desire of avoiding crosses is not so. Besides, you can't avoid them. They will follow and overtake you in every state."

Seeing Williamson coming up, Wesley advised them to have the banns published, exhorted them to love and serve God, and told them that they might always depend on his friendship and assistance. Then he went home, feeling "easy and satisfied."[54]

On Sunday, March 12, 1737, Sophy and Williamson were married in Purrysburg, South Carolina, by one of the ministers of that colony. A month later Wesley, having learned that one of the ministers in South Carolina—perhaps the same one who had married Sophy and Williamson—had been marrying some of his parishioners without either banns or licenses, went to Charles Town by sloop to stop this proceeding. There he saw Reverend Alexander Green, bishop of London's Commissary, who assured him he would "take care no such irregularity should be committed for the future." But Wesley never forgave Sophy for marrying Williamson. On July 13, immediately after Holy Communion, he said to her:

"Mrs. Williamson, have you any reason to believe that from the day I first saw you till this hour, I have dissembled with you?"

"Indeed, I can't believe you have. But you seem to think I have dissembled with you."

He agreed that he thought so and began to explain. But the more he spoke, the angrier she became until, in a few minutes, she turned and abruptly went away. On Sunday, August 7, he "repelled" Sophy from Holy Communion. Forseeing the consequences of his action, he remembered the promise of the Epistle for the day: "God is faithful, who will not suffer you to be tempted above that ye are able; but will with the temptation also make a way of escape, that ye may be able to bear it."[55]

All Savannah was stunned by Wesley's action. Next day William Williamson in great anger went to one of the magistrates and requested him to issue a warrant for Wesley's arrest. The magistrate forthwith issued this order to his constables:

YOU, and each of you, are hereby required to take the body of John Wesley, Clerk:

And bring him before one of the bailiffs of the said town, to answer the complaint of William Williamson and Sophia his wife, for defaming the said Sophia, and refusing to administer to her the Sacrament of the Lord's Supper, in a public congregation, without cause; by which the Said William Williamson, is damaged one thousand pounds sterling; And for so doing, this is your warrant, certifying what you are to do in the premisses. Given under my hand and seal the 8th day of August, *Anno Dom.* 1737.[56]

One of the constables, Noble Jones, served the warrant. Brought before two magistrates, Wesley was charged with defaming Williamson's wife by causelessly denying her Holy Communion. Wesley denied the first charge. The second, he said, was purely an ecclesiastical matter in which the magistrates had no right to interrogate him. One of the magistrates then informed him that he must appear at the next court.[57]

Causton wrote to Wesley, insisting that he give reasons for denying his niece Holy Communion. Whereupon Wesley wrote to Sophy, reminding her that those who intended to take communion were required to notify him the day before. She had failed to do so. By his regulation, anybody who had wronged his neighbor could have an opportunity to declare his repentence to the congregation before he partook of Holy Communion. He would be happy to administer the sacrament to Sophy, he said, as soon as she declared her repentance for the wrong she had done. But he declared contradictorily that he had nothing against her save her failure to notify him of her intention to take Holy Communion.[58]

News of the affair soon reached London, where letters, affidavits, and grand jury presentations on several points against Wesley poured in the offices of the trustees, some of whom found some justification in his procedure. The accusations were sent to him for his reply. The Earl of Egmont, president of the trustees and a large landowner in Georgia, summoned up the affair in a few words that have the ring of truth:

> It appears to me that he was in love with Mrs. Williamson before she married, and has acted indiscreetly with respect to her, and perhaps with respect to others, which is a great misfortune to us, for nothing is more difficult than to find a minister to go to Georgia who has any virtue and reputation.[59]

Though the grand jury found ten counts against Wesley, he was never brought to trial; it was always postponed, perhaps at Causton's instigation. At last, Wesley prepared to return to England. Because his case was pending, the magistrates ordered him to remain in Georgia; but nothing was done to apprehend him when, on the night of December 2, he left the colony and went to Charles Town, where he later took ship for England. He arrived at Deal on February 1, 1738, the anniversary of Oglethorpe's landing in Georgia. On that day, he summarized his experiences in the colony:

> It is now two years and almost four months since I left my native country, in order to teach the Georgian Indians the nature of Christianity. But what have I learned myself in the meantime? Why, what I the least of all suspected, that I, who went to America to convert others, was never myself converted to God.[60]

In writing these words, did he realize he was closer to his inspiring work in Aldersgate Street than when he left for America?

5

In February, 1736, Oglethorpe journeyed southward to St. Simon Island where, on a bluff facing its western shore, he laid out the town of Frederica. It was named in honor of Frederick, Prince of Wales, who died before he could become king, and who claims human remembrance only because he was the father of George III and because Alexander Pope once presented him with a dog bearing this legend on its collar:

> I am his Highness' dog, at Kew,
> Good reader, pray, whose dog are you?

The forty families that followed Oglethorpe there soon lined the streets with houses, some of brick, some of *tabby*, some of wood. The streets were spacious and were surrounded by a moat with banks that formed the ramparts of the town. A wall of cedar posts ten feet high, forming the stockade and palisade, flanked both sides of the moat. On the corner bastions were pentagonal towers, each of which could hold one hundred men defended by a number of cannon. On the eastern end of Broad Street was the Town Gate, through which inhabitants and strangers came and went.[61]

With Frederica rising to protect the eastern coastal region of North America against the possibility of Spanish attack from Florida, Oglethorpe in March journeyed southward with forty Indians under Tomochichi and thirty Highlanders under Captain Hugh Mackay to ascertain where "his Majesty's Dominion and the Spaniard's joyn." On Cumberland Island he selected a site for Fort St. Andrews and left Mackay and his men to build it. Resuming his journey with the Indians, he passed the mouth of the St. Marys and arrived at the island of San Juan, near the mouth of the St. Johns, which Tomochichi described as the threshold of the Spanish possessions. The Indians were so excited that Oglethorpe had difficulty restraining them in their desire to avenge an old grievance against their tribe. Returning to St. Andrews, Oglethorpe found that Captain Mackay was making rapid progress with the fort. The soft sandy soil forced that officer to build the parapets as had Caesar in his Gallic wars: he alternated cut trees with earth. The trees held the earth in place while the earth prevented them from burning. With these posts Oglethorpe was doing his best to provoke a war with the Spaniards or to entrench himself so strongly that they would not dare to attack him.[62]

That autumn Oglethorpe returned to England to secure the men, equipment, ammunition, and supplies to garrison the forts he had built and to employ them in a possible campaign against Florida. In this endeavor he was entirely successful. He was made colonel of an infantry regiment and general and commander in chief of the military forces of South Carolina and Georgia. The first detachment of the regiment reached St. Simon Island in June, 1738. Three months later, Oglethorpe, with the rest of the regiment and the wives and children of the soldiers, arrived at St. Simon Island in five transports. The regiment, which had its headquarters at Frederica, was distributed among the many posts Oglethorpe had established.[63]

Spain had never relinquished her claim to the entire eastern seaboard of North America and had long contemplated against the English an expedition aimed at extirpating them from "the New Colony of Georgia ... which they have usurped." But Georgia was really only one of two bones of contention between the two countries. The other bone, which was larger, was trade and supremacy of the sea. For nearly two centuries, Englishmen had smuggled freely in Spanish waters. Then, by the Treaty of Utrecht, England signed with Spain an *asiento* or contract by which she gained a monopoly in the slave trade to the Spanish colonies, together with the right to send annually to them an armed cargo of five hundred tons. English merchants, dissatisfied with the paucity of trade permitted to them by this agreement, smuggled as before.

Spain protested repeatedly but in vain. So she established a rigorous coast guard which naturally seized scores of English ships and which, not unnaturally, roughly handled English traders. English propaganda, which has always been fruitful in promoting wars, exaggerated and distorted the treatment the traders had received. This powder keg needed only a match to set it off. That match appeared as if by magic in the form of Robert Jenkins, skipper of the slave ship *Rebecca*, who caused a sensation in Parliament by displaying his detached and pickled ear which he said a Spanish captain had slashed off seven years before near Florida. Where had Jenkins been all that time? Nobody knows. Thomas Carlyle speculated that Jenkins had been "steadfastly navigating to and fro, steadfastly eating tough junk with a whetting of rum, not thinking too much of past labours, yet always keeping his lost ear in cotton." In any case, he entered the stage of British politics at the right psychological moment. He related to a furious Parliament that the Spanish captain had slashed off his ear and had handed it back with a gross insult to his king: "Carry it to your king and tell his majesty that if he were present I would serve him in the same manner." The ministers, who were conveniently there to hear him, agreed among themselves that England needed no allies to whip Spain: Jenkins' pickled ear alone could do it. Alexander Pope sneered at English timidity in its attempt to avoid offense:

> And own the Spaniard did a waggish thing,
> Who cropped our ears, and sent them to the king.[64]

But Sir Robert Walpole was a man of peace; he wanted for the present to stem the tide of war by diplomacy. War, he thought, might destroy more trade than it could conquer; furthermore, Newcastle was not quite sure that England had a legal claim to Georgia. So England and Spain in January, 1739, signed the Convention of El Pardo by which mutual claims for damages were balanced and liquidated. While Philip V demanded £68,000 as his profits in the monopoly he had granted to England, he agreed to pay to the English merchants an indemnity of £95,000. The two nations agreed to retain their possessions in Florida and Georgia until commissioners could mark their boundaries. This meant that England was to hold undisputed jurisdiction over the region as far south as the St. Marys River.[65]

But the Convention reckoned without the opposition of the Georgia trustees who, fearing that their province would be sacrificed, bombarded Walpole with demands for protection. Otherwise they would oppose the Convention of El Pardo.

> Sr. Robert hearing this, call'd to Col. Baden, and ask'd him whether England had a right to Georgia? yes, reply'd the Col°. Can you prove it, said Sr. Robert, and will you undertake it? the Col° answer'd he would. Then, said Sr. Robert, By G—d the Spaniards shall not have it.[66]

So the commissioners had not the ghost of a chance. While they deliberated, Englishmen cried for war. In June it came. Sealed orders were hustled to Jamaica and to the mainland colonies authorizing privateers to "commit all sorts of hostilities against the Spaniards." The war that ensued got its ludicrous name from Jenkins' pickled ear and his coached story in Parliament. When war was declared, the English mobs went wild. But Walpole, the man of peace, looked on in alarm. "Ah," he exclaimed, "they are ringing the bells today; they will be wringing their hands tomorrow!"[67]

Meanwhile Oglethorpe took steps to enlist the support of the regional tribes, though he had not yet learned that war had broken out between his country and Spain. Knowing that Spain and France had often offered bribes of various kinds to the Indians to turn them against the English, he planned to hold a personal conference with the representatives of the Creeks, Cherokees, Choctaws, Chickasaws and other tribes who were soon to assemble at Coweta, on the west bank of the Chattahoochee River in western Georgia, five hundred miles away by the route he contemplated. Leaving Frederica on July 8, 1739, with twenty-five persons including a group of the regiment stationed at St. Simon Island and a few Indian guides, he journeyed to Savannah and then ascended the Savannah River to Ebenezer by boat. Thence he proceeded with his party on horseback across the trackless wilderness of Georgia. Frequently the horses mired up knee high, forcing their owners to dismount and wade through swamps to scramble them through. Often the men slept on the ground, sometimes in rain under the cover of trees. Mile after mile they looked in vain for the smoke of a wigwam or listened in vain for the lowing of cattle or the bark of a dog. Mile after mile the only sounds indicating life were those of the turkeys, the deer, and the buffalo that the Indian guides killed for their meals. But, as they neared their destination, they saw signs that more than compensated them for their loneliness and misery: "several strings of Cakes and Bags of Flower, etc., which the Indians had hung up in Trees for our Refreshment." And when they camped within two miles of Coweta the Indians "sent Boys and Girls out from their Town with Fowls Venison Pompions Potatoes Water Melons & Sundry other things."[68]

Chief Chigilly, who had invited Oglethorpe to attend the conference, bore the English flag as he escorted him to the public square, where villagers and dogs gave them a noisy welcome. Oglethorpe participated heartily in their games and dances, ate their food, drank their "black drink," and smoked their pipes, while he won their steadfast support by his plain and firm sincerity, by settling difficulties that had risen between the Indians and the traders, and by his emphatic assertion that the king of England desired no land save that transferred to him in their first treaty of 1733. At Cassista, across the river from Coweta, the Creeks pledged Oglethorpe their full support and declared that they would permit no Spaniard to settle north of the San Juan River and Apalache.

On August 25 Oglethorpe set out for Savannah. Three weeks later, when he reached Augusta, he learned that England and Spain were at war. At the same time he became desperately ill with fever, but his indomitable will and stalwart constitution quickly brought him to his feet. When he reached Savannah, he went to see Tomochichi, who was on his deathbed but who was anxious to hear in detail about his mission with the Indians. On October 5 the old warrier died, counseling his people to remain in everlasting friendship with the king of England and his representative Oglethorpe. Georgia had never seen so large a funeral. In the lead walked Oglethorpe, his head bowed in agonizing grief for the loss of his old friend who had passed ninety-seven years of strife and sorrow and joy. At his request he was buried in Savannah among the people he had learned to love so much.[69]

Immediately after the funeral Oglethorpe sent runners to the Indian chiefs, calling for a thousand braves along the southern boundaries of the colony. Officially informing the people of Savannah of war conditions and obtaining their united loyalty, he departed on November 5 for Frederica, where he learned that a small group of Spaniards had invaded Amelia Island during the night and killed from ambush two unarmed Highlanders. This cowardly deed aroused Oglethorpe to stern purpose and action. Finding on Amelia Island no trace of the enemy, he returned to Frederica, gathered about two hundred Highlanders and Rangers from his regiment and some Indians under Hillispilli and Towanahowi, swept with them up the St. Johns River, invaded Florida, burned three Spanish outposts, and returned to Georgia. Then on January 1, 1740, he ascended the St. Johns with a group of soldiers and Creek riflemen to Fort Picolata, which he reduced to ashes. Advancing on Fort St. Francis de Pupa, he forced its garrison to surrender. Because it stood only twenty miles from St. Augustine and could shelter its men in a planned attack on that town, and because its surrounding fields teemed with great herds of cattle and horses, Oglethorpe repaired and strengthened the fort by raising parapets and a palisade and garrisoning it with twenty Highlanders under Mackay. But though he had swept down to the very gates of St. Augustine, he was not strong enough to attempt to attack that town. So he returned to Frederica, whence he journeyed to Charles Town to enlist the support of South Carolina in his plans.[70]

There he and a naval captain, Vincent Pearce, convinced a committee of the assembly that their plan of attacking St. Augustine was feasible. Pearce even declared "That he would answer for it if the Place should have no Relief by Sea, and that they ought to be hanged if they did not take it in very short Time."[71] The assembly responded with magnificent generosity. It appropriated £120,000, raised four hundred well-armed and well-supplied cavalrymen, furnished a schooner to guard Matanzas Inlet, and called for two hundred men over and above those promised.[72]

On May 9 Oglethorpe, with two hundred and twenty men of his own regiment and one hundred and twenty Carolinians under Colonel Alexander Vander Dussen, landed at Fort St. George, just south of the St. Johns, in Spanish territory. Pushing down to within twenty miles of St. Augustine, he captured Fort Diego, named for Diego de Spinosa, owner of the estate on which it stood in present Palm Valley. Leaving it in charge of Lieutenant George Dunbar, he returned to the St. Johns to await the arrival of more troops and to allow Commodore Sir Yelverton Peyton to blockade the harbor of St. Augustine with his fleet which consisted of four vessels of twenty guns each. When his reinforcements arrived, Oglethorpe dashed down the peninsula to the Inlet of St. Augustine and captured Fort Moosa, which was manned by fugitive Negro slaves who evacuated it and scurried back to St. Augustine, two miles away.[73] To the Carolinians all this marching and countermarching in the sand over palmetto roots under terrific heat was so much "squirrel-shooting," which they performed with much cursing and sweating.

Accelerating his military plans, Oglethorpe held with the naval officers a council of war in which they organized a threefold attack. Peyton with his fleet was to block the inlets and assist Captain Peter Warren with two hundred sailors in bombarding St. Augustine from Anastasia Island, while Oglethorpe, leading the land forces, was to attack it from the rear. Oglethorpe was to signal Peyton when the engagement was to start. He gave the signal but received no reply. After he repeated it in vain, he hurried back to headquarters to ascertain what had gone wrong. He learned that Peyton had found the water too shallow to dislodge the Spanish galleys, which were arranged so effectively that they prevented his barges from advancing and from landing troops from Anastasia Island.[74]

Oglethorpe now had no choice but to besiege the town. He crossed to Anastasia Island, where he set up a strong battery and summoned the Spanish governor, Manuel de Montiano, to surrender. Montiano, a brave and efficient officer, replied after a leisurely wait that, by the holy cross, he would devote the last drop of his blood in defense of the fort where, he added with a glint of urbanity, he would be delighted to kiss General Oglethorpe's hand! Indignant at such a reply, Oglethorpe opened fire on the town, driving its inhabitants into open country instead of crowding the fort, as he expected, with helpless humanity.[75]

Montiano, observing that Oglethorpe at intervals relaxed his attack, sent out a detachment of three hundred men and a party of Yamasee Indians to strike at Captain John Palmer at Fort Moosa. Instead of obeying Oglethorpe's orders to change his camp every night, Palmer remained in the fort. The Spaniards surprised, overwhelmed, and butchered him and twenty-two of his Highlanders, who fought like mad demons. Twenty-seven others surrendered. This was a severe blow to Oglethorpe, not so much because he had lost men but because it gave the Indians an excuse to desert him at the first opportunity. This presented itself when, in an indiscreet moment, he called a Cherokee a barbarous dog for presenting him with the head of a Spaniard slain in battle. Soon after the Indians were gone.[76]

Meanwhile Oglethorpe continued to bombard the town, but he learned to his chagrin that even his nearest battery was too far away to damage its walls. The Carolinians, wilting under the intense heat and complaining of the sandflies and mosquitos, began to desert him in squads. Peyton, fearful of hurricanes and finding his provisions dwindling, was unwilling to remain longer with his fleet. Then on July 3 the English schooner that had been guarding Mantanzas Inlet withdrew, permitting the Spanish defenders to welcome seven hundred additional fighting men and a large supply of provisions from Havana. To Oglethorpe, this was the last blow. He reluctantly called off his men, though with indomitable and patriotic pride he marched them away with colors flying and drums beating. He arrived in Frederica on July 10. His men quickly returned to their homes.[77]

The campaign aroused considerable criticism, both favorable and unfavorable, in England as well as in America. It dealt a terrific blow to Oglethorpe's military pride and to his optimism and vanity. People who had praised him for his courage now damned him for his foolhardiness. Oglethorpe was justifiably embittered by the paucity of aid he had received from England and from South Carolina. He particularly blamed South Carolina for his failure. In a letter to the Duke of Montagu, he affirmed that South Carolina had more than forty thousand Negroes but less than four thousand white men capable of bearing arms, and even these were mere militia. "If they remove us," he wrote, "all that country is at their pleasure; yet there is a kind of stupid security that makes them not believe they are in danger, and not thank those who would prepare against it."[78]

The Carolinians quite naturally resented these insinuations; they urged their assembly to make a full investigation. This eventually cleared their troops and refuted Oglethorpe's contentions. Then the assembly retaliated by hurling a heated charge of incompetency against Oglethorpe. The vehemence by which he attempted to clear himself and the privations and exertions he had sustained during the campaign produced nervous exhaustion with a fever that raged for two months. Then his indomitable spirit reasserted itself and hastened his recovery.[79]

This did not come too soon. Spain was planning a campaign to drive the English out of Georgia and to make good her claim to the region as far north as Port Royal. She hoped to gain by war what she had lost by her diplomatic credulity at El Pardo. In the fall of 1740, Campillo, minister of Philip V of Spain, wrote to Juan Francisco Güemez y Horcasitas, governor of Havana, of his plans to destroy Carolina and Georgia. The king made Montiano leader of the expedition, which left Havana on May 25, 1742, in thirty vessels composed of frigates and bilanders and carrying thirteen hunded men, six hundred of whom were regulars and the rest militia. By June 4 the vessels arrived at St. Augustine, where they were delayed for two weeks by stormy weather and by the necessity of replenishing the water supply. On June 20 the invasion forces sailed for the Georgia coast.[80]

Meanwhile Oglethorpe, learning from Indian spies and from an English sea captain that the Spanish fleet was approaching, made immediate preparations to bolster his defenses and to collect as many men and ships as he could. He wrote to England for assistance, though he knew that this would arrive too late. At the same time he sent an officer to Charles Town to secure the assistance of the English ships stationed there, but Governor Bull told the officer that the arrival of soldiers and ships at St. Augustine was the usual relief sent annually to that garrison and that Georgia had nothing to fear.[81]

On July 5 the lookout at the watchtower on St. Simon saw a long line of ships, thirty-six in number, advancing like an invincible armada toward the island. The alarm gun boomed one for every ship in sight and the approaching Spanish ships answered with brisk firing. The attack began when two Spanish quarter-galleys, carrying nine-pound guns, and a half-galley with two eighteen-pound guns in her bow bore down on the *Success* under Captain Carr who, however, defended himself so bravely that the Spanish commander abandoned his frontal attack.[82]

That afternoon, the Spanish fleet entered the harbor, eluded the batteries of Fort St. Simon, and though badly crippled from the recent fight, gained the extreme southern end of Gascoigne Bluff, below Captain Gascoigne's plantation and above the Pilot House, where it disgorged its forces, a motley crew of regulars, volunteers, and Indians numbering in all about three thousand men. Oglethorpe, leaving his Indians to annoy the Spaniards as they landed and the Rangers to watch their movements and report to him, directed the evacuation of Fort St. Simon, destroyed all his provisions, artillery and most of his vessels, and marched his troops to the defense of Frederica. Three ships, the merchant vessel *Success*, the grand schooner *Walker*, and the prize sloop *St. Philip*, gained the sea in the face of fierce firing from the enemy and escaped to Charles Town, where they demanded assistance in "His Majesty's name."[83]

That evening, the Spaniards lay under arms. Next morning, they marched to the southern end of St. Simon, where they took possession of the abandoned fort, which became Spanish headquarters throughout their stay on the island. Some of the soldiers set fire to the houses, destroying about sixty of them. That same day, Oglethorpe reached Frederica, where he ordered all the women and children evacuated, but few of them agreed to leave for the safety of Darien or Mary Musgrove's trading post at Mount Venture over a hundred miles away. Those who preferred to remain in Frederica and share the dangers of the invasion along with the soldiers were described as "in good heart."[84]

On the morning of July 7 Montiano sent Captain Sebastian Sánchez with one of the companies of the garrison at St. Augustine and a picket of forty men to reconnoiter the road to Gascoigne Bluff while he sent twenty-five men and forty Indians under Captain Nicolas Hernandez to reconnoiter the road to Frederica. Sánchez soon lost his trail and joined Hernandez. As they approached Frederica, they met five Rangers, one of whom they shot in the leg and thigh and then killed. The other Rangers retreated to Oglethorpe in Frederica with word that about two hundred Spaniards were about a mile and a half away. Leaping on the first horse he could find, Oglethorpe put himself at the head of a group of Indians and a company of Highlanders who had been parading, while he ordered four platoons of his Regiment and Rangers and Indians to follow him. Then he galloped away against the Spaniards, who were just entering a treeless meadow to take possession of a ditch which they planned to use as an entrenchment. In the bloody skirmish that ensued, Sánchez was captured and the Spaniards were entirely defeated. Oglethorpe took two prisoners with his own hands while Towanahowi, though wounded in the right arm, drew his pistol with his left hand and shot his attacker through the head. All told, about a hundred Spaniards were killed and sixteen were captured.

Oglethorpe pursued the enemy for about two miles to an advantageous piece of ground where he took his stand to repel any possible attempt against Frederica. When the detachment of his regiment arrived, he posted it on the right of his Highlanders and Rangers on the left of the road to stem the Spaniards should they advance. Then he returned to Frederica to meet a possible invasion from the sea.[85]

Meanwhile Montiano, learning of the defeat of his troops, ordered three hundred grenadiers under Captain Antonio Barba to march to the support of their countrymen. At three o'clock in the afternoon this force reached the place where Oglethorpe had posted his men. In the confusion of battle, while "the air was darkened with the smoak and the shower of rain," the English retreated in disorder. They soon reached a place on the road that formed a crescent with a thick growth of underbrush on one side and a marsh on the other. As they retreated down the road and around the crescent, the rear guard, composed of a platoon of the regiment under Lieutenant Patrick Sutherland, a group of Highlanders under

Lieutenant Charles Mackay, and some Rangers and Indians, laid an ambuscade in the brushwood just a little inside the curve of the crescent. The Spaniards, reaching the crescent, observed by the footprints in the sand that their enemies were in full retreat. Seeing the brushwood on one side of the road and a marsh on the other, they felt they could relax their vigilance. They stopped on the inviting greensward, stacked their guns, and sat down to rest and to make preparations for cooking food.

At a prearranged signal—the raising of a Scotch cap on a stick—a horse, frightened by the gay uniforms of the regulars, gave the alarm by snorting. The panicky Spaniards ran hither and thither to get hold of their arms, but they were too late. The Highlanders poured fire on them from every side. Vainly trying to form, they fled helter-skelter, leaving their accoutrements on the field. So excited were those who secured their arms that they fired over their shoulders as they retreated, pruning the trees instead of hitting the enemy. The battle became known as Bloody Marsh, from the blood that had been spilled on the woodland flowers, among the noble trees, and on the lush greensward.[86]

Oglethorpe marched in the direction of the firing to a causeway over a marsh very near the Spanish camp, where he stopped a retreating detachment that told him that the English had been routed. But soon learning the truth, he marched with contingents down the causeway, hindering the dispersed Spaniards from returning to their camp. Realizing the imprudence of attacking them with his small numbers, he marched his forces back to Frederica, leaving only small parties of Indians and Rangers to harass the enemy. On the afternoon of July 12 Oglethorpe marched with three hundred troops from Frederica to within two miles of the Spanish camp, where a Frenchman who had served with Captain Mark Carr deserted to the Spaniards and told them that Oglethorpe had only a thousand men but that he expected reinforcements from the English colonies. Knowing that the deserter would give the Spaniards valuable information, Oglethorpe worked out a stratagem to discredit him in their eyes. To the deserter he addressed a letter in French as if from a friend, asking him to hold the Spaniards at Fort St. Simon for three days longer, when the English should receive huge reinforcements. He planted the decoy on a prisoner whom he released and sent to Montiano, who called a council of war in which his officers advised him to withdraw as quickly as possible. He took their advice. The Spanish fleet sailed away, leaving Georgia to England.[87]

Word of the Spanish defeat filled the other English colonies with joy. Governor Lewis Morris of New Jersey wrote to express his pleasure at "the great (or rather wonderful) Success God has been pleased to give to His Majesty's arms under your Conduct."[88] Governor William Gooch of Virginia wrote Oglethorpe that the whole continent was eternally grateful to him.[89] George II rewarded him for his services by promoting him to the rank of Brigadier General. Only the governor of South Carolina was silent, though Port Royal, Beaufort, and Charles Town thanked

Oglethorpe for preserving them from the Spaniards.[90] Well did he merit their gratitude. Bloody Marsh was as decisive a defeat for Spain as was the Plains of Abraham for France two decades later and as was Yorktown for England two decades later still. By this victory, Oglethorpe saved the thirteen colonies for England and so preserved the nucleus of the United States for English civilization.

But Oglethorpe's work in Georgia soon came to an end. In 1743 he sailed to England never to return to the frontier utopia he had founded. He had good reasons for abandoning his work. In the past five years multitudinous and perplexing cares had begun to pile up on him. To threatened invasion from Florida had been added the attack of malcontents who had organized themselves against Oglethorpe's policies. In Savannah, one hundred and twenty-one of them, including some of the magistrates, signed and sent to the trustees a petition demanding rum, slaves, and the absolute ownership of property. The trustees, with Oglethorpe's strong approval, denied the petition and dismissed the magistrates who had signed it. So embittered were they by their failure that their leader, Pat. Tailfer, with the corroboration of his comrades wrote a book, *A True and Historical Narrative of the Colony of Georgia in America*, which was published in Charles Town in 1741. It carried a mock dedication to Oglethorpe, whom they called "our Perpetual Dictator" and under whom, they declared, they had "seen something like *Aristocracy, Oligarchy*, as well as the *Triumvirate, Decemvirate* and *Consular Authority* of famous Republicans, which have expired many Ages before us."[91]

They soon sent Thomas Stephens, son of the secretary of Georgia, to appeal their cause directly to Parliament which, however, upheld the trustees and forced Stephen to fall on his knees and receive a reprimand. But the malcontents continued to complain so vehemently that at last their wishes were granted. In 1742 the trustees, observing that rum had long been bootlegged into the colony and that it was sold openly in the grogshops of Savannah, permitted it to be imported, though it could be purchased only with an exchange of products raised in Georgia.[92]

Slavery was prohibited for six years longer. Then it too was admitted with prescribed conditions. The law maintained a semblance of the indenture system by requiring one white male servant for every four slaves a planter owned. The planter had limited power of his slaves. He had to register them in the colonial records, teach them religion and the obligations of marriage, use them only for agricultural purposes, prohibit profanity among them, and teach one female in every four slaves how to wind silk. The malcontents also forced the trustees to introduce land reforms which abolished *tale male*, permitted women to inherit land, and limited the size of property.[93] These reforms spelled the doom of Oglethorpe's utopian colony.

The founder of Georgia lived many years after his return to England. He enjoyed his pleasant estate, his English beer, and his literary friends, including Dr. Johnson, Boswell, and Oliver Goldsmith. He maintained the liveliest interest in significant historical events, especially those pertaining to that region of North America in which he had spent his most productive years.

In 1752 the trustees gave up their charter to the king, who converted Georgia into a royal colony. Four years later the Seven Years' War broke out with Russia, Austria, and Poland on the side of France and Prussia on the side of England. In the last months of the war, Spain entered the struggle on the side of France, but she was too late to save her sinking ally. By the definitive treaty, signed on February 10, 1763, France gave up to England all of her possessions in India save two small colonies, all of Canada save two fishing posts in the Gulf of St. Lawrence, and all of the territory east of the Mississippi save the Island of Orleans. Spain, during the war, had lost Cuba and the Philippines. But England, in the peace treaty, returned the Philippines to Spain and exchanged Cuba for Florida. France compensated Spain for her losses by ceding Louisiana west of the Mississippi and the Island of Orleans. Of all the vast territory that England acquired, none was more gratifying to Oglethorpe than Florida, which England subsequently divided into two provinces, East Florida and West Florida. At last, after waiting for twenty-three years, his country had vindicated his defeat before the gates of St. Augustine.

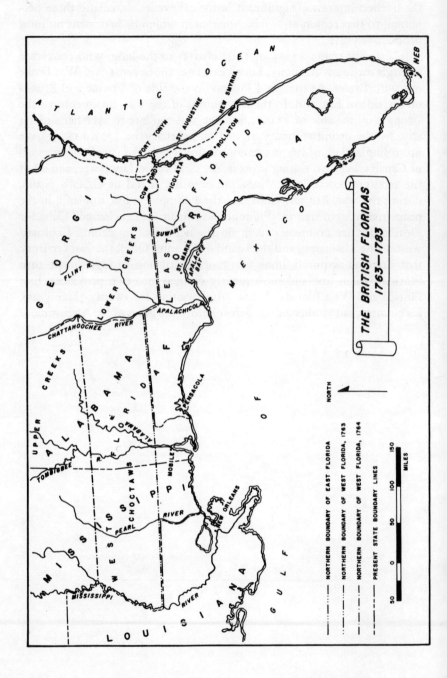

THE BRITISH FLORIDAS
1763—1783

NORTH

NORTHERN BOUNDARY OF EAST FLORIDA
NORTHERN BOUNDARY OF WEST FLORIDA, 1763
NORTHERN BOUNDARY OF WEST FLORIDA, 1764
PRESENT STATE BOUNDARY LINES

MILES
50   0   50   100   150

The British Floridas

LORD EGREMONT, SECRETARY OF STATE, KNEW NOTHING ABOUT THE TERRI-
tory his country had acquired from Spain. He requested information
from the Board of Trade, but it could offer him very little. So he induced
a number of writers to make reports that should describe East Florida
and West Florida as a fertile but neglected region. Basically, these reports
were similar in that they showed each province dominated by a single
sizable settlement: East Florida by St. Augustine and West Florida by
Pensacola. To Great Britain, the importance of the Floridas lay in their
geographical location and their strategic position. St. Augustine and
Pensacola with a few other small places "were excellent vantage points
of trade with the Spanish colonies in time of peace and attacks on this
trade in time of war."[1] Florida, too, commanded the entrance of the
Bahama Channel through which flowed European commerce with the
Spanish colonies adjacent to the Caribbean Sea.[2]

Among several early British descriptions of the Floridas were those of
William Roberts and John Gerard William DeBrahm, a Dutchman who,
as Surveyor General of the Southern District of North America for
George III, received the munificent salary of £150. The purpose of each
report was to encourage English settlement of Florida which the great
majority of its Spanish inhabitants had deserted for Havana. Roberts'
book is largely a pedestrian and inaccurate account of early Florida but it
includes valuable maps by Thomas Jeffreys, "Geographer of His Majesty." Roberts described the soil of Florida as "remarkably rich and fruitful, frequently producing two or three crops of *Indian* corn in the year,
and might, with proper cultivation, be made to bear every sort of grain."
He praised Florida for its excellent limes and plums, though he warned
all comers that it teemed with snakes and alligators.[3]

DeBrahm wrote a fuller and therefore a more valuable account which
covered the three provinces of South Carolina, Georgia, and Florida.
The sections dealing with South Carolina and Georgia have been pub-

lished; the remaining section is still in manuscript. DeBrahm included
bounties on crops, grants of land, and subsidies among the inducements
which the English government offered to settlers of Florida. He praised
the salubrious climate, pointing out that it had blessed with longevity
many of the three thousand former inhabitants of St. Augustine. Yet he
saw fit to advise "new settlers" that they could preserve their health by
taking the following precautions:

> [They] must by all means avoid wetting their Bodies, or even only
> their Feet in rain, and more so in Dew; but *if* by Chance or Necessity
> it will so happen, they who thus become Sufferers, are to increase their
> Motion, until they reach their Habitation, then take a good, and re-
> peated Draught of warm Tea, warm, but weak Coffee; warm Water
> & Rum or Wine; warm Water mixed with sweetened Juice of Limes,
> Lemons or Oranges; but in case none of these Promises are to be had
> conveniently, then warm calibiated Water, uncloath themselves, enter
> their Beds, and provoke, under sufficient Coverts a moderate Perspira-
> tion for the Space of thirty minutes, then dress themselves dry, and
> take a gentle Exercise.[4]

He also advised them to abstain

> ... in hot Seasons from boiled Meat and Fish, from all manner of warm
> Broth, or Liquids, and to eat no warm Victuals, but such as are roasted,
> and drink none but moderately cold Draughts in common Diet, altho'
> in cold Weather both boiled Victuals or warm Liquids may be used;
> and when a Regimen of Perspiration requires them to be warm; ... No
> Draughts should be pure water, but mixed with a little good Rum; if
> good Rum is not at hand, the Water must be corrected by calibiating
> it with quenching in it a red hot Iron.[5]

DeBrahm described the soil, vegetation, crops, and rivers, and included
turpentine, pitch, and lumber among the manufactures. He stated that
he had seen no olives in Florida but that its China oranges, Seville oranges,
lemons, and citron were better than those of Europe and even of those
in other English colonies in America. He was particularly delighted with
the oysters, which were so plentiful that they formed "rocks of one hundred and more Fathoms in Length." He described them as "three times
as long as they are broad; when in Season they are very fat, and of so
agreeable a Tastiness, that they, who have been long in America cannot
relish English oysters on account of their strong copperish Taste."[6] He
admitted that Florida was plagued with mosquitoes but advised that these
could be eluded by covering beds with nets. He warned the settlers to
give Indians no rum but to temper their savagery with small gifts of rice
and salt.[7]

2

Since Florida under Great Britain consisted of two provinces we must, for the sake of clarity, consider them separately. In May, 1763, Major Francis Ogilvie arrived at St. Augustine to accept the transfer of East Florida from the outgoing Spanish governor. A choleric gentleman who disdained Spaniards and liked to boast of his Protestantism, Ogilvie quickly incurred the hatred and fear of the Catholic population which moved en masse to Havana. Out of possibly three thousand persons, only five consented to remain in the province. The Spanish governor, as he departed, destroyed his garden with its beautiful flowers and its rare plants and trees.[8]

Conditions greatly improved with the arrival of Governor James Grant in August of the following year. A typical Highlander, he was proud of his birth, devoted to his men, and enamored of money. He had fought at Culloden Moor in 1746 and served in Ireland before coming to America with General Jeffrey Amherst during the French and Indian War. In 1758 he served with Colonel Henry Bouquet in General John Forbes' expedition against Fort Duquesne. He was captured in battle, gained his release in an exchange of prisoners, served as a lieutenant-colonel of infantry under Colonel Archibald Montgomery in the Carolinas, defeated the Cherokee allies of the French, spent time in Martinique, and, in the last months of the war, commanded the forces that captured Havana. Retiring to Scotland with the reputation of a hero, he was rewarded with the governorship of East Florida in November, 1763, though he did not begin actual administration until August of the following year.[9]

He tempered despotic justice with witty conversation and many gay dinners which won him the lukewarm approval of his people. He described St. Augustine to a friend as "the gayest Place in America nothing but Balls, Assemblies and Concerts, we are too inconsiderable to enter into Politicks & Faction, and as People have little to do the Novelty has catched, and they are all at present Season Musick and dansing Mad. . . ."[10] Despite these distractions he found time to build military posts, to plan schools and churches, to grant a bounty on indigo to increase its output, and to run a road from St. Augustine to New Smyrna and thence to Jacksonville and the St. Marys River. At Picolata in 1765 he and Colonel John Stuart, Superintendent of Indian Affairs for the Southern District, held with the Seminoles a conference in which they guaranteed them a hunting ground that ran down the center of the province from the "Ochkanphanoko" Swamp to the "Oklyahaw" River.[11]

The most interesting event of Grant's administration was the establishment of New Smyrna with non-English immigrants. The founder of this colony was Dr. Andrew Turnbull, a Scotch physician who had served as

British consul at Smyrna in Asia Minor, where he married Gracia Dura Bin, daughter of a Greek merchant. Relinquishing his medical practice, he returned to England, where he planned to establish a colony of Greeks in Florida, whose climate was similar to that of their own country. The Greeks, moreover, had grown "restive under the galling yoke of Turkey." He formed a partnership with Sir William Duncan and Lord Grenville and petitioned the king for a sizable tract of land. The king granted each of them twenty thousand acres.[12]

In November, 1766, Turnbull arrived with his family at St. Augustine and immediately went to see his fellow Scotchman, Governor Grant, who entertained him lavishly. Establishing his family in a typically Spanish house with balconies overhanging the narrow streets and a lovely garden behind high stone walls, he sailed down the coast to Mosquito Inlet, seventy-five miles away, which DeBrahm had recommended to him as the most valuable timber country in the province. He was so impressed with its fertility that he purchased a large cotton plantation there and placed it in charge of an overseer with orders to buy cattle and horses from Georgia and South Carolina. Returning to St. Augustine, he spent a few days with his family, then sailed to England where he requested the Board of Trade to give him a sloop to transport the emigrants he sought. The Board of Trade not only granted his request but gave him £4500 as a bounty on future East Florida products. Early in the spring of 1767 he loaded his sloop and two smaller vessels with tools, seeds, and farming implements and voyaged with them to the Mediterranean.[13]

On his way to Greece he stopped at Leghorn, in northwestern Italy, where, he had heard, many farmers were eager to join his project. The governor of Leghorn allowed some unemployed farm hands and strangers to sign contracts with Turnbull but strictly prohibited Genoese silk manufacturers. One hundred ten Italians joined Turnbull, agreeing to enter his employ for seven or eight years in return for fifty acres and five additional acres for each child in a family. They were free to return home within six months should they become dissatisfied.[14]

Turnbull proceeded to Greece, but there he met great obstacles in the realization of his plans. The Levant Company, which was very active in nearly all the Greek ports, regarded him as a keen competitor and complained to the Turkish authorities that he intended to move to America citizens needed in Turkey. In every harbor he found Turkish soldiers on hand to prevent him from achieving his purpose. For weeks he journeyed with little success hither and thither among the islands in the Aegean Sea. Eventually he arrived at Mani, whose inhabitants lived in about two hundred villages perched like eagle nests on the cliff of a rocky peninsula. Under their leader, Ananias Lambardes, Bishop of Lacedaemon, they had continued their defiance of Turkish authorities who had retaliated by putting him in chains and then beheading him at Mystra on the outskirts of Mani. As they grieved the loss of their leader, they heard that Turnbull had anchored at Coron and that he sought to transport people to the New World, where they would be free from oppression and tyranny. Many sought him in the port and agreed to follow him. There the Turkish commander, in return for a bribe of 1200 piastres, agreed to look the other way while men, women, and children boarded Turnbull's ships with the blessings of Orthodox priests.[15]

From Coron Turnbull sailed perhaps to Crete, then to the volcanic island of Santorin, then to Smyrna, picking up a few persons in each place. In Smyrna he learned that the crops in Minorca had failed for three consecutive years and that most of its farmers were on the verge of starvation. To that island Turnbull quickly sailed. He encountered no difficulty in realizing his aim, for Minorca had been an English possession since 1713. The Minorcans, dissatisfied with English policy of restricting the correspondence and activities of Catholic priests despite its promise of allowing them freedom of worship, crowded the decks, welcomed Turnbull with shouts of joy, and begged him to take them to Florida. They were so near starvation that the bishop had released them from the ecclesiastical law of fast and abstinence. To facilitate his plans, Turnbull persuaded some of the Italians to marry Minorcan girls. When at last he was ready to sail for Florida, he had over fourteen hundred immigrants, three times more than he had originally sought. He had to hire five more ships to accommodate them.[16]

By midsummer 1768 they had all arrived in St. Augustine. Turnbull immediately sent them to his new colony, which he named New Smyrna in honor of his wife's birthplace and which William Bartram, the botanist, located on the west bank of the south branch of the Mosquito River and about thirty miles north of Cape Canaveral.[17] The immigrants were lodged in huts built by Governor Grant in expectation of their arrival. Uniformed in heavy durable material, they were put to heavy labor clearing fields and learning how to raise hemp, cotton, and indigo—articles on which England had placed a bounty.[18]

They derived small compensation for their backbreaking labors. Their English overseers, who had been used to Negro workers, understood neither Spanish nor Italian nor Greek; they made themselves disliked by their arbitrary manners and impatience at what they considered the stupidity and laziness of some of their charges. The colonists, on their part, dreamed, like those who came before and after them, of a life of ease and plenty. Instead of a smiling land, they found a dreary wilderness; instead of fertile soil, they found barren, arid sand; instead of working in such vineyards as they had known in Greece or Italy, they found themselves indentured to men who appeared to them no more humane than the bashaws or the arrogant overseers for whom they had slaved in their native countries.[19]

By August they could stand no more. One morning, Carlo Forni led twenty of his fellow Italians to the town square and began a ranting speech on their trials and tribulations. The other colonists threw down their shovels and picks and gathered around him. Declaring himself commander-in-chief of the Italians and Greeks, he expressed his intention of leading them to Havana where the Spanish authorities would be happy to protect them from the English and where they would be forever free of stultifying and crippling work. The colonists grew more and more excited as Forni rambled on. Clotha Corona, one of the Greeks, broke the door of the store nearby and, with the help of a few of his countrymen, rolled out into the road casks of wine, broke them, and quaffed their contents.[20]

At this juncture Cutler, a brutal overseer, came up, interrupted Forni's speech, and ordered him and his followers to disperse. One of Forni's men replied by seizing Cutler, cropping off his ears and two of his fingers, and locking him up in one of the closets of the store, while Italians and Greeks, numbering three hundred, howled in triumph. Observing that the Minorcans took no part in the uprising, they ordered them to submit to their demands. The Minorcans refused. Whereupon the malcontents plundered the dwellings of the Minorcans and threw their belongings out on the road. Then a richer prize commanded their attention. They seized a ship of provisions that lay in the harbor and began to load her in preparation for their voyage to Havana. They carried clothes, blankets, linen, and fishing tackle down to the shore by the armfuls and, unable to haul casks of rum and oil, staved them in on the road.

Forni threatened with death anybody who dared escape and warn the authorities. Nevertheless, two Italians who were loyal to Turnbull slipped away into the swamp at nightfall and made their way to his plantation four miles away. They found an overseer who hurried with their frantic tale to Turnbull. Thanking God that his wife and children were safe in St. Augustine, where they awaited the completion of their new home, Turnbull wrote to Governor Grant asking for immediate help and sent the letter off by express rider. Then he went with a small group of men to New Smyrna, rescued his wounded overseer, and brought him back to his plantation for medical treatment. While he waited word or action from Grant, he learned that the mutineers, after spending a day feasting and drinking on board the ship they had seized, were preparing to sail for Havana. Riding to the shore, Turnbull saw the ship hoist her sails and move down the inlet to await the eleven o'clock tide. As he wheeled his horse and rode slowly along the bank, he heard the boom of a cannon. With renewed hope he dashed back to the inlet, where he saw two vessels bearing down on the escaping ship on the very tide that was to carry her to Cuba. He knew that Grant had received his letter and had sent the ships posthaste to his rescue. The deck of the rebel ship soon swarmed with terrified men waving white flags. But before the relief ships could reach the rebel ship, thirty-five men under Forni got into an open boat and rowed frantically toward the wooded shore. The other mutineers surrendered. Soon the captain came ashore with the prisoners, whom Turnbull took into custody.[21]

The captain sent against Forni and his comrades one of his ships which chased them four months before she overtook them on the Florida Keys. During all this time, Forni and his men had traveled in their open boat through the fall season of hurricanes, afraid to stay too long on land from fear of Indians and wild beasts and too long on water from fear of storms and their pursuers. They were taken to St. Augustine and tried for their crimes, but their wretched appearance moved the jurors to pity. In a letter to the Earl of Hillsborough, secretary of the colonies, Grant opined that the mutineers had suffered enough by their experiences and that two or three of the most flagrant offenders among them should bear punishment for the rest. Three were finally convicted of piracy. One of these was pardoned on the cruel condition that he serve as hangman to the other two. The doomed men were Carlo Forni, self-appointed leader of the uprising, and Clotha Corona, charged with murdering Cutler, who had died of his wounds. On Hillsborough's recommendation, Grant pardoned three other Greeks who had committed less violent crimes. His leniency proved wise. The mutineers returned quietly to their work and never again disturbed the orderly progress of the colony.[22]

In ensuing years New Smyrna grew into a plantation that extended for four miles along the river banks. The colonists, whose palmetto dwellings stood picturesquely amid their properties, raised ample quantities of maize, sugar, cotton, and rice which they shipped from their great *coquina* wharves. They burned seaweed to make *barilla*; they planted mulberries to raise silkworms; they raised five thousand bushels of corn; they boiled indigo in huge vats that they dug in the fields. Thanks to their diligence, Turnbull imported even the cochineal insects which clung in white webs to the cactus plants in the woods around the colony and which were used to make scarlet dyes.[23]

3

In 1767 another colony, Rollston or Rollstown, was established on a lonely curve of the St. Johns River, about a mile from present San Mateo. Its founder, Denys Roll or Rolle, a member of Parliament and a wealthy landowner of Devonshire, became obsessed with the idea of winning immortality—and perhaps of accumulating more wealth—by founding in the New World a model state composed of poor white people whom he planned to employ in making naval stores for the British government. He made several unsuccessful attempts to purchase land in Georgia and Cumberland Island before he secured a grant of twenty thousand acres— a mere fifth of what he originally sought—from his friend Lord Shelburne, who preceded Hillsborough as secretary of colonies. Roll tried earnestly to put himself in the place of the unfortunates whose lot in life he planned to improve. Eschewing his affluent associates and his comforts, he sailed to America as a steerage passenger on a small schooner and slept under a cart on deck. As soon as he arrived in St. Augustine from Charles Town, he went to dine with Governor Grant who privately pooh-poohed his visionary plans but who, knowing him to be a friend of Shelburne, received him with a show of kindness.[24]

Roll adored beautiful scenery. He journeyed along the St. Johns, building cabins on lovely spots to which he quickly claimed ownership. Eventually, Grant had to inform him that he must take his land, good and bad, in one contiguous tract. Much distressed, Roll searched anew for a choice piece of land. This time he claimed both banks of the St. Johns, asserting that the river should not prevent the land from being described as contiguous. But again Grant disagreed with him. Whereupon Roll in high dudgeon sailed for England, vowing that he would obtain the title to his grant directly from the Lords of Trade and Plantations. In this aim, he was successful. Hillsborough was so anxious to prevent any adverse report about Florida that he requested Grant to let Roll have land wherever and whenever he wanted it.

But Roll's difficulties began anew when he sought worthy citizens for his colony; he found only vagrants, debtors, and beggars willing to exchange their miserable circumstances in London for the unknown dangers of a new country. Inveterate utopian that he was, Roll accepted forty-nine of them and put them on a small ship on which they sailed for Florida, where he chose a tract of land about a mile from present San Mateo on the St. Johns River. Heedless of their unfitness, he put them to work, which they shirked at the first opportunity or unpleasantness. When Roll countered by cutting off their food supply, they ran away to St. Augustine, where they filled the streets with tales of the persecutions they had endured. Though Grant had no love for Roll, he felt obliged to return the runaways to him. Again Roll put them to work; again they ran away. This time he let them go. Later, he hired eighty-nine more men of the same caliber as the first group; they, too, vanished as soon as they were put to work. Roll then bought Negroes; they proved more dependable, or amenable to whip and reprimand; they brought the colony a measure of prosperity. But misfortune hounded Roll to the bitter end. In 1783 the English returned Florida to Spain and Roll was forced to give up his property.[25]

4

In 1770 ill health forced Governor Grant to ask for permission to return to England, but pressing duties kept him at his post until the following spring. Hillsborough submitted to him a list of possible candidates for the governorship of the colony. Though he favored Turnbull he regarded his presence in New Smyrna as so indispensable that he passed him up in favor of John Moultrie, owner of a magnificent estate at Bella Vista, seven miles from St. Augustine. Hillsborough accepted his choice to the extent of appointing Moultrie lieutenant-governor, though most of the colonists persisted in believing that eventually Turnbull would be chosen governor. Moultrie met with powerful opposition from the day he took office. The officers of Fort George thought he lacked force and decision and called for the appointment of Turnbull as governor. Turnbull enjoyed the support of William Drayton, chief justice of the colony, who disliked Moultrie intensely and who never attended any of the social functions at the official mansion. He belonged to a prominent family of South Carolina, where both his uncle and grandfather had served as lieutenant-governors. Moultrie, too, was a South Carolinian, but he and Drayton had never been friends. Moultrie regarded the military, Turnbull, and Drayton with suspicion and waited for an opportunity to discredit them for the purpose of having them removed from the colony.[26]

The resentment which one group felt for the other soon developed into heated disputes. Turnbull and Drayton had long championed representative government for the colony. Its original letters patent, issued in October, 1763, provided for a governor, a lieutenant-governor, a council of twelve members, and an elected assembly. But Grant had never called an assembly, claiming that the sparse population of the colony did not merit it. Turnbull had always disagreed with him on this point. When Moultrie became lieutenant-governor, Turnbull and Drayton urged the election of an assembly in council meetings. Since the population of East Florida was now considered large enough to merit representative government, all parties in the council agreed that it should be instituted. But demonstrations against British rule in the colonies north of Florida alarmed the ministry to the extent that it discouraged representative government anywhere in the empire. This stand precipitated so much debating and quarreling between the two parties in East Florida that those who advocated the election of an assembly accomplished nothing. Moultrie, wishing to control public opinion as long as possible, favored elections every three years. Turnbull and Drayton and many other prominent settlers declared for annual elections.[27]

The disputes between Moultrie on one side and Turnbull and Drayton on the other grew more and more acrimonious until they became irremediable quarrels. Turnbull strongly supported Drayton. This verbal warfare of course killed any possible plans for an assembly. At last Drayton withdrew from the meetings in disgust. Turnbull a little later followed suit, either to show his affiliation with Drayton or because he was too busy to attend any more council meetings in St. Augustine.[28]

Word of these dissensions soon reached Hillsborough, who resolved to stop them by appointing a strong governor for the colony. His choice was Patrick Tonyn, a curmudgeon of forty-nine who had seen much military service and who regarded any mention of representative government in his presence as a personal insult. As soon as he arrived at St.

Augustine, in March, 1774, he defended Moultrie and retained him in his post. For Turnbull and Drayton he expressed utter contempt. Like Moultrie before him, Tonyn awaited an opportunity to discredit the two men and drive them from the colony.[29]

In October such an opportunity presented itself. Tonyn learned in a letter from Sir James Wright, governor of Georgia, that Jonathan Bryan, a friend of Drayton's uncle, who was then governor of South Carolina, had violated the Proclamation of 1763, by negotiating with thirteen Indians for the lease of a tract of land on the Apalache oil fields, lying in northwestern Florida and extending westward to the Apalachicola River and Apalache Bay. But the Indians, in a meeting with Governor Wright, discovered that their transaction with Bryan was illegal and angrily tore their marks and seals from the deed. Wright followed up his letter with another in which he stated that Drayton and Turnbull were implicated in the deal and that they were willing to spend £500 to secure the king's approval of the lease or a grant of the land.[30]

Tonyn sent an officer with a warrant for Bryan's arrest, but he learned that the culprit had been warned by a friend and had fled to the protection of Georgia. Tonyn then suspended Drayton from the council until he could ascertain the royal pleasure. Tonyn warned Turnbull that he too was mentioned in the illegal deal with the Indians, but he failed to call him before the council. Turnbull replied that he and his friend were in their rights and that they were sure of support from the government. Tonyn once had said that the province did not contain six loyal subjects. To disprove this remark, Drayton and his friends, numbering seventy-eight, assembled early in 1776 at Wood's Tavern and, with Turnbull presiding, prepared an address of loyalty to the king. At the bottom of the address Turnbull signed again, on "behalf of upwards of two hundred families of Greeks and other Foreigners at the Symrna settlement." Turnbull's friends chose him to carry the address to England while they appointed a committee to present a copy of it to the governor. At the conclusion of business, most of them remained in the tavern to discuss the chief topic of the day—Drayton's suspension. Turnbull read aloud to them a copy of Drayton's defense. They agreed with him that Drayton had justified himself.[31]

Tonyn attempted to discredit the address by saying that it contained no signatures of propertied gentlemen. Turnbull replied that singly many of them had more property than the governor and council put together. Next day he and a few friends presented the governor with a copy of the address. Tonyn expected the original. When he found it was only a copy without signatures, he upbraided them for insulting him. He countered by sending the king an address of his own. At the same time, he and Turnbull exchanged angry letters. During this correspondence Turnbull's friends warned him that Tonyn planned to suspend him from the council and perhaps to throw him into a dungeon. Whereupon Turnbull made preparations to leave the colony. Tonyn declared that he would be delighted to see him go but that he must request a leave of absence in writing before he left. But the governor received no hint of Turnbull's preparations to depart from Florida until the morning the ship was scheduled to sail. Then he summoned her captain and asked him of Turnbull's intentions. The captain replied that Turnbull had taken passage but later had given it up. Tonyn, learning that Turnbull was in town and perhaps preparing to leave for England, sent an officer to inform him that he wished to see him. Turnbull sent back word that he was going to see his son off to England and that his lawyer, James Penman, was going with him. By this subterfuge Turnbull and Drayton escaped Tonyn's clutches. When Tonyn learned that Turnbull had sailed without requesting a leave of absence, he assembled his council and suspended him from that body.[32]

On May 10 Turnbull presented his address of loyalty to Lord George Germain, new secretary of colonies, with the request that it be delivered to the king. Later, as the result of an interview with Turnbull, the secretary wrote to Tonyn that the Lords of Trade had fully examined the charges brought against Drayton, and that they had reported to the king their opinion that his suspension from his office of chief justice ought to be removed.

Therefore, wrote Germain, "I am commanded by the King to signify to you His Majesty's Pleasure that you do accordingly remove his Suspension and reinstate him in his office of Chief Justice, and that no part of his Salary be withheld on account of his suspension."[33] Germain went on to remind the governor that New Smyrna was a "valuable Settlement" and that he "should be very watchful to prevent any Injury or Detriment happening to the Settlement, and to give every Encouragement in your power to promote its Growth and the Advantage of the Proprietors."[34]

Early in September, 1776, Tonyn, in compliance with orders from England, reinstated Drayton in office. But for this humiliation he wreaked his vengeance on Turnbull by destroying New Smyrna on grounds adroitly calculated to justify his action to Germain. In December, 1779, Turnbull returned to St. Augustine from New York where he had been detained for a month by an embargo on ships. To his boundless distress he found the town filled with his colonists, especially women and children, begging for bread around Tonyn's residence. He learned that Tonyn had persuaded many of the young Minorcans to join the militia by offering them freedom from indentures, land in St. Augustine, and assurances of protection if they ran away. Some of them had joined Indian bands to scalp Americans living on the fringes of Georgia.

Turnbull learned that the court had declared many of his indentured people still bound by their contracts but that Tonyn had disregarded its decision. With his encouragement the colonists of New Smyrna had moved bag and baggage to St. Augustine where, however, no provision whatever had been made to house and feed them. Sixty-five of them died without medical attention after sleeping under trees and beside old walls in the heavy rains of August and September. Though not a single colonist had died during Turnbull's long absence in England, ten of them had died every week after they came to St. Augustine. Those who were too old or infirm to join the militia remained to build hovels for the women and children on the small lots assigned to them north of the town. Having no money with which to buy supplies to begin farming, they led a precarious existence as fishermen along the shore of the inlet. Tonyn was no longer interested in them—they had served his purpose and they must now shift for themselves.[35]

Like most men, Tonyn preferred to invent a virtue rather than admit a vice in excusing himself for destroying the colony. He wrote Germain that he had always protected New Smyrna but that he would never countenance "Injustice, Tyranny, and Oppression." He falsified the financial consequences of his action by affirming that it would in no way be a loss to the colonists, because "the expense of their and their Families' maintenance will ever equal the value of their labor." To Turnbull's criticism that he had sent colonists to help the Indians scalp American settlers in Georgia, he replied that this mission had received the blessing of the Crown. "If this is so," wrote Turnbull, "I cannot expect any redress." He sent Tonyn a note in which he expressed his intention of living in St. Augustine and of continuing to serve as secretary and clerk of the council. Tonyn permitted him to continue to draw his salary but refused to reinstate him in office because of his "extravagant" conduct since his return from England. He wrote Germain recommending Turnbull's dismissal on the ground of his disloyalty to England, meaning probably his strong disapproval of the scalping raid in Georgia.[36]

By this time Turnbull's two partners had died, and their heirs, Lady Mary Duncan and the sons of Lord Grenville, had sued him for debt. Tonyn, serving as their attorney and as judge of the court of chancery, summoned Turnbull before him and forced him to spend more than £400 to defend himself. Then, fearing his departure from the province, he required him to give bond in the sum of £4000. Since Turnbull was unable to raise this large sum, he was placed in the custody of the provost marshal. Protesting vigorously against such a procedure, which he declared was unjust, he was released in May, 1781, when he agreed to surrender most of his share of New Smyrna. Nevertheless, he feared another imprisonment so much that he moved with his family to Charleston, South Carolina, where he spent the rest of his life. Tonyn tried in vain to induce Lord Cornwallis to expel Turnbull from the city.[37]

5

The sister republic of West Florida embraced a large part of the present states of Alabama and Mississippi, extending northward beyond present Montgomery. Its first governor was Captain George Johnstone, who arrived in February, 1764, at Pensacola with a British regiment and many Highlanders from Charleston and New York. He was thirty-four years old and the fourth son of a baronet of Dumfries, Scotland. Entering the navy, he rose to the position of port captain which he enlivened with a few acts of gallantry and many disputes and duels. On November 20, 1763, he was appointed governor of West Florida, probably through the influence of his fellow countryman, Lord Bute, who was then a member of the ministry. The widely read magazine, *North Briton*, announced his appointment with a sarcastic allusion to him and Governor James Grant as a brace of Scotchmen. Johnstone was so incensed at this insult that he challenged the publisher of the magazine to a duel. Meeting one Brooks, a member of its staff, he accused him of being the author of the article. He drew his sword, but bystanders stopped him from running Brooks through. Brooks sued Johnstone, who was ordered to keep the peace.[38]

Johnstone remained pugnacious the rest of his life, though he proved himself an able administrator. He immediately organized a government of effective and honest officials. He planned the town of Pensacola, granting a generous lot to each petitioner who agreed to fence it and build on it a sizable home with a brick chimney. He confirmed the land titles of all Frenchmen who had improved their properties. He invited Swiss and German families to migrate from New Orleans to West Florida. Most of them turned down his generous offer because of the sterility of the soil around Mobile and Pensacola, the uncertain attitude of the West Florida government toward Roman Catholics, and their inability to sell their properties for negotiable funds. To encourage emigration and to strengthen communication with the Illinois country, Johnstone, with the help of fifty Negroes, made the Iberville River navigable by clearing it of uprooted trees and other debris. At the junction of the Iberville and Mississippi rivers he built a military post which he named Fort Bute in honor of his benefactor in England.[39]

Early in his administration Johnstone reported to the Lords of Trade that the boundary of the province at the thirty-first parallel, as designated by the Proclamation of 1763, excluded considerable settlements on the Mississippi and even Mobile, which was a growing village. In consequence of Johnstone's report, the Board of Trade, with the permission of George III, moved the boundary of the province from the thirty-first parallel northward to the junction of the Yazoo and the Mississippi rivers. West Florida now embraced "the former Spanish territory including and adjacent to Pensacola; former French territory including and adjacent to Mobile, Biloxi, and Natchez; and certain land that might have been claimed by Georgia under the Charter of 1732."[40] Soon a British frigate conveyed troops to Fort Rosalie at Natchez which was repaired and rechristened Fort Panmure.

Equally impressive was Johnstone's success in establishing friendly relations with the Indian tribes of the region. In the spring of 1765 he traveled with Colonel John Stuart, superintendent of Indian affairs for the southern department, and a few other men to Mobile where he met the Choctaws and Chickasaws who signified their friendship for the English by giving them Indian names. With these tribes Johnstone and Stuart signed a peace treaty by which they agreed to encourage traders to supply them with goods in return for their promise to prevent incursions on settlements, horse stealing, and other disturbances and to make restitution in case these crimes occurred. Later in the spring Johnstone and Stuart met the Upper and Lower Creeks at Pensacola, where the influential chief, Mortar, presented each of them with a white wing as an emblem of peace and friendship. Notwithstanding these gestures of friendship Mortar demanded presents, saying that he thought the red-crossed banner of the English denoted hostility and that he needed proof to the contrary. Eventually, however, he signed a treaty similar to that negotiated with the Choctaws and Chickasaws.[41]

Unfortunately for Johnstone, he marred his achievements by quarreling unnecessarily with his officers. Always bellicose and litigious, he never permitted anybody to infringe on his prerogatives, which he practiced with more zeal than he did his religion. As Captain-General and Governor-in-Chief of the Province of West Florida, as his commission read, he claimed the right to command garrisons and to grant paroles. "*Imperium in imperio,*" he growled to Captain Robert Machinen, commander of the fort, "cannot exist in a commonwealth, much less within the fortification of a garrison; either you must have the command of the fort or I; this is indubitable." Captain Machinen, however, was as hard-headed as his superior; he refused to surrender control of the fort. Whereupon Johnstone sent an account of the difficulty to the Board of Trade, which referred the matter to Lord Halifax, secretary of state for the southern department. Lord Halifax sided with Machinen, informing Johnstone that the king intended that the orders of the commander-in-chief for North America and after him those of the brigadier generals commanding the northern and southern departments should be supreme in all military matters and should be obeyed by all of the troops in the civil governments of America.[42]

Later in the year Johnstone became involved in a dispute with Major Robert Farmar, commander of the garrison at Mobile. Farmar was preparing an expedition to the Illinois country and needed hard cash to finance it. He tried to persuade merchants in Mobile and New Orleans to accept his New York bills of exchange drawn on General Gage. From a Mobile merchant who reluctantly accepted his bills of exchange, he acquired a considerable number of deerskins which he planned in turn to exchange in New Orleans for cash. Though Johnstone frowned on such a transaction, he agreed, in view of Farmar's great need, to instruct the customs officers to allow a shipment of twelve hundred pounds of the deerskins. The governor also permitted another shipment of twelve hundred pounds on condition that Farmar compensate the customs officers with an amount equal to the import duties he would pay had he shipped the deerskins to England.

Objecting to these restrictions, Farmar wrote to Gage complaining that Johnstone had used every means at his disposal to stall the expedition. Nevertheless, Farmar departed for the Illinois country. Hearing of Farmar's complaints, Johnstone countered them by charging him in a letter to Gage with eight serious offenses, among which were selling the king's flour in New Orleans, misapplying £10,000 that had been reserved to buy presents for the Indians, and selling Fort Tombeckbe to a merchant. On receipt of these charges, Gage ordered Brigadier-General William Taylor, commander of forces in the southern district, to arrest Farmar on his return from the Illinois country and to summon a court-martial as soon as possible to review the offenses with which he was charged. Farmar was subsequently acquitted.[43]

Johnstone had a more serious quarrel with Lieutenant-Colonel Ralph Walsh, commander of the fort at Pensacola, who scoffed at the governor's pretenses of authority over military matters. At the advice of his council, Johnstone ordered Lieutenant Edward Maxwell, who had succeeded Farmar to the post at Mobile, to come to Pensacola with part of his force and arrest Walsh for disobedience and mutiny. While Johnstone awaited Maxwell's arrival, he applied to Gage for a court-martial for Walsh, charging that officer with usurping his prerogative by entertaining an Indian chief, withdrawing sentinels from his house, ordering soldiers to pay him no respect, and disobeying his orders by firing salutes in honor of the queen's birthday, which had already been celebrated. Gage, observing that these charges were manifestations of Johnstone's jealousy for what he regarded as his prerogatives, asked Maxwell to examine Walsh's conduct and give him a private reprimand or, should he prove guilty, bring him to trial.[44]

At last Maxwell, at the head of sixty-five men, arrived by water. Johnstone ordered him to disembark with his men and to take immediate possession of the fort. In obeying Johnstone's orders, Maxwell found that Walsh had locked the gates of the fort and had increased his guard. To avoid bloodshed, Maxwell asked Walsh for a conference during which the two men came to a complete understanding. Undeterred by Maxwell's defection, Johnstone issued a warrant for Walsh's arrest, executed it himself, and then turned his victim over to the provost marshal. Walsh chose as his attorney Edmund Rush Wegg, whom Johnstone had two weeks before suspended from the office of attorney general on a charge of incompetency.

The provost marshal immediately brought Walsh before William Clifton, chief justice, for a hearing. The chief justice found that charges against Walsh had risen from an extended dispute between the officer and the governor over their several powers, which were all derived from the king and which could be decided, therefore, only by the king and his commander-in-chief in America. Clifton ruled that he had no legal reason to prosecute or even detain Walsh and therefore ordered his release. Maxwell persuaded Walsh to restore the governor's sentinels and to show respect to him as governor. Though Johnstone was baffled, he permitted Walsh to return to his troops in Mobile. So the matter ended.[45]

Johnstone closed his turbulent administration with a quarrel with Mortar, chief of the Lower Creeks, who had always regarded the English with suspicion. The governor confronted the chief with the charge that his tribe was responsible for murdering five white men, stealing cattle and horses, and harboring runaway slaves and deserters. To assure safety for the settlements and to retain the respect of the other Indian tribes, Johnstone planned a military campaign against the Lower Creeks. But General Taylor, commander of the forces in the southern department, was unwilling to begin military preparations without orders from General Gage. When word of Johnstone's plans reached Lord Shelburne, he wrote to the governor that the king disapproved extremely of his action in starting a campaign against the Indians without awaiting permission from England. Hillsborough informed him that, since his actions were contrary to the spirit of his instructions and since his administration had caused much disharmony in the province, the king had ordered his recall. Johnstone, perhaps seeing the storm approaching, had availed himself of a leave of absence to depart for England. By his overbearing manner and his unconciliatory attitude he had dissipated much of the good that his progressive measures had achieved.[46]

Lieutenant Governor Montford Browne succeeded Johnstone while Hillsborough sought a new governor. Browne removed much of the dissension in the government and endeavored to promote peace and prosperity in the province. He made some headway in fostering trade with the Spaniards in New Orleans, smoked the calumet with several tribes along the Mississippi, and persuaded Hillsborough to abandon his plans to remove troops from the province. But his political enemies, daily expecting his recall, charged him with peculation in office and denounced him to Hillsborough, who sent a letter to the incoming governor of West Florida ordering an investigation of Browne's accounts. It reached Pensacola while Browne was still in power and fell into his hands.[47]

The new governor, John Eliot, arrived in West Florida in the spring of 1769, but for unknown reasons he soon hanged himself in his study. By this time Hillsborough had ascertained that Browne was innocent of all the charges of which he had been accused and therefore permitted him to continue in office as lieutenant governor. Browne requested the surveyor, Elias Durnford, who was about to depart for England, to carry to Hillsborough an account of affairs in the province. Durnford pretended friendship for Browne but was ambitious to succeed him in office. By disparaging him to the authorities, he realized his aim. When Browne was recalled, he was naturally furious with Durnford for what he considered duplicity. Durnford accused Browne of reluctance in surrendering the papers and archives of the government. Browne countered that Durnford tried to prevent him from obtaining copies of documents that were necessary to establish his innocence in England.[48]

An able executive, Durnford restored a measure of order in the province though his administration was too short to permit him to formulate permanent policies. In August 1770 Peter Chester, whom Hillsborough had chosen as Eliot's successor, arrived. Governor Chester, a professional soldier who had retired from military service because of poor health, served until West Florida was lost to Spain in 1781.

Chester's administration was characterized by rapid and widespread settlement of the province. In August, 1770, seventy-nine whites and eighteen Negroes arrived, led by Daniel Huay, a North Carolinian who had piloted them from Fort Pitt to Natchez and who planned to settle with them in the fertile lands along the Mississippi. Huay delivered to Chester a letter from John McIntyre who announced that he was migrating to the province with a hundred families from his native Pennsylvania and from Virginia and that he planned to establish a saw mill and a grist mill.[49]

By welcoming these emigrants, Chester encouraged others to follow their example. In the following year came Colonel John Clark with two hundred families from the Holston River region of Tennessee. The authorities thought these settlers so fine an acquisition that they allowed each man among them salt and a barrel of corn per month until he could raise his own food. In the spring of 1773 Colonel Israel Putnam, who later won fame in the American Revolution, Lieutenant Rufus Putnam, Captain Roger Enos, and Thaddeus Lyman arrived in Pensacola and informed Chester that they were representatives of the Company of Military Adventurers, a New England organization composed largely of officers who had fought in the French and Indian War and who sought land on which to settle. Chester and his council received them warmly and invited them to choose tracts which would be reserved for them until their agent in England, General Phineas Lyman, obtained a royal grant. Lyman succeeded in his mission, but was forced to allocate three thousand acres to men who advanced the funds necessary for issuing the grant.[50]

Among the first settlers in the Natchez region was Amos Ogden, an impoverished sea captain to whom George III made a grant of twenty-five thousand acres on condition that he locate and permanently settle it with a specified number of families. Unable to comply with these conditions, he sold 19,800 acres of his grant to two wealthy planters from New Jersey, Richard and Reverend Samuel Swayze or Sweesy, with the understanding that they assist him in locating the grant and settle on it with their portion of families. In the spring of 1773 Ogden and the Swayze brothers with their wives, children, apprentices, and slaves arrived in West Florida after a tedious and perilous journey and settled on the Homochitto River near Kingston, which became known as the "Jersey Settlement." Reverend Swayze, who was a Congregational minister, established the first known Protestant church in the present state of Mississippi.[51]

The most prominent of these Tories of the Natchez region was Anthony Hutchins, a South Carolinian planter of the Santee Hills and a younger brother of Thomas Hutchins who became a famous geographer and the surveyor of the Seven Ranges in the Northwest Territory. Dogmatic and tenacious, gaunt and possessed of a high-pitched voice, Hutchins was known to all and sundry as "Squeaky Tony, long and bony."

He was highly unsympathetic toward the aggressive patriots who filled the Santee Hills. In 1777, fearing that the Revolution would succeed and that he would in consequence be deprived of his estate, he resolved to settle in West Florida. He collected a large group of Tories and, with their slaves and livestock and provisions, took them to the Holston River in east Tennessee, where they built a fleet of flatboats in which they planned to float up the Tennessee River and then down the Ohio and Mississippi to their destination over a thousand miles away. All went well until they reached Muscle Shoals on the Tennessee, where they met with a band of Chickamaugas, who wounded Hutchins and seized one of their boats, which was loaded with hogs. Slipping away from their attackers they floated northward to the Ohio, thence down to what later became New Madrid, where, learning that half-breeds intended to deprive them of their property, they left hurriedly for Cole's Creek, above Natchez, their destination.[52]

6

By this time France had transferred the adjacent colony of Louisiana to Spain. The history of the last decades of French domination in Louisiana are not germane to this volume and may, therefore, be told with few words. In 1743 Bienville, old and infirm, retired as governor of Louisiana. His successor, Pierre Rigaud, Marquis de Vaudreuil, characterized his administration with elegant manners and sumptuous entertainments which won him the sobriquet of the Grand Marquis. He placated or outmaneuvered the Indians, kept the levees in safe condition, stabilized the currency, and introduced sugar cane into Louisiana and subsequently in the lower Mississippi country. But his campaign against the pro-English Chickasaws was such a humiliating failure that he soon resigned his office. The new governor, Louis Billouart, Chevalier de Kerlérec, was a fun-loving and honest naval officer who played the Indian tribes against one another in his efforts to obtain favorable trade returns during the difficult period of the French and Indian War. Kerlérec increased diciplinary measures as the morale of the colony declined.

Soon threats of revolt shook the colony. After sixty years of endeavor France was ready to admit her failure in colonizing Louisiana. By 1756 France was spending 800,000 livres a year on the colony without any appreciable returns. Since its establishment in 1699 between 70 and 80 million livres had been invested in it. As we have seen, Pontchartrain had met expenses without profits, Crozat had lost his huge fortune, Law's Mississippi Company had gone bankrupt, and the last French governors had realized only mounting expenses each year.

The military reverses that France had suffered in the French and Indian War only increased her dissatisfaction for her Louisiana burden. Toward the end of the war she realized that she would lose Canada to England. Louisiana, wedged in between the English and the Spaniards, was in a precarious position. Since France could not assure its defense and since its administrative expenses were ruinous, she offered Louisiana to Spain. At first, Spain was not interested in acquiring the colony; but when, in 1762, she declared war on England and in consequence lost Havana she resolved to regain that important city so that she might trade it for Florida. In that case Louisiana would become an important possession which, though expensive, could gradually be developed to become invaluable in protecting the Spanish possessions of Texas and Mexico from possible English encroachment. On November 3, 1762, by a secret treaty signed at Fontainbleau, France ceded to Spain the Isle of Orleans and the rest of Louisiana west of the Mississippi River. A few months later England, by the Treaty of Paris, which ended the French and Indian War, acquired Spanish East and West Florida and the French area north of the Isle of Orleans and east of the Mississippi.

But Spain was in no hurry to take possession of expensive Louisiana. So for four more years France continued to govern the colony. Not until 1766 did Antonio de Ulloa arrive in New Orleans to serve as the first governor of Spanish Louisiana. A nervous, shy, and small man, Ulloa made little impression on the colonists, though he was an eminent scientist who had established an astronomical observatory, Spain's first society of natural history, and the first laboratory for the study of metallurgy.

Ulloa's colorless personality and his scientific gifts proved detrimental to his political office. He was wise where wisdom required study, foolish where wisdom required action. On the day of his arrival he offended the Supreme Council, which was composed of Frenchmen who opposed Spanish rule, by denying it a trifling request. He alienated his soldiers by cutting their salaries, by paying them in depreciated French currency, and by demanding that French ships have their passports approved before they discharged their cargoes. Spain added to his difficulties by failing to send him a strong force which would enable him to enforce his decrees on his reluctant colonists. Intrigue and agitation soon fanned the smoldering discontent into open rebellion. By diligent propaganda, the malcontents effectively spread their feelings of righteous indignation to all parts of Lower Louisiana. The last straw came in 1768 when instructions from Spain ordered the people of the colony to use only Spanish ships in their commerce and restricting their trade to Spanish ports only. The malcontents drew up a petition that contained more than five hundred names and that demanded Ulloa's recall, restoration of their former privileges, and freedom of trade. Then, on October 27, they spiked the guns at the gate of New Orleans, while one of their leaders, Villière, entered the city at the head of four hundred Germans, Acadians, and other farmers.

Seeing that rebellion was about to ensue, Philippe Aubry, who had been acting governor before Ulloa's arrival, advised the governor to take refuge in a Spanish frigate anchored in the river. Ulloa followed his advice. Gathering up his family and official papers, he sailed for Cuba, leaving Aubry in charge of the colony.[53]

The French colonists were so delighted with Ulloa's departure that they thronged through the streets of New Orleans shouting, "Long live the king! Long live Louisiana! Long live Louis! Down with Ulloa! Down with the Spaniards!" The Supreme Council sent one of its members to France with a memorial in which the inhabitants and merchants of Louisiana pledged their allegiance to Louis XV. The French government rejected the memorial. Word of the insurrection soon reached the Spanish government which resolved to avenge the insult to Spain by suppressing the revolt and firmly establishing Spanish control.[54]

Spain assigned this task to General Alejandro O'Reilly. As his name implies, he was of Irish origin. He belonged to one of those persecuted Catholic families who left their native Ireland and offered their services to sympathetic Spain. He had devoted much of his life to military service for Spain in the War of the Austrian Succession, in the war with Portugal, and in the Seven Years' War. He returned to Spain in time to save Charles III's life in the Madrid riot of 1765. Behind mild and suave manners, he concealed a will of iron. Convinced that, in the long run, prompt punishment was the most lenient course to pursue in dealing with the malcontents of Louisiana, he suffered no qualms of conscience in administrating it.[55]

On August 17, 1769, O'Reilly arrived at New Orleans with a large fleet carrying over two thousand of the best troops in the Spanish army. Next afternoon, at five o'clock, as a signal gun announced their presence, they poured out of the ships and marched with military precision to the Place d'Armes where they ranged themselves in front of the cathedral. While sailors and soldiers cried repeatedly, "*Vive el rey!*" fifty cannon roared out salutes that were answered by volleys of Spanish musketry. To the beating of drums O'Reilly descended from his ship, preceded by an escort in resplendent uniforms and bearing silver maces as the symbol of their authority. He advanced to the flagpole in the square where, at his request, Aubry read aloud the proclamations in which the French and Spanish kings had announced the transfer of Louisiana. Then O'Reilly ordered the fleur-de-lis lowered and raised in its stead the dragons and castles of Spain while the soldiery shouted, "*Vive el rey!*"[56]

With this dramatic pageantry O'Reilly restored Spanish control over the rebellious colony. Then he invited the twelve foremost leaders of the insurrection to meet him at his quarters. When they arrived, he arrested them and informed them that they would be tried without delay for having led the people of Louisiana in rebellion against Spanish authority. Their trials, conducted in strict conformity with Spanish laws, lasted three weeks and resulted in verdicts of death by hanging for five of the most important leaders and imprisonment for six others. The twelfth defendant had died in a struggle with his guards before his trial ended. The properties of all twelve men were sequestered.[57]

Since O'Reilly could not find a hangman, he sentenced five of the six men to the firing squad. On October 25, 1769, town criers went through the streets of New Orleans reading the death sentences to the people. That same afternoon the condemned men were shot. A short time later Aubry sailed for France, some say with a fortune; but near his destination a storm wrecked his ship, which took him to the bottom of the sea.[58]

Even before he restored Louisiana to Spanish control, O'Reilly had turned his attention to the political and economic problems of the colony. He reorganized the government, passed laws that prevented merchants from making excessive profits, permitted many French officials to continue in office, revived commerce and trade, and abolished Indian slavery. In December he placated the French Creoles by sending the bulk of his army back to Havana and by organizing thirteen militia companies under native Louisianians. Then, early in 1770, he himself departed for Havana, leaving the colony in charge of Luis de Unzaga y Amérzaga.[59]

Unzaga, a native of Málaga, had left Spain with O'Reilly and had been commissioned to succeed him as governor of Louisiana as soon as the insurrection was put down. A professional soldier, he had seen thirty years of service in Spain, Italy, and Africa and had lived twenty-five years in the New World, where he acquired a wide knowledge of colonial administration. Mild and indulgent, he easily reconciled the French Creoles of the colony and ruled wisely for seven years. Early in 1777 poor health forced him to relinquish his office to Lieutenant Colonel Bernardo de Gálvez, captain of grenadiers in the Regiment of Infantry of Seville. Though only twenty-nine or thirty years old, Gálvez had already shown himself a brilliant commander against the Apache Indians of New Spain.[60]

Though Spain was at this time neutral, Gálvez favored the patriots in the American Revolution. He rendered invaluable assistance to them through Oliver Pollock, a Roman Catholic and a native of Ireland, who had amassed a fortune and had placed it at the disposal of the Revolutionary authorities. The Continental Congress made him a member of its Commercial Committee on which he served in the double capacity of agent for the state of Virginia and "commercial agent" for the United States. He persuaded Gálvez, who was his friend, to assist the Americans with arms, ammunition, and provisions for the frontiers of Pennsylvania and Virginia. Gálvez functioned through James Willing, whose older brother was a business partner of Robert Morris and a member of the first Continental Congress. Willing was familiar with conditions on the lower Mississippi, where he had been an indifferent merchant while he frittered away his fortune in dissolute living. In 1777 he returned to his home in Philadelphia and enthusiastically accepted a commission from the Commerce Committee to procure the supplies and ammunition that Pollock had deposited at New Orleans and bring them to Fort Pitt.[61]

On January 10, 1778, Willing, with a volunteer crew of about thirty men, sailed in the armed boat *Rattletrap* from Pittsburgh down the Ohio and thence down the Mississippi, ruthlessly burning the crops and houses of Tory planters, killing their hogs and cattle, and carrying off their slaves. In the latter part of February, he reached the plantation of Anthony Hutchins, a short distance above Natchez. He captured him, seized his Negroes and property, and, convening the regional planters, wrested from them a promise that they would "not in any fashion take arms against the United States of America, or help to supply, or give any assistance to the enemies of said States." Willing on his part promised that their persons, slaves, and other property would "be left secure and without molestation during [their] neutrality."

A few days later one of Willing's advance detachments seized the armed British sloop *Rebecca* at Manchac and made the inhabitants of that settlement prisoners on their parole. Meanwhile Willing, with a force augmented by several men from Natchez who hated "squeaky Tony" and a goodly number of French and Spanish boatmen, set fire to many houses and buildings on settlements from Manchac to Point Coupée. Thence the raiders proceeded to New Orleans, where, thanks to Pollock, Gálvez extended them the freedom of the city amid the cheers of its inhabitants. The governor assigned a public building to them for a barracks and appointed Pollock to auction off their plunder, which consisted mostly of Negro slaves.[62]

One of Willing's officers, Captain Joseph Calvert, proceeded downstream and captured the English brig *Neptune* and another English vessel, the *Dispatch*, near the mouth of the river. These seizures prompted Governor Chester to send two sloops, the *Sylph* and the *Hound*, to the Mississippi to intercept any rebel craft that might be coming to Willing's support and to demand that Gálvez explain his unneutral conduct of permitting the Americans to enter New Orleans, thereby making of that city a base of operations against the English. Gálvez replied that his policy of protecting the Americans was in keeping with that taken by the leading European powers. Spain, he further explained, was under no obligation to protect British subjects on British soil or off the shore of British territory. He would not release Willing's seizures, therefore, until he could make a complete and official investigation. He agreed, however, to return to their owners certain boats seized below Manchac, where Spain controlled both banks of the river.[63]

Meanwhile, Hutchins had escaped from prison and had hastened to Natchez, where he alarmed the inhabitants by telling them that Willing and his men were planning to attack them again. To protect themselves against this new danger they gathered three hundred strong at White Cliffs, where they defeated a group of Americans under Richard Harrison, because they were outnumbered and far more exposed than their attackers. Five of them were killed; the rest quickly surrendered. Hutchins, having decided that he was no longer bound by his oath of neutrality, applied to Governor Chester for reinforcements. Chester replied by sending him a detachment of seventy-five soldiers from his garrison to fortify Manchac and a small body of loyal Carolina refugees under Michael Jackson to garrison Fort Panmure. These reinforcements blockaded the river, interrupting Pollock's shipping of supplies to Fort Pitt, intercepting some messengers on their way from the United States, and, mindful of Gálvez's sympathy toward the Americans, stopping the passage of goods even under the Spanish flag.[64]

Willing, too, was in danger. He was now unable to sail up the Mississippi from New Orleans to Fort Pitt. And while he tarried he wore out his welcome with both Gálvez and Pollock. Disregarding Spanish sovereignty, he had issued a proclamation to his prisoners. Gálvez upbraided him for taking advantage of the hospitality and favors accorded him. Pollock, too, was disgusted with him for wasting his time in drinking bouts instead of making some effort to return to the states. The more Willing tried to explain and apologize the more Pollock tried to get rid of him to end the expense of maintaining him and his followers and to minimize English antagonism and suspicion of commerce going up the Mississippi.[65]

At last he hit on the scheme of asking Gálvez to fit out the prize ship *Rebecca*, which had been rechristened *Morris*, to take Willing and his men home. The governor consented to the plan, but Willing was reluctant to leave; he feared the fury of the people he had victimized; he wanted to leave northward through Spanish territory and under Spanish protection. Gálvez, suspecting that this was only a pretext to conceal his plans for new ravages on the English settlements, refused him permission, though he made a partial concession by issuing a letter to the Spanish commanders along the Mississippi to allow Willing and twenty-five of his men passage up the river. Willing thought the trip too hazardous to undertake.[66]

A month later Gálvez permitted Robert George to take Willing's men northward through Spanish territory on their oath of honor that they would refrain from raiding any of the settlements they passed. George took them to the Illinois country, where he placed them under George Rogers Clark.[67]

As for Willing himself, he sailed by sloop for Philadelphia, but he failed to reach his destination. An English ship captured his sloop and took him to New York, where he contrived to escape and take refuge in the house of a friend. But he was too well known to escape notice for long. The authorities discovered him, transferred him to Long Island, then took him to New York, where they loaded him with chains for having resented the insult of an English officer. Congress, learning of his depressed circumstances, directed the commissary general of prisoners to supply him with £100 in New York currency for his sustenance. In July, 1779, he was exchanged, perhaps for Colonel Henry Hamilton, the "Hair Buyer General" who had surrendered to George Rogers Clark at Vincennes. Though resolute and compelling, Willing lacked restraint and humanity. His raid did more harm than good. Such benefits as accrued to his country from his raid redounded to Pollock's credit. Yet neither American could have accomplished much for the Revolutionary cause without the fortunate partnership of the Spanish governor of Louisiana.[68]

The Willing raid exposed to Governor Chester the defenseless state of West Florida and prompted him to apply to Sir Henry Clinton, commander of British forces in America, for assistance. Clinton in turn sent to Pensacola twelve hundred men under General John Campbell with orders to establish a post on the Mississippi near Fort Bute and to give all proper protection to the king's subjects in their efforts to carry on lawful commerce and to cultivate their lands.[69]

On June 21, 1779, Spain had entered the American Revolution as an ally of France. The British government ordered Campbell and Admiral Sir Peter Parker to concert their forces for an attack on New Orleans. Campbell replied to Clinton that desertions and diseases among his troops and the lack of naval transport entrenching tools, and artillery precluded the possibility of a surprise attack on the town.[70]

Nevertheless, Campbell ordered Captain Alexander Dickson and Captain Anthony Forster, commanders at Fort Bute and Fort Panmure, respectively, to prepare for war. But Gálvez had received word of hostilities earlier and was already advancing up the Mississippi with a large force. Dickson wisely retreated to make his stand at a more tenable position behind a redoubt on the Watts and Flowers' plantation at Baton Rouge, leaving only twenty of his men to defend Manchac. On September 7 Gálvez stormed Manchac and forced its weak garrison to surrender. He gave his sick men a few days to recover, then advanced up the river to meet Dickson's main force.

To attract the entire attention of the English, he resorted to the ruse of sending a detachment of his troops to cut down trees, throw up earthworks, and, in general, make as much noise as possible, while he planted his cannon unmolested and unobserved in a garden opposite the fort and within musket shot of it. When Dickson discovered his mistake, he ordered a heavy fire against the Spanish batteries which, however, were too well concealed to be greatly harmed. Gálvez retaliated with fire so effective that within two hours Dickson raised a white flag. The victorious Spanish commander forced him to surrender not only Baton Rouge but also Fort Panmure with its garrison of eighty grenadiers under Forster. One of Gálvez' officers, Carlos Grand Pré, with troops drawn from Pointe Coupée, had already seized the British posts on Thompson's

Creek and on the Amite. Gálvez rewarded his good work by placing him in command of the district.[71]

Gálvez' expedition in the lower Mississippi region was only the prelude to his plans to drive the British from Mobile, Pensacola, and other posts in West Florida. To prepare for such a campaign he returned to New Orleans, whence he dispatched one of his officers, Colonel Estevan Miró, to the Captain General of Havana, his superior, for reinforcements. After prolonged arguments with Miró, the captain general, in January, 1780, agreed to send Gálvez five hundred sixty-seven men in four transports which sailed from Havana and reached Mobile Bay after sustaining a strong northwest wind of almost hurricane proportions.[72]

Meanwhile Gálvez, with a little over seven hundred fifty men, descended the river in twelve ships of various sizes and entered Mobile Bay, where a strong wind grounded several of them on the treacherous bar. Nothing daunted, he prepared to attack the fort. He ordered his men to build from the grounded vessels a number of ladders with which to scale the walls of Fort Charlotte. Then, planting a battery on the point to command the entrance of the bay, he moved with most of his men toward Mobile and began to fire on its fort while he sent one of his officers, Bouligny, to request its commander, Colonel Elias Durnford, to surrender. Bouligny and Durnford were old friends. While they wined and dined, each magnified his side's strength. Supported by his men, Durnford determined to fight. He sent his friend back with a dozen bottles of wine, a dozen chickens, a dozen loaves of fresh bread, and a mutton and provisions for prisoners in the Spanish camp. Gálvez, in turn, sent Durnford a case of Bordeaux wine and one of Spanish, a box of tea biscuit, a box of corn cakes, and a box of Havana cigars, with assurances that his prisoners were well treated.[73]

Between these cordial exchanges each commander made preparations for war. Gálvez built a trench and erected a battery. Durnford, seeing these warlike moves, fired on the Spaniards with cannon, both ball and grape, and with carbines and muskets, killing six of them and wounding five others. Gálvez fired back, wreaking so much damage to the parapets and embrasures of the fort that at sundown it raised a white flag. Gálvez accepted Durnford's proposals to surrender the fort in return for the full honors of war. Next day, March 14, the Spaniards occupied the fort.[74]

Hardly had the ink dried on the surrender of Mobile than Gálvez turned his attention to his chief objective—the conquest of Pensacola. He had detailed information that Campbell had concentrated there twenty-five hundred men including regular soldiers, hunters, sailors, settlers, and Negroes. Gálvez had about the same number of men, but he learned that his enemy expected reinforcements from Jamaica. To offset such an advantage he returned to Havana and, after holding a number of war councils with the captain general, secured from him over thirty-eight hundred reinforcements with provisions for three months. Early in October, he put them on forty-nine transports and, accompanied by fifteen ships, sailed for West Florida; but for the third time in as many years nature intervened to disrupt his preparations to drive the English from that province. On October 18 a hurricane that raged for five days struck his fleet and scattered it in all directions. This disaster, however, failed to dampen his determination to undertake the expedition. After vainly striving to reunite his fleet, he returned to Havana, where he persuaded the captain general to grant him a new force, this time of only 1315 men, for the purpose of strengthening Spanish defenses on the mainland and, if opportunity permitted, of advancing against Pensacola.[75]

On March 9, 1781, after an uneventful voyage of ten days, Gálvez landed his men at Santa Rosa Island. Under cover of darkness they marched along the beach to Sigüenza Point, where, however, they found only an abandoned breastwork and three dismounted guns. But between them and victory lay the strong English defenses of Fort George and Fort Barrancas Coloradas. Fort George, which was the strongest of the two posts and which Governor Chester had built in 1772, had barracks for the garrison, powder magazines, and a double stockade. The other post, which was located about seven miles from the town, was a square stronghold with earthen breastworks and a surrounding ditch.[76]

Next day the fleet prepared to enter Pensacola Bay, a task made difficult and hazardous by the sand bars, the guns of Fort Barrancas, and two English frigates in the harbor. As soon as the English frigates discovered the Spaniards, they began to fire on them, with the assistance of the guns at Fort Barrancas. Nothing daunted, Gálvez landed a pair of twenty-four pounders and some lighter guns, as well as one hundred and fifty campaign tents, and erected a battery which forced the two frigates to withdraw out of range. Gálvez then attempted to enter the harbor, but his flagship, the *San Ramón*, grounded on the first bar and, as quickly as she was worked free, returned to her former anchorage.

A week later Gálvez, in defiance of the naval commander, Calbo, who refused to expose his ships to the dangers of the bay, took personal command of a number of small boats from Louisiana, bravely crossed the bar despite heavy fire from Fort Barrancas, and anchored under the shelter of the Spanish battery on Sigüenza Point. Soon the entire fleet save the *San Ramón* followed him into the bay, where his forces from Mobile and New Orleans soon joined him, swelling his ranks to over thirty-five hundred men. He now felt strong enough to ferry his troops from Santa Rosa Island to the mainland behind Fort Barrancas. During this operation Indian allies of the English harassed them constantly, keeping them on guard and hindering them from making preparations to attack the fort.[77]

They spent much of April reconnoitering British positions, building fortified camps on the lagoon just west of the town, and extending their lines north and west to within artillery range of the fort and its outer redoubts. On April 19 they sighted a fleet of twenty ships off the coast. Were they friends or foes? Knowing that Campbell expected reinforcements, they were filled with apprehension until an officer arrived and informed them that the approaching fleet was Spanish and that it carried over thirty-six hundred reinforcements. The elated soldiers then learned that the captain general, fearing that several English frigates sighted off the coast of the island were on their way to raise the siege of Pensacola, had dispatched ships and soldiers to reinforce Gálvez. Though Gálvez now had over seven thousand men, he felt that Fort George was so strong that it could be taken only at the sacrifice of much bloodshed. He therefore intensified his preparations against the fort.

On the last three nights of April he employed hundreds of men to dig a covered trench or tunnel from the Spanish lines to a small hill, where they built a redoubt of earth and timber almost as large as Fort George itself and where they installed a battery of six twenty-four pounders and three thirteen-inch mortars. In the morning, they opened fire on the redoubts of the fort while their mortars ranged on Fort George. The English opened a vigorous barrage and, under its cover, charged the Spaniards in such strength that they were forced to retreat to their redoubt. But they soon rallied, repaired the damages the British had inflicted, and bombarded one of the English redoubts. Early in the morning of May 8 a shot from one of the Spanish howitzers struck the powder magazine in the redoubt. The explosion was terrifying. It ruined the redoubt and killed between eighty-five and a hundred five of the defenders. Gálvez immediately moved his light infantry to the smoking ruins and installed cannon and mortars which fired mercilessly on the terrified enemy. Campbell realized now that his situation was desperate, that he could not hope to sustain himself for long against the heavy fire, and that, when the redoubt fell, Fort George itself would be untenable.[78]

In the morning, therefore, he raised a white flag and asked Gálvez for terms of capitulation. The Spanish commander, who was as anxious to halt the carnage as was his beaten enemy, agreed to negotiations. Campbell surrendered all of West Florida, while Gálvez granted him the honors of war, the protection of noncombatants and unarmed laborers, and the restoration of slaves. The victor took much booty and 1113 prisoners who remained in camp at Pensacola until June 1, when they were taken to Havana in transports. Three days later Gálvez turned over Pensacola to Arturo O'Neill, its new commander, and returned to New Orleans, where in succeeding weeks he became the recipient of many military and political favors. The king rewarded him with the rank of lieutenant-general, the commission of governor of West Florida as well as Louisiana, and the title of count "to perpetuate for your posterity the memory of the heroic action in which you alone forced the entrance of the bay, you may place as the crest on your coat of arms the brig *Galvestown* with the motto '*Yo Solo.*'"[79]

And he alone, by his victory, paralyzed a new danger that broke out in the Natchez district and might well have obviated his well-earned honors. Anthony Hutchins and other leading settlers of the Natchez district, fearing that Spanish rule would blight their prosperity and happiness, sent word to General Campbell that they planned to attack Fort Panmure, which had fallen to Gálvez less than two years before. Campbell encouraged them by optimistically telling them that an English fleet was in the Gulf and that it would soon move against New Orleans. They immediately assembled for action.[80]

Not all of the settlers in the district sided with them. Captain Alexander MacIntosh, a wealthy and intelligent planter who enjoyed prosperous business relations with the Spanish authorities, informed Captain Juan Delavillebeuvre, commander of the garrison at Fort Panmure, of the approaching storm. The commander tried to discourage the rebels from pursuing their plans, warning them of the consequences of such action and offering amnesty to all of them save their leaders. They replied by attacking the fort with light artillery which wrought some damage and wounded a noncommissioned officer who died a few days later.

But the rebels realized that they were too weak to conquer the fort. So they schemed to achieve by subterfuge what they could not hope to win by force of arms. They intercepted MacIntosh's messenger to Delavillebeuvre and forced him by threats of death to deliver a substitute letter which was written by their expert penman, John Alston, over the planter's signature and which warned the Spanish commander that they had undermined the fort and that, therefore, he had better give it up. Convinced that the message was genuine, Delavillebeuvre surrendered with his garrison and took an oath to remain inactive for the remainder of the war. The rebels entered Fort Panmure and hoisted the British flag from its ramparts.[81]

A small group under one of their captains, Jacob Winfree, departed with the prisoners for Baton Rouge, but when they reached Loftus Heights they saw a considerable body of men, both whites and Indians, ascending the river in barges. Discovering that they were French militia and their Indian allies in the service of Spain and under Major Mulligan, Winfree released the prisoners, who made their way to the boats of the rescuing party. Winfree and his comrades fled to his property near the Homochitto River. Surmising that Mulligan would proceed up the river, they took no precautions against a surprise. But Mulligan, leaving his barges at White Cliffs, decided to push with his men after Winfree and his followers. Learning through his scouts that they were engaged in pounding corn and roasting beef, Mulligan fell on them at daylight, killing fourteen of them and capturing several others. A little later, a courier from Pensacola rode up to the surviving rebels and informed them that Campbell had surrendered the port to Gálvez.[82]

The revolt collapsed instantly. Its leaders, fearing Spanish wrath, fled in every direction. About eighty of the rebels took refuge with the Chickasaw and about thirty with the Choctaws. Another group, about a hundred in number, took to the wilderness with a few pack horses and scanty provisions. After five months of intense suffering, they reached

Savannah and security. Anthony Hutchins, leading a small band of his friends and neighbors, also reached Savannah, where he took boat for London. Later, through the intercession of William Panton, the great Scotch merchant of Pensacola, he was allowed to return to his property in Natchez, where he shed his Tory sentiments and became a solid American citizen.

Ironically enough, all this suffering was unnecessary. The Spaniards, wishing to placate the settlers of the district, proved extremely lenient toward those rebels who remained for trial. Though the leaders were imprisoned and deprived of their properties, the ordinary participants of the revolt were pardoned. And, almost as soon as Fort Panmure was recovered, they took a new oath of fidelity to Spain.[83]

On September 3, 1783, the American Revolution closed with the Treaty of Paris. The new republic of the United States stretched magnificently from the Atlantic to the Mississippi and from the Canadian border to the northern boundary of East and West Florida. The preliminary treaty contained a secret clause providing that, should any power other than England receive the Floridas, the boundary of the United States and West Florida would be the thirty-first parallel; but that, should England obtain West Florida, the boundary between it and the United States would be a line drawn due east from the mouth of the Yazoo River to the Apalachicola River. Though Spain failed to receive Gibraltar, one of her main objectives, she retrieved the Floridas with boundaries undefined. This, as we shall see, caused much controversy between the two countries—and of course added to the dramatic content in the history of the Southern Frontier.

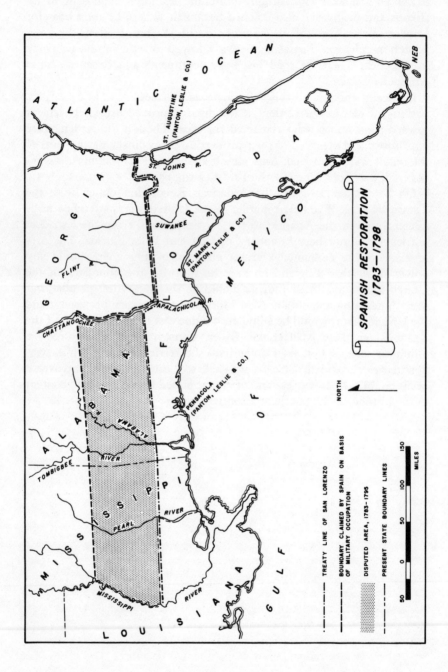

The Spanish Restoration

THE TREATY OF PEACE GRANTED A PERIOD OF EIGHTEEN MONTHS TO THOSE British subjects who wished to sell their property and leave Florida. The dispatch that brought this information also announced the government's plans of evacuation. It had sent four thousand tons of shipping to St. Augustine and had, in addition, ordered the naval commanders at the Leeward Islands and Jamaica to transport British subjects to any part of the empire in Europe, America, and the West Indies. It planned to purchase land in the Bahamas to provide free grants to those who had remained loyal to Great Britain during the American Revolution. It directed Patrick Tonyn to continue as governor of East Florida so that he could regulate the embarkation and assist the people in the disposal or the removal of their property.[1]

In conformity with these orders Tonyn on May 6, 1784, issued a proclamation ordering British subjects to declare their intentions within a designated time. Many had already left East Florida, despite the delay in obtaining small craft to carry them, despite the trouble entailed in assembling the scattered inhabitants, despite the necessity of constructing shelters on the transports against the scorching sun. Others, however, remained in the hope of finding purchasers for their houses and their land. They were bitterly disappointed to learn that at first few Spaniards came to Florida and that these were interested only in buying houses in St. Augustine for a fraction of their value. Some of the English families left their properties in the hands of Francis Philip Fatio, hoping that he would sell them and remit the money later. The government appointed David Yates and John Leslie to supervise and register the sales and to aid in adjudging subsequent claims on the British government for compensation.[2]

Most of the English settlers of West Florida declined the option of remaining in the colony. They had depended for support either directly or indirectly on the government. Gone was the brisk trade that the government had developed in lumber, naval stores, skins, and indigo, which had yielded some $500,000 annually. Only a few Canary Islanders remained to produce a few vegetables in their small gardens in town.[3]

But many British subjects still remained in more populous East Florida when, on June 27, Vizente Manuel de Zéspedes arrived in St. Augustine to assume his duties as governor. Tonyn received him in the square and conducted him to the government house where Zéspedes produced his credentials. Several days, however, slipped by in entertainment before the formal transfer of government took place. Then Zéspedes issued a proclamation announcing the establishment of Spanish government and promising British inhabitants of the colony the choice of remaining in Florida or of retiring within the time specified in the terms of the treaty. Most of them—old residents, Tories from colonies to the north of Florida, and even Negroes—preferred to leave than to remain under an alien government that might impose on them a change of religion. Some took the wilderness trails to the back country, some journeyed to the United States, some sailed to Europe or Jamaica or the Bahama Islands. Most of the Minorcans, Greeks, and Italians remained in St. Augustine and formed the nucleus of its polyglot population.[4]

Among the few Tories who remained in Florida, none was better known than William Panton. With John Leslie and Thomas Forbes he formed the firm of Panton, Leslie and Company which, thanks to his business acumen, became the trading colossus of the Southern Frontier. In 1770, when he was about twenty-five years old, Panton migrated from his native Scotland to Charles Town and later to Savannah where he became a junior partner of the firm Moore and Panton. Perhaps through debts owed to his firm, Panton during the same period acquired an interest in the trading post of James Spalding at Frederica on St. Simon Island. During the American Revolution he remained loyal to the Crown and saw his property confiscated by the patriots. Migrating to Florida, which during Tonyn's administration was a haven for Tories, Panton established Panton, Leslie and Company with two main trading posts about fifty miles apart on the west bank of the St. Johns River. The "lower store" was located near present Palatka and the "upper store" at Astor in present Lake County. Later the company opened two smaller stores at Alachua and at Talahasochte on the Suwannee River.[5]

Having renewed her rule over the Floridas, Spain needed the support of the Indians, many of whom dwelled on the Spanish-American border between the thirty-first parallel and the Tennessee River. To fail in her endeavor meant to drive the Indians to the side of the land-hungry and trade-hungry Americans. Zéspedes, realizing that the Indians had grown accustomed to English goods, permitted Panton, Leslie and Company to remain in Florida. The company expressed its gratitude by granting Zéspedes credit on goods he bought as presents for the Indians. While Spain ordered all those who refused to take the oath of allegiance to leave Florida, she allowed Panton, Leslie and Company to remain merely by pledging their obedience. In May, 1786, a royal decree issued on Zéspedes' recommendation permitted the company to trade directly with England on paying a 6 per cent import and export tax. Since Spaniards seldom entered the fur trade, Panton, Leslie and Company enjoyed a monopoly under the Spanish government for all trade with the Indians in Florida.[6]

In granting this monopoly Zéspedes counted on Panton's close friendship with Alexander McGillivray, influential chief or "emperor," as he called himself, of the Creeks. He was the son of Lachlan McGillivray, a Tory who before the Revolution had been active in the fur trade, and Sehoy Marchand, a half-French, half-Creek princess of exotic beauty and quick intelligence. His father sent him to school in Charles Town, where he learned Greek, Latin, English history, and English literature. He became, too, a skilled penman, perhaps with his father's preliminary assistance, and developed a literary style that combined the classic purity and simplicity of an Addison with the down-to-earth imagery of Indian oratory.

After the Revolution, Lachlan, who had sustained great losses as the result of his loyalty to the Crown, retired to Scotland, leaving his wife and their son with her people. Thanks to his mother's connections and influence with the tribe, Alexander soon became its chief, spokesman, and diplomat. He established himself on the Coosa River, near present Montgomery, Alabama, where on broad, fertile acres he lived like an affluent southern planter. He dressed like a white man, became a Mason, and entertained with lavish hospitality friends and strangers alike. He had two weaknesses—women and rum—which undermined his health and brought him to the grave when he was still a young man.[7]

McGillivray sought Spanish trade and support almost as soon as the English evacuated the Floridas. Because the patriots of Georgia had mistreated and persecuted his father and many of his friends, he regarded the United States as a greater enemy than Spain. He greatly resented the restless and aggressive American frontiersmen with their propensity for encroaching on Indian lands. He had no confidence that they could be restricted. So he naturally reasoned that Spain, too, must defend her possessions and that she would strengthen the Indians to serve as buffer nations against the expanding Americans. He accordingly urged Panton to remain in Florida and continue the Indian trade. Panton agreed when McGillivray pledged to align his tribe with the monopoly. On this stabilizing base Panton, Leslie and Company built its Indian policy. Without Panton's influence over McGillivray, and without McGillivray's influence over the Creeks, Spanish rule over the Floridas would doubtless have failed.[8]

In 1785 the company, finding that its volume of trade in Pensacola was developing four-to-one over that of the other stores, made that town its headquarters. Its enormous warehouse stood on the waterfront. Nearby, Panton built a brick mansion that caught the breezes of the bay and afforded a view of Santa Rosa Island with its snowlike sands. The mansion stood three stories high in the English style. Its bricks, which were lain with a mortar of crushed oyster shells and cement known as *coquina* or tabby, had perhaps been brought over as ballast from England, though Pensacola had several brickyards. Warmhearted and generous, Panton kept a regular table for chiefs, runners of the path, messengers from the tribes, and stray Indians whose horses, when they had any, he stabled and fed. He loved to walk in his garden, among his flowering shrubs and variety of fruit trees, and along his orange grove that in spring perfumed the front of his mansion. His eternally bowing Negro servant, Pompey, attended him at home and on his travels.[9]

At his store he kept a stock of $50,000 to supply the traders and Indians. To John Forbes, brother of his partner Thomas, he once wrote that "our Traders have come down handsomely this month past & we now have in store above 70000 lb. weight of skins."[10] He often bought a variety of articles from the firm of Edwin Gairdner in London. One of its shipments to Panton included "excellent Claret . . . London Duffil blankets . . . Oznaburgs, Callicos, black silk handkerchiefs 20 doz. . . . White bone handled scalping knives, some small iron potts, stocks Locks & Padlocks, mens shoes, knives, spurs, hoes, nails."[11] The fifteen clerks in his Pensacola store were well educated and picked for him by his sister, Mrs. John Innerarity, who always ascertained that their morals were beyond reproach. In dealing with the tribes, Panton used sturdy Indian ponies, each of which could carry a load of one hundred eighty pounds and travel as much as twenty-five miles a day. The rich and abundant pasturage of those days enabled each pony to supply itself with sufficient food at noon and at night. Its load was often an oddity, containing a miniature chicken coop, two kegs of taffi hung to its sides, a pack of merchandise on its back, and "two pendant firkins of honeycomb, with a pile of hides, skins, or beeswax towering between."[12]

A caravan usually consisted of from five to ten companies. Usually ten ponies under a single driver formed a company. The caravan always composed an impressive and colorful procession as it meandered up and down narrow trails and across rivers and streams to each Indian village on its route. At unfordable rivers, drivers ferried their ponies on rafts composed of logs or masses of matted cane. They guided their rafts against strong currents by stretching grapevine ropes across the stream.[13]

The Indians regarded the traders as friends who met their periodical needs and gratified their taste for taffi or firewater. The southern traders, like those in other frontiers, were joyous men, full of fun and jokes, news and gossip, to which they gave full play under the spur of a cup of taffi or at the sight of a pretty Indian damsel. Panton certainly owed much of his success to Alexander McGillivray. Had the great chief seen fit to point his long, slender finger toward Savannah or Charles Town rather than toward Pensacola, Panton's commercial life would have withered and perished "like a tree girdled by the woodman's axe."[14]

Panton's monopoly naturally embittered those British merchants who had hoped for lucrative trade with the Indian tribes of Florida. Miller, Bonnamy and Company of New Providence in the Bahama archipelago planned to ruin Panton, Leslie and Company and supplant it in the Indian trade. John Miller, senior member of the firm, bore one grudge against Spain for damages he had suffered during the siege of Nassau in 1782 and another grudge against Panton, Leslie and Company for depriving him of his trade in Florida. He enlisted the support of Lord Dunmore, governor of the Bahamas and formerly governor of Virginia, by promising him a handsome profit should he succeed in invading Panton's monopoly.

As their agent Miller and Dunmore chose William Augustus Bowles. Soldier, painter, musician, actor, gambler, and lover of Indian women— Bowles swaggers before us as one of the most colorful rogues in the history of the Southern Frontier. Bearing the names of the Norman conqueror of England and of the mighty emperor of Rome, he perhaps felt inspired to emulate each at irregular intervals of his career. A native of Maryland, he found himself at the age of fifteen in faraway Pensacola serving as an ensign with a loyalist regiment during the Revolution. Heedless of military orders, he was soon dismissed. Taking to the woods, he lived with the Creeks for two years, during which time he adopted their customs, learned their language, and married the daughter of one of their chiefs, thereby becoming a chief in his own right. In 1781, when Gálvez threatened Pensacola, Bowles collected a small group of his Indian friends and joined Campbell. He showed such intrepidity that he was reinstated in his commission. At the end of the Revolution he was retired on half-pay. For two more years he knocked about in several occupations, until he fell in with Miller, Bonnamy and Company. Miller was convinced that Bowles, by his marital connection with the Creeks and by his knowledge of their language and customs, would succeed in his mission. Miller instructed him to win their good will with gifts, then gradually wean them away from Panton and the Spaniards.[15]

Circumstances in the tribe favored Bowles. In 1784 McGillivray had placed his people under Spanish protection. In the ensuing four years the Spaniards had armed the Creeks against real or imaginary American encroachments. But in 1788 Spain, unsure of her position in Europe, reversed her old policy; she began to befriend the Americans, allowing them to migrate to Louisiana. McGillivray, still resentful of the United States, refused to go along with Spanish policy. And he showed at the first opportunity that he would not be coerced into permitting the Spaniards to dictate his policies. He received Bowles warmly in the Lower Creek towns. Though Bowles never disclosed his real intentions to McGillivray, he entered into an agreement with him to secure supplies from New Providence. McGillivray even assured Bowles that he would offer no opposition to any activities of the New Providence merchants in Florida.[16]

Bowles returned with this information to New Providence, where Lord Dunmore and Miller immediately made preparations for an armed invasion of Florida. They enlisted over thirty men, placed them under Bowles, and sent them in two ships to East Florida. But the Creeks were disappointed to learn that Bowles, despite his bold promises of innumerable gifts, came with only a few horseloads of ammunition, a small brass cannon, and just enough cloth to trade for food for himself and his companions. And soon after he landed most of his men deserted him and surrendered to the Spanish authorities in East Florida. They explained that they had left their leader because he planned to use them in an attack on one of Panton's stores. McGillivray, who was disgusted with Bowles, surmised that his followers had succumbed to wet weather.

Deprived of their services, Bowles, who later accused them of laziness and cowardice, fled to the Florida Keys, where luckily he found a wrecked schooner. Appropriating its cargo, he found a number of elaborate uniforms in which he dressed his few Indian comrades, whom he took in a fishing boat to Halifax, Nova Scotia. Its governor, believing his tale that he headed a delegate of Creek and Cherokee chiefs bound for London on business vital to the British Empire, sent him and his followers to Quebec, whence they sailed to London. There he represented himself as an official delegate from the "United Nation of the Creeks and Cherokees" seeking recognition of their state, a commercial treaty, and a military alliance. Bowles arrived a little too late to secure favorable negotiations with the government. Spain and England had just settled their controversy over the Nootka Sound on the west coast of North America. Nevertheless, the ministers, regarding him as a useful tool should England and Spain come to blows, received him cordially, while many members of the nobility feted him lavishly. The government opened all its West Indian ports to vessels flying the flag of the new Creek and Cherokee nation which Bowles said he represented.[17]

Returning to New Providence in the summer of 1791, Bowles gave Dunmore and Miller contradictory reports of what he had accomplished in England and of what he planned to do next. In his breathless but compelling manner he spoke of an alliance with England, of an alliance with McGillivray, of his determination to destroy McGillivray, who had forsaken him, of his plans to raid Georgia, and of his designs against one of Panton's stores. Though Miller had lost nearly £2000 in Bowles' first venture, he and Dunmore again supported him in his new enterprise, whatever it entailed.[18]

That fall Bowles landed in Florida, where he arranged for his followers to elect him "Director of Affairs of the Creek and Cherokee nation." To the Count of Floridablanca, Spanish minister, and to Arturo O'Neill, governor of Pensacola, he addressed a memorial in which he offered them a Creek and Cherokee alliance and declared that, as "Director of the Affairs of the United nations of Creek and Cherokee," he intended

> ... to Establish the free ingress & egress of the Vessels of all Nations
> (not at War with us) to the Ports & Rivers of this Coast, & I do also

declare that I have no Intention to Intercept or molest any of his Catholic Majesty's Subjects, unless they or any of them shall give me molestation.[19]

Again circumstances in the tribe favored him. He learned that during his absence McGillivray had signed a treaty at New York which ceded to the United States certain Creek lands along the Oconee River. Bowles cleverly used Creek resentment as a weapon against McGillivray who, having persuaded the Spanish government to renew its subsidy to his people, had no further need of him. Bowles branded McGillivray a puppet of the United States and, on this ground, challenged his right to leadership of the Creeks. And he was able to muster enough support among their warriors to prevent the execution of the Treaty of New York. The American commissioners waited in vain at the specified place for the delegation of chiefs who were to assist in surveying the new boundary line. In high dudgeon McGillivray called Bowles a liar, a rascal, and a vagabond, proclaimed a reward of $300 for his head, and sent three warriors to kill him. In this endeavor McGillivray failed, either because, being afflicted with rheumatism and fever, he was unable to give the matter his close attention, or because he was not powerful enough to nullify the militant group that sided with "Captain Liar," as he called Bowles.[20]

Because Bowles did not recognize Panton as a Spanish subject, he moved quickly against his store at St. Marks in the Apalache country. The storekeeper, Edward Forrester, described the attack, which occurred on the evening of January 16, 1792, in breathless and angry sentences:

... a man now Calling himself William Cunningham, with about nine or more Indians, Came to the Store at Appalachy, and was acoasted in the yard by Mr. John Humbly & my Self by Inviting him in to the House under the name of Major Cunningham of whom we had heard of, and had reson to Expect as a British officer from Detroit to Enquire what Bowles was about—Who after having Sat about a minute or two arose from his Seat & Steping towards the Door drew his Sword or hanger Saying the House & Store were his, & not one Soule Stur a foot, or offer the least Resistance or he would Cut them to pieces, if there should be the least Resistance made; & demanded the Keys of all the Store & House, with vehement threats, that if Refused I Should be Cut to pieces which I thereupon brought & Cast upon the Table; Saying these were all I had in my possession. After which he took the Keys up & ordered me go with him and Shew him the different Houses & Stores, that he wanted to Examin if the Doors were lock'd or not— and on Coming to the Counting House asked for the key to it, on which I told him Mr. Leslie had it & was at the Fort with it, on which he seem'd very Suspicious, & Still threatening Very Severely he would take my life, to which I told him bring in his powder he might do as he pleased, & this I repeated Several times & that he might Cut away; . . .[21]

Cunningham, forcing Forrester to break into the armory, took fifty guns; but Bowles intervened, saying that twenty-five were enough for the present. At this juncture John Leslie arrived at the store, found Bowles in control of it, and delivered its keys to him.[22]

Bowles and his Indians kept some of Panton's employees at their tasks, forcing them to turn over needed supplies. But Cunningham and Bowles soon quarreled over some trifling matter, giving Forrester an opportunity to make his getaway to the fort at St. Marks with the account books. "I thought proper to Take a Dark night," he wrote later, "and come to the Fort with the Books of Panton Leslie & Co and with Such articles or clothing of my own as I could easily get away with."[23]

The garrison, however, was inadequate to recapture the store. McGillivray and Panton were about to act when Bowles found himself in the hands of Baron Carondelet, the new governor of Louisiana. With the pretext that he wished to give him a reply to his memorial to Floridablanca, Carondelet invited him to New Orleans. Against the advice of his men, Bowles boarded the ship that Carondelet had sent to convey him to the town. When he arrived there he was quietly arrested and sent as a prisoner to Spain.[24]

Panton rejoiced, but he was soon to lose the friend from whom his financial blessings flowed. In the fall of 1792 McGillivray, returning home from a conference with Carondelet, contracted a violent fever which hung on for a long time. He had hardly recovered when, in October, he reached home. "On my first Coming home," he wrote later, "I had so much to do that I coud not leave it soon & the Cursed Gout [perhaps rheumatism] seizing me has laid me up these two months nearly. Every periodical attack grows more Severe & longer in Continuance. It now mounts from my feet to my knees & am Still Confined to the fire side."[25] He grew progressively worse, and on February 17, 1793, he died. Because he was not a Roman Catholic, he was denied burial in the regular cemetery. Panton buried him with full Masonic honors in his garden while Creeks expressed their great grief with wails and screams. Panton paid final tribute to his good friend in a beautiful letter to Lachlan McGillivray in Scotland

. . . Your son, sir, was a man that I esteemed greatly. I was perfectly convinced that our regard for each other was mutual. It so happened that we had an interest in serving each other, which first brought us together, and the longer we were acquainted, the stronger was our friendship.

I found him deserted by the British, without pay, without money, without friends, and without property, saving a few negroes, and he and his nation threatened with destruction by the Georgians, unless they agreed to cede them the better part of their country. I had the good fortune to point out a mode by which he could save them all, and it succeeded beyond expectation. . . .

He died . . . of complicated disorders—inflamed lungs and the gout in his stomach. He was taken ill on the path coming from his cow-pen on Little River, where one of his wives, Joseph Curnell's daughter, resided, and died eight days after his arrival here. No pains, no attention, no cost was spared to save the life of my friend. But fate would have it otherwise, and he breathed his last in my arms. . . .

He died possessed of sixty negroes, three hundred head of cattle, with a large stock of horses. . . .

I advised, I supported, I pushed him on, to be the great man. Spaniards and Americans felt his weight, and this enabled him to haul me after him, so as to establish this house with more solid privileges than, without him, I should have attained. This being the case, if he had lived, I meant besides, what he was owing me, to have added considerably to his stock of negroes. What I tended to do for the father, I will do for his children. This ought not to operate against your making that ample provision for your grandson, and his two sisters, which you have it in your power to make. They have lately lost their mother, so that they have no friends, poor things, but you and me. My heart bleeds for them, and what I can I will do. The boy, Aleck, is old enough to be sent to Scotland to school, which I intend to do next year, and then you will see him.[26]

2

About two weeks before McGillivray's death, revolutionary France, which had just guillotined Louis XVI, declared war on England. Soon Spain entered the war on the side of England. The war involved the United States for the first time in serious international relations. Most Americans naturally sympathized with France because she had assisted them in gaining their independence. They had recently been celebrating French victories by singing patriotic songs, putting on cockades, drinking toasts, and setting off fireworks. Now they clamored to rush to her assistance against Great Britain, that common enemy of human liberty. But news of the war between France and England greatly disturbed President Washington who, mindful that the United States was financially in no condition to wage war, determined to maintain her neutrality. Yet the United States had, by her treaty of 1778, bound herself forever to assist France in the West Indies.

Hamilton, who favored England and who had frowned on the treaty with France, argued that it had been negotiated between the United States and Louis XVI and that, since the king was dead, it was no longer binding. But Jefferson, though desiring peace, insisted that the treaty between the United States and France was a treaty between two nations and that, since they still existed, it should be honored. So went the heated arguments between the Hamiltonians and Jeffersonians until on April 22 Washington cooled them by issuing his policy of neutrality. This document, known as Washington's Neutrality Proclamation, stated that the conduct of the United States during the conflict in Europe should be "friendly and impartial" and that any American who illegally aided or abetted hostility against any of the warring powers would be prosecuted.

The proclamation bitterly disappointed those who had expected active intervention in behalf of France. They expressed their sentiments in such toasts as the following: "May the sister republics of France and America be as incorporate as light and heat." "May honour and probity be the principles by which the connexions of free nations shall be determined." "May those who attempt to evade or violate the political obligations and faith of our country be considered as traitors & consigned to infamy." "May all tories have a perpetual itching, and never the gratification of scratching."[27]

On the day that Washington signed the Neutrality Proclamation, the Philadelphia newspapers announced the arrival at Charleston, as it was now spelled, of Citizen Edmond Charles Genêt, first minister from the new French republic. The frigate that bore him, the *Embuscade*, had anchored in the harbor just two weeks earlier. Her contours, her sails, the liberty cap that hung from her foremast head, and the letters "R.F." that adorned her quarter galleries—all proclaimed her French nationality. Immediately ten thousand throats or more roared a loud and zealous welcome. Ardent, passionate, excitable, and stubborn, Genêt unknowingly violated the Neutrality Proclamation again and again. The French government had instructed him to seek with the United States a treaty that would assist him in rapidly freeing Spanish America, in securing navigation of the Mississippi for the frontiersmen of Kentucky, in delivering Louisiana and Florida from Spanish tyranny, and perhaps in adding the "fair star of Canada to the American constellation." Should he find the United States reluctant to support this program, he would take all measures that comported with his position to develop the principles of liberty and independence in Louisiana and other Spanish provinces adjacent to the United States.[28]

In accordance with these instructions Genêt declared Michel Ange Bernard de Mangourit, French consul at Charleston, a court of admiralty so that he could judge prizes caught by French privateers. He set up similar tribunals elsewhere. He dispatched to Canada, to Nova Scotia, and to Louisiana colorful proclamations inviting the inhabitants of these colonies to throw off the British or Spanish yokes and promising them assistance in this endeavor. He instructed Mangourit to plan an expedition of American frontiersmen against Louisiana and Florida, while he interested himself in the details of a similar movement from Kentucky with which Mangourit's corps were eventually to unite. The expedition from Kentucky was to be under George Rogers Clark who, feeling neglected by his own government, gladly accepted a commission to serve France against Spain in New Orleans.[29]

Having prepared these stratagems, Citizen Genêt departed for Philadelphia to present his credentials to President Washington. Instead of taking the easier route by sea he journeyed by coach through the back country, whose small farmers, hating the aristocratic pro-English people of the east, were rabidly pro-French and Jeffersonian. His journey was one long ovation. The beaming young minister bowed to frantically cheering crowds at Statesburgh and Camden, South Carolina, at Salisbury, North Carolina, and at Richmond, Virginia, where, however, he declined a public feast in favor of an interview with merchants who were interested in selling their grain to France. He stretched his journey, which could have been made in a week, to twenty-eight days, during which time Americans burned more powder celebrating French liberty than was used in achieving it. At one place, Genêt served as godfather for an Indian child who was baptized Genêt Republican Frenchman.[30]

On May 16 he arrived in Philadelphia. Bells ding-donged joyfully and throats grew hoarse with cheering and singing and strangers of both sexes hugged and tugged as surging crowds escorted Genêt to Oeller's Tavern—the best in town—where his admirers showered him with bombastic sentiments and regaled him with a civic feast. He sooned learned of the Neutrality Proclamation. He was shocked but not discouraged. His roaring reception fortified his conviction that most Americans favored intervention on the side of France. The newspapers championed him. "Thanks to our God," exclaimed one of them, "the *sovereignty* still resides with THE PEOPLE, and that neither proclamations, nor *royal demeanor and state* can prevent them from exercising it. Of this the independent freemen of this metropolis gave a striking example in their reception to Mr. Genêt."[31]

Washington received Genêt's credentials and acknowledged him as Minister Plenipotentiary from the Republic of France to the United States. But Washington's manner was formal and dignified; his speech of welcome was frigid and short; it formed a painful contrast to the rousing reception Genêt had received from the people. Washington neither wore the red cap of liberty nor called Genêt "Citizen" nor kissed him on both cheeks in the French fashion. Genêt's anger mounted when he saw in one of the president's reception rooms medallions of the recently guillotined Louis XVI and of his ill-starred family. He withdrew in a rage, telling his admirers that "the old man," as he called Washington, wanted to be king and that, therefore, he had lost his love of liberty. Later he told friends that Washington was jealous of his popularity. He continued to send out privateers, some of which were captured British vessels, in defiance of the Neutrality Proclamation, until even Jefferson felt constrained to reprimand him. Fuming with anger, Genêt threatened to take his project directly to the people.[32]

Meanwhile, Governor William Moultrie of South Carolina had supplied Consul Mangourit with letters of introduction to some outstanding
officers of the American Revolution. The consul succeeded in enlisting
their services as agents or leaders of the planned expeditions against Spanish possessions. He wrote Genêt that he had given rank to those who
wanted rank and money to those who preferred money.[33] Among them
were William Tate of South Carolina and Elijah Clarke and Samuel Hammond of Georgia. Mangourit supervised two separate expeditions. The
first, under Hammond, was to attack St. Augustine. The other, composed
of Carolinian backwoodsmen under Tate, was to descend the Tennessee
River and co-operate with George Rogers Clark, who was to lead a force
of Kentuckians down the Mississippi against New Orleans. Clarke collected men in western Georgia, presumably as a free lance, with designs
against West Florida.[34]

All these officers met with Genêt's hearty approval. Mangourit characterized Tate to the minister as having all the virtues and none of the
vices and ignorance of a true adventurer. In the consul's words, Tate
"conceives in a moment, decides in an instant, and carves in the right
joint." Tate soon boasted that he had a force of two thousand men. He
was so elated with his success in recruiting them that he talked of leading
his men in the conquest of South America. Colonel Clarke was a tough,
rugged officer who had shown unlimited endurance and courage in a
number of engagements during the Revolution. Colonel Hammond,
whom Mangourit described to Genêt as "our great pivot," was supreme
commander of the invading expeditions, which were collectively known
as the "Revoluntary Legion of the Floridas."

Born in Virginia, Hammond had served as a cavalry officer in Lord
Dunmore's War in 1774 and at King's Mountain in 1780. He had a
brother, Abner, who was also interested in the movement. As a member
of the trading firm of Hammond and Fowler, he hoped to supercede
Panton, Leslie and Company in the Creek trade. Samuel Hammond, indeed, made a treaty with the Creeks, who agreed to fight Spaniards in
return for liberal gifts of shirts, razors, scissors, salt, and uniforms of the
National Guard. When Washington learned of these plans and arrangements, he naturally accused Genêt of violating the neutrality of the
United States. The minister defended his actions on the ground that the
troops were raised not in the territory of the United States but among
the independent Indian tribes, who were ancient allies of the French.
Jefferson, who expected that the United States would soon be at war with
Spain, decided that, while he formally made a show of preserving the
neutrality of the United States, he would maintain some acquaintance
with Genêt's designs, particularly since they were represented as nothing
more than a plan to liberate Louisiana.[35]

George Rogers Clark entered into Genêt's designs with boundless
enthusiasm. He wrote to the minister in Philadelphia, declaring that with
four hundred men he could drive the Spaniards from upper Louisiana

and with eight hundred men from New Orleans. Expressing his readiness
to raise such a force, he asked for £3000 sterling to promote the project
and for naval assistance consisting of two or three frigates. Genêt accepted Clark's proposals and appointed him "major general of the Independent and Revolutionary Legion of the Mississippi."[36]

From his agent, André Michaux, a French botanist who had traveled
widely on the frontier, Genêt learned that his designs were proceeding
satisfactorily. He unfolded them to Jefferson, "not as Secy. of state, but
as mr. Jeff." Jefferson warned him "that his enticing officers and souldiers
from Kentucky to go against Spain, [was] really a halter about their
necks, for that they [would] assuredly be hung, if they [began] hostilities a[gainst] a nation at peace [with] the US. that leaving out that
article I did not care what insurrection should be excited in Louisiana, . . ."[37] Though he considered a French alliance his "polar star," he
realized that Great Britain and Spain were dangerous neighbors because
of their influence over the Indians and because of their own unfriendli-
ness toward the United States.

Genêt's designs and preparations greatly alarmed Baron de Carondelet,
governor of Louisiana, who, finding himself without an adequate force
with which to stem a possible attack on the colony, alerted the Spanish
representatives in Philadelphia. They in turn communicated their apprehension to Jefferson. The secretary assured them that President Washington "will employ all his power to restrain the citizens of the United
States from . . . sharing in any hostility by land or sea against the subjects
of Spain or its dominions." In conformity with this policy, Washington
sent instructions to Governor Shelby of Kentucky to watch "with the
strictest caution over any attempts that may be made there to incite the
citizens of that state to take part in that enterprise or any other."[38]

Clark planned to march against New Orleans by the middle of February, 1794, providing Genêt would send them the necessary funds. But
Genêt, meeting Hamilton's stubborn opposition, failed to obtain any
advances of the money that the United States owed to France. Then
Washington and his cabinet, disgusted by Genêt's threat to appeal to the
people above their heads, requested the French government to recall him.
By this time, a new faction, the Jacobins, ruled in France. Hating Genêt,
who was a Girondist, they were eager to curtail his diplomatic career
as well as his head. They agreed to his recall, thereby wrecking his designs
against Louisiana and the Floridas. Even his former friend, Governor
Moultrie, turned against him and told him in a letter that he had "deeply
offended the friends of France." But Washington declined to bestow a
martyr's crown on his detractor by sending him back to France. The
"burned-out comet," as Hamilton called him, "retired to New York,
where hand in hand with the daughter of Governor Clinton, he faced the
altar instead of the guillotine."[39]

Acting on his instructions, Genêt's successor, Joseph Fauchet, issued
on March 6 a public statement forbidding Frenchmen to violate the

Neutrality Proclamation and terminating the planned expeditions against Louisiana and the Floridas. Mangourit would not believe that Fauchet's orders were genuine; he called them an English hoax; he urged his agents forward. "In the name of the Republic," he wrote Fauchet, "send us some artillery, some guns with bayonets . . . on the tenth, the tenth [of April] we send the hymns of the Republic echoing through the caverns of royalty."[40] But the movement was wrecked. Elijah Clarke took his disappointed followers to the Oconee, where he established himself among the Indians. Tate and Hammond fled to Amelia Island. And George Rogers Clark, embittered over the failure of his mission, never again took part in any public affair.[41]

3

In their declaration of loyalty to French principles, Genêt's agents doubtless were moved by the spirit of antagonism toward a possible *rapprochement* between England and the United States. On November 19, 1794, after Genêt's designs had been wrecked, the two nations signed Jay's Treaty, by which England promised to surrender the posts in the Northwest Territory which she had illegally occupied since the end of the American Revolution. Spain, faced with military reverses and unpopular taxes, threatened by conspiracy against the government, and fearful of a future Anglo-American alliance that would be directed against Louisiana, decided on a policy of peace with all nations. First she deserted her ally, England, and made peace with France. Then, fearing English wrath, she turned to make peace with the United States and thereby protect her dominions against aggressive frontiersmen who for years had clamored for free navigation of the Mississippi.[42] So on October 27, 1795, Godoy, Spanish minister of foreign affairs, and Thomas Pinckney, envoy extraordinary of the United States, signed at the Spanish village of San Lorenzo el Real a treaty in which Spain conceded everything she had denied for twelve years. She granted the United States free navigation of the Mississippi and the right to deposit goods at New Orleans for transshipment for a period of three years, designated the boundary of Florida at the thirty-first parallel, and promised to restrain the tribes of the Southern Frontier.

This treaty, which was as favorable to the United States as it was detrimental to Spain, removed the rock on which the diplomatic differences of the two nations had been stranded. But Spain considered her concessions as only a temporary expedient that she hoped eventually to evade. Godoy himself admitted that the Treaty of San Lorenzo averted "great latitude to evil designs; it was possible to injure Spain in an indirect manner, and without risk, in her distant possessions."[43] The truth was that the Treaty of San Lorenzo was bound up with the disposal of Louisiana. That colony was useless to Spain, but it was a valuable diplomatic pawn. Godoy had long wanted to sell or transfer it to France, but not before it had served his purpose of gaining the friendship of the United States against a possible Anglo-American attack on Spanish territory. After he signed the Treaty of San Lorenzo, he had no further need of Louisiana. So in December, 1795, he offered the colony to France in return for Santo Domingo, which France had recently acquired from him. But France thought Godoy's price for Louisiana was too steep and, in hopes of striking a bargain, continued negotiations with him for several years.[44]

Meanwhile Carondelet, governor of Louisiana, acted in accordance with Godoy's orders. When negotiations with France blew hot, Godoy ordered the governor to proceed to the punctual execution of the Treaty of San Lorenzo; when negotiations blew cold, he rescinded or reversed his orders without giving his real reasons. Carondelet himself frowned on the Treaty of San Lorenzo. He was intriguing with that colorful bamboozler, James Wilkinson, and some of his fellow Kentuckians to set up their state as an independent nation that would serve as a buffer between the United States and Louisiana. Carondelet felt that this project would fall through if Americans obtained free navigation of the Mississippi, which would put them in the position of attacking Louisiana and even of menacing Mexico and other Spanish possessions. But as a loyal subject of his Catholic Majesty, who was a pitiful puppet of Godoy, he had no choice but to follow orders as he received them.[45]

The wavering negotiations of two great nations over Louisiana threw their full weight, of all places, on tiny Natchez on the lower Mississippi. For in its ramshackle Spanish fort gathered Wilkinson and his fellow intriguers, promoters of land speculation at Muscle Shoals and the fertile Yazoo strip, and officials of Spain and of the United States. Among the latter was Andrew Ellicott, Surveyor General of the United States, whom President Washington had appointed commissioner to represent his country in surveying the boundary established by the Treaty of San Lorenzo. He was past forty years old and had spent many years conducting surveys between Pennsylvania and New York, in the District of Columbia, and at Niagara Falls. Though he professed Quakerism he never permitted its pacifism to stand in his way of fighting for what he thought were his rights. On the eve of his departure for Natchez, where he was to begin his duties, he held a conference with Washington, who told him confidentially that certain Americans, such as Wilkinson, had formed improper associations with the Spanish government and that, therefore, neither Spaniards nor frontiersmen were to be trusted. Washington thought the matter so important to the honor and safety of the country that he asked Ellicott to investigate it privately and to make a report of it for him.

Ellicott, as he departed on his mission, became suspicious of everybody —like a man who has been warned that he can expect to encounter bandits as he walks in the dark. At Pittsburgh, where he arrived in October, 1796, he met Wilkinson himself who was traveling eastward and who placed at his disposal a river boat with "new and spacious cabin." At Cincinnati he heard rumors of Wilkinson's intrigue with Carondelet. At the mouth of the Ohio he enlisted the services of Philip Nolan, a daring young adventurer who was famous for his "athletic exertions and dexterity in taking wild horses" and who is sometimes erroneously regarded as the "Man Without a Country." At New Madrid, in present Missouri, Ellicott received respectful treatment from the commander who, however, informed him that Carondelet forbade him to descend the river "till the posts were evacuated, which could not be effected till the water should rise." The surveyor's suspicions were immediately aroused. He told Nolan that he strongly suspected that something had gone wrong with the Treaty of San Lorenzo.

"Keep your suspicions to yourself," advised Nolan. "By no means let them appear; you may depend on me, whatever I can discover, you shall know, but the utmost caution will be necessary, both for your success and my own safety."[46]

At Chickasaw Bluffs Ellicott received a letter from Manuel Gayoso de Lemos, governor of Natchez and commissioner of the survey for Spain, saying that the forts could not be evacuated for want of ships, which were momentarily expected, and requesting him to leave his military escort, numbering about twenty-five men, at Bayou Pierre to prevent any unfortunate incident between them and the Spanish soldiers. Ellicott agreed, though he questioned the sincerity of Gayoso's reasons and took the precaution of ordering his escort to raise the American flag at the mouth of Bayou Pierre.[47]

On February 24, 1797, Ellicott reached Natchez, where Gayoso received him with great courtesy and promised to begin negotiations regarding the survey on March 19. The governor was quite sincere in his intentions, though Ellicott received them with badly concealed suspicion. Honest, charming, speaking excellent English, and married to an American woman, Gayoso counted many friends among the planters of the region. He not only protected them against their debtors in New Orleans but he encouraged them to lead lives of visiting, eating, drinking, dancing, and card-playing. Their affection for him increased with his chances of bankruptcy.

Ellicott and his few attendants soon camped on the top of a hill about a mile and a half from town and put up the American flag. Within two hours a messenger from Gayoso requested him to take the flag down. He positively refused. The flag, he proudly wrote in his journal, "wore out upon the staff."[48] In the next two weeks he lessened his resentment as Gayoso proceeded with the work of evacuation. Then Gayoso received another countermanding order from Carondelet. And Gayoso hauled back the cannon he had taken from the fort to the river landing. While Ellicott fumed, Gayoso coolly explained that he could not keep the cannon in an exposed place. But in a proclamation that he issued on the following day Gayoso gave new or added reasons for his actions: "His Majesty has offered to support the rights of the inhabitants to their real property, and until this is ascertained I am bound to keep possession of this country, as likewise until we are sure that the Indians will be pacific." He assured the colonists that they would never be molested for their religious principles and that they were free to hold private meetings, but that they were allowed to worship no other faith save Catholicism, the religion "generally established in all His Majesty's dominions."[49]

The Protestant settlers of the region were so infuriated by this portion of the proclamation that they threatened Gayoso with bodily harm. Hutchins went to Ellicott and offered to take the governor by surprise and carry him as a prisoner to the Chickasaws, who hated the Spaniards. Ellicott rejected this proposition, but not with contempt, for Hutchins enjoyed considerable respect among the settlers of the district. Ellicott himself had greatly increased the agitation. He had raised recruits in the district, a measure which Gayoso decried as both improper and impolitic. And Ellicott had written to General Anthony Wayne in the Northwest Territory for reinforcements. Wayne had detached a company under Lieutenant Percy Smith Pope but had ordered this officer to stay at Fort Massac, on the junction of the Ohio and the Mississippi rivers, until he obtained some information respecting the evacuation of the forts. Ellicott induced Pope to descend the river to Natchez. This questionable character, whose drooling habits and unprovoked fits of fury earned him the nickname of Crazy Pope, lacked artillery, tents, money, and medicines, all of which Ellicott had to furnish.[50]

So matters stood until, on the first of May, Gayoso confronted Ellicott with still another excuse for his failure to evacuate the forts. This time the American commissioner was told that the Spanish minister to the United States had informed the king of an attack which the British from Canada planned against Spanish territory in upper Louisiana. Since this British expedition could not succeed without passing through United States territory, the king had decided to "suspend" evacuation of the forts until the danger had passed and to strengthen the defenses of the province. Ellicott was undeceived:

> Having heard nothing respecting the intended British expedition from Canada, but from the officers of his Catholic Majesty, it appeared to us, that it was probably no more than a pretext for putting the country in such a state of defense, as to render our getting possession of it difficult, and expensive, and enable his Catholic Majesty to retain a part of it by the negotiations which Governor Gayoso informed us officially was then carrying on.[51]

To Ellicott's vehement protests Gayoso replied that as an agent to His Catholic Majesty he had no choice but to obey orders. Soon Carondelet issued a proclamation in which he stated that "some evil disposed persons" had forced the king to suspend evacuation of the forts in order to secure the safety of lower Louisiana. After this proclamation, wrote

Ellicott, "the public mind might be compared to inflammable gaz; it wanted but a spark to produce an explosion!"[52]

The explosion soon occurred. About June 1 John Hanna, an itinerant Baptist minister, asked Gayoso's permission to preach a sermon on the following Sunday. Gayoso granted his request but, mindful of the prevailing agitation among the people, cautioned him against discussing political matters. A Protestant sermon was so rare a thing in the region that it drew a considerable crowd. Though Hanna refrained from making political allusions, he became so puffed up with the attention he received that, on the following Friday, he engaged some Irish Catholics in a controversy over certain practices of their faith.

The Catholics, their fervor intensified by liberal draughts of whiskey, took offense at what they regarded as Hanna's deprecations of some of their sacred tenets and gave him a thrashing. The preacher with his bloody nose and blackened eye went to Gayoso, threatening to take his revenge on his attackers with the help of his Protestant friends. The governor listened to his rantings with more than ordinary patience, then coolly had him arrested and had his feet placed in stocks. This enraged the Protestant settlers to the extent that Gayoso, together with other Spanish officials and their families, took refuge in the fort. The malcontents then went to Crazy Pope, who by now was drooling with fury, and demanded that he storm the fort; but Ellicott with great difficulty induced him instead to issue a proclamation requesting the people to hold a meeting to determine what should be done. At the meeting, which they held at Belk's house on the Nashville road eight miles from Natchez, they organized a Committee of Public Safety which included Hutchins, Ellicott, and Pope. The Committee drew up four articles which Gayoso reluctantly accepted:

1st. The inhabitants of the District of Natchez who under the belief & persuasion that they were Citizens of the U.S. agreeably to the late treaty have assembled & embodied themselves are not to be prosecuted or injured for their Conduct on that account but to stand exonerated & acquitted.

2n. The Inhabitants of the Government aforesaid above the 31st degree of North Latitude are not to be embodied as militia or called upon to aid in any military operation except in case of an Indian invasion or for the suppression of riots during the present State of uncertainty owing to the late treaty between his Catholic Majesty & the U.S. not being carried fully into effect.

3rd. The laws of Spain in the above District shall be continued and all occasions be executed with mildness & moderation nor shall any of the inhabitants be transported as prisoners out of this Government on any pretext whatever and notwithstanding the operation of the law aforesaid is hereby admitted yet that the Inhabitants shall be considered to be in actual state of neutrality during the Continuance of their un-certainty as mentioned in the second proposition.

4th. We the Committee aforesaid do engage to recommend it to our Constituents, and to the utmost of our power endeavor to preserve the Peace & promote the due Execution of Justice within the said Govern-ment.[53]

The Committee was a temporary body that dissolved itself as soon as it had completed its work. Carondelet, fearing that the revolution might spread to Louisiana, hastened to placate its leaders by accepting their articles. Early in July the settlers, with Gayoso's approval, appointed a permanent committee that recognized him as governor of the Natchez district.[54]

The king soon rescued him from his humiliating situation by appoint-ing him to succeed Carondelet, whom he promoted to a post in Quito. Four days later Gayoso departed for New Orleans, leaving Captain Stephen Minor, his former secretary, as temporary commander of the fort and as civil and military governor of the Natchez district.

Minor was an American immigrant who had served His Catholic Majesty wisely and well for over a decade; but he found insoluble prob-lems in his new post. No sooner had the settlers united in declaring them-selves citizens of the United States than they divided sharply over their political creeds. Hutchins, who felt that he deserved political leadership of the region by right of his wealth, his long residence, and his influence in both the British and Spanish periods, bitterly resented Ellicott. He and his friends wanted to organize a committee of their own which would elect to Congress a territorial delegate who would work for them in securing their land claims, which were largely pretended. Hutchins addressed to Congress a memorial in which he denounced Ellicott as an appeasor of Spain and as an opponent of democratic government. But Ellicott learned of the memorial and had his men take it away from the messenger sent to deliver it. The infuriated Hutchins then threatened to publish a story of "old Ellicott, young Ellicott, and a housekeeper." This time Ellicott's men chased the scandalmonger deep into the woods. Minor was horrified at the prevailing turmoil. "God send a speedy determina-tion of things," he prayed, "otherwise they will all run mad, with me-morials, certificates, circular letters &ca."[55]

Eventually his prayer was answered. Godoy had, by his wavering ne-gotiations with France over the disposal of Louisiana, unleashed troubles he had never imagined; he now hastened to restore order for the good of Spain. He greeted the revolutionary activities of the colonists "as a good means of pacifying them." Then he ordered evacuation of the forts. Be-hind his change of policy lay weighty considerations of state. His nego-tiations with France had failed. And, furthermore, he feared that if he allowed the turmoil in the Natchez district to continue it might easily spread to other Spanish possessions in North America. So, he wisely decided to surrender the posts in his endeavor to conciliate the United States. This time he could have no reason to change his mind again.[56]

In January, 1798, Gayoso, acting on orders from Spain, informed Ellicott that His Catholic Majesty had decided to surrender the territory north of the treaty line of demarkation. The decision was not too early, for the exasperated American government had sent Captain Isaac Guion with orders to seize the forts. Guion had given Minor until the last day of March to leave Natchez.

In these circumstances the beleaguered garrisons at Natchez and at Walnut Hills, on the present site of Vicksburg, Mississippi, took their artillery, stores, and baggage to their boats and galleys. Then, at four o'clock in the morning of March 30, the troops marched out of the fort toward the river bank to the sound of doleful drums. Andrew Ellicott rose from a few hours of repose to watch the evacuation. His pleasure was intensified when he discovered that the Spaniards had tried to slip away unnoticed. He walked to the fort and found the rear guard just leaving it. He walked past the open gate into the fort and, ascending its parapet, witnessed the departing galleys and boats until, before daylight, they faded from his view. The same day American troops occupied the fort.[57]

Ellicott could now proceed with his task of surveying the boundary established by the Treaty of San Lorenzo. Spain soon appointed a commissioner for the work that was to occupy him and Ellicott for the next two years. But now that the Spaniards were on his side Ellicott was "more sorely tried than ever. Mosquitoes, malaria, canebrakes, torrential rains, and incompetent helpers made his life a nightmare."[58] In Philadelphia, Dr. Benjamin Rush had given him some "precious pills" which had fortified him against malaria and other tropical diseases; but he had furnished him with no antidote against Creek and Seminole bullets, scalping knives, and poisoned arrows, which grew more and more violent the deeper he penetrated their country. When he and his party reached the Apalachicola River, the Indians attacked them so fiercely that they scampered like frightened rabbits to the safety of St. Augustine. Ellicott made some observations on the St. Marys River and then sailed for Philadelphia and safety. Even then, his trouble did not end. Timothy Pickering, secretary of state, scanned his expense account with distrustful eyes and gave him a tongue-lashing for its magnitude.[59]

Mississippi Territory

Early in June, 1797, four months after Ellicott arrived in Natchez to begin his survey, President John Adams sent to Congress a special message, in which he recommended the establishment of a government in the newly acquired region. Congress refused to act until it could reach an amicable settlement with Georgia, which claimed the region by right of a commission that the king had granted in 1764 to Sir James Wright, newly appointed governor of the province. Wright's commission designated a province with its western boundary at the Mississippi and its southern boundary at the thirty-first parallel from the Mississippi to the Chattahoochee and thence down this river to meet the line from the St. Marys River. The king had requested the governors of the southern provinces and Colonel John Stuart, superintendent of Indian affairs for the southern department, to meet with the Creeks and other southern tribes and settle their claims to the region. At this conference, held in Augusta in November, 1763, the Indians had recognized the right of the province to the region and had promised to confine themselves to a specified area within it. Thus Georgia was greatly enlarged to embrace most of the region which later became the states of Alabama and Mississippi.[1]

At the close of the American Revolution the state of Georgia still claimed these boundaries. But Congress declared that this vast region had been won not by Georgians in particular but by Americans in general and that, therefore, it belonged to the United States. But Georgia, relying on her colonial claims, as did every other state with western land, refused to cede her back country to Congress. In 1787 Congress again appealed to Georgia to give up her western land. Next year Georgia offered to sell to Congress a region running for a hundred forty miles from north to south and stretching from the Chattahoochee to the Mississippi. But she accompanied this offer with what Congress regarded as unreasonable conditions. She wanted Congress to pay her over $171,000, which she said she had spent in putting down Indian raids and in confirming her claim to the rest of her territory. Congress rejected these terms,

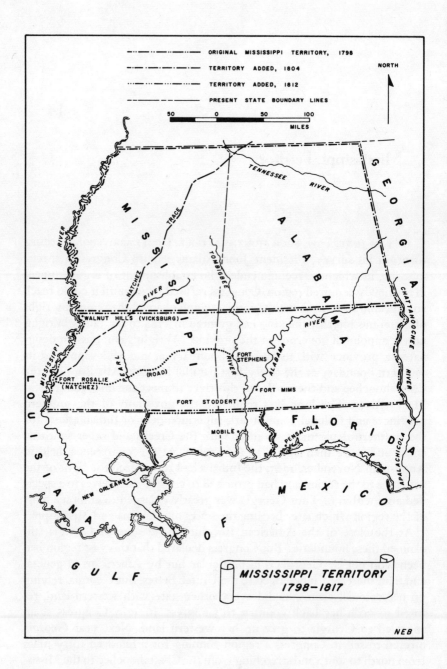

ORIGINAL MISSISSIPPI TERRITORY, 1798
TERRITORY ADDED, 1804
TERRITORY ADDED, 1812
PRESENT STATE BOUNDARY LINES

NORTH

50   0   50   100
MILES

GEORGIA

TENNESSEE   RIVER

M I S S I S S I P P I

A L A B A M A

CHATTAHOOCHEE   RIVER

RIVER

NATCHEZ   TRACE

TOMBIGBEE   RIVER

WALNUT HILLS (VICKSBURG)

RIVER

PEARL

(ROAD)

FORT
STEPHENS

ALABAMA   RIVER

FORT ROSALIE
(NATCHEZ)

RIVER

FORT MIMS

MISSISSIPPI

LOUISIANA

FORT STODDERT

F L O R I D A

MOBILE

PENSACOLA

APALACHICOLA R.

NEW ORLEANS

G U L F

O F

M E X I C O

MISSISSIPPI TERRITORY
1798-1817

NEB

though it agreed to accept them if they were properly modified and if Georgia agreed to cede her land west of the Chattahoochee. Georgia declined these proposals and allowed the matter to drop.[2]

The truth was that Georgia was deeply committed to land speculation by which she hoped to enrich herself. At first she had used her land wisely. To the officers and soldiers who had served her in the American Revolution she had granted generous tracts, with no cost for the first 200 acres save for office and surveying fees. So many settlers poured into Georgia that she saw fit to create new counties which, however, she provided with neither courthouses nor jails for many years. But she soon obviated all the good she had accomplished by allowing speculation that was as dishonest as it was rampant. Perhaps she felt that she could never assimilate her vast domain into the state; perhaps she feared that, with Spain astride it and the United States claiming it, she might lose it all. So, in 1789, she decided to sell vast tracts to three groups of speculators who had organized for the purpose of buying them.

Because some of the land lay in the vicinity of the Yazoo, this name was added to the companies. The Tennessee Yazoo Company, under the leadership of Zacariah Cox and with the support of the Holston settlers, secured the Muscle Shoals area. The Virginia Yazoo Company, including Patrick Henry and a wealthy fur merchant named David Ross, obtained a grant on the Mississippi as close to Chickasaw Bluffs as the claims of the state would permit. The South Carolina Yazoo Company, led by Thomas Washington, whose real name was Walsh, lay on the Mississippi between the Yazoo River and the lands of the Virginia Yazoo Company and included the important site of Walnut Hills, present Vicksburg, at the mouth of the Yazoo. These companies impressed the Georgia legislature with the importance of selling part of the back country to pay off the soldiers and the state debt. The legislature obliged them with a bill authorizing the sale of about 20,000,000 acres for $207,000. The terms required a small down payment with the remaining payments extending over a period of two years, after which title to the land should pass to the companies, or, if they defaulted in payment, should be returned to the state.[3]

The companies soon encountered difficulties. The legislature refused the paper money that the Virginia Yazoo Company gathered to make payment and withheld the title to its grant on grounds that it had failed to comply with the terms of its contract. In ensuing months the legislature turned down the paper money payments of the other companies and, at the end of two years, reclaimed their grants. The South Carolina Yazoo Company sued the legislature; but its efforts failed when its leader, Walsh, was arrested, tried for forgery in his state, and hanged in Charleston.[4]

But Georgia profited nothing from her experience. In 1795 influential members of the legislature accepted bribes from four new groups of speculators, the Georgia Company, the Georgia Mississippi Company, the Upper Mississippi Company, and the Tennessee Company, to introduce a bill authorizing the sale of tracts estimated from 35,000,000 to 50,000,000 acres for $500,000, or about one to one and a half cents an acre. The bill, a prolix and obscure document, mentioned no sale, but it aimed to bribe the citizens by setting aside for them 2,000,000 acres in each tract. Lobbyists from several states flocked to Augusta to hurry the bill through the legislature. Among them were a judge from the supreme court of Pennsylvania, a judge from a district court of Georgia, and a United States senator from Georgia. They offered as much as 75,000 acres to an influential member of the legislature. To others they offered slaves, barrels of rice, and various sums of money as they persuaded or cajoled or threatened them. They induced those who were too honest to vote for the bill to go home. Another group of speculators, the Georgia Union Company, seeing the absurd price that was being offered for the tracts and convinced that the legislature would pass the bill, offered $300,000 more for the land; but its offer was rejected.[5]

At first Governor George Mathews, fearing public wrath, refused to sign the bill; but he changed his mind when the speculators hurriedly modified some of its provisions. His young secretary bitterly opposed the bill. He was horrified that the governor should accept an enormity which he had so recently denounced. He knew that Mathews was a superstitious man. He hurriedly dipped the governor's pen in oil so that it would not write. He hoped that the governor would regard this as a bad omen and would refuse to sign the bill. But the ruse failed. Mathews scowled at the recalcitrant pen and called for a new one. Then he signed the infamous bill.[6]

The bad news touched off a storm of anger over the state. The people, regarding the sale as a theft of property that they felt belonged to them, sought to avenge themselves on the corrupt legislators. At an indignation gathering in Oglethorpe County, a man saw a friend carrying a rope toward the courthouse. Asked to explain the rope, he replied, "To hang Musgrove." This bribed legislator, learning that a man planned to lynch him, fled to South Carolina. One man followed a dishonest legislator into another state, found him sitting alone in a cabin, and shot him dead. Then the murderer became so distraught over his crime that he returned home and sought repentance by shutting himself up in a dark room for eighteen years.[7]

As soon as he learned of the Yazoo sale President Washington asked Congress to take action against it. Before Congress could do so, James Jackson resigned his seat in the United States Senate to accept a nomination to the state legislature and to devote his entire energy to having the infamous bill nullified. The voters turned out the corrupt legislature and, in the ensuing May, held a convention in which they condemned the bill and directed the new legislature to repeal it.[8]

This body, assembling at the new capital of Louisville under Jackson's powerful influence, resolved to eradicate the shame that the bill had heaped on the state. The legislature rescinded the bill, declaring that it was undemocratic, that it aimed at establishing an aristocracy, that it disposed of millions of acres under false title, and that it had accepted $300,000 less than the land was worth. The legislature then made long and elaborate preparations to burn the bill publicly, expunged all references to it from the state records, and decreed that any official who mentioned it thereafter would "be fined $1000 and rendered incapable of holding . . . any office of trust or profit in the state."[9]

On the designated day, February 13, 1796, people gathered from all parts of the state to witness the burning of the bill in front of the courthouse. The members of both Houses of the legislature filed out to the fire which, says tradition, had been drawn from heaven by means of a sun glass to give the ceremony celestial blessing. The president of the Senate examined the bill, then passed it to the speaker of the House, who read it and passed it to the clerk, who passed it to the doorkeeper, who committed it to the flames as he exclaimed: "God Save the State! And Long Preserve her Rights! ! And May every Attempt to Injure Them Perish as these Corrupt Acts now Do! ! !"[10]

In 1798 Georgia received a new constitution which declared that all her territory belonged to her free citizens. But the widespread agitation over the infamous Yazoo companies had led Congress to enquire anew into the claims of Georgia to her back country. To this end the Senate appointed a special committee which studied the matter and emphasized that the Proclamation of 1763 reserved under the sovereignty of the king all lands lying west of the sources of the rivers flowing into the Atlantic Ocean, and that therefore Georgia had no legal claim to her back country. But in this the committee overlooked the commission that the king had granted to Sir James Wright a year later than the Proclamation of 1763 and that extended the limits of Georgia to the Mississippi. Yet the committee had no desire to antagonize Georgia. So it advised the appointment of commissioners to reach amicable agreement with the state and recommended the establishment of a territorial government over the disputed region. In June, 1800, Congress passed an act putting the territorial government into operation.

The mild and obsequious manner in which Georgia remonstrated against the act marked a new era in her relations with the federal government. Congress referred the remonstrance to a House committee, which reported that Georgia had begun negotiations for the cession of the district and that therefore no action would be taken against her. In 1802 the Georgia commissioners, James Jackson, Abraham Baldwin, and John Milledge, met the United States commissioners, James Madison, Levi Lincoln, and Albert Gallatin, and agreed to cede to Congress for $1,250,-000 all the land beyond the present western boundary of Georgia. Even the Yazoo speculators were placated in this deal. They received 5,000,000 acres or the proceeds from the sale of 5,000,000 acres in Mississippi Territory.[11]

2

Mississippi Territory derived its government from the great Northwest Ordinance, which the Congress of the Confederation had passed on July 13, 1787, for the territory acquired from Great Britain at the close of the American Revolution. The Northwest Ordinance, which was applied, sometimes with modifications, to every American territory in its progress toward statehood, provided for three stages of territorial government. The first stage authorized a governor, a secretary, and three judges chosen by Congress to enforce laws and to control the militia. A territory reached the second stage of government when it could show the relative stability of having five thousand white males of voting age. It was then permitted to have a legislature consisting of a house of representatives elected by the people and a council of five members elected by Congress on nomination of the territorial House of Representatives, and a delegate to Congress who could participate in the deliberations but could not vote. A territory attained the third and last stage of government when it could show what the Ordinance considered an established society of sixty thousand people. It could then frame a constitution and apply for admission to the Union "on an equal footing with the original states in all respects whatever." The Ordinance granted religious freedom, guaranteed trial by jury, and declared that "schools and the means of education shall forever be encouraged." The sixth and last article of the Ordinance forbade slavery in the Northwest Territory. In the case of Mississippi Territory, however, this article was replaced by a provision which reads as follows:

> From and after the establishment of the aforesaid government, it shall not be lawful for any person or persons to import or bring into the said Mississippi Territory from any port or place within the limits of the United States, or to cause or procure to be so imported or brought, or knowingly to assist in so importing or bringing any slave or slaves, and every person so offending and being thereof convicted before any court within the said territory having competent jurisdiction, shall forfeit and pay for each and every slave so imported or brought, the sum of three hundred dollars; one moiety for the use of the United States and the other moiety for the use of any person or persons who shall sue for the same; and every slave so imported or brought shall hereupon become entitled to and receive his or her freedom.[12]

While this provision barred the importation of slaves from Africa and other foreign lands, it recognized traffic of slaves among the states.

The first appointed governor of Mississippi Territory was George

Mathews, but because he was implicated in the fraudulent land sales, he aroused so much opposition in the Yazoo district that President Adams saw fit to replace him immediately. Adams nominated Winthrop Sargent, secretary of the Northwest Territory, whom the senate confirmed. The choice of Sargent was even more injudicious than that of Mathews. In the Northwest Territory he had shown himself an unyielding and unimaginative New Englander who "wore his Harvard education on his sleeve" and who made no secret of his contempt for the frontiersmen. They had "frowned on his firm and drastic attitude toward the squatters beyond the Miami settlements and on his connivance with prominent speculators" while they had "laughed at his pompous manners and everlasting jeremiads."[13] His chronic ill health had hardly sweetened his temper. At last his physicians and friends, perhaps alarmed as much by his increasing boorishness as by his deteriorating health, impressed on him the necessity of "a change of air." President Adams went to the rescue of his fellow Federalist by nominating him for the governorship of Mississippi Territory.[14]

In June, 1798, Sargent left Cincinnati on a boat provided by General James Wilkinson. As he descended the Ohio and the Mississippi he was so ill that his companions repeatedly despaired of his llfe. Arriving at the Natchez district early in August, he sought convalescence at Concord, the handsome residence that Governor Gayoso had built, which stood about two miles from Fort Panmure. The southern climate partially restored his health, but it failed to change his personality. Though he stated in what he called his inaugural address that "only merit can entitle a man to office," he promptly filled all important posts with Federalists, most of whom belonged to the creditor class. Disdained or ignored, the Jeffersonian planters and mechanics expressed their dislike for him by dubbing him "His Yankeeship." He countered by calling them "the most Abandoned of Vilains who have escaped from the Chains and Prisons of Spain and been Convicted of the Blackest Crimes."[15]

He awaited the arrival of one of the three territorial judges, Daniel Tilton, who was to bring the Great Seal of the Territory as well as a set of laws of the original states from which must be fashioned a code of laws for the territory. Only one of the judges, Peter Bryan Bruin, a resident of the Natchez district, "was constantly present"; the other two judges "were slow to arrive, rapid to leave, and loath to remain on the job."[16] William McGuire of Virginia had the sole legal experience, and he unfortunately arrived too late and left too early to temper his muddling colleagues with his cautious wisdom. Early in January, 1799, arrived Tilton, a native of New Hampshire. He announced that he brought the Great Seal of the Territory but that his boat was too small to carry stationery, let alone bulky law books. So Sargent and the two judges sat down without any law books, without any legal experience, and without any understanding of frontier conditions and needs, to form a code for the territory. The result of their lucubrations was "Sargent's Code," most of which could be reconciled neither to the Constitution of the United States nor to the Northwest Ordinance.

Sargent's Code decreed that any person convicted of treason incurred the death penalty and forfeited all his property, real or personal, to the territory. It punished arson and burglary with cropping, pillorying, and whipping, and with confinement for not more than three years and forfeiture of all property. It imposed a tax on the two counties of Adams and Pickering, which Sargent had established, without determining their populations or their incomes. It provided fat fees for the governor, including five dollars for a passport, eight dollars for a tavern license, and ten dollars for a marriage license.[17]

These tyrannies immediately engendered violent resentment from the unprivileged Republicans. Such intelligent men as Cato West, Thomas Marston Green, and Anthony Hutchins resigned their civil offices to plot against Sargent for popular elections of military officers and, eventually, of civil officers as well. They attacked the governor in grand jury presentments of Adams and Pickering counties, then promulgated their grievances throughout the territory by addressing to Congress a number of petitions in which they denounced Sargent's Code and his appointment of men "well known to be hackneyed in Spanish duplicity and drudgery, whose former conduct is prophetic of their future, and who only wish and wait for an opportunity of aggrandizing themselves on the ruins of their Country."[18] As they repeated their demand for a greater voice in territorial affairs, they pointed out that even under the "despotic" Spaniards they had enjoyed the "privilege" of serving as advisers to the government.[19]

Sargent and his followers, of course, defended their policies. In an address to an Adams County jury, Daniel Clark deplored the unwillingness of many of the "Yeomanry" to support the territorial militia on the "ill-grounded belief that they have a right to chuse their leaders."[20] Sargent himself assured his detractors that he possessed all the necessary qualifications for his office, that the constitution required him to appoint all officers, and that he had no reason to be disappointed with any of his appointments. He said he would consider any removal not by innuendoes and insinuations but by "direct charges of Malconduct Substantiated by Facts."[21]

Meanwhile, West and his associates learned that their petitions had never reached Congress. They had entrusted them to Sargent, who patiently forwarded them to the state department, where Secretary Pickering carefully filed them away in his office. Now the wary Republicans adopted the plan of sending one of their ablest colleagues, Colonel Narsworthy Hunter, to Congress with two petitions, one requesting confirmation of the people's land rights and the other deploring Sargent's improper and oppressive measures and praying for the second stage of

territorial government, which would grant them a legislature and a delegate to Congress. Hunter wasted no time in introducing himself to William Charles Cole Claiborne of Tennessee and Thomas T. Davis of Kentucky—young frontier representatives who, anxious to ingratiate themselves with older members of their party, gladly offered to help him
realize his aims. As chairman of a House committee, Claiborne pushed
through a bill which the Senate, though dominated by Federalists,
adopted on May 10, 1800, and which President Adams quickly signed.[22]

But the Republicans regarded this as only a partial victory; they continued their attacks on Sargent and on the Federalist administration.
While Claiborne demanded repeal of Sargent's criminal codes and laws
regulating taverns and fees, several other frontier Republicans "attempted to abridge the power of the territorial governor, a move aimed
exclusively at Sargent."[23] Though the Senate refrained from proceeding
against complaints of maladministration against Sargent, it abolished
many of the objectionable provisions in his code, including those relating
to treason and arson and establishing exorbitant fees. Congress later confirmed the claims of the settlers to their lands.[24]

The more Sargent was maligned, the more was he determined to vin-
dicate his honor. He could not tolerate, he wrote, "the idea of being
vanquished in the way of well doing by a lot of miscreants *here* or *elsewhere.*"[25] At last he journeyed from New Orleans to Washington, new
capital of the United States, to defend his conduct and to seek reappointment. But he arrived too late. Thomas Jefferson had succeeded John
Adams to the presidency. And no sooner did Jefferson assume his duties
than he became convinced that Sargent must go. To please his Republican friends in Mississippi, he gave the post to Claiborne, who had kept his
native Tennessee for him during the balloting for president in the House
of Representatives. Jefferson requested James Madison, Secretary of
State, to notify Sargent of his dismissal:

That from the various and some of them delicate considerations
which mingled themselves with the designation of the individual for
the government of Mississippi Territory, it was expedient, in his judgment, to fill with another than yourself, whose administration, with
whatever meritorious intentions conducted, had not been so fortunate
as to secure the general harmony and the mutual attachment between
the people and the public functionaries so particularly necessary for
the prosperity and happiness of an infant establishment.[26]

In the autumn of 1801, while the Republicans of Mississippi Territory
anxiously awaited word of the triumph of their party, two men journeyed toward Natchez. Claiborne was going south to assume the duties
of governor of a turbulent territory. And Sargent was returning to his
estate and his wife, hoping to find peace at last.[27]

3

Claiborne was only twenty-six years old when, in November, 1801, he assumed his duties as governor of Mississippi Territory. Despite his youth he showed many of the qualities of a seasoned politician. Though born in Virginia, he had in his early years migrated to Tennessee, where his tact and good manners won him the admiration of John Sevier, popular states-man and Indian fighter, who persuaded him to study law. In 1796, when he was twenty-one, he served as a delegate from Knoxville to the conven-tion summoned to draw up a constitution for Tennessee, which had applied for admission into the Union. His friend Sevier, who had been elected governor of the new state, appointed him a judge of the supreme court. In the following November he was elected to Congress, where he supported Thomas Jefferson for the presidency. On May 25, 1801, his victorious friend rewarded him for his loyalty with the governorship of Mississippi Territory.

That autumn Claiborne and his bride journeyed by boat from Nash-ville to Natchez. Having braved the high winds and the hazards of low water in the Cumberland, the Ohio, and the Mississippi rivers, he was ready to master the turbulent politics of the territory. But the assembly, impressed or flattered by his conciliatory address, acceded gladly to his request to improve the judiciary and to organize a militia. It adopted, too, a code of laws which, however imperfect, had the saving grace of being more liberal than the old. In another session the assembly divided the territory into five counties and removed evidence of former Federalist control by changing the name of Pickering County to Jefferson County.[28]

To make the territory safe from the influence of the wealthy Natchez merchants, most of whom were rabidly Federalist, Claiborne, with the approval of President Jefferson, moved the territorial capital from Natchez to the village of Washington, six miles away. The governor further strengthened the territory by establishing on high ground near Washington a formidable stronghold, Fort Dearborn, where arms and ammunition could be stored for militia as well as regular American troops against spasmodic Indian raids or possible assaults from France or Spain.[29]

The importance of Fort Dearborn became evident when, on October 16, 1802, Juan Ventura Morales, intendent of New Orleans, convinced that Americans and Louisianians were carrying on a contraband trade highly detrimental to Spanish interests, suspended the right of deposit at that port without naming another place. This was a violation of the Treaty of San Lorenzo, signed seven years before. The Mississippi flat-boatmen, who were handling a large quantity of wheat and corn and whiskey for the American farmers and manufacturers as far away as Kentucky, found themselves deprived of a deposit for their cargoes while these awaited ocean-going ships. "The Mississippi," wrote Madison to

Pinckney, "is to them everything. It is the Hudson, the Delaware, the Potomac, and all the navigable rivers of the Atlantic States, formed into one stream."[30] The news from New Orleans, traveling slowly up the river and penetrating the valleys, infuriated the American frontiersmen: they demanded war. And war surely would have ensued had the United States been stronger. But the frontiersmen, though infuriated, were willing to see what President Jefferson could accomplish by diplomacy.

Matters were bound to change. Spain had in October, 1800, signed a preliminary treaty at San Ildefonso to transfer Louisiana to Napoleon, who wished to use the colony as a granary to feed the West Indian empire he planned to establish. He waited to make sure, however, that neither war with the United States nor with England would spoil his plans. On the day after Morales suspended the right of deposit, Spain signed the order to deliver Louisiana to France.

That made matters worse for the United States. She was much more afraid of France than of Spain in Louisiana. Claiborne learned, through some talkative ladies who had received their information from Morales, that Napoleon had ordered General Claude Victor to occupy the colony with 3000 men and that he planned to send 7000 more men to it within a month or two. To the territorial assembly Claiborne suggested an invasion of New Orleans. Jefferson urged the union of Great Britain and the United States in case Napoleon's troops occupied New Orleans and Louisiana. In December, 1802, Claiborne, addressing the assembly, treated the subject in these words:

> That anxious solicitude of the people of this Territory occasioned by the difficulties under which our commerce is placed in consequence of the Spanish Government withholding from citizens of the United States the privilege of depositing their merchandize and effects at the port of New Orleans, has not escaped my observation, and it is with regret that I inform you that the last advices are unfavorable to the prospect of immediate relief. We may, however, rest in confidence that on this occasion such measures will be adopted by the executive and legislature of United America to promote and protect the general interests of our common country, as wisdom shall dictate.[31]

In regard to the right of deposit, Claiborne had addressed a letter of protest to Morales, who replied that he was merely following the orders of his king. But His Catholic Majesty thought better of the matter. As soon as he learned that his subjects in New Orleans had "put their noses out of joint" by denying themselves American articles which they appreciated, he rescinded Morales' interdiction and, on March 1, 1803, restored the right of desposit to American farmers.

Three weeks later Pierre Clement de Laussat landed in New Orleans to make arrangements for the transfer of Louisiana to France. He was unaware that his master Napoleon was already negotiating with Robert Livingston to sell Louisiana to the United States. Later James Monroe arrived in Paris to assist Livingston in the negotiations. By now Napoleon had lost all hope of establishing a West Indian empire. In the previous year he had sent a splendid army of veterans under Leclerc, his brother-in-law, to subdue the rebellious blacks in Santo Domingo. Leclerc defeated the black liberator, Toussaint L'Ouverture, captured him, and sent him as a prisoner to France, where in the Jura Mountains he died of exposure. But a deadly scourge of yellow fever came to the rescue of the blacks; Leclerc's army melted away; he asked for reinforcements in vain; then he himself succumbed to the disease. His prestige suffering at home and abroad, Napoleon could not afford to send another army to Santo Domingo and risk the possibility of another defeat. Abandoning Santo Domingo, he had no further need of Louisiana. To avert war with the United States and to avoid driving her into the arms of England, he sold the vast colony to the American commissioners for $15,000,000.

By this time Claiborne had grappled mightily with a social menace—a menace which had brought and was still bringing ruin and sometimes death to many good citizens of a large section of the Southern Frontier and which was terrifying those who yet remained free of its clutches. For a number of years outlaws had been infesting the Natchez Trace, a narrow Indian trail that wound from Natchez through cane thickets and swamps and forests of oak and hickory and pine to Nashville on the Cumberland River, five hundred fifty miles away. John Swaney, who began to carry the mail over the trace in 1796, described it as a mere bridle path winding through an almost endless wilderness. The mail consisted of a few letters, newspapers, and government dispatches. Riding a sturdy horse, Swaney traveled the trace for eight years at about twenty-five miles a day, making a round trip every three weeks. At night he would build a fire and sleep under a blanket with a pistol at his side. At dawn he would feed his horse from the bushel of corn he brought with him. At every Indian village or white settlement he would blow his tin trumpet to announce his arrival to those who had something for him to carry. At Colbert's Ferry on the Tennessee River he could almost always count on some trouble from the "contrary" Indian ferryman who refused to cross for him if he arrived after bedtime. At Chickasaw Agency, halfway to his destination, he would change horses. Every forty or fifty miles he would meet a settler or a traveler returning to the north.[32]

The most notorious highwayman of the Natchez Trace during Claiborne's administration was Samuel Mason. Nothing in his background or early career presaged the criminal activity of his later years. He was born about 1750 of a good Virginia family; he served with George Rogers Clark's "Long Knives" in the Illinois country; he participated in the frontier defense of the upper Ohio; he proved himself one of General Edward Hand's best officers during Indian raids against Fort Henry, at present Wheeling, West Virginia. When the American Revolution ended, he opened a tavern in Wheeling and ran it successfully, until he drifted with his wife and children to eastern Tennessee, then to western Kentucky, presumably to take up the land which his state granted him for his military services. The Kentucky assembly, in its efforts to maintain law and order, commissioned him a justice of the peace.

He was a tall man who had grown somewhat portly and pompous with age. The mail carrier Swaney, who unfortunately encountered him several times on the Natchez Trace, described him to a writer of the frontier as "a fine looking man" with a protruding tooth that gave him a wolfish look and that he always tried to cover with his lip. But he was not without charm as he swaggered "a little in the light of his martial glory" or paced "the town landing, parleying with the merchants."[33]

Then his character changed completely. Or rather his aggressive nature, which in a law-abiding society made him a brave soldier, changed him on the bleak and lawless frontier into an outlaw. So he could lean "almost fearfully on his ancient manhood: he tried, as one might wrap a bundle with rotten twine, to tie up his present degradation with his former glory."[34] When he was drunk, he liked to boast that he was one of the boldest soldiers of the American Revolution, and that nobody excelled him in stealing Negroes. Did his great anger rise from his protruding tooth, which he felt spoiled his looks?

Mason and his men operated from the cavern of Cave-in-Rock on the northern bank of the lower Ohio River, in present Hardin County, Illinois, about twenty miles below Shawneetown and twenty miles above Golconda. Its location, with its large and dark funnel-like mouth extending into a gray limestone bluff partly hidden by shrubbery and small trees, was unknown to all white men save the outlaws.

Operating from this inaccessible hideout, Mason and his gang in the summer of 1801 committed their first famous robbery. Their victim was Colonel Joshua Baker, a merchant and planter of Hardin County, Kentucky. He had had a good year. He loaded several flatboats with wheat and vegetables and horses and lazied down the Mississippi to New Orleans, combining business with pleasure. He sold his cargo and started homeward with four men, each of whom rode a horse. With them were their five pack-mules laden with provisions and with the gold coins of their profit rolled tight in buckskin bags and concealed among their supplies. All went swimmingly until they reached the ford across a small, clear stream known today as Baker's Creek, where they dismounted to wash themselves. Mason and three of his men appeared with blackened faces, got between Baker and his companions and their horses, and demanded that they surrender their money and property. The surprised travelers handed over their horses, their utensils, and about $2300 in cash. The outlaws left as quickly as they had appeared. One of the pack-mules, which carried a considerable sum of money, became frightened at the sudden appearance of the bandits and ran off so fast that they were unable to pursue it. Baker and one of his companions eventually caught the animal, mounted it, and rode to the first settlement, where they obtained assistance in pursuing the bandits, but they found no trace of them.[35]

Soon one of Mason's sons, John, was arrested, perhaps in Natchez, and jailed as a possible participant in the robbery. He was tried, convicted, and punished with Moses' law of forty lashes save one. Somehow Samuel Mason learned that one of the jurors had expressed the wish to all and sundry that John Mason be hanged. A few weeks after the trial this juror, returning to Natchez from one of the settlements, had occasion to ride over a bridle path through a canebrake. Suddenly Samuel Mason, armed with a tomahawk and a rifle, sprang from the canebrake. He pointed the rifle at the rider, who instantly threw up his hands. Mason very calmly told him that he had waited for two days "to blow your brains out." The terrified man begged that his life be spared for the sake of his wife and children. Mason replied that he, too, had children, that he loved them as any other father loved his, and that he now wanted to reciprocate for the mercy shown to his son John.[36]

"Did John Mason ever do you any harm?" he asked. "Did I myself ever do you any injury? Did you ever hear of me committing murder, or suffering murder to be committed?" Mason failed to add, "except when necessary."

"Never in my life," replied the juror.

"Thank God, I have never shed blood," said Mason emphatically. "But now, come down off your horse, sir. If you have anything to say to your Maker, I'll give you five minutes to say it."

The man sank off his horse, fell on his knees, and began to utter a fervent prayer addressed less to his Maker than to the bandit who stood beside him with gun cocked. But his words failed and, expecting death, he began to weep violently. Mason kicked him and spat at his face.

"You ain't worth killing!" he said disdainfully. And he turned quickly and disappeared in the canebrake.

Mason had a friend in Natchez named Anthony Glass or Gass. He operated a general store; he was prosperous, affable, a good mixer; he not only stored or marketed what Mason robbed along the river, but also informed him when a rich prize was coming up the trace. Sometimes Glass was Mason's partner in crime. Once he rode north with a rich Kentuckian named Campbell. Somewhere along the wooded trace Mason held them up, depriving them of several horses, saddles, and some money. Later a crude sign was found on a tree near the scene of the robbery: "Done by Mason Of the Woods." A month or two later, Glass turned up in present Vicksburg and started business anew.[37]

Soon after he became governor of Mississippi Territory, Claiborne began a thorough investigation of the robberies. Then, on February 10, 1802, he wrote to Manuel de Salcedo, governor of Louisiana, informing him that many Americans had been robbed as they descended the river on their way to Natchez, and that he was unable to ascertain whether they were Americans or Spaniards. In his reply, Salcedo admitted the difficulty of trying to determine the nationality of the delinquents and informed his correspondent that he had given his officers:

> ... the most positive orders ... to take the most efficacious means of discovering and apprehending the criminal or criminals that can be adopted ... and I assure your Excellency that if the criminals are taken they will be punished in such a manner as to serve as an example to others.

He complained, however, that American frontiersmen had availed themselves of free navigation of the Mississippi to come down into Spanish territory in large numbers and that they had among them "vagabonds ... who had fled from, or who do not or cannot return to the United States."[38]

Samuel Mason knew that either governor would arrest highwaymen and river pirates on his side of the river but that neither would suggest free passage of the other side to a pursuing party without a special license. So the bandit avoided committing crimes on the Spanish side. Realizing that his notoriety would eventually result in his being hunted along the Natchez Trace, he moved to the Mississippi, where he confined his operations to the American bank of the river, within easy reach of refuge in Spanish Louisiana.[39]

That spring Colonel Baker, undaunted by his loss of money and by his failure to capture Mason, again started down the river in a flatboat loaded with merchandize. This time he supplied himself with guns, not only to protect his boat but also to protect himself on his return over the trace. When he reached a point below Vicksburg, he met Mason and some of his men, but he succeeded with the assistance of a few of his companions in driving them off. Baker sent an account of the attack to Claiborne, who quickly wrote to the commanders of the military posts along the river and the trace, informing them of the numerous robberies and urging them to search out the outlaws and capture them.[40]

These letters stated that Wiley Harpe, one of the most brutal outlaws of Tennessee and Kentucky, had joined Mason's gang. Wiley had been partner to his older brother Micajah who, after committing numerous robberies and murders, had been discovered, shot, captured, and beheaded by a member of an angry posse. Wiley had escaped with his women and children and had eventually joined Mason. In contrast to Micajah, whose tall and muscular frame earned him the nickname of Big Harpe, Wiley or Little Harpe was meager of face and body, though he equaled his brother in his paranoid suspicions and in his "fierce and sinister countenance." The citizens of the region, terrified by his crimes, in which he often mutilated or killed as well as robbed his victims, hoped that he had left the country for good or had been killed. Claiborne had probably heard from Baker that Wiley was one of Mason's gang. But though he may not have been convinced of Harpe's presence on the

Mississippi, he knew that by linking the names of these two ferocious outlaws together, he could the more readily obtain the support of the public in capturing them and bringing them to justice.[41]

The governor issued a proclamation in which he offered rewards totaling $2000 for the capture of Mason and Harpe. This sizable sum had the desired effect: Indians as well as whites formed themselves into bands and plunged into the wilderness to the gang's new hideout near Rocky Springs on the trace, forty miles north of Natchez. They found the camp deserted. The outlaws had fled across the river to Little Prairie, twenty miles downstream from New Madrid, in Spanish territory. There they rented ten acres and a house from John Ruddell and bought a cow and sundry provisions. The nervous manner in which the outlaws guarded the house aroused Ruddell's suspicions. He hastened to Henri Peyroux de la Coudrenière, commander of New Madrid, who immediately sent four men under Captain Robert McCoy to join a dozen regulars already detailed to Little Prairie.[42]

McCoy walked to Mason's house and requested him and his companions, consisting of six men, one woman, and three children, to go to the house of one Lesieur, an American citizen, for a hearing. The Masons had no idea that McCoy had surrounded Lesieur's house with militia. Before they realized what was happening, they were handcuffed and chained. McCoy asked them their names, which they readily gave: Samuel Mason and his four sons, Thomas, John, Samuel, and Magnus. The other man, Little Harpe, called himself John Taylor. The woman gave her name as Marguerite Mason, wife of John Mason. McCoy ordered an inventory of their belongings: eight horses, new and old clothes, many yards of silk, muslin, and cotton, old and new pistols and guns, "a field stove," a box of salt, three horns of powder, six barrels of flour, English cutlery, various other imported goods and more than a hundred other items, and $7000 in United States currency of various demominations.[43]

On January 17, 1803, the prisoners were brought to trial, a curious blend of judicial pomposity and frontier laxity. The magistrates conducted court in Spanish; the testimony was taken down in French; the deponents heard their own stories in secondhand English. The only evidence of cross-examination was in occasional interjections of the magistrates. Eight of the fifteen witnesses declared knowledge of Mason and his family; the other seven witnesses were the prisoners themselves, who testified in their own behalf. Each of the witnesses took an oath "on the cross of his sword" to tell the truth; Mason, his sons, and Little Harpe, being less addicted to Christian guilt, were obliged to add "by the Holy Scriptures." Before he signed his testimony, each witness had to maintain that it contained the truth, to which nothing could be added or unsaid.[44]

Mason was heard first. He denied with vehemence that he had been involved in any robberies; he had not robbed Colonel Baker; indeed, he had been far from the scene when the robbery occurred. But he was highly disturbed when Captain McCoy told him that Baker would appear in a few days. How, asked the captain, did he come by so much money? Mason started, then pretended he had not understood. When McCoy repeated the question, the prisoners stared at each other until Little Harpe came to Mason's rescue:

"The banknotes were found in a bag hanging in a bush near the road where we happened to be camping."[45] A case of money growing on trees?

The next witness was Little Harpe—now calling himself John Taylor. Unlike Mason, he was sullen and reticent. But he gradually grew talkative and indiscreet as he neatly grafted lie after lie onto those of Mason in his desperate attempt to establish his innocence. He admitted that his name was not Taylor; it was Setton—John Setton. He was a native of Ireland; he had come to America in 1797; he had joined the army only to desert it. But he was an honest man and a hard worker: he had worked three weeks for His Catholic Majesty; he had worked a whole winter as a carpenter in New Orleans. Then he had hunted with the Chaquetaw Indians in Arkansas Territory until one of his former officers recognized him and jailed him as a deserter. In jail he had met another deserter, Wiguens, who escaped with him and introduced him to Mason.

Coudrenière asked him if he knew a man named Harpe. The bandit answered that in Cumberland he had heard of somebody by that name who had been killed but who had left a brother whose whereabouts were unknown to him. He deprecated the Masons; they had made life miserable for him and he had tried repeatedly to escape. But he was unlucky; they never allowed him more than two rounds of powder at a time; and he was always caught, always recaptured. Furthermore, John and Thomas Mason had taken everything he owned, had encouraged him to stay with them by promising him land on which he could move with his family. Then they had grown crueler: they had forced him to sign a statement declaring that he, under the name of John Taylor, and a few other men were implicated in one or more of three robberies but that they themselves were in no way connected with these crimes.[46]

The trial became a perfect round-robin of perjury and counter-accusations. It lasted eleven days. Mason had told Setton that he was the leader of fifty highwaymen; Setton had told Mason that he could muster as many as five hundred Choctaw braves to defend him against the law. Mason's sons testified that he led "a decent life" and that he had spent two years away from home trying "to discover men who were committing the robberies." All the Masons agreed that Setton was the great villain. Mason told Coudrenière that he had detained Setton because he wanted to trick him into making a public confession of his crimes. He desired, he said, to clear his own fair name.[47]

The more the magistrates heard, the more confused they became. At last, on January 31, Coudrenière had heard enough. He directed that the proceedings of the trial

> originally set down in writing on ninety-one sheets of paper written on both sides, as well as the pieces of evidence tending to conviction, together with seven thousand piasters in U.S. banknotes, be forwarded to the Honorable Governor General by Don Robert McCoy, Captain of the Militia, whom we have charged to conduct the prisoners, Mason and consorts, to New Orleans with the view of their trial being continued and finished, if it so please the Honorable Governor General.[48]

Early in the following month McCoy, with his guard and his prisoners and their loot, crowded into a flatboat and started toward their destination. Setton, who was considered a more dangerous criminal than any of his comrades, was chained in the most conspicuous place on the boat, not only to prevent his escape, but also to prevent Samuel Mason from trying to persuade him to plot against the crew. His captors regarded the sullen outlaw as "nothing more than a vicious dog whose life was being spared solely that he might later give Mason a long-deserved, fatal bite."[49]

On arriving in New Orleans, the captain submitted the long report of the trial to the governor, who ruled that since the outlaws had committed no crime on Spanish soil they should be turned over to the American authorities. So McCoy took them aboard a small sloop and sailed toward Natchez. The March wind that came clapping down in gusts delayed them; then, as they were passing Pointe Coupée—still a hundred miles from their destination—it shattered the mast of their ship. McCoy sent some of his men to the shore to make a new mast, keeping the rest to guard the prisoners. They quickly threw off their chains, seized a few pistols, and fired on the guard. McCoy, hearing the alarm, ran out of his cabin. Mason shot him through the breast and shoulder. Though hardly able to stand, the officer shot Mason in the head. The bandit fell and rose, fell and rose, while one of his sons, though covered with blood, shot off a Spaniard's arm and repulsed the guard. Then the bandits seized and held the ship until, in the evening, they saw approaching the men who had been making the mast. They fled with the woman and three children into the forest.[50]

The commander of the village offered a reward of one thousand dollars to any man who would take Samuel Mason, dead or alive. A large group of Frenchmen or Spaniards pursued him and his comrades in vain. In June the bandits, armed to the teeth, returned to the trace. Claiborne sent against them two detachments of the Jefferson County militia which, however, failed to find them.[51]

At this juncture James May, a rough character who had been driven out of Henderson County, Kentucky, appeared in Hunston, later Greenville, Mississippi, twenty-five miles northeast of Natchez, and delivered to a magistrate a number of small articles which he said he had taken from Samuel Mason. May said that Mason had robbed and captured him but that he had shot the bandit in the head, had taken the articles on board a skiff, and had headed for Hunston. He claimed the reward. But the magistrate wanted more positive proof; he told May to bring in Mason or his dead body. So May took fresh supplies and plunged into the wilderness in search of the bandit. Several months later he returned with Setton. This time the magistrate was more skeptical than before; he clapped both men in jail. But they soon gained their release by guaranteeing to bring in Mason. They found him, perhaps in the swampy region around Lake Concordia, gained his confidence, and succeeded in convincing him that they had returned to follow him as their leader. That night, while he was counting out to them some ill-gotten money, they buried a tomahawk in his brain. Then they cut off his head, rolled it up in blue mud to keep it from stinking, and took it in a canoe to a magistrate in Natchez. They broke the clay ball, revealed its gruesome burden, and asked for the reward. But while they were talking, in walked a man who requested the magistrate to arrest them. He said he had just arrived in town and had recognized in the stable two horses which the two men had stolen from him some time before. Hardly had the magistrate enquired into the matter than Captain Frederick Stump, an old friend of Claiborne, moved closer to Setton and stared at him.

"Why," he exclaimed, "that man's Wiley Harpe!"

Until now nothing was known of the bandit save that Mason had abused him. Some may have known that he traveled under assumed names, but none suspected that he was Little Harpe. Stump's identification, therefore, was exciting news! But apparently he was not quite sure of his man, for the magistrate saw fit to post a proclamation at the landing in Natchez, inviting any Kentucky boatman with knowledge of Harpe to come to the town jail and identify him. Soon several boatmen appeared.

"If he is Harpe," said one of them before he saw the bandit, "he has a mole on his neck and two toes grown together on one foot." This identification proved accurate.

John Bowman of Knoxville, Tennessee, recognized Little Harpe. The bandit denied his own name. Bowman persisted:

"If you are Harpe you have a scar under your left nipple where I cut you in a difficulty we had at Knoxville." Bowman tore the bandit's shirt open; the scar was there![52]

He had planned to save himself by turning state's evidence against the Masons, but now he realized that escape was his only salvation. And he and May did escape—how, nobody knows. But they were soon recaptured in Jefferson County and returned to jail. In due time they were tried before Judges Peter Bryan Bruin, David Ker, and Thomas Rodney in the Circuit Court of Greenville. Needless to say, they were convicted.

In those days the official hangman would usually drive condemned prisoners in a wagon, with their coffins serving as a seat, to the place of execution, where he would prepare a gallows by fastening a beam between two forked trees. He would use a coffin as the platform and the wagon as the trap for his gallows. Then he would loop the noose around each prisoner's neck and rush the horses forward.[53]

But Harpe and May were no ordinary criminals; they deserved a more elaborate procedure in keeping with their barbarity. The hangman tied two ropes to a heavy pole between two trees. Harpe and May walked to Gallows Field, as their place of execution was called, each with his hands tied behind him. Each in his turn climbed a ladder until his neck came under the rope. Each said his last words while the hangman stood by to knock the ladder away. Harpe made a confession of some sort that implicated several hitherto innocent persons. May complained of the hardships of his fate, protested his innocence, and spoke of the benefit he had rendered society by killing "old Mason." Then each swung until he was "dead, dead, dead."[54]

Their heads were cut off and placed on poles, one a short distance to the north, the other a short distance to the west of Greenville. Tradition says that some people objected to having their kinsmen share their resting place with the decapitated and despised outlaws. So they dug up their own dead and carried them away beyond the town to a field which became known as Bellegrove Church Yard.[55]

This proved propitious. In a few years, as the trace widened and deepened under wagon wheels and horses' hoofs, it encroached on the graveyard. Eventually whitish fragments, "mixed indiscriminately with dust," began to protrude along the banks of the trace. Dogs and other animals dragged out the crumbling bones and scattered them until the trace widened beyond the graveyard. The future would discard that small section of the trace of which the graveyard was a part. And a jungle of briar and brush would obliterate the last vestiges of the burial place of the two bandits. But the wave stirred by their barbarous operations would continue as a ripple of human interest down to our own time.

4

In the late summer of 1803 President Jefferson appointed Claiborne to the governorship of Orleans Territory, which was part of the Louisiana Purchase. Toward the end of that year he departed for his new post in New Orleans, leaving Cato West as acting governor of Mississippi Territory. That old Jeffersonian Republican had been serving as territorial secretary and had been considered Claiborne's logical successor. But eventually national politics bestowed the office on Robert Williams, member of a distinguished and influential North Carolina family. Nevertheless, West, who was greatly loved by his people, showed that he felt the pulse of the Mississippi frontiersmen far better than did Williams.

And he had the distinction of governing a far larger territory than Claiborne. In 1804 Congress added to the territory the old Georgia cession, which included the land lying north of the territorial boundary and south of Tennessee. Mississippi Territory thus "embraced all of Alabama and comprised in all one of the richest sections of the Union."[56]

On May 10, 1805, Robert Williams assumed his active duties as governor of Mississippi Territory. In the fall of that year the Choctaws ceded to the United States a rectangular region that ran roughly one hundred twenty miles long and fifty-five miles wide along the thirty-first parallel. This tribe had in the past decade bought on credit from Panton, Leslie and Company a quantity of goods priced at over $46,000. The company proposed that, for the sake of expediency, the Choctaws discharge their obligation to it by ceding a tract of land. Though the Choctaw agent, John McKee, and the chiefs favored this proposal, Henry Dearborn, Secretary of War, declared it invalid, pointing out the "extreme impropriety" of a foreign firm holding land within the United States. But he was willing to help the firm secure payment of its claims, though he emphasized that the United States was in no way obligated to do so.[57]

Anxious to obtain control of the riverfront, most of which was held by the Choctaw and the Chickasaws, the American government decided to negotiate with these tribes for a cession. Since the Choctaws held virtually all of the southern section of present Mississippi, a cession from them was deemed especially important. Their contiguity to West Florida, moreover, portended future trouble in view of their large indebtedness to Panton, Leslie and Company.[58]

Secretary Dearborn, mindful that the coveted region would serve the double purpose of attracting American citizens to the area and of eliminating Panton, Leslie and Company as rivals of the American factorage system, instructed General James Wilkinson to persuade the Choctaws to cede it. But Wilkinson found the tribe intractable; it preferred to sell an area in the forks of the Alabama and the Tombigbee. John Forbes, successor of Panton, Leslie and Company, eventually persuaded them, however, to cede the riverfront region. In August 1804 they signified their willingness to negotiate with the American government.[59]

In June of the following year the American commissioners, James Robertson and Silas Dinsmoor, held a conference with the tribe. The chiefs recoiled at the ridiculously low price offered for the 4,400,000 acres that the tract embraced. The commissioners then turned to buy a piece of ground from the Chickasaws, who also desired to discharge their indebtedness to Panton, Leslie and Company. This tribe ceded a grant in south central Tennessee and northern Alabama for $20,000 and an annuity of $100 for the tribal chief. Later that summer the commissioners reopened negotiations with the Choctaws and this time found them more tractable. On November 16, 1805, they signed a treaty by which they agreed to cede part of the desired region for $50,000

in cash and an annuity of $3,000. Jefferson was so disappointed over his
failure to acquire all of the tribe's riverfront that he waited two years
before he submitted the treaty to the Senate for ratification. In 1807 it
was approved. The cession was thrown open to settlement and organized
into three counties, Wayne, Greene, and Marion, which were subsequently divided into the counties of Lawrence, Pike, Covington, Perry,
Lincoln, Lamar, Forrest, Jefferson Davis, and Walthall.[60]

While the American government strove to open more of the territory
to Mississippians, Mississippians plotted to seize Spanish territory, or territory still governed by Spain, beyond their borders. Spain still held the
Baton Rouge and Manchac districts, between the Island of Orleans and
the Natchez district, as well as the gulf district of Mobile. The American
government made serious claim to all this region as part of Louisiana
and therefore as part of the territory it had recently acquired from
France. The Baton Rouge district, moreover, was mainly American in
population and was bound to become a part of the United States.

The Americans in the region showed their resentment at having been
excluded from the Louisiana Purchase by disobeying and even by threatening the Spanish officials. The insurgent leaders were three gigantic
Kemper brothers, Reuben, who lived in New Orleans, and Nathan and
Samuel, who lived in Pinckneyville, a settlement in the Natchez district.
Samuel kept a tavern in which he and his brothers and their followers
held their seditious meetings. With four of their armed companions they
seized property at Bayou Sara, in Spanish territory, and dared the governor of nearby Baton Rouge, Captain Carlos de Grand Pré, to oust
them. Mindful that most of the settlers in the district were Americans
who were "inclined to insubordination and prone to insurgency," Grand
Pré decided to follow a policy of caution. Furthermore, he found himself in the predicament of having an uncertain militia and of being able
to muster only fifty-six men, including his drummer boy and his in-
valids. Beyond him were Americans "who looked upon his jurisdiction
as their next acquisition and were only too ready to initiate the necessary
measures to acquire it."[61]

Since he deemed Pensacola and Havana too distant to assist him, he
applied to the Marquis de Casa Calvo, who, despite American occupation of Louisiana, still remained in New Orleans as Spanish governor,
for men and gunboats with which "to exterminate all these vagabonds
at one blow." But, feeling that reinforcements, if and when he received
them, would be too tardy to assist him, he resolved on a bold stroke. He
sent an improvised gunboat under Thomas Estevan who, supported by a
few loyal militiamen, drove the Kempers from Bayou Sara into American
territory.[62]

Casa Calvo, who regarded the Kempers as outlaws, asked Governor
Claiborne to prevent them from taking refuge in Mississippi Territory.
Claiborne replied that they "had received no encouragements from the
United States or its officers."[63] In these circumstances Casa Calvo

urged Grand Pré to be lenient toward the misguided rebels. Accepting this advice, Grand Pré offered amnesty to the Kempers if they and their seditious followers would promise to stay out of Spanish territory. Instead of complying with this request, they threatened to burn and pillage the houses of all those who sympathized with Spanish rule and encouraged their slaves to escape. A provincial patrol under Vizente Pintado, observing that they were about to invade Spanish territory again, fired on them and wounded and captured two of them. But Grand Pré, fearing that Americans from other states would replace "these white Indians and river pirates," renewed his plea to Casa Calvo for men, money, and munitions. The rebels tried to set fire to Pintado's house, then departed for Bayou Sara. Pintado naïvely ordered them to surrender and leave the region, while he requested new instructions from Grand Pré. The Kempers, ignoring threat or pardon, resumed their raids, in which they stole horses and slaves with impunity.[64]

Early in August, 1804, thirty rebels under Nathan and Samuel Kemper seized Pintado and other Spanish officials, mistreated them, burned Pintado's house and cotton gin, and advanced on Baton Rouge, for the purpose of surprising and capturing Grand Pré and thereby forcing him to surrender the fort. Aiming to overthrow Spanish rule in the region, they issued a proclamation of independence and unfurled a flag composed of seven white and blue stripes with two stars in a blue field. Grand Pré, learning of the revolt from one of Pintado's slaves, readied his slender garrison and summoned his militia. Early next morning he exchanged shots with two small bands skulking near the fort and drove them away. This reverse convinced the Kempers that, though they were superior in numbers to the enemy, they were not strong enough to capture the fort without artillery. Discouraged by their failure and by the unwillingness of most of the people to rush to their standard, they retreated on August 9 to Bayou Sara, where they resumed their depredations which, far from helping their cause, only drove their fellow Americans to seek Spanish protection. The people even volunteered for military service and, "in relays of a hundred each, . . . manned the fort, kept the patrols, garrisoned strategic points, and loaned their slaves to the common cause."[65]

By the middle of August Grand Pré had mustered a force of nearly one hundred fifty volunteers. Presenting them with a small flag and "an analogous discourse," he sent them to scour the roads passing through Feliciana, an American settlement. At the same time he secured the roads leading into American territory and blockaded the Bayou Sara to prevent the rebels from escaping in that direction.[66]

Dumfounded by these military preparations and precautions, the Kempers saw the wisdom of curtailing their depredations temporarily and of making some pretense of peace. They sent one of their followers, Daniel Clark, to Grand Pré with a penitent letter in which they asked him "to pardon them on the plea that they were now ready to lay aside their arms and refrain from further molesting persons and property."[67] Grand

Pré saw through their ruse. He upbraided Clark for asking him to pardon them, pointing out that even the Americans of Feliciana regarded them as outlaws. Persuading himself that only the extensive property interests in Feliciana of some of their leaders and his own military preparations had impelled them to ask for peace, he was not inclined to be lenient with them. Yet his men were unable to apprehend them. While the roads and byways that passed through nearby American territory were numerous enough to favor the rebels, they were almost impassable to organized pursuit. So Grand Pré had no choice but to keep his jurisdiction on the alert and to thank his officers and men for their military services, which had enabled him to survive his troubles.[68]

But his troubles with the Pinckneyville gang were far from ended. In the spring of 1805 he heard that Reuben Kemper, with some companions, had departed for the Bahama Islands to seek British assistance in an invasion of the Baton Rouge district. One of the chief conspirators was said to be Edward Randolph, who had probably written the proclamation of independence which the Kempers had issued during their invasion of the previous year and who, like Daniel Clark, claimed extensive property in Feliciana. Finding himself in poorer circumstances than before to cope with the purported invasion, Grand Pré appealed to Casa Calvo, who immediately went to see Claiborne. The governor doubted that the invasion would occur but agreed to warn Governor Robert Williams of Mississippi Territory. Williams, too, was skeptical, though he promised to co-operate with Casa Calvo and Grand Pré in suppressing all border lawlessness and especially the raids of the Kempers. Grand Pré furnished Williams with a list of the rebel leaders and their abettors. Governor Vizente Folch of West Florida, however, counseled him to rely on his own resources rather than those of American officials.[69]

Whereupon Grand Pré moved with the boldness of desperation against the Kempers. During the night of September 3 he sent about twelve white men with blackened faces and seven Negroes under two Horton brothers, who hated the Kempers, across the border to Pinckneyville. Judge Thomas Rodney later left this description of the incident in his journal:

> Reuben Kemper, Says it was on the 3d. of September 1805. at his House about Two Miles from Pin[c]kney Ville at Midnight he awoke and found a Negro of the defendt. had him by the foot and when he got up the House was full of armed Men, and Two of Hortons Negros draged him out into the gallery (after Tying him with a rope) where they had his brother Reuben and were beating him most unmercyfully Till he Interposed & prevailed on him To Cease the party were chiefly Negros—Ruben was also Tied then The party Took them both To where Their horses were Tied where he Saw A Horton and another person sitting on horse & Horton Hailed the Party who Comes there, They answd. friends. he replied advance friends, Then they all Moved

off along the Road Towards Hortons and J Horton was with them Till they got near Hunter's [?] House and then J Horton left them—on the road they often Struck R. Kemper whose face was very bloody with their beating him—after this they passed Joseph Hunters where they called out and Told Him Situation and they came out but did not pursue—they went on Till near Hortons House & then A. Horton left them They went on To the road that led to Pinkney Ville where Several of the party left them They then went Some Distance on the road & were taken into the woods where they Stayed Till the Party that went to Pinkney Ville came to them with his brother Sam who was Tied also—[70]

The kidnapers took the Kempers below the border, where they delivered them to a group of Spanish soldiers under Captain Solomon Alston, who took them in a pirogue by way of Tunica Bayou toward Baton Rouge. The pirogue approached so near the west bank of the Mississippi that the Kempers were able to inform a passerby of their need for help. Captain William Wilson, commander of the American garrison at Pointe Coupée, rescued them, then took the Spanish subjects in the escort to Captain Richard Sparks at Fort Adams in American territory. Sparks turned them over to Governor Williams.[71]

At the same time the governor prepared to defend the territory against a possible counterattack from the Spaniards by calling out a company of militia for patrol duty at Pinckneyville and another at Ticfay Bayou. Then he lectured Grand Pré for invading American territory. Grand Pré replied that the Kempers had, by their depredations, forced him to set up the border patrol that had apprehended them. He emphasized that Americans, not Spaniards, had seized the troublemakers. He reminded him that Captain Wilson had, by arresting the guard and prisoners on the Mississippi, violated Spanish rights to navigate on the river. So he requested the governor to release the patrol and to extradite the Kempers so that they could be tried and punished for the crimes they had committed on Spanish territory. Williams released the patrol but refused to comply with the rest of Grand Pré's request. Instead, he turned the Kempers over to Judge Rodney, who released them under bond to keep the peace "especially with subjects of the Spanish crown." The Hortons, whom the Kempers recognized and sued as their kidnapers, were bound over to the court. To prevent further disturbances, Williams ordered Colonel John Ellis to place two companies on duty at Pinckneyville. Ellis furnished each of his men with twelve rounds of cartridges and instructed them to repel with force any hostile intent by any party.[72]

For some time Governor Williams had planned to return to North Carolina to bring his family back to Mississippi Territory. But one thing or another had forced him to postpone his trip until the spring of 1806. On May 31 William Cowles Mead, secretary of the territory, assumed the duties as acting governor in the absence of Governor Williams.

5

To this exuberant Virginian fell the task of dealing with the last and most dramatic phase of the Aaron Burr conspiracy. Many historians have written about this event, but none have succeeded in ascertaining Burr's ultimate objectives. After killing Alexander Hamilton, whom he blamed for his political ruin in New York, Burr retired from the vice-presidency and resolved to seek fame and fortune on the frontier. Most southern frontiersmen were still hostile toward Spain. They regarded her domains as a possible field of conquest. Did Burr dream of carving an empire for himself in Mexico as compensation for his loss of political power in his own country? Did he hope to liberate the Mexican people from Spanish tyranny? Did he plan to establish a buffer state between Louisiana and Mexico? All these are moot questions, for Burr unfolded a different scheme to each of his associates. To Harman Blennerhassett, a wealthy Irishman who lived in regal splendor on an island in the Ohio below present Parkersburg, West Virginia, he spoke of establishing a new state in Louisiana. He promised to name him its minister to the Court of St. James.

Fired by political ambition, Blennerhassett furnished his friend with armed flatboats and men for the expedition, which sailed from Blennerhassett Island for New Orleans. Burr joined it further down the Ohio. General James Wilkinson, commander of American forces in New Orleans, seemed to have been deeply involved in Burr's conspiracy until its significance became known to the Federal government. Then he deserted Burr and turned informer. He himself was a veteran of intrigue. In 1788, posing as an agent for his fellow Kentuckians, he had sailed down the Mississippi to New Orleans and had obtained from Governor Miró a monopoly of trade. In return he had promised to use his influence to detach Kentucky from the Union and to convert it into an independent buffer state that should serve to shield Louisiana from possible American aggression. Actually, he was interested neither in obtaining benefits for Kentuckians nor in urging them to establish a separate state. While he let Miró think he was working in the interest of Spain, he was doing the same thing with respect to his friends and associates in Kentucky. His aim was obviously to profit from both parties without siding with either. In 1792 Spain rewarded him for his "services" by granting him an annual pension of $2,000. Four years later President Washington appointed him to succeed Anthony Wayne as commander-in-chief of American forces, a post which, despite his continuing intrigues, he held for nineteen years.[73]

Such was the man who, to divert attention from himself, warned President Jefferson that he had "discovered . . . a powerful association, extending from New York through the Western States, . . . for the purpose of leading an expedition against Vera Cruz."[74] Convinced by this information that Burr meant trouble, if not treason, Jefferson on November 27, 1806, issued the following proclamation:

Whereas information has been received that sundry persons . . . are conspiring and confederating together to begin . . . a military expedition or enterprise against the dominions of Spain; that for this purpose they are fitting out and arming vessels to the western waters of the United States, collecting provisions, arms, and military stores, and means; are deceiving and seducing honest and well-meaning citizens, under various pretenses, to engage in their criminal enterprises; are organizing, officering, and arming themselves for the same, contrary to the laws in such cases made and provided: I have therefore thought proper to issue this, my proclamation, warning and enjoining all faithful citizens who have been led without due knowledge or consideration to participate in the said unlawful enterprise to withdraw from the same without delay.[75]

As soon as Acting Governor Mead received word of Jefferson's proclamation he issued one of his own, in which he stated that Burr's conspiracy was "directed by men of secret and profound intrigue for the aggrandizement of themselves and their minions, to the oppression of the great mass of the people." He requested the soldiers and officers of the territory to help apprehend the conspirators and their agents. He required every local officer to take an oath of allegiance within fifteen days on pain of dismissal.[76]

Next day he wrote Claiborne asking for a supply of arms and expressing confidence in the willingness of his militia to fight and in its ability to stop the expedition. "If Burr passes this Territory with two thousand men," he said, "consider him a traitor, and act as if certain thereof. You may save yourself by it." Next day he mustered his militia and, in the scarcity of military arms, furnished it with shotguns and fowling pieces.[77]

On January 10, 1807, Burr, who had pushed ahead of his main party in a keelboat, arrived with twelve men at the house of his friend Judge Peter Bryan Bruin in Bayou Pierre above Natchez. To counteract Mead's proclamation he issued a public letter in which he asserted that his aims had been misconstrued:

If the alarm which has been excited should not be appeased by this declaration, I invite my fellow citizens to visit me at this place, and to receive from me in person, such further explanations as may be necessary to their satisfaction, presuming that when my views are understood, they will receive the countenance of all good men.[78]

On January 16 Mead sent his aides-de-camp, William B. Shields and George Poindexter, United States attorney for Mississippi Territory, to interview Burr. On their heels followed a detachment of militia under Colonel Thomas Fitzpatrick. Acting on Mead's orders, Shields and Poindexter asked Burr to meet the governor next day at Thomas Cavit's house near the mouth of Cole's Creek. Burr agreed when they assured him that no hostile moves would be taken against him and that, after the interview, he could return to his boats. Early next morning Burr had himself rowed some distance down the creek, where he met a company of dragoons who escorted him to Cavit's house. Mead informed him that he and his men would have to surrender unconditionally to the civil authorities or be taken into custody by the militia. Next day Burr surrendered. He and his men were taken to Washington, capital of the territory.[79]

In those days Washington was a pleasant village with a main street about a mile long. There Burr counted many friends among the wealthy planters and among a group of officers who disliked President Jefferson because he had retired them when he reduced the army in 1802. No charges were brought against the prisoners; indeed, they appear to have enjoyed complete freedom of the village. Some of the young men liked it so well, they decided to settle down in it.[80]

On January 26 Governor Robert Williams returned to the territory from his trip to North Carolina. Unlike Mead, who now descended reluctantly "from the clouds of glory in which he had literally been wallowing," Williams assumed a milder attitude toward Burr. He thought like most local jurists that, whatever the distinguished prisoner might have done elsewhere, he had committed no crime in Mississippi Territory and could not, therefore, be tried in it. Whereupon Judge Harry Toulmin of the Tombigbee District brought charges against Burr and his followers, for the purpose of sending them to a jurisdiction where their cases could be cognizable. But Judge Rodney maintained that Toulmin had no jurisdiction outside his own district. And he proceeded to arraign Burr before the territorial supreme court, despite the protests of Burr's bibulous friend, Judge Bruin, who maintained that its functions were appellate and that, therefore, it enjoyed no original jurisdiction. In the privacy of his journal Judge Rodney drew this frank picture of his mulish colleague:

> Judge Bruin Is a friendly Hospitable good Man; and a Man of Good Education and good Sense, and when Sober, Upright in his Judgments—But has suffered himself To acquire Such a Strong habit of Drinking Spiritous Lyquoirs, That he cannot restrain himself—This kept him from the last Supreme Court—but being determined To Attend The fall Courts, he Came down from the Jefferson Court and Attended the Adams Circuit with me, but was obliged To Stay off the Bench Two days—Then he Set off with me to Wilkinson Court, but only got to Col. Eliss Plantation, Buffalo—and came back with me on my return. And Today he went on the bench of the Supreme Court

quite Intoxicated, So that the barr applied To me To Adjourn the Court, which was done. Bruin when Sober is a very pleasant Companion—but habit has become So Uncontrolable and the public business has been So much Interrupted by it, that Everybody, & Especially his best friends, Think it high Time for him To resign—[81]

Before a large crowd of jurors, witnesses, and spectators the grand jury, which consisted largely of Federalists and friends of Burr, cleared the prisoner of all charges. But it charged the territorial government with various irregularities in its dealings with him. The governor, for example, had called out the militia and had made

. . . military arrests without warrant and as they conceive, without other lawful authority; and they do seriously regret that so much cause should be given to the enemies of our glorious Constitution, to rejoice in such measures being adopted in a neighboring Territory, and if sanctioned by the Executive of our country, must sap the vitals of political existence, and crumble this glorious fabric into the dust.[82]

All of which was tantamount to whitewashing Burr and indicting Mead, Williams, and even Jefferson!

But the Homeric comedy continued. Though the court had cleared Burr, it was still so jealous of him as a prize that, instead of releasing him, it bound him in the sum of $5000 to appear day after day as long as the court saw fit. Seeing that he had friends, Burr failed to comply with court orders and in consequence forfeited his bond. Williams issued a proclamation offering a reward of $2000 for Burr's arrest. Burr, fearing that Wilkinson would seize him and knowing that the general had commissioned various persons, both civilian and military, to arrest him and bring him to New Orleans, wrote to Williams expressing his willingness to submit to the civil authorities in return for the rights granted to any citizen and a guarantee against military arrest.[83]

He doubtless would have been granted all he asked had he been discreet. But on February 10 he wrote to two of his principal agents, David Floyd and Comfort Tyler. Though the note was unsigned and undated it was clearly in his handwriting: "If you are yet together, keep together, and I will join you tomorrow night. In the meantime put all your arms in perfect order. Ask the bearer no questions, but tell him all you think I should know. He does not know that this is from me, nor where I am."[84]

He was staying with Dr. John Cummins, who had given him refuge after his failure to appear in court. Stitching the note in the cape of his surtout, he sent one of Cummins' slaves to deliver it. At the house of William Fairbanks, near the mouth of Cole's Creek, the slave stopped to enquire his way. Fairbanks recognized Burr's horse, searched the slave, and discovered the note. Fairbanks sent the slave to Governor Williams, who immediately placed guards on Burr's boats and on the roads leading to Cummins' house, and arrested Floyd, Blennerhassett, Tyler, Ralston, and about forty other members of Burr's party. Next day all of them were released save Floyd, Ralston, and Blennerhassett, who were turned over to the territorial supreme court.[85]

No longer conciliatory toward Burr, Williams told him "that from the judicial proceedings of this Territory you cannot be considered in any other light than as a fugitive from the laws of your country." Burr now realized that his only hope was in flight. He returned to his boats, where he addressed his followers in a long speech in which he told them that, though the authorities had acquitted him, they were going to take him again and that he planned to "flee from oppression." His bills, he told them, had been protested; he had nothing to give them; but they might sell the boats and supplies and retire, if they wished, to his Ouachita lands. They sold some of the boats and supplies and divided the money among themselves. The boats, being of unusual size and construction, brought $75 each instead of the customary $25 or $30.[86]

On the night of February 18 two strangers rode in the moonlight into the village of Wakefield. A recent downpour had turned the surrounding countryside into a number of quagmires and had swollen the streams. One of the men rode a short distance ahead of the other on "a small tackey of a horse." He had covered his saddle with a bearskin and had disguised himself as a river boatman in a tattered blanket coat. He had stuck a butcher's knife in one side of his leather belt and had dangled a tin cup from the other. He wore a misshapen white hat that flopped down and hid a part of his face. Nicholas Perkins, registrar of the local land office, was standing in the doorway when the men approached. The first rider passed without looking up. But the second stopped and asked Perkins for directions to the home of Major John Hinson, whom Burr had known in Natchez and with whom he planned to stay for a week. Perkins explained that the stream they must cross on the way to Hinson's house was swollen and that, furthermore, the major was away. Nevertheless, they followed Perkins' directions.[87]

He thought that honest men would hardly be prowling through the wilderness at that late hour. Robbers, perhaps; then he started; could one of the horsemen be the man named in Governor Williams' recent proclamations: Burr—Aaron Burr? Perkins rushed to Sheriff Theodore Brightwell and rode with him to Hinson's house, where they could see the two men with Mrs. Hinson inside. Brightwell entered the house, but Perkins, strongly suspecting that one of the strangers must be Burr, rode to Fort Stoddert and notified its commanding officer, Lieutenant Edmund Pendleton Gaines. Next morning Gaines, with four of his men and Perkins, set out for Hinson's house. Presently they saw Burr and Brightwell approaching. Gaines arrested Burr, took him to the fort, and placed him under guard.[88]

The man who had ridden with Burr to Wakefield on the previous night was Major Robert Ashley. Leaving Hinson's house just before

Burr's arrest, he met Thomas Malone and went with him to the house of Colonel John Caller, who hated Spaniards intensely and who had tried in vain to raise a force to capture Mobile. Ashley told Caller that he and Burr had planned to march against Baton Rouge until General Wilkinson frustrated their purpose by deserting them. Ignorant of Burr's arrest, he told Caller that they planned to move next against Mobile, where they counted many friends including even a Spanish abbé and a disgruntled Spanish officer. Caller pledged his full support to the undertaking.[89]

Meanwhile, Burr was waiting for an opportunity to escape from Fort Stoddert. Gaines was fully aware of his intention, though he treated him well and even allowed his wife to play chess with him. He learned that Major Ashley had been arrested but that he had escaped and had made friends among the people of the district. He knew that Burr was trying to bribe the guards. He feared that some of the prisoner's Spanish friends might try to free him. Convinced that he could not keep his captive for long, he engaged Nicholas Perkins to take him to Washington, D.C. and turn him over to the Federal authorities. On March 5 Burr, surrounded by a guard of six men under Perkins, departed on his journey of a thousand miles. He was given so much freedom on the road that in South Carolina he tried to escape by jumping from his horse, but the alert guard disarmed and remounted him. Thereafter he was not permitted to speak to anybody. Presently, Perkins put him in a gig and took him to Fredericksburg, Virginia. There he received a messenger directing him to take his prisoner to Richmond for trial. Chief Justice John Marshall cleared Burr as well as Blennerhassett of treason for want of sufficient evidence.[90]

Burr's presence in Mississippi Territory put its politics in a terrible muddle. One faction attached the stigma of "Burrism" on the other. The Mead faction, which flowered during Williams' absence in North Carolina, had started proceedings against Burr. Its leaders included George Poindexter, William B. Shields, Colonel F. L. Claiborne, brother to the governor of Orleans Territory, and Judge Rodney. These aristocratic planters hated Williams. Though erstwhile prime movers in the persecution of Burr, they poked fun at those who feared Burr's "formidable flotilla" when Williams, returning from North Carolina, took up the case. And when the governor ordered a number of arrests, the Mead faction condemned him loudly and even "indicted him," as we have seen. Williams retaliated by demoting every officer in the Mead camp who had participated in Burr's arrest and persecution.

How did Burr fare with the people? Once arrested, he became in the public mind a kind of hero—"a pleasant fellow, harmless and persecuted." No faction could now afford to "risk popular disapproval by being too hard on him." While Williams obeyed Jefferson's wishes, he made amends by firing Mead, Claiborne, and others "who had preceded him in the same course." Burr found most of his friends among the Federalists, who supplied the "backbone of his support in all sections of the country." To Jefferson, Federalism and Burrism were synonymous terms. Neither the Mead faction nor the Williams faction had any great interest in Burr other than for political purposes, which each promoted "no matter how friendly to Burr [it] might have been at one time or another, by making the bald assumption that he had been a traitor." Each imputed treason to the other by the simple expedient of growling "B-u-r-r-r-r!" when they met.[91]

The territorial assembly became so relentless in its opposition to Williams that it rejected nearly all of his appointments. Some of its members, including Poindexter, resigned. In November, 1807, Williams refused to recognize it on the ground that it had met in disregard of congressional law and without the governor's consent. So many of its members stayed home that it lacked a quorum to transfer business. So Williams gleefully prorogued it until December. Its infuriated members countered by addressing Jefferson a memorial in which they expressed disapproval of Williams' possible reappointment for a second term. They charged him with political treason and with Burrism. They cited "as special instances of apostasy" his removal of important officials and his attempts to monopolize the judges of elections with Federalists. Jefferson must have regarded these charges as expressions of prejudice or malice, for he renominated Williams for a second term.

Far from submitting to this humiliation, the governor's enemies secured a majority in the territorial House of Representatives to renew their fight against him with replenished strength. At the same time, they re-elected George Poindexter as delegate to Congress. Poindexter wasted no time in introducing a bill to deprive the governor of the right to dissolve the assembly. This failed. Undaunted, Poindexter bent all his efforts toward obtaining the governor's removal from office. Knowing that his success depended less on his forensic skill than on his aptitude at "buttonhole" politics, he worked, not in the House of Representatives itself but in the cloakrooms and committee rooms. But all this proved needless. On November 10, 1808, Williams communicated to Jefferson his intention of "going out of office with you." Jefferson left the presidency on March 4, 1809. Williams did him one better by leaving the governorship of Mississippi Territory a day earlier.[92]

6

The last and best governor of the territory was David Holmes, a Pennsylvanian who had moved to Virginia, where he practised law and became commonwealth attorney for Rockingham County. He was serving as a representative in Congress when, on March 7, 1809, he was appointed to succeed Williams. He was an honorable and mild mannered man who owed his success less to brilliance and aggressiveness than to "kindness, persuasiveness, and even gentleness combined with true courage, intelligence of a high order, culture and good breeding."[93]

Early in his administration, the chaotic condition of adjacent West

Florida, which still remained under Spanish rule, occupied most of his attention. He learned that its regular authorities had ceased to exercise their functions, and that its voluntary police service was wholly ineffective. Most of its inhabitants were Americans, who regarded it as a part of the territory the United States had purchased from France in 1803. Holmes felt that they would rather run the risk of revolt than submit longer to anarchy or to foreign rule. Though he favored annexation of the province to the United States, he thought it should come through invitation of the people.[94]

The inhabitants of Baton Rouge in particular were critical of their commander, Carlos Duhault de Lassus, who had succeeded Grand Pré in 1807. A dawdling gourmand, he was exceedingly lax in suppressing crimes and in punishing his corrupt officials. Since Spain was too far away and was, moreover, engrossed in her titanic struggle with Napoleon, she could give little attention to her dominions in America. All grievances, therefore, fell in the lap of local officials who, regarding them as reflections of their own incompetence, more often than not frowned on them or ignored them altogether. Amid the great discontent, rumors spread that Napoleon was about to claim the province and that he would send troops to take possession of it.[95]

Though the Americans of West Florida preferred the government of the United States, they were willing to tolerate Spanish rule as long as it showed some regard for their interests. But the thought of French domination, which they realized would be much more stringent, was entirely repugnant to them. So they resolved to abort any possibility of a change of jurisdiction to France by giving formal assurance of their fealty to Spain. But how could they provide themselves with a more effective government and still maintain their attitude of loyalty to the king of Spain?

The people of Feliciana answered this question by calling a convention composed of delegates from every section of the province. Meeting at St. John's Plains on July 20, 1810, with John Rhea as chairman, they declared in a formal set of resolutions their unswerving allegiance to Spain as against possible French jurisdiction. They accepted Lassus as governor of West Florida and sent a committee which conveyed to him a memorial explaining the need for the reorganization of the government of the province. The committee assured him that the convention had no intention of jeopardizing the sovereignty of Ferdinand VII over the province and pledged him the leadership of the new government.[96]

Lassus appeared complaisant and acquiesced to the proposed reforms. But his subsequent actions disclosed that he was merely biding his time. On August 25 a second convention organized a new government and issued a proclamation to that effect in the name of Lassus and of the people of Baton Rouge. It named its officers, including Philemon Thomas as commander of militia for the district.[97]

Everything seemed serene and harmonious until Philemon Thomas learned that Lassus was playing a game of duplicity; that, while he pretended to comply with the insurgent program, he was laying treacherous plans to crush what he had considered all along outright rebellion against his king. The militia leader had intercepted a letter that Lassus had sent to Juan Folch, Spanish governor of West Florida at Pensacola, urging him to come to Baton Rouge with a force strong enough to quell the rebellion, which he described as "desperate and determined."[98]

The discovery of this duplicity convinced the insurgent leaders that they would never achieve good government as long as they remained under Spanish rule. Consciously or unconsciously, they had longed for this opportunity to declare their independence. They assembled their followers and raised the standard of a new sovereign state—a piece of blue woolen blanket with a silver star in the center. Though only about eighty strong, they felt fit to fight a battle for the freedom of the world. On September 23 they advanced against the fort, a ramshackle building with two large gaps in the stockade, which constituted its chief defense. The absence of an outer ditch invited attack from every direction. The gate served as a guard station rather than as a point of defense. The fort had twenty cannon in workable order, but most of its ammunition had been spent saluting American gunboats and American officers passing up and down the river. Lassus, fearing an American attack, deserted the fort for the house of a friend only two hundred paces away and remained there all morning long, despite repeated messages warning him of what was about to occur. The second in command, Luis de Grand Pré, son of the old Natchez commander, had assembled his small force and was attempting to unite it with the handful of militia when the attack began. "Hurrah, Washington!" shouted the insurgents as they swung into the fort through the undefended gate and the gaps in the palisade. Grand Pré ordered his men to fire on them. The insurgents followed suit, mortally wounding Grand Pré and a soldier and wounding two militiamen. Not a single member of the attacking party was injured. At this juncture, Lassus ran with one of his officers toward the fort, but, just as they reached it, they learned that the rebels were already in possession of it and were gleefully shouting: "Uurra Waschintown!"

Several parties of horsemen coming from the fort met Lassus face to face. "Alas, what is this?" he exclaimed. He quickly found out. They seized him roughly and pushed him into the fort, where they forced him to surrender the keys of the magazine. One of the insurgent officers pulled down the Spanish flag and dragged it through the village dust, while another sent up the lone star flag of the republic of West Florida. It fluttered in the breeze amid the thunderous shouts of the victors: "Uurra Waschintown!"[99]

Three days later the insurgent leaders assembled and formed a provisional government for their new state. Emulating the original thirteen colonies in their revolt against George III, they soon promulgated a Declaration of Independence:

Being ... left without any hope of protection from the mother country, betrayed by the magistrate whose duty it was to have provided for the safety and tranquility of the people and government committed to his charge, and exposed to all the evils of a state of anarchy, which we have so long endeavored to avert, it becomes our duty to provide for our own security, as a free and independent state, absolved from all allegiance to a government which no longer protects us.

We, therefore, the representatives aforesaid, appealing to the Supreme Ruler of the world for the rectitude of our intentions, do solemnly publish and declare the several districts composing this Territory of West Florida to be a free and independent State; and that they have a right to institute for themselves such form of government as they may think conducive to their safety and happiness.[100]

They sent a copy of the declaration to Governor Holmes with the request that it be forwarded to President Madison. They chose Fulwar Skipwith, a lawyer with diplomatic experience in France and a flair for political rhetoric, governor or president of the republic. At the request of the convention, John Rhea, its president, applied for admission of the republic into the Union without delay, "since our weak and unprotected situation will oblige us to look to some foreign government for support, should it be refused by the country which he had considered our parent State."[101]

The president peremptorily refused their request. Annex West Florida? Preposterous! Why, that region was already a part of the United States—had been since the Louisiana Purchase! But he considered the time ripe to proclaim American ownership. On October 27 he issued a proclamation ordering Governor Claiborne of Orleans Territory to take possession of the revolted territory as far as the Perdido River, establish courts, organize the militia, and take every measure necessary to secure to the people the "peaceful enjoyment of their lives, property, and religion."[102]

Presently Claiborne scattered copies of the president's proclamation throughout West Florida, much to the indignation of Fulwar Skipwith, who in the previous month had been inaugurated and had, for that occasion, delivered an address typical of his resplendently turgid style:

Wherever the voice of justice and humanity can be heard our declaration and our just rights will be respected. But the blood which flows in our veins like the tributary streams which form and sustain the father of rivers, encircling our delightful country, will return if not impeded to the heart of our parent country. The genius of Washington, the immortal founder of the liberties of America, stimulates that return, and would frown upon our cause should we attempt to change its course.[103]

Though he had accepted the presidency with reluctance, he now felt that he deserved some recognition of his elevated office, and that Claiborne should have officially apprised him of the proclamation before circulating it indiscriminately. Proud as a pouter pigeon, he took off for Baton Rouge, vowing that he "would, with twenty men only, if a greater number could not be produced," rather "surround the Flag-Staff and die in its defense," than "surrender the country unconditionally and without terms."[104]

Meanwhile Claiborne, with a small force, had journeyed to West Florida, where he read the president's proclamation and replaced the Lone Star of the West Florida Republic with the Stars and Stripes. When he learned of Skipwith's opposition, he sent for reinforcements and ordered gunboats up the river from New Orleans. When the gunboats arrived, Skipwith suddenly sobered down. Though he protested Claiborne's actions as an outrage to the flag and constitution of West Florida, he declared that, as a citizen of the United States, he would never sign an order that would lead to the shedding of American blood. Though he refused to order his troops to lower the flag of the new republic, he commanded them to accept Claiborne's measures. As a conciliatory gesture, Claiborne offered to make him a justice of the peace—a humiliating post which he declined with badly concealed anger. The fort quickly surrendered; the Lone Star came down; in its place flew the Stars and Stripes. With the surrender of the fort the whole district of Baton Rouge fell to the United States.[105]

The Republic of West Florida had lasted less than three months. But in that brief time it had accomplished much. Its convention had deposed the Spanish authorities in and around Baton Rouge. But in its success it envisaged the possibility of Spanish retaliation from Mobile and perhaps from Pensacola. This it attempted to forestall by posting sentinels along the banks of the Pearl River, which formed the boundary of the insurgent section of West Florida. It soon found these precautionary measures uncertain as well as expensive, so it resolved to seize the rest of the province. To this end it commissioned Reuben Kemper to raise a force with which to attack Mobile.

Far from being cowed by Judge Rodney's order to keep the peace, Kemper had quickly wreaked vengeance on Keeland and the Horton brothers, who had kidnaped him and his brothers. He captured Keeland, inflicted on his bare back a hundred lashes, then one hundred more for brother Nathan, who was absent, cut off his ears with a dull knife, and sent him home. Reuben preserved his bloody trophies in strong wine and hung them up in his parlor. Sometime later he caught James Horton and lashed him within an inch of his life. Then he seized Barker, one of Horton's accomplices, in a courthouse under the very nose of the judge and dragged him on the rough ground until most of his skin was torn off his body. Captain Alston, who had seized Kemper and his brothers with the help of a Spanish guard, avoided their attacks only by lying in an open boat every night until he contracted pneumonia and died.

In his endeavor to raise a force with which to seize Mobile, Reuben proved as resolute as he was implacable in his resentments. He soon realized a sizable body of frontier roughnecks, but it was so poorly equipped that it was forced to defer its attack. Eventually Reuben received arms from a rich merchant of New Orleans and a flatboat load of food from the convention. But again he was cheated of his ambition. The presence of Americans just across the border demoralized Governor Folch to the extent that he appealed to President Madison to send the garrison of nearby Fort Stoddert to help him drive Reuben Kemper back to Baton Rouge. In addition he asked for commissioners with power to treat for the transfer of Mobile and the rest of the province of West Florida to the United States. Opposed by Judge Toulmin of the Tombigbee region, by Governor Holmes of Mississippi Territory, and by President Madison, Kemper grumblingly disbanded his men and returned to his home in New Orleans.[106]

7

On June 18, 1812, the United States declared war on Great Brtiain. Madison, believing that the ports of Mobile, Pensacola, and St. Augustine were likely to prove too tempting for England, Spain's ally, asked Congress for authority to occupy them. Factional disputes in the Senate, however, defeated this proposal until January 1813, when Congress authorized Madison to occupy all of Florida west of the Perdido River.[107] East Florida remained in Spanish hands for six years longer. Acting on orders from John Armstrong, secretary of war, General Wilkinson in March 1813 occupied Mobile with six hundred men. On April 13 the Spanish commander, Cayetano Pérez, evacuated Fort Charlotte, which commanded the town, leaving his artillery to Wilkinson. Late that afternoon, amid a salvo of batteries from Wilkinson's gunboats, the American flag rose over Fort Charlotte.[108] Congress added the region of Mobile to Mississippi Territory.

Governor Holmes could now turn his full attention to the Creeks, who saw in the struggle between Great Britain and the United States the possibility of driving the Americans from the region. In this endeavor they were inspired by the great Shawnee chief, Tecumseh, who in the previous year ranged among the tribes in his mission to secure a solid front against the white man's greed for their lands. He visited them at Coosawada, where the Coosa and Tallapoosa rivers join to form the Alabama, informing them that Detroit had fallen to the British and Indians. The enthusiasm with which they received his message encouraged him to move on to Toockabatcha, capital of the Creek confederacy, where he urged them in a long speech to return to their primitive customs, to disdain the plow and the loom, and to abandon their agricultural life in favor of joining England in relentless war against their enemies. His speech had such an overpowering effect on them that, despite their comparative wealth and comfort, they clamored for war against the whites. Their war chief was William Weatherford, a half-breed who proudly bore the Indian name of Red Eagle. The son of Charles Weatherford, a shrewd Scotch merchant who had migrated from Georgia, and Sehoy, the beautiful half-sister of Alexander McGillivray, he inherited wealth, handsome features, unusual intelligence, and a noble bearing. Yet he never learned to read or write. Though his station in life would have permitted him education, culture, and comfort, he preferred to lead the wretched and dirty existence of a Muskogee Indian, hunting and riding with great skill and boasting that he had "not a drop of Yankee blood in my veins."[109]

Tecumseh had advised him to obtain military stores from the friendly Spaniards or from the British fleet off Pensacola. Thither in July, 1813, Red Eagle sent three chiefs—Peter McQueen, a half-breed from the Tallahassee region, Prophet Josiah Francis, and High Head Jim—with three hundred warriors to trade a herd of cattle, which they had stolen during raids on white settlements, for whiskey, guns, and ammunition. On arriving at the port they met the Spanish governor, who treated them kindly but who, fearing violence, gave them only "a small bag of powder each for ten towns, and five bullets to each man." With this supply, which the governor represented as a friendly present for hunting purposes, they started homeward.[110]

The white settlers above Mobile, fearing imminent Indian raids, took refuge in stockades. They soon learned that McQueen's Indians had, on their way to Pensacola, burned a corn crib belonging to a half-breed named Cornells, and that they would return to that place, which became known as Burnt Corn, on their journey homeward. Colonel James Caller and Captain Sam Dale, intrepid Indian fighters, joined their forces, totaling a hundred eighty men, and led them toward Pensacola to meet the returning Indians. On July 27, a little before noon, they found them encamped and eating by a large creek near Burnt Corn. They charged them while they poured on them a withering fire. The Indians took refuge in a canebrake across the creek. But while the Americans were plundering the Indian baggage, McQueen rallied his braves who, uttering terrifying war whoops, charged them with war clubs, tomahawks, and guns. The dumbfounded Americans retreated to a hill so far away from Caller that his orders could not reach them. About eighty of them, under Captain Dale, remained on the hill, desperately fighting the Indians until, overwhelmed by superior numbers, they turned and fled, some on horses, some on foot. Dale and twelve of his men were wounded; two were killed. Each man mustered himself out of service and returned as fast as he could to defend his own home. Colonel Caller and another officer, retreating on foot, were lost in the wilderness and were eventually separated. Cold, hungry, and tired, Caller wandered for fifteen days before friends found him and restored him to health. The Indians lost most of their supplies and ammunition. Those who survived the battle returned to Pensacola for more military supplies.[111]

The tussle at Burnt Corn signaled the beginning of hostilities between the Americans and the Creeks. Frontiersmen hurried to the safety of stockades with their families and hunting dogs and what of their live-stock they could gather quickly. One of these stockades was Fort Mims, named for its half-breed owner, Samuel Mims, which lay on Tensaw Lake, about ten miles above the junction of the Alabama and Tombigbee rivers. Here Mims ran a trading post and a ferry across the Alabama. During the summer of 1813, when the surrounding settlers feared the possibility of Creek raids, Mims added to his property a spacious planta-tion, which he surrounded with a high picket fence that enclosed about an acre of ground.[112]

To the defense of the fort Governor Holmes sent a force of 265 men, who were put under the command of Major Daniel Beasley. On August 7 Frederick L. Claiborne, now a general, visited the fort to inspect its defenses. He advised Beasley to respect the bravery of the enemy, to send out scouts frequently, and to allow ample provisions to anybody who should seek the protection of the fort. But Beasley, fearing no further hostilities from the Creeks, paid small attention to Claiborne's military advice. And in the ensuing days his complacency seemed justified. When no Indians appeared, he relaxed his vigilance altogether; he allowed sand to accumulate before one of the gates of the fort so that it could not be closed quickly in case of an attack; he ignored warnings of impending danger from experienced and cautious fur traders and Indian scouts. In vain did a hostile warrior apprise some of his relatives in the fort of an impending attack; in vain did two Negroes who had been rounding up cattle outside the fort declare that they had seen a large body of painted Indians hiding in an adjacent canebrake and swamp. Vain, rash, inexperi-enced, Beasley listened to no remonstrance. He steadfastly refused to keep the gate of the fort closed. He permitted men, women, and children to wander unrestrained along the banks of the lake. He had one of the Negro slaves flogged for falsely alarming the garrison by reporting that Indians were near the fort. Another Negro slave, seeing Indians skulking in the wilderness, fled to Fort Pierce from fear that he would be whipped should this information be communicated somehow to Beasley.[113]

By August 30 five hundred fifty-three persons, of whom about a hun-dred were children, had gathered inside Fort Mims. Free of alarm, they abandoned themselves to fun and frolic. Major Beasley was playing cards with some of his officers. A roll of the noon drum summoned the garrison to dinner. At that moment a thousand warriors under Red Eagle were lying flat on the ground in a thick ravine four hundred yards from the fort. The drumroll was the signal for which they had been waiting. Yell-ing and yelping, they swept toward the fort, where they met Beasley who, sword in hand, was trying to close the gate and defend himself at the same time. They struck him down with their tomahawks and clubs and swarmed over his body to the fort, leaving him to crawl and soon to die behind the gate. Officers and soldiers died in vain attempts to rectify the evil of their own complacency. The mangled and bloody bodies of men, women, and children fell in heaps. The young men, who had been dancing with their girls, fought the unrelenting Indians with desperate fury. Captain Dixon Bailey assumed command of the fort and animated its defenders to a resolute resistance. The women loaded the guns, brought water from the well, nursed the wounded, and encouraged the soldiers to fight on with greater courage.[114]

At last Red Eagle himself expressed disapproval of the terrible slaughter. He was in love with Lucy Cornells, a beautiful and spirited half-breed girl of eighteen whose father had taken refuge in the fort, and he wanted to impress them with his humanity. He reproached his men for their barbarity and implored them to spare the women and children; but they were so infuriated by their heavy losses that they threatened to kill him if he interfered. Disgusted with them and anxious to show Lucy and her father that he opposed the massacre, he mounted a beautiful black horse and rode away from the horrid scene.[115]

By now the survivors, driven from building to building, had taken refuge in a second line of pickets, which they called the bastion, near an unfinished blockhouse. Some of the Indians climbed to its roof and, after trying in vain to dislodge its defenders with bullets and flaming arrows, set fire to a house near it. The flames soon spread to the kitchen of the house and to the adjacent picket. Most of its defenders, including Bailey, perished in the enveloping holocaust. Not more than twenty-five or thirty persons escaped, and even these were badly wounded. The rest, including most of the women and children, fell, victims of the Indians or of the flames. A little before sunset the Indians withdrew with what booty they could salvage.[116]

Among the survivors was a Negress named Hester who, though gravely wounded, broke through the line of Indian warriors, reached a canoe in the lake, and paddled to Fort Stoddert, where she apprised General Claiborne of the massacre. Claiborne immediately despatched a detachment under Captain Joseph P. Kennedy to bury the dead at Fort Mims. This force found the bodies of two hundred forty-seven men, women, and children. While it searched the adjacent woods for more bodies, it found those of about a hundred Indians.[117]

Nothing in the entire War of 1812 shocked the American people more than did the massacre at Fort Mims. Everywhere they demanded immediate vengeance. In the Southern Frontier, horror changed to fear that Red Eagle, emboldened by his victory, would ravage the more densely settled states of Georgia, Tennessee, and Louisiana. The chief was contemplating an attack on Mobile, which he knew the Spanish governor at Pensacola yearned to recapture from the Americans. Though the governor welcomed Red Eagle's plan, he admonished him not to burn the town, "since the houses and properties do not belong to the Americans, but to true Spaniards." To arrest the possibility of further Creek massacres or even depredations, Governor Holmes with characteristic promptness called out the Mississippi Dragoons, an intrepid force of two hundred cavalrymen which he put under the command of Major Thomas Hinds. Marching to the frontier, the Dragoons found that the Creeks had already attacked Fort Sinquefield and had forced its garrison to seek safety in Fort Madison. Meanwhile, Governor Holmes and General Claiborne had won the friendship of the Choctaw chief, Pushmataha, who offered them his full support against Red Eagle. The Americans and their Choctaw allies held the field against the Creeks until in October twenty-five Tennesseans under Andrew Jackson marched from Nashville to Huntsville, north of the Tennessee River, where he established his headquarters.[118]

Though he had risen just a few days before from bed with a shattered shoulder and a bullet received in a duel with Thomas Hart Benton, Jackson showed the boundless energy and invincible will that was leading him to greatness. But for the present these qualities could not rescue him from the difficulty in which he found himself. Indeed, his difficulty increased with his energy. He had brought no supplies with him. He hoped they would be sent to him by the river, but it was too low to move them. Without food, without forage, he could neither advance, remain in Huntsville, nor hope to keep his men even with half of their horses. So he sent General John Coffee with his mounted men, numbering nine hundred, to forage Indian corn on the banks of the Black Warrior River, many miles away from any Creek villages. Then he himself moved twenty-four miles along the Tennessee to its southernmost bend, where on October 23 he established a camp which he called Fort Deposit and which was to become his main base of supplies.[119]

Jackson waited until Coffee returned with his mounted men. Then, intending to raid the Creek villages for food, he marched his men to the upper waters of the Coosa, where he put them to work cutting down trees for a stockade which he called Fort Strother. Among his soldiers was Davy Crockett, "the merriest of the merry, keeping the camp alive with his quaint conceits and marvelous narratives." Thirteen miles away was the village of Tallasehatche, which he learned contained two hundred eighty-four Creek warriors. He sent Coffee to destroy them. "We shot them like dogs," exulted Davy Crockett. No brave survived the battle. Coffee lost five killed and forty-one wounded. Jackson said the slaughter of Tallasehatche avenged the massacre of Fort Mims. Among the eighty-four prisoners was a boy of three years whose parents had died. "Kill him, too," said the prisoners.[120] But Jackson, who could be as tender toward the helpless as he was relentless toward the enemy, kept the child alive by coaxing him to drink brown sugar water. Jackson sent him to Huntsville and paid for his nursing there. Licoyer, as they named the boy, was destined to live with Andrew and Rachel Jackson in the

Hermitage, where they watched over him with paternal care. When, in late adolescence, he died of tuberculosis, they buried him in the family vault.

While waiting for supplies Jackson received an appeal for help from Talladega, a Creek village thirty miles away, which Red Eagle was besieging with a thousand braves because it had refused to join him in war against the Americans. To its defense hurried Jackson with twelve hundred infantry and eight hundred cavalry. Though he was so weak from dysentery and lack of sleep that he had to prop himself up against a tree, he deployed his men for battle in the form of a crescent with the points toward the village. Then he sent three companies of cavalry under Captain Russell to lure Red Eagle's warriors to battle. The men forming the crescent saw their comrades ride warily through the brush and dead grass, saw them exchange signs with their red friends in the village, saw two Indians receive Captain Russell's horse and point to their enemies hidden among trees along a creek. At this juncture Red Eagle's naked warriors fired a volley; then, "screaming like devils," they burst from their hiding places "like a cloud of Egyptian locusts." Pursued, Russell's men galloped back to the crescent. As soon as the Indians came within range of his cannon, Jackson attacked them with deadly fire. This slackened their charge but not their fury; they fought their enemies with guns, arrows, and tomahawks until the crescent advanced and joined, encircling them with superior arms that mowed them down in heaps. Only one detachment gave way to their blind fury; it opened up a gap through which seven hundred of them escaped. The remaining three hundred perished as the gap closed again around them. Jackson lost only fifteen men.[121]

He burned to press forward to win fresh laurels, but the lack of supplies and the burden of his eighty-seven wounded men forced him to return to Fort Strother. There his soldiers, hungry and exhausted, were about to desert him when General John Cocke arrived with fourteen hundred fifty fresh troops. But he soon learned that their time of service would expire within ten days and that they yearned to return home. Old Hickory, as his men called him, denied them rations and wounded their pride by sending them home within twenty-four hours after their arrival. Soon he sustained a harsher blow. Harkening to public opinion, Governor William Blount ordered him to evacuate Fort Strother and return to Tennessee. Jackson refused. In an indignant letter he reminded the governor that the Tennessee assembly had promised the president to keep thirty-five hundred men in the field until the Creeks should be destroyed.

And you my Dear friend sitting with yr. arms folded, . . . recommending me to retrograde to please the whims of the populace. . . . Let me tell you it imperiously lies upon both you and me to do our duty regardless of consequences or the opinion of those fireside patriots, those fawning sycophants or cowardly poltroons who after their boasted ardor would . . . let thousands fall victims to my retrograde. . . .

Arouse from yr. lethargy—despite fawning smiles or snarling frowns —with energy exercise yr. functions—the campaign must rapidly progress or . . . yr. country ruined. Call out the full quota—execute the orders of the Secy of War, arrest the officer who omits his duty, . . . and let popularity perish for the present. . . . Save Mobile—save the Territory—save yr. frontier from becoming drenched with blood. . . . What retrograde under these circumstances? I will perish first.[122]

This reproof had its effect. Blount decided to support Jackson in the campaign and, with the consent of the secretary of war, sent eight hundred recruits to join him.

At about the same time—December, 1813—General Thomas Flournoy, who had succeeded Wilkinson as commander of the southern forces, ordered Claiborne to invade Creek country and "kill, burn, and destroy all their negroes, cattle, and other property that could not be conveniently brought to the depots." With a thousand Mississippi militiamen, some infantry troops, and fifty-one Choctaw braves under Pushmataha, Claiborne marched on the Holy City of the Creeks, a fortress of two hundred houses lying on a bluff on the southern bank of the Alabama River, just below Powell's ferry in present Lowndes County, Alabama. There Red Eagle had built on a wooded peninsula that jutted out into the river a rude citadel surrounded by impassable swamps, canebrakes, and ravines. The Holy City served the Creeks as a refuge in time of defeat, at a hospital for their wounded, and as a shrine where their prophets, Josiah Francis and Sinquista, sometimes burned prisoners at the stake. The Creeks believed that no white man could survive in the Holy City.[123]

At daybreak on December 23 Claiborne led his army in three columns over a winding trail toward the Holy City which the Creeks kept secret but which friendly Indians disclosed to him. The Creek warriors, encouraged by Red Eagle and blessed by their prophets, poured a storm of bullets and arrows on their enemies from the brink of an impassable ravine and from behind a redoubt of heavy logs. Undaunted, the Americans, closely supported by Pushmataha's braves, pressed steadily on the city. The Indians, seeing their foes were about to enter it with impunity, lost all faith in their own invincibility and fled into the forest through a gap in the American lines. Red Eagle fought on until he found himself alone. On three sides pressed the Americans; on the remaining side was the bluff with the Alabama River fifteen feet below. Red Eagle mounted his strong and swift gray horse, Arrow, galloped to the edge of the bluff, and—in the twinkle of an eye—leaped into the swirling river. The pursuing Americans saw horse and rider sink beneath the rushing current, saw Red Eagle rise with Arrow, saw him grasp his horse's mane with one hand and his rifle in the other, saw him regain his saddle, saw him ride defiantly up the opposite bank—and their eyes bulged with mingled awe and admiration. The feat inspired a number of Mississippi and Alabama historians to describe it with charming variations—any of which may be entirely true.[124]

Claiborne entered the great square of Holy City, where he found a number of half-breeds tied to stakes with wood piled around them. They had unwisely shown friendship toward the Americans. By his timely arrival Claiborne snatched them from death. On Christmas Day he and his men dined on parched corn. In Red Eagle's house he discovered a number of letters that proved that the chief enjoyed close ties with the Spanish authorities in Pensacola. Claiborne sent the letters to the secretary of war with this advice: "Seize Pensacola and you disarm the Indians. It is the real heart of the Creek Confederacy."[125]

Jackson concurred in the belief that the capture of the city was paramount to the successful conclusion of operations against the secretly inimical Spaniards and the openly hostile British and their Creek allies. Later his quick decision against the city proved a master stroke in defense of the Gulf Coast. For the present, however, his attention was directed elsewhere. In January, 1814, having received more reinforcements from Governors Blount and Holmes, he attacked the Creeks at Emuckfau and forced them into headlong flight. Two days later he attacked them again at Enotachopco Creek. All of his men save twenty-five suddenly panicked and fled precipitously; but an officer turned defeat into victory by firing a six-pounder which scattered the Indians in all directions. In the following month friendly Indians advised Jackson that Red Eagle had concentrated his braves in Tohopeka or Horseshoe, a peninsula of about a hundred acres at the great bend of the Tallapoosa River, in the northeastern part of present Tallapoosa County, Alabama. Across the neck of the peninsula the chief had built a kind of stronghold composed of five huge logs, one above the other, with two rows of portholes. With fallen timber protecting him along the river bank and with trees and underbrush sheltering him in the interior, Red Eagle considered Tohopeka impregnable to infantry attack. Yet he took no chances. Along the river his men, at his command, moored hundreds of canoes in which they hoped to escape in case of defeat.[126]

On March 26 Jackson, with two thousand men, camped within five miles of the Horseshoe. Early next morning General Coffee, in accordance with military plans, crossed the Tallapoosa two miles below the Horseshoe, occupied the high ground along the river, seized the canoes, and paddled them back to the opposite bank. Meanwhile, Jackson moved two six-pounders to within eighty feet of the stronghold and fired on it. The round balls sank harmlessly in the giant soft pine logs. Red Eagle's men replied with scornful shouts.[127]

Meanwhile Coffee with two hundred dismounted cavalrymen had crossed the river in canoes, had captured the town, and had set fire to it. The fire and smoke that rose to the bright sky signaled to Jackson the success of Coffee's task. He gave him time to carry the Creek women and children across the river to safety. Then, as drums beat a long roll, he charged the stronghold with his infantry. The first man to reach it was Major Lemuel Purnell Montgomery who fell dead instantly with a bullet in his brain. Tears gathered in Old Hickory's eyes as he looked at Montgomery's body. "I have lost the flower of my army," he said.

The first soldier to scale the stronghold was a mere youth in the blue and brass uniform of a regular. He was Ensign Sam Houston, who was destined to cover himself with glory twenty-two years later at San Jacinto, where he won Texan independence by defeating the Mexicans and by capturing their leader Santa Anna. Though wounded by a bullet in his thigh and by a barbed arrow in his body, he charged the stronghold and fought with leonine courage in the ensuing battle that drove the Indians to the safety of the wooded area in the center of the peninsula. Thence, suffering fearful losses with every yard of their retreat, they sought protection in the thickets and under the bluff until they were hunted or burned out or killed. Toward the end of the day Jackson sent to the remaining warriors an interpreter offering clemency to all those who would surrender. They received the interpreter with scorn, abused him, sent him back to Jackson, and resumed the battle. When it ended at the close of day, few Creeks remained alive to recount the terrors of the Battle of Horseshoe Bend, which practically wiped them out as an Indian nation. Next morning Jackson counted five hundred fifty-seven Indian bodies on the peninsula. Many more had drowned in the river. About twenty, including the chief, Peter McQueen, escaped to Florida, where they later fought the Americans anew under the magnificent Osceola. Jackson lost forty-nine killed and one hundred fifty-seven wounded.[128]

Next day Jackson moved down toward the junction of the Tallapoosa and the Coosa rivers, where he heard Red Eagle had rallied his few remaining braves. But the beaten chief offered him no more resistance. Four miles beyond the junction of the aforementioned rivers Jackson came on the crumbling ruins of Fort Toulouse, which Bienville had built in 1717 —not 1715 as some historians state.[129] He cleaned its trenches, rebuilt its stockades, and rechristened it Fort Jackson. Here one day he saw approaching his tent a tall, handsome, light-complexioned Indian. Naked to the waist, he was wearing only dirty and torn breeches and moccasins. He had no arms, no horse, no attendant.

"General Jackson?"

"Yes."

"I am Billy Weatherford," said Red Eagle, no longer esteeming his Indian name.

"I am glad to see you *Mr.* Weatherford. How dare you show yourself at my tent after having murdered the women and children at Fort Mims!"

They went inside.

"I have come," said Red Eagle, "to give myself up. I can oppose you no longer. I have done you much injury. I should have done you more ...

[but] my warriors are killed. . . . I am in your power. Dispose of me as you please."

"You are not," replied Jackson, "in my power . . . I had ordered you . . . brought to me in chains. . . . But you have come of your own accord. . . . I would gladly save you and your nation, but you do not even ask to be saved. If you think you can contend against me in battle go and head your warriors."

"Ah," said Red Eagle, "well may such language be addressed to me now. . . . There was a time when I . . . could have answered you. . . . I could animate my warriors to battle; but I can not animate the dead. My warriors can no longer hear my voice. Their bones are at Talladega, Tallasehatche, Emuckfau, and Tohopeka. General Jackson, I have nothing to request . . . [for] myself. But I beg you to send for the women and children of the war party, who have been driven to the woods without an ear of corn. . . . They never did any harm. But kill me, if the white people want it done."[130]

Old Hickory thought that anybody who would kill such a brave man as Red Eagle would rob the dead. As he poured him a cup of brandy he promised to send food to the Creek women and children and to help them return to their homes. Red Eagle in turn pledged his people to peace. Then, taking Jackson's extended hand, he "strode from the ruined fort in which his mother had been born—vanished from the view of the astonished soldiery, and from history, a not entirely graceless figure."[131]

Now that all was quiet again on the Creek front, Jackson returned to the Hermitage for a well-earned rest. President Madison promoted him to the rank of major-general, made him commander of American forces in the south, and empowered him to arrange a treaty with the tribe he had vanquished. On August 9 he met some Creek chiefs at Fort Jackson and exacted from them a brutal peace: they gave up 23,000,000 acres of their domain between the Chattahoochee on the east and the Coosa on the west—a territory that comprised one-fifth of the present state of Georgia and three-fifths of the present state of Alabama. This treaty represented the fulfillment of a combined military and political policy: it isolated the Creeks from the Seminoles and Spaniards on one side and from the Choctaws and Chickasaws on the other, and it completely surrounded them with a white population.[132]

On Christmas Eve the war ended. In the previous month Jackson had realized his long-range ambition of conquering Pensacola. And two weeks after the United States and Great Britain signed a treaty of peace in Ghent, Belgium, and before word of it could reach the United States, Jackson won the most brilliant victory of his military career. On January 8, 1815, he routed the British in the Battle of New Orleans.

8

His victories over the Creeks greatly augmented the flow of migration into Mississippi Territory. By now all of it was open to settlement save two isolated islands of territory in eastern Alabama and in northern and central Mississippi.[133] Many of the immigrants were Highlanders from the Carolinas, Georgia, and Tennessee who sought not trade and adventure among the Indians but permanent homes for their wives and children.[134] Some of them were leaders from well-to-do classes who longed to improve their fortunes in the freer opportunities of a new region. The indenture law then in operation permitted them to bring their slaves with them. They crowded fords and bad roads as they journeyed toward the sunset in heavy schooner-shaped wagons drawn by four or six horses. The poor classes walked, often carrying their meager possessions in a cart drawn by themselves. Those in better circumstances usually took their horses, cattle, and sheep with them and sent their household goods by wagon or by flatboat down the Mississippi River.[135]

They came in two successive waves. The first wave consisted of herdsmen who subsisted primarily by hunting and by raising a few vegetables. Like the pioneers of the Appalachian Frontier or the Great Lakes Frontier, they depended for subsistence on the natural growth of vegetation and on their luck in hunting. With his agricultural implements, which he himself crudely fashioned, each frontiersman, as soon as he settled, directed his efforts mainly toward realizing a crop of corn and a few vegetables. He found that only a few sections of the territory favored livestock, but he knew that southern settlements were nearer to the markets than were northern settlements west of the mountains. Furthermore, his cattle and hogs needed no shelter for the winter. The best grazing section of the territory was perhaps the piney woods east of the Pearl River, where the grass grew three feet high and the valleys were studded with flowers of every hue. Here, as the territory progressed toward statehood, thousands of cattle grazed for the market. Here, years later, a herdsmen described to Judge William H. Sparks, who dwelled in the Natchez district, how his grandfather had migrated from Emanuel County, Georgia:

> He carried with him a small one-horse cart pulled by an old gray mare, one feather bed, an oven, a frying-pan, two pewter dishes, six pewter plates, as many spoons, a rifle gun, and three deer-hounds. He worried through the Creek Nation, extending then from the Oconee River to the Tombigbee River.
>
> After four months of arduous travel he found his way to Leaf River, and there built his cabin; and with my grandmother, and my father, who was born on the trip in the heart of the Creek Nation, commenced to make a fortune. He found on a small creek of beautiful water a little bay land, and made his little field for corn and pumpkins upon the spot; all around was poor, barren woods, but he said it was a good range for stock; but he had not an ox or cow on the face of the earth. The truth is it looked like Emanuel County. The turpentine smell, the moan of the wind through the pine-trees, and nobody within fifty miles of him, was too captivating a concatenation to be resisted, and he rested here.

About five years after he came, a man from Pearl River was driving some cattle by to Mobile, and gave my grandfather two cows to help drive his cattle. It was over one hundred miles, and you would have supposed it a dear bargain; but it turned out well, for the old man in about six weeks got back with six other head of cattle. From these he commenced to rear a stock which in time became large.[136]

The second wave of settlers in Mississippi Territory were farmers and planters who desired to own land rather than to use a portion of the public domain. Unlike the herdsman, the agricultural immigrant sought a country that was as similar as possible to that in which he had formerly lived. In the new country, he aimed to pursue the same tillage methods and marketing, to grow the same crops, fruits, and vegetables, and to employ the same tools he had known in the old. These early farmers and planters of Mississippi Territory were largely the children or grandchildren of Carolinians, Georgians, and Tennesseans. The Carolinian and Georgian cotton planters sought in the territory soil similar in its clay and sand content to that of their native regions. Small wonder that Carolinians from the York, Abbeville, and Fairfield districts settled on the similar soil and topography of Blount, Jefferson, and Pickens counties, Alabama. The cotton farmers who settled in Newton County, Mississippi, "preferred the poorer sandy lands to the richer prairies and clay soils."[137]

So they moved into Mississippi Territory by the thousands, usually in parties composed of friends and relatives. Like the children of Israel, "they sent their Calebs and Joshuas ahead to spy out the land and prepare the way."[138] The rapidly increasing migration encouraged William Lattimore, territorial delegate, to work in Congress for the admission of the entire territory as a state in the Union. In March, 1816, the Senate advised him that it could not seriously consider the matter without a census of the territory. The census, taken in December, showed 75,502 people, of whom 45,085 were free whites, 356 free Negroes, and 30,061 slaves. Mindful of the "unprecedented magnitude" of the territory, Lattimore, now chairman of a committee seeking admission for Mississippi, proposed it be divided by a north and south line. The western or more populous part would become a state and the eastern part would remain a territory. Eventually Congress adopted this plan.

On March 1, 1817, President Monroe signed an enabling act which defined the present boundaries of Mississippi and which permitted the territorial delegates to meet in convention for the purpose of drafting a constitution. Under the able chairmanship of George Poindexter, the committee of twenty-one men appointed to draft a constitution concluded its labor in just seven days. Believing perhaps that the best government needs the least laws, Poindexter and his committee produced a lucid, simple, conservative, and dignified document that contained a required Declaration of Rights. Congress declared it republican and in conformity with the Ordinance of 1787. On December 10, with Monroe's signature, Mississippi added a star to the Stars and Stripes.[139] David Holmes was unanimously elected governor of the new state, George Poindexter its sole representative, and Walter Leake and Thomas H. Williams its senators.

Alabama remained a territory a little more than two years. On July 5, 1819, a constitutional convention, meeting in Huntsville, drafted a constitution that Congress approved. Late that summer Alabama entered the Union as the twenty-first state. Its first governor was William Wyatt Bibb, who also had served as its only territorial governor.

Masters and Slaves

LATE IN AUGUST, 1619, WHILE THE SETTLERS OF JAMESTOWN, IN THE colony of Virginia, were busy building their homes on the rim of civilization, they saw a strange ship sail with the tide up from the sea. To a settlement as weak as Jamestown, the approach of such a ship was the occasion for much alarm. In those days Spain claimed all of North America. Many times she had threatened to destroy the English settlement as an encroachment of her rights. In view of these circumstances, the settlers of Jamestown readied their muskets to protect themselves against possible attack. At first something about the approaching ship seemed unfriendly to them. Her stern was bluff-bowed and round; her sails were like great bags bellying before the wind; from the bulwarks on each of her sides protruded a row of black-muzzled cannon. But, as she drew near, the colonists saw many signs that allayed their fears. She was flying the Dutch, not the Spanish flag; her cannon were neither manned nor cast loose for action; her crew, by its friendly attitude, bespoke trade, not war. The colonists laid aside their muskets and accorded the strange ship a friendly welcome.[1]

John Rolfe, who married Pocahontas, tells us that the ship was "a Dutch man-of-Warre" and that she sold "20 negars" to the colonial government. The nameless ship was really a privateer that had taken the Negroes from a captured slaver. The colonial government sold them to settlers, who used them either as domestics or in expanding tobacco fields. The ship may have been the first to carry slaves to an English colony in North America; but she was not the first ship to carry slaves to what is now the United States. We have seen that Lucas Vásquez de Ayllón in 1527 took a small number of slaves with him on his expedition to the Cape Fear River. The Dutch privateer, however, has as much claim to fame as the *Mayflower* that arrived a year later. For the twenty Negroes she carried were the antecedents of all that their race contributed to American wealth and culture. They foretold Carolina rice,

Louisiana cane, the system of labor on the Southern Frontier, the Aboli-
tion Society, the Missouri Compromise, and the Civil War. And beyond
that unique conflict they presaged Reconstruction, the Solid South, Jim
Crow, and, in our own day, the struggle for integration.

For many years the trade was small. No vessel carried slaves exclusively on the high seas until 1630, when an English ship, the *Fortune*, fell
in with an Angola ship loaded with slaves and captured her. The *Fortune*
carried the slaves to Virginia, where they were exchanged for eighty-five
hogsheads and five butts of tobacco, which in turn were sold in London.
By 1650 Virginia had only some three hundred slaves—certainly less than
would have made a single cargo in later years. Most of the slave ships
weighed about a hundred tons. The first American slaver, the *Desire*,
built at Marblehead in 1636, weighed one hundred twenty tons. Another
slaver, the *Oak Tree*, "Jansen Eykenboom, from Hoorn, master under
God," which trafficked between New York and the Atlantic coast of
Africa in 1659, had a poop deck and a magnificent length of one hundred
twenty feet.[2]

The English colonists obtained their slaves largely from the Atlantic
coast of Africa between Cape Verde and Cape St. Marta. Here the sea
scoops into the land, as though the hump of Brazil had broken away to
form the hollow on the continent of Africa. Here two large rivers and a
number of smaller streams flow into the sea. The beach is so low that
distant hills and mountains may be seen clearly. The rivers meander
through numberless valleys covered with masses of mangrove and palm
trees and infested with poisonous reptiles. The sand along the shore and
the washings of the uplands mingle to form a kind of yellow-and-black
crazy quilt of beaches and dunes where the omnipresent and treacherous
surf repels the currents of the rivers. Here, in Goree and Gambia, in
Sierra Leone and Liberia, in Bonny and Calabar, in Congo and St. Paul de
Loango dwelt countless thousands of men, women, and children who
were sent as slaves to work in the plantations of the New World.

Their primitive society enabled the strong to dominate the weak.
Stalwart chiefs of mentally and physically superior tribes rose as heroes
among the people, subdued weaker tribes, and reduced them to slavery.
The destructive influence of their environment impelled these superstitious and savage people to believe in a host of malevolent spirits, which
they associated with such evil creatures as the poisonous snakes, the fierce
robber birds, the ravenous beasts, and those human beings who showed
cunning and stealth rather than courage and physical strength. But in at
least one respect blacks and whites met on common ground: they both
loved rum. The white man mixed his rum with lime juice or with sugar
and water; the black man took his rum straight. The white man preferred
madeira wine and, when he could afford it, usually after a voyage to
Africa, drank it for his health. The black man drank madeira because he
liked it.

The white man wanted slaves; the black man wanted rum, madeira, presents. So they agreed to barter. After a tribal war, a formidable chief always found himself with many young and healthy prisoners of both sexes and of various ages. Instead of killing them, why not trade them for spiritous liquors and presents?

Enterprising slavers found ways of enlivening their trade. They would seek out a chief and would tell him that certain stout, well-built young men in a neighboring tribe planned to deprive him of his authority. Incited to revenge, the chief would make war on his neighbors, would capture the presumed offenders, and would sell them to the slavers. To strengthen their chances of success, slavers would sometimes make friends with medicine men and urge them to charge young members of their own tribe with witchcraft, which invariably led to enslavement. Sometimes slavers would tell an influential old man that some of his wives were lovers of younger men. Whereupon the old man would lay in wait for the presumed lovers, would capture them, and would sell them to the slavers.[3]

In their desperate effort to obtain as many slaves as possible, slavers often encouraged coast tribes to make piratical raids into the interior. One John Bowman had charge of an agency established on the Scassus River for the purpose of supplying the warlike tribes with arms for raids. Once a chief came to the agency for a supply of guns and ammunition. With a blast of his trumpet, he collected a band of men, gave them arms, and started with them for the interior. Bowman accompanied them. Late that afternoon they all collected near a branch of the Scassus River and waited until midnight. Then, leaving Bowman, who was too afraid to go along, they crept away through the jungle. Later Bowman heard shouts and screams and saw the jungle light up with the flames of burning huts. Presently the raiders returned, bringing thirty men, women, and children. Bowman learned that they had attacked a small village while it was asleep. Some of its inhabitants they had killed; some had escaped to the jungle; but thirty captives were alive and unhurt. These they bound securely and, when day arrived, carried down to the agency.[4]

Another slaver, Captain Theodore Canot, saw a raid led by Negresses. He found them neither as decent nor as merciful as the beasts of the wilderness:

> Their malignant pleasure seemed to consist in the invention of tortures that would agonise but not slay. . . . A slow, lingering, tormenting mutilation was practised on the living, as well as on the dead; and in every instance the brutality of the women exceeded that of the men. They passed from body to body, digging out eyes, wrenching off lips, tearing the ears, and slicing the flesh from the quivering bodies; while the queen of the harpies crept amid the butchery gathering the brains from each severed skull as a *bonne bouche* for the approaching feast.[5]

A slaver required from three to six months to complete his cargo. Each slaving voyage was composed of three passages—the passage from the home port to the slave coast, the passage from the slave coast to the market, and the passage from the market back to the home port. Thus the passage in which the slaves were carried was called the Middle Passage. The male slaves were chained two by two by their ankles and sent to the hold or lower deck or, as it was called at the end of the eighteenth century, the "house," which the sailors had built on deck. The women and children were permitted the freedom of the ship, though they had to spend the night apart from the men. The irons on the men were usually secured to chains or iron rods on the deck or to the ceilings of the ship. The slaves slept without covering on the unplaned boards of the deck.[6]

As the trade grew, slavers studied economy of space. So great was the profit they derived from each slave that they seldom missed an opportunity to load the ships to their utmost capacity. The Liverpool ships, which began to be widely used in the latter part of the eighteenth century, had two decks five feet apart. The slaver frowned on this waste of space. So he built a shelf or platform between the decks. When he had covered the decks with slaves he packed another row on the platform. If even the platform proved inadequate for his cargo, he built another above it, leaving about twenty inches of headroom for the slaves.[7]

The slaver reached the height of his diabolical ingenuity at the end of the eighteenth century, when the trade was outlawed. Then he adopted what was called the "spoon fashion," that is, the slaves were compelled to lie on their sides, breast to back. Or, when space between the decks permitted, the slaves were stowed away sitting up in rows, one crowded into the lap of another, with legs on legs, like riders on a crowded toboggan. During storms, when the openings into the cesspools were sealed, naval officers stationed on the coast complained that they could smell a slaver farther away than they could see her on a clear night.[8]

The most heartless tale of the slave trade was perhaps that of the *Zong*, Captain Luke Collingwood. This ship left San Thomé, off the African coast, on September 6, 1781, bound for Jamaica with a cargo of four hundred forty slaves and a white crew of seventeen. During the voyage the water supply ran short and Collingwood, fearing that it would be exhausted before he could reach the home port, denied it to the slaves. Many died of thirst. On arriving in Jamaica, Collingwood made the mistake of supposing he was in Haiti. By this time so many slaves had died that he despaired of making any profit from the voyage. He found that he had only two hundred gallons of water left and that this quantity was insufficient for the voyage he thought he must resume to the home port. On November 29 he summoned his officers and informed them that the insurance company was obliged to pay for any cargo thrown overboard either to lighten the ship or to safeguard the remaining cargo, but that it would not reimburse the owners of the ship for the slaves who died of thirst or illness. Then, rationalizing that he would be less cruel if he threw his sick slaves into the sea than if he allowed them to die eventually of thirst, he ordered his sailors to bring them on deck in groups or "parcels." The first group, numbering fifty-four, was almost immediately bound and thrown overboard. The forty-two who formed the second group met the same fate a few days later. On the same day a heavy rainfall enabled the sailors to collect six casks of water, enough to carry the *Zong* to the home port. Yet Collingwood went on with his plans. At his orders his sailors brought another group of slaves to the deck. Twenty-six of them were handcuffed and jettisoned. But the last ten struggled to their feet and, despite their cramps and pains, staggered to the rail. Then they plunged over to show the others how to die.[9]

On December 22 the *Zong* anchored at her home port after a voyage of three months and sixteen days. As soon as he sold the slaves he had not drowned, Collingwood sailed for England, where the ship owners claimed thirty pounds of insurance money for each of the one hundred thirty-two jettisoned slaves. The insurance company refused to pay, and the case went to court. The jury decided in favor of the owners, since "they had no doubt . . . that the case of slaves was the same as if horses had been thrown overboard."[10]

The insurance company then appealed the case to the Court of Exchequer. The presiding judge, Lord Mansfield, disregarded the obvious meaning of the law, which he had not made, and yielded to his sense of humanity. "This is a very shocking case," he said. He granted a new trial which ended in favor of the insurance company. Thus the English court violated or disregarded a law that it considered unjust.[11]

Not all slavers were as heartless as Collingwood. Captain Hugh Crow, a one-eyed slaver of Liverpool, alleviated the suffering of the slaves by providing them with good food, by having them washed daily, and by having musical instruments played to them.[12]

2

In the spring of 1793 young Eli Whitney, a recent graduate of Yale College, arrived by water in Savannah from his home in Massachusetts for the purpose of finding employment as a tutor in a planter's family. While he was sojourning at Mulberry Grove, residence of General Nathanael Greene's widow, whom he had met on shipboard, he listened to a conversation between a group of men from up the river on the great need of a machine to expedite the cleaning of the upland variety of cotton. Mindful of Whitney's mechanical skill, Phineas Miller, tutor to Mrs. Greene's children, manager of her estate, and later her husband, urged him to apply it to a solution of the problem.

When Miller offered to finance the project, Whitney went to work. Within ten days he produced a box with a slatted side against a wooden cylinder studded with wires that resembled the quills of a porcupine. As the cotton was fed into the box, the wires of the revolving cylinder passed between the slats and caught and separated it from its seeds which, being too large to pass through, remained in the hopper. When nearly all of the cotton was torn off, the seeds would fall through a crevice on the farther side. When the wires became clogged with lint, Mrs. Greene cleaned them with a hearth broom. Seizing on this principle, Whitney equipped his machine with a second cylinder studded with brushes that swept the wires clean as soon as they emerged from the hopper. This was Whitney's famous cotton gin.[13]

But a series of accidents prevented him and his partner from manufacturing the large number of gins which the southern planters demanded. In 1794 an epidemic prostrated Whitney's workmen at his factory in New Haven. In the following year a fire destroyed the factory. Meanwhile, competitors brought out a gin with saw-toothed discs in place of the less satisfactory wires in Whitney's model. This improved machine involved Whitney in litigation over patents, while he and his partner incurred public wrath by attempting to monopolize the operations of gins. In consequence, juries rendered decisions in favor of the opponents.[14]

Nevertheless, the cotton gin had revolutionized the economy of the south. The tobacco industry, which had been the mainstay for half of the people in the South since early colonial days, had reached such low prices that the opening of a new plantation was often offset by the closing of an old one. Exports remained stationary at about half a million hogsheads. The indigo industry was stagnant; the rice culture had reached an unpredictable stage of development. By 1794 slave prices had dropped so drastically that George Washington advised a friend to convert his slaves into a more lucrative form of property. "Were it not that I am principled against selling negroes," he wrote, "as you would cattle in a market, I would not in twelve months hence be possessed of a single one as a slave. I shall be happily mistaken if they are not found to be a very troublesome species of property ere many years have passed over our heads."[15]

Whitney's gin changed all that. Soon improved into a cheap and efficient operation, it brought about a wonderful expansion of upland cotton. It fostered King Cotton, though nobody at the time knew how extensive his realm would become. India no longer needed to provide Western nations with calico from Calcutta, madras from Madras, and muslin from the Moslems. These cloths as well as osnaburgs and gingham, twills and drills, duck and denim could be produced from American cotton, thanks to Whitney and to such English inventors of the Industrial Revolution as Hargreaves and Arkwright and Crompton and Cartwright.

The whole Southern Frontier gradually witnessed a renaissance of cotton. In 1792, just before the gin was invented, the entire cotton crop amounted to only 13,000 bales; in two decades, it leaped to 461,000 bales —a thirty-five-fold increase.[16] Before the invention of the cotton gin, settlers roamed constantly and aimlessly in search of choice lands on which they might eke out a living. Now they rushed like a torrent over every part of the Southern Frontier in their frantic endeavor to engross as much land as possible. Of course, the cotton gin could not by itself increase the output of cotton; but, working with better soil, with better methods and implements, and with increased Negro labor, it wrought an economic miracle. Prospective cotton growers made extensive clearings, bought new good land, added to the number of their field-hands. But unfortunately the white population was too small to cope with the cotton boom. This depended on two circumstances: the great abundance of suitable and cheap land and the large and increasing, though still inadequate, supply of slaves.[17]

By their use of Negro slave labor the planters precipitated among scholars a controversy that rages to this day. Ulrich Bonnell Phillips, an apologist of southern slavery, regarded the weather as "the chief agency in making the South distinctive." The torrential rains, the searing droughts, the "bakingly hot" temperatures, the richness of the soil—all these in his opinion determined the nature of southern institutions and society, which gravitated around Negro slaves, whose traits enabled them to "become largely standardized into the predominant plantation type."[18] He attempted to substantiate his arguments by pointing out that the prevailing traits of the Negro

> ... were an eagerness for society, music and merriment, a fondness for display whether of person, dress, vocabulary or emotion, a not flagrant sensuality, a receptiveness toward any religion whose exercises were exhilarating, a proneness to superstition, a courteous acceptance of subordination, an avidity for praise, a readiness for loyalty of a feudal sort, and last but not least, a healthy human repugnance toward over-work.[19]

The planters generally rationalized that the miasmic environment and intense heat of the south would ever render them helpless to raise a corn or cotton crop and that an "all-wise Creator" had purposely given to the Negro race the traits to turn the south from "a howling wilderness" into an agricultural paradise.

In a more recent work Kenneth M. Stampp has ably challenged these contentions. He doubts that human institutions are formed by natural forces, though he admits that environmental conditions demand certain adjustments in a variety of forms. He points out that the plantation system was quite possible without slavery, that it existed before slavery, and that it survived slavery. He states that southern agriculture without slavery would have had a slower growth, but that it would have depended on small farmers interested in a large variety of crops. Slavery was by no means indispensable to the cultivation of any crop. Since the founding of Jamestown white men have done much of the heavy agricultural labor of the south; since the Civil War, they have tended their own cotton fields in every part of the Deep South. Southern weather, therefore, had no bearing on slavery. As for the belief that Negroes possess certain traits that fitted them to slavery, it controverts the findings of modern biologists, physiologists, and sociologists, who see no evidence that they are intellectually inferior to any other race. Stampp concludes that southern planters deliberately used slave labor because it brought greater returns than their own labor, and because other forms of labor were too expensive. Southern planters championed slavery, not because they needed it but because they wanted it.[20]

In the latter part of the eighteenth century, southern planters, desirous of keeping prices up and competition down, and fearful of too high a proportion of slaves in the entire population and of receiving rebellious slaves from the West Indies, made their first attempts to control or abolish the slave trade. Delaware led the way in 1776. Virginia followed in 1778, Maryland in 1783, South Carolina in 1787, North Carolina in 1794, and Georgia in 1798. In 1803 South Carolina resumed her slave trade, importing 39,310 Negroes before Congress declared it illegal five years later. Thereafter southern planters were forced to rely on the slaves already in the country and on those smuggled in.[21]

The slave trade between the states immediately assumed the aspect of a regular business. Migrating farmers and planters began to buy slaves for the purpose of reselling them at much higher frontier prices, which enabled them to defray the expenses of their new homesteads. In 1810 William Rochel, a migrant farmer of Natchez, advertised in a local newspaper that he had "upwards of twenty likely Virginia born slaves now in a flat bottomed boat lying in the river at Natchez, for sale cheaper than has been sold here in years. Part of said Negroes I wish to barter for a small farm. My boat may be known by a large cane standing on deck."[22]

At first interstate slave trade was small. Most auctioneers sold other property as well as slaves. Every sizable town had its broker, who bought slaves to sell them again at a handsome profit. Sometimes planters who wished to buy slaves would pass the word around to their neighbors or would publish advertisements in newspapers. A southern planter who was moving westward advertised in a Washington, D.C. newspaper as follows: "NEGROES WANTED.—A GENTLEMAN from the South wishes to purchase 40 or 50 effective Slaves, of good character, for his own service, and among them it is desirable to have a blacksmith, carpenter, coachman, and a man cook."[23]

After Jackson's campaign against the Creeks in 1814, the trade became more enterprising and profitable. In the South this trade was considered as lawful as any other business. Slaves, said a southern newspaper, "are as much and as frequently articles of commerce as the sugar and molasses they produce." The slave trade "was as common in the cotton belt of the South at this period as the buying and selling of horses and cattle, or any other merchantable line product."[24] Yet, paradoxically enough, many cultured southerners regarded the slave trader with abhorrence. David R. Hundley, a defender of slavery from Alabama, pictured the slave trader somewhat unjustly as a southern Shylock, a heartless villain, "a coarse ill-bred person, provincial in speech and manner, with a cross-looking phiz, a whiskey-tinctured nose, cold hard-looking eyes, a dirty tobacco-stained mouth, and shabby dress." Though "he is . . . one of the jolliest dogs alive," he habitually separates mothers from their children, husbands from their wives, brothers from their sisters. Most of the slaves

> . . . he buys and sells are vicious ones sold for crimes and misdemeanors, or otherwise diseased ones sold because of their worthlessness as property. These he purchases for about one half what healthy and honest slaves would cost him; but he sells them as both honest and healthy, mark you! So soon as he has completed his "gang" he dresses them up in good clothes, makes them comb their kinky heads into some appearance of neatness, rubs oil on their dusky faces to give them a sleek healthy color, gives them a dram occasionally to make them sprightly, and teaches each one the part he or she has to play; and then he sets out for the extreme South. . . . At every village of importance he sojourns for a day or two, each day ranging his "gang" in a line on the most busy street, and whenever a customer makes his appearance the oily speculator button-holes him immediately and begins to descant in the most highfalutin fashion upon the virtuous lot of darkeys he has for sale. Mrs. Stowe's Uncle Tom was not a circumstance to any one of the dozens he points out. So honest! so truthful! so dear to the hearts of their former masters and mistresses! Ah! Messrs. stockbrokers of Wall Street—you who are wont to cry up your rotten railroad, mining, steamboat and other worthless stocks—for ingenious lying you should take lessons from the Southern Negro trader![25]

A slaveowner told Frederick Law Olmsted, whose works on slavery are well known, that in a few southern states "as much attention is paid to the breeding and growth of Negroes as to that of horses and mules." He also learned that farther south "we raise them both for use and for market. Planters command their girls and women (married and unmarried) to have children; and I have known a great many negro girls to be sold off, because they did not have children. A breeding woman is worth from one-sixth to one-fourth more than one that does not breed."[26] Olmsted observed, however, that "gentlemen of character seem to have a special disinclination to converse on the subject." Slaveholders, indeed, resented greatly the accusation of slave breeding. Phillips stated that his vigorous research found very little evidence of it. The truth seem to be that many slaveholders encouraged breeding but that, from feelings of guilt engendered by a conflict between their secret practises and their Christian upbringing, left no written records of it. The account of most southern travelers indicate that slaveowners counted the fecundity of Negro women as an economic blessing. Olmsted learned

... that the cash value of a slave for sale, above the cost of raising it from infancy to the age at which it commands the highest price, is generally considered among the surest elements of a planter's wealth. Such a nigger is worth such a price, and such another is too old to learn to pick cotton, and such another will bring so much, when it has grown a little more, I have frequently heard people say, in the street, or the public houses. That a slave woman is commonly esteemed least for her laboring qualities, most for those which give value to a breeding-mare is, also, constantly made apparent.[27]

That this was largely true is borne out by numerous advertisements in southern newspapers. In offering for sale fifty prime Negroes, an advertisement in a Charlestown, South Carolina, newspaper emphasized that they were not "selected out of a larger gang for the purpose of a sale, but are prime, their present Owner, with great trouble and expense, selected them out of many for several years past. They were purchased for stock and breeding Negroes, and to any Planter who particularly wanted them for that purpose, they are a very choice and desirable gang."[28] The most familiar terms in such advertisements were "breeding slaves," "child-bearing women," "breeding period," and "too old to breed."

Thomas Jefferson Randolph said in a speech before the Virginia House of Delegates that the exportation of slaves from his state to states in the Deep South averaged 8500 annually. "It is ... an increasing practice in parts of Virginia," he said, "to rear slaves for market. How can an honorable mind, a patriot, and a lover of his country, bear to see this ancient dominion, rendered illustrious by the noble devotion and patriotism of her sons in the cause of liberty, converted into one grand menagerie where men are to be reared for market like oxen for the shambles[?]"[29]

He complained in vain. The advertisements offering Negresses for breeding purposes continued:

A GIRL about 20 years of age (raised in Virginia), and her two female children, one 4 and the other 2 years old. She is ... remarkably strong and healthy, never having had a day's sickness, with the exception of the small pox, in her life. The children are fine and healthy. She is very prolific in her generating qualities, and affords a rare opportunity for any person who wishes to raise a family of strong and healthy servants for [his] own use. Sold for no fault.[30]

Frances Anne Kemble, who became the wife of Pierce Butler, a wealthy Georgia planter, found that

... many indirect inducements [are] held out to reckless propagation, which has a sort of premium offered to it in the consideration of less work and more food counterbalanced by none of the sacred responsibilities which hallow and ennoble the relation of parent and child; in short, as their lives are for the most those of mere animals, their increase is literally mere animal breeding, to which every encouragement is given, for it adds to the master's live-stock and the value of his estate.[31]

Overseers were constantly reminded that they must state the number of actual and prospective infants in their reports or in their rules for plantation management. To Negresses who bore children regularly the master gave delicacies from his kitchen or a muslin or a calico frock. One planter gave a Negress a small pig with every child she bore. Another planter promised freedom to his female slaves as soon as they should bear a specified number of children. Some planters even provided their young Negroes with a motto for procreation: "Look, missis! Little Niggers for you and massa; plenty little niggers for you and little missis!" Little or no attention was given to the paternity of these children. One Negress, Nancy, bore seventeen children by different men in eighteen years; another, Hannah, fourteen or fifteen; still another, thirteen, three of whom were sold; still another left ten children, one of whom was sold. For a few hundred dollars a man could buy a girl who in six or eight years had a family worth as much as $10,000. A planter named Cobb boasted that his slaves multiplied "like rabbits." He expected them to double in number every ten or twelve years. One of his father's female slaves had been so fecund that in her old age she could call together more than a hundred of her lineal descendants. DeBow knew of a plantation which boasted fifty or sixty persons descended from a single female in the course of her master's lifetime. Slave breeding was like "a magical orchard that bore regularly, gathered and cared for its own fruit, and steadily enlarged its own area and production."[32]

A restricted kind of slave trading was slave hiring as household servants for private families, for boardinghouses, and for hotels. Most of those who hired slaves were small farmers, merchants, contractors, drovers, and mechanics. They hired them for permanent or temporary work because they could not afford to buy them. And, at the same time, they could claim that they belonged to the influential slaveholding class, for in the popular mind no distinction was made between a hirer and an owner of slaves. The despised pariahs of the land were the "poor whites" who, far from owning a slave, could not even afford to hire one.[33] In this "peculiar institution" little restriction was made against separating mothers and children or husbands and wives or selling children of any age.[34]

Some planters sent some of their slaves to work on their new cotton plantations in that section of present Alabama and Mississippi which is known as the Black Belt because of the color of its fertile loose loam. The planters themselves usually remained at their old homesteads until their overseers or some relative or relatives investigated the new land. Some ebullient planters, however, tugged westward with all they had without any regard for consequences. In 1811 an Augusta, Georgia, newspaper sarcastically announced the departure for Mississippi Territory of "Brigadier General" Wade Hampton, "Commander in chief of the western army, preceded by a division of fifty ragged, meager looking negro infantry. Should his Excellency fail in obtaining laurels before Mobile, he will be able to make sugar at New Orleans."[35] Edward Talbot of Talbot County, Maryland, sent a part of his many slaves to a cotton plantation he had purchased in present Mississippi. Another Marylander who moved to Louisiana sent back home a report in which he described that state as so rich that a man with ten slaves could make a fortune: "With you," he wrote, "the seasons are so irregular your crops often fail; here the crops are certain, and want of the necessities of life never for a moment causes the heart to ache—abundance spreads the table of the poor man, and contentment smiles on every countenance."[36]

The migration of any responsible planter from his old home to his distant new one always entailed elaborate plans. And they were seldom final. Owsley compares these migrant planters to "a great drove of blackbirds lighting in a grain field, with each bird milling about, making short flights within the field in search of a more satisfactory location."[37] Such were Senator Charles Tait and his son James Asbury, who in 1816 made plans to migrate from Elbert County, Georgia, to the public domain in Alabama Territory. In February, 1817, James journeyed with his wife's brother and father to explore in the territory for a suitable piece of ground. There he received from his father a letter describing his ideal of a location. It must combine fertility with salubrity and have, in addition, such "minor advantages" as:

> . . . a stream near at hand for a mill and machinery—a never failing spring at the foot of a hillock, on the summit of which a mansion house can be built in due time; . . . an extensive back range where our cattle and hogs [can] graze and fatten without the aid of corn houses, [and] on the right and left . . . an extensive body of good land where will settle a number of good neighbors and from whom the pleasure and benefits of society will soon be realized.[38]

James sought this agricultural paradise in vain. The land he eventually purchased must have been somewhat malarious, for he and his father contemplated removal to the more salubrious climate of the piney country in the interior. But their favorite slave, Hercules, whose "noble and disinterested example has mainly effected this temper and disposition among our people," persuaded them to stay. The Taits eventually established two great plantations, "Weldon," and "Springfield," and employed a number of overseers on them. One of the overseers, J. B. Grace, who was himself a slaveholder, seems to have been much concerned with the health of his charges. "The helth of ower negrowes is impruvin," he wrote to Charles Tait, "thow thar is 8 field hands not abel to worke yet." Later he reported that "ower hans seemes as they cant git helthy." And still later: "I have had 5 hands dowen with the chill and fever all this week." Tait chided him for working his slaves too hard. The overseer replied that "you nede not be one esy the new handes worken to hard becase ower work is lite and they git out of task by 10 and 11 oclock A.M." When James Tait approved the purchase of three young girls, Grace expressed regret that they were not older:

> I wish the three girls you purchest had been all grown. They wold then bin a wife a pese for Harise & King & Nathan. Harris has Jane for a wife and Nathan has Edy. But King & Nathan had sum difuculty hoo wold have Edy. I promist King that I would in dever to git you to bey a nother woman sow he might have a wife at home. He is envious that you wold git a nuther woman, as he has quit his wife that he had at Netoles, thinking that he wold git Edy for a wife. I am willing to take Vilet at the same price you give for her and pay you the expence in bringing her from Mobile, or eny other expense you were at. As she is too young for eney of your men a wife and you have small girls enough for your young boys, and then you can by a woman in her place for King a wife.[39]

Another immigrant to Mississippi Territory was General Leonard Covington, owner of Aquasco plantation and other lands in Maryland. Finding himself in debt because of falling tobacco prices, he planned to sell his property and migrate with his sixty slaves to Mississippi, where he hoped to hire out some of them until he could establish a plantation of his own. In addition to his slaves he planned to take to the territory ten or fifteen families of non-slaveholding whites for the purpose of employing them until they could find other work. Covington accordingly sent a letter to his brother Alexander, who had settled in Mississippi, enquiring about the manner and terms of hiring out slaves:

> It would certainly be material to the owner of slaves, whether their treatment in many respects was such as would be desirable, and in what manner the payments for hirelings were made; if in advance, or punctually at the months end. Whether the slaves were well fed; and only compelled to work from "sun to sun." It is possible that so much labor may be required of hirelings and so little regard may be had for their constitutions as to render them in a few years, not only unprofitable, but expensive. In your case, who pays the doctor, abides the loss from death or running away? Do the negroes in that country generally look as happy and contented as with us, and do they as universally take husbands and wives and as easily rear their young as in Maryland?[40]

He received satisfactory replies, but he failed to sell some of his property. In consequence, he could take with him only a small part of his slaves. In October, 1809, he departed for Mississippi Territory with his wife, five children, a neighbor named Waters, three other white men, and five or six slaves. To a friend named Rawlings, who had gone to Mississippi, he described his party as

> ... the damnedest cavalcade that ever man was burdened with: not less than seven horses compose my troop: they convey a close carriage (Jersey Stage) a gig and horse cart, so that my family are transported with comfort and convenience, though at considerable expense. All these odd matters and contrivances I design to take with me to Mississippi if possible. Mr. Waters will also take down his wagon and team.[41]

At Wheeling, present West Virginia, they boarded a boat and dragged "through shoals, sandbars and ripples" to Cincinnati, where he wrote to his brother, announcing that he should arrive by the end of the year. The boat on which he traveled was so crowded that he was forced to limit his supplies to a few hundred pounds of pork and a few barrels of flour. On arriving in Mississippi he established a plantation with part of his slaves and hired out the rest. But he was not destined to enjoy his new homestead for long. In 1813 the secretary of war called him to military service. He was killed while he led a regiment of dragoons in the invasion of Canada.[42]

The travel writer, Basil Hall, left a pathetic picture of a migrating farmer's caravan which he overtook in South Carolina in 1828. The caravan consisted of about thirty persons, most of whom were slaves. The women and children were stowed away in wagons that moved slowly up a steep hill. The drawn curtains permitted Hall to catch only occasional glimpses of dark eyes and rows of teeth seemingly whiter than snow. In the rear a light wagon carried the planter and his wife. In front and along the roadside trudged the male slaves in scattered groups. Hall noticed that two of them had apparently clasped hands in carefree camaraderie. But something about the pair seemed constrained. When he and his companions came nearer, they found that a short chain or bar bolted the two slaves together at their wrists.

"What have you been doing, my boys," asked Hull's coachman as he passed them, "to entitle you to these ruffles?"

"Oh, sir," replied one of them gaily, "they are the best things in the world to travel with."

Mystified by this reply, Hall stopped his carriage and asked one of the slave drivers why the two men were chained and why they took their misfortune so cheerfully. The slave driver explained that one of the men was married but that his wife belonged to another master and had been forbidden to go with him. Because he was unwilling to leave his wife his master had him "shackled to a young unmarried man who having no such tie to draw him back might be more safely trusted on the journey."[43]

3

The size of a plantation ranged from several square miles to much less than a hundred acres. And its "big house," as the slaves loved to call their master's home, might be a double log cabin with rough interiors or a colonnaded mansion with many elegant rooms. The average house was a roomy and rambling dwelling surrounded by a primeval forest or by a well-tended garden. The hall by day and the veranda by night "served in all temperate seasons as the receiving place for guests and the gathering place for the household at all its leisure hours." The house derived its beauty, if it could claim any, not from its own quality and design but from its surrounding live oaks if it stood on the rich and sugar coasts or from its hickories and cedars if it stood in the uplands. A small building that flanked the house usually contained the administrative headquarters, a schoolroom, and "apartments for any bachelor overflow whether tutor, sons or guests." The kitchen stood as far behind the house as was necessary to isolate its noises and odors. Near the kitchen was the "well with its two buckets dangling from the pulley," and near the well stood the dairy and the open-air laundry with its pots and tubs. In the back yard were the smoke house, the chicken coops, the sweet potato pit, the pigeon cote, the carriage house, the cabins for the domestic servants, the overseer's house, the blacksmith shop, the wagon sheds, the corn cribs, the stables, the tobacco house, the gin and press, and the threshing and pounding mills. Beyond all these lay the master's orchard, his sweet potato field, his watermelon patch, and his forage plots of millet and sorghum. Phillips, on whose work this hypothetical picture of a plantation is based, describes the countryside as a cornucopia of delicious fruits and nuts:

> From June to September every creature, hogs included, commonly had as many peaches as he cared to eat; and in addition great quantities might be carried to the stills. The abandoned fields, furthermore, contributed dewberries, blackberries, wild strawberries and wild plums in summer, and persimmons in autumn, when the forest also yielded its muscadines, fox grapes, hickory nuts, walnuts, chestnuts, and chinquapins, and along the Gulf coast pecans.[44]

No less abundant was the edible game, including

> . . . squirrels, opossums and wild turkeys, and even deer and bears in the woods, rabbits, doves and quail in the fields, woodcock and snipe in the swamps and marshes, and ducks and geese on the streams. . . .

The creeks and rivers yielded fish to be taken with hook, net or trap, as well as terrapin and turtles, and the coastal waters added shrimp, crabs and oysters.[45]

The master's table groaned under a daily banquet that included all the favorite southern dishes. Because the pastures were poor, beef and mutton were scarce; but fried chicken and baked, broiled, or fried ham, prepared in a number of overwhelmingly aromatic guises and served with roasted, fried, or candied sweet potatoes, butter beans, radishes, turnip greens, asparagus, and artichokes were omnipresent in gargantuan quantities. This meal they washed down with wine or brandy or whiskey and coffee.[46]

But the slaves knew no such feasting. Usually they received an ample supply of pork and bacon. While the master always kept the shoulders, sides, hams, and lard for himself, he often distributed the spare ribs, backbone, jowl and feet, souse and sausage, liver and chitterlings among his slaves. The usual weekly portion of bacon for each slave was three or four pounds, depending on the generosity of his master, and a peck and a half of corn meal. Some masters permitted their slaves to raise pigs and poultry, and in summer they could grow as many vegetables as they pleased. But more often than not they neglected to provide for themselves. They subsisted mainly on the food which their overseer distributed to the heads of families or to single Negroes either on Saturday night or, in better managed plantations, in the middle of the week, to prevent them from using it extravagantly or selling it for whiskey on Sunday. In large plantations the cooking was done in a "cook-house," which was furnished with an oven and a large copper for boiling. Every night the slaves took to the cook their "mess" for the next day's breakfast and dinner. Each Negro marked his meat by cuts so that he could identify it from that of the other slaves, an observance which he practised with punctilious regularity.[47]

The master believed that the most perfect relationship between himself and his slaves was that in which he governed absolutely and they obeyed implicitly. His aim was to instill in them a sense of inferiority. They must understand that slavery was their natural destiny, must know and keep their places, must feel that their African ancestry tainted them, must believe that their color was a mark of degradation. They were trained to lift their hats to any white man and to make way for him in the street. To show familiarity to a slave was to encourage his impudence. This he expressed in a number of ways: by the tone of his voice, by answering a question, by refusing to answer it, by his grimaces or frowns, by the motion of his head, by his gait, his manner, and his bearing. The master derived enormous power by instilling his slaves with fear and awe. Frederick Douglass believed that most of them stood in awe of all white men, and that few could free themselves from the fixation that their masters were endowed with a kind of sacredness. Olmsted observed

that most white men maintained a constant, habitual, and instinctive surveillance and authority over slaves. In a district where the slave population was fifty to one of the free he saw a girl of twelve

> . . . stop an old man on the public road, demand to know where he was
> going, and by what authority, order him to face about and return to
> his plantation, and enforce her command with turbulent anger, when
> he hesitated, by threatening that she would have him well whipped if
> he did not instantly obey. The man quailed like a spaniel, and she
> instantly resumed the manner of a lovely child with me, no more ap-
> prehending that she had acted unbecomingly, than that her character
> had been influenced by the slave's submission to her caprice of su-
> premacy; no more conscious that she had increased the security of
> her life by strengthening the habit of the slave to the master race, than
> is the sleeping seaman that he tightens his clutch of the rigging as the
> ship meets each new billow.[48]

But human instincts are stronger than man-made conventions or pretenses of superiority, as any discerning person knows. The barrier of
color proved no barrier whatsoever to sexual relations. Some of these
were open and constant; some were clandestine and casual. Miscegenation, as the mixing of any two races is called, was widespread in the Old
South, though defenders of slavery have strongly denied this. Mrs. Douglass, a Virginia woman who was jailed for teaching slaves how to read
and write, wrote that miscegenation pervaded the entire social structure
of the Old South:

> Its followers are to be found among all ranks, occupations and profes-
> sions. The white mothers and daughters of the South have suffered
> under it for years—have seen their dearest affections trampled upon—
> their hopes of domestic happiness destroyed, and their future lives
> embittered, even to agony, by those who should be all in all to them,
> as husbands, sons, and brothers. I cannot use too strong language in
> reference to this subject, for I know that it will meet with a heart-felt
> response from every Southern woman.[49]

Most miscegenation involved white males and slave females, but occasionally white females reversed the situation. A number of white men
sought divorce on the ground that their wives had sexual relations with
slaves. In one such case the woman admitted that her black lover had
made love to her better than "any body in the world"; she grew so
ecstatic, she said, that she believed he had given her a strong love potion.[50]
Such a woman irretrievably lost the respect of society.

But the white men paid no such price. Overseers, unmarried slaveowners, and adventuresome adolescents particularly indulged these illicit affairs. One Louisiana planter complained that his overseer caused

him no end of trouble by constantly pursuing Negro girls, who provided him with a numerous progeny.[51] Occasionally we hear of a female slave resisting the attention of her overseer. In Mississippi a slave named Alfred killed his overseer for forcing his wife, Charlotte, into sexual relations with him. Alfred was convicted and hanged. The counsel of the defendant declared that "the servile condition . . . has not deprived him of his social and moral instincts, and he is as much entitled to the protection of the laws, when acting under their influence, as if he were free . . . and the white man degrades the species to which he belongs in denying them to him."[52] The wife of one planter sought a divorce because, she said, he had a higher regard for his maid than for her. Another woman in North Carolina divorced her husband because he had "bedded with Lucy," whom he had placed in charge of the entire household.[53] A respectable "Christian lady" kept a handsome mulatto female for the use of her "genteel" son as a means of deterring him "from indiscriminate and vulgar indulgences."[54] Harriet Martineau tells of a young man who, on visiting a southern lady, became insanely enamored of her intelligent quadroon maid. He tried in vain to buy her from her owner. The young man persisted, saying he could not live without her. Thereupon the lady, fearing that the young man would take his own life, heeded his pitiful appeal.[55]

The plantation system involved many instances of harsh treatment inflicted by cruel masters or their overseers on their slaves. Slavery disclosed its worse aspect on a large plantation where the master was unable to give his personal attention to the humane treatment of his slaves. Slaveholders or their overseers devised a number of punishments for slaves accused of failing or neglecting to finish their tasks, stealing, running away, showing impudence or insolence, and attacking fellow slaves. They whipped field hands, sometimes severely, denied passes to unfaithful domestics, demoted foremen, and sent Negro drivers to work in the field. Often they excluded incorrigibles from participating in Saturday night dances, penalized them by confiscating the crops in their "truck patch," and reduced their wages. Sometimes they put them on short rations or deprived them of bacon and pork for several months. Occasionally they sold them away from their families and friends. At a "corn shucking" in South Carolina the American poet William Cullen Bryant heard slaves sing a song illustrative of their fear of being sold to distant regions:

> Johnny, come down de hollow.
> Oh hollow.
>
> . . .
>
> De nigger-trader got he.
> Oh hollow.
> De speculator bought me.
> Oh hollow.

I'm sold for silver dollars.
  Oh hollow.
Boys, go catch de pony.
  Oh hollow.
Bring him round de corner.
  Oh hollow.
I'm goin' 'way to Georgia,
  Oh hollow.
Boys, good-bye forever.
  Oh hollow.[56]

And yet relations between masters and slaves seem to have been cordial
in many regions of the Southern Frontier. On some of the large plantations, especially in Alabama and Mississippi, "master and slaves frequently
lived together under conditions that were genuinely patriarchal."[57] The
special link between them were their children, who could hardly distinguish their mothers from their mammies, their uncle by blood from their
"uncles" by courtesy. Steadfast playmates, they took possession of orchard and kitchen, of sand yard and cabin, of quarters and "big house,"
where their elders regaled them with folklore and songs, with Bible and
fairy tales, with grapes and peaches and melons. But with maturity they
began to separate, each pursuing a different pattern of living. During the
day fox hunts were diversions only for the planters and their sons and
guests; but at night blacks and whites mingled as they had in childhood
to seek 'possum and 'coon, and in "spare times by day they hied their curs
after the fleeing B'rer Rabbit, or built and baited seductive traps for
turkeys and quail."[58]

And during the last of November or the beginning of December,
whites and blacks would join in corn-shucking bees, which were a kind
of prelude to the festivities of the Christmas season. After the slaves had
piled up the corn, sometimes thousands of bushels in the shape of a
mound fifty or sixty feet high, the master would send out an invitation
to the neighboring masters to attend the corn-shucking with their slaves.
The invitation would usually marshal several hundred men, women, and
children of both races. As they assembled around the great mound of
corn, one of them, usually a singer of some reputation, would climb to
its top and, in a clear, loud voice, would begin one of the many songs of
the corn-shucking season in which a chorus of about a hundred would
soon join:

Massa's niggers am slick and fat,
  Oh! Oh! Oh!
Shine just like a new beaver hat,
  Oh! Oh! Oh!

Turn out here and shuck dis corn,
  Oh! Oh! Oh!

Biggest pile o' corn seen since I was born,
   Oh! Oh! Oh!

Jones' niggers am lean an' po';
   Oh! Oh! Oh!
Don't know whether dey get enough to eat or no,
   Oh! Oh! Oh!

Turn out here and shuck dis corn,
   Oh! Oh! Oh!
Biggest pile o' corn seen since I was born,
   Oh! Oh! Oh![59]

On Saturday nights and on holidays, the slaves would gather in their quarters and indulge their favorite pastime of dancing or, as they called it, "shake-down." To the strumming of a banjo or guitar they would contort, spring, fling, kick, and caper, or with thumping ecstasy, loose elbows, pendulous paws, angulated knees, heads thrown back and backs arched forward they would dance "Jim Crow" or shuffle while their friends would beat out the rhythm with sticks or tin pans or clap their hands or tap their feet and sing:

Ol' Mars'r had a pretty yaller gal,
   He brought her fum de Souf;
Her hair it curled so berry tight
   She couldn't shut her mouf.

Way down in Mississippi
Where de gals dey are so pretty,
W'at a happy time, way down in old Car'line!
Dis darky fell in love
Wid a han'some yaller Dinah.
Higho—higho—higho!

He took her to de tailor,
   To have her mouf made small.
She swallowed up the tailor
   Tailorshop and all.

Way down in Mississippi
Where de gals dey are so pretty, . . .[60]

The same headlong zeal characterized their religious practises. The belief in evil spirits, which regulated the rituals and dogmas of their African ancestors, had evaporated within a generation; the urgent needs engendered by their bondage and experiences in the New World necessitated a new set of religious beliefs. They sought faiths that would trans-

port them from their stultifying routine to promises of a better life. Like
many of the white frontiersmen of the Appalachian and Great Lakes
regions, they were attracted to the Methodist and Baptist faiths, which
sympathized with the poor and downtrodden, which promised them
personal participation, and which filled "their lonely and hungry souls
with all the fervor and zeal they could command."[61] One Negro preacher
shouted his preference for the Baptist faith and his objection to free-will
Methodism in this manner:

"De Methodiss, my bruddren, is like de grasshopper—hoppin', all de
time hoppin'—hop into heaven, hop out, hop into heaven, hop out. But,
my bruddren, de Baptiss, when he get to heaven, *he's dar!* De Baptiss is
like de 'possum. Hunter get after him, he climb de tree; he shake de
limb, one foot gone; he shake de limb, anudder foot gone; he shake de
limb, ebbery foot gone; but tink you, my bruddren, *'possum fall?* You
know, my bruddern—you cotch too many—you know *'possum hang on
by de tail*, and de berry debbil can't shake him off!"[62]

They usually poured into their religion an intensity and excitement
that white men often found terrible to witness. "It is not at all uncommon
to hear them refer to conversations," wrote Olmsted, "which they allege,
and apparently believe themselves to have had with Christ, the apostles,
or the prophets of old, or to account for some of their actions by attribut-
ing them to the direct influence of the Holy Spirit, or of the devil."[63]
Supporting Olmsted's observation is the legend of Old Jupiter who described to his master in his own words how he had a vision of heaven,
where Jesus received him with great deference and bestowed on him
many kindnesses:

Den de blessed Jesus tell anurruh angel fuh bring me some milk an
honey fuh drink. Eh bring um een a nice glass tumbler, an eh gen me
fuh drink. Me tase um, an eh sweet mone anything me ebber drink een
me life. Eh tell me fuh drink um down, an wen me drink all outer de
glass, an me yeye ketch sight er de bottom er de tumbler, me see some
speck. De ting trouble me, fuh me dunno wuh mek speck day een de
bottom er dat clean tumbler. Den de blessed Master notus me, an eh
say: "Don fret, Jupter; dem speck duh you sin, but now dem all leff
behine."

All dis time me bin er set wid me face tun way from de Lord an
eh trone, cause eh so great an bright me could'nt look pon topper um.
Mossa, me cant scribe wuh me see an yeddy een dat Hebben. Eh yent
fuh tell. De blessed Jesus tek me tru de gaden, down by de ribber, an
een de orchid way de bigges peach, an fig, an orange, an pomegranate,
an watermillion, an all kin der fruit der grow. Me see heap er good
people wuh me bin know befo eh dead. . . .

Arter me bin in Hebben good while, de blessed Master, him say:
"Come, Jupter, I gwine show you way de bad people go." Den eh lead
me down to one bottom wuh dark an kibber wid cloud. In de fur een

me see smoke duh rise, an me yeddy people duh cry an duh holler so bad. Wen we git ter that spot, lo an behole! day was de mouf er Hell. Satan, him bin day wid eh pitchfork, an eh black head wid screech-owl yez, an eh red yeye, an eh claw-han, an eh forky tail. Eh tan right at de mouf er de big hole way de smoke an de fire duh bile out. Fas as de tarruh debble bring sinner ter um, eh push um wid eh pitchfork an eh trow um een de fire. Lord Amighty! Mossa, how dem sinner did kick an holler an try fuh pull away! But twant no use. De minnit ole Satan graff eh claw on him eh gone, an you could yeddy um duh fry een de fire same luk fat een me pan yuh. Me bin rale skade. De ting mek me sick. Me hole on ter me Jesus, an him tell me not teh fade, dat nuttne shill troble me.[64]

And he woke up.

A Negro funeral procession was as touching as it was bizarre. Twenty or thirty men and women would follow the hearse, which was drawn by two horses and followed by a number of dilapidated coaches, to the place of rest, where they would set the coffin while they joined in a wild chant. Olmsted, who was present at the burial of a child, observed that the grave digger concluded his work with a deep sigh:

"Lord Jesus, have mercy on us—now! You, Jim—*you—see yar*, you jes lay dat yar shovel cross the grave—so fash—dah—yes, dat's right!"

Olmsted saw them lay the coffin on the shovel and a hoe handle across the unfilled grave, pass lines under it, and lower it to the bottom. He was touched by their unaffected feeling, their simplicity, their rude truthfulness, and their absence of any attempt at formal decorum. But he never heard such ludicrous language as was sometimes uttered by the speaker, who said:

"We do not see the end here! Oh no, my friends! There will be a putrefaction of the body!"

He failed to indicate whether he meant "putrefaction" or "purification." Olmsted doubted that he attached any definite meaning to the word. The speaker quoted several times from the Bible, several times from hymns, which he always introduced with "in the words of the poet, my brethren." He threw a few handfuls of earth on the coffin, then, with the assistance of six or seven other men, proceeded to fill the grave, while an old Negro raised a confused chant.[65]

Sometimes a dying slave spurned all thought of glorification. When Jeff, a colored preacher, heard that Old Uncle Caleb was dying, he went with his congregation to pay him a visit. He read a passage from the Bible and his companions sang a hymn. Uncle Caleb, lying motionless with closed eyes, made no sign for Jeff to approach. Jeff took his hand.

"Uncle Caleb," he said, "de doctor says you are dying; and all de bredderin has come in for to see you de last time. And now, Uncle Caleb, dey wants to hear from your own mouf de precious words, dat you feels prepared to meet your God, and is ready and willin' to go."

Uncle Caleb suddenly opened his eyes and in a peevish voice proudly scolded the preacher:

"Jeff, don't talk your nonsense to me! You jest knows dat I an't ready to go, nor willin' needer; and dat I ain't prepared to meet nobody."

Whereupon Jeff expiated largely on the mercy of God, on the glory of heaven, and on its eternal bliss. But Uncle Caleb was unmoved.

"Dis ole cabin suits me mon'sus well!" he muttered. So saying, he died.[66]

Florida: From Spanish Province to American State

WILLIAM AUGUSTUS BOWLES WAS NO SHIRKER OF TROUBLE. HE PUR-
sued it everywhere; he made it a basic and unpleasant concomitant of
the fabulous life he had fashioned for himself. So he was much in his
element when in September, 1799, his ship, the *Fox*, met a savage gale
that split her in two and sent her aground on the eastern end of St.
George's Island. Learning that Andrew Ellicott, the American surveyor,
was in the vicinity, he sent him a letter requesting permission to land
with his companions. Ellicott, who was having troubles of his own with
regional Indians as he marked the boundary between Florida and the
United States, had himself rowed to the shore where, during an idle
week occasioned by high winds and much rain, he held several interviews with Bowles. He judged him correctly as "a man of enterprize,
and address" with "considerable talents" for trouble. Even now Bowles
was up to no good. Ellicott refused his request on the ground that the
United States was neutral in the war then in progress between Great
Britain and Spain. He did, however, give him needed provisions. And
as partial compensation he received some charts that he found helpful
in his route around the treacherous Florida Cape.[1]

In the past seven years Bowles' bad luck had had a rewarding side: it
had enabled him to see several remote parts of the world without cost
to himself. When we saw him last, in 1792, he was a prisoner on his way
to Spain. He spent more than a year in the Madrid jail while the Council
of the Indies debated on his fate. At last its endless judicial proceedings
annoyed the impatient king who, following the recommendation of one
of his ministers, deported the culprit to the Philippines. In Manila the
Spanish governor informed him that his sentence would consist of his
being detained indefinitely at Tondo on the island of Luzon. Though he
gave him his freedom to enable him to work for his living, he required

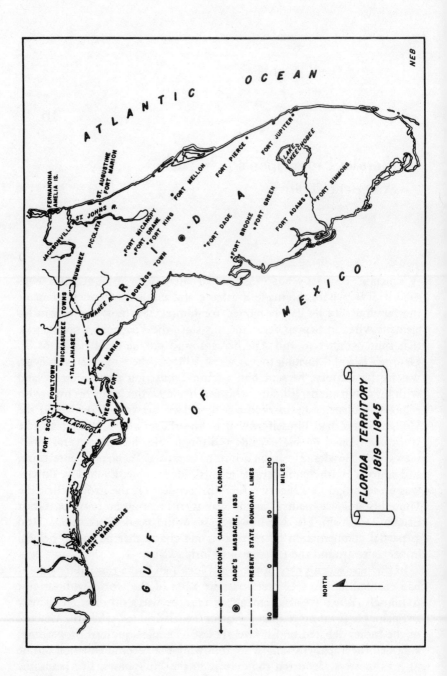

FLORIDA TERRITORY
1819—1845

ATLANTIC OCEAN

GULF OF MEXICO

NEB

NORTH

MILES
50   0   50   100

JACKSON'S CAMPAIGN IN FLORIDA
DADE'S MASSACRE, 1835
PRESENT STATE BOUNDARY LINES

FERNANDINA
AMELIA IS.
JACKSONVILLE
ST. AUGUSTINE
FORT MARION
PICOLATA
ST. JOHNS R.
SUWANEE
FORT MICANOPY
FORT DRANE
FORT KING
BOWLEGS TOWN
SUWANEE R.
MICKASUKEE TOWNS
TALLAHASEE
FORT SCOTT
FOWLTOWN
APALACHICOLA
ST. MARKS
NEGRO FORT
APALACHICOLA R.
PENSACOLA
FORT BARRANCAS
FLORIDA
FORT MELLON
FORT PIERCE
FORT JUPITER
LAKE OKEECHOBEE
FORT SIMMONS
FORT GREEN
FORT DADE
FORT BROOKE
FORT ADAMS

him to report daily to the *corregidor*. That local official of finances found him intractable. He refused to report; he loudly denounced the king and his ministers; he demanded a pension that should enable him to live in a style commensurate with his talents and culture. The governor, fearing that he would attempt to escape or to communicate with one of his henchmen who had been captured with him and confined under similar orders to nearby Cavite, deported him to Cádiz.

As his ship sailed with a convoy around the Cape of Good Hope on her way home, Bowles hatched a plot to seize her by murdering her captain, crew, and passengers. But the ship's chaplain somehow discovered the plot and went with it to the captain, who removed the troublemaker and twelve of his friends to another ship in the convoy. Bowles escaped and made his way to the British colony of Sierra Leone, where he convinced its governor, Zachary Macaulay, that "he was an important instrument of British policy in America." Macaulay sent him on to England.[2]

There his flamboyant personality, his Indian dress, and his astonishing adventures, which he artfully exaggerated, endeared him to nobleman and commoner alike. They hailed his courage in defying Spanish oppression—or did they regard him as a useful agent to enlist Creek support in case of war between England and Spain? Greatly encouraged, he became more cocksure than before; he revived his plans to establish an independent Indian nation with himself as its ruler. Though the British government refrained from recognizing him as an Indian prince, it encouraged him in his plans and facilitated his return to the West Indies. In Jamaica he met Thomas Hugh Ferguson, a young man whose services he obtained by offering to make him collector of a port he hoped to build on the Ochlockonee River, which flows into the Gulf of Mexico between St. Marks and the Apalachicola River. The highest officials of the island paid Bowles every mark of respect and attention. With their praises still ringing in his ears, he sailed on His Majesty's schooner, the *Fox*, for Nassau, whose merchants he found just as anxious to break Panton's monopoly as they had been a decade earlier. Thence he sailed with a handful of white men for the Ochlockonee, but before he could reach it he found himself shipwrecked on St. George's Island, where we renewed our acquaintance with him.[3]

Leaving Ferguson and another man in charge of his supplies, Bowles went to the mainland. He eventually sent them canoes in which they joined him. Bowles and his men spent the rest of the winter in the woods instead of in the palace he had promised them. They built a hut and huddled around a fire. Their only solace was the hatred they felt for the rogue who had lured them into their difficulties. But while they complained and shivered, their leader kept himself busy establishing temporary headquarters on the Ochlockonee and rallying his old supporters among the Seminoles and Lower Creeks. He called a congress which established the independent state of Muskogee and which elected him "Chief and Director General." He immediately turned his attention to the problem of clarifying Muskogee's policy toward her two neighbors, Spain and the United States. Resolving to take on the stronger of them first, he wrote to the American government a long letter in which he reviewed its relations with the southern tribes. He grew bolder with each sentence he wrote. Without specifying the boundaries of Muskogee, he criticized the Treaty of San Lorenzo, which established the surveying of the boundary between the United States and the Floridas; he attacked the Treaty of New York, which Alexander McGillivray had signed in 1790; and he denounced American usurpations of Indian lands. But, he said, he was willing to forgive all these serious aggressions, in return for a treaty which would recognize the independence of Muskogee and would terminate the work of the boundary commission. He warned that any further effort to run the boundary line, or any attempt to alter or subvert the sovereignty of Muskogee, would be regarded "not only as a rejection of the proposed treaty but as grounds for a declaration of war against the United States."[4]

He followed this representation with an insolent and bombastic proclamation in which he directed his people to drive out of Muskogee any person who held a commission under the United States. The representation as well as the proclamation greatly worried Benjamin Hawkins, American agent to the Creeks, who was unable with his few assistants to influence his widely scattered red charges against joining Bowles. Hawkins characterized that adventurer and his cronies as "mischief makers who are by every opportunity poisoning the minds of the Indians with their abominable lies and misrepresentations."[5] Bowles' feeling toward Hawkins was no less acrimonious. To Chief Little Prince, one of his warmest supporters, he vowed that he would "seize Hawkins, if I find him, for not obeying the proclamation, and proceed against him according to law."[6]

Even more critical were Bowles' relations with Spain. In view of his capture, imprisonment, and escape he must have realized the hopelessness of any *rapprochement* with that nation. Furthermore, Governor Folch had put a price of $4,500 on his head. But, for the present, he knew he was too weak militarily to force a showdown with either Spain or the United States. So he contented himself with implementing the internal structure of Muskogee. By a series of acts and decrees, he equipped that country with all the trappings and machinery of sovereignty. He designated Mikasuke, a Seminole village near Tallahassee, as the national capital. He adopted the motto, "God Save the State of Muskogee," for his state papers, in which he assumed the royal "We" after the manner of European monarchs. He designed an impressive national flag. Lyle N. McAlister described this as "divided into four quarters by crossed vertical and horizontal broad blue bars bordered by thinner white stripes. The upper left and the lower left and right quarters were red. The upper right quarter was blue and had in its left center a sun to which was added human features."[7]

As his ministers, Bowles appointed fellow filibusters who either had followed him from Nassau or had joined him subsequently. One of them, William McGirt, served as Minister of State, as Commissary of Marine, and as Judge of the Court of Admiralty. Another, James Devereux Delacy, a renegade Irishman of obscure antecedents, represented Muskogee in the Bahamas.[8]

To stimulate interest in agriculture and in the crafts, Bowles placed in the *Nassau Gazette* a number of advertisements praising Muskogee as a country of rich opportunities and offering free tracts to farmers who wished to settle there permanently. Few persons, however, answered the advertisements, and those who did found that the opportunities were much less attractive than Bowles had pictured them and that he was unwilling or unable to keep his promises.[9]

With the intention of striking against his unfriendly neighbors, Bowles gave much of his attention to building an army. Appointing himself supreme military chief, he recruited in the Tallahassee region a group of Seminole warriors, whom he augmented with his handful of white men and a number of Negroes and mulattoes who had deserted from the Spanish garrisons at St. Augustine and Pensacola. But Governor Folch anticipated his plans and struck the first blow. In February, 1800, two hundred Spaniards surprised Bowles' military headquarters at Wekiwa, burning it to the ground and capturing several of his men. Ferguson escaped by diving into the harbor, where he spent the night. For the next five days he wandered, hungry and cold, in the woods, an experience which hardly lessened the hatred he felt toward his leader.[10]

Bowles, too, eluded the Spaniards, though at the expense of most of his wardrobe and all of his library. They found a green jacket, a blue cloak which was embroidered and was braided in gold, a fur turban adorned with glass pearls, a sheet, an empty pocketbook, and a watch. The books indicated that their erstwhile owner was either an ostentatious or an actual lover of good literature: Milton's *Paradise*—whether *Lost* or *Regained* the Spaniards failed to specify and thereby slurred an important literary distinction; Abbé Raynal's *Indies* in seven volumes, which was then hailed as a masterpiece but which has since been reduced to a mere collector's curiosity; the *Letters of Junius;* the works of Molière and Boileau; treatises on physics, algebra, and painting; a volume of classical mythology; a French, a Spanish, and an English dictionary; and several English grammars. Some of his miscellaneous belongings bespoke his many-sided talents in the past: an octant, two saddles, some hydrographic plans, a pair of spurs, two fragments of a flute, a picture of Venus and Cupid, and a bar of soap.[11]

Disdainful of his own troubles, Bowles took refuge in his capital, where he assembled his scattered forces. A day's march away, at St. Marks, was Panton's store, which he had held up once before. In sore need of supplies and weapons, and unable to receive them from the Bahamas, he prepared a repeat performance. With three hundred of his men, most of whom were Indians, he took the store, seemingly with shameless ease.[12]

On April 5 he declared war on Spain. In the previous month that country had ordered her colonial officials "to make every effort to capture him and to execute him on the spot."[13] Bowles, of course, was as yet unaware of this order, but he knew full well what punishment Spain had in store for him. He resolved to save himself by attacking first Spain and then the United States. He swooped down with his entire force of four hundred men on the fort of St. Marks and began to besiege it, while he called for reinforcements from among his Indian friends. Though the fort contained only a little more than a hundred officers and men, it enjoyed an impregnable position against Bowles' force, which was armed only with muskets. Built of solid stone, it stood on a narrow peninsula at the juncture of the Apalache and Wakulla rivers. A stone wall and a canal connecting the two rivers protected it from its only approach by land. On its walls were several serviceable cannon. Its water supply was ample and its provisions sufficed for a long siege. Had the garrison performed its military duties with moderate diligence, it could easily have repulsed its enemies; but it was so demoralized that its commander, Tómas Portell, offered only token resistance. Receiving no reply to his appeal for relief from the nearby galleys of the Louisiana fleet and learning that Bowles had captured one of Panton's ships, which purportedly was heavily armed, Portell concluded that further resistance was suicidal. On May 19 he surrendered. Bowles boasted that he had gained his victory without the loss of a man.[14]

But his undoing was almost as swift as his triumph. At the end of April a Spanish vessel captured one of his ships from the Bahamas, depriving him of badly needed reinforcements. The Spaniards, retrieving their courage, attacked Bowles in his recently won fort. This gave Ferguson an opportunity to revenge the many wrongs his leader had inflicted on him. Obtaining permission to go on a fishing trip, he boarded instead one of Panton's ships and sought out Folch in Pensacola. The governor had assembled his forces, but, fearing defeat, was reluctant to lead them against Bowles. Ferguson gradually convinced him that Bowles, having a smaller force and inferior arms, could not win. Whereupon Folch hesitated no longer; he launched against Bowles his entire armada, which consisted of five well-armed ships with a complement of one hundred fifty officers and men and four schooners carrying a company of grenadiers. On the morning of June 23 he arrived before St. Marks. To divert Bowles' attention from the fleet, he entered into negotiations with him.

Under cover of a white flag the fleet stole to within firing range of the fort. Folch then declared Bowles' replies unsatisfactory and ordered his men to battle. For an hour Bowles replied by a lively and well-directed fire; but his men became frightened when one of the powder magazines exploded. Seizing on this advantage, Folch again assaulted the fort. At the same time his largest ship, which had run aground earlier in the day, returned to action. Her big guns thoroughly discouraged Bowles' men;

they threw down their guns and fled. Bowles made off up the river in two boats that carried powder, guns, and a recent batch of mail from Madrid. Folch sent a detachment after him. It soon recaptured the boats and recovered the Madrid mail; but it failed to find Bowles. Among the recaptured dispatches were two royal orders showing that, in the past, Spain had used Indians against Americans. Had Bowles seen fit to reveal this information to American authorities, he doubtless would have caused Spain no small embarrassment.[15]

Despite his defeat Bowles remained a grave threat to Spain and the United States. With provisions and munitions he received from the Bahamas he was able to organize another force with which he conducted a series of depredations over a large part of Florida. Carlos Martínez de Irujo, Spanish minister to the United States, remarked to the American authorities that Bowles' raids were "highly discreditable to Spain," for she was at peace with the rest of Europe. Benjamin Hawkins blamed Spain as much as Bowles. Estimating the adventurer's force at no more than sixty men "more attentive to frolicking than fighting," the American agent criticized Spain for her supineness, saying that she must either fight for the Floridas or give them up altogether.[16]

Irujo had several times reminded the American authorities that, in accordance with the Treaty of San Lorenzo, each party was responsible for maintaining peace and order on its side of the line. His appeals gradually stirred President Jefferson to action. In June 1801 Secretary of War Henry Dearborn wrote Hawkins to be on his guard

> . . . against the improper views of that adventurer [Bowles]; to counteract them as effectually as possible by all suitable means; to watch all his movements attentively, and to persevere in endeavoring to fortify the minds of the Indians against his artful schemes.
>
> Should Bowles at any time come within the limits of the United States, every exertion must be made to apprehend him, taking care only not to compromise the peace of the United States.[17]

In the spring of the following year stronger representations from Irujo resulted in imperative instructions to Hawkins:

> No exertion should be wanting on your part for securing him if he should venture within our limits; if there has been one or more thousand dollars offered for him by the Spanish government, as stated by the minister, I should suppose that a knowledge of that circumstance among the Creeks, or some particular individuals of them would induce them to make an exertion to apprehend him. His being secured is so important to the peace and harmony of the Spanish and American frontiers that every justifiable measure should be taken for placing him in such a situation as will prevent his being mischievous.[18]

Hawkins needed no further instructions to goad him to action. With the object of seizing Bowles, he connived with Folch; he plotted with Jacopo DuBreuil, newly appointed commander of St. Marks; he intrigued with those few chiefs who were known to be hostile toward the adventurer. Folch, realizing that Bowles derived his influence with the tribes from his promises of supplying them with goods and munitions, established a blockade of the West Florida coast, which soon interrupted his communications with his backers in the Bahamas. At the same time DuBreuil intrigued with a few chiefs, promising them a reward for their assistance in seizing Bowles. Hawkins' role in his own grand plot, which came last in May, 1803, proved efficacious and the most dramatic of all. For the purpose of considering a common policy on land cessions, the southern tribes held a general congress on the Hickory Ground, where Alexander McGillivray had once dwelled with his father and where Andrew Jackson was to win a smashing victory over the Creeks.[19]

Hawkins, learning that Bowles planned to attend the congress, made preparations to seize him. He now had a new and powerful ally, John Forbes, who had recently succeeded Panton as head of Panton, Leslie and Company. The adventurer, attended by a retinue of Seminoles and Upper Creek chiefs, presently appeared, as confident as ever that nothing or nobody could harm him and hopeful that he could unite all the southern tribes in active support of his schemes. Even when he learned that Hawkins and Forbes planned to trap him, he trusted in the devotion of the Cherokees, in the bravery of the Creeks, and in the cherished Creek custom which forbade any act of violence in a peaceful town. He reckoned ill. The Seminoles, hoping that Forbes would restore their trade, which his predecessor had curtailed, offered him a land cession in payment of their debts and in reparation of their robberies. Seizing on this offer, Forbes stipulated as a prerequisite their separation from Bowles which they reluctantly accepted. The Cherokees, too, early abandoned Bowles. They asked him to show them his English credentials, of which he repeatedly boasted. When he failed to do so, they became convinced that he was an imposter. Gradually even his warmest friend, Chief Opoie Micco, deserted him for a substantial bribe from Hawkins. Shorn of his supporters, Bowles bowed graciously to his fate. Hawkins arrested him, then had him bound with handcuffs made by a blacksmith whom the American government maintained among the Creeks in pursuance of its program to civilize them. At Hawkins' request, the chiefs took Bowles to Governor Salcedo in New Orleans and collected the reward. This time Bowles made no spectacular escape. His talent for intrigue, his feats of derring-do, his sheer audacity—all failed to break his shackles and secure his liberty. Salcedo sent him to Havana, where the authorities threw him into a dungeon in Morro Castle. There he died three years later, either of disease or undernourishment or, as some historians infer or suggest, from the result of foul play. Though he was doubtless a rogue, his vaunted aims, his variegated talents, and his personal magnetism seem to suggest that he deserved, "if not a better end, at least something more heroic than a lingering death in a Spanish dungeon."[20]

2

The impunity with which Bowles invaded Florida bespoke the impotency of Spanish authority in that province. In the ensuing decade, when Spain fell to Napoleon and her overseas colonies began their wars of independence, her authority in Florida disintegrated altogether. We have seen how, in 1810, the American immigrants in West Florida succeeded in wresting that province from Spanish control and how Governor Folch, in a moment of desperation over the Kemper depredations, offered it to President Madison provided no Spanish aid reached him from Cuba or Mexico within a specified time. In that communication perhaps lies the best explanation for the revolution which broke out in East Florida in 1812. Inspired or strengthened by Folch's communication, Madison, on January 3, 1811, sent to Congress a secret message in which he requested authority to take temporary possession of any part of the Floridas in accordance with any arrangement that might be made with the Spanish authorities or in case any part of the Floridas should be seized by any foreign power. Less than two weeks later Congress obliged him with a resolution which declared that

> . . . taking into view the peculiar situation of Spain and her American provinces; and considering the influence which the destiny of the territory adjoining the southern border of the United States may have upon their security, tranquility, and commerce, . . . the United States, under the peculiar circumstances of the existing crisis, cannot, without serious inquietude, see any part of the said territory pass into the hands of any foreign power; and that a due regard to their own safety compels them to provide, under certain contingencies, for the temporary occupation of the said territory; they, at the same time, declared that the said territory shall, in their hands, remain subject to future negotiations.[21]

An act passed by Congress at the same time empowered the president to take possession of all or part of the territory lying east of the Perdido River and south of Georgia and Mississippi Territory, with the approval of "the local authority" or in case of any attempt by a foreign power to occupy the aforementioned territory. The act also empowered the president to use the army and navy of the United States to maintain order in the region, once it was occupied. Congress appropriated $100,000 to defray the expenses of the occupation and authorized the president to establish a temporary government in the territory. On March 3 Congress passed another act which forbade the publication of the resolution and the first act. They remained secret documents until the spring of 1818.[22]

The commissioners whom Secretary of State Robert Smith chose to carry out the provisions of the act were Colonel John McKee, the Indian agent, and George Mathews, the superstitious and almost illiterate former governor of Georgia. Smith instructed them to set out secretly for West Florida and ascertain Folch's intention or inclination or that of any other local authority in regard to the peaceful surrender of that province to the United States. If necessary to the success of their mission, they were to assume payment of Spanish debts to the people of the Floridas, to guarantee them in their land titles, to permit Spanish officials to retain their positions under the government of the United States, or, if they wished to move, to advance money for their transportation out of the country. They must respect all Spanish property as well as the liberties and properties of the people. Should they fail in their negotiations, they were to remain at their headquarters and, in case of the approach of a foreign power, were to seize the province with troops from Georgia under Mathews' command.[23]

On arriving in West Florida, McKee and Mathews found that Folch had completely changed his mind. He had received funds from his superiors with orders to hold the province at all costs. Conveniently ignoring his message to Madison, Folch told Mathews that the American government had, by taking possession of West Florida, administered an unforgivable insult that released him from his previous offer. So the commissioners, at Secretary Smith's request, entrusted their mission, so far as West Florida was concerned, to Governor Claiborne, and departed for St. Marys, in present Georgia, to work for the possible acquisition of East Florida.[24]

There Mathews found private individuals, whose names he had submitted to Secretary Smith, ready to help him in his mission. But the promised military aid had not yet arrived. To Smith he wrote the only letter ever found in his own handwriting: "I found the Gentelmin hows names I give you well disposid to sarve our Government. But thare has not one solder arived or one armed vesil or a Gun Boat in this rivar, from this cause its thought not propar to attemp Eney thing at present."[25] Later he was somewhat heartened to receive from James Monroe, who had replaced Smith, a letter authorizing him to continue his mission in East Florida, "especially if you entertain any reasonable hope of success there."[26]

Mathews made every effort to enlist in his scheme as many inhabitants of Florida as he could possibly find. To each white man he offered fifty acres of land and guarantees of his religion and his property. To soldiers and officers of Spanish garrisons he offered positions in the army of the United States or removal to places of his own designation. But most of the men he approached were so prosperous in the illicit border trade that they ignored his offers. Infuriated by his failure, he resolved to journey to St. Augustine and enlist the support of Governor Enrique White of East Florida. At the St. Johns River he imparted his mission to an innkeeper named Atkinson, who dissuaded him from undertaking it.

"As sure as you open your mouth to White on the subject," said Atkinson, "you will die in chains in Morro Castle, and all the devils in hell can't save you!"

Next day Mathews retraced his steps to St. Marys.[27]

Among the wealthy planters of East Florida, however, Mathews met with some success. He found a kindred spirit in John H. McIntosh, a veteran of the Revolutionary War. After that conflict he had filled a number of minor posts in the Spanish government. He lived in a pretentious house on the St. Johns River, where he enjoyed a prosperous lumber trade. Closely associated with him were Ludowick Ashley, a cattleman and lumber dealer on the St. Marys, and one captain Wylly, a former British officer who ingeniously pursued his new affiliation as well as his old. In his spare time he sent A. J. Foster, the British minister at Washington, important information concerning social and economic conditions in Florida. None of these names carries convincing evidence of Spanish blood, just as the names of their followers suggest little of Iberian ancestry. McIntosh's recruiting party of eight included only one Spanish subject. His name was Haddock.[28]

By the middle of March these "patriots," as they liked to call themselves, had completed their plans. Nothing remained but for Mathews to receive the military and naval aid that the government had promised him. To expedite matters he wrote to Monroe, imparting his military plans. He received no reply. At last, persuading himself that Monroe's silence signified tacit approval of his plans, he resolved to make a surprise attack on St. Augustine with the aid of the gunboats and land forces at Point Peter, an American arsenal just below the town of St. Marys. Its commander, Colonel T. A. Smith, had been ordered to prepare for action. Mathews went to the post to arrange for the use of the troops, but he learned that Smith was on leave of absence. The officer in charge, Major Jacint Laval, refused to let his men participate in the campaign, explaining that "secret service" was to him a seemingly wrong undertaking for American regulars. Without Laval's assistance, Commodore Hugh Campbell, of course, refused to use his gunboats. Several times Mathews and McIntosh tried by cajolery, by bluster, by threats to move Laval from his resolution until with mounting anger he ordered them out of camp, "in a manner," complained Mathews, or rather his more literate letter writer, "marked by rudeness and ungentlemanlike behavior."[29]

Unable to carry out their project against St. Augustine, Mathews and his associates resolved on the less spectacular campaign against Fernandina, on Amelia Island, center of the illicit trade in cotton between the United States and Great Britain. To this end they assembled their followers at Rose's Bluff, on the south side of the St. Marys River, where they organized an insurgent government with McIntosh as "director" and Ashley as military commander. The less articulate Mathews preferred to remain in the background as a kind of impresario. On the bluff they raised a white flag, embellished with the figure of a soldier in blue, bayonet at charge, and with the inscription *Salus populi, supreme lex.* But since they promised little law and less security to anybody outside of themselves, the inscription aroused no little merriment among their more educated members. Eventually they persuaded their superiors to change the *salus* to the less definite *vox populi.*[30]

Next day the insurgents moved down the river two miles to Lower Bluff, only seven miles from Fernandina, and began preparations to capture Amelia Island. The commander of Fernandina, Justo López, had a garrison of only ten men. Naturally alarmed by the activity of the insurgents along the St. Marys, he had written to several justices of Fernandina, inquiring about its meaning. The justices had disclaimed any knowledge of it. Now, on March 15, McIntosh, under a flag of truce, sent López a message informing him of the progress of the insurgents and requesting him to surrender or join their "glorious cause." Since the United States was bent on conquering the island, he said, he and his associates had resolved to seize it themselves in the interest of their country. He claimed that they already controlled the region between the St. Johns and the St. Marys rivers and that they would have possessed St. Augustine too, had Laval supported them. But, he concluded, their numbers were "increasing like a snow-ball," assuring them of eventual success. Though his simile was hardly seasonable for a Florida springtime, it seemingly confirmed its claim when recruits from Georgia swelled his force to over two hundred men. This, however, failed to stir López one step toward surrender. Instead, he bulwarked the fort with bales of cotton, mounted a few small and rusty cannon, and mustered a force of some fifty or sixty men. Then he sent Laval a message inquiring about the disposition of his forces. The testy officer scribbled this emphatic reply:

> You desire to know for me, sir, if the United States are to be considered as principals or auxiliaries? I have the greatest satisfaction in informing you that *the United States are neither principals or auxiliaries*, and that I am not authorized to make any attack upon East Florida; and I have taken the firm resolution of not marching the troops of the United States, having no instructions to that effect.[31]

Encouraged by the tenor of Laval's message, López grew confident that he could contend with Mathews and his followers, but he hesitated to provoke the intervention of Campbell's gunboats. Mathews had obviously persuaded the commodore to change his mind and to draw five of his gunboats before the makeshift fort. Observing them, López sent two commissioners to Mathews who, however, insisted on the peaceful surrender of the island. When they prepared to return from their fruitless mission, Ashley handed them a note in which he apprized López that the insurgents would soon land on Amelia Island and that they would not fire a shot unless they were provoked. Before López received the note, he ascertained that eight of the gunboats had drawn up before the town, and that three of them lay within pistol shot of the guard house with springs on their cables, tampions removed from their guns, and their crews at quarter. On reading Ashley's note, López saw the futility of further resistance. He surrendered the island to the United States. Presently the insurgents landed in Fernandina, marched through its streets, and triumphantly raised their flag. The articles of capitulation, which López signed under protest, stipulated that the inhabitants were to maintain their existing privileges, could remain on the island or leave it, and could enlist in the American army. Next day Colonel Smith, commander of the arsenal at Point Peter, returned to his post, overruled Laval's policy, placed him under arrest, and, "as God would have it"—so piously wrote Mathews—sent fifty of his soldiers to assist in the occupation of the island.[32]

Mathews' next objective was St. Augustine. On April 1 he sent Smith by boat against Picolata, on the St. Johns River, which they seized four days later. Then he led his men up Six Mile Creek, one of the tributaries of the St. Johns, left most of his supplies there, and marched against Moosa Old Fort, an abandoned outpost two miles from St. Augustine. Colonel Smith sent Estrada, the acting governor of Florida, a message demanding the immediate surrender of the town and fort of St. Augustine. Though Estrada had scarcely enough of a garrison to defend them, he mounted some guns on a Spanish schooner and sent her against Moosa Old Fort. The Americans, seeing her approach, fired on her; but when she replied with a twenty-four pounder that almost demolished the fort, they retreated to their positions along the St. Johns.[33]

Notwithstanding this reverse, Mathews, who had followed Smith, sent President Madison a glowing report of his success. But just when he thought his prospects were bright, just when he expected official recognition of his great services, disaster fell on him. He firmly believed that Secretary Monroe had, by his silence, given tacit approval to his plans. But, though the government could pursue secret negotiations in its endeavor to acquire East Florida, it could not permit the open and flagrant use of troops against a friendly nation without risking the censure of the nation and perhaps of the world. Such a policy, indeed, would have been particularly harmful to the country at that time. In March, 1812, John Henry, a British agent, had published his papers, in which he reported the attachment of the Federalist leaders to England. To discredit his political rivals and at the same time expose British chicanery in New England, President Madison bought the papers for $50,000 and laid them before Congress, which found that Henry had deleted the names of the

Federalist leaders. This deception had aroused a great wave of popular anger against England. The American government could not be found sanctioning in Mathews what it had decried in Henry.

While the Democratic newspapers praised the Florida affair, Federalist newspapers denounced Madison and Monroe for complicity in it. So they saw the advisibility of extricating themselves from a dilemma of their own making. This explains Monroe's failure to answer Mathews' letters. But on April 4, Monroe did write a letter to Mathews, the kind of letter that left him speechless—not with wisdom, but with anger. He was informed that he had exceeded both the secret act of January, 1811, and his own instructions and that, therefore, he must give up his duties to Governor David B. Mitchell of Georgia. Senator W. H. Crawford of Georgia knew Mathews to the core of his being. "Poor old Mathews," he said, "I am fearful will die of mortification and resentment when he is made sensible of the utmost extent of his disappointment." These words proved prophetic. Gradually Mathews' anger became quite audible. At last he resolved to depart for Washington in an effort to clear himself. "I'll be damned," he roared, "if I don't blow them all up!" Fortunately for Monroe and Madison, Mathews never reached his destination. Worn out by his incessant activities and crushed by his disappointment, he died on September 1 at Augusta.[34]

Monroe asked Mitchell to restore East Florida to its former status by withdrawing the United States troops as slowly as he deemed feasible and by securing from the Spanish authorities an amnesty for those who had joined Mathews. The new Spanish governor, Sebastián Kindelan, insisted on the immediate withdrawal of the United States troops before he would consent to enter negotiations with Mitchell. To this view he succeeded in enlisting the support of the regional Indians, who immediately took the warpath against the helpless settlers. The result was even more advantageous to Kindelan than he had anticipated. Most of the insurgents left their ranks to protect their families and property. The rest of them, a leaderless rabble, retired, together with the United States troops, to their positions on the St. Johns River, where they could maintain communications with Georgia.[35]

At this juncture the War of 1812 broke out, giving Mitchell an opportunity to withdraw for the purpose of dealing with the war session of the Georgia assembly. That fall Monroe sent Major General Thomas Pinckney to negotiate a settlement with Kindelan. In March, 1813, they agreed to the withdrawal of the United States troops. At about the same time Luis de Onís, newly appointed Spanish minister at Washington, sent Monroe an act of amnesty for the East Florida insurgents "who had been induced to revolt by an agent of the United States, whose proceedings in that respect were unauthorized." Accordingly, Kindelan published an act of amnesty and arranged with Pinckney for the withdrawal of the United States troops from East Florida. What remained of the insurgents continued to threaten Spanish authority; but, denied official

American support, they accepted Spanish citizenship in return for self-government for the region in which they lived.[36]

3

By the Treaty of Ghent, which ended the War of 1812, Great Britain and the United States agreed to evacuate the places they had occupied in the Floridas. But Great Britain feared American expansion in the Caribbean and planned to prevent it, or at least retard it, by sustaining Spain in her endeavor to retain the Floridas, and by sending agents to incite the Indians of that region against American settlements across the line or to organize alliances with them along the Southern Frontier. Some officials in Washington, as well as in the south, believed that the numerous British subjects who appeared in East Florida after the War of 1812 had definite instructions from their government. Others were convinced that Great Britain planned to reoccupy the Floridas. How many of them were actual British agents and how many were mere adventurers or fortune seekers will, of course, never be known.

One of the most intrepid British officers of the war was Colonel Edward Nicholls, who had served in East Florida and in Pensacola. Instead of sailing home with his regiment after the war, he returned to East Florida with fifty-five slaves he had either stolen or lured away from the plantation of John Innerarity, one of the wealthiest citizens of Pensacola. In East Florida he negotiated an alliance with the Indians, and gave it substance by rebuilding an old fort some fifteen miles from the mouth of the Apalachicola River. He equipped it with three thousand small arms and a thousand barrels of powder, and manned it with the slaves he had brought from Pensacola. His aims, however, were purely defensive. He urged his Indians to remain peaceful. He punished severely those who crossed the line to murder and steal. Indeed, he complained to Benjamin Hawkins by letter that the depredations were committed not by Indians but by Americans. He expected Hawkins to stop them. As proof of their guilt, he cited the bloody clothes which one of the chiefs, Bowlegs or Boleck, had found in their camp, which they had evacuated hastily in their endeavor to escape detection. Nicholls went on to inform Hawkins that the chiefs had given their consent

. . . to await your answer before they take revenge; but, sir, they are impatient for it, and well armed as the whole nation now is, and stored with ammunition and provisions, having a strong hold to retire upon in case of a superior force appearing, picture to yourself, sir, the miseries that may be suffered by good and innocent citizens on your frontiers, and I am sure you will lend me your best aid in keeping the bad spirits in subjection. Yesterday in a full assembly of the chiefs, I got them to pass a law for four resolute chiefs to be appointed in different parts of the nation, something in the character of our sheriffs, for the purpose of inflicting condign punishment on such people, as broke the law, and I will say this much for them, that I never saw men execute laws better than they do.

He concluded his letter by informing the Indian agent that the chiefs had "signed a treaty of offensive and defensive alliance with Great Britain, as well as one of commerce and navigation, which as soon as it is ratified at home you shall be made more fully acquainted with."[37]

Hawkins replied that Bowlegs had complained to him personally that white men from Georgia had gone into East Florida and had driven off his cattle and destroyed some of his property. "All that is wanted," added Hawkins sarcastically, "is proof against the aggressors." As for the treaties that Nicholls had signed with the Creeks, Hawkins dismissed them as a novelty "with the authority created by yourself." He would be greatly surprised, he concluded, "to see your sovereign ratify such as you have described them to be, with the people such as I know them to be, in the territories of His Catholic Majesty."[38]

Nicholls soon sailed to England with his white troops, the Indian prophet Francis, and several Creeks. When he arrived, he learned much to his chagrin that the Foreign Office disavowed his conduct in arranging an alliance with Indians living in a province of a foreign nation. The government naturally repudiated the alliance, though it saw fit to placate Francis by appealing to his vanity. It made him a brigadier-general and presented him with the scarlet uniform of his new rank.[39]

Meanwhile Nicholls' stronghold, which became known as Negro Fort, had fallen into the hands of fugitive slaves under the intrepid leadership of one of their number named Garçon. The slaves were soon joined by Indians and free Negroes who held grazing lands and farms along the Apalachicola in each direction from the fort. Often Garçon sent his men out to raid the region and even to plunder and fire on the boats that passed up and down the river. Disturbed by these depredations, the secretary of war instructed Andrew Jackson, commander of American forces in the south, to ask the Spanish governor in Pensacola to suppress them. Governor José Masot, who had just arrived in Pensacola, extended much politeness but few promises, declaring that he was helpless to act without the permission of his superior in Havana. Jackson did not wait. He ordered Brigadier-General Edmund Pendleton Gaines to build near the junction of the Flint, Chattahoochee, and Apalachicola rivers, in present Georgia, a stronghold named Fort Scott, which would serve the double purpose of defending the region against marauding Indians and Negroes and of providing it with a depot of supplies brought up the Apalachicola from New Orleans with the permission of the Spanish authorities.

When Gaines learned that the first boatload of supplies was coming up the river, he sent Colonel Duncan L. Clinch to the region of Negro Fort to capture its marauding Indians, free Negroes, and slaves, and to restore the latter to their owners. They hurriedly took refuge in their fort. Angered by the failure of his mission, Clinch destroyed their grazing fields, their cornfields, and their melon patches. Then, with Gaines' permission, he prepared to destroy Negro Fort. On July 26, 1816, he bombed it from two boats and from the shore. One of the cannon balls struck a powder magazine. The explosion was terrifying; the havoc it caused, terrific. In an instant, hundreds of lifeless bodies lay on the surrounding plain or were buried in the rubbish or suspended from the tops of southern pines. Large heaps of sand, broken guns, and accoutrements covered the site of the fort. "The brave soldier," wrote an eyewitness, "was disarmed of his resentment, and checked his victorious career, to drop a tear on the distressing scene." Two hundred seventy men, women, and children were killed, and sixty others escaped with injuries, some of which proved fatal. The surviving slaves and some free Negroes were taken to Georgia, where they were delivered up to men who claimed to be their masters or the relatives or descendents of their masters.[40]

But East Florida was too tempting a region for too many kinds of adventurers to remain peaceful for long. As Kathryn Abbey Hanna eloquently says, "If one liked a fight, there was plenty of opportunities for the soldier; if one was an idealist, there was satisfaction in breaking a lance for liberty; or if more tangible and immediate gains were an objective, smuggling and contraband trade presented a fertile field."[41] Especially inviting to any of such characters was Amelia Island. In the summer of 1817 it became the stage of activity for another of the innumerable colorful and dramatic seekers of fortune that fill the annals of the Southern Frontier. His name was Gregor MacGregor, a Scotsman who had joined the British army and, according to his own account, had moved to Venezuela to settle and help that region secure her independence from Spain. There he married Josefa Lovera, who accompanied him in many of his astonishing escapades. In 1812 a terrible earthquake devastated large areas of Venezuela and temporarily paralyzed the movement for independence. When this was renewed, MacGregor fought under that precursor of Latin American freedom, Francisco Miranda, who rewarded his military gifts by promoting him to the command of a brigade. Later, when Simón Bolívar succeeded the defeated Miranda, MacGregor joined him and distinguished himself in many battles. Bolívar promoted him to general of a division in the Venezuelan army and rewarded him with special thanks and the insignia of the Order of Liberators.[42]

Yet Gregor MacGregor was dissatisfied. Envious of Bolívar's glory and realizing that he could never hope to rival it as long as he stayed in South America, he resolved to leave that continent for the United States, where he would plan a descent on East Florida. In New York he requested, from a group of revolutionary agents of Latin America known as "the deputies of free America," a commission to liberate the Floridas. The agents were greatly impressed by his military record and by his personal charm, which he seems to have inherited from his grandfather, whose name in Gaelic was "MacGregor the Beautiful" and whose dexterity with the broadsword and Lochabar ax had earned him the admiration of his king. They granted his request. With his commission in his pocket he solicited aid in Philadelphia; but, refusing to disclose his specific aims, he failed miserably. Undaunted, he went to Baltimore, where he sought the friendship of J. Skinner, the postmaster, who he supposed had influence with the Federal government. Skinner and his friends provided MacGregor with small sums of money and induced some young men to join the projected expedition. With these MacGregor went to Charleston, South Carolina, where he enlisted the support of quite a number of respectable citizens and recruited some young men who had fought in the War of 1812. Under a borrowed name he purchased a sizable schooner and cleared her for New Orleans, though he sailed with her to the mouth of the Altamaha River, where he planned to concentrate his supplies for his planned seizure of Amelia Island. At Savannah he recruited from among sailors and stevedores the rest of his force, paying each man $12 in advance and $10 a month. He interested in his cause a large mercantile company, which promised to buy 30,000 acres in Florida at a dollar an acre once that province was conquered.[43]

Boarding his force of about one hundred fifty men on two schooners, MacGregor sailed down the inside passage along Cumberland Island, crossed the channel of St. Marys, and anchored on the northern end of Amelia Island. There he landed fifty-five of his musketeers and marched them to a thick forest bordering on Egon's Creek across from Fernandina. Its commander, Francisco Morales, believing that MacGregor had a force several times its actual size, surrendered without firing a shot. Whereupon MacGregor hoisted over the fort a flag that he himself had recently designed. Inspired by the flag of Great Britain, it was white, with one vertical and one horizontal green stripe intersecting in the center to form a St. George's cross. He called it the Green Cross of Florida. He sent his prisoners to the mainland, whence they embarked for St. Augustine. José Coppinger, a fiery Irishman currently serving as governor of the province, suspected Morales of cowardice. He clapped him in irons and conducted a court-martial that sentenced him to death. Morales, however, was never executed, thanks either to the negligence or to the humanity of the Governor General of Cuba, who never sent Coppinger permission to impose the sentence.[44]

MacGregor now issued one of his many grandiloquent proclamations, which in phrasing and sentiment is suspiciously similar to some of those penned by Napoleon early in his career:

SOLDIERS AND SAILORS!

The 29th of June will be forever memorable in the annals of the independence of South America. On that day, a body of brave men, animated by a noble zeal for the happiness of mankind, advanced within musket shot of the guns of Fernandina, and awed the enemy into immediate capitulation, notwithstanding his very favorable position. This will be an everlasting proof of what the sons of freedom can achieve when fighting in a great and glorious cause against a Government, which has trampled on all the natural and essential rights which descend from God to man. . . . I trust that, impelled by the same noble principle, you will soon be able to free the whole of the Floridas from tyranny and oppression.

Then shall I hope to lead you to the continent of South America to gather fresh laurels in freedom's cause. Your names will be transmitted to the latest posterity, as the first who formed a solid basis for the emancipation of those delightful and fruitful regions, now in a great part groaning under the oppressive hand of Spanish despotism. The children of South America will re-echo your names in their songs; your heroic deeds will be handed down to succeeding generations, and will cover yourselves and your latest posterity with a never-fading wreath of glory. The path of honor is now open before you. Let those who distinguish themselves look forward with confidence to promotion and preferment.[45]

As a port on the Atlantic so close to the United States, Fernandina was of great importance to the swarms of pirates and smugglers who infested the West Indies and who sailed with impunity under the flags of such emerging republics as Mexico, Buenos Aires, Venezuela, and Granada. Having an excellent eye for business, which he greatly needed, MacGregor invited them to make Amelia Island "the depot of their prizes and the vent of their cargoes."[46] But what he gained by cultivating their friendship, he lost by sending out parties that committed excesses on planters and inhabitants. And by failing to advance on St. Augustine, he sacrificed that enthusiasm which accompanies a quick victory and which would have attracted to his side sufficient numbers to make it respectable. He preferred to tarry in Fernandina, spending much of his time eating and drinking and savoring the delicious phraseology of his Napoleonic proclamations. These soon earned him the contempt which their frequency deserved. Then he further alienated what little sympathy he had gained for his cause by selling thirty-one slaves he found on the island and pocketing the proceeds. The planters, recalling the excesses of Mathews' "patriots," were greatly alarmed.[47]

In time MacGregor's soldiers degenerated into roving bands of marauders. Governor Coppinger, learning that a group of them were approaching St. Augustine in an open boat, sent his soldiers against them. Ten of them were killed. The rest landed on a plantation and began to plunder it. In their endeavor to find money and valuable articles, they broke down the doors of the master's house and wrecked a chest of drawers and a trunk. They fled as soon as Coppinger's men arrived.[48]

By this time most of MacGregor's soldiers had melted away. When only twenty-five of them remained, he decided to quit the island and seek another field of adventure. Turning the affairs of Fernandina over to two of his most trusted followers, Jared Irwin and Ruggles Hubbard, formerly sheriff of New York, he put his baggage on board one of his boats and sailed to Nicaragua, where he attempted in vain to establish a colony among the Indians.[49]

To a council of his few soldiers and officers Irwin declared his intention of holding out against the "Damn Spaniards." Coppinger, having welded the garrison of St. Augustine, Negro reinforcements from Havana, and militiamen into a formidable force of four hundred men, sent it against the insurgents. Superior to them in quality and quantity, his men defeated them in a short but sharp naval engagement; but they became demoralized when a bomb accidentally exploded among their concentrated numbers, killing a small number of soldiers and officers and wounding many others. The rest returned to St. Augustine.[50]

A few days later Louis Aury, the famous or infamous French pirate, appeared in the harbor of Fernandina and proclaimed himself master of Amelia Island. Running a Spanish blockade with a part of his fleet at Cartagena, in present Colombia, he had sailed to Santo Domingo, thence to Galveston Island, on the coast of Texas. There he had collected a gang of desperadoes, including Frenchmen who had fought under Napoleon, some of Laffite's pirate band, freebooters and smugglers, and mulattoes from Santo Domingo. With the consent of Manuel de Herrera, an insurgent who called himself minister plenipotentiary of the "Republic of Mexico" to the United States, Aury had established a government of which he himself was civil and military governor. Learning of conditions in Florida, he planned with Herrera's blessing to go to that province and, if he found that MacGregor was no longer in possession of it, annex it to Mexico, which was then fighting for her independence. Sailing into the harbor of Fernandina on his flagship the *Mexico Libre*, which carried a prize of $60,000, he ordered Irwin and Hubbard to give up the island to him. Though they protested with great indignation, they yielded to his wishes because they needed his financial backing. Aury made himself commander-in-chief of the military and naval forces, and chose Hubbard as civil governor and Irwin as adjutant general of Amelia Island. Then, on September 21, 1817, amid the boom of cannon, "and with the buccaneer nobility of the high-seas and the land forces of iniquity lined up in attention," he annexed Amelia Island to the "Republic of Mexico."[51]

But factional strife among the leaders soon obviated any possibility of success in their arrangement. Hubbard, leader of the American party, and Aury, leader of the French party, were soon enmeshed in a bitter quarrel over whether Negroes should be permitted to serve in the garrison. Another quarrel broke out among Aury's one hundred thirty mulattoes, whom McIntosh described as "a set of desperate, bloodthirsty dogs." The dispute between Aury and Hubbard ended on October 19, when the latter died of yellow fever. Deprived of leadership, the American party became a mob. This situation enabled Aury to strengthen his control of the island by declaring it under martial law. He banished troublesome members of the American party and tried British officers by martial law with predetermined sentences of death.[52]

Word of conditions on the island soon reached the American government which, seeing that Aury's government was in no way interested in conquering Florida from Spain but that it existed purely for its own aggrandizement, directed that it be destroyed. Acting under the secret resolution of January, 1811, President Monroe ordered naval Captain J. D. Henly and Major James Bankhead to evacuate Aury as quickly as possible. Aury refused to leave. Instead he proclaimed Amelia Island an independent republic and named Irwin its president.

Then he addressed to Monroe a lengthy message inferring that the United States had become subject to Spain and reminding him to respect the rights of Amelia Island as a sovereign nation. But he quickly surrendered when American troops landed on the island, though he fired a single cannon shot in protest. The Americans marched into Fernandina to the tunes of "Hail Columbia" and "Yankee Doodle" and took possession of the fort without encountering the slightest resistance. Aury and his officers were placed on parole, his white troops under strict surveillance. The black troops were sent to Santo Domingo. Early in 1818 Aury departed for Nicaragua, where, like MacGregor, he tried in vain to establish an independent colony.[53]

No sooner was quiet restored in one part of Florida than trouble broke out in another. The Seminoles, joined by runaway slaves and goaded by British traders or agents, made sporadic raids into American territory, burning farmhouses and livestock and sometimes murdering men, women, and children. They had good reasons for their hostility. After 1808 further importation of Negro slaves was forbidden. The consequent rise of prices for runaway slaves attracted many slave-catchers to Seminole country. At last Chief Neamathla, whose principal village lay near present Tallahassee, felt constrained to advise the soldiers at Fort Scott that he would tolerate no trespassing of his hunting grounds. The soldiers answered this effrontery by attacking a Seminole village. Its inhabitants resisted as long as they could, then fled. But they were so inflamed by this raid, which they considered unprovoked, that nine days later they retaliated by attacking and killing most of a boatload of forty soldiers, seven women, and four children on the Apalachicola River. A little later they looted one of the stores of Forbes & Company—successors to Panton, Leslie and Company—near the mouth of the river, and carried its clerks into captivity.[54]

Though the whites had committed as many depredations in Seminole country as the Seminoles had committed on American soil, most frontier newspapers printed only lurid reports of the sufferings that the Indians had inflicted on American settlers. No doubt the Seminoles were incited by British agents who operated in Florida but who had their headquarters in New Providence. Among them was Captain George Woodbine who, with one eye for his own pocketbook and the other for his king, acquired from the Seminoles a large grant of land which he could enjoy only if Florida remained Spanish or became British or independent. A more honest trader was Alexander Arbuthnot, an elderly Scotsman from Nassau. He charged the Indians honest prices, took an interest in their welfare, and gave them legal advice in which he told them repeatedly that the Americans had robbed them at the Treaty of Fort Jackson in 1814. On the Southern Frontier he had the reputation of being the evil genius behind the Seminole attacks. The widely read *Niles' Register*, which was printed in Baltimore, thought that Arbuthnot was Woodbine in disguise and that he deserved to die like a sheep-killing dog.[55]

In December, 1817, President Monroe sent Andrew Jackson to clean up the Seminole country once and for all. Old Hickory never received an assignment more attractive to his prejudices. He could not conceive of a war against the Seminoles without a war against the Spaniards, though he had specific orders to respect all posts that flew the Spanish flag. Nevertheless, his general instructions were broad: he was to "adopt the necessary measures to terminate . . . [the] conflict."[56] Later, when he faced censure on grounds of having exceeded his instructions, he claimed that he had received, through Congressman John Rhea, instructions from Monroe approving his recommendation for the seizure of Florida within sixty days. Monroe denied that he had ever empowered Rhea to convey any such approval. The truth seems to be that Jackson, in the words of Secretary of War Calhoun, felt he was "vested with full power to conduct the war as he may think best."[57]

With militia collected in Tennessee and Kentucky, Old Hickory, early in March, 1818, arrived at Fort Scott, where he assumed command of eight hundred regulars and nine hundred Georgia militia. Allowing one quart of corn and three rations of meat for each of his men, he advanced through high streams and quagmires to the site of Negro Fort, where he ordered Lieutenant James Gadsden to build a new fort to which that officer gave his name. As soon as his supplies permitted, Jackson proceeded toward St. Marks, attacking all Indians who came in his way, even those who were peacefully engaged in herding cattle. On April 6 he arrived at St. Marks, seized it in the face of protests from its commander, Francisco Casa y Luego, and replaced the Spanish flag with the Stars and Stripes. There he found that one of Casa's guests was none other than Alexander Arbuthnot, whom he immediately arrested. Next he swooped down on Suwannee, Chief Bowlegs' main village, where Arbuthnot and his son operated a store. He found Suwannee deserted. As soon as the Scotch merchant learned of Jackson's invasion he had sent a letter to his son, urging him to warn Bowlegs and to remove the goods from their store. The chief had fled to the swamps with his women and children.[58]

That night Robert Cristy Ambrister, a captain in the Royal Colonial Marines and a veteran of the Napoleonic wars, and another Englishman, Peter B. Cook, stumbled into the American camp. On one of their Negro servants, Jackson found Arbuthnot's letter to his son. He considered its message an overt act of war against the United States.[59]

Enraged by his failure to capture Bowlegs, Jackson dashed back to St. Marks, where on April 26 he ordered a court-martial for Arbuthnot and Ambrister. The court, under the presidency of General Gaines, arraigned Arbuthnot on charges of spying for the Indians and of inciting them to war. Two days later the court charged Ambrister with assuming command of the Indians in war against the United States. At his defense Arbuthnot avoided any appeal to sympathy. He admitted that he had sold powder to Bowlegs, but he contended that it was no more than the chief and his men needed for hunting. Nevertheless, he was found guilty and sentenced to be hanged. Ambrister by his sociability and charming manners won the sympathy of many of Jackson's men. Summoned to offer his defense, he pleaded guilty, asked for mercy, and expressed his appreciation for all the courtesies the soldiers had extended him. He was sentenced to be shot. But at the last moment one of the members of the court reconsidered his vote, which resulted in the reduction of the sentences to fifty lashes and confinement with ball and chain for one year. Unfortunately for Ambrister, Jackson disapproved of the reconsidered vote and insisted that the original sentence be carried out. So a drum summoned a platoon to conduct the executions. Arbuthnot died stoically. And Ambrister was no less brave. "There," he said at the drum roll of death, "a sound I have heard in every quarter of the globe, and now for the last time."[60]

Four days later Jackson marched to Fort Gadsden, where he heard that Governor Masot in Pensacola had given refuge to Indians. Dropping his plans to return to Tennessee, he marched two hundred seventy miles in two weeks through rain-soaked terrain that "destroyed our horses, and next our shoes," leaving him and his men "literanny barefoot." Ignoring Masot's protests and orders to withdraw, Jackson captured the town in the face of heavy Spanish fire, deposed the fuming governor, seized and signed for royal property in the town and its outskirts, declared American revenue laws in force, established a military and civil government, installed garrisons in the forts, and issued a proclamation guaranteeing protection of public and private property, freedom of worship, and freedom of trade. Then, arranging for the evacuation of the Spanish garrison, staff, and governor, he departed for Tennessee, leaving diplomats "to disentangle the situation he had created."[61]

Luis de Onís, Spanish minister to the United States, was so incensed with Jackson's invasion of Florida that he awoke Secretary of State John Quincy Adams in the middle of the night to demand indemnity "for all injuries and losses and punishment for Jackson." His angry and persistent protests precipitated cabinet meetings for three days from noon to five in the afternoon to determine whether Jackson should be supported or repudiated. At last, president and cabinet settled on a compromise: Jackson should neither be punished nor censured. They simply agreed to restore to Spain the posts Jackson had taken. For this purpose Spain commissioned Juan Maria Echavarría who, early in 1819, arrived in Pensacola with Lieutenant Colonel José de Callava, the new governor, and a garrison of twenty-four officers and four hundred eighty-three enlisted men. Four days later Pensacola was returned to Spain.[62]

But Pensacola as well as the rest of Florida was soon to become forever a part of the United States. Far from apologizing for Jackson's invasion, Secretary Adams justified it on the ground of self-defense in a memorable instruction to the American minister in Madrid. He charged the Spaniards with having incited the Indians against settlers on American soil and with having sheltered them in their flight. He warned that, if Indians returned to the warpath, the United States would again chastise them. Spain, he concluded, must either protect her territory with an adequate force and fulfill her agreement with the United States in accordance with the Treaty of San Lorenzo, or she must cede to the United States a province "of which she retains nothing but the nominal possession, but which is, in fact, a derelict, open to the occupancy of every enemy, civilized and savage, of the United States, and serving no other earthly purpose than as a post of annoyance to them."[63]

Adams and Onís had long before opened negotiations for the possible cession of Florida. These broke down during Jackson's invasion but were resumed when the United States restored Pensacola and, a little later, St. Marks. Onís then offered Florida to the United States on condition that she refrain from recognizing the new Latin American nations, which had won or were winning their independence from Spain. Adams refused. But Spain, faced with many troubles at home, with revolution in her colonies, and with inability to secure effective aid from her ally England, realized the uselessness of trying to hold Florida. So she decided to cede the province while she could for a monetary consideration, rather than face the eventuality of losing it in a conflict that would be humiliating as well as expensive. On February 22, 1819, therefore, Onís signed a treaty of cession, which most American historians erroneously call the Purchase of Florida. Actually, the United States paid Spain nothing for the province; she simply agreed to pay the claims of her own citizens against Spain up to $5,000,000. But Spain, still fearing that the United States would recognize the independence of the Latin American nations, refused to ratify the treaty. In 1820, however, army and naval officers, unwilling to leave Cádiz to fight against the insurgents in the New World, revolted against Ferdinand VII, forcing him to adopt the liberal constitution of 1812. The new government advised the cession, which the king signed. On February 19, 1821, the United States Senate ratified the treaty. President Monroe approved it two days later.[64]

4

Early in the morning of July 17, 1821, Major General Andrew Jackson entered Pensacola with his wife Rachel and his staff, breakfasted with them, and, at the appointed time, advanced with some of his officers between saluting ranks of Spanish and American troops to the Government House, where Callava would tender him the formal surrender of Florida. Presently the governor, a tall, well-proportioned, blond man of about forty, appeared, smiled, bowed graciously, and signed the agreement of transfer. Then the dignitaries again passed by saluting troops to the plaza, where the Fourth Infantry band struck up "The Star-Spangled Banner," while the red and yellow banner of Castile and León fluttered to half-staff. The Stars and Stripes was raised to the level of the Spanish flag, then above it to the tune of "long may it wave, o'er the land of the free and the home of the brave," while an American vessel in the bay boomed the first of twenty-one guns. Florida had become American.[65]

Next day most of the Spanish garrison left for Havana. Only thirty-six officers, including Callava, remained on condition that they leave within six months. To Rachel and Andrew Jackson everybody and everything in Pensacola seemed symbolic of Spanish decadence. The heavy traffic and torrential rains had turned the streets into quagmires which soiled the clothes of passing speculators, swindlers, gamblers, and soldiers. Rachel surmised that the dilapidated houses must be "as old as time." The general found the Government House propped up by hewn logs, the barracks uninhabitable, and the morals of the people disturbing to Rachel's Presbyterian upbringing. "I think the Lord had a controversy with them," she wrote. "They were very far from God." Andrew hastened to salve her indignation. Assuming the duties of a stern constable, he destroyed the gambling houses and closed the shops and bazaars on Sunday. Rachel was delighted. "Fiddling and dancing not heard any more on the Lord's day," she exulted. "Cursing not heard. What, what has been done in one week!"[66]

Under Jackson's uncompromising rule Pensacola began to take on the complexion of an American town. He issued proclamations organizing the local government; he made ordinances for the preservation of health and for the creation of a territorial judiciary; he created two new counties—St. Johns to the east side of the Suwannee and Escambia to the west side of that stream—and organized for each a court consisting of five justices of the peace who had jurisdiction over all criminal cases and in civil cases over twenty dollars.[67]

In August he became entangled with former Governor Callava in a controversy which disclosed his dislike for Spaniards and his inability to conceal what was temperamentally alien to him. Mercedes Vidal, a free octoroon, told Henry M. Brackenridge, American mayor of Pensacola and one of her attorneys, that her father, Nicolas Maria Vidal, who had been a Spanish official until his death in 1806, had left her large tracts of land in the vicinity of Baton Rouge. She charged that Forbes & Company, administrators of the estate, had records of the case but that John Innerarity, resident manager of the firm in Pensacola, had ignored court orders to deliver them. She suspected that Innerarity and Callava were in collusion to remove the records from Florida. But, she said, she had by various means obtained enough copies of the records to substantiate her story. The originals had been spirited from the municipal archives to the residence of Lieutenant Domingo Sousa, one of Callava's clerks. Brackenridge went with the story to Jackson, who immediately suspected that all the papers in Sousa's possession must be important and thought, therefore, that they should be examined. He sent Brackenridge to demand them from Sousa, who, however, refused to give them up without Callava's sanction. Next morning Jackson sent Colonel Robert Butler to bring Sousa and the papers, but the clerk had already transferred them to Callava's residence for safekeeping.

More convinced than before that Callava and Innerarity had formed a conspiracy to defraud Mercedes Vidal of her property, Jackson sent a delegation of officials, including Brackenridge, to demand the records from the former governor and to tell him that, if he refused to give them up, Sousa would be jailed. Learning that Callava was dining at the house of one of the American officers, Colonel George M. Brooke, the delegation proceeded thither and stated its errand. Jumping up from his place at the table, Callava protested that, as royal commissioner in the transfer of Florida, his person was inviolate, and that he would never surrender the records. When Brooke, too, protested the intrusion of his home, the delegation left. Later, however, it found Callava in his own residence with Innerarity, and it repeated its request. Callava replied he was too ill to discuss the matter. As the delegation was about to depart, Innerarity exclaimed: "The die is cast!"

When these words were repeated to Jackson, he interpreted them as a challenge. He sent about twenty armed men to Callava's residence, where they found him half-dressed in bed. They again demanded the records. When he still refused to give them up, they arrested him and brought him before Jackson. In the ensuing interview neither man understood a word of the other's language. But Jackson, through Brackenridge, his interpreter, asked Callava whether the records were in his possession. Instead of replying, Callava in a low voice began to dictate to his secretary a protest against his arrest. Informed of what Callava was doing, Jackson shouted at the secretary to stop writing. Whereupon Callava again sought refuge behind his commission until Jackson told him he had summoned him as a private citizen whom he charged with refusing to surrender papers belonging to Mercedes Vidal and with scheming with others to remove them from Florida. Callava began to harangue his spectators on the indignities he had suffered as a royal commissioner. This time Jackson told him in an angry voice not to use the word commissioner again. When Callava continued to rant about indignities and to beseech his friend Innerarity to help him, Jackson, quivering with rage, picked up a pen and signed a paper remanding him to prison.[68]

Next day Jackson had the records seized. Then he signed an order for Callava's release. But before this could be executed, Judge Egilius Fromentin, one of Callava's best friends, had granted him a writ of habeus corpus. Jackson immediately rejected the writ and ordered the judge to appear before him to explain his attempted interference with authority that belonged to him alone as supreme judge of the territory. No sooner did Fromentin arrive than Jackson upbraided him for issuing a writ without an affidavit and, indeed, without any authority. He told him that his action was "unaccountable, indecorous, and unjustifiable," and that it bespoke his general ignorance of legal knowledge. The frightened judge meekly admitted that his writ had been ill-advised. To Secretary Adams the tempestuous general explained that Fromentin's jurisdiction extended only to revenue laws and to acts pertaining to the importation of slaves. Jackson later heard the case himself. It furnished a tragi-comic anticlimax to the whole episode. When the Vidal records were examined and all accounts settled, they showed that Mercedes Vidal owed Forbes & Company one hundred fifty-seven dollars![69]

Jackson had accepted his office of military governor reluctantly and only until he could organize a government for the territory. Now that this had been achieved, he informed Monroe that he was returning to Tennessee. The president sent him a letter asking him to remain at his post; but before it could reach him, says Marquis James, "the handsome carriage, drawn by four white horses, had emerged from the Government House gate and crossed the flowering Plaza. A sentry presented arms, and the Gargantuan quit the land of Lilliput."[70]

In March, 1822, Congress established civil government in Florida Territory. Its first governor was William Pope DuVal. He remained at his post for twelve years, a witty and charming man, grappling with vigor and unflinching courage the enormous task of trying to change Florida from a Spanish to an American territory. Like his Huguenot ancestors, who had been driven from France by the revocation of the Edict of Nantes and had settled in Virginia, he showed in his youth an avid taste for high adventure and nomadic living, which took him to the wilderness of Kentucky, where he spent much of his time hunting. But with maturity came a need for the security of a profession; abandoning his hazardous and uncomfortable existence, he turned to the study of law with hardly more than the rudiments of an education. But his ignorance proved no match for his persistence and diligence: in 1804 he was admitted to the bar. Then he had the good fortune to meet Washington Irving who, seeing in him all the virtues and none of the vices of the ideal frontiersman and therefore the personification of America, wrote several stories admirably depicting his career under the name of Ralph Ringwood. He was serving as a judge of East Florida when, on April 17, 1822, he was commissioned to succeed Jackson as the first civil governor of Florida Territory.

In the first meeting of his legislative council DuVal discovered that Pensacola was in an inconvenient location for the territorial capital. Because of the lack of roads, the delegates from East Florida had to travel by water and did not reach Pensacola for six weeks after the meeting was scheduled to begin. For the next meeting, the delegates tried St. Augustine; but their delight in its charms did not blind them to the hard reality that it was just as inconvenient for the delegates of West Florida as Pensacola had been for those of East Florida. They agreed that they needed a permanent capital somewhere between the two towns, which would enable them to preserve for their labors the energies they had been expending on their journeys, to lessen the risk of damaging their records, and to obviate the possibility of jealousy between the two sections. Thereupon DuVal appointed two commissioners, Dr. W. H. Simmons of St. Augustine and John Lee Williams of Pensacola, to locate a site for a new capital. After considerable search they found, just south of the deserted fields of Tallahassee, an elevated tract that invited immediate occupation. On March 24, 1824, DuVal proclaimed it the new seat of government. He allowed it to retain its Indian name, Tallahassee, meaning "sun town" in the Seminole tongue. Congress approved it, donating a quarter-section of land on which to build the town and permitting the surrounding quarter-sections to be sold to provide funds for public buildings. The first edifice of the new town was a log cabin, which served the delegates as their place of meeting. Presently settlers, realizing the political and economic advantages of living in the territorial capital, migrated to it in increasing numbers from all parts of Florida and from adjacent states. By the time the council convened in the fall of the year Tallahassee was well on its way to becoming a thriving town, though for some years longer it continued to press close to the great wilderness and to the Seminole villages, which regarded it with unfriendly eyes.[71]

The increase of white population in northern Florida, where the government expected to raise the cession price of $5,000,000, forced DuVal to come to some decision in regard to the Seminoles. At first he was conciliatory toward them; but, sensing the unpopularity of his stand, he reverted to Jackson's policy of removing them from the territory, either to join the Creeks or to resettle west of the Mississippi. The Seminoles were a composite tribe of Muskogee and Hitchiti, of Upper and Lower Creeks and Yamasees, and of Negroes or the descendants of Negroes who had run away from South Carolina to Florida and became Spanish subjects. Calling themselves Seminoles, meaning "separatist" or "runaway," they cultivated the soil and raised herds under the irresponsible freedom of decadent Spanish rule. When in 1790 the Creeks signed their first treaty with the United States, they promised to placate the people of Georgia by promising to restore all the Negroes who lived among the Seminoles. But the latter repudiated the Creek promises on the ground that they were an independent tribe. This claim of the whites and the promise of the Creeks and their pretense of authority over the Seminoles produced the tragic Indian wars that run practically throughout the annals of territorial Florida.[72]

The number of runaway Negroes increased with the white settlers, who in turn increased their raids into Seminole country in search of their slaves and other property. Now that Florida was a part of the United States, the federal government resolved to remove this long-standing and vexatious situation. In September, 1823, it sent a commission to negotiate a treaty with the tribe. The commission met seventy Indians under Neamathla at Moultrie Creek, seven miles south of St. Augustine, and told them that they must remove from their cultivated fields on the Suwannee and Apalachicola rivers to the interior country below Tampa Bay. Neamathla objected to the move to this reservation, because the soil was too poor to sustain him and his people:

> We are poor and needy; we do not come here to murmur or complain; . . . we rely on your justice and humanity; we hope you will not send us south, to a country where neither the hickory nut, the acorn, nor the persimmon grows. . . . For me, I am old and poor; too poor to move from my village to the south. I am attached to the spot improved by my own labor, and cannot believe that my friends will drive me from it.[73]

The allusion to the acorn and the hickory nut was by no means idle talk. Like other Indian tribes, the Seminoles needed oils, which they derived from nuts. As for Neamathla's abject humbleness, it was calculated to impress not his own people but the commissioners. He sought as favorable terms as he could possibly get. His plea for humanity and justice may have influenced the commissioners to modify the instructions they had received from the federal government.[74]

To remove the opposition of Neamathla and some other chiefs, the commissioners bribed them with reservations of from two to eight square miles in the valley of the Apalachicola River, so they were not forced to move to the interior Neamathla professed to detest. This enabled the commissioners to persuade the remaining chiefs to sign the treaty. By its principal provision, the Seminoles agreed to prevent runaway slaves from entering their country and to restore to the Indian agent those who were living among them. For $6000 worth of agricultural equipment and livestock and an annuity of $5000 for twenty years, they gave up all of their best lands to the federal government. The treaty provided $2000 for their transportation to the reservation assigned to them.[75]

No American agent saw this reservation for two years after the treaty was signed. Then DuVal sent an agent to examine it. He found it so poor that no part of it could be cultivated or settled, that a fire had ravaged one of the villages, and that its "burned and blackened pines, without a leaf, added to the dreary poverty of the land," which presented "the most miserable and gloomy prospect I ever beheld."[76] Under such circumstances, how could the Seminoles hope to sustain themselves? Many of them were forced to return to their old homes, where they soon became involved again in troubles with their white neighbors. More runaway slaves joined them. The whites complained to the secretary of war, who permitted them to search the Seminole country for their slaves. The Seminoles, incensed that their own slaves or the freedmen with whom they had intermarried should be taken from them, went on the warpath. And the whites, of course, resumed their rapacities. They flogged and killed Indians, seized their slaves, killed their livestock, burned their villages. Again misery stalked the land; again Indian agents sought a treaty with the Seminoles. This time they urged them to move with their slaves west of the Mississippi, where they would be forever free of outrages by their white neighbors. But the Seminoles, suspecting that the American government planned to send them back to the Creeks, refused to negotiate with its commissioners.[77]

On May 28, 1830, Congress, through the powerful influence of President Andrew Jackson, enacted the Indian Removal Law. Though it neither enforced their removal nor menaced them, it empowered the president to initiate steps to secure exchanges of land with any tribe "residing within the limits of the states or otherwise." He sent commissioners to make the new law known to the tribes and to persuade them to move to the west. The commissioner to the Seminoles, James Gadsden, now a colonel, joined by Indian agent Major John Phagan, summoned the tribe to a conference at Payne's Landing on the Oklawaha River. There on May 9, 1832, they signed a treaty by which they agreed to relinquish their lands in the "Big Swamp" and to migrate to the reservation already assigned to the Creeks west of the Mississippi. Before they signed the treaty, they requested and obtained from the commissioners permission to take an exploratory party consisting of seven of their own chiefs to the country in which the American government wished them to locate. The treaty specified that they were to migrate in three shifts, one-third in 1833; one-third in 1834, and the rest in 1835.[78]

Early in November, 1832, the Seminole explorers arrived by steamboat at Little Rock, in Arkansas Territory, and proceeded on horseback to Fort Gibson, where they allowed John Blunt, head of the Apalachicola band, and the American commissioners for the region to bamboozle them into signing another treaty in which they were made to say that they were satisfied to settle with the Creeks on the part of the reservation between the Canadian and the North Fork rivers. They did not know that Blunt had accepted from his American friends a bribe of $3000 in cash and a promise of $10,000 when they had moved. The preamble in the Treaty of Payne's Landing stated that, should "they"—obviously meaning the Seminoles—be satisfied with the country their explorers examined, they would agree to leave; but in the Treaty of Fort Gibson the preamble was made to read, "should this delegation be satisfied," with the aim of getting them to sign for something they had never considered. The government then insisted that the Treaty of Fort Gibson had become effective and demanded that the Seminoles prepare to move within the specified time to the reservation in Arkansas Territory.[79]

No sooner had the Seminole explorers returned to their homes in Florida than they realized they had been tricked. They refused to heed either treaty. They found a champion in Osceola, undoubtedly the greatest man their tribe has produced and one of the most admired chiefs in American history. Born perhaps east of the Chattahoochee River, in present Georgia, about the beginning of the nineteenth century, he was regarded by many whites as the son of a Creek woman and an English fur trader named Powell. But George Catlin, whose masterful pictorial documentary record of portraits and scenes of Indian life is justly famous, knew Osceola well, painted his portrait twice, and informs us that the chief spoke only his native tongue and that his general appearance and actions were "those of a full-blooded and wild Indian."[80] Osceola himself always claimed that he was a full-blooded Muskogee Indian.[81] But though historians disagree about his parentage, they generally agree about his personal appearance. One of the best contemporary descriptions of him is that of Jacob Rhett Motte, an army surgeon who served "in camp and field" during the Seminole Wars:

. . . his person, rather below than above the common height, was elegantly formed, with hands and feet effeminately small. He had a countenance expressive of much thought and cunning, and though when captured evidently sad and care-worn, the fire of his flashing eyes was unsubdued. His forehead was tolerably high, and cast in an intellectual mold—the upper portion which was generally concealed by his hair being worn low and hanging out in front expressed dignity and firmness, while the full arched brow indicated a man who thought much and intensely. His eyes were black and piercing; and when animated were full of dark fire, but when in repose they were softer than the soft eye of woman. His mouth, when relieved by a smile, wore an expression of great sweetness;—and his lips were chiselled with the accuracy of sculpture. His address was easy, and his bearings affable and courtly; in his salutations full of smiles, and like most of the Indians, hearty in the shake of his hand.[82]

He was not a hereditary chief. He owed his elevation to his energy and talent. By his shrewdness and sagacity he exercised over his followers an autocratic power that enabled him to organize a band of laggards into a formidable military force. In eloquent addresses he repeatedly told them that their primary duty was to resist any effort to take them away from their Florida lands.[83]

In 1834 the American government, insisting that the Seminoles comply with the treaties they had signed, sent General Wiley Thompson to summon them in the fall, when their annuity became available for distribution. He told the assembled Indians that the government expected them to move by the following spring. Perhaps acting on Osceola's instructions, they obtained permission to discuss the matter in private. When they reassembled they told Thompson that in their opinion the

Treaty of Moultrie Creek had seven more years to run. Thompson sent them away for further deliberation. On their return they reiterated their belief that the treaty was valid for twenty years and that their assent to the later treaties had been obtained by fraud. Thompson then drew a gloomy picture of their future if they insisted on remaining in Florida, saying that their annuity would be stopped. Osceola replied with great firmness that he did not care whether it was ever paid. Thompson then closed the conference with the hope that, on more mature reflection, they would act like honest men and not force him to report them as faithless to their promises.[84]

In the following spring Thompson, joined by Duncan L. Clinch, now a general, called the Indians to another conference. This time Thompson read to them a forceful and admonitory message from President Jackson; but it failed to sway them in their determination to remain in Florida. Clinch then warned them that he had been sent to enforce the treaty, and that he had with him enough soldiers to realize his mission. This veiled threat enraged Osceola. Suspecting Thompson of instigating it, he insulted him "by some insolent remarks." This furnished Thompson with an opportunity to deprive the Seminoles of their leader. He had Osceola arrested, put in chains, and confined to Fort King. For hours Osceola remained in a state of frenzy; then, collecting himself, he sent for Charley Amathla, who was less averse to migration than any of the other chiefs, and solicited his intercession. Thompson, believing Osceola's protests of repentance, freed him and presented him with an expensive rifle as token of their reconciliation.[85]

Of course Osceola had no intention of respecting the treaty. Soon after his release he held a secret meeting of the chiefs in which he persuaded most of them to adopt a policy of armed resistance. Of the leading chiefs only Charley Amathla expressed a reluctant inclination to comply with the wishes of the government. Osceola, regarding him as a potential traitor, resolved to kill him. With twelve followers he surprised the chief, two of his daughters, and one of his Negro slaves as they made their way homeward from Fort King, where they had declared their willingness to migrate.[86]

Having consolidated his position by ridding himself of a potential enemy in his ranks, Osceola resolved on armed resistance. He turned to avenge the wrongs Thompson had inflicted on him and his people. With fifty of his followers he lurked around Fort King for several days, waiting for the agent to show himself. On December 28, 1835, they saw Thompson strolling with Lieutenant Constantine Smith a few hundred yards from the fort. They fired from ambush, killing both men. Howling in triumph, they next attacked a nearby store; but its owner, Erastus Rogers, had anticipated them and had moved his merchandise to Fort King. Rogers' cook, hiding in the empty store, identified Osceola, while a few friendly Indians at the fort recognized his shrill war cry.[87]

On the same day a company of troops, consisting of eight officers and one hundred two noncommissioned officers and privates under Major Francis L. Dade, rode from Fort Brooke toward Fort King to assist in the enforced removal of the Seminoles. Near the Great Wahoo Swamp, six or seven miles north of the Withlacoochee River, Dade and his men were ambushed by a large group of Indians and Negroes. All of them were killed save three who, despite their serious wounds, bore news of the massacre individually and successively to Fort Brooke. The massacre struck such terror in the soldiers that none of them dared to visit the spot until February, 1836, when Captain Ethan Allen Hitchcock ventured there to bury the dead.[88]

In the previous month Osceola wrote to Clinch, saying that he was ready to wage war for five years. "You have guns, and so have we—you have powder and lead, and so have we—you have men, and so have we—your men will fight, and so will ours, till the last drop of the Seminole's blood has moistened the dust of his hunting ground."[89]

The government answered this challenge by ordering regulars and volunteers to Florida from neighboring states. At New Orleans, General Gaines took command of eleven hundred men, including seven hundred volunteers, and sailed with them in three steamboats to Tampa Bay. Joined there by seventy-seven friendly Indians, he marched through the country to Fort King, where, however, he found no provisions for his men and horses. Disgusted, he turned back toward Tampa Bay; but when, on February 27, he was about to cross the Withlacoochee, he was attacked by several hundred Indians under Osceola and two of his confederates, Jumper and Alligator. Gaines fortified his camp, which later was named in honor of one of his officers, James Izard, and sent to Clinch for reinforcements. While he waited, his provisions gave out. He was forced to order his men to kill some of their horses for food.[90]

On the night of March 5 they heard a stentorian voice, which some of them identified as that of the Negro, Abraham, asking for an interview in the morning. Gaines assented. Next day the soldiers saw the enemy defiling to the rear of the camp under a white flag. Major Barrows, with Hagan as his interpreter, also under a white flag, approached and asked them what they wanted to communicate. Jumper replied through Abraham that the Indians were tired of fighting and wanted Gaines to go away. The general instructed one of his officers, Hitchcock, to tell them that he lacked authority to make terms, but that they could show their desire for peace by refraining from further hostility and by withdrawing to the south bank of the Withlacoochee to await summons of a council from the great chief, Winfield Scott, who was soon expected. At this juncture Clinch arrived with reinforcements and, ignorant of what was taking place, fired on the Indians, who fled in the belief that they had been betrayed.[91]

Scott arrived in Florida only to be transferred to direct operations against hostile Indians in Alabama. His successor in Florida was Richard Keith Call, a Virginian and a veteran of the Battle of New Orleans who in March, 1836, had been appointed governor of Florida Territory. In October of that year the governor with a small force of Florida militia and Tennessee mounted volunteers surprised a small band of Indians near Fort Drane; but his military reputation dwindled when he failed to win any other victory or to persuade the Indians to make a peace treaty. So in December President Jackson replaced him with Major General Thomas S. Jesup, who began a brutal campaign against Seminole bands lurking along the Withlacoochee. He burned villages, killed hundreds of cattle and horses, captured ponies often loaded with packs for a quick getaway, and destroyed stores of coontie root, from which the Seminoles made bread by scraping, mashing, and placing it in a sack and draining off its liquor which, settling, left a flourlike powder. At one place the Indians, seeing Jesup's men approaching, took alarm and plunged into a thick growth of palmettos and small trees immediately beyond their camp. The soldiers found three pots of coontie root and palmetto cabbage boiling on the fire and wooden spoons in a small wooden bowl, a rifle, bow and arrows, two shot pouches and powder horns, a tomahawk, two axes, scalping knives, blankets, skins, and several ornamental trinkets of silver and beads. "The poor devils," wrote one of the officers, "are driven into the swamps and must die next summer if not before, from the effects of being constantly in the deep, low, and foggy ground. And yet they will not go. . . . There is a charm, a magic . . . in the land of one's birth." In January, 1837, some of Jesup's mounted men and Indians took sixteen prisoners whose families had been slain. Among them were two widows, each with a child on her back and another at her breast. One of the officers could not look at them without pity and compassion. His heart bled, he wrote, when he recalled that the sun "rose upon them with peace in their cabins, and in company of the husbands of their youth; but ere the noon arrived, they were bereft and desolate, and their children fatherless."[92]

Jesup's ruthless campaign produced the desired effect. In February a faction of the tribe sent Abraham to tell Jesup that it was tired of fighting and that it wanted peace. The general summoned the chiefs to meet him in conference at Camp Dade, where on March 6 they signed what he called a capitulation. They agreed to immediate peace, immediate migration, immediate withdrawal to the south of the Hillsborough River. They agreed to assemble by April 10 at a designated place near Tampa Bay, where they would be fed and clothed until they should board transports. Jesup assured them that their lives and properties would be protected, and that they would be allowed to keep their slaves, whom they regarded as their legitimate property. As a guarantee for the performance of their promises, they surrendered old chief Mikanopy, who on March 18 came to Camp Dade and said he was ready to go west. Gradually seven hundred Seminoles assembled near the post. Among their chiefs were Jumper, who, suffering from tuberculosis, was in low spirits; Alligator, a shrewd, active man with an inexhaustible fund of good humor; and young Wild Cat, whose father, Philip, was the most influential chief on the St. Johns River. Many Indians, heeding the reports of mischievous whites that they would be executed, fled in terror. Others stayed away because they were afraid of contracting measles, which had spread to the camp from the army.[93]

Osceola spurned any thought of surrender. While the old chiefs "came in," he "folded his arms and walked away." Gathering around him two hundred braves—all that remained to him—he planned to invade the Indian camp, abduct the chiefs, and lure and force their followers to escape. On the night of June 2 he and Sam Jones, a Negro, surrounded the camp with some braves and easily accomplished their purpose. Mikanopy refused to go, saying that he had signed a treaty and that he proposed to abide by it. Ignoring his objections, Osceola had him put on a horse and taken away. He forced Jumper, who had sold his mount, to walk. By daylight the camp was empty.[94]

Depressed by what he regarded as his failure, Jesup offered to give up his command in Florida; but he reconsidered and stayed on. During the rest of the summer the unhealthful weather prevented him from beginning another campaign against the escaped Indians. And now even Osceola longed for peace. In the previous year he had contracted malaria; he "suffered severely from chills and fever which, with an injury he received by a shot through the hand at the Withlacoochee, . . . prevented him from taking much part in the war."[95] Too weak from disease and undernourishment to meet the rigors of warfare and unwilling to prolong the intense sufferings of his people, he resolved to remain inactive unless he was attacked. And in September an event occurred which increased the possibility of peace. One of the American officers, Joseph A. Hernandez, captured Philip and his band by a surprise night attack on his camp. He brought his prisoners to St. Augustine, where he permitted Philip to send to the members of his family a message requesting them to come and share in his captivity. His son, Wild Cat, responded with his presence, telling Hernandez that, since he had come voluntarily, he should be permitted to visit his father and then to depart without hindrance. He promised to use his influence to persuade his people to surrender with their Negroes and their cattle. Hernandez granted his request. Wild Cat was as good as his word. Two weeks after his departure he returned with his uncle and his youngest brother. He also brought word that Osceola, with some other chiefs and about a hundred braves, was about a day's journey away. Osceola desired to come in for a conference.[96]

Two days later two Indians appeared in Hernandez' headquarters. The spokesman announced that he represented Jumper and Mikanopy, and that he bore from Osceola a message requesting a peace conference and expressing his regrets for the errors he had committed in the past. Osceola asked Hernandez to visit him alone at his camp near Fort Peyton; but Jesup, who had recently arrived in St. Augustine, suspected treachery; he forbade Hernandez to visit Osceola without an escort. At the same time he ordered Lieutenant Peyton, commander at Fort Peyton, to seize Osceola and his party should they come in. Hernandez himself, with an escort of two hundred men, proceeded toward the Indian camp, which he could discern from a distance by its flying white flag. Standing under it, Osceola shook hands with Hernandez and the members of his staff.

"What people have come with you?" asked Hernandez.

"All that are well and could gather," replied the chiefs.

"I speak to you as a friend: what induced you to come?"

"We came for good . . . "

"What do you expect from me?"

"We don't know."

"Have you come to give up to me as your friend?"

"No, we did not understand so; word went from here, and we have come; we have done nothing all summer, and want to make peace."

"In what way to make peace?"

"They thought they would come in and make peace, with liberty to walk about."

"Are you ready to give up all the property that you have captured?"

"We intend to do so, to bring in what is due to the white people; we have brought a good many Negroes in now."

"Why did not Mikanopy, Jumper, and Cloud come, instead of sending a message?"

"They all got the measles and could not come."

"What word did they send by you?"

"When they get stronger they will come and see you."

"I am an old friend of Philip's and wish you all well; but we have been deceived so often, that it is necessary for you to come with me; you can send out a messenger; you shall stay with me and none of you shall be hurt."[97]

Before they could reply, Hernandez had them surrounded, disarmed, and made prisoners. With Osceola were thirteen other chiefs, seventy-one warriors, six women, and four Negroes, with forty-seven rifles. Of the Indians, only Osceola and two other chiefs rode horses as they marched between a double file of soldiers to St. Augustine. One of the officers, Jarvis, rode beside Osceola and observed that the chief, though far from despondent, was so weak that he could scarcely sit on his horse. The prisoners were confined in Fort Marion. Jesup, noticing the absence of children and the meager number of women in the party, believed that Osceola's purpose in coming to Fort Peyton was not to make peace but to gain Philip's release either by stratagem or assault.[98]

But that piece of white cloth under which Osceola was seized made him immortal, while it brought down on the head of his captor a deluge of condemnation from every part of the United States. Soon after his capture, Osceola died. He became a martyr to what most Americans regarded as Jesup's treachery. A score of states named towns in Osceola's honor; Iowa, Michigan, and Florida each bestowed his name on one of their counties. Only those Floridians who lived in the region of the Seminoles seem to have approved of Jesup's violation of the flag of truce, though they had lived on good terms with the Indians for many years and counted some of them among their friends. Sentiment against Jesup seems to have increased with distance. So bitter were the innumerable editorials in American newspapers that Congress felt constrained to ask the secretary of war for an explanation. The secretary of war submitted to Congress Jesup's own explanation of his conduct:

> As I had informed the chiefs at Fort King that I would hold no communication with the Seminoles unless they should determine to emigrate; as I had permitted no Indian to come in for any other purpose but to remain; as they were all prisoners of war, or hostages who had violated their parole; as many of them had violated the truce entered into at Fort King, by occupying the country east of the St. Johns, by allowing predatory parties to go to the frontier, and by killing at least one white man, and as the white flag had been allowed for no other purpose than to enable them to communicate and come in without danger of attack from our parties, it became my duty to secure them on being satisfied of the fact that they intended to return to their fastnesses. . . . I accordingly required General Hernandez to seize them.[99]

On November 30 Wild Cat complicated matters for his captive friends by escaping from Fort Marion with nineteen men and two women. This convinced the insecure Jesup that the old fort was too weak to hold his savage charges. He ordered them removed to Charleston, South Carolina. Accordingly, on December 31, Mikanopy, Osceola, Philip, and other chiefs, together with one hundred sixteen warriors and eighty-two women and children, were put on board the *Poinsett*, which took them to their destination on the first day of 1838. They were soon transferred to Fort Moultrie on Sullivan's Island. On his arrival Osceola, as well as the other chiefs, were permitted the freedom of the enclosure. On January 6 they attended a play in a Charleston theater.[100]

Learning that Osceola was at Fort Moultrie, George Catlin arrived there to paint his portrait. He found the chiefs talkative and fond of his company, though they complained bitterly, through an interpreter, of the manner in which they had been captured. In about a week Catlin had finished one portrait of Osceola and had started another. Day by day the artist noticed Osceola's face and body sinking under the onslaughts of disease. He consulted Dr. Frederick Weedon, physician at Fort Moultrie, who told him that Osceola did not have long to live. Before Catlin could finish the second portrait, Osceola developed quinsy or putrid sore throat, "a topical diagnosis which has several etiological implications, but which could not have been related to his chronic malaria infection, which however, had probably lowered his vitality."[101]

Dr. Weedon prevented him from suffocating by setting him up in bed. His pulse was full, quick, hard. At that moment an Indian prophet, or conjurer, entered the room. Thenceforth Osceola refused all medication. Alarmed, Weedon called in Dr. B. B. Strobel to help him try to persuade Osceola to submit to treatment. Osceola permitted Strobel to examine his throat. The doctor found that the tonsils were so much enlarged that they impeded breathing and that the mucous membrane of the pharynx was greatly inflamed. He asked the patient to allow him to arrest the disease by scarifying his throat. Osceola referred to his conjurer, who was sitting on the floor with his blanket wrapped around him. "No!" he replied with imperial dignity. Then Strobel proposed that he apply leeches to the throat and back of the ears. "No!" thundered the conjurer. Then Strobel asked for permission to apply medication to Osceola's throat. Again the conjurer strenuously refused. Next day Osceola, sensing that he was dying, signified that he wanted Weedon to send in the chiefs and officers. Then he made signs to his two wives to fetch him his war dress. He put on the shirt, leggings, and moccasins, and girded on the war belt with its scalping knife. Holding his looking-glass before him, he painted red one-half of his face, his neck and throat, his wrists and backs of his hands, and the handle of his knife. He placed the knife in its sheath and carefully fixed on his head his turban with its three ostrich feathers. For a few minutes he lay flat to recover what strength remained to him; then, sitting up, he smiled as he extended his hands to Weedon, to the officers, to the chiefs, to his two wives, and to his two fine little children. Signaling for them to lower him on his bed, he slowly drew his scalping knife and laid it on his breast. Then, without a struggle, without a groan, he smiled away his last breath.[102]

When Weedon was alone with the body, he cut off the head, though he left it in the coffin with a scarf which Osceola habitually wore around his neck. Shortly before the funeral Weedon removed the head from the coffin and took it to St. Augustine, where he embalmed it. What was his motive in severing Osceola's head? His granddaughter, May McNeer Ward, offers this explanation:

It is hard to know his motives, for we are so far removed by time from the events and the way of thinking of those days. However, doctors then thought nothing of collecting heads of savage tribesmen. Medical museums had collections of heads brought in by sailors from South America, Africa and the South Seas. Phrenology was considered important, for the shape of the skull was thought by scientists to show intelligence as well as talents and aptitudes. Dr. Weedon was an unusual man, and his methods of child training would not find favor today, for he used to hang the head of Osceola on the bedstead where his three little boys slept, and leave it there all night as punishment for misbehavior.[103]

The death of Osceola by no means brought peace to Florida Territory. Wild Cat, who, we will recall, had escaped from Fort Marion, resumed hostilities, confounding by his intrepidity and resourcefulness the strategies of some of the most experienced officers in the American Army. In 1838 the hated Jesup gave way to Zachary Taylor, who built roads deep into Seminole country, where he erected seventy stockades at strategic points. Yet Wild Cat and his associates proved so elusive that they were able to pick off many of Taylor's soldiers with impunity. Though a good many Seminoles with their chiefs surrendered and accepted migration, some of them because of illness, enough remained to cause Taylor much fretting and frowning. He succeeded in finding and destroying only a small part of the Seminole huts and cornfields. At last, in desperation, he asked Governor Call for permission to use bloodhounds in scenting down the invisible warriors, though he promised not to use them against women and children. The governor granted his request, purchasing from Cuba thirty-three bloodhounds at over one hundred fifty dollars each and having them trained under combat conditions. The dogs proved useless. The numerous bogs, swamps, lakes, and streams of Florida prevented them from scenting anything at any considerable distance from their noses. They became a standing joke as far away as Georgia. One newspaper of that state alluded to them as "Cuba curs," good for nothing save to feast "upon their six pounds of fresh beef per day. . . . As to their ferocity, it is all humbug—a child may fondle with them. They have been more grossly misrepresented than any set of animals in the world."[104]

Meanwhile, in April, 1839, General Alexander Macomb had arrived in Florida to supercede the frustrated Taylor as commander in the territory. The president hoped that Macomb's superior rank as commander-in-chief of American forces would impress the Indians with the desirability of making peace. On May 22 Macomb called the chiefs to a conference, at which he received them with every mark of friendship. He uttered not a word about removal. Instead he urged them to retire to the country near Lake Okeechobee, with a guarantee of protection from the whites as long as they remained there. But his treaty proved vain when the whites, having enjoyed considerable prosperity in keeping and feeding the American soldiers, demanded for the Indians "nothing short of absolute removal or annihilation."[105] The Indians, suspecting treachery, surprised Colonel William S. Harvey, who, in agreement with the treaty, had been sent to establish a trading post at Charlotte Harbor. Eighteen of Harvey's party were killed.[106]

The struggle continued for four years more. By 1842 American troops had, by hook or crook, succeeded in rounding up all of the Seminoles in the territory save about three hundred. Weary of the struggle, Colonel William J. Worth, now commander of the territory, offered from $200 to $500 and a rifle to any warrior who would surrender. No longer dominated by Wild Cat, who had surrendered in the previous year, some Indians accepted the bribe, whereupon Worth announced that the war was over. But not quite. A few months later, when one of the imprisoned chiefs escaped with some of his band, Worth ordered Colonel Ethan Allen Hitchcock to "reopen" hostilities. But Hitchcock treated the Indians with such kindness that in a short time he gained their complete confidence. At last Chief Pascofa accepted peace on one condition: would Hitchcock give him a blanket—even an old horse blanket—for his wife? He was ashamed, he explained, of seeing her going around almost naked. Hitchcock presented him with the best blanket he owned. And Pascofa there and then surrendered and accepted migration together with his band. The remaining Seminoles agreed to retire to a reservation in southern Florida, where the descendants of some of them may be seen to this day.[107]

Coinciding with the long and bloody Seminole wars was the rapid economic development which led to the movement for statehood. The eastern and western regions of the territory joined for the first time when in 1826 John Bellamy and John Robinson, two wealthy planters, completed a road from St. Augustine to Pensacola. The opening of branch lines to this road attracted so many prospectors and travelers that in a decade both towns were flourishing with the lumber industry and the beginnings of the citrus industry. Even more engrossing in the field of speculative activity were the numerous projects for canals and railroads, though few were completed during the territorial period. The Tallahassee-St. Marks Railroad, completed in 1837, operated intermittently with mules and then with a steam engine providing the locomotion. Later, by reducing its rates on building materials and fertilizer during the dull months, it gained enough freight to run continually. The internal improvements led to the establishment of many banks which, "organized on speculative principles and supported by territorial or 'faith' bonds, grew into paper giants."[108] Most of them collapsed in the panic of 1837.

At this time Governor Call sent to the territorial council a message urging it to take specific measures toward statehood. The council responded by calling for the election of delegates to a constitutional convention to meet at St. Joseph in December, 1838. Call then appointed persons in each county to determine by a census whether the territory had sufficient population to assume the responsibility of statehood. The census, completed in May, showed 48,223 persons, of whom 21,132 were slaves and 958 free Negroes. Though this was about twelve thousand below the number required for statehood by the Northwest Ordinance of 1787, the council completed its plans for a constitutional convention. Its forty-six delegates spent most of their sessions in fiery and prolonged oratory and in debating banking and the banking laws. But at last on January 10, 1839, they adopted a constitution. No sooner was the convention adjourned, however, than the people of the territory became divided into supporters and detractors of statehood and the constitution. The constitution won by a slight margin; on October 21 it was ratified.

But soon active opposition to admission developed in East Florida, which, economically tied to the Atlantic seaboard, favored two states with the Suwannee River as the dividing line. Furthermore, it believed that statehood should wait until the Indians were removed. Under these circumstances Congress could hardly consider the numerous petitions praying for admission into the Union. But, eventually, statehood found a champion in David Levy, territorial delegate to Congress. On October 22, 1844, he published in a widely read newspaper a circular letter in which he pleaded for Southern solidarity. Pointing out the preponderance of Northern over Southern strength in the Senate, he urged his fellow Floridians to prevent further increase by supporting the admission of Florida as a slave state against the imminent admission of Iowa. His plea produced the desired effect. Backed by the majority of the people, statehood could no longer be delayed. By March 3, 1845, a bill for the admission of Florida and Iowa had passed the House of Representatives and the Senate, despite the opposition of some Northern senators who objected to the clauses favoring slavery in the constitution submitted by Florida.

Don Juan Ponce de León might well have pondered the inscrutability of history had he lived to learn that the first discovered and settled region of the Southern Frontier was the last to enter the Union.

Notes

CHAPTER I

1. Antonio de Herrera y Tordesillos, *Historia General de los Hechos de los Castellanos* . . . , II, 207; T. Frederick Davis, "History of Juan Ponce de León's Voyages to Florida," in *Florida Historical Quarterly*, XIV (1935), 11; T. Frederick Davis, "The Record of Ponce de León's Discovery of Florida," in *Florida Historical Quarterly*, XI (1932), 13, 26.

2. Woodbury Lowery, *The Spanish Settlements Within the Present Limits of the United States, 1513-1561*, p. 131. Hereinafter cited as Lowery, *Spanish Settlements*.

3. Bartolome de las Casas, *Historia General de las Indias*, II, 540; Edward W. Lawson, *The Discovery of Florida and Its Discoverer Juan Ponce de León*, p. 2.

4. *Ibid.*

5. Gonzalo Hernandez de Oviedo y Valdés, *Historia General y Natural de las Indias*, I, 547.

6. Herrera, II, 207.

7. F. Zarncke, "Der Priester Johannes," in *Abhandlingen der phil. hist.*, VII (1879), 912-13.

8. John Ashton, ed., *The Voiage and Travayle of Sir John Maundeville, Knight*, p. 128; Malcolm Letts, *Sir John Mandeville*, pp. 58, 110, 164.

9. Pedro Mártir de Angleria [Peter Martyr], *Decadas del Nuevo Mundo*, pp. 7, 8, 17, 535. Hereinafter cited as Martyr. Lawson, p. 12.

10. Contract of Ponce de León in regard to his discoveries in Brooks Transcripts, I (1500-1580), September 23, 1513. Lowery, *Spanish Settlements*, p. 135; T. F. Davis, "Ponce de León's Voyages," XIV, 10.

11. T. F. Davis, "Ponce de León's Discovery," XI, 10.

12. T. F. Davis, "Ponce de León's Voyages," XIV, 28.

13. Lawson, p. 38.

14. *Ibid.*

15. Lowery, *Spanish Settlements*, p. 142.

16. Herrera, II, 210.

17. *Ibid.*; Lawson, p. 40.

18. Herrera, II, 210; Lawson, p. 41; T. F. Davis, "Ponce de León's Voyages," XIV, 44.

19. Lowery, *Spanish Settlements*, pp. 146-47.

20. *Ibid.*, p. 148.

21. Oviedo, II, 622-23; Lowery, *Spanish Settlements*, p. 160; Garcilaso de la Vega, *The Florida of the Inca*, p. 638.

CHAPTER 2

1. Philip Ainsworth Means, *The Spanish Main*, pp. 105-06.

2. Lowery, *Spanish Settlements*, p. 154.

3. Martyr, pp. 407-08, 457, 507; Francisco López de Gómara, "De la Historia General de las Indias," in Enrique de Vedia, ed., *Historiadores Primitivos de Indias*, I, 179.

4. Oviedo, III, 629.

5. Bernal Díaz del Castillo, *The True History of the Conquest of Mexico*, pp. 213-66; Lowery, *Spanish Settlements*, p. 174.

6. *Ibid.*, p. 175; Morris Bishop, *The Odyssey of Cabeza de Vaca*, pp. 3-4; Álvar Nuñez Cabeza de Vaca, "Naufragios," in Enrique de Vedia, ed., *Historiadores Primitivos de Indias*, I, 517.

7. *Ibid.*

8. *Ibid.*, 518; Oviedo, III, 583. Author's translation.

9. *Ibid.*

10. *Ibid.*

11. *Ibid.*; Lowery, *Spanish Settlements*, p. 181; Bishop, p. 39.

12. Cabeza de Vaca, I, 520.

13. *Ibid.*; Herbert Eugene Bolton, *The Spanish Borderlands*, p. 21.

14. Cabeza de Vaca, I, 520-21.

15. *Ibid.*, 521.

16. *Ibid.*; Bishop, pp. 44-45.

17. Cabeza de Vaca, I, 521-22.

18. *Ibid.*, 522.

19. *Ibid.*

20. *Ibid.*, 523.

21. *Ibid.*

22. *Ibid.*, 524.

23. *Ibid.*, 525; Bishop, p. 55.

24. Cabeza de Vaca, I, 526.

25. *Ibid.*

26. *Ibid.*; Bishop, p. 57.

27. Cabeza de Vaca, I, 527.

28. *Ibid.*, 528.

CHAPTER 3

1. Bishop, p. 167; Lowery, *Spanish Settlements*, pp. 210-11.

2. *Ibid.*, pp. 213-15.

3. *See* Buckingham Smith, trans., "Concession Made to Hernando De Soto," in *Florida Historical Quarterly*, XVI (1938), 179.

4. The Fidalgo [Gentleman] of Elvas, "True Relation of the Vicissitudes That Attended the Governor Don Hernando de Soto and Some Nobles of Portugal in the Discovery of the Province of Florida," in Edward Gaylord Bourne, ed., *Narratives of the Career of Hernando de Soto*, I, 10.

5. *Ibid.*, 11; Bolton, *Spanish Borderlands*, pp. 48-49.

6. Elvas, I, 21.

7. John R. Swanton, "The Landing Place of De Soto," in *Florida Historical Quarterly*, XVI (1938), 150; Mark F. Boyd, "Arrival of De Soto's Expedition in Florida," in *ibid.*, 188; Theodore Maynard, *De Soto and the Conquistadores*, p. 141; *Final Report of the United States De Soto Expedition Commission* (1939), pp. 118-19; hereinafter cited as *U.S. Soto Commission*.

8. Bolton, *Spanish Borderlands*, p. 50.

9. Luis Hernandez de Biedma, "Relation of the Conquest of Florida," in Bourne, ed., *Narratives of the Career of Hernando de Soto*, II, 3-4; Rodrigo Ranjel, "Relation," in *ibid.*, II, 56-57.

10. Elvas, I, 34-35; La Vega, pp. 96-98.

11. Ranjel, II, 63-64; Maynard, pp. 159-60.

12. *Ibid.*, p. 160.

13. Elvas, I, 40.

14. Ranjel, II, 74; Maynard, pp. 164-68.

15. Elvas, I, 42-44; Ranjel, II, 76-77.

16. Maynard, p. 172; Bolton, *Spanish Borderlands*, p. 56; Elvas, I, 48; *U.S. Soto Commission*, p. 166.

17. Elvas, I, 53.

18. *Ibid.*, 64; Maynard, p. 187.

19. La Vega, pp. 297-301; Maynard, p. 189; Biedma, II, 13; *U.S. Soto Commission*, p. 171.

20. Elvas, I, 66; Biedma, II, 14; Ranjel, II, 98-100.

21. Elvas, I, 70; Bolton, *Spanish Borderlands*, p. 58.

22. Maynard, p. 197; Elvas, I, 71-72; *U.S. Soto Commission*, pp. 198-99.

23. Ranjel, II, 120-21; Elvas, I, 87-88; Maynard, pp. 204-05; *U.S. Soto Commission*, p. 200.

24. Ranjel, II, 122.

25. *Ibid.*, 124; Biedma, II, 16-17; Maynard, p. 206.

26. Ranjel, II, 125; Maynard, pp. 207-09; *U.S. Soto Commission*, pp. 216-17.

27. Elvas, I, 92-98; Ranjel, II, 126; Maynard, p. 211.

28. *Ibid.*, p. 212; Ranjel, II, 127.

29. *Ibid.*; Maynard, p. 212.

30. *Ibid.*; Ranjel, II, 127.

31. *Ibid.*; Maynard, p. 213.

32. *Ibid.*, p. 217; Elvas, I, 98-106.

33. *U.S. Soto Commission*, pp. 217-19; Maynard, p. 220; Elvas, I, 110-15.

34. *U.S. Soto Commission*, p. 220; Maynard, pp. 226-27; Elvas, I, 110-15.

35. Bolton, *Spanish Borderlands*, pp. 242-43.

36. Lowery, *Spanish Settlements*, pp. 242-43.

37. *Ibid.*, p. 244.

38. Bolton, *Spanish Borderlands*, pp. 74-78.

CHAPTER 4

1. Lowery, *Spanish Settlements*, p. 351; Bolton, *Spanish Borderlands*, p. 121.

2. Francis Augustus MacNutt, *Bartholomew de las Casas*, p. 188; Lowery, *Spanish Settlements*, p. 412.

3. *Ibid.;* Bolton, *Spanish Borderlands*, p. 123.

4. V. F. O'Daniel, *Dominicans in Early Florida*, pp. 47-49; Brooks Transcripts, I (1500-1580).

5. Bolton, *Spanish Borderlands*, p. 124; Lowery, *Spanish Settlements*, p. 417; O'Daniel, p. 61.

6. *Ibid.*, p. 61; Henri Ternaux-Compans, ed., *Recueil de Pièces sur la Floride*, pp. 107-144.

7. Andrés Gonzalez de Barcia Carballido y Zúñiga, *Chronological History of the Continent of Florida*, p. 27; John Gilmary Shea, *The Catholic Church in Colonial Days*, p. 125.

8. Buckingham Smith, ed., *Colección de Various Documentos, para la Historia de la Florida y Tierras Adyacentes*, pp. 190-202, gives Father Cancer's account of his expedition.

9. *Ibid.*

10. *Ibid.*

11. *Ibid.*

12. Augustin Dávila Padilla, *Historia de la Fundación y Discurso de la Provincia . . .*, pp. 225-26.

13. John Lothrop Motley, *The Rise of the Dutch Republic*, I, 148-57; William Hickling Prescott, *Philip II*, I, 25-28.

14. Means, *The Spanish Main*, pp. 58-60; Herbert Ingram Priestley, *Tristan de Luna*, pp. 56-58.

15. *Ibid.;* Shea, p. 127.

16. Priestley, *Tristan de Luna*, p. 74.

17. *Ibid.*, p. 64-79; Herbert Ingram Priestley, ed., *The Luna Papers*, I, xxviii-xxxii; Charles W. Arnade, "Tristan de Luna and Ochuse (Pensacola Bay) 1559" in *Florida Historical Quarterly*, XXXVII (1958), 208-210.

18. Priestley, *Tristan de Luna*, pp. 97-99; Velasco to Luna, Mexico, October 25, 1559, in Priestley, ed., *Luna Papers*, I, 57-79.

19. Luna to Philip II, Port of Santa Maria, September 24, 1559, in *ibid.*, II, 245-47.

20. *Ibid.*

21. Priestley, *Tristan de Luna*, p. 109; Priestley, ed., *Luna Papers*, II, 281-88; Arnade, "Tristan de Luna," XXXVII, 215.

22. Lowery, *Spanish Settlements*, p. 362.

23. Barcia, p. 36; Dávila, p. 249.

24. Lowery, *Spanish Settlements*, p. 365.

25. Barcia, pp. 36-37.

26. *Ibid.*, pp. 37-38; Dávila, p. 255.

27. Barcia, p. 38.

28. Dávila, pp. 265-67; Lowery, *Spanish Settlements*, p. 368.

29. Priestley, *Tristan de Luna*, p. 146.

30. Barcia, p. 39.

31. *Ibid.*, p. 40.

32. *Ibid.*

33. *Ibid.*, p. 42; *see also* Michael Kenny, *The Romance of the Floridas*, p. 86.

34. Barcia, p. 42.

35. Dávila, p. 273.

36. Bolton, *Spanish Borderlands*, pp. 134-35.

CHAPTER 5

1. Woodbury Lowery, *The Spanish Settlements Within the Present Limits of the United States. Florida, 1562-1574*, pp. 30-31; hereinafter cited as Lowery, *Florida*.

2. Jean Ribaut, "Voyage," in Richard Hakluyt, ed., *The Voyages, Traffiques & Discoveries of Foreign Voyagers*, X, 16.

3. *Ibid.*, 17.

4. *Ibid.*, 20.

5. *Ibid.*, 26-27; *see* Charles E. Bennett, "Fort Caroline, Cradle of American Freedom," in *Florida Historical Quarterly*, XXXV (1956), 4.

6. Ribaut, X, 31-32.

7. *Ibid.*, 33-35.

8. *Ibid.*, 37.

9. *Ibid.*, 37-38.

10. *Ibid.*, 39-40.

11. Lowery, *Florida*, pp. 37-38; J. Leitch Wright, Jr., "Sixteenth Century English-Spanish Rivalry in Florida" in *Florida Historical Quarterly*, XXXVIII (1960), 267-71.

12. Lowery, *Florida*, pp. 53-54; Jacques Le Moyne de Morgues, "Narrative," in Stefan Lorant, ed. and trans., *The New World*, p. 36.

13. Lowery, *Florida*, pp. 54-55; René Laudonnière, "Voiage," in Hakluyt, ed., X, 47.

14. *Ibid.*

15. *Ibid.*, 48.

16. Quoted in Lowery, *Florida*, p. 56.

17. Laudonnière, X, 53-54.

18. Lowery, *Florida*, pp. 60-61.

19. *Ibid.*

20. *Ibid.*, pp. 63-64.

21. *Ibid.*, p .67.

22. *Ibid.*, p. 68.

23. *Ibid.*

24. *See* Francisco Pareja, "*Confessionario*," in A. S. Gatschet, "The Timucuan Language," in *Proceedings of the American Philosophical Society*, XVII (1878), 500-01.

25. Lowery, *Florida*, pp. 69-70.

26. *Ibid.*, pp. 70-71.

27. *Ibid.*

28. *See* picture and explanation in Le Moyne, p. 57.

29. *Ibid.*, p. 59.

30. Lowery, *Florida*, p. 73; *see* picture in Le Moyne, pp. 63, 67.
31. Lowery, *Florida*, p. 74.
32. Laudonnière, X, 56; Francis Parkman, *Pioneers of France in the New World*, p. 53.
33. Laudonnière, X, 94.
34. Parkman, *Pioneers of France*, pp. 63-64.
35. Laudonnière, X, 70-71.
36. Parkman, *Pioneers of France*, pp. 59-61.
37. *Ibid.*, pp. 63-64.
38. Barcia, p 58.
39. *Ibid.*, p. 59; Laudonnière, X, 72f.
40. Parkman, *Pioneers of France*, p. 66; Laudonnière, X, 77.
41. Parkman, *Pioneers of France*, p. 67.
42. Laudonnière, X, 90.
43. *Ibid.*, 91.
44. Parkman, *Pioneers of France*, p. 73.
45. Laudonnière, X, 94-95; Parkman, *Pioneers of France*, p. 75.
46. *Ibid.*, pp. 76-78.
47. *Ibid.*
48. Laudonnière, X, 104; Lowery, *Florida*, pp. 88-89.
49. Laudonnière, X, 105-07.
50. Parkman, *Pioneers of France*, p. 82.
51. Laudonnière, X, 107.

CHAPTER 6

1. Lowery, *Florida*, pp. 116-17.
2. *Ibid.*, p. 121.
3. *Ibid.*, pp. 122-26.
4. *Ibid.*, p. 133.
5. *Ibid.*, pp. 134-35.
6. Barcia, p. 69.
7. Lowery, *Florida*, p. 143.
8. Parkman, *Pioneers of France*, p. 94.
9. Gonzalo Solís de Merás, *Memorial*, pp. 86-88; Barcia, pp. 80-81; Parkman, *Pioneers of France*, p. 100.
10. *Ibid.*, p. 102.
11. Barcia, p. 82.
12. Parkman, *Pioneers of France*, p. 107; Eugenio Ruidíaz y Caravia, *La Florida su conquista y colonización por Menéndez de Avilés*, II, 208.
13. Barcia, pp. 83, 84.
14. Merás, pp. 96-98; Barcia, p. 85.
15. Lowery, *Florida*, p. 173; Barcia, p. 86.
16. Nicolas le Challeux, "Discourse," in Lorant, ed. and trans., p. 100; Lowery, *Florida*, p. 173.
17. Le Moyne, p. 74.
18. Le Challeux, pp. 102, 104.
19. *Ibid.*
20. Le Moyne, p. 76.

21. Lowery, *Florida*, p. 175.
22. Le Challeux, p. 104.
23. Parkman, *Pioneers of France*, p. 116; Lowery, *Flordia*, p. 176.
24. *Ibid.*, p. 177.
25. Le Challeux, pp. 106, 108, 110; Lowery, *Florida*, p. 183.
26. Le Challeux, p. 112; Lowery, *Florida*, pp. 184-86.
27. Solís de Merás, pp. 113–14.
28. Lowery, *Florida*, p. 193.
29. Parkman, *Pioneers of France*, pp. 128-29.
30. Barcia, pp. 94-95.
31. Menéndez to Philip II, October 15, 1565, in Ruidíaz, II, 103; Lowery, *Florida*, p. 200.
32. *Ibid.*, pp. 198-199.
33. *Ibid.*, p. 204; Bartolomé Barrientos, "*Vida y hechos de Pero Menéndez de Auiles, Caballero de la Horden de Santiago, Adelantado de la Florida,*" in Genaro Garcia, ed., *Dos Antiguas Relaciones de la Florida*, p. 72.
34. Parkman, *Pioneers of France*, p. 137; A. M. Brooks Transcripts, I (1500-1580).
35. Philip II to Avilés, May 12, 1566, in Ruidíaz, II, 362; also quoted in Lowery, *Florida*, p. 206.
36. *Ibid.*, p. 314.
37. Bolton, *Spanish Borderlands*, pp. 155-56; Dominique de Gourges, "Voyage," in Hakluyt, ed., X, 123-24; Parkman, *Pioneers of France*, pp. 143-47.
38. *Ibid.*, p. 148; Gourges, X, 125.
39. *Ibid.*, 126.
40. Parkman, *Pioneers of France*, p. 152; Gourges, X, 127.
41. Parkman, *Pioneers of France*, pp. 155-56.
42. *Ibid.*, p. 157; Gourges, X, 131.
43. Parkman, *Pioneers of France*, p. 158.
44. Gourges, X, 132; Lowery, *Florida*, p. 335.

CHAPTER 7

1. *Colección de documentos inéditos*, XIII, 307-08.
2. John Tate Lanning, *The Spanish Missions*, p. 36.
3. *Colección de documentos inéditos*, XIII, 308.
4. Barcia, p. 131.
5. *Ibid.*
6. Lanning, *Spanish Missions*, p. 41.
7. *Ibid.*, p. 44; Shea, p. 144.
8. Lanning, *Spanish Missions*, p. 44.
9. *Ibid.*, pp. 44-45.
10. Barcia, p. 152.
11. *Ibid.*
12. *Ibid.*, p. 153.
13. Clifford M. Lewis and Albert J. Loomie, *The Spanish Mission in Virginia*, pp. 15-18.
14. Lanning, *Spanish Missions*, p. 50; Lewis and Loomie, p. 36.
15. Luis de Quirós and Juan Bautista de Segura to Juan de Hinistrosa, Ajacan, September 12, 1570, in *ibid.*, pp. 88-91.

16. *Ibid.*, p. 89.

17. *Ibid.*, pp. 90, 92.

18. Luis Geronimo de Oré, *The Martyrs of Florida*, p. 21.

19. *See* "Relation of Juan de la Carrera" in Lewis and Loomie, pp. 131-39.

20. Lanning, *Spanish Missions*, p. 54; Lewis and Loomie, p. 48.

21. *Ibid.*, p. 50.

22. *Ibid.*, pp. 51-53; Shea, p. 150.

23. Maynard Geiger, *The Franciscan Conquest*, p. 55.

24. Barcia, pp. 172-73.

25. Geiger, pp. 64-65, 75; Charles W. Arnade, *Florida on Trial, 1593-1602*, p. 21. During Canzo's administration, the Spanish crown sent Valdes to determine if Florida and St. Augustine should be abandoned.

26. Barcia, pp. 181-82; Geiger, p. 88; Lanning, *Spanish Missions*, p. 83.

27. Barcia, pp. 181-82.

28. *Ibid.*, p. 182.

29. Geiger, p. 92.

30. Lanning, *Spanish Missions*, p. 87.

31. *Ibid.*, p. 88; Geiger, pp. 93-94; Kenny, p. 345.

32. Lanning, *Spanish Missions*, p. 89; Kenny, p. 345.

33. Lanning, *Spanish Missions*, p. 90.

34. *Ibid.*, p. 91.

35. Quoted in Geiger, p. 101.

36. *Ibid.*, pp. 102-04.

37. *Ibid.*, pp. 104-08.

38. Quoted in Lanning, *Spanish Missions*, p. 103.

39. *Ibid.*, pp. 104-05.

40. *Ibid.*; Kenny, p. 346.

41. *"Relación del Viaje que hizo el Señor Pedro de Ibarra, gobernador y capitán general de la Florida, a visitar los pueblos indios de las provincias de San Pedro y Guale,"* in Manuel Serrano y Sanz, ed., *Documentos historicos de la Florida ye la Luisiana, siglos XVI al XVIII*, pp. 165-79.

42. *Ibid.*

43. *Ibid.*

44. *See Carta a Sr. M. del fraile Fray Alonzo de Peñaranda, al Pedro de Ibarra*, January, 1608, in Lowery MSS, VI (1608-1620); *see also* arrival of monks in St. Augustine on July 24, 1612, in Lowery MSS, VI (1608-1620).

45. Diego de Rebolledo to the Spanish Crown, October 24, 1656, in A. M. Brooks Transcripts, III (1621-1689).

46. *Carta de los Religiosos de la Provincia de Santa Elena a S.M. en gueja de la Mal a Conducta y Agravios que hace el Gobernador de la Florida Don Diego de Rebolledo a aquella naturales*, September 10, 1657, in Lowery MSS, VII (1621-1657).

47. Lanning, *Spanish Missions*, p. 208.

Chapter 8

1. Verner W. Crane, *The Southern Frontier*, p. 108.

2. Henry Woodward, "A Faithfull Relation of My Westoe Voiage," in

Alexander S. Salley, Jr., ed., *Narratives of Early Carolina*, p. 131.

3. *Ibid.*, p. 132.

4. *Ibid.*, pp. 133-34.

5. Langdon Cheves, ed., *The Shaftesbury Papers*, pp. 13, 52, 93, 130, 217-18; Robert Sandford, "A Relation of a voyage on the Coast of the Province of Caroline, 1666," in Salley, Jr., ed., *Narratives of Early Carolina*, p. 89.

6. *Ibid.*, p. 91.

7. *Ibid.*, pp. 92-93.

8. *Ibid.*, p. 105.

9. Herbert Eugene Bolton, *Arredondo's Historical Proof of Spain's Title to Georgia*, p. 31, hereinafter cited as Bolton, *Arredondo's Proof*.

10. Crane, *Southern Frontier*, pp. 19, 29.

11. Herbert Eugene Bolton, "Spanish Resistance . . . in . . . Georgia," in *The Georgia Historical Quarterly*, IX, 121; Lanning, *Spanish Missions*, p. 178: John Archdale Papers.

12. Bolton, *Arredondo's Proof*, pp. 50-54; Serrano y Sanz, *Documentos*, pp. 193-98; Lanning, *Spanish Missions*, p. 179.

13. Bolton, *Arredondo's Proof*, pp. 50-54.

14. Serrano y Sanz, *Documentos*, pp. 219-21.

15. *Ibid.*

16. *Ibid.*

17. Quoted in Verner W. Crane, "The Southern Frontier in Queen Anne's War," in *The American Historical Review*, XXIV (1919), 386; John Archdale Papers (1690-1706).

18. David Ramsay, *History of South Carolina*, I, 71-72; John Archdale Papers.

19. Lanning, *Spanish Missions*, pp. 186-87.

20. Shea, p. 462.

21. Crane, "Southern Frontier," XXIV, 389.

22. *Ibid.*, 391-92.

23. *Ibid.*, 392-93.

24. Thomas Cooper, ed., *Statues at Large*, III, 152-55.

25. *Ibid.*

26. Ramsay, I, 89-90.

27. Chapman J. Milling, *Red Carolinians*, p. 140.

28. *Ibid.*, pp. 141-42; Crane, *Southern Frontier*, p. 168; Ramsay, I, 90.

29. *Ibid.*, 91.

30. Milling, p. 145.

31. Thomas L. Stokes, *The Savannah*, p. 68-72; Milling, pp. 149-50.

32. Stokes, p. 71.

33. Milling, p. 152.

34. Crane, *Southern Frontier*, p. 211; C. C. Jones, *History of Georgia*, I, 70-75; *South Carolina Historical Society Collections*, II, 232-33; E. Merton Coulter, *Georgia, A Short History*, p. 13.

35. *See* Crane, *Southern Frontier*, pp. 212-13.

36. Bolton, *Arredondo's Proof*, p. 69; Crane, *Southern Frontier*, pp. 229-33; *South Carolina Historical Society Collections*, II, 232-43; John Tate Lanning, *The Diplomatic History of Georgia*, pp. 9-11.

37. *Ibid.*, pp. 13-22.

CHAPTER 9

1. William Edward Dunn, *Spanish and French Rivalry in the Gulf Region of the United States, 1678-1702*, pp. 185-89.
2. Dunbar Rowland, *History of Mississippi*, I, 139.
3. *Ibid.*, 135-39.
4. T. J. Campbell, *Pioneer Laymen of North America*, II, 62-63.
5. *Ibid.*, 65.
6. *Ibid.*, 66.
7. Pierre François Xavier Charlevoix, *Histoire et Description Générale de la Nouvelle France* ... III, 227.
8. *Ibid.*
9. Nellis M. Crouse, *Lemoyne d'Iberville, Soldier of New France*, pp. 40-66.
10. *Ibid.*
11. *Ibid.*, pp. 90-117; T. J. Campbell, II, 79.
12. *Ibid.*, 83.
13. Crouse, pp. 119-138.
14. T. J. Campbell, II, 87-88; Crouse, pp. 152.
15. *Ibid.*
16. Dunn, pp. 171-84; Alcée Fortier, *A History of Louisiana*, I, 34-35.
17. Crouse, pp. 169; Pierre Margry, ed., *Découvertes et Établissements des Français dans l'Ouest et dans le Sud de l'Amérique Septentrionale*, V, 312.
18. André Pénicaut, edited and translated by Richebourg Gaillard Mc-Williams as *Fleur de Lys and Calumet*, pp. 1-3.
19. Crouse, p. 176.
20. *Ibid.*, pp. 178-82; Pénicaut, pp. 21-23.
21. Crouse, p. 182; Pierre Lemoyne, "Journal," in Margry, ed., IV, 101 ff.
22. A. C. Albrecht, "The Origin and Settlement of Baton Rouge, Louisiana," in *Louisiana Historical Quarterly*, XXVIII (1945), 5-68.
23. Crouse, p. 186.
24. Pénicaut, pp. 29-30; Crouse, p. 190; Lemoyne, "Journal," IV, 190.
25. Pénicaut, p. 30; Fortier, I, 42.
26. Charles Gayarré, *History of Louisiana*, I, 59; Peter Hamilton, *Colonial Mobile*, p. 80.
27. Crane, *Southern Frontier*, p. 57; Gayarré, I, 60; T. J. Campbell, II, 206.
28. Gayarré, I, 72-74; for a study of the wretched economic conditions of early Louisiana, *see* Marcel Giraud, "France and Louisiana in the Early Eighteenth Century," in *Mississippi Valley Historical Review*, XXXVI (1950), 657-74.
29. Gayarré, I, 69.
30. Souvole to Pontchartrain, Biloxi, August 4, 1701, in Dunbar Rowland and Albert Godfrey Sanders, eds., *Mississippi Provincial Archives*, II, 9-18.
31. *Ibid.*
32. Lemoyne, IV, 206.
33. *Ibid.*
34. Rowland, *History of Mississippi*, I, 175.
35. *Ibid.*

36. Margry, ed., IV, lix, 501-04, 512, 530; Peter Hamilton, p. 53.

37. Margry, ed., IV, 362, 406, 418; Crouse, pp. 238-40.

38. Fortier, I, 48-49.

39. Rowland, *History of Mississippi*, I, 189.

40. Nicolas de la Salle to Pontchartrain, Fort St. Louis, August 31, 1704, in Rowland and Sanders, eds., II, 20.

41. Gayarré, I, 87.

42. *Ibid.*, 95.

43. *Ibid.*, 96.

44. *Ibid.*

45. *Ibid.*, 101-02.

46. Georges Oudard, *Four Cents an Acre*, p. 112; Gayarré, I, 88.

47. *Ibid.*, 99.

48. Artaguette to Pontchartrain, Massacre Island, February 12, 1710; Artaguette to Pontchartrain, Fort St. Louis, June 20, 1710, in Rowland and Sanders, eds., II, 52-55; 56-59.

49. Rowland, *History of Mississippi*, I, 192.

50. Gayarré, I, 102-03.

51. *Ibid.*, 111.

52. *Ibid.*, 119.

53. Oudard, p. 116.

54. Francis Parkman, *A Half-Century of Conflict*, I, 17.

55. Gayarré, I, 108.

56. Cadillac to Pontchartrain, Fort St. Louis, October 26, 1713, in Rowland and Sanders, eds., II, 166.

57. *Ibid.*, 167-68.

58. Quoted in Gayarré, I, 129.

59. *Ibid.*, 131.

60. *Ibid.*

61. *Ibid.*, 133.

62. Duclos to Pontchartrain, Mobile, October 25, 1713, in Albert Godfrey Sanders, ed., "Documents Concerning the Crozat Regime in Louisiana, 1712-1717," in *Louisiana Historical Quarterly*, XVI (1933), 305.

63. Ross Phares, *Cavalier in the Wilderness*, p. 38; Gayarré, I, 88.

64. Phares, pp. 43-66.

65. *Ibid.*, p. 68.

66. Pénicaut, pp. 184-90; Phares, pp. 78-86. The latter is critical of "romancers" who portray St. Denis as "a man madly in love."

67. *See* St. Denis's conversation with the viceroy in Pénicaut, pp. 86-88.

68. Gayarré, I, 136; Agnes C. Laut, *Cadillac*, p. 224.

69. Bienville to Longueuil, October 2, 1713, in Grace King, *Jean-Baptiste Le Moyne*, p. 205.

70. *Ibid.*, p. 211-12.

71. *Ibid.*, p. 217.

72. *Ibid.*, p. 224-25.

73. Oudard, p. 126.

74. Quoted in Gayarré, I, 158-59.

75. *Ibid.*, 160.

76. *Ibid.*, 161.

77. *Ibid.*, 184-85; King, p. 228-29.
78. Gayarré, I, 192.
79. *Ibid.*

CHAPTER 10

1. Oudard, p. 142.
2. *Ibid.*, p. 134.
3. Adolphe Thiers, *The Mississippi Bubble*, p. 46.
4. *Ibid.*, p. 68; Gayarré, I, 201.
5. *Ibid.*, 209-10.
6. *Ibid.*, 211; John K. Bettersworth, *Mississippi: A History*, p. 78.
7. Gayarré, I, 213-14.
8. H. Montgomery Hyde, *John Law*, p. 114.
9. *Ibid.*, pp. 114-15.
10. Gayarré, I, 235.
11. *Ibid.*; Pierre Heinrich, *La Louisiane sous la Companie des Indes, 1717-1731*, p. 10.
12. *See* Oudard, pp. 153-54; J. H. Schlarman, *From Quebec to New Orleans*, p. 186.
13. Oudard, p. 150; *see* letter by Father Poisson in Reuben Gold Thwaites, ed., *Jesuit Relations*, LXVII, 281.
14. J. Hanno Deiler, *The Settlement of the German Coast of Louisiana and the Creoles of German Descent*, pp. 12, 14.
15. Oudard, pp. 158-59; Deiler, p. 23.
16. Barcia, pp. 379-82.
17. *Ibid.*, p. 386.
18. *Ibid.*; Phares, pp. 156-57; Gayarré, I, 238-41; *see* Bienville to the Navy Council, September 25, 1718, in Rowland and Sanders, eds., II, 232-36.
19. Phares, p. 156.
20. T. J. Campbell, II, 231.
21. Phares, p. 157; Barcia, pp. 387-88.
22. Phares, pp. 158-60.
23. Hyde, pp. 125-30 ff; Schlarman, pp. 188-89.
24. Hyde, p. 135.
25. Thiers, pp. 181-92; Hyde, p. 141; Gayarré, I, 223-24.
26. Schlarman, p. 189; Hyde, p. 142.
27. Gayarré, I, 226.
28. Deiler, pp. 38-41; Oudard, p. 160.
29. Marc de Villiers du Terrage, "A History of the Foundation of New Orleans," in *Louisiana Historical Quarterly*, III (1920), 177; Charlevoix, IV, 196.
30. Henry E. Chambers, *A History of Louisiana*, I, 107-08; Antoine Simon Le Page du Pratz, *Histoire de la Louisiane*, I, 83; Villiers, "New Orleans," III, 189-90.
31. *Ibid.*, 232, 233, 235, 237.
32. *Ibid.*, 236.
33. *Ibid.*, 237-38.
34. Quoted in *ibid.*, 246.
35. Quoted in *ibid.*, 250.

36. Pénicaut, pp. 249-50.

37. Marc de Villiers du Terrage, *Les Deniers Années de la Louisiane Française; le Chevalier du Kerlérec, d'Abbadie Aubry, Laussat*, p. 18.

38. Heinrich, pp. 181-85; Schlarman, p. 232.

39. Heinrich, p. 192.

40. Louis François Benjamin Dumont de Montigny, *Mémoires Historiques sur la Louisiane*, II, 118-22, 125, 127-28; Le Page du Pratz, III, 231-33; John R. Swanton, *Indian Tribes of the Lower Mississippi Valley*, pp. 223, 224, hereinafter cited as Swanton, *Indian Tribes*.

41. Mathurin le Petit to d'Avaugour, New Orleans, July, 1730, in Thwaites, ed., *The Jesuits Relations*, LXVIII, 165-167; Swanton, *Indian Tribes*, p. 226; W. Adolphe Roberts, *Lake Pontchartrain*, p. 55; Jean-Bernard Bossu, *Travels in the Interior of North America, 1751-1762*, pp. 45-46.

42. Charlevoix, VI, 84-85.

43. Le Petit, LXVIII, 171, 179, 181; T. J. Campbell, II, 246.

44. Charlevoix, VI, 89-92.

45. Le Page du Pratz, III, 283, 289-90; Bettersworth, p. 82.

46. Swanton, *Indian Tribes*, pp. 243-48; Charlevoix, VI, 114-18.

47. *Ibid.;* Rowland, *History of Mississippi*, I, 236; Bossu, p. 47.

48. Rowland, *History of Mississippi*, I, 236-37; Adolphe Roberts, p. 59.

Chapter 11

1. John R. Swanton, *Early History of the Creek Indians and Their Neighbors*, pp. 108-09.

2. Stokes, pp. 73, 83.

3. James Ross McCain, *Georgia as a Proprietary Province*, pp. 57-59.

4. Coulter, *Georgia*, p. 15; Amos Aschbach Ettinger, *James Edward Oglethorpe: Imperial Idealist*, pp. 109-10; Henry Bruce, *Life of General Oglethorpe*, pp. 45-46.

5. Coulter, *Georgia*, pp. 15-16; Ettinger, p. 110.

6. *Ibid.*, pp. 111-12.

7. *Ibid.*, pp. 120-32.

8. Oglethorpe to Trustees, January 13, 1732/33, Egmont Papers, 14200, p. 13; Thomas Causton to his Wife, March 2, 1732/33, Egmont Papers, 14200, p. 53.

9. Oglethorpe to Trustees, July 13, 1732/33, Egmont Papers, 14200, p. 93; William Houston to Oglethorpe, January 26, 1732/33, Egmont Papers, 14200, p. 21.

10. Samuel Eveleigh in *South Carolina Gazette*, March 24, 1732/33. *See also* Samuel Eveleigh to Trustees, South Carolina, April 6, 1732/33, Egmont Papers, 14200, pp. 61-62.

11. Oglethorpe to Trustees, June 9, 1732/33, Egmont Papers, 14200, p. 86; Bruce, pp. 112-13.

12. *Ibid.*

13. *Ibid.*, p. 113.

14. *South Carolina Gazette*, February 16, 23, 1734.

15. *Gentleman's Magazine*, September, 1734.

16. Bruce, pp. 152-53.

17. *Ibid.*, p. 147.

18. *Gentleman's Magazine*, August, 1734.

19. *Ibid.*

20. Bruce, p. 147.

21. Ettinger, p. 155.

22. *Gentleman's Magazine*, October, 1734.

23. *Collections of the Georgia Historical Society*, I, 80.

24. *Ibid.*

25. *Ibid.*

26. Pat. Tailfer and Others, *A True and Historical Narrative of the Colony of Georgia*, pp. 46-47.

27. James G. Johnson, "The Colonial Southwest, 1732-1763," in *The University of Colorado Studies*, XIX (1932), 22.

28. Sarah B. Gober Temple and Kenneth Coleman, *Georgia Journeys*, p. 197; Bruce, p. 100.

29. *Ibid.*, p. 99.

30. *Collection of the Georgia Historical Society*, I, 85.

31. P. A. Strobel, *The Salzburgers and Their Descendants*, pp. 29, 41-42; George Bancroft, *History of the United States*, II, 284-85; Earl of Egmont, *Diary*, I, 305, 378.

32. Strobel, pp. 54-56; Oglethorpe to Trustees, April 2, 1734, Egmont Papers, 14200, p. 169.

33. Strobel, p. 66; *South Carolina Gazette*, March 23, 1734.

34. *Ibid.*

35. Temple and Coleman, p. 61; Strobel, pp. 86-91; Oglethorpe to Trustees, March 16, 1735, Egmont Papers, 14201, pp. 340, 342.

36. Strobel, pp. 125-48.

37. John Anthony Caruso, *The Appalachian Frontier*, p. 31; Coulter, *Georgia*, p. 28; Adelaide L. Fries, ed., *Records of the Moravians in North Carolina*, I, 13-14.

38. Earl of Egmont, II, 413; James Etheridge Callaway, *The Early Settlement of Georgia*, p. 25.

39. Reba Carolyn Strickland, *Religion and the State in Georgia in the Eighteenth Century*, pp. 41-43.

40. Temple and Coleman, p. 26.

41. Earl of Egmont, *Diary*, I, 441.

42. Charles Wesley, *Journal*, p. 4.

43. John Wesley, *Journal*, I, 189; Howell, I, 198.

44. John Wesley, I, 190n.

45. Charles Wesley, p. 5.

46. *Ibid.*, pp. 19-20; Howell, I, 195.

47. *Ibid.*, 198.

48. Charles Wesley, p. 35.

49. John Wesley, I, 317.

50. *Ibid.*, 318.

51. *Ibid.*, 318-19.

52. *Ibid.*, 325.

53. *Ibid.*, 330, 333.

54. *Ibid.*, 336.

55. *Ibid.*, 337, 376; John Wesley, *Excerpts from a Journal*, Egmont Papers, 14203, p. 100.

56. Howell, I, 205; Egmont Papers, 14203, p. 100.

57. John Wesley, I, 377-78.

58. John Wesley to Sophia Williamson, August 31, 1737, in *ibid.*, 379; Egmont Papers, 14203, p. 100.

59. *Earl of Egmont*, II, 450-51.

60. John Wesley, I, 421-22.

61. *Collections of the Georgia Historical Society*, I, 128-9, 188, 257; Egmont Papers, 14201, pp. 389-90.

62. Howell, I, 164-65.

63. Margaret Davis Cate, "Fort Frederica and the Battle of Bloody Marsh," in *Georgia Historical Quarterly*, XXVII (1943), 123-24.

64. Bancroft, II, 294.

65. John Tate Lanning, *Diplomatic History of Georgia*, pp. 126-53.

66. *Ibid.*, p. 153.

67. Bolton, *Arredondo's Proof*, p. 82.

68. William Bacon Stevens, *A History of Georgia*, I, 157-58; Earl of Egmont, III, 121.

69. *Ibid.*

70. Oglethorpe to Lieutenant Governor Bull, Frederica, January 23, 1740, in John Tate Lanning, ed., *The St. Augustine Expedition of 1740*, pp. 94-95.

71. *Ibid.*, p. x.

72. *Ibid.*, pp. x, 101-02.

73. *Ibid.*, p. xi; William W. Dewhurst, *The History of Saint Augustine, Florida*, pp. 89-90.

74. Lanning, ed., *St. Augustine Expedition*, pp. 15, 16, 28, 55.

75. Lanning, *Diplomatic History*, p. 225.

76. Dewhurst, p. 94.

77. Lanning, *Diplomatic History*, pp. 225-26.

78. Quoted in Ettinger, pp. 234-35.

79. Allen D. Candler, ed., *Colonial Records of the State of Georgia*, IV, 295, 323, 653.

80. *Collections of the Georgia Historical Society*, VII, Part III, 48, 52, 55, 65, 89.

81. Candler, ed., XXXV, 455.

82. *Collections of the Georgia Historical Society*, III, 134-35.

83. *Ibid.*, III, 135; Candler, ed., XXXV, 500, 501.

84. *London Magazine*, 1742, p. 515.

85. *Collections of the Georgia Historical Society*, VII, Part III, 70, 72, 90, 91; Cate, XXVII, 148.

86. *Ibid.*, 149-50.

87. *Collections of the Georgia Historical Society*, III, 136.

88. Cate, XXVII, 173.

89. *Ibid.*

90. Ettinger, p. 249.

91. Tailfer and Others, p. 5.

92. Bolton, *Arredondo's Proof*, p. 91. *See* William Stephens, *Journal*, I, 123. Edited by E. Merton Coulter. Candler, ed., I, 431, 440.

93. Temple and Coleman, pp. 261-63; Coulter, *Georgia*, p. 68.

CHAPTER 12

1. Kathryn Abbey [Hanna], *Florida, Land of Change*, p. 77.

2. *Ibid.*

3. William Roberts, *An Account of the First Discovery and Natural History of Florida*, p. 34.

4. John Gerard William DeBrahm MS, Report on East Florida, p. 300.

5. DeBrahm MS, pp. 299-300.

6. DeBrahm MS, p. 319.

7. DeBrahm MS, pp. 201, 305.

8. Dewhurst, p. 108.

9. Philip C. Tucker, "Notes on the Life of Governor James Grant," in *Florida Historical Quarterly*, VIII (1929), 112-18.

10. Clarence E. Carter, ed., *The Correspondence of General Thomas Gage*, I, 139; Charles L. Mowat, "St. Augustine Under the British Flag," in *Florida Historical Quarterly*, XX (1941), 133-34.

11. Hanna, *Florida*, pp. 78-79; John Richard Alden, *John Stuart and the Southern Colonial Frontier*, pp. 230-31.

12. Carita Doggett [Corse], *Dr. Andrew Turnbull and the New Smyrna Colony of Florida*, pp. 16, 18, 21, hereinafter cited as Corse, *New Smyrna Colony*. E. P. Panagopoulos, "The Background of the Greek Settlers in the New Smyrna Colony," in *Florida Historical Quarterly*, XXXV (1956), 97, 98.

13. Corse, *New Smyrna Colony*, pp. 27-28.

14. Panagopoulos, XXXV, 101; Corse, *New Smyrna Colony*, pp. 30-31.

15. Panagopoulos, XXXV, 101-104.

16. Corse, *New Smyrna Colony*, p. 40; Panagopoulos, XXXV, 114.

17. William Bartram, *Travels*, pp. 91-92.

18. Corse, *New Smyrna Colony*, p. 45.

19. Dewhurst, p. 114.

20. Corse, *New Smyrna Colony*, pp. 54-55.

21. *Ibid.*, p. 60.

22. *Ibid.*, p. 76.

23. *Ibid.*

24. Carita Doggett Corse, "Denys Rolle and Rollestown, A Pioneer For Utopia," in *Florida Historical Quarterly*, VII (1928), 115-16.

25. *Ibid.*, 117-18.

26. Corse, *New Smyrna Colony*, p. 89.

27. *Ibid.*, p. 90.

28. *Ibid.*

29. Wilbur Henry Seibert, *Loyalists in East Florida*, I, 14; II, 316-17.

30. Corse, *New Smyrna Colony*, pp. 116-18; Seibert, I, 34.

31. *Ibid.*, pp. 131-32.

32. *Ibid.*, p. 139.

33. *Ibid.*, pp. 139-40; Seibert, *Loyalists in East Florida*, I, 43.

34. Germain to Tonyn, Whitehall, April 14, 1777, in *ibid.*, pp. 155-56.

35. *Ibid.*, pp. 157-65.

36. *Ibid.*, pp. 168-69, 170.

37. Seibert, *Loyalists in East Florida*, II, 326-27.

38. Cecil Johnson, *British West Florida, 1763-1783*, pp. 3, 24-25.

39. *Ibid.*, pp. 29, 30, 32, 33, 36.

40. *Ibid.*, p. 6.

41. Alden, pp. 199-206; Clarence E. Carter, "The Beginnings of British West Florida," in *Mississippi Valley Historical Review*, IV, 330.

42. Johnson, *British West Florida*, pp. 49-50.

43. *Ibid.*, pp. 50-51.

44. Carter, ed., *Correspondence of Gage*, I, 341-42.

45. Johnson, *British West Florida*, pp. 55-56.

46. *Ibid.*, pp. 57-59.

47. *Ibid.*, pp. 61-62, 63, 65, 66-67, 68-69.

48. *Ibid.*, pp. 69-75.

49. *See* deposition of Daniel Huay in Mrs. Dunbar Rowland, "Peter Chester," in *Publications of the Mississippi Historical Society*, V, 26-27, hereinafter cited as Dunbar, "Peter Chester." *See also* Bettersworth, pp. 93-94.

50. Cecil Johnson, "The Distribution of Land in British West Florida," in *Louisiana Historical Quarterly*, XVI (1933), 543-44.

51. *See* Peter Chester to the Earl of Dartmouth, Pensacola, May 16, 1773, in Dunbar, "Peter Chester," V, 167-68, which, however, mentions no names.

52. Dunbar, *History of Mississippi*, I, 266-67.

53. Gayarré, II, 190-91.

54. *Ibid.;* Edwin Adams Davis, *Louisiana*, p. 84.

55. John Walton Caughey, *Bernardo de Gálvez in Louisiana*, pp. 20-21, hereinafter cited as Caughey, *Gálvez*.

56. *Ibid.*, pp. 21-22.

57. *Ibid.*, pp. 23-28.

58. *Ibid.*, pp. 26.

59. *Ibid.*, pp. 29-42.

60. *Ibid.*, pp. 43-57.

61. James A. James, *Oliver Pollock*, pp. 113-14; John Caughey, "Willing's Expedition Down the Mississippi, 1778," in *Louisiana Historical Quarterly*, XV (1932), 6-7, hereinafter cited as Caughey, "Willing's Expedition."

62. *Ibid.*, 8-9, 10; Wilbur H. Seibert, "The Loyalists in West Florida and the Natchez District," in *Mississippi Valley Historical Review*, II (1916), 469-70, hereinafter cited as Seibert, "Loyalists of West Florida." Draper MSS, 32J140-47; 59J288-289; 4J116-124.

63. Seibert, *Loyalists in East Florida*, I, 470-71; James, *Oliver Pollock*, pp. 120-21.

64. Seibert, "Loyalists of West Florida," II, 470-71; Caughey, "Willing's Expedition," XV, 27; Garland Taylor, "Colonial Settlement and Early Revolutionary Activity in West Florida Up to 1779," in *Mississippi Valley Historical Review*, XXII (1935), 359.

65. Caughey, "Willing's Expedition," XV, 28-30.

66. *Ibid.*, 32.

67. Seibert, "Loyalists of West Florida," II, 472.

68. Caughey, "Willing's Expedition," XV, 33-34.

69. Seibert, "Loyalists of West Florida," II, 472-73. *See also* Kathryn T. Abbey [Hanna], "Peter Chester's Defense of the Mississippi After the Willing Raid," in *Mississippi Valley Historical Review*, XXII (1935), 31.

70. Caughey, *Gálvez*, p. 149; Johnson, *British West Florida*, pp. 211-12.

71. For an illuminating article on Gálvez' source of information about the

English, *see* Kathryn Abbey [Hanna], "Efforts of Spain to Maintain Sources of Information in the British Colonies Before 1779," in *Mississippi Valley Historical Review*, XV (1928), 56-68; Caughey, *Gálvez*, pp. 155-59.

72. *Ibid.*, p. 174.

73. *Ibid.*, pp. 174-78.

74. *Ibid.*, pp. 180-85.

75. *Ibid.*, pp. 187-93; Bernardo de Gálvez, "Diary," in *Louisiana Historical Quarterly*, I (1917), pp. 42, 44.

76. *Ibid.*, 47-48; L. N. McAlister, "Pensacola During the Second Spanish Period," in *Florida Historical Quarterly*, XXXVII (1959), 282-83.

77. Caughey, *Gálvez*, pp. 200-07.

78. Gálvez, I, 66-74.

79. *Ibid.*, 74-75; Caughey, *Gálvez*, pp. 210-14.

80. *Ibid.*, p. 216.

81. *Ibid.*, pp. 217-18.

82. Rowland, *History of Mississippi*, I, 288-89.

83. *Ibid.*, 289-91.

CHAPTER 13

1. Charles Loch Mowat, "East Florida as a British Province, 1763-1783," in *University of California Publications in History*, XXII (1943), 144.

2. *Ibid.*, 145.

3. *Ibid.*, 147.

4. *Ibid.*

5. J. A. Brown, "Panton, Leslie and Company, Indian Traders of Pensacola and St. Augustine," in *Florida Historical Quarterly*, XXXVII (1959), 329.

6. *See* McGillivray to Zéspedes, Little Tallassie, January 5, 1787, in John Walton Caughey, *McGillivray of the Creeks*, pp. 141-42, hereinafter cited as Caughey, *McGillivray*. Lawrence Kinnaird, "The Significance of William Augustus Bowles' Seizure of Panton's Apalachee Store in 1792," in *Florida Historical Quarterly*, IX (1931), 157-58.

7. McAlister, "Pensacola," XXXVII, 295; Caughey, *McGillivray*, pp. 9-17.

8. *Ibid.*, pp. 22-26.

9. Marie Taylor Greenslade, "William Panton," in *Florida Historical Quarterly*, XIV (1939), 112-13.

10. William Panton to John Forbes, Pensacola, June 4, 1794, in "Panton, Leslie Papers," *Florida Historical Quarterly*, XIV, 220.

11. Edwin Gairdner to William Panton, Charleston, December 9, 1798, in *ibid.*, XV, 127.

12. Richard L. Campbell, *Historical Sketches of Colonial Florida*, pp. 155-56.

13. *Ibid.*, p. 156.

14. *Ibid.*, p. 157.

15. Kinnaird, IX, 158-59.

16. *Ibid.*, 159-61.

17. Caughey, *McGillivray*, p. 37; McAlister, "Pensacola," XXXVII, 397-98.

18. Caughey, *McGillivray*, p. 48.

19. Quoted in Kinnaird, IX, 165.

20. Caughey, *McGillivray*, p. 48; Draper MSS, V 5.

21. Statement of Edward Forrester, February 28, 1792, in "Panton, Leslie Papers," *Florida Historical Quarterly*, XIV (1939), 171-72.

22. *Ibid.*

23. *Ibid.*, 176.

24. Caughey, *McGillivray*, p. 50.

25. McGillivray to Panton, November 28, 1792, in *ibid.*, p. 348.

26. Panton to Lachlan McGillivray, Pensacola, April 10, 1794, in Greenslade, XIV, 114-15.

27. Philadelphia *National Gazette*, July 13, 1793.

28. John Bach McMaster, *A History of the People of the United States*, II, 98; "Correspondence of Clark and Genet" in *Annual Report*, American Historical Association, I (1896), 957-67, hereinafter cited as "Correspondence of Clark and Genet."

29. "Mangourit Correspondence," in *Annual Report*, American Historical Association (1897), pp. 570-71.

30. Meade Minnegerode, *Jefferson, Friend of France*, pp. 192, 193.

31. *Ibid.*, pp. 195-96.

32. McMaster, II, 101; Minnegerode, pp. 208-11.

33. *Ibid.*, p. 250; Mangourit to Genet, June 17, 1793, in "Mangourit Correspondence," pp. 583-84.

34. *Ibid.*, pp. 571-72.

35. Draper MSS, V 1g.

36. Draper MSS, 55J2, 5, 6.

37. "Correspondence of Clark and Genet," I, 984-85; *see* Michaux to George Rogers Clark, Philadelphia, December 27, 1793, in Draper MSS, 55J8.

38. Thomas Jefferson to Spanish Agents, Philadelphia, Augusut 29, 1793, in "Correspondence of Clark and Genet," I, 1005; Isaac Shelby to Thomas Jefferson, January 13, 1794, in Draper MSS, 55J12.

39. Thomas A. Bailey, *A Diplomatic History of the American People*, p. 78.

40. Minnegerode, p. 359.

41. Draper MSS, V 22.

42. Arthur Preston Whitaker, "New Light on the Treaty of San Lorenzo: An Essay in Historical Criticism," in *Mississippi Valley Historical Review*, XV (1929), 449. Hereinafter cited as Whitaker, "Treaty of San Lorenzo."

43. Quoted in Franklin L. Riley, "Spanish Policy in Mississippi After the Treaty of San Lorenzo," in *Annual Report*, American Historical Association (1897), p. 178.

44. Whitaker, "Treaty of San Lorenzo," XV, 437, 438, 448, 450, 452.

45. Arthur Preston Whitaker, *The Mississippi Question*, pp. 53-54.

46. Andrew Ellicott, *Journal*, p. 35; *see* Bettersworth, p. 117.

47. Ellicott, p. 39.

48. *Ibid.*, pp. 43-44.

49. *Ibid.*, p. 66.

50. *Ibid.*, p. 80.

51. *Ibid.*, p. 86.

52. *Ibid.*, p. 96.

53. *Ibid.*, p. 100; Committee of Public Safety to Manuel Gayoso de Lemos,

June 22, 1797, in Clarence E. Carter, ed., *Territorial Papers of the United States*, V, 11-12; hereinafter cited as Carter, ed., *Territorial Papers*.

54. Whitaker, *Mississippi Question*, p. 64.
55. Quoted in *ibid.*, p. 65.
56. *Ibid.*
57. Ellicott, p. 176.
58. Whitaker, *Mississippi Question*, p. 66.
59. *Ibid.*, p. 67.

CHAPTER 14

1. Coulter, *Georgia*, p. 91; for a detailed description of the Conference of Augusta, *see* Alden, pp. 186-91.
2. U. B. Phillips, *Georgia and State Rights*, p. 29; William Estill Heath, "The Yazoo Land Fraud," in *Georgia Historical Quarterly*, XVI (1932), 278; Arthur Preston Whitaker, *The Spanish American Frontier*, pp. 129-33.
3. Heath, XVI, 279.
4. Coulter, *Georgia*, p. 200.
5. George White, *Statistics of the State of Georgia*, p. 51.
6. *Ibid.*; Heath, XVI, 281.
7. White, p. 50; Howell, I, 432.
8. Stevens, II, 479.
9. Heath, XVI, 282; Stevens, II, 492.
10. Coulter, *Georgia*, p. 203.
11. Heath, XVI, 283-84; Coulter, *Georgia*, pp. 204-05.
12. Quoted in Rowland, *History of Mississippi*, I, 340.
13. John Anthony Caruso, *The Great Lakes Frontier*, p. 184.
14. Rowland, *History of Mississippi*, I, 347.
15. *Ibid.*, 348-49; Sargent to Timothy Pickering, December 20, 1798, in Rowland, ed., *Mississippi Territorial Archives, 1798-1803*, I, 89; Bettersworth, p. 123.
16. Robert V. Haynes, "The Revolution of 1800 in Mississippi," in *Journal of Mississippi History*, XIX (1957), 236.
17. *See* Clarence E. Carter, ed., *Territorial Papers*, V, 87-88, 94-95.
18. Presentment of the Grand Jury, Pickering County, June 17, 1799, in *ibid.*, 63-66, 67-68.
19. Haynes, XIX, 241.
20. *Ibid.*
21. Sargent to Marshall, June 15, 1800, August 25, 1800, in Rowland, ed., *Mississippi Territorial Archives*, I, 247-77.
22. Carter, ed., *Territorial Papers*, V, 95-98.
23. Haynes, XIX, 244.
24. *See Annals of Congress*, Sixth Congress, 2nd Sess., pp. 837, 838-54.
25. Quoted in Haynes, XIX, 248.
26. Rowland, *History of Mississippi*, I, 373.
27. Haynes, XIX, 251.
28. Rowland, *History of Mississippi*, I, 380-81.
29. *Ibid.*, 384-85.
30. James Madison to Timothy Pickering, November 27, 1802, in *American State Papers, Foreign Relations*, II, 527.

31. Quoted in Rowland, *History of Mississippi*, I, 394-95.

32. J. C. Guild, *Old Times in Tennessee*, p. 93; Lena Mitchell Jamison, "The Natchez Trace: A Federal Highway of the Old Southwest," in *Journal of Mississippi History*, I (1939), 82-99.

33. Robert M. Coates, *The Outlaw Years*, p. 117.

34. *Ibid.*, p. 115.

35. *The Kentucky Gazette*, September 14, 1801.

36. Otto A. Rothert, *The Outlaws of Cave-in-Rock*, pp. 189-90.

37. Coates, p. 139.

38. Dunbar Rowland, ed., *Official Letter Books of W. C. C. Claiborne, 1801-06*, I, 91-94.

39. Rothert, p. 195.

40. *Ibid.*, pp. 195-96.

41. Rowland, ed., *Official Letter Books*, II, 40.

42. Coates, pp. 151-52; Rothert, p. 211.

43. *Ibid.*, p. 215.

44. Coates, p. 154.

45. Rothert, p. 217.

46. *Ibid.*, pp. 219-22.

47. Coates, p. 158.

48. Rothert, pp. 239-40.

49. *Ibid.*, p. 244.

50. *The Western Spy*, May 4, 1803.

51. *Ibid.*

52. Rothert, pp. 249, 250, 253; Draper MSS, 31S55, 56.

53. Coates, p. 163.

54. *The Palladium*, March 3, 1804.

55. Rothert, p. 263.

56. Rowland, *History of Mississippi*, I, 403.

57. Rowland, ed., *Official Letter Books*, I, 158-59, 163.

58. Martin Abbott, "Indian Policy and Management in the Mississippi Territory, 1798-1817," in *Journal of Mississippi History*, XIV (1952), 164.

59. *Ibid.*, 165.

60. *Ibid.*, 165-66.

61. Isaac Joslin Cox, *The West Florida Controversy, 1798-1813*, p. 153.

62. *Ibid.*

63. Rowland, *History of Mississippi*, I, 411.

64. Cox, *West Florida Controversy*, p. 154.

65. *Ibid.*, p. 157.

66. *Ibid.*, p. 158.

67. *Ibid.*

68. *Ibid.*, pp. 159-60.

69. *Ibid.*, pp. 163-64.

70. William Baskerville Hamilton, *Anglo-American Law on the Frontier*, p. 246.

71. *Ibid.*

72. Cox, *West Florida Controversy*, pp. 167-68.

73. For a detailed account of Wilkinson's conspiracy, *see* Caruso, *Appalachian Frontier*, pp. 322-38.

74. Thomas Perkins Abernethy, *The Burr Conspiracy*, pp. 150-51.

75. Walter Flavius McCaleb, *The Aaron Burr Conspiracy*, pp. 167-68.

76. Abernethy, *Burr Conspiracy*, pp. 203-04.

77. Natchez *Mississippi Messenger*, January 6, 1807.

78. McCaleb, p. 219.

79. Natchez *Mississippi Messenger*, January 20, 1807.

80. Thomas Perkins Abernethy, "Aaron Burr in Mississippi," in *The Journal of Southern History*, XV (1949), 10-11.

81. Hamilton, p. 78.

82. Quoted in Mack Buckley Swearingen, *The Early Life of George Poindexter*, p. 78.

83. Abernethy, "Aaron Burr in Mississippi," XV, 12.

84. *Ibid.*, 13.

85. *Ibid.*

86. McCaleb, p. 232; Abernethy, "Aaron Burr in Mississippi," XV, 14; Abernethy, *Burr Conspiracy*, p. 221.

87. Abernethy, "Aaron Burr in Mississippi," XV, 15-16.

88. Abernethy, *Burr Conspiracy*, p. 222.

89. *Ibid.*, p. 223.

90. *Ibid.*, pp. 224-26.

91. Swearingen, pp. 79-80.

92. Carter, ed., *Territorial Papers*, V, 661; Swearingen, pp. 81-83.

93. Rowland, *History of Mississippi*, I, 445.

94. Cox, *West Florida Controversy*, p. 339.

95. *Ibid.*, p. 335.

96. *Ibid.*, pp. 345-46.

97. *Ibid.*, pp. 378-79.

98. *Ibid.*, pp. 384, 394.

99. *Ibid.*, pp. 396-403; Henry Eugene Sterkx and Brooks Thompson, "Philemon Thomas and the West Florida Revolution," in *Florida Historical Quarterly*, XXXIX (1961), 381-82.

100. *American State Papers, Foreign Relations*, III, 396.

101. *Ibid.*, 395-96.

102. Chambers, I, 487-88.

103. Quoted in Cox, *West Florida Controversy*, p. 434.

104. Quoted in *ibid.*, p. 501.

105. *Ibid.*, pp. 501-03.

106. Dunbar Rowland, ed., *Encyclopedia of Mississippi History*, I, 996-98; 999-1000.

107. Rowland, *History of Mississippi*, I, 451.

108. *Ibid.*

109. *See* Draper MSS, V60 (2), V62 (1), V62 (4); Glenn Tucker, *Poltroons and Patriots*, II, 444-45; Draper MSS, V62.

110. Draper MSS, V61 (3).

111. Draper MSS, V66 (53).

112. Tucker, II, 449.

113. T. H. Ball, *The Great South-East*, pp. 142-45.

114. Draper MSS, V66 (63).

115. Draper MSS, V66 (65).

116. Tucker, II, 450-51.

117. Rowland, *History of Mississippi*, I, 459.

118. *Ibid.*, 460; *Washington Republican*, October 6, 1813.

119. Marquis James, *The Life of Andrew Jackson*, pp. 153-60.

120. Tucker, II, 453; Marquis James, p. 159.

121. *Ibid.*, pp. 160-61; *Washington Republican*, December 8, 1813.

122. John Spencer Bassett, ed., *Correspondence of Andrew Jackson*, I, 416.

123. Draper MSS, V66 (70).

124. Draper MSS, V66 (71), V62 (18).

125. Draper MSS, V66 (72); Rowland, *History of Mississippi*, I, 464.

126. *Washington Republican and Natchez Intelligencer*, February 16, 1814; Natchez *Mississippi Republican*, April 20, 1814.

127. Draper MSS, V66 (82).

128. Natchez *Mississippi Republican*, April 20, 1814.

129. *See* Daniel H. Thomas, "Fort Toulouse—in Tradition and Fact," in *The Alabama Review*, XIII (1960), 243-57.

130. Marquis James, pp. 172-73.

131. *Ibid.*

132. *Ibid.*, pp. 176-78; William B. Hamilton, "The Southwestern Frontier," in *The Journal of Southern History*, X (1944), 391.

133. Thomas Chalmers McCorvey, *Alabama Historical Sketches*, p. 74.

134. *Ibid.*

135. *See* William O. Lynch, "The Westward Flow of Southern Colonists Before 1861," in *The Journal of Southern History*, IX (1943), 303-27.

136. William H. Sparks, *The Memories of Fifty Years*, pp. 332-33.

137. Frank L. Owsley, "The Pattern of Migration and Settlement on the Southern Frontier," in *The Journal of Southern History*, XI (1945), 164, 165, 170, 171; Frank L. Owsley, *Plain Folk of the South*, pp. 60-61.

138. Owsley, "Pattern of Migration," XI, 172.

139. Rowland, *History of Mississippi*, I, 472, 494-97.

CHAPTER 15

1. John R. Spears, *The American Slave-Trade*, pp. 1-3.

2. *Ibid.*, pp. 9, 36.

3. *Ibid.*, p. 50.

4. *Ibid.*, pp. 55-56.

5. Theodore Canot, *Adventures of an African Slaver*, p. 359.

6. Spears, pp. 68-69.

7. *Ibid.*, pp. 69-70.

8. *Ibid.*, pp. 70-71.

9. *Ibid.*, pp. 72-74; Daniel P. Mannix and Malcolm Cowley, *Black Cargoes*, pp. 125-27.

10. Quoted in *ibid.*, p. 126.

11. Spears, p. 73.

12. *Ibid.*, p. 72.

13. U. B. Phillips, *American Negro Slavery*, pp. 156-58.

14. *Ibid.*, p. 158.

15. Quoted in *ibid.*, p. 150.

16. Frederic Bancroft, *Slave-Trading in the Old South*, p. 10.

17. *Ibid.*, p. 11.

18. Phillips, *American Negro Slavery*, p. 291.

19, *Ibid.*

20. Kenneth M. Stampp, *The Peculiar Institution*, pp. 4-10, 13, 20, 32. For a detailed explanation of the Phillips-Stampp views, *see* Stanley M. Elkins, *Slavery: A Problem in American Institutional and Intellectual Life*, pp. 9-23.

21. Phillips, *American Negro Slavery*, pp. 132-38.

22. Natchez *Weekly Chronicle*, April 2, 1810.

23. Washington, D.C., *National Intelligencer*, August 19, 1833.

24. David R. Hundley, *Social Relations in Our Southern States*, pp. 139-42.

25. *Ibid.*

26. Frederick Law Olmsted, *A Journey in the Seaboard Slave States*, p. 55n.

27. *Ibid.*

28. U. B. Phillips, ed., *Plantation and Frontier*, II, 57.

29. Quoted in Frederic Bancroft, pp. 69-70.

30. Quoted in *ibid.*, p. 74.

31. Frances Anne Kemble, *Journal of a Residence on a Georgia Plantation in 1838-39*, p.122.

32. Frederic Bancroft, p. 87.

33. Phillips, *American Negro Slavery*, pp. 356-57.

34. Frederic Bancroft, p. 199.

35. Phillips, ed., *Plantation and Frontier*, II, 196.

36. *Ibid.*, 207.

37. Owsley, *Plain Folk of the Old South*, p. 66.

38. Owsley, "Pattern of Migration," XI, 173.

39. U. B. Phillips, *Life and Labor in the Old South*, pp. 277, 278.

40. Phillips, ed., *Plantation and Frontier*, II, 201-02.

41. *Ibid.*, 215.

42. Phillips, *American Negro Slavery*, p. 178.

43. Basil Hall, *Travels in North America*, III, 128, 129.

44. Phillips, *American Negro Slavery*, p. 311.

45. *Ibid.*

46. *Ibid.*, pp. 311-12.

47. Frederick Law Olmsted, *A Journey in the Back Country*, pp. 49-51.

48. Frederick Douglass, *My Bondage*, pp. 250-301; Olmsted, *Back Country*, pp. 444-45.

49. Quoted in Olmsted, *Seaboard*, p. 601.

50. Helen Tunncliff Catterall, ed., *Judicial Cases Concerning American Slavery and the Negro*, I, 357.

51. Stampp, p. 354.

52. Catterall, ed., III, 362.

53. *Ibid.*, II, 139.

54. Quoted in Carter G. Woodson, *The Negro in Our History*, p. 232.

55. Harriet Martineau, *Society in America*, II, 123.

56. H. M. Henry, *The Police Control of the Slave in South Carolina*, p. 56.

57. Booker T. Washington, *The Story of the Negro*, I, 153.

58. Phillips, *American Negro Slavery*, p. 314.

59. Washington, I, 160.

60. Dorothy Scarborough, *On the Trail of Negro Folk-Songs*, pp. 66-67; *see also* Newman I. White, *American Negro Folk-Songs*, p. 154.

61. Caruso, *Appalachian Frontier*, p. 221.

62. Quoted in Everett Dick, *The Dixie Frontier*, p. 186.

63. Olmsted, *Seaboard*, 449.

64. Charles Colcock Jones, *Negro Myths from the Georgia Coast*, pp. 161-64, reprinted in B. A. Botkin, *A Treasury of Southern Folklore*, pp. 108-10.

65. Olmsted, *Seaboard*, pp. 24-25.

66. William H. Holcombe, "Sketches of Plantation Life," in *Knickerbocker Magazine*, LVII (1861), 631.

CHAPTER 16

1. Ellicott, *Journal*, pp. 226-33.

2. Whitaker, *Mississippi Question*, p. 166.

3. *Ibid.*, pp. 166-67.

4. Lyle N. McAlister, "William Augustus Bowles and the State of Muskogee," in *Florida Historical Quarterly*, XL (1962), 322-23.

5. Merritt B. Pound, *Benjamin Hawkins—Indian Agent*, p. 191.

6. *Ibid.*, p. 192.

7. McAlister, "Bowles," XL, 323-24.

8. *Ibid.*, 324.

9. *Ibid.*

10. Whitaker, *Mississippi Question*, p. 168.

11. *Ibid.*

12. *Ibid.*

13. McAlister, "Bowles," XL, 323; Whitaker, *Mississippi Questions*, p. 169.

14. *Ibid.*

15. *Ibid.*, pp. 171-72.

16. *Augusta Chronicle*, July 12, 1800.

17. Quoted in Pound, p. 193.

18. Quoted in Whitaker, *Mississippi Question*, pp. 172-73.

19. R. S. Cotterill, *The Southern Indians*, pp. 137-38; McAlister, XL, 326; Whitaker, *Mississippi Question*, pp. 172-73.

20. *Ibid.*, pp. 174-75; McAlister, "Bowles," XL, 327-28.

21. *United States Statutes at Large*, III, 471.

22. *Ibid.*, 471-72.

23. Julius W. Pratt, *Expansionists of 1812*, p. 75.

24. Isaac J. Cox, "The Border Missions of General George Mathews," in *The Mississippi Valley Historical Review*, XII (1925), 317.

25. Quoted in Pratt, pp. 81-82.

26. *Ibid.*, p. 82.

27. *Senate Miscellaneous Documents*, No. 55, 36 Cong. 1st Sess., pp. 17-18.

28. Cox, "Border Missions," XII, 319.

29. Quoted in Pratt, pp. 93-94.

30. Cox, "Border Missions," XII, 324-25; Pratt, p. 94.

31. *Senate Miscellaneous Documents*, No. 55, 36 Cong. 1st Sess., p. 72. *See also* Rufus Kay Wyllys, "The East Florida Revolution of 1812-1814," in *The Hispanic American Historical Review*, IX (1929), 433.

32. *Ibid.*, 434-36; Cox, "Border Missions," XII, 329.

33. Wyllys, IX, 436-39.

34. Cox, "Border Missions," XII, 332.

35. Wyllys, IX, 441.

36. *Ibid.*, 441-43.

37. Edward Nicholls to Benjamin Hawkins, May 12, 1815, in *National Intelligencer*, June 20, 1815.

38. Benjamin Hawkins to Edward Nicholls, June 10, 1815, in *Niles' Weekly Register*, VIII, 285.

39. Marquis James, p. 286.

40. *Army and Navy Chronicle*, II, 116.

41. Hanna, *Florida*, pp. 126-27.

42. T. Frederick Davis, "MacGregor's Invasion of Florida, 1817," in *Florida Historical Quarterly*, VII (1928), pp. 3-5.

43. *Ibid.*, 4-7.

44. *Ibid.*, 10-14.

45. *Ibid.*, 17.

46. *Ibid.*, 18.

47. *Ibid.*, 19.

48. *Charleston Courier*, August 4, 1817.

49. T. F. Davis, "MacGregor's Invasion," VII, 28.

50. *Ibid.*

51. *Niles' Weekly Register*, XI, January 24, 1818.

52. T. F. Davis, "MacGregor's Invasion," VII, 34.

53. *Ibid.*, 53-55.

54. Grant Foreman, *Indian Removal*, p. 317.

55. Abbey, *Florida*, p. 131; Marquis James, p. 287.

56. John Spencer Bassett, ed., *Correspondence of Andrew Jackson*, III, 342.

57. Marquis James, p. 285.

58. *American State Papers, Military Affairs*, I, 721-28.

59. Marquis James, p. 289.

60. *Ibid.*, p. 290.

61. *Ibid.*, p. 291.

62. John Quincy Adams, *Diary, 1794-1845*, pp. 199-201.

63. *American State Papers, Foreign Relations*, V, 542.

64. For a detailed account of the Adams-Onis Treaty, *see* Charles Carroll Griffin, *The United States and the Disruption of the Spanish Empire*, pp. 161-90, 221-43.

65. Herbert J. Doherty, Jr., "The Governorship of Andrew Jackson," in *Florida Historical Quarterly*, XXXIII (1954), 10; Marquis James, p. 318.

66. Doherty, XXXIII, 11; Marquis James, p. 320.

67. Doherty, XXXIII, 12.

68. *American State Papers, Miscellaneous*, II, 829; Marquis James, pp. 323-25.

69. *Ibid.*; Hanna, *Florida*, pp. 145-46.

70. Marquis James, p. 327.

71. Hanna, *Florida*, pp. 158-59.

72. Foreman, *Indian Removal*, p. 315.

73. *American State Papers, Indian Affairs*, II, 438-39.

74. John K. Mahon, "The Treaty of Moultrie Creek, 1823," in *Florida Historical Quarterly*, XL (1962), 367.

75. *Ibid.*, 368-69.

76. *American State Papers, Indian Affairs*, II, 664.

77. Foreman, pp. 319-20.

78. *Ibid.*, p. 22; Hanna, *Florida*, p. 205.

79. Foreman, p. 321.

80. *See Florida Historical Quarterly*, XXXIII (1955), 205.

81. *Ibid.*

82. Jacob Rhett Motte, *Journey Into Wilderness*, pp. 140-41.

83. Foreman, p. 329.

84. Mark F. Boyd, "Asi-Yaholo or Osceola," in *Florida Historical Quarterly*, XXXIII (1955), 268-69.

85. *Ibid.*, 274.

86. *Ibid.*, 277-78.

87. Foreman, p. 327.

88. *Army and Navy Chronicle*, II, 55, 168.

89. *Ibid.*, II, 99.

90. Foreman, p. 330.

91. Boyd, "Osceola," XXXIII, 283-84.

92. *Army and Navy Chronicle*, VIII, 94.

93. *Ibid.*, IV, 234.

94. *Ibid.*, 200, 236.

95. Boyd, "Osceola," XXXIII, 299n.

96. *Ibid.*, 295.

97. *See Florida Historical Quarterly*, XXXIII (1955), 229-30.

98. Boyd, *ibid.*, 297.

99. *See* Thomas S. Jesup to Joel Roberts Poinsett, Washington City, July 6, 1838, in *ibid.*, 222.

100. Boyd, *ibid.*, 303.

101. *Ibid.*, 304.

102. May McNeer Ward, "The Disappearance of the Head of Osceola," in *ibid.*, 197-98.

103. *Ibid.*, 198-99.

104. James W. Covington, "Cuban Bloodhounds and the Seminoles," in *ibid.*, 118.

105. Foreman, *Indian Removal*, p. 373.

106. *Ibid.*

107. *Ibid.*, p. 382.

108. Rembert W. Patrick, *Florida Under Five Flags*, p. 33.

Selected Bibliography

PRIMARY WORKS

MANUSCRIPTS

Archdale, John, Papers, Library of Congress, Washington, D.C.

Brooks, A. M., Transcripts, Library of Congress, Washington, D.C.

Clark, George Rogers, Papers, Series J, Lyman C. Draper Collection, Wisconsin State Historical Society, Madison, Wisconsin.

DeBrahm, John Gerard William, Report on East Florida, Widener Library, Harvard University, Cambridge, Massachusetts.

Draper's Notes, Series S, Lyman C. Draper Collection, Wisconsin Historical Society, Madison, Wisconsin.

Egmont Papers, University of Georgia, Athens, Georgia.

Lowery, Woodbury, Manuscripts, Library of Congress, Washington, D.C.

Papers Relating to South Carolina, Alabama, and Mississippi, Series V, Lyman C. Draper Collection, Wisconsin State Historical Society, Madison, Wisconsin.

JOURNALS AND NEWSPAPERS

Army and Navy Chronicle (1836-1838).

Augusta Chronicle (1800).

Charleston Courier (1817).

Gentleman's Magazine (1734).

Kentucky Gazette (1801).

London Magazine (1742).

Natchez Mississippi Republican (1814).

Natchez *Weekly Chronicle* (1810).

Niles' Weekly Register (38 vols., Baltimore, 1811-1842).

Palladium (1804).

Philadelphia *National Magazine* (1793).
South Carolina Gazette (1734).
Washington *National Intelligencer* (1815, 1833).
Washington *Mississippi Republican and Natchez Intelligencer* (1814).
Western Spy (1803).

Books

Adams, John Quincy, *Diary*, 1794-1845. Edited by Allen Nevins (New York, 1929).

American State Papers, Foreign Relations (Washington, 1832-1861).

Annals of Congress, Sixth Congress, Second Session.

Ashton, John, ed., *The Voiage and Travayle of Sir John Mandeville, Knight* (London, 1887).

Bartram, William, *Travels*. Edited by Francis Harper (New Haven, 1958).

Bassett, John Spencer, ed., *The Correspondence of Andrew Jackson* (6 vols., New York, 1926-1933).

Biedma, Luis Hernandez de, "Relation of the Conquest of Florida," *see* Edward Gaylord Bourne.

Bossu, Jean-Bernard, *Travels in the Interior of North America*, 1751-1762. Translated and Edited by Seymour Feiler (Norman, Oklahoma, 1962).

Bourne, Edward Gaylord, ed., *Narratives of the Career of Hernando de Soto* (2 vols., New York, 1922).

Cabeza de Vaca, Álvar Nuñez, "Nafragios," *see* Enrique de Vedia.

Candler, Allen D., ed., *Colonial Records of the State of Georgia* (26 vols., Atlanta, 1904-1916).

Carter, Clarence E., ed., *The Correspondence of General Thomas Gage* (2 vols., New Haven, 1933).

——, *The Territorial Papers of the United States* (26 vols., Washington, D.C., 1934-1962).

Castillo, Bernal Díaz de, *The True History of the Conquest of Mexico*. Translated by Maurice Keatinge (New York, 1927).

Catterall, Helen Tunncliff, ed., *Judicial Cases Concerning American Slavery and the Negro* (4 vols., Washington, D.C., 1932).

Charlevoix, Pierre François Xavier, *Histoire et Description Générale de la Nouvelle France* ... (3 vols., Paris, 1744).

Cheves, Langdon, ed., *The Shaftesbury Papers* (Charleston, South Carolina, 1897).

Coleccion de Documentos Inéditos (41 vols., Madrid, 1864-1884).

Collections of the Georgia Historical Society (9 vols., Savannah, Georgia, 1840-1842).

Collections of the South Carolina Historical Society.

Cooper, Thomas, ed., *Statutes at Large of South Carolina* (7 vols., Columbia, South Carolina, 1837).

Coulter, E. Merton, ed., *The Journal of William Stephens* (2 vols., Athens, Georgia, 1958-1959).

Dávila Padilla, Augustin, *Historia de la Fundación y Discurso de la Provincia* ... (Madrid, 1596).

Douglass, Frederick, *My Bondage* (New York, 1855).

Dumont de Montigny, Louis François Benjamin, *Mémoires Historiques sur la Louisiane* (2 vols., Paris, 1753).

Egmont, Earl of, *Diary* (3 vols., London, 1920-1923).

Ellicott, Andrew, *Journal* (Philadelphia, 1803).

The Hidalgo [Gentleman] of Elvas, "True Relation of the Vicissitudes . . . ," *see* Edward Gaylord Bourne.

Fries, Adelaide L., ed., *Records of the Moravians in North Carolina* (8 vols., Raleigh, North Carolina, 1922-1954).

García, Genero, ed., *Dos Antiguas Relaciones de la Florida* (Mexico, 1902).

Gourges, Dominique de, "Voyage," *see* Richard Hakluyt.

Hakluyt, Richard, ed., *The Voyages, Traffiques & Discoveries of Foreign Voyagers* (12 vols., London, 1928).

Hall, Basil, *Travels in North America* (3 vols., Edinburgh, 1829).

Herrera y Tordesillos, Antonio de, *Historia General de los Hechos de los Castellanos* . . . (4 vols., Buenos Aires, 1945).

Kemble, Francis Anne, *Journal of a Residence on a Georgia Plantation in 1838-39* (New York, 1863).

Lanning, John Tate, ed., *The St. Augustine Expedition of 1740* (Columbia, South Carolina, 1954).

Las Casas, Bartolome de, *Historia General de las Indias* (4 vols., Madrid, 1875).

Laudonnière, René, "Voiage," *see* Richard Hakluyt.

La Vega, Garcilaso de, *The Florida of the Inca.* Translated by John Grier Varner and Jeannette Johnson Verner (Austin, Texas, 1951).

LeChalleux, Nicolas, "Discourse," *see* Stefan Lorant.

Lemoyne, Pierre, "Journal," *see* Pierre Margry.

Le Moyne de Marques, Jacques, "Narrative," *see* Stefan Lorant.

Le Page du Pratz, Antoine Simon, *Histoire de la Louisiane* (3 vols., Paris, 1758).

Lewis, Clifford M. and Loomie, Albert J., *The Spanish Mission in Virginia* (Chapel Hill, North Carolina, 1953).

Lorant, Stefan, ed. and trans., *The New World* (New York, 1946).

Margry, Pierre, ed., *Decouvertes et Établissements des Français dans l'Ouest et dans le Sud de l'Amerique Septentrionale, 1614-1698, mémoires et documents inédits* (6 vols., Paris, 1879).

Martineau, Harriet, *Society in America* (2 vols., New York, 1837).

Mártir de Angleria, Pedro [Peter Martyr], *Decades del Nuevo Mundo* (Buenos Aires, 1944).

McWilliams, Richebourg Gaillard, ed. and trans., *Fleur de Lys and Calumet* (Baton Rouge, Louisiana, 1953).

Motte, Jacob Rhett, *Journey Into Wilderness.* Edited by James F. Sunderman (Gainesville, Florida, 1953).

Olmsted, Frederick Law, *Journey in the Seaboard Slave States* (New York, 1856).

———, *A Journey in the Back Country* (New York, 1863).

Oviedo y Valdes, Gonzalo Hernandez de, *Historia General y Natural de las Indias* (4 vols., Madrid, 1851-55).

Pénicaut, André, *Narrative, see* Richebourg Gaillard McWilliams.

Phillips, Ulrich Bonnell, ed., *Plantation and Frontier* (2 vols., Cleveland, 1910).

Priestley, Herbert Ingram, ed., *The Luna Papers* (2 vols., Deland, Florida, 1928).

Ranjel, Rodrigo, "Relation," *see* Edward Gaylord Bourne.

Ribaut, Jean, "Voiage," *see* Richard Hakluyt.

Roberts, William, *An Account of the First Discovery and Natural History of Florida* (London, 1763).

Rowland, Dunbar, and Sanders, Albert Godfrey, eds., *Mississippi Provincial Archives* (3 vols., Jackson, Mississippi, 1927-1932).

Rowland, Dunbar, ed., *Mississippi Territorial Archives*.

———, ed., *Official Letter Books of W. C. C. Claiborne* (3 vols., Jackson, Mississippi, 1917).

Salley, Alexander S., Jr., ed., *Narratives of Early Carolina* (New York, 1911).

Senate Miscellaneous Documents, No. 55, 36th Congress, 1st Session.

Serrano y Sanz, Manuel, ed., *Documentos historicos de la Florida y la Luisiana* (Madrid, 1912).

Smith, Buckingham, ed., *Colección de Various Documentos, Para la Historia de la Florida y Tierras Adyacentes* (London, 1857).

Solis de Merás, Gonzalo, *Memorial*. Translated by Jeannette Thurber Conner (Deland, Florida, 1923).

Sparks, William H., *The Memories of Fifty Years* (Philadelphia, 1870).

Tailfer, Pat. and Others, *A True and Historical Narrative of the Colony of Georgia* (Athens, Georgia, 1960).

Ternaux-Compans, Henri, ed., *Recueil de Pièces sur la Floride* (Paris, 1841).

Thwaites, Reuben Gold, ed., *Jesuit Relations and Allied Documents* (73 vols., Cleveland, 1896-1901).

United States Statutes at Large.

Vedie, Enrique de, ed., *Historiadoes Primitivos de Indias* (2 vols., Madrid, 1946).

Wesley, Charles, *Journal*. Edited by Thomas Jackson (London, 1849).

Wesley, John, *Journal*. Edited by Nehemiah Curnock (2 vols., New York, 1909?).

JOURNALS AND MAGAZINE ARTICLES

"Correspondence of Clark and Genet," in *Annual Report*, American Historical Association, I (1896).

Gálvez, Bernardo de, "Diary," in *Louisiana Historical Quarterly*, I (1917).

"Mangourit Correspondence," in *Annual Report*, American Historical Association (1897).

Oré, Luis Geronimo de, "The Martyrs of Florida," in *Franciscan Studies*, XVIII (1936).

"Panton, Leslie Papers," in *Florida Historical Quarterly*, XIV (1939) and XV (1940).

Pareja, Francisco, "Confessionario," *see* A. S. Gatschet.

Sanders, Albert Godfrey, ed., "Documents Concerning the Crozat Regime in Louisiana, 1812-1817," in *Louisiana Historical Quarterly*, XVI (1933).

Smith, Buckingham, trans., "Documents of the King of Spain to De Soto," in *Florida Historical Quarterly*, XVI (1938).

SECONDARY WORKS

Books

Abernethy, Thomas Perkins, *The Burr Conspiracy* (New York, 1954).

Alden, John Richard, *John Stuart and the Southern Colonial Frontier* (Ann Arbor, Michigan, 1944).

Bailey, Thomas A., *A Diplomatic History of the American People* (New York, 1946).

Ball, T. H., *The Great South-East* (Tuscaloosa, Alabama, 1962).

Bancroft, Frederic, *Slave-Trading in the Old South* (Baltimore, 1931).

Bancroft, George, *History of the United States* (6 vols., New York, 1888).

Barcia Carballido y Zuñiga, Andrés Gonzales de, *History of the Continent of Florida*. Translated by Anthony Kerrigan (Gainesville, Florida, 1951).

Bettersworth, John K., *Mississippi: A History* (Austin, Texas, 1959).

Bishop, Morris, *The Odyssey of Cabeza de Vaca* (New York, 1937).

Bolton, Herbert Eugene, *The Spanish Borderlands* (New Haven, 1921).

——, *Arredondo's Historical Proof of Spain's Title to Georgia* (Berkeley, California, 1925).

Botkin, B. A., *A Treasury of Southern Folklore* (New York, 1949).

Bruce, Henry, *Life of General Oglethorpe* (New York ,1890).

Callaway, James Etheridge, *The Early Settlement of Georgia* (Athens, Georgia, 1948).

Campbell, Richard L., *Historical Sketches of Colonial Florida* (Cleveland, 1892).

Campbell, T. J., *Laymen of North America* (2 vols., New York, 1915-1916).

Canot, Theodore, *Adventures of an African Slaver*. Edited by Malcolm Cowley (New York, 1928).

Caruso, John Anthony, *The Appalachian Frontier* (Indianapolis and New York, 1959).

——, *The Great Lakes Frontier* (Indianapolis and New York, 1961).

Caughey, John Walton, *Bernardo de Gálvez in Louisiana* (Berkeley, California, 1934).

——, *McGillivray of the Creeks* (Norman, Oklahoma, 1959).

Chambers, Henry E., *A History of Louisiana* (2 vols., Chicago, 1925).

Coates, Robert M., *The Outlaw Years* (New York, 1930).

[Corse], Carita Doggett, *Dr. Andrew Turnbull and the New Smyrna Colony of Florida* (Jacksonville, Florida, 1919).

Cotterill, R. S., *The Southern Indians* (Norman, Oklahoma, 1954).

Coulter, E. Merton, *Georgia, A Short History* (Chapel Hill, North Carolina, 1960).

Cox, Isaac Joslin, *The West Florida Controversy* (Baltimore, 1918).

Crane, Verner W., *The Southern Frontier* (Ann Arbor, Michigan, 1959).

Crouse, Nellis M., *Lemoyne d'Iberville, Soldier of New France* (Ithaca, New York, 1954).

Davis, Edwin Adam, *Louisiana* (Baton Rouge, 1959).

Deiler, J. Hanno, *The Settlement of the German Coast of Louisiana and the Creoles of German Descent* (Philadelphia, 1909).

Dewhurst, William W., *The History of Saint Augustine, Florida* (New York, 1881).

Dick, Everett, *The Dixie Frontier* (New York, 1948).

Dunn, William Edward, *Spanish and French Rivalry in the Gulf Region of the United States* (Austin, Texas, 1917).

Elkins, Stanley M., *Slavery: A Problem in American Institutional and Intellectual Life* (Chicago, 1959).

Ettinger, Amos Aschbash, *James Edward Oglethorpe: Imperial Idealist* (Oxford, 1936).

Final Report of the United States De Soto Commission (Washington, D.C., 1939).

Foreman, Grant, *Indian Removal* (Norman, Oklahoma, 1932).

Fortier, Alcíer, *A History of Louisiana* (4 vols., New York, 1904?).

Gayarré, Charles, *History of Louisiana* (4 vols., New Orleans, 1903).

Geiger, Maynard, *The Franciscan Conquest of Florida* (Washington, D.C., 1938).

Griffin, Charles Carroll, *The United States and the Disruption of the Spanish Empire* (New York, 1937).

Guild, J. C., *Old Times in Tennessee* (Nashville, 1878).

Hamilton, Peter, *Colonial Mobile* (Boston, 1897).

Hamilton, William Baskerville, *Anglo-American Law on the Frontier* (Durham, North Carolina, 1953).

Hanna, Kathryn Abbey, *Florida, Land of Change* (Chapel Hill, North Carolina, 1948).

Heinrich, Pierre, *La Louisiane Sous la Companie des Indes* (Paris, n.d.).

Henry, H. M., *The Police Control of the Slave in South Carolina* (Emory, Virginia, 1914).

Howell, Clark, *History of Georgia* (2 vols., Chicago, 1926).

Hundley, David R., *Social Relations in Our Southern States* (New York, 1860).

Hyde, H. Montgomery, *John Law* (London, 1948).

James, James A., *Oliver Pollock* (New York, 1937).

James, Marquis, *The Life of Andrew Jackson* (Indianapolis and New York, 1938).

Johnson, Cecil, *British West Florida* (New Haven, 1943).

Jones, Charles Colcock, *History of Georgia* (2 vols., Boston and New York, 1883).

——, *Negro Myths from the Georgia Coast* (Boston, 1888).

Kenny, Michael, *The Romance of the Floridas* (New York, 1934).

King, Grace, *Jean-Baptiste Le Moyne* (New York, 1892).

Lanning, John Tate, *The Diplomatic History of Georgia* (Chapel Hill, North Carolina, 1936).

——, *The Spanish Missions of Georgia* (Chapel Hill, North Carolina, 1935).

Lawson, Edward W., *The Discovery of Florida and Its Discoverer: Juan Ponce de León* (St. Augustine, Florida, 1946).

Letts, Malcolm, *Sir John Mandeville* (London, 1949).

Lowery, Woodbury, *The Spanish Settlements Within the Present Limits of the United States, 1513-1561* (New York, 1911).

————, *The Spanish Settlements Within the Present Limits of the United States, 1562-1574* (New York, 1911).

McCain, James Ross, *Georgia as a Proprietary Province* (Boston, 1917).

McCaleb, Walter Flavius, *The Aaron Burr Conspiracy* (New York, 1936).

McCorvey, Thomas Chalmers, *Alabama Historical Sketches* (Charlottesville, Virginia, 1960).

McMaster, John Bach, *A History of the People of the United States* (5 vols., New York, 1888).

MacNutt, Francis Augustus, *Bartholomew de las Casas* (New York, 1909).

Mannix, Daniel P., and Cowley, Malcolm, *Black Cargoes* (New York, 1962).

Maynard, Theodore, *De Soto and the Consquistadores* (New York, 1930).

Means, Philip Ainsworth, *The Spanish Main* (New York, 1935).

Milling, Chapman J., *Red Carolinians* (Chapel Hill, North Carolina, 1940).

Minnegerode, Meade, *Jefferson, Friend of France* (New York, 1930).

Motley, John Lothrop, *The Rise of the Dutch Republic* (3 vols., Philadelphia, n.d.).

O'Daniel, V. F., *Dominicans in Early Florida* (New York, 1930).

Oudard, George, *Four Cents an Acre*. Translated by Margery Bianco (New York, 1931).

Owsley, Frank L., *Plain Folk of the Old South* (Baton Rouge, 1949).

Parkman, Francis, *Pioneers of France in the New World* (Boston, 1865).

————, *A Half-Century of Conflict* (2 vols., Boston, 1893).

Patrick, Rembert W., *Florida Under Five Flags* (Gainesville, Florida, 1960).

Phares, Ross, *Cavalier in the Wilderness* (Baton Rouge, 1952).

Phillips, Ulrich Bonnell, *Georgia and State Rights* (Washington, D.C., 1902).

————, *Life and Labor in the Old South* (Boston, 1929).

————, *American Negro Slavery* (New York, 1952).

Pound, Merritt B., *Benjamin Hawkins—Indian Agent* (Athens, Georgia, 1951).

Prescott, William Hickling, *History of the Reign of Philip the Second* (3 vols., Philadelphia, 1882).

Priestley, Herbert Ingram, *Tristan de Luna* (Glendale, California, 1936).

Ramsay, Davis, *History of South Carolina* (2 vols., Spartenburg, South Carolina, 1959).

Roberts, W. Adolphe, *Lake Pontchartrain* (Indianapolis and New York, 1946).

Rothert, Otto A., *The Outlaws of Cave-in-Rock* (Cleveland, 1924).

Rowland, Dunbar, ed., *Encyclopaedia of Mississippi History* (Madison, Wisconsin, 1907).

Rowland, Dunbar, *History of Mississippi* (2 vols., Chicago, 1925).

Ruidíaz y Caravia, Eugenio, *La Florida Su Conquesta y Colonización por Pedro Menéndez de Avilés* (2 vols., Madrid, 1894).

Scarborough, Dorothy, *On the Trail of Negro Folk-Songs* (Cambridge, Massachusetts, 1925).

Schlarman, H. H., *From Quebec to New Orleans* (Belleville, Illinois, 1930).

Seibert, Wilbert Henry, *Loyalists in East Florida* (2 vols., Deland, Florida, 1929).

Shea, John Gilmary, *The Catholic Church in Colonial Days* (New York, 1886).

Spears, John R., *The American Slave-Trade* (New York, 1907).

Stampp, Kenneth M., *The Peculiar Institution* (New York, 1956).

Stephens, William Bacon, *A History of Georgia* (2 vols., 1847-1859).

Stokes, Thomas L., *The Savannah* (New York, 1951).

Strickland, Reba Carolyn, *Religion and the State in Georgia in the Eighteenth Century* (New York, 1939).

Strobel, P. A., *The Salzburgers and Their Descendants* (Athens, Georgia, 1953).

Swanton, John R., *Indian Tribes of the Lower Mississippi Valley* (Washington, D.C., 1911).

——, *Early History of the Creek Indians and Their Neighbors* (Washington, D.C., 1922).

Swearingen, Mack Buckley, *The Early Life of George Poindexter* (Chicago, 1934).

Temple, Sara B. Gober, and Coleman, Kenneth, *Georgia Journeys* (Athens, Georgia, 1961).

Thiers, Adolphe, *The Mississippi Bubble*. Translated and edited by Frank S. Fiske (New York, 1859).

Tucker, Glenn, *Poltroons and Patriots* (2 vols., Indianapolis and New York, 1954).

Villiers du Terrage, Marc de, *Les Deniers Années de la Française; le Chevalier du Kerlérec, d'Abbadie Aubry, Lausat . . .* (Paris, 1904).

Washington, Booker T., *The Story of the Negro* (2 vols., New York, 1940).

Whitaker, Arthur Preston, *The Spanish-American Frontier* (Boston, 1927).

——, *The Mississippi Question* (New York, 1934).

White, George, *Statistics of the State of Georgia* (Savannah, 1849).

White, Newman I., *American Negro Folk-Songs* (Cambridge, Massachusetts, 1928).

Woodson, Carter G., *The Negro in Our History* (Washington, D.C., 1928).

MONOGRAPHS AND MAGAZINE ARTICLES

Abbott, Martin, "Indian Policy and Management in the Mississippi Territory, 1798-1817," in *Journal of Mississippi History*, XVI (1952).

Abernethy, Thomas Perkins, "Aaron Burr in Mississippi," in *The Journal of Southern History*, XV (1949).

Albrecht, A. C., "The Origin and Settlement of Baton Rouge, Louisiana," in *Louisiana Historical Quarterly*, XXVIII (1945).

Arnade, Charles W., "Tristan de Luna and Ochuse," in *Florida Historical Quarterly*, XXXVII (1958).

——, *Florida on Trial, 1593-1602* (Coral Gables, Florida, 1959).

Bennett, Charles E., "Fort Caroline, Cradle of American Freedom," in *Florida Historical Quarterly*, XXXV (1956).

Bolton, Herbert Eugene, "Spanish Resistance . . . in . . . Georgia," *Georgia Historical Quarterly*, IX (1925).

Boyd, Mark F., "Arrival of De Soto's Expedition in Florida," in *Florida Historical Quarterly*, XVI (1938).

——, "Asi-Yaholo or Osceola," in *Florida Historical Quarterly*, XXXIII (1955).

Brown, J. A., "Panton, Leslie and Company, Indian Traders of Pensacola and St. Augustine," in *Florida Historical Quarterly*, XXXVII (1959).

Cate, Margaret Davis, "Fort Frederica and the Battle of Bloody Marsh," in *Georgia Historical Quarterly*, XXVII (1943).

Caughey, John Walton, "Willing's Expedition Down the Mississippi," in *Louisiana Historical Quarterly*, XV (1932).

[Corse], Carita Doggett, "Henry Rolle and Rollestown, A Pioneer for Utopia," in *Florida Historical Quarterly*, XXXIII (1955).

Covington, James W., "Cuban Bloodhounds and the Seminoles," in *Florida Historical Quarterly*, XXXIII (1955).

Cox, Isaac J., "The Border Missions of General George Mathews," in *Mississippi Valley Historical Review*, XII (1925).

Crane, Verner W., "The Southern Frontier in Queen Anne's War," in *The American Historical Review*, XXIV (1919).

Davis, T. Frederick, "MacGregor's Invasion of Florida, 1817," in *Florida Historical Quarterly*, VII (1928).

———, "History of Juan Ponce de León's Voyages to Florida," in *Florida Historical Quarterly*, XIV (1935).

———, "The Record of Ponce de León's Discovery of Florida," in *Florida Historical Quarterly*, XI (1932).

Doherty, Herbert J., Jr., "The Governorship of Andrew Jackson," in *Florida Historical Quarterly*, XXXIII (1954).

Gatschet, A. S., "The Timucuan Language," in *Proceedings of the American Philosophical Society*, XVII (1878).

Giraud, Marcel, "France and Louisiana in Early Eighteenth Century," in *Mississippi Valley Historical Review*, XXXVI (1950).

Greenslade, Marie Taylor, "William Panton," in *Florida Historical Quarterly*, XIV (1939).

Hamilton, William B., "The Southwestern Frontier, 1795-1817," in *Journal of Southern History*, X (1944).

[Hanna], Kathryn Abbey, "Efforts of Spain to Maintain Sources of Information in the British Colonies Before 1779," in *Mississippi Valley Historical Review*, XV (1928).

———, "Peter Chester's Defense of the Mississippi After the Willing Raid," in *Mississippi Valley Historical Review*, XXII (1935).

Haynes, Robert V., "The Revolution of 1800 in Mississippi," in *Journal of Southern History*, XIX (1957).

Heath, William Estill, "The Yazoo Land Fraud," in *Georgia Historical Quarterly*, XVI (1932).

Holcombe, William H., "Sketches of Plantation Life," in *Knickerbocker Magazine*, LVII (1861).

Jamison, Lena Mitchell, "The Natchez Trace: A Federal Highway of the Old Southwest," in *Journal of Mississippi History*, I (1939).

Johnson, Cecil, "The Distribution of Land in British West Florida," in *Louisiana Historical Quarterly*, XVI (1933).

Johnson, James G., "The Colonial Southwest, 1732-1763," in *The University of Colorado Studies*, XIX (1932).

Kinnaird, Lawrence, "The Significance of William Augustus Bowles' Seizure of Panton's Apalachee Store in 1792," in *Florida Historical Quarterly*, IX (1931).

Lynch, William O., "The Westward Flow of Southern Colonists Before 1861," in *Journal of Southern History*, IX (1943).

McAlister, L. N., "Pensacola During the Second Spanish Period," in *Florida Historical Quarterly*, XXXVII (1959).

Mahon, John K., "The Treaty of Moultrie Creek, 1823," in *Florida Historical Quarterly*, XL (1962).

———, "William Augustus Bowles and the State of Muskogee," in *Florida Historical Quarterly*, XL (1962).

Mowat, Charles L., "St. Augustine Under the British Flag," in *Florida Historical Quarterly*, XX (1941).

———, "East Florida as a British Province," in *University of California Publications in History*, XXII (1943).

Owsley, Frank L., "The Pattern of Migration and Settlement on the Southern Frontier," in *Journal of Southern History*, XI (1945).

Panagopoulous, E. P., "The Background of the Greek Settlers in the New Smyrna Colony," in *Florida Historical Quarterly*, XXXV (1956).

Riley, Franklin L., "Spanish Policy in Mississippi After the Treaty of San Lorenzo," in *Annual Report*, American Historical Association (1897).

Rowland, Mrs. Dunbar, "Peter Chester," in *Publications of the Mississippi Historical Society*, V (1925).

Seibert, Wilbert H., "The Loyalists in West Florida and the Natchez District," in *Mississippi Valley Historical Review*, II (1916).

Sterkx, Henry Eugene, and Thompson, Brooks, "Philemon Thomas and the West Florida Revolution," in *Florida Historical Quarterly*, XXXIX (1961).

Swanton, John R., "The Landing Place of De Soto," in *Florida Historical Quarterly*, XVI (1938).

Taylor, Garland, "Colonial Settlement and Early Revolutionary Activity in West Florida," in *Mississippi Valley Historical Review*, XXII (1935).

Thomas, Daniel H., "Fort Toulouse—In Tradition and Fact," in *The Alabama Review*, XIII (1960).

Tucker, Phillip C., "Notes on the Life of Governor James Grant," in *Florida Historical Quarterly*, VIII (1929).

Villiers du Terrage, Marc de, "A History of the Foundation of New Orleans," in *Louisiana Historical Quarterly*, III (1920).

Ward, May McNeer, "The Disappearance of the Head of Osceola," in *Florida Historical Quarterly*, XXXIII (1955).

Whitaker, Arthur Preston, "New Light on the Treaty of San Lorenzo: An Essay in Historical Criticism," in *Mississippi Valley Historical Review*, XV (1929).

Wright, J. Leitch, Jr., "Sixteenth Century English-Spanish Rivalry in Florida," in *Florida Historical Quarterly*, XXXVIII (1960).

Wyllys, Rufus Kay, "The East Florida Revolution of 1812-1814," in *Hispanic American Historical Review*, IX (1929).

Zarncke, F., "Der Priester Johannes," in *Abhandlingen der phil. hist.*, VII (1879).

Acknowledgments

So far as I know, this volume is the first narrative history of the frontier of Florida, South Carolina, Georgia, Alabama, Mississippi, and Louisiana. Professor Verner W. Crane's splendid book, which is primarily a critical study, embraces the states of the Deep South together with those of the Appalachian region, but it covers only a part of the frontier period. My book is based on manuscripts, printed sources, secondary works, monographs, and magazine articles. Only some of the manuscript collections that I examined were suitable for my purpose; others would be excellent for use in writing dissertations, monographs, or statistical studies. In this earliest and most romantic of American frontiers, much of the spade work from important manuscript collections has already been done in specialized fields by reputable scholars; I saw no good reason why I should not avail myself of their labors, for which I am profoundly grateful.

I would never have completed the seemingly endless research and tremendously difficult task of writing this book without the experience, knowledge, and patience of many persons. I owe a debt of gratitude to staff members of the following institutions for their cheerful and invaluable help: the Ohio County, West Virginia, Public Library; the Library of West Virginia University; the Library of the University of California; the Library of the University of Michigan; the Library of Louisiana State University; the Library of the University of Georgia; the Library of the University of Florida; the Library of the University of Mississippi; the Library of the University of Alabama; the Library of Congress; the Widener Library of Harvard University; the Florida Historical Society; the Mississippi Historical Society; and the Louisiana Historical Society.

For many kinds of help I am indebted to Virginia Ebeling, Virginia Perry, Charles Shetler, Agnes Patton, Ethel Gaston, Lorice Boger, Ellen Sumner, Marilee Wilhoit, Ann Day, Frances Teter, Carol Ralston, Professor Edward M. Steel, Professor Armand Singer, and Professor Patrick Ward Gainer. I am especially grateful to Dr. C. Percy Powell, Dr. Elizabeth McPherson, Roger Preston, Richard Leach, and John McDonough, all of the Library of Congress, for graciously placing a number of manuscript collections at my disposal; to Michael Reynolds, Associate Director of Libraries, West Virginia University, for obtaining for me microfilm of the DeBrahm Manuscript from the Widener Library of Harvard

University; and to William Porter Kellam, Director of Libraries, University of Georgia, for microfilm of a portion of the invaluable Egmont Manuscripts.

I herewith offer thanks to the following for permission to reproduce copyrighted material: Professor Thomas A. Bailey for quotations from his *Diplomatic History of the American People,* copyrighted 1946, Century, Crofts & Company; Stefan Lorant for quotations from his excellently edited and translated work, *The New World,* copyrighted 1946, Duell, Sloan & Pearce; Alfred A. Knopf, Inc., for a quotation from Everett Dick, *The Dixie Frontier,* copyrighted 1948; Duell, Sloan & Pearce for selections from Ulrich Bonnell Phillips, *American Negro Slavery,* copyrighted 1918; and Little, Brown & Company for quotations from Ulrich Bonnell Phillips, *Life and Labor in the Old South,* copyrighted 1929, © 1957 by Mrs. Ulrich Bonnell Phillips. I beg the forgiveness of any author or publisher if by some inadvertence I have failed to obtain permission to quote from any work protected by copyright. If brought to my attention, I promise to make amends in any new printing of this book.

I am grateful to my wife, Marie, and my two little daughters, Johanna and Camille, for their patience, forbearance, and sacrifices while this book inched toward completion. I rejoice, too, in the friendship of Andrée Fé Coers and Harry Platt who, since the publication of the first volume of this series in 1959, have continued to give me generous encouragement, wise counsel, and even perspicacious literary guidance. I can never repay them for their devotion. Last but not least, I acknowledge my appreciation of the unfailing kindness and patience of the Bobbs-Merrill editorial, publicity and production departments and their personnel in answering my queries and finding solutions to my problems.

John Anthony Caruso

Morgantown, West Virginia

INDEX

Current boundary lines have been observed in locating towns, villages, forts, etc., within states. Non-Christian names of Indians are set in full and small capitals.